D0537229

# THE OXFORD JUNIOR
# COMPANION TO MUSIC

# THE OXFORD JUNIOR COMPANION
## TO
# MUSIC

SECOND EDITION
by Michael Hurd

based on the original publication
by Percy Scholes

London
OXFORD UNIVERSITY PRESS
New York   Toronto
1979

LIBRARY
WESTERN OREGON STATE COLLEGE
MONMOUTH, OREGON 97361

#780
JH
1979

JUV.
ML
100
.H96
1979

*Oxford University Press, Walton Street, Oxford OX2 6DP*

OXFORD  LONDON  GLASGOW  NEW YORK  TORONTO
MELBOURNE  WELLINGTON  CAPE TOWN  IBADAN  NAIROBI
DAR ES SALAAM  TOKYO  KUALA LUMPUR  SINGAPORE  JAKARTA
HONG KONG  DELHI  BOMBAY  CALCUTTA  MADRAS  KARACHI

© Oxford University Press 1979

All rights reserved. No part of this publication may be reproduced, stored
in a retrieval system, or transmitted, in any form or by any means,
electronic, mechanical, photocopying, recording, or otherwise, without
the prior permission of Oxford University Press

First published 1979
ISBN 0 19 314302 X

Designed and produced by QED Publishing Limited
*Art Editor* Marnie Searchwell
*Designer* Heather Jackson
*Illustrators* Elaine Keenan, Edwina Keene, Abdul Aziz Khan, David
Mallott, Jim Marks, Nigel Osborne, John Woodcock, Martin Woodford,
Kai Choi, Perry Taylor, Tony Merritt, Simon Roulstone
*Production Director* Edward Kinsey
*Art Director* Alastair Campbell
*Picture research by* Elisabeth Agate
*Captions by* Jenny Mulherin

Filmset in Britain by Filmtype Services Ltd
Colour origination in Italy by Starf Photolitho SRL, Rome
Printed in Hong Kong by Leefung-Asco Printers Ltd

# CONTENTS

# FOREWORD

**D**r Percy Scholes's *Oxford Junior Companion to Music* was first published in 1954 and, as the natural pendant to his popular and enormously influential *Oxford Companion to Music*, has enjoyed a lasting and deserved success with the readers for whom it was designed. But all works of this kind must continue to reflect contemporary values and interests. *The Oxford Junior Companion to Music* has reached the stage of needing a complete revision.

The present edition is completely new. Though based on Scholes's original, scarcely a word remains of what he wrote in 1954. Entries which were relevant then have been dropped in favour of those that are relevant now – who, for example, in 1954 knew or cared about folk instruments or medieval music! Minor composers who were living and influential then have made way for new lions. And, perhaps most important of all, a more international view has come in to replace what were often narrowly parochial interests.

One special feature of the new edition is worthy of comment. This is the placing of certain key articles in 'boxes' as a means of drawing attention to a subject of particular interest. Opera, for instance, is so important and absorbing a topic that such treatment was literally demanded, if the information was not to become obscured in the general alphabetical arrangement of the text. The articles themselves are liberally cross-referenced by means of bold type and an arrow ( → ).

Finally, I have tried to approach the writing of this new edition in something of the spirit that informed Percy Scholes's original, and have sought to present objective, useful information in a way that is personal, readable, and entertaining. Probably here and there, as in his writings, the wry touch of mild prejudice and the excitement of special enthusiasms have crept in to colour the factual recital. If so, I cannot truly say I am sorry.

*Michael Hurd*

# Notes and notation

## 1. Note values

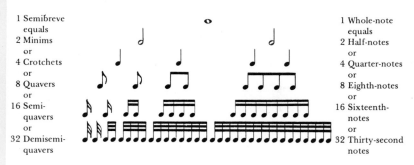

| | |
|---|---|
| 1 Semibreve equals | 1 Whole-note equals |
| 2 Minims or | 2 Half-notes or |
| 4 Crotchets or | 4 Quarter-notes or |
| 8 Quavers or | 8 Eighth-notes or |
| 16 Semi-quavers or | 16 Sixteenth-notes or |
| 32 Demisemi-quavers | 32 Thirty-second notes |

After this come Hemidemisemiquavers (sixty-fourth notes ♬), and, occasionally, Semihemidemisemiquavers (notes of 128 to the semibreve ♬). *Semi* is Latin for 'half', *hemi* is Greek for 'half', and *Demi* is French for 'half', so these ponderous terms are thorough mongrels.

A dot after a note increases its value by half. Thus ♩· = ♩ ♪ . A double dot after a note increases its value by a half plus a quarter, thus ♩·· = ♩ ♪ ♩ .

The rarely used breve (Double whole-note) ⫤ is equal to two semibreves.

## 2. Rests

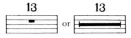

Note that the semibreve (whole-note) rest hangs below the line, while the minim (half-note) rest sits above it.

The semibreve (whole-note) rest is often used to indicate a bar's rest, whatever the note-value of the bar.

A silence of several bars is often indicated like this:

13 or 13

Rests can be dotted and double dotted, just like notes – the effect is the same.

## 3. Clefs

| G or TREBLE CLEF On 2nd line up, fixing that as Treble G | F or BASS CLEF On 2nd line down, fixing that as Bass F |
|---|---|

| C (SOPRANO) CLEF On 1st line, fixing that as middle C | C (ALTO) CLEF On 3rd line, fixing that as middle C |
|---|---|

| C (TENOR) CLEF On 4th line, fixing that as middle C |
|---|

The above shows the one note, middle C, represented in five different ways. (→ **Great Stave**)

The alto clef, formerly used for the alto voice and certain instruments, is still in use for the viola. The tenor clef, formerly used for the tenor voice, is still in use for the higher notes of the violoncello, for the tenor trombone, etc.

## 4. Notes and their pitch names

| | C | D | E | F | G | A | B♭ | B |
|---|---|---|---|---|---|---|---|---|
| English | C | D | E | F | G | A | B♭ | B |
| German | C | D | E | F | G | A | B | H |
| French | ut | ré | mi | fa | sol | la | si bémol | si |
| Italian | do | re | mi | fa | sol | la | si bémolle | si |

## 5. Sharps and flats

| SHARP Raising the note a half-step or semitone ♯ | DOUBLE SHARP Raising the note a full step or tone 𝄪 |
|---|---|

| FLAT Lowering the note a half-step or semitone ♭ | DOUBLE FLAT Lowering the note a full step or tone ♭♭ |
|---|---|

After a sharp or flat the natural sign ♮ restores the note to its normal pitch.

After a double sharp or double flat the sign ♯ or ♭ (or ♮♯ or ♮♭) changes the pitch of the note to that of a single sharp or flat.

After a double sharp or double flat the sign ♮ (rarely given ♮♮) restores the note to its normal pitch.

These signs affect not only the notes before which they occur, but also any other notes on the *same* line or space in the bar. If the last note in a bar is tied to the first note of the next bar, any sharp, flat or natural (sometimes called ACCIDENTAL) continues to take effect.

## 6. Major and minor key signatures

| C maj. | G maj. | D Maj. | A maj. | E maj. | B maj. | F♯ maj. | C♯ maj. |
| A min. | E min. | B min. | F♯ min. | C♯ min. | G♯ min. | D♯ min. | A♯ min. |

| C maj. | F maj. | B♭ maj. | E♭ maj. | A♭ maj. | D♭ maj. | G♭ maj. | (seldom used) |
| A min. | D min. | G min. | C min. | F min. | B♭ min | E♭ min. | C♭ maj. |
| | | | | | | | A♭ min. |

In the table above the white note represents the major key, and the black note the minor key with the same key signature. Two keys which share the same key signature are said to be 'relative' to one another. For example, E minor is the 'Relative Minor' of G major; and G major is the 'Relative Major' of E minor.

The Relative minor key is always three notes lower than the major key with the same key signature.

Here is an easy way to remember the order of sharps and flats: the sharp keys follow in order of *rising* fifths; the flat keys follow in order of *falling* fifths. The one is the reverse of the other:

Sharps → F C G D A E B ← Flats

## 7. Time signatures

Each Simple time has a corresponding Compound time. The beat in simple times always has the value of a plain note; the beat in compound times has the value of a dotted note.

The notes in simple times can therefore be divided into halves, quarters, etc. Those in compound times divide by thirds, and sixths, etc. The notes are always grouped so as to make this clear.

Composers nowadays often use irregular time signatures, such as 7/4, 11/8, and so on. These can always be broken down: thus, 7 = 3 + 4, or 4 + 3.

## 8. Irregular rhythmic groupings

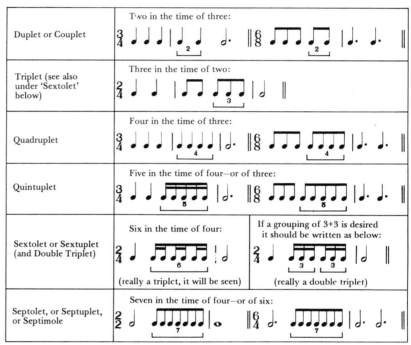

| Duplet or Couplet | Two in the time of three: |
| Triplet (see also under 'Sextolet' below) | Three in the time of two: |
| Quadruplet | Four in the time of three: |
| Quintuplet | Five in the time of four—or of three: |
| Sextolet or Sextuplet (and Double Triplet) | Six in the time of four: (really a triplet, it will be seen) | If a grouping of 3+3 is desired it should be written as below: (really a double triplet) |
| Septolet, or Septuplet, or Septimole | Seven in the time of four—or of six: |

Many other groupings are possible. When an unusual one occurs, add up the notes in the bar, subtract them from the value of the bar, and the remainder will be the note-value of the irregular grouping.

| | | | |
|---|---|---|---|
| Simple Duple | 2/2 or ₵ | 2/4 | 2/8 |
| Compound Duple | 6/4 | 6/8 | 6/16 |
| Simple Triple | 3/2 | 3/4 | 3/8 |
| Compound Triple | 9/4 | 9/8 | 9/16 |
| Simple Quadruple | 4/2 | 4/4 or C | 4/8 |
| Compound Quadruple | 12/4 | 12/8 | 12/16 |

# Ornaments and grace-notes

These tables explain how to interpret the most common signs for ornaments and grace notes. It must be understood, however, that such signs have carried different meanings at different periods of history and in different countries – sometimes even among different composers of the same period. When playing early music, it is therefore necessary to make a special study the practice of the times.

## 1. Acciaccatura and mordent
### (a) The acciaccatura

The main note keeps its accent and practically all its value. The auxiliary note is played on the same beat, squeezed in as quickly as possible before the main note is heard.

The Acciaccatura always has a stroke through its tail:  . Double and Triple Acciaccaturas are also possible, but these are written without a stroke through the tail. They too are squeezed in on top of the main note:

An Acciaccatura can be combined with a spread chord, thus:

performed as though notated:

### (b) The lower and upper mordents

Lower mordent
(or merely 'mordent')

Lower mordent with sharp or flat.

Upper mordent
(or 'inverted mordent')

Upper mordent with sharp or flat.

Like the acciaccatura, the mordent is also squeezed in on top of the main note as quickly as possible. In the case of the Lower Mordent the decoration consists of the note itself, and the note below it; while the Upper Mordent consists of the note, and the note above. If the lower note is to be sharpened, a sharp is written below the sign. If the upper note is to be flattened, a flat is written above the sign.

## 2. The appoggiatura
Unlike the acciaccatura, the Appoggiatura robs the note which it decorates of part of its value. If the note is plain, then the Appoggiatura takes half its value. If the note is dotted, it takes two-thirds.

The Appoggiatura looks very like the acciaccatura – the only difference being that it has no stroke going through the tail:

### (a) With ordinary and dotted notes

When the Appoggiatura 'leans upon' two tied notes, it usually takes the time value of the whole of the first note:

### (b) With tied notes

The Appoggiatura can also be combined with a chord, but it only affects the note to which it is attached:

### (c) With a chord

## 3. The turn
A Turn is an ornament consisting of the main note, the note above and the note below. If the sign is placed *above* the note, the turn must be played *instead* of the note – that is to say, it takes the whole value of the note:

If the sign is placed *after* the note, then the turn must be played *after* the note has been struck, and therefore takes half of its value:

As with the acciaccatura, the Turn can be combined with sharps or flats, etc.:

The Inverted Turn is similar to the Turn, except that it begins on the note *below* the main note, instead of on the main note or note above:

(The commonest sign)

(With three alternative signs for it)

## 4. The trill or shake

The Trill consists of the rapid alternation of the written note and the note above it:

Nowadays the Trill always begins on the written note. But in earlier times (up to and including early Beethoven) it generally began on the note above:

If, nowadays, the composer wishes the Trill to begin on the upper note, he adds an acciaccatura to the sign:

The Trill usually ends on the written note, and this may involve adding a triplet or quintuplet as a finishing touch:

Some writers indicate the Turn in their notation, thus:

or even

The number of alternating notes played in a Trill must depend upon the speed of the music and the taste of the performer. If the music is fast, then there may only be time to insert a turn, even though a trill is written in the notation:

Sharps and flats, etc., are shown like this:

A Trill is often indicated with a wavy line and the abbreviation 'tr':

# Interpretation

## 1. Signs for loudness and softness

| *pp*<br>pianissimo<br>or<br>very soft | *p*<br>piano<br>or<br>soft | *mp*<br>mezzo piano<br>or<br>moderately soft | *mf*<br>mezzo forte<br>or<br>moderately loud | *f*<br>forte<br>or<br>loud | *ff*<br>fortissimo<br>or<br>very loud |
|---|---|---|---|---|---|

Some composers have also used *ppp*, *pppp*, *fff*, and *ffff* – more, perhaps, to frighten performers into reacting positively than actually expecting that degree of loudness or softness.

Here are two very important signs:

*Crescendo*, i.e. increasing gradually in power.

*Decrescendo*, or *Diminuendo*, i.e. decreasing or diminishing gradually in power.

## 4. Various uses of the curved line

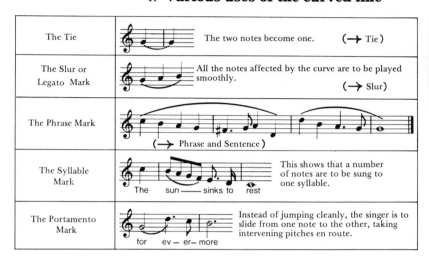

| The Tie | | The two notes become one. (→ Tie) |
|---|---|---|
| The Slur or Legato Mark | | All the notes affected by the curve are to be played smoothly. (→ Slur) |
| The Phrase Mark | | (→ Phrase and Sentence) |
| The Syllable Mark | | This shows that a number of notes are to be sung to one syllable. |
| The Portamento Mark | | Instead of jumping cleanly, the singer is to slide from one note to the other, taking intervening pitches en route. |

## 2. Staccato marks

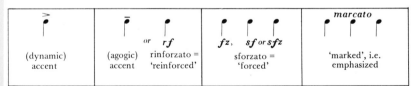

| | MEZZO-STACCATO<br>(shorten the notes by about ¼) | STACCATO<br>(shorten the notes by about ½) | STACCATISSIMO<br>(shorten the notes by about ¾) |
|---|---|---|---|
| Written | | | |
| Played (Approx.) | | | |

## 3. Accentuation signs

| (dynamic) accent | (agogic) accent | *or* *rf*<br>rinforzato = 'reinforced' | *fz*, *sf* or *sfz*<br>sforzato = 'forced' | *marcato*<br>'marked', i.e. emphasized |
|---|---|---|---|---|

The 'dynamic' accent implies a sharp attack at the very start of the note. The 'agogic' accent means a lingering pressure all through the note. (→ **Agogic**)

# Useful abbreviations

## 1. Repeat marks (for notes)

The following abbreviations are often used in orchestral scores:

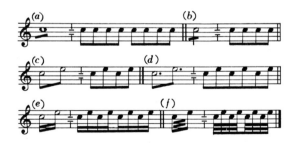

If the word *Tremolo* (or *Trem.*) is added, the notes must be repeated very rapidly and not measured out as strict quavers, etc.

## 2. Repeat marks (for passages)

| 𝄇 means return to 𝄆 or, if that does not occur, to the beginning of the composition. | *D.C.* or *Da Capo*, literally 'From the head', i.e. return to the beginning. | *D.S.* or *Dal Segno* i.e. from the sign, meaning return to the mark 𝄋 | *A.S.* (rare) *or Al Segno*, i.e. to the sign. Usually the expression is *D.C. al Segno e poi la Coda* i.e. 'From the beginning to the 𝄋 and then the Coda'. | *Bis* means perform the passage twice. |
|---|---|---|---|---|

When a complete figure, or a whole bar has to be repeated exactly, the following signs are useful:

When a whole section has to be repeated, two 'endings' must be provided. The first leads neatly back to the beginning of the section, and the second either leads on to the next section or provides a satisfactory final ending. This is shown by the figure 1, for the first ending, and 2 for the second:

When only part of a complete section is to be repeated, the word *Fine* ('end') shows the performer where to stop.

### 3. **Octave signs**

| *8va* or *8* | *8va bassa / 8va sotto* | *loco* | *con 8* |
|---|---|---|---|
| 'Ottava', i.e. perform an 8ve higher than written. | Perform an 8ve lower than written ('sotto' = under). | 'Place', i.e. (after playing an 8ve higher or lower) resume the playing as written. | Play the passage not in single notes, as marked, but in octaves.[1] |

[1] The added line of 8ves will be above if the passage is in the treble of a pianoforte piece, and below if it is in the bass.

### 4. **Pause signs**

| ⌢ Pause | *lunga pausa* long pause | *G.P.* 'General Pause' — an indication in an orchestral score that the whole orchestra is silent. |
|---|---|---|

# Signs in piano music

### 1. **Arpeggios**

Written        Played

If the wavy line is not continuous, the arpeggio must be played by both hands simultaneously:

### 2. **Left and right hands**

| L.H. Left Hand Linke Hand (German) | M.S. Mano Sinistra (Italian) | M.G. Main Gauche (French) | R.H. Right Hand Rechte Hand (German) | M.D. Mano Destra (Italian) or Main Droite (French) |
|---|---|---|---|---|

# How to write music

### 1. **Clefs**

a. Remember that the Treble Clef (or G Clef) curls around *the second line from the bottom* (making it the G line). Do not curl it round any other lines:

b. Remember, too, that the Bass Clef (or F Clef) curls around *the second line from the top* (making it the F line). And do not forget the two dots, one on each side of that line:

c. Remember that the Alto Clef (or C Clef) curls around the *middle* line (making it the C line).

or    *etc.*

### 2. **Leger lines**

a. On upper leger lines notes on spaces have the lines *under* them:

b. On lower leger lines notes on spaces have the lines *over* them:

### 3. Key signatures

a. Learn on which lines and spaces the sharps and flats are written in the Treble Clef:

b. Then remember that in the Bass Clef they take *just the same shape as in the Treble Clef*, the two signatures running parallel, so to speak:

### 4. Accidentals

a. Remember that, though in words we say, 'F sharp', 'B flat', etc., when writing in notation we put 'Sharp F', 'Flat B', etc. That is, all accidentals (sharps, flats, naturals, etc.) are placed *before their notes:*

b. If after an accidental the same note, *in the same octave*, recurs in the same bar we do not, of course, need to repeat the accidental:

(All those E's are understood to be flattened.)
If a note that has been given an accidental occurs in another octave in the same bar, then an accidental must be added to the second note as well as the first:

c. The DOUBLE-SHARP sign is a single sign

(×), whereas the DOUBLE-FLAT sign is a double sign (♭♭):

d. To reduce a double-sharp or double-flat to a single sharp or single flat it is best to write as follows:

e. To reduce a double-sharp or double-flat to a natural it is best to write as follows:

f. Be careful to make all sharps, flats, double sharps, and naturals exactly as they are printed above. Do not 'scamp' them, and be especially careful that your ♯ and ♮ do not resemble one another. And place all these signs clearly on their proper lines and in their proper spaces — not a little above or below these, as is often carelessly done.

### 5. 'Stems up or stems down: Stems to right or stems to left'

a. The general rule is: Notes *below* the middle line have their stems up; Notes *above* the middle line have their stems down; notes *on* the middle line follow the fashion of their companions:

b. But if there are passages of which the stems of the notes are joined, we may have to depart from this rule and to go by the majority, so as not to break the join:

c. The above refers to the cases where there is merely one 'part' to a stave. When, as in hymn-tunes for instance, there are two parts on a stave they have to be made distinct from one another by turning the stems of the upper part up and those of the lower part down. In the following, for instance, we see Soprano and Alto parts on one stave and Tenor and Bass parts on the other:

d. Up-stems are usually placed to the right of the note, and down-stems to the left. The hooks to the stems are always placed on the right-hand side:

## 6. Rests

a. The semibreve rest and minim rest are (in ordinary circumstances) placed in the top space but one, the semibreve hanging from the upper shelf (so to speak) and the minim lying on the lower shelf:

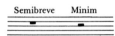

b. The crotchet and quaver rests have their heads in that same space – the crotchet rest turning to the right and the quaver rest to the left:

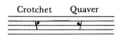

The usual printed crotchet rest is not easy to imitate by hand, but a little experiment may help you to find a reasonable approximation.

c. The semiquaver rest, demisemiquaver rest, etc., are like the quaver rest but with extra heads added in the spaces below:

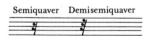

## 7. Ties and dots

a. We can lengthen a note by half by dotting it, or lengthen it by three-quarters by double-dotting it, *and we can do the same with a rest*. We can also lengthen a note by tying another note or other notes to it, but *we never use ties with rests*:

b. Be careful to put dots *in spaces*, not on lines, where they would not be so clearly seen.

   If the note to be dotted is in a space, put the dot in that space. If it is on a line, put the dot in the space above.

## 8. **The pause sign**

This can be placed either over or under the stave, but in the case of notes with tails is generally placed against the head:

## 9. **Time signatures**

Time signatures should be written so that the figures lie on either side of the middle line of the stave:

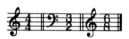

## 10. **Making the beats clear**

a. In writing music we should always try to *avoid confusing the performer as to where the beats fall*. Here is a simple example:

But never as follows:

which would give the idea of compound duple time, instead of simple triple. On the other hand, we should write:

Not:

It will be realized that the last example gives the idea of simple triple time, instead of compound duple.

b.  Here are some more examples:

(In the last four examples the three 'good' ones divide the bar into its *natural halves*, each with its accent, whilst the 'bad' example conceals the halves.) ( → **Notes and notation**)

c.  With RESTS, too, we have to be careful to guide the eye correctly:

The second example is bad because it not only hides the second and third beats, but disguises the fact that the third beat is a strong one.

d.  There is, however, no objection to the following:

Here there is no disturbance of the division of the bar into two halves, each with its accent.

e.  So in a COMPOUND TIME we may have:

Or:

Or:

The principle is always the same: to show the beats, or the main divisions of the bar as clearly as possible, so that the performer can tell exactly where he is.

11.  **The whole-bar rest**

a.  The semibreve rest is not only a rest of a semibreve value; we also use it as a WHOLE-BAR REST, whatever the value of the bar (which may be that of a semibreve, or less, or greater):

b.  There is one exception to the above – in 4/2 time, where the bar amounts to exactly the value of a breve, we use the breve rest:

# The music manuscript

Unless you are a composer, hastily jotting down a rough score *entirely for your own benefit*, you must assume that a piece of manuscript music is to be read by someone else with a view to performance. It is therefore essential that what you write should be clearly legible. It is worth spending a great deal of time and thought on this matter, and practising – as carefully as you did when you first learned to write. What you end up with may not be as perfect as a printed score (indeed, it is better not to imitate the printed style slavishly), but it is well within anyone's powers to write a manuscript that is easy and pleasant to read. Here are a few tips:

1.  **The nib**
This is partly a matter of taste, but the nib you choose must be capable of making thick lines *and* thin lines. You will find the OSMIROID range of nibs at any good stationers. Try an *Italic Straight*. You will

find it is better to *dip* the pen in ink rather than use it as a fountain pen: for in this way it is easier to control the flow of ink. Pencils, biros and felt-tip pens should only be used for private sketches.

## 2. **The ink**

Always use a good quality black ink, capable of making a nice solid effect. Some 'black' inks dry out as grey, and these are not satisfactory. Again it is a matter of taste and experiment. Both Quink and Pelikan make a useful permanent black ink. Indian ink is rather difficult to control and calls for special pens.

## 3. **The paper**

A good quality *white* paper is best, with a smooth surface that will not trip the pen. Your local music shop will advise you. Always use the size of paper that suits the job in hand. For example, an orchestral score written on the kind of large twelve stave paper normally used for piano music always looks rather silly. Manuscript paper can be bought in a variety of shapes and sizes, so it is worth investigating the possibilities.

## 4. **Bits and pieces**

You will need a decent ruler, with a bevelled edge (look along it and make sure it is straight!); erasers (the typist's pencil-shaped eraser can be very useful); blotting paper; and a smooth surface on which to work – one with a slope is best of all, as it helps you avoid backache and smudges. A clean adhesive paste may also come in handy if you prefer to correct any mistakes by sticking a small piece of specially trimmed manuscript paper over the offending passage. Don't use a very wet glue for this, as it will spoil the surface on the other side of the paper and make your ink run.

## 5. **Making the shapes**

Note heads should be slightly oval. They must be absolutely central on the line or in the space. Try to make the stem and the head without taking the nib from the paper. For a note with an upward stem, start with the stem. For a note with a downward stem, start with the head. Here, greatly magnified, is the kind of direction your pen will travel:

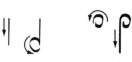

Stems and heads *must* be joined. Nothing looks worse, or is more difficult to read, than this kind of thing:

Plan each bar (and each page) carefully. However many notes there are, the bar should look balanced. It is much more difficult to grasp the musical sense of this:

than this:

Rule your bar lines, but plan in advance where you are going to need them. It is better to put them in as you write the notes – though you can safely pencil them in, very lightly, in advance.

If you have a page which has several sets of staves (as in piano music, for example) try not to put the bar lines of one set immediately underneath the bar lines of the set above – otherwise the eye will run them together and see columns up and down the page.

Take special care over leger lines and make sure they are in proper relation to one another. For example, this is wrong:

but this is right:

When writing rests, make sure the hooks go *in* the spaces, and not across the lines.

Be very careful not to make the natural look like a sharp, and vice versa. The natural is made up of two pen strokes:

$$♭ + ¬ = ♮$$

The sharp needs four:

$$‖ + = = ♯$$

The flat, of course, is simply a rather pointed b: ♭ .

**A** in Italian (or **à** in French) has several meanings, such as 'at', 'by', 'with', 'in', 'in the manner of'. Various expressions beginning in this way will be found throughout this book, placed alphabetically according to the main word.

In musical scores the direction '*a 2*' (It. *a due*, 'by twos') has two precisely opposite meanings. Only the context in which it is used will make the meaning clear, thus:

1. Where music for a whole group of voices or instruments is written on one stave (as, for example, in choral music, or music for the string section of an orchestra) and single notes are replaced by double notes, '*a 2*' means that the performers must divide into two equal groups, each taking one note.
2. Where a single stave is used for two instruments of the same kind (for example, Clarinets 1 and 2), '*a 2*' means that they must play in unison. If only one is to play, the direction is *1* or *Solo*.

**A.B.A.** One of the formulas used to describe musical forms. Each letter stands for a section of the music. In this case the first section (**A**) is repeated at the end, after something new (**B**) has happened in the middle. This form is known as TERNARY which means 'three part'.

Working on the same principle, other formulas can indicate BINARY form (**A.B.**), RONDO (**A.B.A.C.A.D.A.**), and so forth. When a section is repeated in a way that is slightly varied the letter may be modified thus: **A.B.A**¹.

**Abbandono** (It.) Passionately. Used to indicate that the music must be played in a free, impassioned style.

**Abel, Karl Friedrich** German composer, 1723–87. He was a pupil of J. S. Bach, but settled in London as a viola da gamba player. In 1762 he joined forces with J. C. Bach and together they successfully promoted concerts for twenty years. His sonatas, symphonies and concertos are still sometimes performed.

**Abendlied** (Ger.) Evening song. *Abend* is German for 'Evening'.

**Abendmusik** (Ger.) Evening music. A term that describes the evening performances of serious music that became popular at the Protestant church of Lübeck in North Germany (under the direction of Buxtehude) from 1673, and continued into the 19th century.

**Absolute music** (or **abstract music**) Music that has been composed simply as music and not to represent any imaginary picture or story, etc. Music which does attempt to represent such things we call **Programme music →**.

**Absolute pitch** The sense which some people possess which enables them to name any note they hear, or sing it without first hearing it played. Though many great musicians have been born with this gift, it is not an essential requirement. What is important is a sense of *relative pitch* – the ability to recognize notes *in relation to each other*. Thus if you are told what C is, you can automatically sing G or D or any other note.

It is very important to cultivate the sense of relative pitch, and this can be done by careful practice. The sense of absolute pitch can sometimes be a nuisance, especially if you are required to sing or play with an instrument that is tuned slightly too high or low.

Many people acquire a sense of absolute pitch for certain notes. A violinist, for example, who always tunes to the note 'A' can often do this from memory. You may find you can remember accurately the pitch of a well-known tune which is usually played in the same key – such as *God save the Queen*, which is mostly sung in G major.

**Abstract music** Another name for **Absolute music →**.

**A Cappella → Cappella**

**Accelerando** (It.) Accelerating (getting gradually quicker). Also **accelerato**.

**Accent → Rhythm** and **Agogic**. For accent signs **→ Notes and notation**.

**Karl Friedrich Abel**
1723-1787 He had unusual skill as a player of the viola da gamba and was one of the last great players of that instrument. This pastel drawing of the composer is by Thomas Gainsborough.

**Acciaccatura → Notes and notation.**

**Accidental** The name given to a sharp (♯), flat, (♭) natural (♮), etc, which for the moment contradicts the key-signature. For instance, in the key of C an F sharp would be an accidental.

An accidental, if not contradicted, holds good not only for the particular note before which it is placed but also for any further appearances of that note in the same bar— that is, of that *very same* note (not of that note in another octave). Sometimes, however, composers help performers by repeating the accidental in brackets, just as a tactful reminder.

When the last note in a bar has an accidental and happens to be tied to the first note in the next bar, the accidental applies to both notes. (→ **Notes and notation**)

**Accompaniment** This cartoon by Hoffnung shows one of the hazards of the piano accompanist's job.

**Accompaniment** When a song or an instrumental work has a part for a pianist to play, we call the piano part the accompaniment, and the pianist the accompanist. Sometimes the accompaniment is for some instrument other than the piano, or for several instruments, or for a whole orchestra.

It is a mistake to think that the accompaniment is unimportant. Often it is just as interesting and just as difficult to play as the solo part itself – and in any case, the one is useless without the other.

In the same way the art of accompanying is a very difficult one since it depends upon the ability to give and take – in other words to provide the soloist with a sensitive support that positively helps his interpretation, and yet know the precise moment when to take the lead.

# Accordion (Piano accordion)

A portable free-reed (→ **Free-reed**) instrument invented in Germany in about 1822. It consists of a pair of bellows with a keyboard fixed to the righthand end and, nowadays, a series of buttons on the left. The player squeezes the two ends together and draws them apart, thus operating the bellows, while at the same time pressing the keys and buttons. These open a series of valves and allow air to pass over a set of metal reeds. Each key sounds two notes – one when the bellows are squeezed together, the other when they are drawn apart. The buttons enable the player to sound complete chords to accompany the tune being played on the keyboard.

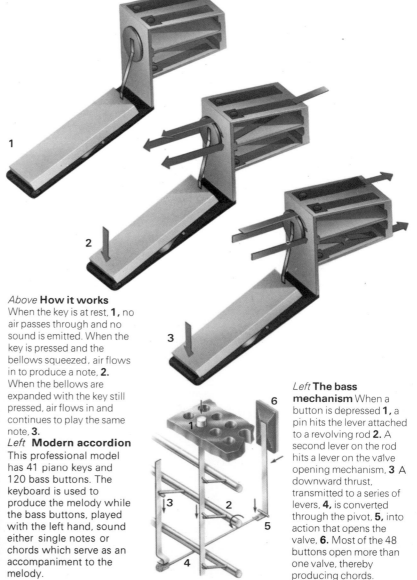

*Above* **How it works**
When the key is at rest, **1,** no air passes through and no sound is emitted. When the key is pressed and the bellows squeezed, air flows in to produce a note, **2.** When the bellows are expanded with the key still pressed, air flows in and continues to play the same note, **3.**

*Left* **Modern accordion**
This professional model has 41 piano keys and 120 bass buttons. The keyboard is used to produce the melody while the bass buttons, played with the left hand, sound either single notes or chords which serve as an accompaniment to the melody.

*Left* **The bass mechanism** When a button is depressed **1,** a pin hits the lever attached to a revolving rod **2.** A second lever on the rod hits a lever on the valve opening mechanism, **3** A downward thrust, transmitted to a series of levers, **4,** is converted through the pivot, **5,** into action that opens the valve, **6.** Most of the 48 buttons open more than one valve, thereby producing chords.

# Acoustics

Acoustics is the science of sound. It is therefore an important aspect of music – for music, scientifically speaking, is the creation and arrangement of sounds.

### The nature of sound

Every sound, from the whisper of the breeze to the roar of a great waterfall, from the hum of a bee to the whine of a circular saw, from the whistling of an errand boy to the climax of a great opera, reaches our ears as the result of changes in the pressure of the air around us. These changes, however, are minute. For example, the change of pressure corresponding to the *loudest* sound the ears can stand is no more than you would get from a bicycle pump if you pushed the plunger an inch.

The important point about these pressure changes is that they travel from place to place as 'waves' in the air. You will probably have played the game with dominoes in which you stand them on end, fairly close together, in a line. When you knock down the first, the rest fall down in turn. This is how a wave works. Each domino has only moved a small amount, yet *something* has travelled from one end of the line to the other. In sound, that 'something' is the pressure change.

However, pressure changes do not simply travel in one straight line. They spread out in every possible direction. Moreover, just as it took a definite time for the movement of

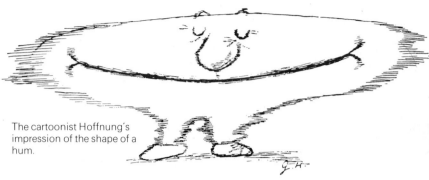

The cartoonist Hoffnung's impression of the shape of a hum.

the dominoes to travel along the line, so it takes time for sound to travel. Sound waves travel at about 330 metres per second (about 740 miles per hour). Light waves travel about a million times faster, and so, for example, you see a flash of lightning long before you hear the crack of thunder.

### Measuring musical sounds

There are a great many ways in which sounds can be measured, but perhaps the most useful in trying to understand the connections between sound waves and music is the cathode-ray oscilloscope. This has a screen rather like a television set. A spot of light travels from one side of the screen to the other in a straight line. If the pressure changes in a sound wave are changed into varying electric currents (by being fed through a microphone), these currents can be used to move the spot of light up and down on the screen and so draw a graph of the pressure changes (right).

**How a sound wave works** From the initial impetus the movement of sound waves continues ad infinitum, like these dominoes, with little resistance. Sound waves are conducted by air until dissipated by distance from the sound source or by meeting with an obstacle.

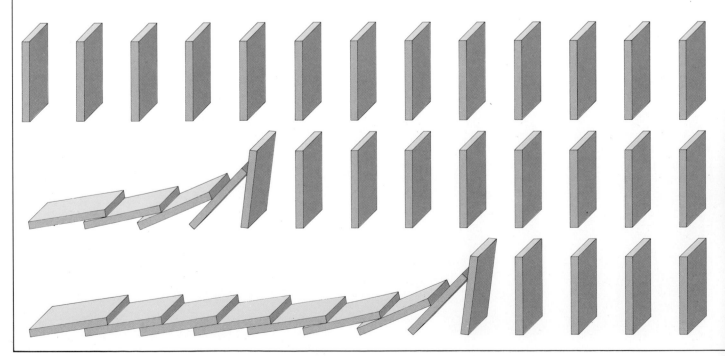

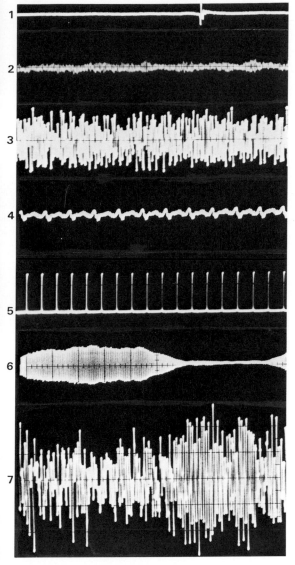

**Oscilloscope readings**
The screen shows a straight line with one bleep at regular intervals when the device is waiting to be fed sound signals, **1**. The regular cycles of a breeze, **2**, are smaller than those of the louder, therefore deeper, patterned waterfall, **3**. The regular beats of a bee's wings, **4**, and the whine of a circular saw, **5**, have a definite pitch. The trace for the whistling boy **6**, and the opera, **7**, show an irregular pattern indicating variations of pitch.

Consider, however, the pressure changes made by the three pairs of sounds mentioned at the beginning of this article. The *size* of the pressure change for the waterfall is greater than that of the breeze – for the sound is much *louder*. But in both instances the *kind* of change is irregular. This is because the sound of the breeze and the waterfall is entirely non-musical.

Again the larger variations correspond to the louder sound, but now the variations are regular. This is because the bee's wings beat regularly, at about 200 times a second, and the teeth of the saw hit the wood regularly, at about 360 times a second. The sounds are not exactly musical, but they do have a *definite pitch*. In fact, whenever pressure changes are regular there is a definite pitch. The faster the changes occur, the higher the pitch goes. If we double the rate of change (the 'frequency'), our ears

tell us that the pitch goes up one whole octave. The circular saw therefore produces a note of higher pitch than the bee.

Finally, we have the graphs for the whistling boy and the opera. The whistle graph is quite regular, but there is a change in the middle which corresponds to the different notes of the tune. For the opera there are a great many notes happening at once (from the voices and instruments of the orchestra). Each is regular in itself, but when they are all added together the result is something of a jumble.

It is at this point that the most remarkable thing of all takes place. Our ears and brains can actually disentangle the jumble, so that we can hear not only the combined effect of voices and orchestra, but every individual sound as well!

## Making musical sounds

If we wish to make *musical* sounds, the changes in the air pressure must be *regular*. In most musical instruments this regularity is achieved by making something vibrate. The string of a guitar or violin vibrates regularly back and forth when plucked or bowed; the air in the pipe of a recorder or clarinet vibrates up and down when it is blown. But how do we get notes of *different* pitch?

There are three basic ways. We can use a separate vibrator for each note. Each vibrator will be different in size and shape. This is how the notes of a harp, a piano, an organ, or a xylophone are produced. Or we can use a limited number of vibrators and make changes to them while we are actually playing. For example, in woodwind instruments we change the length of the air that is vibrating by opening and closing holes in the side of the tube. In stringed instruments we alter the length of the string that is vibrating by pressing our fingers down at different points along its length. The third way is a bit more complicated and is used by brass instruments. It involves blowing harder and tightening the lips, and thus changing the pattern (or 'mode') of vibration inside the pipe and so changing the pitch.

## The effect of the surroundings

When we listen to music in a concert hall, the sound we hear is influenced by the 'acoustic properties' of the hall itself. Sound waves, as we know, travel in every possible

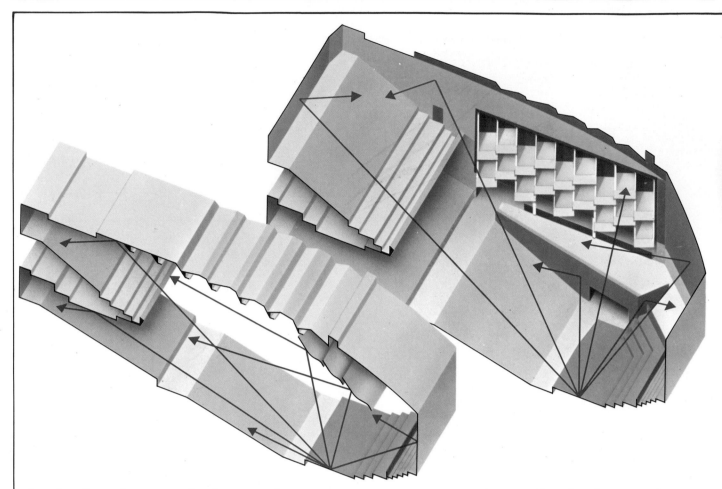

direction from the source. In the open air they spread out over a wide area, gradually losing their energy as they go. If we are too far away, the sound waves will not reach us. In a concert hall, however, we can hear everything quite clearly because the walls and the ceiling prevent the waves from spreading out indefinitely. Some of them are absorbed by the materials of the building, and therefore lose much of their energy; but others are reflected back again towards us with very little loss.

This is where the problem lies. Soft furnishings, such as carpets and curtains, upholstered seats and human bodies, all tend to absorb sound waves. Hard surfaces, such as walls and ceilings, metal and glass, all tend to reflect them. A concert hall that absorbed most of the sound waves would feel very 'dead'. But one that reflected sound waves too readily would seem far too 'alive' – the sounds would become mixed up, and we would say that that hall was too 'reverberant' for music to be heard clearly.

The designer of a concert hall must therefore choose the materials very carefully so as to achieve a balance between too much reflection and too much absorption. He

**Modern concert hall** This diagram is based on London's Royal Festival Hall. The design makes use of an angled suspended ceiling, suspended deflectors and boxes set at a particular angle to the supporting walls to direct sound from the orchestra dais to the auditorium with as little distortion as possible.

must also consider the shapes and curvatures of the surfaces (particularly those near the players), for they will act like mirrors and influence the direction in which the sound waves are reflected.

Unfortunately, we expect our concert halls to be used for many different kinds of music-making. The kind of acoustic that suits a solo singer is different from that which is appropriate to a whole orchestra. In trying to satisfy every musical demand, the designer faces an almost insoluble problem.

### The quality of musical sounds
Why do instruments sound different from each other? And what is the difference between good and bad instruments? Here are three clues that go some way towards answering these difficult questions.

First look at the graphs of the pressure variations for a recorder, a violin, and a clarinet (opposite page, left). Each is playing a steady note. Notice that although each is quite regular and repeats at a constant rate (thus giving a constant pitch), the actual *pattern* of pressure changes is different. This is one of the important

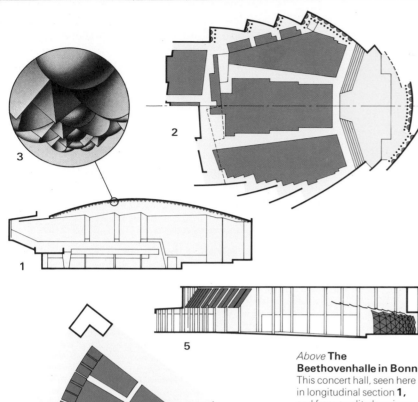

factors, and it depends on the kind of vibrator used to make the sound.

Now look at the graphs for a piano, a violin, and a trumpet (below, right) . The spot of light has been slowed down so that we can see the changes that occur in the first one and a half seconds of playing. The piano starts very steeply, and then dies away. The violin starts more slowly, but stays fairly steady. The trumpet has a sort of 'bulge' before it settles down.

Our ears are very sensitive to this kind of difference, and so the first 1/10 sec or so of a note can give very important information about the instrument. This is one reason why the 'attack' at the beginning of a note is so important and often very difficult for players to get right. In the same way, the *consonants* we use in speaking or singing can often give us more clues about the word than the vowels. For example, the words '*c*od', '*r*od', '*n*od', '*g*od' depend entirely on the first consonant for their different meanings.

Nearly all instruments have at least two parts: something that creates the vibrations in the first place, and something that makes them larger and more effective as sound waves. For example, strings on their own would be very quiet. They need the body of the guitar or violin to amplify the sound waves. The reed of a clarinet is very squeaky and unstable. It needs a pipe to give it stability and make the vibrations longer. But these partnerships must be carefully planned. The body of a violin must treat every note in the same way. In a bad violin some notes are louder than others, regardless of how the performer plays. Instrument makers therefore try to design the whole instrument so that the partnership works smoothly and uniformly at all pitches. This is why instrument-making is an art. ( → **Harmonics**)

*Above* **The Beethovenhalle in Bonn** This concert hall, seen here in longitudinal section **1,** and from a split plan view, **2,** was completed in 1955 and seats 1,387 people. A remarkable feature of the design is the suspended 'egg crate' ceiling, **3,** comprising 1,760 elements to both scatter and absorb sound. The colours indicate structure (light blue), stage (yellow), acoustic devices (red) and audience seating (red-mauve) *Left* **Tanglewood Music Shed in Lennox, Massachusetts** This fan-shaped auditorium, **4,** holds 6,000 listeners. An additional 6,000 can be seated on the lawns outside and hear the music through the partly open sides of the Shed, **5.** The orchestra and part of the hall are enclosed in an acoustic canopy. The colour coding here is as above.

**Sound quality** Different instruments produce different sounds for a number of reasons. One depends on the kind of vibrator used to make the sound. The violin, for example, makes use of strings, the clarinet of a single reed, **1.** The bodies of the instruments amplify the sound and produce the different reverberations noticeable in the first few seconds of playing, in this example, a piano, violin and a trumpet, **2.**

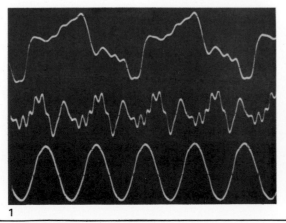

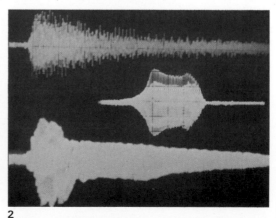

**Acoustic guitar** → **Guitar**

**Acute** A word often used as meaning 'high' in pitch.

**Adagietto** (It.) Slowish. Not quite so slow as *adagio*. It can also mean a short movement in Adagio tempo.

**Adagio** (It.) Slow. (Literally 'at ease' *ad agio*.) Also used as the title of a slow composition. For example, Mozart's Adagio and Allegro in F minor (K.594), for mechanical organ.

 **Adagissimo** means 'very slow'.

**Added sixth chord** This is a frequently-used chord consisting of the chord of the subdominant with the interval of a sixth added to it. In the keys of C major and minor it is as follows (the chords marked × ):

The root of the chords shown above is considered to be D, so that they are really first inversions of the chord of the seventh upon the supertonic (D-F-A-C and D-F-A♭-C).

**Additive rhythms** The kind of rhythm that does not stick to a regular beat that can be measured out in bars of equal length, but cheerfully adds or subtracts a note or two when needed. Patterns that have to be notated as 3/8, 2/4, 5/8, 6/8, 7/8, 3/8 etc, are common. Examples can be found in the music of Stravinsky, Bartók, Michael Tippett, etc., as well as in certain types of folk music.

**Ad libitum** (Lat.) At pleasure. Usually shortened to 'Ad lib'. In music it means that the performer can do one of the following things:

1. Vary discreetly from the proper tempo or the strict rhythm, if so inclined.
2. Omit or include (according to the resources available) the music for some voice or instrument over whose part these words are printed.
3. Omit or include the passage so marked, as preferred.
4. Add a **cadenza** → at the point indicated, if so inclined.

**A due corde** → **Due corde**

**Æolian harp** Æolus, in Greek mythology, was the God of the Winds. So an Æolian harp means one played by the wind. We do not see

# Aerophone

Any instrument whose sound is produced by the vibration of a column of air – everything from a penny whistle to a church organ. Such instruments are classified according to the way in which the vibrations are generated – as, for example, by blowing across a hole (flute), through a reed (oboe), into a cup-shaped mouthpiece (horn), etc. The following instruments, all described in this book, are aerophones: Accordion, Bagpipe, Bassoon, Clarinet, Concertina, Crumhorn, Euphonium, Flute, Harmonium, Horn, Mouth organ, Oboe, Organ, Rackett, Recorder, Saxophone, Serpent, Shawm, Trombone, Trumpet, Tuba.

**Aerophone mouthpiece**
A blow hole, **1**, or whistle mouthpiece, **2**, causes air to vibrate against a sharp edge. In the cup type, **3**, air vibrates by action of the player's lips. In a tube, vibrations can be produced through single, **4**, double, **5**, or free, **6**, reeds. **7**, is a free aerophone.

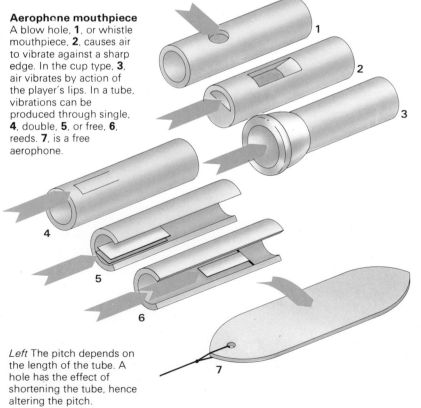

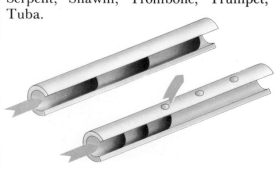

*Left* The pitch depends on the length of the tube. A hole has the effect of shortening the tube, hence altering the pitch.

such harps now, but at one time they were fairly common. They were flat boxes with strings stretched over them, and people used to hang them up outside or put them on their window-ledges. Then when the wind blew it made the strings sound and so there was a sort of pleasant music – without, of course, any tune to it.

**Æolian mode** → **Modes**

**Aerophone** → page 24

**Affections** The 'Doctrine of Affections' is a theory that was popular during the first half of the 18th century, especially in Germany. It held that the different human emotions and feelings (the 'affections') could be expressed through particular kinds of music. Thus, a slow melody in a minor key might express melancholy, while a brisk tune in the major would suggest joy. It was also believed that each movement of a work should only express one mood ('affect'). This belief in 'one emotion at a time' is quite different from the attitude adopted by composers in the second half of the century, where the idea of Sonata Form depends very much upon the contrast of different moods within a single movement.

**After-beat** is the term applied to the last

**Aeolian harp** Though simple to make, complicated forms of the instrument do exist, for example the Aeolians in Strasburg Cathedral.

two notes of a shake (→ **Ornaments and grace-notes**), that is, the 'lower auxiliary' and the principal note.

**Agiatamente** (It.) Comfortably, freely. Not to be confused with **agitatamente**. (→ **Agitato**)

**Agitato** (It.) Agitated. **Agitatamente** is the corresponding adverb 'agitatedly'.

**Agnus Dei** → **Mass**

**Agogic** This adjective describes a type of accent that occurs as part of the music's 'expressiveness'. For example, a sudden high note, or a sudden discord can give the feeling of an extra accent – the note or chord sticks out. Agogic accents are therefore different from the regular accents in music, as indicated by time signatures. These are known as DYNAMIC ACCENTS. (→ **Notes and notation**)

**Air** A tune or a song, or any simple melody. Though the word usually implies a piece of vocal music, it can also be used to describe instrumental music written in a simple melodious style. The Italian term *aria* has the same literal meaning, but arias are always much more elaborate than airs. (→ **Aria**)

# Air with variations

This is one of the oldest forms of European instrumental music. It was popular in England as long ago as the reign of Queen Elizabeth I and since then has been used by many great composers.

The composer takes a simple tune and then repeats it many times, each time making certain changes. Thus, in an Air and Variations for Piano, he may have one variation in which the tune is in the right hand and a running accompaniment in the left, with another in which the tune is in the left hand with a running accompaniment in the right. If the original tune is in a major key, he may make a minor variation.

As an illustration here is J. C. Bach's variations for piano on the British National Anthem, *God save the Queen*.

After giving out the tune just as it stands, Bach varies it in five different ways, and then closes with a short 'Coda'. These extracts are from the first and fifth variations.

Up to the end of the 18th century the way in which variations were composed was usually fairly straightforward, so that it is easy to recognize the original tune 'behind'

the variation. Later composers began to make their variations rather more elaborate, sometimes ignoring the complete tune and concentrating on one aspect of it – the first few notes, say, or a particular rhythm. Such variations wander away from the tune, yet are still obviously 'related' to it.

**Famous variations**
Handel's *Harmonious Blacksmith*, Beethoven's *Diabelli Variations*, Brahms's *Variations and Fugue on a theme by Handel*, and Britten's *Variations and Fugue on a theme of Henry Purcell*.

**Albéniz, Isaac** Spanish (Catalan) composer and pianist, 1860–1909. He appeared as a prodigy pianist at the age of four. At 13 he ran away to America, but gradually, after many adventures, made his way back to Europe to study in Leipzig, Brussels, and Budapest (under Liszt). He was much admired as a pianist, wrote several operas and a great deal of piano music (for example, the piano suites *Iberia* and *España*). His music was much influenced by folksong and was important in helping to establish a truly Spanish national style.

**Albert Hall, The Royal** → below

**Alberti bass** Named after a minor Italian composer, Domenico Alberti, who died in 1740, this is a type of bass that takes a chord and splits it up into a simple pattern of notes. The ear hears a complete chord, but the note-pattern provides a sense of movement:

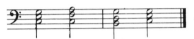

**Isaac Albéniz** 1860–1909

Alberti may not have invented the device, but he certainly over-used it in his harpsichord sonatas and thus ensured for himself a kind of immortality.

**Albinoni, Tommaso** Italian composer, 1671–1750. Born in Venice to wealthy parents, Albinoni had no need to earn a living from music. He wrote many fine concertos that are still played, and 48 operas, but is known to the general public for an *Adagio* that he did not in fact write.

**Alborada** (Spa.) Dawn. A piece to be played beneath somebody's window in the early morning. In Spain it was often played on a bagpipe (or oboe), accompanied by a small drum. (→ **Aubade**)

**Albumblatt** (Ger.) Album leaf. Originally a short piece of music written to go into an autograph book, but later used as a title for any short piece, usually for piano.

# The Royal Albert Hall

This great London concert hall was built on a site near to that of the Great Exhibition of 1851 (→ **Crystal Palace**). The Exhibition was the brain-child of Prince Albert, Queen Victoria's husband, and after his death in 1861 the concert hall was built in his memory. It was opened in 1871.

As it is a very large building many events other than concerts have taken place in it, including boxing matches, fancy dress balls, and political rallies. After the destruction of Queen's Hall in 1941, it became the home of Sir Henry Wood's Promenade Concerts. It holds about 10,000 people, and has a fine

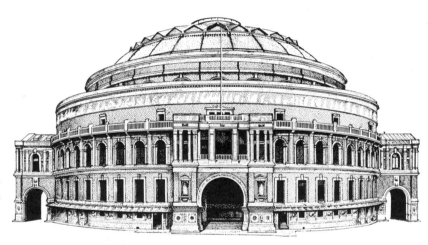

and appropriately large 19th–century organ. Because of its size and oval shape, the hall has suffered from acoustic problems (it has been said that in certain positions you could hear a concert twice over!), but these have largely been cured in recent years.

*Above* **The Royal Albert Hall** This view is from the Victoria and Albert Memorial, Kensington Gardens.

*Left* This engraving of 1871 shows the Hall's interior. The lowest level, without seating, is where promenaders now stand.

**Aldeburgh Festival** Founded by Benjamin Britten and his friends in 1948 in the small Suffolk coastal town which was his home. Though the annual festival revolves round his music, and strongly reflects his personality and taste, it is a showcase for English music generally and attracts artists of international repute. Concerts take place in halls and churches in and around Aldeburgh and in the magnificent concert hall and opera house built in 1967 at the Maltings, Snape.

**Aldeburgh Festival**
The Maltings Concert Hall at Snape, which is credited with near perfect acoustics.

**Aleatoric** A word derived from the Latin *alea* (a dice), used from about 1950 to describe music that deliberately allows a degree of chance during performance. No two performances of an aleatoric piece are therefore ever quite alike. For example, the performers may be given several short passages of music which they may play in any order – so that, like the dice player, no one knows exactly which section will turn up. The word INDETERMINACY, used by the American composer John Cage, describes a similar but even more extreme attitude to composition. For example, he has used several radio sets tuned at random to different stations and all playing simultaneously to create a piece of 'music'. The idea behind all this is the belief that any musical event, if it is made in a truly creative spirit, is just as valuable as music carefully thought out and written down. Music has always valued improvisation within certain limits, but aleatoric methods go far beyond this and try to make a virtue out of the totally unexpected.

**Alkan, Charles** French composer and pianist, 1813–1888. His real name was Morhange. He lived a very secluded life, but

# Allemande

A dance of German folk origin (the word means 'German') which became popular in the late 16th century and was later adopted as one of the main ingredients in 17th- and 18th-century dance suites. It is a processional dance in duple time, each phrase beginning on a quaver up-beat. In the following example the four crotchets (eighth-notes) are to be played *alla breve* (as two main beats in the bar).

There are various alternative spellings of the word: *Almain, Alman, Almayne,* for example; but these belong mostly to the 16th and 17th centuries – by the 18th, 'Allemande' is the most common.

**Allemande** This 18th-century French engraving shows the dancing of the allemande at a fashionable ball. It was the only German court dance to be taken up by other European courts until the arrival of the waltz. The dance was disapproved of by the American Puritans of New England and those wishing to learn it had to do so in secret. An echo of the dance remains today in the square-dance called 'allemande'

Henry Purcell

wrote a great deal of fine piano music – much of it extremely difficult to play. He died tragically, crushed to death when a bookcase fell on him.

**All', alla** (It.) To the, at the, on the, with the, or in the manner of.

**Alla breve** → **Breve 2**

**Allargando** (It.) Broadening. Indicates that the music must become fuller and more dignified, as well as slower. Compare with *rallentando*, which applies to speed alone.

**Allegretto** (It.) Fairly fast. Not quite so fast as *allegro*, but faster than *andante*.

**Allegro** (It.) Literally 'cheerful', but now used to indicate a quick tempo. Also used to describe a complete movement.

**Allemande** → page 27

**Alphabet pieces** Sometimes, as a tribute to a friend or in honour of another musician, composers have written pieces of music based on notes which spell out that person's name. For example, because our B natural is called H in German, and our B flat is called plain B, pieces have been made out of the following:

Schumann's Op. 1 is named *Variations for the Pianoforte on the name 'Abegg'. Dedicated to Miss Pauline, Countess Abegg* (not really a countess, by the way). The theme is as follows:

More recently, Shostakovich has used the notes D, E flat, C and B to spell out **D.S.C.H.** (the initial letter of his first name, Dmitri, and the opening of the Russian spelling of his surname). It occurs in the scherzo and finale movements of his Tenth Symphony (1953), and again in all the movements of his Eighth String Quartet (1960), which is meant to be autobiographical.

**Alphorn** A wind instrument played by the peasants of the Swiss Alps to call their cattle home. Its length is anything from two to four

metres. Only simple tunes can be played as it has few notes at its command.

**Al Segno** (It.) 'To the Sign' – that is, to the sign :𝄋:. It is used in two senses:
1. 'Go *back* to the sign' and start again from there. (→ **Useful abbreviations**)
2. 'Go *forward* with the performance until you see the sign', and then stop.

G in alt.   G in altissimo

**Alt (1).** High. **Altissimo** means 'very high'. These words are generally used in reference to music for the soprano voice. We speak, for instance, of '*G in alt*' or '*G in altissimo*'.

All the notes between these two G's are spoken of as '*In alt*' ('*A in alt*', '*A♯ in alt*', '*B in alt*', etc.), and all those above the second G are spoken of, similarly, as '*In altissimo*'.

Of course sopranos who can sing '*In altissimo*' notes are very rare, but Mozart in 1770 said that he had heard the famous Italian opera singer Lucrezia Aguiari end a passage on the '*C in altissimo*', that is, 5 semitones above the G shown on the left. (→ **Helmholtz**)

**2.** The word **alt** has also another meaning. It is the German for the alto (or contralto) voice and when it is applied to instruments it means that their range is more or less the range of that voice. For instance the **altgeige** ('alto fiddle') is the viola.

**Alternativo** This word is sometimes found in old dance music, meaning a section in the middle of the piece, contrasting with the main section that comes before and after it.

A minuet usually has what is called a trio (see that word) as an alternativo, so that the order is minuet–trio–minuet again.

**Alto** (It.) High. Used to denote various types of human voice:
1. the lowest unbroken boy's voice
2. the lowest female voice (more often called Contralto)
3. the high male adult falsetto voice (not the same as the Counter-tenor).

The male alto is not a natural voice like the tenor or bass, but a falsetto (→ **Falsetto**) voice that has to be specially cultivated. It is in use in English cathedral and church choirs, and has been revived among singers who wish to perform madrigals, glees, and early part songs in an authentic manner.

**Alphorn** This is probably the largest of the Aerophones. Its range is one harmonic series, simple (like the bugle), but with a powerful tone. In Switzerland it attracts the attention not only of cattle but also tourists.

**Alto clef** → **Notes and notation**

**Alto Flute** → **Flute**

# American musical terms

Here are some terms which differ in their meaning as used in Great Britain and the United States respectively, so that British musicians reading American books and American musicians reading British books need to be aware of them.

| British | American |
|---|---|
| **1** Note (as used not only by British musicians today but throughout English literature – Chaucer, Shakespeare, etc.). | *Tone* (this creates some confusion for a British reader, since by Tone he understands the interval of 2 semitones). |
| **2** Tone and Semitone. | Sometimes the terms *Whole step* and *Half step* are used. |
| **3** Bar | *Measure* (sometimes also used by British musicians). |
| **4** Semibreve, Minim, Crotchet, Quaver, Semiquaver, Demisemiquaver. | *Whole-note, Half-note, Quarter-note, Eighth-note, Sixteenth-note, Thirty-second-note* (these practical names are being increasingly adopted in Great Britain). |
| **5** Natural (the sign contradicting a sharp or flat). | *Cancel* (an appropriate term) is sometimes used. |
| **6** To flatten and to sharpen. | *To lower* and *To raise, to flat* and *to sharp*. |
| **7** Organ. | Sometimes in America called *Pipe Organ*. |
| **8** Stave. | *Staff*. |
| **9** American Organ. | *Cabinet Organ*. |
| **10** Leader (chief First Violin of an orchestra). | *Concert Master*. |

**Amati family** This great family of violin-makers, of Cremona, in Italy, was active for nearly 200 years – from about 1550 to 1740. The most famous member of the family was Nicola (1596–1684), and his violins are very valuable nowadays.

The other two famous violin-making families of Cremona are those of **Guarneri** and **Stradivari** (→) and the founders of both learnt their craft in the workshop of Nicola Amati.

**Ambrosian chant** The collection of chants used in Milan Cathedral. Named after Saint Ambrose (c.340–97), who was Bishop of Milan, but composed after his death. They are not as old as **Gregorian chant** → .

**American organ → Harmonium**

**America the Beautiful** The poem of this national song was written in 1893 on the top of Pile's Peak, Colorado, by Katharine Lee Bates. Ten years later she re-wrote it in a simpler style. Very many tunes have been written for it – 60 at least. Of these the most widely known are, perhaps, those by Will C. Macfarlane and S. A. Ward.

**Amoroso** (It.) In a loving style.

**Anacrusis** An unstressed note, or group of notes at the beginning of a musical phrase – in other words, the 'upbeat'.

**Ancora** (It.) Still, yet. So *ancora forte* means 'still loud', whilst *ancora più forte* means 'Yet more loud'. The word is also used for 'Again',

**Amati** This violin by Hieronymous Amati was made in Cremona in 1618.

**Ambrosian chant** In this Gothic Cathedral of Milan the chant has been preserved since the 14th century and is still in use today.

that is, 'Repeat'.

(It will be seen that this word has the same meanings as the French *encore*.)

**Andante** From It. *andare*, 'to go'. It really means 'moving along' – that is, slowish but not slow (generally about 72 or 76 beats to a minute). **Andante con moto** indicates a speed rather quicker than mere *andante* (*con moto* = 'with motion'). **Andante sostenuto** indicates a speed rather slower than mere *andante* (*sostenuto* = 'sustained'). There is also a 'diminutive' of the word – **andantino**. This, usually, means *less slow* than *andante*, but unfortunately a few composers have used it as meaning *more slow*; thus the performer must be guided by the spirit of the music. The word *andantino* has also another 'diminutive' meaning. A slowish piece of music is sometimes given the title of 'Andante' (for example, Beethoven's 'Andante in F') and the word *andantino* is sometimes applied to a *short* Andante.

**Anfang** (Ger.) Beginning. **Anfangs** means 'at the beginning' and **wie anfänglich** 'as at the beginning'.

**Anglaise** This French word (which of course means 'English'), when used as a title for a composition, does not seem to have any very fixed meaning. The earliest 18th-century composers, such as Bach, use the term for a piece in some sort of dance style – sometimes like a hornpipe and sometimes like a country dance, or something similar (generally fairly bright and lively).

# Anglican chant

Since the time of the Reformation, the Anglican Church (the 'Church of England') has used short harmonized melodies for chanting the Psalms and Canticles. These melodies are repeated for each verse of the text and are sung by the choir in four-part harmony, with the congregation joining in with the melody.

The texts themselves, however, do not have lines of an equal length. The number of syllables in each line varies, therefore. To allow for this, the first note of each musical phrase is treated as a 'Reciting Note' – that is to say, it can be used to sing as many syllables as need be, before the singers pass on to complete the chant (and the text) in strict time, with one syllable, usually, for each of the remaining notes.

There are SINGLE CHANTS and DOUBLE CHANTS (and, more rarely, Triple and Quadruple Chants). The Single Chant has 7 bars, split into two unequal sections of 3 and 4 bars. The Double Chant is twice the length (3 + 4 + 3 + 4).

Here is a Single Chant by Samuel Wesley. Reciting notes are marked R.N.:

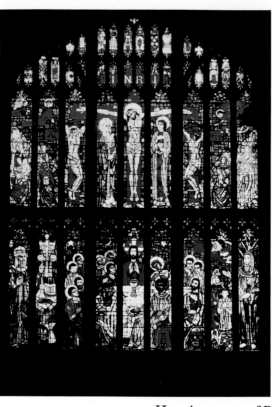

**Eton College Chapel**
Until the mid-19th century Anglican chant was heard mainly in collegiate churches, like this one, or in cathedrals. Today it is also used in some parish churches and a few village churches. In the hands of a good choir it can be very effective, but is considerably less successful with an untrained choir.

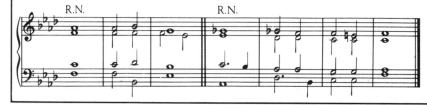

Here is a verse of Psalm 102, set out with appropriate bar lines to show how it would be fitted to Wesley's chant:

Hear my | prayer O | Lord ‖
And let my | crying | come unto | thee. ‖

The method of dividing up the words is known as 'pointing'.

**Anima** (It.) Soul. **Con anima** means 'with soul', in the sense of 'with emotion'. It should never be translated as 'with animation', although some composers have made this mistake.

The word *anima* is also used to describe the sound-post of a stringed instrument (→ **Sound-post**). The reason for this is that the sound-post connects the back and the belly of the instrument, and thus increases the tone quality. Without it, the sound would be lifeless – lacking in 'soul'.

**Animato** (It.) Animated, lively.

**Animo** (It.) Spirit, or boldness. Used mainly in the form *con animo* – 'with spirit'. **Animoso** means 'spirited'. The word is often confused with *anima* (see above).

**Anna Magdalena's Notebook** A collection of simple two-part keyboard pieces which Johann Sebastian Bach wrote in 1722 for his second wife, Anna Magdalena, to play. He made another collection, which includes vocal pieces, in 1725.

**Answer** → **Fugue**

**Anthem** An anthem is a piece of choral music, usually accompanied by the organ, sung in a Protestant church service by the choir. Unlike the Canticles and Psalms, it is not an essential part of the service and may be omitted. It grew up in the Anglican Church after the Reformation.

A FULL ANTHEM is one in which the whole choir sings throughout. A VERSE ANTHEM has sections for solo voices which contrast with the choir. (→ also **Motet**)

The word 'anthem' is also used in the special sense of National Anthem – presumably because the term sounds more dignified than National Song. Church Anthems praise God; National Anthems praise the country. (→ **Antiphon**)

**Antiphon** In the Roman Catholic Church

this is, properly, a verse or other passage intoned or sung before and after a Psalm or Canticle.

But Antiphons are sometimes sung by themselves (without any Psalms or Canticles) and so the English word 'anthem' has been derived from 'antiphon'. (→ **Anthem**)

**A piacere** (It.) At pleasure. The same as *ad libitum*, it means that the performer may use his discretion as to the manner of performance.

**Appassionato** (**Appassionata**) (It.) Impassioned. Beethoven has a piano composition called (by the original publisher, not by Beethoven himself) *Sonata Appassionata*, that is, a sonata full of high emotion.

**Appoggiando** (It.) Leaning. **Appoggiato**, 'leaned'. When used in music the usual intention is that each note is to lean against the following one, that is, the notes are to pass on smoothly from one to another (the same as *portamento*).

But there is another meaning. 'Leaning' is sometimes used in the sense of 'putting weight on', that is, 'stressing'.

**Appoggiatura** → **Ornaments and grace-notes**

**Appreciation of music** Though attempts were made in the 19th century to help the ordinary listener to listen to music with intelligence and understanding, the idea of *Music Appreciation* as a study in its own right only began to appear, in the United States and Britain, about the year 1910. Since then it has become very common.

Stated quite simply: Music Appreciation teaches you how to use your ears. It aims to show you *why* the composer has written a piece of music, and *how* he has written it, and *why* it is good (or bad!). It believes, quite rightly, that the more you know about a piece of music, the greater your enjoyment of it will be. It is, in a way, like map-reading: it prepares you for the journey ahead.

The kind of things Music Appreciation concerns itself with include: a knowledge of musical history; a knowledge of the lives and personalities of composers; a knowledge of musical form; a knowledge of the orchestra and its instruments; and so on.

Music, after all, is a kind of language, and we shall only learn the finer points of what it has to say if we are prepared to pay it the attention it deserves.

**Arabesque** (Eng. and Fr.) and **Arabeske**

**Arabesque** This tiled niche from the Lotfollah Mosque in Isphahan, Iran shows the complex twining curves typical of Arab architecture.

(Ger.) come from the word 'Arab'. The Arabs in their architecture and decoration love to introduce a fanciful intertwining of curves and this we speak of as 'Arabesque', sometimes also applying the term musically to florid, decorative, melodic passages, or to some composition that abounds in passages of this kind (for instance Schumann's well-known *Arabeske* for piano). The term is also used to describe a step in classical ballet.

**Archet** (Fr.) Bow (of a stringed instrument).

**Archi** → below

**Arco** (It.) Bow (of a stringed instrument). The plural is *archi*. Also used as a direction to cancel a *pizzicato* passage, instead of the more grammatical *arcato* (meaning 'bowed').

**Arensky, Anton** Russian composer, 1861–1906. He showed early gifts for music and studied at the conservatory in St Petersburg (now Leningrad). Later he was a Professor of Composition at the Moscow Conservatory and then Director of Music in the Tsar's Chapel at St Petersburg. He wrote operas, symphonies, chamber music, and songs. His *Variations on a Theme by Tchaikovsky* are still sometimes played.

**Aria** (It.) Air or song. It is the name given to the long vocal solos found in opera and oratorio. In the 18th century most arias were '*da capo*' arias: that is to say, they had three sections – a first section, a contrasting middle section, and then the first section again. Singers were expected to add vocal decorations to the final section, partly for variety, and partly to show off their virtuosity.

Arias in later operas (19th century) vary in form and tend to follow whatever pattern best suits the drama.

Composers have also written 'concert' arias, which, as the name implies, are intended for concert performance and are not attached to any opera or oratorio.

**Arioso** Either (1) a short aria, or (2) a melodious recitative.

**Armstrong, Louis 'Satchmo'** → page 32

**Arne** Father and son. English composers.
1. **Thomas Augustine Arne**, 1710–1778. Though his father intended to make a lawyer of him, he studied music secretly and was eventually allowed to become a professional musician. Finding that his sister, Susanna Maria, had a fine voice, he

**Thomas Arne 1710-1778** This caricature shows the composer playing his most famous work, 'Rule Britannia'. Wagner said of this song that the opening eight notes expressed the whole English character.

# Louis Armstrong ('Satchmo')

American jazz trumpeter and composer, 1900–1971. Generally considered to be one of the greatest musicians to grow out of the New Orleans style of folk jazz. He began playing, in New Orleans, when he was twelve, moved to Chicago in 1922 and New York, to join Fletcher Henderson's big band, in 1924. Here he began to shine as solo trumpet, making many recordings (1925–28) under the name of Louis Armstrong's Hot Five and Hot Seven, including the brilliant *West End Blues*. He then made extensive tours in Europe, but after 1946 began to concentrate more on singing and general entertainment.

**As he will be remembered** Satchmo, as he appeared in the great jam session sequence in the film *The Glenn Miller Story*.
His nickname is derived from 'satchel-mouth', a reference to his wide mouth. He will also be remembered for his gravel-toned voice and his style of 'scat' singing.

**As he was** This photograph of Louis Armstrong in his twenties was taken for a record catalogue.

trained her and in 1733 wrote an opera, *Rosamond*, which brought them both success. She later became famous as a tragic actress, Mrs Cibber; but Thomas remained true to music. He composed many pieces for the theatre, most of which were Ballad Operas, such as *Thomas and Sally* (1760) and *Love in a Village* (1762), and were very popular. He is also known for the oratorio *Judith* (1761), and the opera *Artaxerxes* (1762).

Arne's tuneful songs are still sung, and in recent years orchestras have begun to explore his many delightful concertos and overtures. One of his tunes is known to everybody, even if they never bother to ask who wrote it. It comes from a masque called *Alfred* (1740) and its title is '*Rule, Britannia!*'.

2. **Michael Arne,** 1740–1786.
Although a talented composer, he ruined himself by experiments to find the 'Philosopher's Stone' that was traditionally supposed to turn all metals into gold. His song 'The Lass with a delicate Air', often wrongly attributed to his father, is still sung.

**Arnold, Malcolm** English composer, b. 1921. Trained at the Royal College of Music and worked for several years as a leading orchestral trumpet player. He has written music of all kinds, including several fine symphonies and concertos. His film scores, such as 'The Bridge on the River Kwai' and 'The Inn of the Sixth Happiness', are much admired. Although his musical style is traditional and makes use of bold tunes, simple harmonies, and lively rhythms, it is also very subtle and always extremely effective. His orchestration is particularly brilliant and colourful. Good examples of his style can be heard in the *Second Symphony* (1953), and the *Eight English Dances* (1950).

**Arpeggiare** (It.) To play in arpeggio fashion. **Arpeggiato** means played in that fashion.

**Arpeggio** (It.) A chord played 'harp-wise', that is, with the notes spread out. All piano students practise arpeggios (or arpeggii – the proper plural) like these:

**Arrangement** (or **Transcription**) Sometimes we find an orchestral piece rewritten so that it can be played on the piano, or a piano piece rewritten so that it can be played by an orchestra, or a song rewritten so that it becomes a violin piece; or we may find a piano piece rewritten in a form easier to play – and so on.

This we call 'arranging' or 'transcribing', and any piece of music so 'arranged' or 'transcribed' is called an 'arrangement' or 'transcription'.

**Ars antiqua** (Lat.) Old art. A term used to distinguish the music of the late 12th and 13th centuries from the music of the 14th century, which was called the *Ars nova* (the 'new art'). The musicians of the ars antiqua belong mainly to northern France and Germany, whereas those of the ars nova came from southern France and Italy.

**Ars nova** (Lat.) New art. A term used to describe the music of the 14th century, as distinct from that of the 12th and 13th, which was considered an **Ars antiqua →**, an 'old art'. The most important composers of this period were the Frenchman Guillaume de Machaut, and the Italian Francesco Landini.

**Assai** (It.) Very. Used in such phrases as **allegro assai** – Very quickly. Some composers (Beethoven, for example) seem to have confused it with the French *assez* (see below).

**Assez** (Fr.) Moderately. Used in such phrases as **assez vite** – Moderately quick. ( → also **Assai**, above)

**A tempo → Tempo**

**A.S.C.A.P.** The American Society of Composers, Authors, and Publishers. Founded in 1914. The equivalent of the British **Performing Right Society →.**

**Athematic** Athematic music is music that does not make use of themes or tunes as such, but explores instead such things as different textures, contrasting harmonic colours, different dynamics, isolated sounds, etc. Music of this kind does not always seem to 'go' anywhere, in the sense that traditional music has an obvious beginning, middle, and end. It can, however, be very fascinating. Composers who work with electronic equipment often create music that is athematic. ( → **Electronic music**)

**Atonal music** Music that makes no reference to a key or a mode, but uses all 12 notes of the chromatic scale quite freely. Though many composers in the late 19th century (such as Wagner) caused their music to modulate (change key) so frequently that all sense of key was often lost from time to time, it was not until the beginning of the 20th century that composers began to explore the serious possibilities of keyless music. The great pioneer in these explorations was Schoenberg.

**Attacca** (It.) Attack. A direction added at the end of a movement to indicate that the next must follow almost without a break.

**Attack** In musical performance this is the prompt and decisive beginning of a passage.

**Attendant keys** The same as **Related keys**. ( → **Modulation** )

**Attwood, Thomas** English composer, 1765–1838. He was educated as a choirboy at St Paul's Cathedral, and then went to Vienna to study with Mozart. He wrote many operas, but is now remembered for his church music. He became organist of St Paul's and was a close friend of Mendelssohn.

**Aubade** (Fr. from **aube**, dawn). Music to be played in the morning, perhaps to awaken somebody – the counterpart of the evening 'serenade' or 'nocturne'.

Composers have used the word very loosely to describe a light, cheerful work – an individual movement, or even a complete suite. ( → **Alborada** and **Serenade**)

**Auber, Daniel** French composer, 1782–1871. When he was a youth he came to London and whilst earning his living in a business office took part in all sorts of musical activities. At 22 he went back to Paris and soon became known as a gifted composer. In his long life he wrote about 40 operas (all very tuneful), some of which are still remembered by their bright, vigorous overtures.

**Aufführung** (Ger.) Performance.

**Augmentation** The 'augmentation' of a passage means its change into longer notes – perhaps double the original ones. (The corresponding term for the contrary is 'diminution'.)

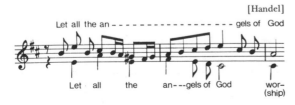

[Handel]

Let all the an - - - - - - - - - - - - - - gels of God

Let all the an- --gels of God wor-
(ship)

**Daniel Auber**
1782–1871 This composer was musical director to Napoleon III from 1857. It is interesting that he never attended a performance of his own works.

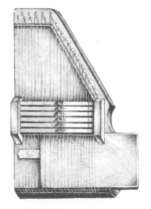

**Autoharp** This is a simple instrument of German origin which can be played on the lap or on a table.

Here upper and lower voices have the same passage (at different pitches), but in the lower voice, as compared with the upper, the passage is 'augmented', whilst in the upper, as compared with the lower, it is 'diminished'.

**Augmented sixth, Chords of** → **Chromatic chords**

**Augmented triad** → **Harmony**

**Auld Lang Syne** → **Scales**

**Auric, Georges** French composer, b. 1899. One of the group known as *Les Six*. He has written a great deal of music of all kinds, including ballets and film scores. From 1962 to 1968 he was administrator of the Paris Opéra.

**Ausgabe** (Ger.) Edition.

**Autoharp** A type of zither invented towards the end of the 19th century and often used by folk musicians. It has a series of chord bars that lie across the strings. When these are pressed down, the unwanted strings are damped, leaving the notes free to vibrate.

**Automatic instruments** → **Mechanical instruments**

**Auxiliary note** A variety of passing note, which instead of passing on to another note, passes back to the note it has just left. Augmented notes can be diatonic or chromatic. In the following example, the first auxiliary note (A) is diatonic, while the second and third (E flat and A sharp) are chromatic:

**Avant-garde** Originally a French military term to describe the 'advance guard', this is now used to describe any group of composers, painters, writers, film-makers etc, who believe themselves to be blazing a new trail in their respective arts.

**Avison, Charles** English composer, 1709–1770. He spent most of his life working as an organist in his native city of Newcastle upon Tyne, but was widely admired as a scholar and composer. He published five sets of concertos (50 in all) and a quantity of chamber and harpsichord music, some of which is now being played again; and was the author of an important and controversial treatise, *An Essay on Musical Expression*.

**B.** In German this means not our 'B' but 'B flat'. For our B (natural) the Germans use 'H'. → **Alphabet pieces**

**Babbitt, Milton** American composer, b. 1916. Began writing music in the style of Webern, but from 1947 explored the possibilities of 'total serialisation' (→**Serialism**) and then, after 1960, moved on to electronically produced music. He is a pupil of Roger Sessions.

**Baby Grand** A small grand piano. → **Piano**

**Bach, Carl Philipp Emanuel and Bach, Johann Christian** → **Bach's sons**

**Bach, Johann Sebastian** → page 36

**Bach's sons**
1. **Wilhelm Friedemann** – generally known simply as 'Friedemann' (1710–84).

He was Johann Sebastian Bach's second child and eldest son, and a learned and able musician. His life was spoilt by an unsteady disposition and he died poor and miserable.

His fugues and polonaises are sometimes played.

2. **Carl** (or **Karl**) **Philipp Emanuel**, often called 'C. P. E. Bach', 1714–88.
He was J. S. Bach's fifth child and third son. He was a remarkably precocious and gifted child and soon became an able composer and harpsichordist. In 1740 he was appointed keyboard player to the young, and very musical, king of Prussia, Frederick the Great, and spent 28 years at Berlin in his service. He was not very happy in this post, however, and

**Wilhelm Friedemann Bach**
1710–1784

**Carl Philipp Emanuel Bach**
1714–1788

**Johann Christian Bach**
1735–1782

**Mily Balakirev**
1837–1910

eventually escaped to become Telemann's successor in Hamburg (1767), where he was able to give concerts and direct the music in the city's five main churches.

As a composer he is very important for his daring experiments with the new Sonata Form and he must be regarded as one of the chief founders of the symphony. His symphonies, concertos, and keyboard sonatas are quite often played.

3. **Johann Christian** often called '**J. C. Bach**', 1735–82.
He was J. S. Bach's 18th child and 11th son. He is known as the 'London Bach' because he settled in England in 1762 and became famous as a composer, keyboard performer, and teacher. He worked for many years with the composer and viol-player Abel, and together they promoted a whole series of successful concerts which, among other things, introduced Haydn's symphonies to London. Like his brother, C. P. E. Bach, he helped to bring the early symphony into existence. His music is particularly elegant and tuneful and had a great influence on the young Mozart, whom he met in 1764. He wrote many operas, symphonies, and concertos which are still much admired.

**Bach trumpet** → **Trumpet**

**Badinage** or **Badinerie** These French words mean 'playfulness' or 'joking'. Sometimes a light-hearted piece of music is given this title.

**Bagatelle** This is both a French and a German word meaning a 'trifle'. Sometimes a short piece of music has that name as a title.

The plural in French is *bagatelles* but in German *Bagatellen*.

**Bagpipes** → page 38

**Balakirev, Mily** Russian composer, 1837–1910. He was much influenced by Russian folksong, and a meeting with the composer Glinka (sometimes called 'the Father of Russian music') confirmed this interest and led him to write music with a strong Russian flavour. He started the Free School of Music in St Petersburg (1862) which gave many public concerts, at which he figured both as a pianist and conductor. He wrote two symphonies, two piano concertos (the second of which was completed by another composer after his death), and many songs and piano pieces, of which the 'Oriental Fantasy' *Islamey* is one of the most interesting. He was one of the group of Russian composers known as '**The Five**' →

# Bach

Johann Sebastian Bach. Born at Eisenach, in Saxony, in 1685. Died at Leipzig in 1750.

## 1. Bach's life

Of all great musical families, that of the Bachs is the most remarkable. They were active in various branches of German musical life from the middle of the 16th century to the middle of the 19th – seven generations, spread over three centuries!

The names of about 60 Bach musicians have been recorded. Some were church organists; some played in municipal bands; some were fiddlers; and some were capable composers.

The most gifted of all the Bachs belonged to the fifth generation – Johann Sebastian. He was the youngest son of one of the town musicians of Eisenach.

When he was nine years old his father and mother died within months of each other and he was adopted by his eldest brother, Johann Christoph, who was organist at Ohrdruf. This brother now became his music teacher; but he also attended the town school, where he learnt Latin, Greek, theology, and arithmetic.

When he was 15 he obtained a post in the choir at the Church of St Michael at Lüneburg, but his voice soon broke and he stayed on as rehearsal accompanist, occasional violinist, and member of one of the town bands. He was now, in fact, a professional musician.

When he was 18 he was offered a post at Weimar, as one of the musicians of the brother of the reigning Duke, and a few months later a better post as organist at Arnstadt. Then, in 1707, he moved again – this time to Mühlhausen as organist. In the same year he married his cousin, Maria Barbara.

After a year at Mühlhausen Bach returned to Weimar, this time as court organist and chamber musician to the Duke himself. He now had the opportunity to compose a great deal of organ music, and later, after promotion, music for the Duke's chapel.

He spent nine years at Weimar, and then, in 1717, moved on to the court of Prince Leopold of Anhalt-Cöthen, who was himself an excellent amateur musician. Here Bach acted as 'Kapellmeister'; he had the

**Johann Sebastian Bach**
1685–1750, the most illustrious of this great musical family.

**St Thomas's Church, Leipzig**
This 18th-century engraving shows the church's interior and (*below*) the portico of the church with some of its fashionable congregation arriving by carriage and sedan chair.

direction of all the Prince's singers and instrumentalists, and was therefore encouraged to write a great deal of music for the orchestra.

He remained at Cöthen for six years, during which time his wife died and a year later (1721) he married again. Prince Leopold married in the same year, but his bride had no taste for music, and Bach began to look for a new post.

He was 38 when he moved to Leipzig (1723). After all his wanderings he had finally come to rest, and here, as 'Cantor' of the ancient St Thomas School, he stayed until his death 27 years later.

Altogether he wrote five complete sets (295) of Church Cantatas, each containing a cantata for every Sunday in the church's year. About two hundred of these have survived.

He also composed a Christmas Oratorio and some wonderful settings of the 'Passion' (that is to say, the story of Christ's crucifixion). Two of these Passions remain: the great *St Matthew Passion* and the *St John Passion*; and together with the *Mass in B minor* they contain some of his finest music.

At the end of his life Bach became blind – as did his contemporary Handel. His death attracted little attention and his widow was left to live out her life in great poverty: she died in 1760, aged 59, and was given a pauper's funeral.

## 2. His music

Bach lived at a time when composers had largely turned away from polyphony – that is to say, weaving their music from many lines of independent melody – and were interested more in working with a single melodic line (the 'tune') and a supporting harmony underneath it. His greatness lay in his ability to combine the best of both styles. And so, although his 'tunes' are superb, the harmonies underneath are themselves woven from independent parts that are also very melodious. Thus, when you listen to Bach's music, you find that there are several 'layers' of interest going on at one and the same time – the texture is very rich and exciting.

In certain works Bach deliberately exploits his great skill in writing intricate counterpoint. The two books of *Preludes and Fugues* in all the major and minor keys (known as 'The 48') contain wonderful examples of this skill.

## Summary of Bach's main works

a. His vocal music includes:

| | |
|---|---|
| Magnificat in D major | 1723 |
| St John Passion | 1723 |
| St Matthew Passion | 1729 |
| Christmas Oratorio | 1734 |
| Mass in B minor | 1738 |

b. Orchestral music includes:

| | |
|---|---|
| Suites (Overtures) | 1717-23 |
| No 1 in C major | |
| No 2 in B minor | |
| No 3 in D major | |
| No 4 in D major | |
| Brandenburg Concertos | 1718-21 |
| No 1 in F major | |
| No 2 in F major | |
| No 3 in G major | |
| No 4 in G major | |
| No 5 in D major | |
| No 6 in B flat major | |

c. Solo Concertos (1717-23) include:
Violin Concerto in A minor
Violin Concerto in E major
Concerto for two violins, in D minor

d. Keyboard music includes:

| | |
|---|---|
| The '48' Preludes and Fugues | |
| Book I | 1722 |
| Book II | 1744 |
| Chromatic Fantasy and Fugue | 1720-23 |
| Italian Concerto | 1735 |
| Goldberg Variations | 1742 |

## 4. Bach the man

Bach was regarded by a great many of his employers as a rather difficult man to get on with. And judging by the number of times he changed his job, and the known occasions on which he openly quarrelled with his employers, it seems that this was very likely. The reason must surely have been that he often had to undertake duties which he found boring (such as choir-training) and which robbed him of the time to compose or show off his gifts as a virtuoso organist. He often found rather reprehensible ways of avoiding these duties – as for instance at Arnstadt, when he begged for four weeks' leave to walk the two hundred miles to Lübeck to hear the great organist and composer Buxtehude, and stayed away for sixteen weeks!

**St Thomas's Church, Leipzig**
As Lutheran Cantor of this church Bach gave a singing lesson each morning to the 55 boys that made up the choirs of the four city churches. The churches of St Thomas and St Nicholas took turns, Sunday by Sunday, to perform a Cantata which Bach composed and conducted.

He was a deeply religious man – as many of his greatest works prove. Indeed, his last composition, dictated from his death-bed, was an organ prelude on the chorale 'Before Thy throne, my God, I stand'. Though respected as a composer, he was admired during his lifetime as a great organist and keyboard performer, and it was only many years after his death that his real importance came to be recognized.

Bach enjoyed a happy married life (particularly in his second marriage) and produced, in all, 20 children, of whom only 11 survived childhood. The boys became musicians, and three at least are still regarded as 'great' in their own right.

Little of his music was published during his lifetime, and though the more perceptive musicians went out of their way to study his methods (Haydn and Mozart both learned a great deal from studying the fugues, and so did Beethoven), it was not until Mendelssohn performed the *St Matthew Passion* in 1829 that the general public awoke to Bach's true greatness.

**Bach's Prelude and Fugue in C** This music for a keyboard instrument is from Book II of *The Well-Tempered Clavier*, 1744.

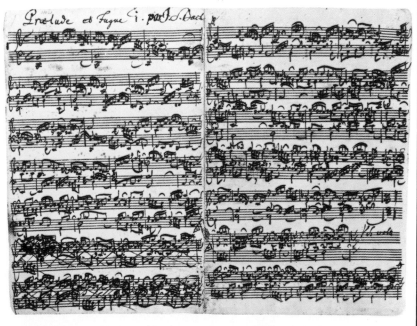

# Bagpipe, or Bagpipes

This is one of the most ancient and widely used of all instruments. The Romans had it in their armies, and nowadays it is found in Northumberland, Scotland, and Ireland; in Brittany and other parts of France; in Italy, Spain, and Portugal; in Norway, Finland, Poland, and Russia; in the Balkan countries and in Greece; in Persia, China, and India.

It takes different forms in different parts of the world. But there is always a 'bag' from which flows the air which blows a pipe or pipes – hence the name. In some instruments, such as the Northumberland Bagpipe and the Scottish Lowland Bagpipe, the bag is filled with air by a bellows held under the arm. In others, such as the Scottish Highland Bagpipe, the bag is filled from the player's mouth.

Attached to the bag there is always one pipe on which tunes can be played. This is called the CHANTER. It has a 'reed' (a slip of cane) in its mouthpiece, and it is this that sets up the vibrations. The different notes are obtained by the player opening and closing holes in the tube with his fingers – as one does with a recorder.

In most countries the instrument has another pipe, or pipes, called DRONE pipes. These play all the time without being touched by the player. If there is only one, it sounds the keynote (*Doh*); if there are two or three, they sound the keynote and the fifth note of the key (*Doh* and *Soh*). This primitive accompaniment fits all the other notes that the chanter can produce.

**Scottish bagpiper** This piper of the Scots Guards is dressed in full Highland regalia and wears the kilt, sporran and dirk. The bagpipes are recognized, throughout the world, as the symbol of Scotland. The 'skirl', or shrill piercing flourish of the pipes in massed bands or lone and plaintive has stirred the hearts of generations of Scots.

Some bagpipes have their own peculiar kind of scale. For instance, the Scottish Highland bagpipe has a scale that we could not play on any piano – the scale of A, but with a G natural, and with a C and F very slightly sharp. It is this scale that gives the Scottish bagpipe its characteristic sound.

In France there used to be two kinds of bagpipe. One, the MUSETTE, had a gentle sound and was often imitated by the keyboard composers of the 17th and 18th centuries. Another kind of keyboard piece which imitated the bagpipe was the LOURE (Bach wrote both Musettes and Loures).

Bagpipes have always been used as military instruments, simply because their sound will carry for miles. It is also said to rouse the fighting soldier's spirits. Some people, however, make jokes about it, and there is a splendid medieval wood carving at Boston in Lincolnshire which shows musicians playing bagpipes – but the bagpipes are live cats, and the musicians are biting their tails!

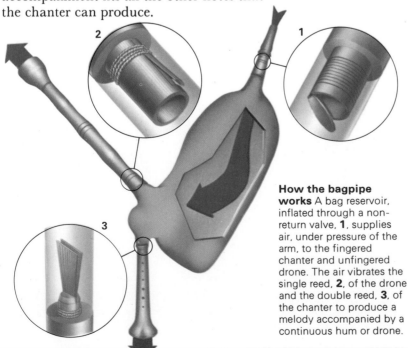

**How the bagpipe works** A bag reservoir, inflated through a non-return valve, **1**, supplies air, under pressure of the arm, to the fingered chanter and unfingered drone. The air vibrates the single reed, **2**, of the drone and the double reed, **3**, of the chanter to produce a melody accompanied by a continuous hum or drone.

## The bagpipe throughout the ages

The origins of the bagpipe are obscure but it probably appeared in the Near East at the beginning of the Christian era. It was known in Roman times but may have been re-invented in the Middle Ages when its use was widespread throughout Europe. Regional variations abound, some primitive, others highly sophisticated like the Italian *zampogna*.

*Above* A map of the Western Hemisphere shows, with shaded area, those parts of Europe, Asia and Africa where the bagpipe is still played today.

*Above* This 14th-century English pipe has a chanter but only one drone. (*Below*) A piper leads these 16th-century Irish foot soldiers.

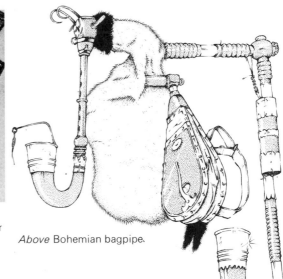

*Above* Bohemian bagpipe.

*Above* Majorcan bagpiper

*Above* Highland sword-dance

*Above* Polish *Dudy* (bagpipe)

*Right* 18th-century musette

# Ballet

1. When pronounced 'Ballay' this means any dance intended for the theatre rather than the ballroom.

Ballet as we understand it today, however, developed out of an elaborate form of ballroom dancing practised in the courts of France and Italy during the 16th and 17th centuries. These dances were performed by the courtiers themselves (even the King joining in) and were part of a general entertainment known as the **Masque →**. The heyday of the Court Ballet was during the reign of Louis XIV, when Lully was in charge of the king's music. Gradually, however, courtiers began to appear in fewer and fewer of the dance-numbers and their place was taken by professional dancers. At much the same time, ballets began to play an important part in opera – Lully and Rameau, for example, made particular use of them. In this way the art of formal dancing moved out of the courts and into the theatre.

Ballets as works in their own right appeared during the 18th century. Gluck's *Don Juan* (1761) is probably the first ballet to tell a story by means of dancing alone.

The idea of ballet as a theatrical entertainment soon spread far beyond France and Italy. In 1735, for example, a State School of Dancing was founded in St Petersburg, and at much the same time a Royal Danish Ballet was set up in Copenhagen. But France remained the home of ballet, and it was from her that the finest dancers and dancing masters came.

It was not until the 19th century, however, that ballet came to be accepted as an important form of theatrical entertainment. Ballets that told a definite story and which would occupy a whole evening in the theatre rapidly became very popular. The earliest of them which is still frequently performed today is *Giselle* (1841), with music by Adolphe Adam (1803–1856). Fine examples came later in the century from another French composer, Léo Delibes: *Coppélia* (1870), and *Sylvia* (1876).

In the meantime ballet developed in Russia – largely through the efforts of a French dancing-master Marius Petipa (1822–1910), who took over the Imperial Ballet School at St Petersburg in 1847. And it was here that Tchaikovsky showed that in the hands of a great composer ballet music could be of genuine artistic importance. His three full-length ballets, *Swan Lake* (1877), *Sleeping Beauty* (1890), and *The Nutcracker* (1892), are considered to be masterpieces.

It should also be remembered that the development of a ballet owed a great deal to certain outstanding dancers, such as Marie Camargo (1710–1770) and Marie Taglioni (1804–1884). Through their grace and skill they transformed the art of dancing and made it deeply expressive. For true ballet is not just the mastering intricate dance-steps, but of conveying also emotions and ideas.

Although the style of Petipa's Imperial School was artistic and extremely effective, it was also classical and stylized. Two men decided that something less formal was needed. They were the dancer Mikhail Fokine, and the wealthy amateur Serge

*Below* **Louis XIV** The 15 year old King of France appeared as Apollo in the *Ballet de la nuit* in 1653. This role gave him the nickname 'Le Roi Soleil' (Sun King).

*Right* **Pas de deux** Two principal dancers rehearse.
*Far right* **Marie Taglioni**, the Italian dancer in *La Sylphide*, a ballet written especially for her by her father, in 1832.
*Below* **Corps de Ballet** The Corps of the Royal Ballet Covent Garden, dance *Swan Lake*. The ballet, choreographed by Petipa, was first produced in St Petersburg in 1895. It is perhaps the best known and loved of all ballets.

*Below* **Vaslav Nijinsky**
This great artist danced the role of the Golden Slave in the Diaghilev ballet *Scheherezade* when it was first performed in Paris in 1910. The music was by Rimsky-Korsakov and the choreography by Fokine.

*Below* **Billy the Kid**
Aaron Copland composed the evocative music for this ballet about the legendary hero of the Wild West. It was first performed in Chicago in 1938.

*Left* **Alvin Ailey dancers**
These principal dancers of the Alvin Ailey Theatre Company perform a scene from the ballet *The Lark Ascending* during a recent tour of Budapest. This black American company produces both classic and modern dances.

Diaghilev. Together they founded the Russian Ballet Company and in 1909 took Paris, and the world, by storm. Diaghilev's particular genius was for bringing together great artists and making them work together – dancers, such as Tamara Karsavina and Vaslav Nijinsky; composers, such as Stravinsky and Ravel; painters, such as Leon Bakst and Picasso; choreographers (to invent the dance steps and direct the ballet), such as Fokine and Massine. These he welded into a remarkable team, capable of producing ballets with a degree of artistic unity never before attempted. The style of dancing, also, was revolutionary. Based partly on the ideas of an American dancer Isadora Duncan (1878–1927), it was much more natural and informal than classical ballet. In such works as Stravinsky's *Firebird* (1910), *Petrouchka* (1911), and, above all *The Rite of Spring* (1913), the Diaghilev company revolutionized the art of ballet.

Stimulated by their example, ballet began to prosper in other countries, in England, with the foundation of the Vic-Wells Ballet Company at Sadler's Wells Theatre (1931), which eventually developed into the Royal Ballet Company, based at Covent Garden, in America, with the foundation of the American Theatre Ballet and the New York City Ballet – both of which developed a more athletic style of dancing. Composers such as Vaughan Williams (*Job*, 1931) and Sir Arthur Bliss (*Checkmate*, 1937) wrote fine new works – as did the American Aaron Copland (*Billy the Kid*, 1938; *Rodeo*, 1942; *Appalachian Spring*, 1944).

Equally flourishing ballet companies now exist in most European countries. In Russia itself the ballet has remained true to a more conservative style of dancing, in which the Bolshoi company in particular attain the highest standards. Here, too, great composers have contributed important new scores – as, for example, Prokofiev (*Romeo and Juliet*, 1940).

Ballet is now recognized throughout the world as an art-form of the greatest importance, capable of attracting the greatest talents – whether of composers, such as Benjamin Britten (*The Prince of the Pagodas*, 1957) and Hans Werner Henze (*Ondine*, 1958); choreographers, such as Sir Frederick Ashton and Jerome Robbins; or dancers, such as Dame Margot Fonteyn and Rudolph Nureyev. At the same time many 'experimental' ballet companies have come into existence, eager to explore new possibilities of dancing and mime, which in due course enter and enrich the accepted traditions of a very lively art.
2. When pronounced (and frequently spelt) 'Ballett' this is a type of madrigal popular in the 16th century. It was usually rather simple in style, with repeated verses, each ending in a 'fa la la' refrain.

*Right* **Nikolais Dance Theatre** This modern American company is boldly experimental.
*Below* **Martha Graham Company**, one of the oldest and best-known modern dance groups.

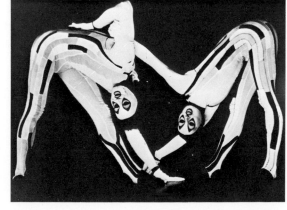

**Balalaika** A Russian instrument something like a guitar. It has a triangular body and three strings, which are plucked. There are several different sizes of instrument and balalaika orchestras are very popular in Russia.

**Balfe, Michael William** Irish composer, 1808–70. He was the son of a Dublin dancing-master and made his first public appearance as a solo violinist when he was nine. After working in England, Italy, and France, and discovering himself to be a capable operatic baritone, he settled in London to a highly successful career as operatic composer and opera manager. His operas were very tuneful and were popular throughout Europe. The most famous is *The Bohemian Girl* (1843).

**Ballabile** From the Italian word *ballare*, 'to dance', this term can be applied to any piece of music suitable for dancing, without regard to differences of rhythm or dance steps. The dances in some of Meyerbeer's operas have this title.

**Ballad opera** An opera that has spoken dialogue, interspersed with simple songs that often make use of well-known tunes. The first ballad opera appeared in London in 1728. It was written by John Gay and was called **The Beggar's Opera →**. It was enormously successful and other pieces in the same style soon followed. The tunes for these later pieces were not traditional, but were composed in the same simple style.

**Balalaika** This instrument comes in several sizes, the largest of which rests on the ground like the double-bass. A popular Russian opera, *Dreams on the Volga* by Privalof is entirely accompanied by a balalaika orchestra. This example is from 19th-century Russia.

**Ballad →** below

**Ballade** A title sometimes given by composers to a piece of music that seems to them to resemble a ballad in poetry. Chopin, Brahms, and Grieg have used the title for some of their piano pieces.

**Ballet →** page 40

**Ballett →** Ballet

**Balla** (It.) Ball, or dance. The direction *tempo di ballo* (at dance speed) is often found in music of a waltz-like character.

**Ballroom dancing →** page 43

**Bamboo pipe** This is a simple instrument, blown at the end like a recorder. **→ Flute**

**Band** Although any large body of instrumental players may be called a 'band', the term is usually applied only to **Brass bands**, **Military bands**, **Dance bands**, and **Jazz bands**.

**Bandmaster** The man who conducts and trains a military band, or a civilian brass band, or any kind of wind band.

**Banjo →** page 44

**Bantock,** (Sir) **Granville** English composer, 1868–1946. He began his career as the conductor of a touring theatrical company, but eventually became Principal of the Birmingham School of Music (1900) and then, in 1907, Professor of Music at

---

# Ballad

From the Italian *ballata*, meaning 'a dance', this word has changed its significance over the ages.

In 15th century Italy a *balletta* was a song that also involved dancing.

In England, from the 16th to 19th centuries, a ballad was a song that told a real, or imaginary, story. When sung in the streets by ballad-singers, the stories were often about recent events – a particularly exciting murder, or the exploits of a daring highwayman – and were thus an early form of newspaper. They are also known as BROADSIDE BALLADS because they were printed on a single long sheet (a 'broadside') with a crude woodcut at the top by way of illustration.

In 19th-century Germany the word *Ballad* was used by Schubert, Schumann, and particularly Brahms to describe such of

A 19th-century ballad singer

their songs as told a story (**→ Lied, Lieder**). And a little later, in England and Germany, we find composers writing choral works which they call CHORAL BALLADS – for example, Elgar's *The Black Knight*. These also told a story and were sometimes settings of the best of the old ballad poems.

Towards the end of the 19th century the word, in England, had also come to mean a type of simple, melodious, and rather sentimental popular song suitable for amateurs to sing at home. Such songs were also called 'Drawing-room Ballads'. In order to publicize them, promoters gave BALLAD CONCERTS consisting entirely of such items, sung, of course, by some famous singer. The word is still used in 'pop' circles to describe simple, melodious songs.

# Ballroom dancing

Although dancing has existed throughout human history, the idea of a special 'ballroom' to which anyone might go, provided that he could afford the ticket and the right clothes, dates from the beginning of the 19th century. Before that time, dances were either the country dances of ordinary people, or the elaborate court dances of the nobility. The rise of ballroom dancing is therefore closely linked with the rise of the middle class and the creation of a widespread 'polite society'.

In the 19th century the most important ballroom dance was the **Waltz** →. When it first appeared, at the beginning of the century, it was thought to be somewhat immoral – for it was the first dance in which a gentleman was required to hold a lady close to him. Other dances of the period include the **Polka** and the **Quadrille** → .

Ballroom dancing did not change much until the 1920s, when there came into existence a whole series of complicated new dance steps, all stemming from the arrival of American **Ragtime** → . The four main dances of this period were the SLOW FOXTROT (later known as the Foxtrot), the QUICK FOXTROT (later known as the QUICKSTEP), the WALTZ (a slow version of the 19th century dance), and the TANGO. The variety of possible steps in these dances was so great, and the art of mastering them

**Waltz** *Above* This 19th-century lithograph from Austria shows a couple dancing the waltz. The great waltz composer of the early 19th century was Johann Strauss the younger who created the Viennese Waltz, the best known of which is the *Blue Danube*.
**Modern ball-room dancing** *Right* These competitors take part in the British ballroom dancing competition *Come Dancing*.

so difficult, that people went to considerable lengths to learn them, often attending instruction classes.

Ballroom dancing of this complexity began to lose popularity in the 1950s, with the arrival of the freer styles of dancing associated with **Rock 'n Roll** →. It still exists, however, and is still very popular with older people. International competitions are held in which the competitors are professional ballroom dancers. Similar competitions, on a more modest scale, are also held regularly for amateurs.

**Waltz** *Left* The dance was initially regarded as improper, but by the end of the 19th century it was a commonplace dance in most ballrooms.
*Below* These identically dressed couples dance in formation.

# Banjo

A stringed instrument with a long neck and a round body, rather like a frying pan in appearance. The body consists of a parchment skin stretched over a metal hoop. There are five, six, or sometimes nine strings, and they can be plucked with the fingers or a small piece of wood, ivory, or metal known as a PLECTRUM.

The banjo is supposed to be of African origin. When the slave trade took thousands of African natives to North America the instrument became very common there. And when, in the 19th century, 'minstrels' (white men with blacked faces) became popular in Europe, they imitated the American negroes by adopting their instruments.

Banjos play an important part in **Country and Western music →**, where players use a particularly elaborate form of 'finger picking'. (**→ Pick**)

*Left* **Playing the banjo**
This elderly negro strums a five string banjo. The instrument was used in much early jazz. George Gershwin featured it in his negro folk opera *Porgy and Bess*.

**Minstrels** (*far left*) Two banjos are used by this 19th-century group of minstrels. Bands like this were common in America and England in the early part of this century.

Birmingham University.

He wrote a great deal of music, mostly using large orchestras and choruses, and often based on Oriental or Gaelic subjects. He was a great champion of English music, and also helped to popularize Sibelius's music.

**Bar** (or **Measure**) Most European music of the past four or five centuries falls into regular groups of beats – groups of two, three, or four beats, etc. with a strong accent on the opening beat of each group. In musical notation these groups are marked off from one another by vertical lines called BAR-LINES, and the space between any two bar-lines is called a 'bar' or a 'measure'.

A time signature at the opening of a composition shows the number of beats in each bar.

Note that a double-bar is a quite different thing. It merely marks the end of a section of a piece and has nothing to do with the time or rhythm of the piece.

**Barber, Samuel** American composer, b. 1910. He studied at the Curtis Institute, Philadelphia, won the American Rome Prize (1935), and then, in 1935, 1936, and 1958, the Pulitzer Prize. He has written all kinds of music, including two operas, *Vanessa* (1958) and *Antony and Cleopatra* (1966), and a number of symphonies and concertos. His *Adagio for Strings* (1936) has become very popular and is typical of his melodious and highly romantic style. *Knoxville: Summer of 1915* for soprano and orchestra (1947) shows him at his best.

**Barber's shop music** In 17th-century London, most barbers kept musical instruments (usually **citterns →**) for the use of their customers, who entertained themselves while waiting their turn. These performances, though lively, were usually rather rough and ready, and the term 'barber's shop music' later came to be used in condemnation of a professional player's poor performance.

The 'Barber's shop quartet' is a style of singing in **close harmony** → that arose, in similar circumstances, in America towards the end of the 19th century. Again, customers entertained themselves by singing popular songs of the day. Their methods of close harmonization came to be recognized as a style in itself.

**Barbirolli,** (Sir) **John** English conductor, 1899–1970. His parents were Italian, but he was born in London. He became an excellent cellist and then a world-famous conductor, directing, among others, the Hallé Orchestra, Manchester (1943).

**Barcarolle** From the Italian word *barca*, 'a boat', and thus a 'boating song' – particularly the kind sung by the gondoliers in Venice. Such songs usually have a gentle lilt and are in 6/8 time. Composers sometimes imitate them in piano pieces (Chopin and Mendelssohn, for example) and use the same title. Probably the most famous orchestral example occurs in Act 3 of Offenbach's opera *The Tales of Hoffmann*.

**Bard** The traditional poet-musician of the Celtic peoples of the British Isles (the Irish, Welsh, and Scots). He composed and sang songs, usually in honour of the nobleman who employed him, accompanying himself on the CRWTH, a type of lyre. Their music, however, was not written down and has therefore not survived. Bards were less important after 1284 (when Edward I conquered Wales), but lingered on into the 17th and 18th centuries as a kind of folk art. In Wales during the 19th century a determined effort was made to revive bardic gatherings, and nowadays the annual Eisteddfod is a popular and thriving event.

**Bar form** A musical form that was popular in medieval times. It consisted of three sections: **A.A.B.**, and was based on a type of German poem known as the **Bar**. Each stanza of the **Bar** was divided into two **sections** (**A.A.**) and a refrain, **B**. Thus, the music of both **A** sections was the same, while different music was used for **B**. Forms of this kind were used by the troubadours, trouvères, and mastersingers. (→ **Minstrels**)

The 18th-century da-capo aria (→ **Aria**) is really a variant of bar form.

**Bare fifth** A common chord with the third

**Sir John Barbirolli** 1899–1970

**Baryton** This instrument was popular for a brief time in the 18th century.

**'Count' Basie** b.1904 This band leader, who conducts from the keyboard, has a unique piano style.

omitted. In old music it is sometimes found at the very end of a piece in a minor key. Known also as an 'open fifth'. (→ **Tierce de Picardie**)

**Baritone** → **Voice**

**Barn dance** Originally an occasion for dancing, rather than a dance in its own right. In the country areas of America it was customary to celebrate the building of a new barn by holding a dance. Various types of country dance were performed on these occasions, usually to a fiddle accompaniment. Towards the end of the 19th century a ballroom dance with this name became popular in England.

**Baroque** A term borrowed from the world of architecture, where it is used to describe a highly ornate style of building found in the palaces and churches of Germany and Austria during the 17th and 18th centuries. Musical historians use the term to describe the music of the same period. Bach and Handel are thus 'Baroque' composers.

**Barraqué, Jean** French composer, 1928–1973. He was a pupil of Olivier Messiaen and pushed still further his methods and theories, writing in particular a quantity of piano music that involves complex rhythms and very precise changes of dynamics. His Piano Sonata, completed in 1952, is a good example of his very intricate and challenging style.

**Barrel organ** → **Mechanical instruments**

**Bartók** → page 48

**Baryton** 1. A bowed instrument somewhat similar to a bass viola d'amore. It had six gut strings, a fretted fingerboard, and a series of 16 (or more) thin wire strings that ran behind the neck in such a way that they could be plucked by the thumb. It was the favourite instrument of Haydn's patron Prince Esterházy, and Haydn wrote more than 100 sonatas for him to play. It is also known as the Viola di bordone.

2. The name by which the Euphonium is known in Germany.

**Basie, William ('Count')** American jazz pianist and composer, b. 1904. He began his career as a vaudeville (variety show) pianist in New York, but soon turned to jazz, forming his own band in 1935. His first recordings appeared two years later and the band quickly became famous for its fast pace and driving rhythms, as well as for its remarkable soloists.

# Band

*Top Left to right*
**Bandstand** Ornate Gothic bandstand at Vauxhall Gardens in the early 19th century.
**Jazz band**, New Orleans. Street marching bands like this played in New Orleans from the end of the last century.
**Indian Naubat band** This 19th-century miniature shows the band playing kettledrums, trumpets, cymbals and shawm.
**John Philip Sousa** The 'king of marches' with the band of the U.S. Marine Corps, 1890.

*Bottom Left to right*
**Pandean band** This group at Vauxhall Gardens in 1805 plays panpipes (pandean pipes) of different sizes as well as percussion instruments.
**Brass band** This engraving shows a 19th-century brass band from Boston, U.S.A.
**Austrian brass band** The brass band is found all over Europe and in countries settled by Europeans. It usually plays in the open air and is made up of amateur musicians.

*Middle Left to right*
**Benny Goodman** The 'King of Swing' and his band in the late 1930s.
**Street musicians** This group, 'Yuck City Jug Band' play in San Francisco.
**Military band** The band of the Grenadier Guards gives an open air concert in London's Regent's Park.
**One-man band** This musician with a variety of percussion instruments plays in New York's Greenwich Village.

# Bartók

Béla Bartók, Hungary, 1881–1945. He received his first piano lessons from his mother when he was five, and even though his father died a few years later and they were very poor, she did everything she could to help his career. When he was 18 he went to Budapest to study piano and composition at the Academy of Music. Though he created a great stir in 1904 with a patriotic symphonic poem called *Kossuth*, he was at this time better known as a brilliant pianist.

In 1905, encouraged by another young Hungarian composer, Zoltán Kodály, he began to study folksong, travelling all over the country, recording and noting down what he heard. The more he studied it, the more he learned and, as a result, his own musical style began to change and become much more personal and much more Hungarian.

But he was still regarded mainly as a pianist, and in 1907 he was appointed Professor of Piano at the Budapest Academy. The tide did not turn until 1917, when his ballet *The wooden Prince* was performed in Budapest. His opera, *Duke Bluebeard's Castle*, was heard in the following year. Though not everybody liked his music

**Béla Bartók** 1881–1945

**Recording folksongs**
The composer records a Slovak song on a phonograph during his travels in 1908.

– they thought it very noisy and modern – they could no longer ignore or deny his talent.

From this point onward his fame increased steadily. He made many lengthy concert tours as a pianist, often playing his own concertos and piano pieces. He continued his folksong studies, and all the time developed a very individual style of composition. He was soon regarded as one of Europe's leading composers.

In 1940, he decided to leave his beloved Hungary as a protest against her alliance with Nazi Germany. He settled in America, but after a while he fell ill, suffered many hardships and died.

Bartók's music is percussive and often harshly dissonant; but it is also tuneful and highly imaginative. Besides the works already mentioned, he wrote six remarkable String Quartets (among the greatest by any 20th-century composer), three Piano Concertos, a *Divertimento for Strings* (1939) *Music for Strings, Percussion and Celesta* (1936), and a *Concerto for Orchestra* (1943). He also wrote a large quantity of very fine piano music, and several choral works, including the *Cantata Profana* (1930).

**Bass** This word is generally pronounced 'base', but sometimes we hear it pronounced as spelt. It is applied to the lowest kind of voice, to the lowest note in a chord, and to one of the clefs. (→ **Voice**)

**Bassa** (low) Thus the term *Ottava bassa* means that the passage to which it is attached should be played an octave lower than is shown in the notation.

**Bass bar** This is a part of a violin (or other member of the violin family). It is the strip of wood glued inside the belly, along the line of the lowest string. One of its purposes is to help to support the pressure of the bridge.

**Bass clef** → **Notes and notation**

**Bass clarinet** → **Clarinet family**

**Bass drum** → **Drum family**

**Basse danse** (Fr.) One of the most important dances of the late 15th century, so called because of its low, gliding steps (in contrast to the high, leaping steps of the

**Basset horn** This is a German example dated 1793.

GALLIARD). Early examples use a number of traditional bass tunes above which a melody and accompaniment would be improvised. It originated in France, but also became very popular in England. There are generally two beats to each bar.

**Basset horn** A tenor member of the clarinet family, invented in Bavaria towards the end of the 18th century. Early examples were often sickle-shaped, with a box device just before the bell. Modern examples have long, straight tubes, with an up-turned bell. The sound is sweet and very mellow, but not very brilliant. Mozart made considerable use of it, but it has never found a place in the standard orchestra.

**Bass flute** → **Flute family**

**Basso continuo** (It.) Continuous bass, or Thorough bass. In music of the 17th and early 18th centuries the bass line often continued without a break throughout a piece of music, so we may speak of a 'through' bass. This is not quite the same as a **Figured bass** →, for in this it is possible to have rests.

# Bassoon

Though really the tenor member of the oboe family, the bassoon usually plays the bass part in any normal woodwind group. It is a double-reed instrument (→ **Oboe family**) and was developed during the 17th century from an instrument called a curtall. It consists of two separate tubes, set parallel to each other and joined at one end by a U-tube. The total sounding length of the modern bassoon is about three metres. Early bassoons had only two keys, but in the 19th century (thanks to the German instrument maker Wilhelm Heckel) many more were added so that the instrument could play chromatic music with ease. For practical purposes the range of the bassoon can be taken as:

*Above* **Making the bassoon** A 17th-century craftsman works on a two-key instrument; a three-key bassoon is to his right.
**Modern bassoon** (*right*) The **double bassoon** lies adjacent.

Bassoon players read from the bass and tenor clefs.

The CONTRABASSOON, or DOUBLE BASSOON, is, as its name implies, a larger version of the bassoon. It has a sounding length of more than six metres and its range is therefore:

**Basso ostinato** (It.) Obstinate bass. This is the same as a **Ground bass →**.

**Baton** The French word for 'stick', used by musicians to describe the slim wand the conductor uses to control a choir or orchestra (→ **Conducting**). In the early 19th century batons were thick and clumsy, but nowadays they are delicately shaped, often with a small cork handle to help the grip.

**Batterie** (Fr.) 'Beaten'. A roll played on the side drum. Also, a method of playing the guitar by striking the strings instead of plucking them. In early keyboard and harp music the term is also sometimes found when chords are to be played in arpeggio.

**Battuta** (It.) This usually means 'beat' and its plural is *battute*. Thus after a passage has been marked to be played *accelerando* (getting gradually quicker), or *ritardando* (getting gradually slower), or *a piacere* (in irregular time according to the performer's taste) we may find the term *a battuta*, meaning 'to the beat', that is 'return now to strict time'.

But *battuta* has also another meaning. Occasionally it means 'bar'. Thus when Beethoven writes *Ritmo di tre battute* (Three-bar-rhythm) he is calling the performer's attention to the fact that his phrases in the passage in question have only three bars each instead of the more usual four.

**Bax,** (Sir) **Arnold** English composer, 1883–1953. He was trained at the Royal Academy of Music, where he proved to be an excellent pianist and a brilliant score-reader. As he enjoyed a private income he was able to settle to a life of undisturbed composing. He wrote seven large-scale symphonies and a number of impressive symphonic poems – including the very popular *Tintagel* (1917). He also wrote songs, piano music, and a quantity of chamber music. He was appointed Master of the King's Musick in 1942, and knighted in 1937.

Bax's music is very romantic, tends to employ large orchestras, and often runs to considerable length. It is still admired, though not quite so widely as during his lifetime.

# The Beatles

British pop group, consisting of John Lennon (b. 1940), Paul McCartney (b. 1942), George Harrison (b. 1943), and, eventually, Ringo Starr (Richard Starkey, b. 1940). The original 'fourth' member was Pete Best.

They began in Liverpool in 1956 as *The Quarrymen*, developed as *The Silver Beatles* (1959), and after a spell in Hamburg (1960), were eventually 'discovered' at The Cavern in Liverpool by Brian Epstein, who became their manager (1961). Fame came in 1963 with their fourth record *She loves you*. From that moment until they broke up in 1970 they enjoyed a world-wide success almost without parallel. They have also made several films.

What distinguishes them from other groups is the quality of their songs, mostly written by John Lennon and Paul McCartney. Both words and music are, by any standards, highly imaginative and memorable. Their three best-selling long-playing records are: *Revolver* (1966), *Sergeant Pepper's Lonely Hearts Club Band* (1967), and *Abbey Road* (1969).

*Above* **The Beatles** with their cartoon counterparts from the film *Yellow Submarine*. From the beginning (*left*) they influenced a whole generation not only by their music, but also by their behaviour (*below*)

**Bayreuth festival** Founded by Richard Wagner, who wished to see his music dramas performed under ideal conditions. He therefore designed a remarkable theatre, and chose the small Bavarian town of Bayreuth as a suitably tranquil spot to build it. The first performances took place in 1876 and have continued annually, each summer, ever since. After Wagner's death in 1883 the festivals were directed by his widow, Cosima, and then, from 1908 to 1930, by his son, Siegfried. Winifred Wagner, Siegfried's widow (an Englishwoman) continued the festivals until 1944, when the progress of the Second World War forced the theatre to close. It was reopened in 1951 under the direction of Wagner's grandsons, Wolfgang and Wieland.

**Beat → Pulse**

**Bebung** (Ger.) Trembling. A special effect in clavichord playing, not possible (or

**Sir Thomas Beecham**
1879–1961

necessary) on the piano. It is really a form of vibrato. The player agitates the key, but does not remove his finger from it to strike fresh blows. This, in turn, keeps the string of the clavichord in motion and prolongs the sound.

**Beecham,** (Sir) **Thomas** English conductor, 1879–1961. Son of a wealthy manufacturing chemist and patron of music. His conducting career, which began in 1906, centred on London where he staged many unusual operas (1909–20) and introduced the Russian Ballet (1911). He founded two orchestras: the London Philharmonic in 1932, and the Royal Philharmonic in 1947. Though especially fond of Delius's music, Beecham was also a brilliant interpreter of Haydn, Mozart, and Berlioz. He had a lively personality and was famous for his wit.

**Beethoven → page 52**

# The Beggar's Opera

The first Ballad Opera (→ **Ballad**). It is a play with songs. The words were written by John Gay, and the music was chosen from popular melodies and folksongs and arranged by the German-born composer John Christopher Pepusch. It was produced by John Rich in January 1728 and took London by storm – it was said that its success made 'Gay rich, and Rich gay'. Although it is a lively story of highwaymen and London low-life, *The Beggar's Opera* is also a satire, attacking not only the government of the day and the society of the time, but also the artificialities of Italian opera. A sequel, *Polly* (1729), went even further and was eventually banned.

*The Beggar's Opera* has been successfully revived in recent times. New versions have been made by Frederick Austin (1920), and Benjamin Britten (1948), while a film version was prepared by Sir Arthur Bliss in 1953. Kurt Weill's *Die Dreigroschenoper* (The Threepenny Opera) (Berlin 1928), with words by Bertholt Brecht, was written in the same spirit as Gay's opera, but does not quote from it.

**The Beggar's Opera**
William Hogarth, the English painter, did several versions of this painting from 1729, the year after the enormous success of Gay's opera in London.

# Beethoven

**Ludwig van Beethoven 1770-1827**

Ludwig van Beethoven. Born at Bonn in 1770 and died at Vienna in 1827.

## 1. Life

Beethoven was born and brought up in Bonn, on the Rhine, where his father and grandfather were employed as musicians at the court of the ruling prince, the Elector of Cologne. His grandfather, Louis van Beethoven (1712–73), was of Flemish origin. He was a very able musician and eventually became the Elector's Director of Music. Ludwig's father, Johann (1740–92), was different. Though appointed as a tenor singer, he had little of Louis's musical ability and none of his character. He drank heavily, chased after women, and was a spendthrift and a bully. Beethoven's mother, Maria Magdalena, was quiet and affectionate and did her best to make the home a happy one, but she could do little to control her husband's excesses.

There were seven children in all; but four, perhaps fortunately, died in infancy. Beethoven was the second child and the first to survive. He had two brothers, Caspar and Nicholas, but he was the only one to inherit his grandfather's musical gifts. As soon as his father realized this he set about teaching him to play the harpsichord and violin. His general schooling was neglected, for what Johann had in mind was to turn his young son into a prodigy like Mozart, and then set him to earn as much money as possible.

In this he failed. The young Beethoven's talents were there, but they developed slowly and had to await the help of the right teacher. This happened in 1783 with the appointment of Christian Gottlob Neefe to the court's music staff. He was kind, helpful, and knowledgeable, and within a year the young Beethoven had been appointed second court organist, and assistant harpsichord player. Three years later, in 1787, he was sent to Vienna for further studies and seems to have had a few lessons from Mozart himself. But he was soon in Bonn again, for in July 1787 his mother died.

At home things now went from bad to worse, and Beethoven, at 17, found himself forced to take charge of everything – including his father's salary. All this helped to make him very determined and self-reliant, but it also made him anxious and constantly on guard lest he too should waste his life and become like his father. Strange as it may seem, Johann van Beethoven's shiftlessness helped to build in his son the driving force and energy that is the outstanding feature of his life and music.

By now, however, it had become clear in Bonn that he was a remarkable pianist and a very promising composer. And so, when Haydn passed through on his way to London, it was agreed that Beethoven should go to Vienna when he returned and take lessons from him. He set out in November 1792. A year later he was joined by his brothers (his father was now dead). They never returned to Bonn.

In Vienna Beethoven soon made influential friends – Prince Lichnowsky, Prince Lobkowitz, Count Razumovsky, and even the Archduke Rudolph himself. These men became his patrons. With their help, and with his own gifts as a brilliant pianist, he was soon a force to be reckoned with. But although he wrote a great deal of music, it was not until he was about 30 that his gifts in this direction began to be recognized as outstanding.

What turned him from a fashionable pianist and teacher into a great composer was the simple fact that from about 1796 he began to go deaf. By the end of 1802 he knew there could be no cure. At first he despaired, but then his determination and true greatness showed themselves. If deafness was to cut him off from a normal happy life, he would make a virtue out of necessity, retire in upon himself and devote his life to the creation of a totally new kind of music.

The first fruit of this change of attitude came in 1803 with his Third Symphony, the *Eroica*. Fine as his first two symphonies had been, they were still very much part of the 18th century – you could, as it were, see Mozart and Haydn behind them. But the *Eroica* was quite different – vaster, infinitely more powerful and expressive: it was the dawn of a new world in music.

From now until his death, Beethoven's life centred on his compositions. External events mean very little – the real growth is within the music itself, and to find out what happened to Beethoven it is to the music you must turn.

There were, of course, certain incidents,

and perhaps the most important concerned his nephew, Karl. When Beethoven's brother, Caspar, married in 1806, Beethoven, rightly or wrongly, took a dislike to his wife, whom he regarded as an immoral woman. Somehow he persuaded Caspar to make him Karl's guardian. When Caspar died in 1815, Beethoven claimed his legal rights. After a great deal of bitter wrangling, the boy came to live with him.

Though Beethoven loved his nephew, their relationship was doomed to failure. How could any ordinary, high-spirited young man cope with a deaf, domineering, eccentric old man who happened also to be a genius? Karl tried his best, but found the situation impossible. In 1826 he tried to shoot himself. Beethoven, bewildered and full of remorse, never really got over the shock, and some have claimed that it contributed to his death.

It is said that when he died his last act was to shake his fist at a thunderstorm raging outside. If so, it was a gesture utterly in keeping with his whole life – an act of heroic defiance against all that misfortune could bring.

## 2. His music

Beethoven was born at exactly the right time and came to live in exactly the right place. Vienna, in the middle of Europe, was open to influences from every quarter. It was a cultured, musical city, eager for new ideas. He came to maturity just as the 18th century was ending and the restrained 'classical' attitude to art was giving way to something more exciting, expressive and 'romantic'. The musical language he inherited from Haydn and Mozart was ready to express these new attitudes.

Almost everything Beethoven wrote was based on the Sonata Form. But in his hands it changed from being the neat, logical formal design of the 18th century, into something that could be intensely dramatic – a kind of battleground for conflicting ideas. Beethoven's music is so expressive that it forces the listener to become involved in what it is saying.

Certain musical fingerprints are particularly characteristic of this quality in his music. The powerful, driving rhythms, for instance; and the way in which he will build up a vast movement from a tiny musical

**Beethoven's studio**
This sketch shows the room as Beethoven left it when he died in 1827. Here, isolated by his deafness, which was total by 1824, he spent the last years of his life completely immersed in his work. A difficult and absent-minded man, he was a great trial to his housekeeper. In hot weather he was known to throw a bowl of water over his head rather than take the time to cool down. This room saw the completion of the Choral Symphony and his five string quartets.

idea. Examples of both can be found in the four pounding notes that open the Fifth Symphony.

Such is the power of his music, that Beethoven must be considered to be one of the greatest artists of all time.

## 3. Summary of Beethoven's main works

a. His vocal music includes:

| | |
|---|---|
| *Fidelio* (opera) | 1814 |
| Mass in C major | 1807 |
| Mass in D major 'Missa Solemnis' | 1823 |

b. Orchestral music includes:
Symphonies:

| | |
|---|---|
| No 1 in C major | 1800 |
| No 2 in D major | 1802 |
| No 3 in E flat (*Eroica*) | 1803 |
| No 4 in B flat | 1806 |
| No 5 in C minor | 1807 |
| No 6 in F major (*Pastoral*) | 1808 |
| No 7 in A major | 1812 |
| No 8 in F major | 1812 |
| No 9 in D minor (*Choral*) | 1825 |

Overtures:

| | |
|---|---|
| *Coriolanus* | 1807 |
| *Egmont* | 1810 |
| *Leonora*, No 1 | 1807 |
| *Leonora*, No 2 | 1805 |
| *Leonora*, No 3 | 1806 |
| *Fidelio* | 1814 |

c. Concertos include:
   Piano Concerto No 1, in C major 1797
   Piano Concerto No 2, in B flat 1795-98
   Piano Concerto No 3, in C minor 1800
   Piano Concerto No 4, in G major 1806
   Piano Concerto No 5, in E flat
      (*Emperor*)              1809
   Violin Concerto, in D major    1806

d. Chamber music includes:
   | | |
   |---|---|
   | 16 string quartets | 1798-1826 |
   | 16 piano trios | 1791-1815 |
   | 10 violin sonatas | 1797-1812 |
   | 35 piano sonatas | 1783-1822 |
   | 29 sets of piano variations | 1783-1823 |

## 4. Beethoven the man

Though he was born at a time when composers were regarded simply as servants of the nobility, Beethoven was an intensely proud man, fully aware of his own worth. When he moved among aristocrats he behaved as their equal and expected them to treat him as such. And so obvious was his genius that they did exactly that.

He was a man of iron determination (stubbornness, if you like), and had enormous courage – his ability to triumph over deafness would prove this, even if there was nothing else in his life to suggest it. But he was not easy to get on with. He was quarrelsome and, because he was absorbed in creating music, not always very considerate of other people. He sometimes even indulged in rather doubtful financial schemes against his publishers! He never married, though he seems to have admired, and been admired by, several beautiful women. He was almost certainly very lonely. But he never gave in to self-pity. Instead, he threw himself into the task of creating a world of his own, in music, in the way he liked it. And one of the most wonderful things about the world that Beethoven created is its optimism – the feeling that however hard the struggle, the outcome is positive and triumphant. It is not possible to listen to Beethoven's music without feeling uplifted and somehow better for the experience.

## 5. Beethoven's Sketch Books

Throughout his life Beethoven was in the habit of carrying small music notebooks, in which he would jot down his thoughts as they occurred to him. Later he would go over these musical ideas, polishing and repolishing until they were exactly suited for the work he had in mind.

**Beethoven in late middle age** this sketch of the composer leaving his house was published in 1833, six years after his death.

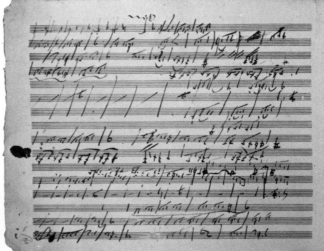

**Pastoral Symphony**
*Above* One of Beethoven's sketches for the Pastoral Symphony (1807–8).

*Left* This lithograph shows the composer working on the symphony in the valley of Nussdorf near Vienna. 'There I wrote the *Episode of the Brook* and the ... quails ... and cuckoos ... helped me compose.'

Many of these sketch books have been preserved (some of them are in the British Museum, London) and they give us a wonderful insight into the way his mind worked, and the enormous pains he took in shaping music that seems, in performance, spontaneous and inevitable.

### 6. Beethoven's Conversation Books
As he became deaf, Beethoven's friends were forced to write down what they wanted to say to him. Some of these 'conversation books' still exist and they tell us a good deal about his friendships and quarrels, and the people he met.

### 7. Beethoven's only opera
This, as has already been mentioned, is called *Fidelio*. It is about a nobleman, imprisoned for political reasons, whose wife dresses up as a youth in order to get into the prison and help him escape.

Beethoven took great pains over this opera and wrote no fewer than four overtures for it. Three of them are called by the original name of the opera: *Leonora Overture No 1, No 2,* and *No 3*. The fourth is called by the opera's final name, *Fidelio*. This is the name that the heroine takes when she disguises herself as a young man. It means 'Faithful'.

Beethoven was right in thinking that his first three overtures would not suit the opera. The trouble is that they are too good! They are so dramatic and descriptive that they steal much of the opera's thunder. The *Fidelio* overture is exactly the right weight: a perfect introduction to the opera, no more and no less.

The *Leonora Overture No 3* is often used as an interlude in the opera, at a point where we are already so deeply involved in the action that it can only add to the effect. It is also a very popular concert piece.

### 8. Beethoven and Britain
An Edinburgh man, George Thomson, who persuaded Haydn to write accompaniments for old Scottish and Welsh songs (→ **Haydn**), employed Beethoven in the same task. Altogether Beethoven treated over 60 songs in this way, for which Thomson paid him more than £500. These song settings can still be obtained, but are not often performed.

In 1818, when Beethoven was nearing his 50th year, he received a fine present from England – a grand piano which the firm of Broadwood sent him. Beethoven was delighted with it and kept it until he died. Then after a time it came into the possession of Liszt and now it is in the Hungarian National Museum at Budapest.

The famous Philharmonic Society more than once invited Beethoven to come to London and conduct his own works at their concerts, and offered him a large fee. He agreed, but never managed to do so. He wrote his ninth Symphony for the Society, and sent them the score, which they still possess. It has on it, in the composer's handwriting, the words (in German) *'Written for the Philharmonic Society in London'*. When Beethoven was dying the Society sent him £100, as he was thought to be short of money, and he sent them his 'most sincere thanks'.

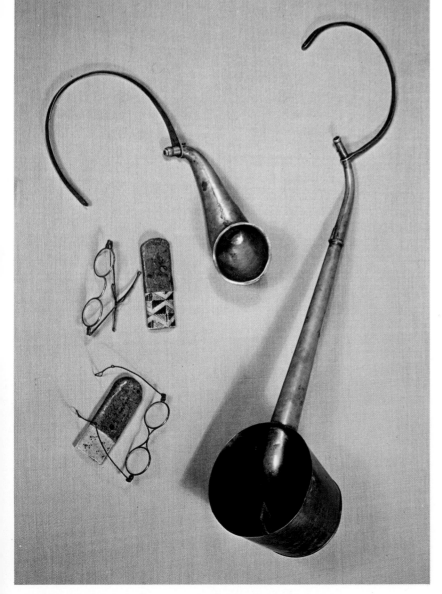

**Ear trumpets and spectacles** After 1824 when Beethoven became totally deaf these crude hearing aids ceased to be useful. Beethoven then relied on his conversation books (in which the visitor would write down what he wished to say), in order to communicate with people.

**Bel** The unit for measuring the intensity (loudness) of sound. It is named after the inventor Alexander Graham Bell (1847–1922). One bel represents a tenfold increase in loudness, therefore it is usual to measure such changes in DECIBELS (one-tenth of a bel). The decibel is the smallest change in loudness that the average ear can detect.

**Bel canto** (It.) Beautiful song. A method of voice production that flourished in Italy from the 17th to 19th centuries. The sound was clear, sustained, and very smooth. Great care was taken over the phrasing and articulation. Although the art of bel canto declined towards the end of the 19th century, the recent revival of interest in Italian opera (particularly that of Rossini, Bellini, Donizetti and early Verdi) has led a number of important singers, such as the soprano Joan Sutherland, to return to its ideals.

**Bellini, Vincenzo** Italian composer, 1801–35. He was a very popular composer of opera. His masterpieces, such as *La Sonnambula* (1831), *Norma* (1831), and *I Puritani* (1835), were introduced into the repertory in the 1950s by among others, the Greek soprano Maria Callas, and are now frequently performed. They are full of beautiful melodies and call for great artistry on the part of the singers. Bellini's kind of melody greatly influenced Chopin, who produced an equivalent 'singing style' in his piano music.

**Bells and bell-ringing** → page 58

**Belly** (of a violin, etc) This is the name given to the top surface. Sometimes it is called the 'Table'.

**Belyayev, Mitrofan** Russian music publisher, 1836–1904. The son of a wealthy timber merchant. His enthusiasm for the cause of Russian music led him to found a publishing house (1885) which greatly helped the young Nationalist composers (Borodin, Mussorgsky, Rimsky-Korsakov, etc.). He also initiated concerts of their works and was, in every sense, a benefactor to them.

**Ben, Bene** (It.) Well (in the sense of 'much'). So *ben marcato* means 'well marked', that is, well accented.

**Benedict,** (Sir) **Julius** German composer, 1804–85. After a successful career in Vienna and Italy, he settled in London in 1835 as a composer and conductor, eventually taking British nationality. He wrote two symphonies and two piano concertos, several oratorios and many operas. Of these, only one is still remembered: *The Lily of Killarney* (1862).

**Vincenzo Bellini**
1801–1835

**Richard Rodney Bennett**
b.1936

**Alban Berg**
1885–1935 Oil painting by Schoenberg.

**Benedictus → Mass**

**Benjamin, Arthur** Australian composer, 1893–1960. He came to London as a student of the Royal College of Music, and after a few years in Australia returned and lived there for the rest of his life. He was a fine pianist and wrote a considerable quantity of music, including some very effective film scores. He was well known to the public for his *Jamaican Rumba* (1938), but his two comic operas, *The Devil take Her* (1931) and *Prima Donna* (1933), show him at his best.

**Bennett, Richard Rodney** English composer, b. 1936. He was a pupil of the Royal Academy of Music and has written a great variety of music in a great variety of styles, from serial techniques (in his serious concert and chamber works) to 'popular' tunes in his many film scores – such as *Nicholas and Alexandra* and *Murder on the Orient Express* – and children's pieces, such as the opera *All the King's Men* (1969). He has also been much influenced by jazz and is an excellent jazz pianist. Of his four large-scale operas, the first, *The Mines of Sulphur* (1965), made the deepest impression.

**Bennett,** (Sir) **William Sterndale** English composer, 1816–75. He came of a musical family and was very precocious. After studying at the Royal Academy of Music he spent some time in Germany, where his music was much admired by Mendelssohn and Schumann. On returning to London in 1837 he settled down to a life of teaching, conducting, and performing (he was a fine pianist), composing in what little time was left to him. It is probably for this reason that he never quite fulfilled the promise of his early years. Even so, he wrote many important things, including a symphony, six piano concertos, five overtures, an oratorio *The Woman of Samaria* (1867), a cantata *The May Queen* (1858), and a considerable quantity of piano music.

**Berceuse** (Fr.) Cradle song. Many instrumental pieces have been written in the Berceuse style – quiet, flowing pieces, generally with six beats to the bar.

**Berg, Alban** Austrian composer, 1885–1935. He studied privately (1904–10) with Arnold Schoenberg, but for the first two years did not have to pay any fees because his family was so poor and Schoenberg was so impressed by his talent. Together with Anton von Webern, Berg remained one of Schoenberg's closest friends and disciples, eventually accepting his 12-note theory of composition (→ **Serialism**). However, he always remained the most lyrical and approachable of the three revolutionaries, and though his music was sometimes received coldly, certain works eventually became almost popular and helped to convince other musicians that there was something to be said for the new theory.

Berg's early works, such as the *Five orchestral Songs* (1912) and the *Three orchestral Pieces* (1914), were not well received, but in 1925 he achieved world fame with his opera *Wozzeck*. He began a second opera, *Lulu*, shortly afterwards and it was thought to have been left unfinished at his death. The first two acts were performed in 1937 (and many times since), but it was later found that the last act was virtually complete, and the complete work was performed in Paris in February 1979.

The first of Berg's works to use the 12-note system was the *Lyric Suite* (1926), and this was also well received. His last, and possibly greatest composition, was the Violin Concerto, completed a few months before his death and first performed in 1936. It was written on the death of Manon Gropius, the 18-year-old daughter of Mahler's widow by her second marriage, and is dedicated 'To that Memory of an Angel'. It is generally considered to be one of the masterpieces of 20th-century music.

**Bergomask** (Eng.), or **Bergamasque** (Fr.), or **Bergamasca** (It.).

This was a peasant dance that came originally from the district of Bergamo, in North Italy. Its music had two beats in a bar. Sometimes the title *Bergamasca* is given to instrumental pieces in the style of this dance.

**Beiderbecke, Leon ('Bix')** American jazz cornet player and composer, 1903–31. One of the few white musicians ever to be admired and imitated by Negro jazzmen. Famous for his smooth legato and beautiful tone, he was also a pianist and composer, and was one of the first to introduce complex modern harmonies into jazz.

**Berio, Luciano** Italian composer, b. 1925. He is a pupil of the influential Italian composer Dallapiccola. In 1953 he founded a studio in Milan to study the problems of musique concrète and electronic music. His compositions are often very unconventional, and many of them involve visual effects. In *Circles* (1960), for example, the actual movement of the performers is very important. Needless to say, his music arouses much heated discussion.

Luciano Berio
b.1925

Sir Lennox Berkeley
b.1903

Leonard Bernstein
b.1918

**Berkeley,** (Sir) **Lennox** English composer, b. 1903. He is partly of French descent and, after studying modern languages at Oxford University, he went to Paris for composition lessons with Nadia Boulanger. His early works were influenced by Stravinsky, but he soon developed a more personal style, and such works as the *Serenade for Strings* (1939), the *Divertimento* for small orchestra (1943), and the song cycle *Four Poems of St Teresa of Avila* (1947) have become very popular.

Berkeley has written four operas and his music is elegant and tuneful.

**Berlin, Irving** American composer, b. 1888. Though born in Russia (his name was originally Isidore Balin) he came to America as a child. After working as a 'singing waiter' he began to write such hits as *Alexander's Ragtime Band* and *Everybody's doin' it* and was soon set fair for an enormously successful career. His most famous stage show was *Annie get your Gun* (1946). His patriotic song, *God bless America*, is also much admired and won him a citation of merit from President Eisenhower in 1954.

**Berlioz** → page 60

**Berners, Lord (Gerald Tyrwhitt-Wilson)** English composer, 1883–1950. Besides possessing a title and a beautiful estate at Farringdon, he served in the Diplomatic Corps, wrote a number of amusing books, painted rather well, and composed a small quantity of delightfully witty music. He was also somewhat eccentric in his personal behaviour. He is best known for his ballets: *The Triumph of Neptune* (1926), and *The Wedding Bouquet* (1936).

**Bernstein, Leonard** American composer and conductor, b. 1918. He was trained at Harvard and the Curtis Institute and then became well known as a conductor, composer, pianist, and television personality. His music is very tuneful, colourful, and lively, and frequently makes use of jazz. He has written ballets, such as *Fancy Free* (1944); musicals, including *Candide* (1957) and *West Side Story* (1958); and two symphonies: *Jeremiah* (1944), and *The Age of Anxiety* (1949). He is the conductor of the New York Philharmonic Orchestra.

**Berwald, Franz** Swedish composer, 1796–1868. He came from a long line of musicians and is now remembered as the first Swedish symphonist and the greatest Swedish composer of his time. He wrote six symphonies, several concertos, and a considerable quantity of chamber music, as well as several operas. He spent many years in

# Bells and bell-ringing

1. Bells come in all shapes and sizes and have been used all over the world for many thousands of years.

The earliest known bells were of two kinds. The oldest are those that are sounded by a striker that is not a part of the bell itself. In this case the bell is either held in one hand and struck by a mallet held in the other, or it is suspended in a frame and then struck. Bells of this type were known in China four thousand years ago, where they were usually found in temples. Eastern music still makes use of struck bells, often employing a whole series hung on a frame and making up a scale. Sometimes the bells are graded in size (according to the note required), sometimes they are the same size but have different thicknesses of metal.

The other type of ancient bell, dating back some three thousand years, has a sounding device actually attached to it. This can either be in the form of a pellet that rattles freely inside the bell – in which case the bell is an almost complete sphere, with only a small slit cut in the end (we see tiny versions of such bells on dog collars); or the bell is an ordinary open-ended kind with a clapper suspended inside (or sometimes outside). Most bells of this type are untuned (but → HANDBELLS, below).

2. If you listen carefully to any large church bell you will notice that it not only has what we may call its proper note (the STRIKE NOTE), but also a jumble of other, softer notes. The deepest of these soft notes persists long after the others have died away. It is called the HUM NOTE, and its sound is usually an octave below the Strike Note.

There are two main ways of sounding the ordinary church bell: CHIMING and RINGING. A bell is said to have been chimed when the clapper is moved by a mechanism so that it strikes the side. When a bell is rung, it is swung round in a full circle by one man pulling on a bell-rope.

A set of church bells is called a RING. The number of bells in a ring will vary from church to church, but anything from 5 to 12 is usual. They can be rung in any order, and these variations are called CHANGES. With a ring of five bells, 120 changes are possible. But with a ring or 12 bells, the number of changes rises to nearly 480 million! There are many 'patterns' for change-

**Types of bells** There are three basic sorts of bells open; suspended, struck from without; or closed, containing a sounding device. The three pictures on the far right are clapper bells which may be fixed, rotated, or be rung by hand.

Bells like these are often used to accentuate rhythm in dance.

**How the bell is made** Whitechapel Foundry, London

**Making the core** Clay loam forms the core on a brick foundation, gauged smooth.

**Making the cope** The cope is made like the core. Both are later oven-dried.

**Inscribing the cope** Dates or letters are engraved to appear in relief.

**Putting the two together** The cope is lowered onto the core and clamped.

**Pouring the molten metal** Bell metal is 13 parts copper, 4 parts tin.

**Tuning** A bell is tuned and finished to five partial tones over two octaves.

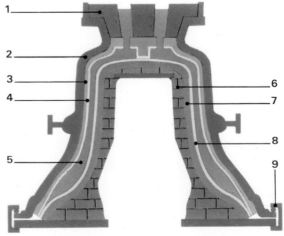

**Bell mould** This cross section shows the crown of the mould, **1**; the cast iron outer casing, **2**; the cope, a clay loam outer skin, **3**; graphite finishing coat to the cope **4**; bronze bell-metal, **5**; brickwork foundation, **6**; clay loam inner skin to the core (yellow London clay in this example), **7**; graphite finishing coat to the core, **8**; and the rim of the outer casing at base level, **9**, to which clamps are applied.

**Change-ringing** To begin, the bell is pulled from the 'down', **1**, to the 'set' position, **2**, inverted and just off-balance. A pull starts the bell-wheel in rotation (*circle below, clockwise*). It swings down, strikes and continues up until stopped at the inverted position. The next pull reverses the process. Changes depend on the timing of the ringers.

*Below* **'Down' position** This bell rests 'down' and the rope hangs down to the ringing chamber below.

ringing (ringing the changes), and they are known by traditional names, such as 'Grandsire Triple', 'Oxford Treble Bob', 'Bob Major', and so forth.

It needs years of practice to become a good ringer, able to follow the scheme of a particular change-ringing pattern without making a mistake. And if the changes are very long, then they also turn into an athletic feat. In some churches you will find old painted boards proudly recording the date when difficult changes were rung and how long it took.

Change-ringing is now a flourishing hobby with many people, but there are a number of very old societies or clubs – one, the Society of College Youths, was founded in London in 1637.

3. Change-ringing is an English art and is not known on the continent of Europe. But Belgium and Holland have the CARILLON. This is a set of bells (sometimes as many as 70) which are struck by clappers operated from a keyboard. In fact there are two keyboards: one for the feet and one for the hands. It is therefore possible to play several notes at once. On certain days the Carilloneur will give recitals to the whole town. In between times, at the hours, half-hours and quarters, by day and night, tunes are played by a clockwork mechanism.

4. Instead of real bells, some churches now have TUBULAR BELLS. These are tubes of metal, each note having a different length of tube. They are played electrically from a small keyboard. A smaller version of the same thing (played, by hand) can be found in the orchestra. ( → **Tubular bells**)

5. HANDBELLS are small bells with leather handles. They are made in sets, tuned to the chromatic scale. They are placed on a table and rung by a number of Handbell Ringers, each taking two or four different notes. If the ringers are skilful, and the bells of good quality, such concerts can be very enjoyable.

6. Many composers have introduced bell sounds into their music. Sometimes they use actual bells, real or tubular; and sometimes they make the orchestra, or piano even, imitate the sound.

(For another use of the word Bell → **Brass**)

# Berlioz

Hector Berlioz. France 1803-69. He was born near Grenoble, where his father was a doctor; and though he insisted, from a very early age, that he wished to be a composer he too was sent to Paris to study medicine. He soon abandoned this for music and eventually persuaded his father to let him study at the Paris Conservatoire.

Even at this date (1824) he was something of a revolutionary, and his imaginative ideas brought him into conflict with the teachers, with the result that he did not gain the coveted Prix de Rome until 1830 – on the fifth attempt! By the end of that year, however, he had become famous, for in December his Fantastic Symphony *(Symphonie Fantastique)* was performed with great success.

The Fantastic Symphony is a 'programme' symphony: that is to say, besides being logical simply as music, it also tells a story. In this instance the story reflects Berlioz's love for an Irish actress, Harriet Smithson, whom he eventually married. The audience knew about his passion, for he had taken care to publicize it, but even so they must have been astonished by the music. It is intensely dramatic, and filled with novel harmonies, long expressive melodies, and exciting orchestral effects. Altogether it suggests a quite new approach to music. And this indeed is what it was: one of the first truly great and original masterpieces of the Romantic era.

After a year in Rome (1831–32), Berlioz returned to Paris to begin the difficult task of earning his living as a composer. He wrote a number of very fine, highly original works which were nearly always well received. They brought him considerable fame, and were much talked about, but they did not bring him enough to live on. He therefore had to do other musical jobs, including work as a critic (which he hated) and conducting (which he liked). He was in fact an excellent critic and a very witty writer and, among other things, published a splendid book of *Memoirs* (privately printed in 1865). He was a fine conductor and made several tours in Germany, Russia, and England. And, as his music shows, he had an unrivalled understanding of the orchestra and its instruments. In 1843 he wrote a book about the art of orchestration which is still regarded as a classic.

**Hector Berlioz**
1803–1869

The last years of Berlioz's life were rather sad. His first marriage was never a success and in 1854, after his wife's death, he married again. His second wife died in 1862, and then, five years later, his only son died of yellow fever far away in Havana, where he was working as a sea-captain. Berlioz, already ill and exhausted by worry and over-work, now felt there was little left to live for.

## Summary of Berlioz's main works

a. Operas:

| | |
|---|---|
| *Benvenuto Cellini* | 1838 |
| *The Trojans* | 1859 |
| *Beatrice and Benedict* | 1862 |

b. Choral:

| | |
|---|---|
| *Requiem* | 1837 |
| *The Damnation of Faust* | 1846 |
| *Te Deum* | 1849 |
| *The Childhood of Christ* | 1854 |

c. Symphonies:

| | |
|---|---|
| *Fantastic Symphony* | 1830 |
| *Harold in Italy* | 1834 |
| *Romeo and Juliet* | 1839 |

d. Overtures:

| | |
|---|---|
| *Les Francs-Juges* | 1827 |
| *Le Carnaval Romain* | 1844 |
| *Le Corsaire* | 1855 |

He also wrote many shorter choral works, including the delightful *Sara la Baigneuse* (1834) and *La Mort d'Ophélie* (1848), both for women's voices; and a number of songs, including the marvellous song-cycle *Nuits d'Été* (1856).

**Berlioz and orchestra**
This contemporary cartoon ridicules the composer's use of extravagant orchestration and effects. Though many of his contemporaries thought he was mad, or at least wildly eccentric, it is now clear that Berlioz was one of the most remarkable and original composers of the 19th century. While his works are often very long and call for vast orchestras and choruses, now that we have come round to performing them as he intended, it is evident that he knew what he was doing – he was simply years ahead of his time.

Germany and Austria and pursued a number of non-musical activities – such as managing a clinic, running a saw-mill, and directing a glass-blowing factory.

**Big band** The classic 'big band' of the 1935–45 'swing' era consisted of four trumpets, three or four trombones, five saxophones (two altos, two tenors, one baritone), and a rhythm section (piano, bass, drums, and sometimes a guitar). Melodies are usually scored for one section of the orchestra at a time – say massed trumpets, or massed saxophones – and are often thickened out with block chords.

Among the famous big bands are those of Benny Goodman, Woody Herman, and Artie Shaw. (→ **Swing**)

**Billings, William** American composer, 1746–1800. He was born in Boston, where he lived and worked as a tanner, composing music in his spare time. Though his knowledge of musical theory was limited, he was a lively and fearless composer, and his music is the first by an American that is not based directly on European models. He

**Harrison Birtwistle**
b.1934

wrote mainly hymns, anthems, and songs – some of which are 'fuguing tunes' (songs in which the voice parts come in one after another, somewhat in the manner of a fugue).

**Birdsong →** page 62

**Birtwistle, Harrison** English composer, b. 1934. He studied at the Royal Manchester College of Music, and at the Royal Academy of Music, and came into prominence as a composer in 1957, with a wind quintet *Refrains and Choruses*. Though much of his music is 'composed', it also contains aleatory elements (as in *Verses for Ensembles*, 1969), as well as synthesised, pre-recorded sounds (*Chronometer*, 1971). His compositions include dramatic pieces, such as *Down by the Greenwood Side* (1969), and the opera *Punch and Judy* (1967), as well as large-scale orchestral works, such as *The Triumph of Time* (1972).

**Bis** (Fr.) 'twice'. If found in a score it means that the passage to which it is attached is to be performed twice: if heard shouted by the audience in a French concert hall it indicates the demand for which the English-speaking

# Binary Form

'Binary' means 'dual', or 'in a pair'. Thousands of short pieces of music consist of two balanced sections, and so we say they are in Simple Binary Form. Here is a brief piece in Binary Form composed by Mozart – In this piece Mozart has begun the first part in G major and ended it in D major (the key of the dominant).

In the second part, after a couple of bars of A minor, he has returned to G major and ended in that key.

This is what is generally done in *Simple* Binary Form. If the piece begins in a major key, the first part moves either to the dominant or the relative minor, and then the second part returns to the original key. If the piece begins in a minor key, the first part usually moves to the relative major (though it can move to the dominant), and then the second part returns to the original.

In Mozart's piece you will see that the last four bars of the second part are exactly the same as the last four bars of the first part (except that they are in a different key). This sort of effect is sometimes called *Rhymed* Binary.

Besides *Simple* Binary Form there is *Compound* Binary Form. Turn to the article on sonata form, where you will find it fully explained. (→ **Sonata Form**)

K.15e

# Birdsong

Though birds may seem to be singing for sheer joy, they are for the most part behaving in a very practical, matter-of-fact way. Birds sing in order to communicate with other birds. Sometimes it is a warning of danger, sometimes it is to attract a mate, sometimes it is to show the extent of their territory. Their song varies enormously, from a few simple notes to the elaborate song of the blackbird and the nightingale.

Composers have always been fascinated by these sounds and have often made use of them in their compositions. Sometimes they have imitated them more or less exactly in order to suggest a country scene – for example, Beethoven's *Pastoral* Symphony has a passage at the end of the slow movement which imitates the Nightingale, the Quail, and the Cuckoo. Sometimes they invent a musical phrase which suggests a particular bird without imitating it exactly – for example, the 'crowing' tune that Rimsky-Korsakov uses throughout his opera *The Golden Cockerel*, and Delius: *On hearing the first Cuckoo in Spring*. The French composer Olivier Messiaen, however, has used birdsong in a much more elaborate way and many of his works are literally modelled on it.

**Song birds** The best of British song birds are said to be the nightingale, blackbird, blackcap (shown as 'summer' birds on the calendar right) and the skylark. Most song birds have dull plumage.

**Cuckoo's song** *Below* This notation of the cuckoo's cry is from Kircher's *Musurgia Universalis*, 1650. The songs of the cuckoo and the nightingale (*below right*) have been much imitated by composers, notably Handel, Haydn, Purcell, Vivaldi and Delius.

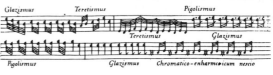

people, strangely, use another French word, 'Encore!' The Italians also use the word in this sense.

In German, **bis** has a quite different sense: it means 'until'.

**Bishop,** (Sir) **Henry** English composer, 1786–1855. He was famous as a London conductor and composer. He wrote many operas, and 'adapted' operas by composers rather greater than himself! A song from one of his operas, *Clari, or The Maid of Milan* (1823), is still sung: 'Home, sweet Home'. He was the first English composer to be honoured with a knighthood.

**Bitonality** Literally 'using two keys at once' – an effect to be found in the work of many 20th-century composers, where two lines of music are combined, even though each is 'in' a different key. The same effect can be obtained with two chords which are clearly in different keys. For example, the first scene of Puccini's opera *Turandot* uses the following 'bitonal' effect:

The chord in the bass is clearly in D minor, and the chord in the treble is clearly in C sharp major. The resulting combination is very pleasant, but it is not in any 'key'.

**Bizet, Georges** French composer, 1838–75. His father was a singing teacher and his mother a pianist and when he was only four they encouraged him to study music seriously. He became a student at the Paris Conservatoire when he was ten and eventually won the famous Prix de Rome (1857). Some of his early works, such as the Symphony in C (1855), are still played.

Though he wrote many different kinds of music, opera was Bizet's real love. He made his first successful attempt, *Dr Miracle*, in 1857 while still a student. His first important opera, *The Pearl Fishers*, was completed in 1863, but it was not a great success. *The fair Maid of Perth* (1867) was rather more successful, but *Djamileh* (1872) failed completely.

Despite his great gift for melody, his colourful harmony and brilliant orchestration, Bizet's operas failed to please. Even his masterpiece, *Carmen* (1875), only became really popular after his death.

Bizet wrote a great deal of music of all kinds, including many fine songs and piano pieces (such as the suite *Children's Games*), but it is *Carmen*, the last of his many operas, and the incidental music he wrote for Alphonse Daudet's play *L'Arlésienne* (The girl from Arles) (1872) that have kept his name alive so far as the general public is concerned. Musicians, however, have begun to realize how good his other operas are, and they too are now being performed. He was only 37 when he died, and there can be no doubt that had he lived he would have written many more operas, and perhaps have enjoyed the success he deserved.

**Blanche** ('white') is the French name for a minim (half-note).

**Bliss,** (Sir) **Arthur** English composer, 1891–1975. He studied at Cambridge University and the Royal College of Music and fought during the 1914–18 war as an officer in the Grenadier Guards. After the war he became known as a rather daring 'modernist', somewhat influenced by Stravinsky and Ravel, but, with the *Colour Symphony* (1922), he settled into a more 'English' romantic tradition.

Bliss lived for a while in America (1923–25) and wrote several works for American patrons, including the *Oboe Quintet* (1927). From 1942 to 1944 he was Director of Music at the BBC, and from 1953 he was Master of the Queen's Musick. He was knighted in 1950.

He wrote music of all kinds, including an opera, *The Olympians* (1949), several important ballets (*Checkmate*, 1937; *Miracle in the Gorbals*, 1944; *Adam Zero*, 1946), a choral symphony, *Morning Heroes* (1930), several concertos and many chamber works. He was also an early contributor to film music, with a very famous score for the H. G. Wells film *The Shape of Things to come* (1935).

**Bloch, Ernest** Jewish Swiss-American composer, 1880-1959. He was born in Switzerland, studied in Brussels and Frankfurt, and lived in Paris and Geneva. He became an American citizen in 1916, retired to live in Switzerland in 1930, but returned permanently to America in 1938.

Bloch made a deep study of Jewish music and this influenced his own style – such works as the popular *Schelomo* (a Hebrew Rhapsody for cello and orchestra, 1916), and the *Sacred Service* (1933) show this very clearly. He

**John Blow** 1649–1708
His opera *Venus and Adonis* is one of the earliest surviving English operas.

wrote a great deal of music of all kinds, including an impressive opera *Macbeth* (1910).

**Block harmony** This term describes music where all the parts in a series of chord progressions move at the same time. You can find examples in simple hymns – the harmony of which moves 'in blocks' along with the tune.

**Blomdahl, Karl-Birger** Swedish composer, 1916–68. He was a pupil of Hilding Rosenberg and wrote music of all kinds, including an impressive choral work *In the Hall of Mirrors* (1953) and a controversial 'space-opera', *Aniara* (1959). His musical style was very adventurous and thought nothing of mixing jazz, traditional, serial, and even electronic elements.

**Blow, John** English composer, 1649–1708. Along with Purcell he was a choir boy of the Chapel Royal and later became organist of it, and of Westminster Abbey. He wrote many fine anthems and services, a number of choral odes (to celebrate court occasions, and for St Cecilia's Day), a quantity of harpsichord music, and a charming opera *Venus and Adonis* (c. 1683).

**Blues** → page 64

**Boccherini, Luigi** Italian composer, 1743–1805. He was taught first by his father, a double-bass player, and then made a name for himself in Rome both as a cellist and composer. He toured Italy and France (1768) with great success and in the following year visited Spain. He later spent ten years (1787–97) in Berlin, thereafter returning to Spain and settling in Madrid, where he died. Although he wrote several operas and 20 symphonies, he is mainly known for his contribution to the development of chamber music – for which he has sometimes been ranked alongside Haydn. He wrote more than 150 quintets of various kinds, more than 100 string quartets, and 60 trios.

**Boehm system** An ingenious system of keys and levers invented by a flute player, Theobald Boehm (1793–1881). It enables the flute-maker to cut the holes in the correct acoustic position, yet leave them in easy control of the player's fingers. The keys and levers are thus flexible extensions of the fingers. This system is now used by all flutes and oboes, and can sometimes be found on clarinets and bassoons.

# Blues

This is a 20th-century jazz song or dance-song. It is in 4/4 time and moves at a moderately slow pace over an unvarying 12-bar bass consisting of Tonic, Subdominant, and Dominant chords. Thus a 'blues' in C major would have four bars on C, two on F, two on C, two on G, and two on C. This structure can, however, be elaborated upon.

In a 'blues' tune the third and seventh notes of the key are flattened. They are known as 'blue notes'. The words often tell of some personal misfortune, but always with a touch of humour.

**Blues singers** *top left* Blind Lemon Jefferson, aged about 30, in the 1920's. A remarkable musician, he also taught Leadbelly the blues. *Top right* Sonny Terry and Brownie McGhee, one of the famous blues duos of the 1940's. *Right* Howling Wolf and his band in a Chicago club, 1959. *Middle* Muddy Waters, who with Howling Wolf dominated the Chicago blues scene in the mid-1950's. *Far right* Junior Wells (harmonica) and Buddy Guy (guitar), two of the popular 'soul' musicians of the late 1950's and early 1960's.

**King Biscuit Time** *below* was a blues radio show which began in the 1940's. Sonny Boy Williamson and James Peck Curtis stayed with the show for over thirty years. With them here is Houston Stackhouse.

**Boito, Arrigo** Italian composer and author, 1842–1918. He was a great admirer of German music and wrote many articles about it in the hope of 'reforming' the Italian opera of his day. His own opera, *Mefistofele* (1868), caused a riot at its first performance, but was later accepted as a classic. He wrote music for only one other opera, *Nerone*, which was performed in 1924 after his death. However, he wrote many excellent libretti for other composers, and two of them, Verdi's *Otello* and *Falstaff*, are considered to be masterpieces. He also published several books of poetry and was an elected member of the Italian Senate.

**Bolero** This is a Spanish dance very like the *cachucha* ( → **Cachucha**). It is performed to the accompaniment of the dancers' own singing and the snapping of castanets.

Sometimes music in this style, and with this name, is written purely for instrumental performance. One such piece, Ravel's *Bolero*, is very famous.

**Bones** This is a very simple instrument – two pieces of bone that can be held between the fingers and clacked together. It used to be a common instrument in the days of the 'Minstrels' ( → **Banjo**), and the man who played it was always addressed by the others as 'Mr. Bones'.

**Bongos** Pairs of small Cuban drums seen in some dance bands. They are played with the fingers and the heel of the hand, not with drumsticks.

**Boogie-woogie** A style of jazz piano playing which became popular in America in the 1930s. It is a method of playing blues – the left hand keeping up a steady, rhythmic bass accompaniment (usually a quaver ostinato figure), while the right hand plays the melody.

**Bop** Short for 'bebop' or 'rebop' – a jazz style of the 1940s, which takes its name from the nonsense syllables sometimes sung by its performers in imitation of instruments. Bop uses complex rhythms, intricate melodic lines, and a more adventurous kind of harmony than earlier jazz. It features a soloist, to whom all other players in the group are an accompaniment. The saxophonist Charlie ('Bird') Parker was a pioneer in developing the bop style.

**Borodin, Alexander** Russian composer, 1833–87. He was a medical man and founded a School of Medicine for Women, and was also a Professor of Chemistry, so as a composer he may be called an amateur. But

**Alexander Borodin**
1833-1887 He was a nationalist composer and drew on Russian history, literature and folk music.

he wrote some fine music and was a respected member of 'The Five' – the group of composers who helped to establish a distinctly Russian type of music.

Borodin's music includes the opera *Prince Igor*, which was completed by Rimsky-Korsakov and Glazunov and produced in 1890; two symphonies, of which the second in B minor (1869–76) is deservedly popular. An orchestral piece, *In the Steppes of Central Asia* (1880), is also frequently heard, as are his two string quartets.

**Bouche fermée** (Fr.) Mouth closed. Sometimes in choral music a passage is so marked and it then has to be hummed instead of sung.

**Boughton, Rutland** English composer, 1878–1960. He studied at the Royal College of Music and was then on the staff of the Birmingham School of Music.

After early success as a choral composer he founded a series of festivals at Glastonbury (1914-27) where he staged his own and other people's operas. His dream was to create a cycle of Arthurian music dramas. He completed the five in 1945, but only three have been performed so far.

Boughton achieved a tremendous success with an opera called *The Immortal Hour* (1913), and three other operas, *Bethlehem* (1915), *Alkestis* (1922) and *The Queen of Cornwall* (1924), were also well received. His music is very simple and melodious, owing much to folksong, and his operas make considerable use of the chorus.

**Boulanger, Nadia** French composer and teacher, b. 1887. Though she has written a certain amount of music, as did her sister Lili (1893–1918), she is better known as a teacher of other composers – including the Americans Aaron Copland, Roy Harris, Walter Piston, Roger Sessions, and Virgil Thomson, and the Englishman Sir Lennox Berkeley. Her teaching methods are based on a rigorous study of the classics and such neo-classic composers as Stravinsky. ( → **Neo-classicism**)

**Boulez, Pierre** French composer and conductor, b. 1925. He is a pupil of Messiaen and came into prominence as an avant-garde composer immediately after the 1939–45 war. His experiments with Total Serialism ( → **Serialism**) have been very influential – such works as *Polyphonie X* for 18 instruments (1951) and *Structures 1* for two pianos (1952)

**Pierre Boulez** b. 1925 He has done less conducting since 1977 in order to direct the work of a centre of acoustic research in Paris.

follow these lines. But later works, such as *Le Marteau sans Maître* (1954), and *Pli selon Pli (Portrait de Mallarmé)* (1960), are less rigid and allow for a certain amount of improvisation (→ **Aleatoric**). In recent years, however, he has given more time to conducting than composing, and is much admired as an interpreter of contemporary music.

**Boult,** (Sir) **Adrian** English conductor, b. 1889. He studied music at Oxford University and the Leipzig Conservatory. He has been the conductor of many great orchestras, including the Birmingham City Orchestra (1924–30), the BBC Symphony Orchestra (1941–49), and the London Philharmonic (1949–57). From 1930 to 1942 he was Musical Director of the BBC. Boult has made a special study of English music, in particular Elgar and Vaughan Williams (many of whose symphonies he premièred).

**Bourrée** A dance of French origin which was popular in the 17th and 18th centuries and is often found in the dance suites of the time. It is a quick dance with two main beats to the bar and beginning with an up-beat. It is not unlike the Gavotte, but this has four beats to the bar and starts on the third beat. In the following example, the four crotchets (quarter-notes) of each bar are to be played *Alla breve* (as two beats to the bar).

*Fine*

*Da Capo al Fine*

J. S. Bach

**Bouzouki** A type of mandolin used by the folk musicians of Greece. It has a long neck, with two courses of three metal strings, tuned like a guitar.

Also a type of popular music which features this instrument, usually played together with an accordion and drums. Bouzouki music, and the instrument, originated in Turkey, but it has played an important part in the popular music of Greece since about 1900. Composers try to recreate the style of ancient folksongs and dances, using a fascinating mixture of Western scales and Eastern rhythms.

**Sir Adrian Boult**
b. 1889

**Bowing techniques**
Violin, viola and cello players usually use the overhand hold on the bow, **1**. Modern double bass players often hold the bow with the palm upwards, as did all players of the earlier viol, **2**.

**William Boyce**
1710–1769

**Branle** This was the first formal dance with alternating quick and slow rhythms. It was similar to the gavotte.

**Bowing** Bowing of a stringed instrument means one of two things:

1. The use of the bow by moving it across the strings ('up-bowing' and 'down-bowing').

2. The playing of a group of notes with one motion of the bow. For instance, in playing a scale, instead of playing one note with each motion of the bow backwards or forwards we can group the notes two to each motion or three to each – and so on. And then we say the scale is 'bowed' in that particular way.

**1**  **2**

**Boyce, William** English composer, 1710-69. He was a chorister of St Paul's Cathedral, and later held organist posts in several important London churches. In 1736 he was appointed composer to the Chapel Royal (and organist in 1758), and in 1757 he was appointed Master of the King's Musick – though he had done the work since 1735!

Boyce wrote many fine anthems and services, a number of 'symphonies' (in the early 'overture' style), several choral odes, and the music for a number of theatrical entertainments. He is remembered as the composer of the song 'Heart of Oak', and in recent years musicians have begun to rediscover his symphonies. He is also important for having collected and published a collection of the best English cathedral music.

**Brace** This is the perpendicular line with a bracket which joins the two staves in music for piano, etc., showing that the two are to be played together.

**Brahms** → page 68

**Branle** (or **Bransle**) A French country dance that also became very popular in the 16th century as a court dance. Its name comes from *branler*, 'to sway', which tells us something of its general character. The branle has two beats to the bar. In English it is sometimes called 'brawle'.

**Brass** The chief brass instruments in the orchestra are those belonging to the families of the TRUMPET, HORN, TROMBONE, and TUBA. In military bands and brass bands we also find the CORNET and the SAXHORN (and its relative the FLÜGELHORN).

A brass instrument does not have 'reeds',

# Bow

A slender, curved wooden stick which carries and keeps tight the strands of horsehair that the string-player uses to set his strings in vibration. The modern bow for the violin family curves slightly inwards *towards* the horsehair. The old bow, and all viol family bows, curve outward.

The wood of the bow is springy and is beautifully tapered to give the proper balance and control. The horsehair has thousands of tiny teeth which grip the strings and make them vibrate.

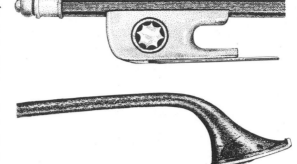
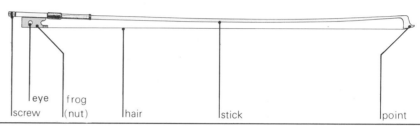

**Types of bow** *left*
These parts of an 18th-century violin bow show an ivory screw button and frog with mother-of-pearl star inlaid into an ivory background (*top*). The head of point (*bottom*) is slightly upturned. *Below* 18th-century bows for viola and viols (*left*); and parts of the modern violin bow (*right*).

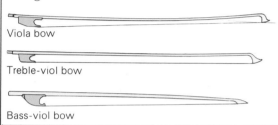

Viola bow

Treble-viol bow

Bass-viol bow

eye
screw | frog (nut) | hair | stick | point

# Brass band

The normal full brass band consists of 25 players, plus drums and any other percussion 'effects' needed.

Here are the instruments, in the order in which they appear in the score, together with the number of players to each part:
1 E flat soprano cornet
3 or 4 solo B flat cornets
1 Repiano B flat cornet
1 or 2 2nd B flat cornets
1 or 2 3rd B flat cornets
1 B flat Flügel
1 solo E flat tenor horn
1 1st E flat tenor horn
1 2nd E flat tenor horn
1 1st B flat baritone
1 2nd B flat baritone
1 or 2 1st B flat tenor trombones
1 2nd B flat tenor trombone
1 G Bass trombone
1 or 2 B flat euphoniums
2 E flat basses (or bombardons)
2 B flat basses (or contrabasses)
Drums – as required

Though the brass band began as a popular 'working class' institution (and there are still many fierce competitions for supremacy among the leading bands, mostly in the North of England), its popularity has spread, particularly in schools. Many fine composers, such as Holst and Vaughan Williams, have written special pieces for it.

**Brass band** This group of East German miners open the Festival of Joy and Light, a traditional Christmas event in the Aue county, Germany.

# Brahms

Johannes' Brahms.    German composer, 1833–97.

Though Brahms was born into a musical household in Hamburg, where his father worked as a double-bass player, it was also an impoverished one and rather unhappy. His mother was 17 years older than her husband and they do not seem to have been very well-suited to each other. Nevertheless, when it became obvious that their young son had genuine talent they did what they could to help.

He trained at first as a pianist, under the celebrated Eduard Marxsen, but soon he began to write music. By the time he was 14 even his stern teacher was convinced of his exceptional ability. At the same time, however, to make ends meet, he was obliged to play the piano in the kind of low dives you find in any great port. The experience left a mark on him, and in later years he sometimes surprised people with sudden outbursts against the worthlessness of human nature. As a child he had seen too much.

In 1853 Brahms met the Hungarian gipsy violinist Eduard Reményi and became his accompanist on a tour which took them, among other places, to Hanover, where the great violinist Joseph Joachim worked. Joachim was impressed by his playing and his compositions and gave him introductions not only to Liszt, but also to Schumann.

When at last they met, Schumann was delighted with Brahms and instantly published his opinion that here was a young man destined to become a great composer in the finest traditions of German music.

Schumann's praise was a great help and soon Brahms had found a publisher. But there were clouds on the horizon. Schumann began to show signs of madness and was placed in an asylum. He died there in 1856. Brahms did everything he could to help his widow, Clara. They became devoted friends, and for the rest of her life she treated him almost as a son.

In 1857 Brahms took part-time employment as musical director to the court at Detmold. It was an unexacting job which brought him conducting experience but left him plenty of time to compose. He was now widely accepted as an important composer – so important, in fact, that musicians who

**Johannes Brahms**
1833–1897

**Brahms with a hedgehog** The composer's association with this animal is based on his own 'prickly' temperament, coupled with the fact that he is said to have dined regularly at a restuarant called 'The Red Hedgehog'

**Johann Strauss with Brahms** The elderly Brahms was photographed, two years before his death, with the composer of *The Blue Danube* and *Tales from the Vienna Woods*.

disliked Wagner adopted him as their hero. Quite against their own wills, the two composers became the leaders of rival parties – Wagner as champion of a 'new' kind of music, and Brahms a defender of traditional values.

He left his native Hamburg in 1860 and, after two years in Switzerland, settled in Vienna where he remained happily for the rest of his life. Little happened to him. He never married. He was not much given to society. He seldom travelled far. But he wrote great music and his fame spread wide.

He was already seriously ill, from cancer, when he attended Clara Schumann's funeral (May 1896). He caught a chill and this brought matters to a head. Within a year he too was dead.

Brahms came to maturity when music was changing and the old methods that had served composers from Bach to Beethoven were giving way to something much more flexible and unpredictable. His greatness lay not so much in the fact that he deliberately tried to halt the change (which, of course, was impossible), but that even while swimming against the tide he managed to produce a series of master-pieces.

## Summary of Brahms' main works

a. Choral: *A German Requiem* 1868
   Many fine motets and part-songs.

b. Symphonies:
   No 1  in C minor          1876
   No 2  in D major          1877
   No 3  in F major          1883
   No 4  in E minor          1885

c. Concertos:
   Piano Concerto No 1,
      in D minor             1858
   Piano Concerto No 2,
      in B flat major        1881
   Violin Concerto, in D major   1878
   Double Concerto (violin & cello) 1887

Brahms also wrote several overtures and smaller orchestral works, a great deal of excellent chamber music, and many songs and piano pieces. Among the most popular of these are the *Academic Festival Overture*, *Variations on a theme of Haydn (the St Anthony chorale)*, the *Hungarian Dances*, and the two sets of *Liebeslieder* waltzes.

like those of the **Oboe family** and the **Clarinet family** →. It is simply a long tube with a MOUTHPIECE at one end (in which the player's lips vibrate like a reed), and what is called a BELL at the other – that is to say, a widening-out at the end of the tube. The various notes are obtained partly by blowing in different ways, and partly by increasing or decreasing the length of tube in use by means of VALVES (or in the case of the trombone by pulling out the tube to greater length or pushing it in again). (→ **Trumpet, Horn, Trombone, Tuba, Cornet, Saxhorn and Flügelhorn**)

**Bravura** (It.) Skill. A bravura passage in music is one that is very showy and difficult to perform. Certain brilliant arias in opera are known as ARIE DI BRAVURA.

**Break, the** In wind instruments, and in human voices, there is a slight change of tone-quality between the different registers. This is known as the 'break'. You can hear it very clearly on a clarinet, which has its low 'chalumeau' (the name of an old 17th-century type of clarinet) register, and its brighter, clearer, higher sounds. A skilled performer will pass from one register to another quite smoothly, but beginners may find trouble. But even skilled performers do not like music which spends its time dodging about on either side of the break!

**Breit** (Ger.) Broad. Used in music to indicate that the tempo should be slow, the performance swinging along in a steady, rhythmic way. In the music of bowed instruments it sometimes applies to the bowing, for instance, *breit gestrichen* means 'broadly bowed', that is, using the full length of the bow and swinging out the tone.

**Breve** 1. (Pronounced 'breeve'.) This word, of course means 'short' (like 'brief') and originally meant the shortest note used in musical notation. But notation has changed, what were the signs for the longest notes in it being dropped, so that the breve ($\|\circ\|$) is now the longest note of all. Its time value is that of two semibreves (whole notes). The corresponding rest is ▆ . (→ **Notes and notation**)

2. There is an Italian expression *alla breve* (pronounced 'brayvay') which means 'in a short manner', that is 'make your notes shorter'. When this term is used the speed is to be double what it would otherwise have been.

When in a piece that has the value of four crotchets (quarter-notes) in every bar we see the term *alla breve*, or the sign ¢ (instead of C),

**Dave Brubeck** b.1920, whose sophisticated piano style and work with the MJQ had an outstanding influence on jazz in the 1950s.

or ₂ (instead of ⁴₄) it means that we are to count two beats in every bar instead of four.

But sometimes *alla breve* is (confusingly) used as a name for ⁴₂ time. Anyhow, whenever we see it we should take the minim (half-note) as our beat.

**Brian, Havergal** English composer, 1876–1972. He was self-taught and after a degree of success in his early days was largely forgotten, until it was discovered that he was remarkably old and had written five operas and no fewer than 32 symphonies, besides a great many other works. A fair number of these have now been performed including the massive Symphony No 1, 'The Gothic' (1919–27).

**Bridge** This is the piece of wood on a stringed instrument over which the strings pass. A string, when it is played, vibrates (that is, waves to and fro) and the bridge carries its vibrations to the body of the violin, so that the sound (which from the string alone would be hardly heard) is made louder.

The vibrating length of the string lies between the bridge and the nut of the fingerboard. (→ **Nut**)

**Bridge, Frank** English composer, 1879–1941. He studied under Sir Charles Stanford at the Royal College of Music and then became known as a fine viola player and conductor. He wrote music of all kinds, including a number of large-scale orchestral works, of which the symphonic suite *The Sea* (1911) is the most famous. He was perhaps more widely admired for his songs and chamber music (which includes four string quartets). He was an excellent teacher and Benjamin Britten was one of his pupils.

**Bridge passage** → **Sonata Form**

**Brio** (It.) Vigour, or spirit. Hence **con brio**, 'with spirit'.

**Brisé** (Fr.) Broken. Used in music to describe a chord played in arpeggio fashion, and in string music to indicate that the notes must be played in a detached fashion with short motions of the bow.

**Britten** → page 70

**Broadcasting** → page 72

**Brubeck, Dave** American jazz composer and pianist, b. 1920. He formed the Modern Jazz Quartet in 1951. It brought into jazz such 'classical' devices as fugue and canon, as well as 'orchestral' instruments such as harp and cello. Brubeck has also taken a delight in 'jazzing the classics' – usually Mozart.

# Britten

Benjamin Britten (Lord Britten of Snape). English composer, 1913–1976. Like many great composers, Benjamin Britten began to write music when he was a child. From the age of seven he studied the piano, and a few years later the viola. When he was 12 he went to Frank Bridge for composition lessons.

He was 17 when he went to the Royal College of Music, 19 when he made a mark as a composer (with a *Sinfonietta*), and 21 when he began to earn his living. At this stage he enjoyed two strokes of good fortune: he was offered a contract by a publisher, and he was invited to write music for the General Post Office's documentary film unit. The first gave him a sense of confidence, the second taught him his trade.

His first important work, the choral variations *A Boy was Born*, appeared in 1934, and his first really great success, the *Variations on a Theme of Frank Bridge*, was heard at the 1937 Salzburg Festival.

There followed a period of some uncertainty, which continued when he went to live in America in 1939 and lasted until 1942 when he decided to return home again. The works he wrote in the meantime, however, all added significantly to his reputation. But real fame came in 1945 with the performance of his opera *Peter Grimes*. It was the first English opera to achieve international success and seemed, to many, to usher in a new era in British music.

From now on, anything that Benjamin Britten cared to write was of world interest. His earlier works, successful enough in the past, were now re-examined and found to be even more admirable. It also became clear that he was about to do what few Englishmen had ever done: write successful operas!

*Above* **Noye's Fludde** The composer talks to a 'squirrel' during a rehearsal of this operatic work, which was first performed in 1958.
*Right* **Britten at the piano**
*Below* **The Maltings, Snape** This concert hall was opened in 1967.

But opera in England has always had a hard struggle, and Britten wisely thought it would be sensible to found his own opera company. Out of this decision came The English Opera Group and the Aldeburgh Festival (1948).

The Festival began in a small way, using the resources of the Suffolk fishing town where he now lived, and the talents of the great artists who were now his personal friends. Since then it has grown and is now famous throughout the musical world. In 1967 its success was crowned with the opening of a magnificent concert-hall, The Maltings, at Snape.

Britten's music covers a wide range. He wrote large-scale operas suitable for major opera houses, and small-scale operas for his own opera group, as well as 'Church Parables' – operas for performances in church. He wrote music for children and amateurs, and for important national occasions, such as the opening of the new Coventry Cathedral – for which he composed the great *War Requiem* (1962). He wrote song cycles and symphonies, cantatas and concertos. In many respects he was one of the most successful composers of his time.

His music is quite simple. He used traditional materials: common chords abound. But he put these simple ideas together in a way that was totally fresh and unexpected. He could write memorable tunes and had a keen ear for new orchestral colours. His way of setting the English language to music was remarkable. Above all, he was able to write operas in which the characters and the dramas spring to life through the music.

*Above* **Peter Grimes**
This opera, first produced in London in 1945, is based on Thomas Crabbe's poem *The Borough* and is named after its fisherman hero. This scene is from the 1958 production of the opera at Covent Garden.

*Below* **Let's Make an Opera!** This 'entertainment for young people' was first produced at Aldeburgh in 1949. In the first section the cast, mostly made up of children, rehearse an opera which is then performed, with the participation of the audience, in the second half.

*Above* **Britten in 1976**
In the year of his death the composer was made a life peer – Lord Britten of Snape.

## Summary of Britten's main works

a. Opera:
  (i) Full-scale operas:

| | |
|---|---|
| *Peter Grimes* | 1945 |
| *Billy Budd* | 1951 |
| *Gloriana* | 1953 |
| *A Midsummer Night's Dream* | 1960 |
| *Death in Venice* | 1974 |

  (ii) Chamber operas:

| | |
|---|---|
| *The Rape of Lucretia* | 1946 |
| *Albert Herring* | 1947 |
| *The little Sweep* | 1949 |
| *The Turn of the Screw* | 1954 |

  (iii) Church Parables:

| | |
|---|---|
| *Curlew River* | 1964 |
| *The Burning Fiery Furnace* | 1966 |
| *The Prodigal Son* | 1968 |

b. Ballet:

| | |
|---|---|
| *The Prince of the Pagodas* | 1957 |

c. Choral:

| | |
|---|---|
| *Ceremony of Carols* | 1942 |
| *Rejoice in the Lamb* | 1943 |
| *St Nicholas* | 1948 |
| *Spring Symphony* | 1949 |
| *Noyes Fludde* | 1958 |
| *War Requiem* | 1962 |

d. Orchestral:

| | |
|---|---|
| *Variations on a Theme of Frank Bridge* | 1937 |
| *Sinfonia da Requiem* | 1941 |
| *Diversions (piano & orch)* | 1942 |
| *Young Person's Guide to the Orchestra* | 1946 |
| *Cello Symphony* | 1963 |

# Broadcasting

The first popular word for what we now call the 'radio' was 'wireless'. Although this did not describe the radio receiver itself (which was full of wires!), it exactly described the fact that electric signals were being transmitted from one place to another without having to pass through wires like the telephone and telegraph.

Radio signals are electro-magnetic waves which travel through space at the speed of light (299,793 km per second). In the broadcasting studio sound waves fall on a microphone which contains a mechanical device that can vibrate in sympathy with them. This device (usually a metal ribbon or coil, suspended in a magnetic field; or a special crystal) generates a small electric current which corresponds exactly to the pattern of the sound waves.

The current is now fed to the radio transmitter, where it is amplified and combined with a high frequency electro-magnetic wave called a 'carrier wave'. When this is done a variation takes place in the amplitude of the carrier wave (amplitude modulation, or A.M.). Thus, what was originally a sound wave can now be sent out by the transmitting aerial in the form of an electro-magnetic wave of varying amplitude.

At the receiver, the weak electric currents are picked up by a receiving aerial, amplified, and then processed in a way which extracts the 'modulation' from the carrier wave. These varying signals are therefore an exact replica of the electric signals from the microphone. After further amplification the signals are fed to a loudspeaker, which acts like a microphone in reverse. The electric signals vibrate a diaphragm, which in turn creates sound waves. We then hear an almost exact copy of what was taking place in the broadcasting studio.

A great many scientists of different nations have helped to bring broadcasting into existence, but perhaps the most famous is the Italian Guglielmo Marconi (1874–1937). He began to make successful experiments with wireless telegraphy in 1895, transmitting messages in morse code. Three years later he sent messages across the English Channel, and in 1901 across the Atlantic.

Radio waves radiate in all directions and

An ionized layer in the earth's upper atmosphere reflects sound waves transmitted on long wave frequencies.

At a lower level the ionized band reflects transmission on medium and VHF frequencies.

*Above* This diagram shows the way in which sound is beamed on various wave lengths to ionized layers in the earth's atmosphere. Sound waves are reflected in much the same way as light is reflected from a polished surface. In this way radio waves may travel directly from a transmitter, reflected in turn by the charged (ionized) layer and the earth's crust, to a receiver hidden by the earth's curvature.
*Below* Paul Burnett, a disc jockey of BBC's Radio 1, sits at the studio control panel with record turntables to hand on either side.

can therefore be received in many different places. This fact led to the idea of Radio Broadcasting to many different listeners – the word itself means that signals are 'cast abroad'. Experimental services began in 1920 and within the next few years many countries had developed at least one service of regular public broadcasting.

In those early days the quality of reproduced sound was not very good because the equipment could not respond to the wide range of frequencies needed to give a faithful copy of the human voice or an orchestra. At first people had to wear headphones in order to hear the sound; but loudspeakers soon made their appearance, thus enabling a whole group of people to listen at the same time. The amplification needed to drive these loudspeakers was carried out by thermionic valves, which looked rather like electric light bulbs. A three or four-valve receiver was quite a large piece of furniture – the age of portable radios had not arrived.

During the second world war there were important advances in radio technology, and the new receivers were able to give a much better reproduction of all sounds. There were corresponding improvements in studios, microphones, the gramophone, recording apparatus, and all the other broadcasting equipment.

In the 1950s there were two more important steps forward. In the first place, the invention of the transistor provided an electronic device no bigger than a pin's head that could do most of the jobs previously done by the thermionic valve. Pocket radios soon became common.

Secondly, there was a new system of broadcasting using Very High Frequency radio waves. V.H.F. transmission permits a different form of modulation to be used where the frequency of the electro-magnetic wave is varied (frequency modulation, or F.M.) in sympathy with the electric signals from the microphone. F.M. broadcasting has two great advantages: it allows a greater range of sound frequencies to be transmitted, thus improving the clarity and quality, and it is also more effective in suppressing electrical interference. With the best equipment it is now possible to reproduce sound which is nearly indistinguishable from the original performance. Further-

*Above* **Guglielmo Marconi** 1874-1937. *Below* the broadcasting sequence. A performance **1,** may be recorded for editing or storage **2,** directed to a remote studio for inclusion in another programme **3,** or it may go direct to a continuity mixer **4,** for live broadcast. The mixer can combine the input from the performance with others from separate studios **5,** or with previously recorded material **6.** A continuity announcer **7,** takes responsibility for the whole process. The signal from the continuity mixer is beamed out by a transmitter **8,** to the listener's receiver **9.**

more, V.H.F. allows the broadcasters to send stereophonic signals which greatly add to the realism of the reproduced sound.

In 'stereo' two separate signals are broadcast. One of them corresponds to sounds picked up by the microphones on the left hand side of the studio, and the other to sounds coming from the right. The two signals are combined in such a way that they can be separated again by the listener's receiver and reproduced through two loudspeakers spaced some distance apart – one for the left hand signals, and the other for the right. This recreates something of the effect we normally hear with our own two ears.

It is now possible to expand the stereo principle to the use of four or more speakers which give 'quadrophonic' or 'surround sound' reproduction.

It need hardly be added that broadcasting, together with the gramophone record and the tape recorder, has created a revolution for the music lover, who can now listen to great music at any time of the day or night.

**Bruch, Max** German composer, 1838–1920. Although he wrote a great deal of music, including choral works, three symphonies, many concertos (three for the violin), and three operas, he is largely remembered for his tuneful but slightly sentimental Violin Concerto in G minor. He spent three years in Liverpool as conductor of the Philharmonic Society.

**Bruckner, Anton** Austrian composer and organist, 1824–96. He was born in humble circumstances in a small village and would have followed his father's profession of teacher, but showed signs of an exceptional talent both as an organist and as a composer. He underwent a severe and lengthy training and only felt able to become a full-time musician in 1856, when he was appointed organist to Linz cathedral.

Even though several of his compositions had been performed successfully, Bruckner continued to study. By 1865 he had become an ardent admirer of Wagner, and this in turn influenced his own music.

His Symphony No 1 was first performed in 1868 and shortly afterwards he took up a new post as a teacher of Theory and Organ at the Vienna Conservatory. Three years later he was appointed Professor, and from 1868 he was an organist at the court chapel.

Bruckner's life was very quiet and uneventful, and, apart from a number of successful tours as a virtuoso organist (including visits to Paris and London), was spent mostly in Vienna, teaching and composing. His symphonies were not always well received, but gradually his fame grew and he eventually came to be regarded as a worthy successor to the great German symphonic composers.

In all he wrote ten symphonies – the first of which is numbered 0, and the last, the ninth, was left unfinished at his death. He also wrote many important motets, five settings of the Mass, a Requiem Mass, a Magnificat, and a Te Deum.

Though Bruckner was a modest, simple man, he had great strength of purpose and was deeply religious. His music has exactly the same qualities and is now much admired as the culmination of the kind of large-scale symphonic writing that began with Beethoven.

**Buffa** (It.) Comic. **Opera buffa** is comic opera. A *buffa* role in opera is a comic role. We speak also of an *aria buffa* – as in many of Rossini's operas.

**Anton Bruckner**
1824–1896 This silhouette shows the composer at the organ.

**Bugle** A signalling instrument used mainly by the armed forces.

**John Bull**
1562–1628

**Bugle** This is a very simple brass instrument. It can only produce the first few notes of the harmonic series.( → **Harmonics**)

It is used for simple march tunes and for 'calls' in the army. Even so, it is surprising the number of changes that can be rung on these few notes. Certain 'calls' such as *Sunset*, (above) are very elaborate.

Nowadays most bugles are in B flat, though a few older ones in C may still exist.

**Bull, John** English organist, virginal player, and composer. About 1562–1628.

He was a choirboy in the Chapel Royal of Queen Elizabeth, then organist of Hereford Cathedral, and later organist of the Chapel Royal. He became a Doctor of Music of both Cambridge University and Oxford University, and was made Professor of Music at Gresham College, London.

He got into some trouble (nobody knows what) at the court of James I and slipped away to Brussels. Here he became one of the organists of the royal chapel, and then he went to Antwerp, where, for the last eleven years of his life, he was organist of the cathedral.

Bull enjoyed a high reputation as a player of and composer for the keyboard instruments, and wrote many fine pieces for the virginals.

Oxford University has a collection of old portraits of British musicians. There is one of John Bull, and round the frame are these lines:

'The Bull by force
In field doth Raigne,
But Bull by Skill
Goodwill doth Gayne'.

**Bull, Ole Bornemann** Norwegian violinist and patriot, 1810–80.

He was famous all over the world for his wonderful violin playing. In Britain he gave nearly 300 concerts and in the United States possibly still more. For the most part he played music that he himself had made out of

Norwegian folk tunes.

With the huge sums he earned he tried to found a Norwegian Colony in the United States and a School of Music in his own country. In the end these fine schemes came to nothing, for he fell into the hands of some swindlers and so lost a lot of his money.

**Bülow, Hans von** German conductor, pianist, and composer, 1830–94. He trained at first to become a lawyer, but was so impressed by Wagner's music that in 1850 he decided to concentrate on music and soon became known throughout Europe as a fine pianist and an exceptional conductor. He married Liszt's daughter, Cosima; but in 1869 she left him to live with Wagner, whom she eventually married. Despite this, von Bülow remained an ardent champion of Wagner's music. His own compositions are seldom played now.

**Burla** (**Burlesca**) (It.) A musical joke – a playful kind of composition, as, for example, in Bach's Partita No 3 in A minor.

**Burletta** (It.) A type of musical comedy, originating in 18th-century Italy. It is half way between true comic opera and ballad opera.

**Burney, Charles** English musician and historian of music, 1726–1814.

He was born in Salisbury. When he was a youth he went to London to be an apprentice and assistant to Arne. He was at different times organist at King's Lynn, in Norfolk, and at various London churches.

Burney travelled in France, Italy, Germany etc., to examine the state of music there, and afterwards wrote books about his travels. His four-volume History of Music (1776–89) is of great importance.

He was a friend of George III, Dr. Johnson, Reynolds the painter, Burke, and nearly all the leading men and women of his day.

Fanny Burney, the famous novelist, was his daughter.

**Button** (of a violin or viola) This is the name of the little projection to which is attached the **tail piece**. Also of the projection at the upper end of the back of such an instrument, where it is glued to the neck.

**Busoni, Ferruccio** Italian composer and pianist, 1866–1924. His first teacher was his mother and he achieved considerable fame as a child prodigy. Later he studied in Leipzig,

**Hans von Bülow** 1830–1894 He studied piano under Liszt and learnt conducting from Wagner. He became the first 'virtuoso' conductor and travelled extensively in Europe, Britain and the U.S.

**Byzantine chant** This mosaic *Christ Pantocrator* is from the Byzantine church at Daphni, Greece.

and taught at Helsingfors (now Helsinki) and Moscow. He made many successful concert tours in Europe and America and was widely regarded as one of the finest pianists of his day. He wrote music of all kinds, including many pieces for the piano. Three of his four operas are much admired, though not often performed: *Arlecchino* (1916), *Turandot* (1917) and the unfinished *Doktor Faust*. He was responsible for editing the works of Bach – the '48 Preludes and Fugues' for example – in a style which conforms more to the ideals of late Romantic piano music than to those of Bach's own time.

**Buxtehude, Dietrich** Danish composer and organist, 1637–1707. He was regarded by his contemporaries as one of the greatest organists of his time (Bach walked 200 miles to hear him!) and he helped lay the foundations for the kind of organ composition that came to its climax in the work of J. S. Bach. He spent most of his life in Lübeck and there introduced the idea of evening concerts (1673). (→ **Abendmusik**)

**Byrd, William** English composer, 1542–1623. He was born probably in Lincolnshire and though little is known of his early life and training it seems probable that he was a pupil of Thomas Tallis. He was appointed organist at Lincoln Cathedral in 1563 and a Gentleman of the Chapel Royal in 1570.

In 1572 he went to London to share the post of organist of the Chapel Royal with Tallis. The two musicians were soon granted a 20-year monopoly on music publishing, and in 1575 they produced a collection of their motets, the *Cantiones sacrae*.

Byrd, as can be seen, was a considerable man of business as well as being the finest English composer of his time. His fame was acknowledged on all sides – he was even allowed to retain his Catholic faith at a time of great religious persecution.

His music includes many fine madrigals and motets, songs and keyboard pieces, three splendid masses, and a considerable number of English anthems.

**Byzantine chant** The form of chant used by the Christian church of the Byzantine Empire (founded by Constantine the Great, c. 330, and conquered by the Turks in 1453). It is not unlike Gregorian Chant, and may have sprung from the same (ancient Jewish) source. It had a great influence on the music of the Orthodox Christian churches of Greece, Bulgaria, Russia, etc.

**C.A.** Short for **coll' arco** (It.). With the bow. A direction used after a pizzicato passage when normal bowing is to be resumed.

**Cabinet organ** Another name for the American organ.

**Caccia** (It.) Hunt. Used as a direction in music: *alla caccia*, 'in the hunting style'. But also, more importantly, the name of an early type of Italian madrigal in which the two upper voices were in **Canon** → (chasing each other, as in a hunt). The word **Catch** → comes from the same source.

**Caccini, Giulio** Italian composer, c. 1545–1618. He was one of the members of the Camerata group in Florence whose theories led to the birth of opera. He contributed music to the first opera to survive, Jacopo Peri's *Euridice* (1600). Many of his songs and madrigals were very popular, and both he and his daughter Francesca (1587–c. 1640) were singers of some repute.

**Cachucha** A graceful Spanish dance in triple time. It is similar to the Bolero, and is danced by a single performer.

**Cacophony** A word borrowed from the ancient Greek, meaning 'ill sound', and used to describe any discordant muddle of sounds. The opposite is EUPHONY.

**Cadenza** (It.) Cadence. But when we use the word it generally has one of two special meanings:
1. An elaborate and showy passage performed by the singer near the end of an operatic aria (or near the end of each section of it). This was an 18th-century custom. The composer's music ceased for the moment and the singer extemporized his or her own passage to fill the gap.
2. A passage of a similar kind by the solo performer in a piano concerto, violin concerto, etc. In old days this also was of the performer's own extemporization, but since about 1800 the composer has generally written it out just as he wants it to be. (→ | **Concerto**)

# Cage

John Cage. America, b. 1912. He was a pupil of Henry Cowell and Schoenberg, but soon outstripped his masters by experimenting with sounds not usually classed as 'music'. He invented the 'prepared piano' (1938), and the idea of Indeterminate Music (*Music of Changes*, for piano: 1951). One of his most famous works, *4'33"* for piano (1954), consists of exactly four minutes and thirty-three seconds of silence – the pianist closes the lid at the beginning and opens it at the end, and the music consists of whatever may happen during that period.

Cage has explained his ideas in witty, thought-provoking lectures and essays. He has been very influential – partly because he challenges musicians to think deeply about the very nature of music. He is much influenced by Zen Buddhism. (→ **Aleatoric; Indeterminacy**)

John Cage b.1912 On his 'prepared' piano the strings are doctored with various materials to produce abnormal tone qualities. In his *Sonatas and Interludes* (*right*) he uses screws, bolts and rubbers to produce this effect.

# Cadence

Just as we punctuate the written word with commas and full-stops that mark off the phrases and sentences and help to make their meaning clear, so also we can use certain chord progressions to mark off the phrases and sentences in music. Musical 'punctuation marks' are called CADENCES.
The four most important are:

### 1. The perfect cadence (Full close)
Most pieces of music end with this cadence, where it acts like a full-stop. But it can frequently be found elsewhere in a piece – where a modulation takes place, for example. It consists of a dominant chord followed by a tonic chord.

### 2. The plagal cadence
This is also used to close a piece, but it is much less common than the perfect cadence. It is often found after the last verse of a hymn, for the 'Amen'. It consists of a subdominant chord followed by a chord.

### 3. The imperfect cadence (Half close)
Very frequently used during the course of a piece of music, since it acts rather like a 'comma' and suggests that there is more to come. It reverses the procedure of the perfect cadence and consists of a tonic chord followed by a dominant chord.

### 4. The interrupted cadence
This gives the impression that it is going to be a perfect cadence, for it begins with a dominant chord; but it is 'interrupted' by moving to the submediant instead of the tonic chord.

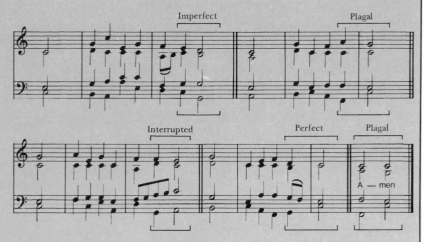

Above is an example, the hymn-tune *St. David*, slightly altered so as to include an example of every type of cadence.

In all the examples above, the cadences move from weak beats to strong beats. This is the most common form of cadence. If, however, the beats are strong to weak, we have what is called a FEMININE CADENCE:

Cadences do not necessarily have to employ chords in their root position. When inversions are used, as on the right, the cadence is said to be INVERTED.

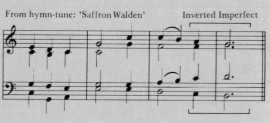

**Calando** (It.) Waning, diminishing. Used to indicate a decreasing volume of tone and a slackening pace. (→ **Diminuendo**)

**Calcando** (It.) Pressing forward. Used to indicate an increase of speed. (→ **Accelerando**)

**Calmando** and **Calmato** (It.) Calming, and calmed.

**Camera** (It.) Chamber. Used in music to describe compositions suitable for performance in a room, as opposed to a church – hence the distinction between the **sonata da camera** (the chamber sonata) and the **sonata da chiesa** (the church sonata). The word is nowadays used rather more loosely to describe music-making on a small scale – thus an *orchestra da camera* would be a small orchestra.

**Calypso** The Mighty Sparrow, one of the best known of West Indian calypso singers.

**Calypso** A type of West Indian popular song which originated in Trinidad. The words usually poke fun at a notable person, or some newsworthy event. The main accents in the music are often made to fall on the weak accents of the words – A*meri*ca, rather than A*me*rica. The music is syncopated and repetitious and is accompanied by guitars and percussion.

**Camerata, The** The Italian for 'fellowship' or 'society'. In music when we speak of 'The Camerata' we mean the society of musicians and poets who met together in Florence about 1600 and whose speculations about the role that music played in ancient Greek drama led to the birth of opera. Among them were Vincenzo Galilei (father of the great astronomer) and Caccini. (→ **Opera**)

**Canaries** This was an old dance, which (one would guess) came originally from the Canary Islands. It was once popular in England (Shakespeare mentions it in *All's well that ends well*).

The music was in three-beats-in-a-bar rhythm or six-beats-in-a-bar rhythm, and all the phrases began at the opening of a bar with a note a beat-and-a-half long.

We sometimes find a canaries in the harpsichord suites of Purcell and Couperin.

**Cancan** A 19th-century French popular dance, usually performed in music-halls, theatres, and night clubs. It is in 2/4 time and is based on the quadrille. It was considered very daring because it involved the dancers (all women) in making very high kicks, and therefore revealing more underwear and leg than was considered proper at the time. Examples of the cancan occur in Offenbach's operettas.

**Cancan** These professional dancers were photographed against a studio backdrop in 1898. This vigorous dance was a symbol of Parisian gaiety in the period known as *La Belle Époque*.

**Cancrizans** From the Latin word for 'crab', and used in music to describe anything designed to make sense when played backwards (crabs actually walk *sideways*!). (→ **Canon**)

**Cannabich, Christian** German composer and violinist, 1731–98. The most prominent member of a very musical family. He was a member of the famous Mannheim Orchestra, a fine violinist and a skilful leader and conductor. Mozart much admired his abilities. He wrote a great many symphonies (nearly one hundred), ballets, and chamber music, and generally contributed to the development of the early symphony. (→ **Symphony**)

**Cantabile** (It.) Songlike. A direction found in instrumental music when a smooth, singing style is required. The same as **Legato** →.

# Canon

The word itself means 'rule' and when a piece of music is called a Canon it means that it obeys the rule of 'Follow-my-leader'. For example, here is the well-known hymn tune called *Tallis's Canon*. The soprano is the leader, and the tenor part follows it throughout:

Thomas Tallis

*Tallis's Canon* is a 'canon at the octave' – the voices are eight notes apart. But it is possible to have canons at the unison, or fifth or fourth – or, indeed, any interval, though it becomes more difficult to make a satisfactory canon if the interval is an awkward one.

Canons can also take place between more than two parts – though again, the larger the number of parts the greater the problems involved.

There are many different kinds of canon, some of which call for great ingenuity. For example:

**Double canon:** two canons at once: each for a pair of voices.

**Canon by augmentation:** the voice that imitates does so in longer notes than the voice it is imitating.

**Canon by diminution:** the opposite of canon by augmentation.

**Canon cancrizans:** the imitating voice gives out the melody backwards.

**Infinite canon:** the end and the beginning are dovetailed, so to speak, and the canon can go on for ever.

**Canon by inversion:** the imitating voice is a mirror version of the main voice – if the main voice goes up a 3rd, the imitating voice descends a 3rd, and so on.

Short vocal canons for singing are called ROUNDS or CATCHES. The idea behind the word 'round' being that the melody comes 'round' again and again, and that behind the word 'catch' being that the singers 'catch' up the melody one after the other. *Three blind Mice* is an example. (→ **Catch club**)

**Cantata** In the general sense, this Italian word means something that is sung, as opposed to 'sonata', which implies an instrumental piece.

As a particular type of musical composition, however, it describes a vocal work, for one or two voices and with instrumental accompaniment, that tells some kind of story by means of brief arias and recitatives. It is therefore closely related to the opera and oratorio. Indeed, in the 17th and 18th centuries there were two distinct types of cantata: the Chamber Cantata (*Cantata da camera*), and the Church Cantata (*Cantata da chiesa*) – the one being on a secular subject, and the other on a sacred subject, suitable for performance in church.

Cantatas were written by composers all over Europe, but they came to be of particular importance to the Protestant church composers of Germany – men such as Heinrich Schütz and J. S. Bach. Here they developed an elaborate form, consisting of arias, recitatives, ensembles, and different kinds of choruses – ranging from simple **Chorale →** settings, to intricate fugal movements. They were often accompanied by a small orchestra. Bach's Church Cantatas are the high-point of this kind of cantata.

In the 19th century these kinds of cantata gradually died out and the word came to be used to describe short choral works which told some kind of story (sacred or secular). These might also include arias, recitatives, and ensembles for soloists, and they were often accompanied by a full-scale orchestra. Cantatas of this kind were immensely popular with the many choral societies that sprang up in England, Germany, and America during this period. One of the most frequently performed cantatas is Coleridge-Taylor's *Song of Hiawatha* (1898–1900), to words by Longfellow.

**Canticle** Any biblical hymn, other than a psalm. For example, the **Magnificat →** and **Nunc Dimittis →**.

**Cantus firmus** (Lat.) **Canto fermo** (It.) Fixed song. From the 12th to the 15th centuries many religious works were built round a plainsong tune, spun out in long notes in one of the voice parts (usually the tenor). This was the 'fixed song', the *Cantus firmus*. It is often abbreviated to C.F.

The term was later adopted by teachers, to describe the 'given part' to which the student would add other voices and so complete the exercise. (**→ Counterpoint**)

**Carnegie Hall** The entrance, the foyer and the auditorium. These engravings are from *Harper's Weekly*, May 1891.

**Canzone** This Italian word has three main meanings in music:
1. A musical setting of the canzona-type of poem, popular at the time of the troubadours.
2. A short instrumental piece in the style of fugal choral music. Sometimes there were several such movements strung together. Works of this kind were popular in the 16th and 17th centuries.
3. In the 18th century short arias were often called *canzoni* – as were brief instrumental pieces in a similar singing style.

**Canzonet** Originally a shorter kind of canzona; but the word is also used to describe a type of madrigal, and a simple solo song.

**Cappella, A** (It.) 'In chapel style' – that is to say, choral music sung without any instrumental accompaniment (as in the Vatican Chapel in Rome). It also means *alla breve* in tempo indications.

**Capriccio** (It.) 'Caprice'. A title sometimes given to a short, lively piece of music.

In 17th-century harpsichord music it described lively pieces in a fugal style. In the 18th century it described exercises for stringed instruments (what we would now call 'studies'). In the 19th century the term is applied to piano pieces in a free rhapsodic style, particularly those by Mendelssohn and Brahms.

**Carezzando** (It.) Caressing.

**Carillon → Bells and bell-ringing**

**Carissimi, Giacomo** Italian composer, 1605–74. He is chiefly remembered as a composer of chamber cantatas and oratorios in which he contributed greatly to the development of the art of recitative. His method of setting words to music is most expressive and dramatic. Though he did not invent the idea of oratorio, it was his genius and resource that turned it into a worthwhile art form. And even Handel sometimes borrowed from his works. His masterpieces are probably *The History of Jonah* and *Jepthah*.

**Carnegie Hall** One of New York's most famous concert halls. It stands on 57th Street and Seventh Avenue and was opened in May 1891. It consists of a main concert hall with 2760 seats, and a small hall for recitals and chamber music. It was named after the Pittsburg millionaire Andrew Carnegie, who was born in Scotland but made his fortune in America and gave away a great deal of money in helping the arts and sciences.

# Carol

Carols, in the strict sense of the word, are not simply Christmas songs, but songs to celebrate almost any religious festival. Some of the earliest may be of pagan origin – for they celebrate such matters as the coming of

**Carol singers** The group below is gathered under St Wenceslas's statue in Prague. The Victorians (*right*) often used versions of ancient carols but with different words.

Spring, and so on.

In 15th-century England the word carol (or carole, as it used to be spelt) meant a part-song, usually with a recurring 'burden' (refrain). Most of them were concerned with religious celebrations, but not all – one, for example, is the famous Agincourt Song, celebrating the victory of the English over the French in 1415.

The present-day practice of singing carols from door to door dates from the middle of the 19th century.

**Carpenter, John Alden** American composer, 1876–1951. Up to the age of 60 he was a successful Chicago business man, writing important compositions in his leisure time. Then he retired from business and gave his whole time to music.

One of his orchestral works is called *Adventures in a Perambulator* (1915), and there is a jazz pantomime called *Krazy Kat* (1921).

**Carter, Elliott** American composer, b. 1908. He studied at Harvard University and with Nadia Boulanger in Paris. He began to call attention to himself as an important composer with the *Piano Sonata* of 1946, in which he began to explore the idea of a controlled cycle of speeds operating throughout the work. His *Double Concerto* for harpsichord and piano (1961) and *Concerto for Piano and Orchestra* (1966) are much admired.

**Casella, Alfredo** Italian composer, 1883–1947. He studied at the Paris Conservatory under Fauré, and then became known as a fine pianist and conductor. As a composer he felt strongly that Italy had devoted too much of its talent to writing sensational operas and argued in favour of a more dignified kind of music. He became an influential teacher.

**Elliott Carter** b.1908 This composer also writes on music and was at one time the musical director of a ballet company.

**Cassation** A type of 18th-century orchestral or chamber work in several short movements, similar to a divertimento or serenade, but usually simpler in design (i.e. the movements seldom fall into Sonata Form).

**Castanets** These are a favourite Spanish instrument. They consist of two small hollow-shaped pieces of wood, to be attached to a finger and thumb of each hand and clacked together. But sometimes in the orchestra they are fastened at the end of a stick which can be taken up and shaken when needed.

**Castrato** Castrati singers were popular in Italy and elsewhere in Europe, during the 17th and 18th centuries. They were male sopranos (or sometimes contraltos), whose voices were obtained by the barbarous custom of castrating boys before their voices broke. A successful castrato might expect to earn vast sums of money, but there was no way of telling before the operation whether the voice would develop to this degree.

Many early operas, such as those of Handel, were written with this kind of voice in mind, and nowadays the part must either be sung by a woman or transposed to suit a male voice.

The last professional castrato was Alessandro Moreschi, who died in 1922. His voice was recorded in 1902–3.

**Catch** → **Canon**

**Catch club** The Noblemen and Gentlemen's Catch Club was founded in London in 1761 and is still functioning. It offered prizes for the best catches, canons and glees and thus stimulated a great deal of composition. The members met, dined and drank and sang in a relaxed atmosphere – women were not admitted. The words of some of the catches, alas, were not always fit for innocent ears. A similar society, the Glee Club, was founded in 1787. Clubs of this kind sprang up all over 18th-century England. ( → **Canon**, **Glee**)

**Cathedral music** → **Choirboys**

**Cavalieri, Emilio di** Italian composer, c. 1550–1602. He was one of the adventurous group of Florentine composers who brought opera into existence. His *Representation of the Soul and the Body* (1600) is sometimes described as the first oratorio, but it is in fact a Sacred Drama intended to be acted and staged.

**Cavalli, Pietro** Italian composer, 1602–76. He became a singer in the choir of St Mark's, Venice under Monteverdi and, after holding organist posts, eventually became its director of music (1668). He wrote many operas (well over 40) for Venice's six operatic theatres, and now that these are being revived he can be seen to be almost the equal of Monteverdi himself. *L'Ormindo* (1644) and *La Calisto* (1651) are two operas that have been successfully restaged in modern times.

**Cavatina** This means either (*a*) a short song or (*b*) a short and rather slow instrumental piece.

**Cebell** A 17th-century English dance similar to the gavotte ( → **Gavotte**), based on a tune associated with the goddess Cybèle in an opera by Lully. Purcell has a cebell in one of his Harpsichord Suites.

**Cecilia, Saint** Martyred in Sicily, A.D. 175. Since the 15th century she has been regarded as the patron saint of music and many pictures have been painted showing her playing the organ or some other instrument, or singing, or composing, and festivals have been held in her honour.

But it is impossible to find out why 1,200 years and more after St Cecilia's death she came to be considered a musician. It really seems as though her association with music is

**Castanets** These percussion instruments held by Copeo dancers of Majorca are named after the Spanish word for 'chestnut'. Their use is most commonly associated with flamenco dancing, although they are also used in other Spanish folk dances.

**St Cecilia** This early 16th-century altarpiece shows the saint (now no longer recognized by the Roman Catholic Church) playing a portative bellows-blown organ, a medieval instrument used in processions and chamber music.

after all a myth.

Many composers (Purcell, Blow, Handel, Wesley, Parry, Britten, etc.) have written choral *Odes* for St Cecilia's Day celebrations (22 November), which in England, date back as early as 1683.

**Ceilidh** (pronounced something like 'Caylee'). An all-night meeting of friends and neighbours, popular in the Scottish Highlands. Songs, instrumental music, and storytelling are part of the entertainment, but it was originally the custom to work at the various crafts at the same time (spinning, weaving, wood-carving, mending fishing nets, and so on). In this way the young learned from the old.

**Celesta** → **Glockenspiel**

**Cello** → page 82

**Cembalo** Though originally the Italian word for dulcimer, it came to be used also for the harpsichord (in full **clavicembalo**, that is, 'keyed-dulcimer').

**Cesti, Marc Antonio** Italian composer, 1623–69. Though he was for some time a Franciscan monk, this does not appear to have interfered with his career as an operatic composer, which began in 1649 with the production of *Orontea*, or with his rather scandalous personal behaviour. However, he was later released from his vows!

He wrote, in all, some 15 operas. They were very successful, and he is one of the most important and interesting composers in this field in the period immediately after Monteverdi when opera was becoming something of a popular industry.

**Chabrier, Emmanuel** French composer, 1841–94. He trained both as a lawyer and a musician and worked, rather reluctantly, in the Ministry for the Interior for 18 years. He was a brilliant pianist, an ardent admirer of Wagner, and the composer of several works that instantly became, and have remained very popular. Chief among them is the orchestral rhapsody *España* (1883), the *Joyeuse Marche* (1888), and the comic opera *Le Roi malgré lui* (1887). His music, at its best, is brilliant and colourful, highly rhythmic and cheerfully melodic. It is 'light' music, and pleasant to listen to.

**Chaconne** and **Passacaglia** These were dances, probably Spanish in origin. Both of them were slow, with three beats in a bar, and the music used at first to be built up on a **Ground bass** → .

# Cello

The short form of *violoncello*. The bass member of the violin family. It was developed in the 16th century and existed alongside the tenor viola da gamba, gradually ousting it in popularity. It was particularly important in the 18th century as part of the Continuo group.

The overall length of the cello is about 120 cm, its body being about 75 cm. It has four strings, tuned in fifths to C, G, D, and A. Its practical range is therefore:

It is a particularly expressive instrument and a number of fine concertos (by Dvořák and Elgar, for example) have been written for it.

**Cellist**, (*above*) with bow fully extended. The 20th century has been rich in virtuosi cellists, notably Pablo Casals, Mstislav Rostropovich, and Paul Tortelier (*right*) the French cellist, conductor and composer.

Both words are often used as names for instrumental pieces, and it seems hardly possible to distinguish between them. The Ground Bass is generally a feature, but sometimes its notes are transplanted into the treble. There are some chaconnes and passacaglias that have no Ground Bass at all though they contain some of the features of the Ground Bass type, e.g. they fall into lengths of four or eight bars.

Bach wrote some magnificent pieces under these two names – especially a wonderful Chaconne for solo violin, and a great Passacaglia and Fugue for harpsichord (it is nowadays played on the organ).

The Italian word *ciaccona* and the French word *passecaille* are sometimes seen.

**Chalumeau** French word derived from *calamus*, meaning a 'reed'. This term is now used to describe the lowest register of the clarinet (roughly D in the bass clef to F sharp in the treble):

The tone is rich and dark. It is also the name given to an early form of clarinet. ( → **Clarinet**)

**Chamber music** This really means music to be performed in a room of a house – as distinct from music to be performed in a concert hall, theatre, or church.

But nowadays when we speak of chamber

**Chamber music** This small group of musicians perform in the music-room of the Schloss Wallerstein Castle in 1791. Noble families in Europe frequently maintained musicians like these for private entertainments and small parties.

music we do not include vocal music (solo or choral) or music for a single instrument or for an orchestra. What we do include is music for any two instruments (for instance violin and piano, or flute and piano), or instrumental trios, quartets, quintets, etc.

The most important of all chamber music is that for the string quartet (two violins, viola, and violoncello).

A CHAMBER CONCERT is one where chamber music makes up the programme.

**Chaminade, Cécile** French composer, 1857–1944. She was an excellent pianist and wrote a considerable quantity of charming, 'light' music which became very popular – particularly her songs and piano pieces.

**Champêtre** (Fr.) Rustic, rural. Often used in a way that suggests that something is only pretending to be rustic, when in reality it is very sophisticated. Thus Poulenc's Harpsichord Concerto has as its title: *Concert champêtre*.

**Change-ringing** The English way of ringing a peal of church bells. (→ **Bells and bell-ringing**)

**Changing notes** These are a kind of passing note (→ **Harmony**). Here are some examples of them (the changing notes marked 'C'):

It will be seen that in every case there is the interval of a third between the changing notes, and that these two notes are respectively a step above and a step below the harmony note to which they are proceeding.

**Chanson** (Fr.) Song. In music this describes different types of composition according to the historical period. Thus in France and Italy from the 14th to 16th centuries it meant a work for several voices, something like a madrigal. In more recent times it has simply meant any kind of verse-repeating solo song.

**Chanson sans paroles** (Fr.) Song without words.

**Chant** → **Anglican chant** and **Plainsong**

**Chanter** → **Bagpipe**

**Chanterelle** (Fr.) The name given to the highest string on any bowed instrument. For example, the E string on a violin. It means, literally, 'the singing one'.

**Chapel Royal** This means, properly, the musicians and clergy employed by a monarch for the religious services of his court, though we also call by the same name the building in which the services are held.

The records of the English Chapel Royal go back a long way – to the first year of King Stephen's reign (1135).

From the reign of Richard III (1483–5), for about two centuries, there was a press-gang system by which officials could go about

**Chapel Royal** These Gentlemen and Children of the Chapel form part of the funeral procession of Queen Elizabeth I in 1603.

the country listening to the singing in all the cathedrals, etc., and robbing them of any boys who seemed fit to sing before the king.

Henry VIII (who was himself a good musician) had 79 musicians in his Chapel, and Edward VI and Mary each had 114.

Elizabeth I (1558–1603) had a wonderful Chapel. It included such fine musicians as Tye, Tallis, Byrd, Gibbons, and Morley.

During the Commonwealth and Protectorate no choirs or organs were allowed in the church service, so the Chapel Royal was disbanded, though Cromwell had a small body of singers who performed to him in his palace. Work was resumed once more after the Restoration of the monarchy in 1660.

Today the Chapel Royal is chiefly engaged in the chapel of St James's Palace, London.

The altos, tenors, and basses of the Chapel Royal have always been known as the 'Gentlemen of the Chapel Royal' and the boys as the 'Children of the Chapel Royal'.

**Characteristic piece** A fanciful title that some composers use for a piece (generally one for piano) that has a distinct character of its own – that is, expresses a mood. In German the word is *Characterstück* (plural *Characterstücke*).

**Charpentier, Gustave** French composer, 1860–1956. Though he wrote very little music after the failure of his second opera, *Julien*, in 1913, two of his earlier works are still heard: the orchestral *Impressions of Italy* (1890) and the opera *Louise* (1909).

**Charpentier, Marc-Antoine** French composer, 1634–1704. He studied with Carissimi and became known as a leading French opera composer after Lully. He wrote a number of masses and motets, etc. that are much admired.

**Chausson, Ernest** French composer, 1855–99. He was a pupil, briefly, of Massenet, and later of César Franck, whom he greatly admired and who influenced his work deeply. A wealthy man, he used his fortune to further the cause of French music. He wrote many fine songs, including the beautiful *Poème de l'Amour et de la Mer* (1892). Of his larger works the *Poème* for Violin and Orchestra (1896) and the Symphony in B flat (1890) are still sometimes performed.

**Chávez, Carlos** Mexican composer, 1899–1978. He developed early as a composer, and, after a period in Europe and America (1922–28), became Director of the

National Conservatory of Mexico. In 1928 he also founded his country's first symphony orchestra, which he conducted until 1949. His compositions were much influenced by folksong and the history and mythology of Mexico, but his style was also often rather austere and neo-classical. He wrote four symphonies and a number of descriptive orchestral works, such as the *Sinfonia India* (1936) and *Xochipili-Macuilxochitl* (1940), both of which use Mexican instruments.

**Cherubini, Luigi** Italian composer, 1760–1842. His musical talent developed early and he had established himself as a composer by the time he was 16. He studied in Venice and wrote his first opera, *Quinto Fabio*, in 1780.

From 1784 to 1786 he was in London, writing Italian operas and actually holding the post of 'Composer to the King' for one year. But in 1788 he settled in Paris and, apart from a short stay in Vienna (1805–6), became to all intents and purposes a French composer.

Cherubini was much admired as a composer (particularly by Napoleon) and became very influential – though some people felt his style was a little too dry and monumental. Nevertheless his many operas met with great success, particularly *Les deux Journées* (1800) (known in England as *The Water Carrier*) which influenced even Beethoven, and *Médée* (1797). In his later years he wrote much fine church music, for he was a great master of polyphony.

Though it is unlikely that he will ever be regarded with the kind of awe he met with in his lifetime, there are signs that his music is being appreciated once more.

**Chevalier, Albert** English music-hall entertainer and composer, 1862–1923. His full name was Albert Onesime Britannicus Gwathreoyd Louis Chevalier. He composed humorous and pathetic songs about London costermongers and sang them in costume in the music halls – for example, 'My Old Dutch'.

**Chitarrone** A type of double-necked lute. It was very large (often nearly 2 m long) and carried some 20 wire strings. It was very popular in the first half of the 17th century, particularly as an instrument for accompanying the solo voice.

**Choeur** (Fr.) Choir, or chorus. In organ music **Grand Choeur** means 'Full Organ'.

**Luigi Cherubini**
1760–1842 In this painting by Ingres the composer is shown with Euterpe, the Muse of music. Beethoven admired Cherubini's music and was influenced by him in his opera *Fidelio*.

**Chitarrone** This instrument, which was also called the Roman theorbo, was not widely used as a solo instrument.

**Choir** or **Chorus** → page 85

**Choirboys** The tradition of using boys' voices to sing the upper parts in church music has persisted longer in England than in any other country. Choir schools, charged with the special purpose of training young singers, were set up by the cathedrals and monasteries as long ago as c. 600 A.D., and their descendants still exist today.

Boys' voices were preferred because it was not thought fitting that women should take any active part in church services, and because nobody in those days believed that women need be given any kind of formal education.

To be selected for the choir school was something of an honour, for it meant that poor boys, who otherwise had no hope of an education, would have a chance to improve themselves. Boys were often 'pressed' into the choir schools – that is to say, taken away (by force if necessary) from their parents because it had been noticed that they possessed a good natural voice. Few seem to have complained. Haydn, who was plucked from the church choir of his obscure native village and taken to Vienna to train at the choir school of St Stephen's cathedral, is a good example of the kind of asset such an event might be to a talented boy.

So far as ordinary parish churches are concerned, the sung service did not come into general existence in England until the 19th century. Here too, all-male choirs were the rule, and remained so until very recent times. Today, unfortunately, it seems to be becoming increasingly difficult to raise any sort of church choir. In those that do exist, women invariably play a most important part. Only in cathedrals is the all-male tradition maintained. Many people maintain that an all-male choir does have a firmness of line, and a purity and consistency of tone that mixed choirs sometimes lack.

In a cathedral school, the choirboy's life is bounded by the services he has to sing. These are, usually, the services of Matins (Morning Prayer) and Evensong (Evening Prayer) and Holy Communion. At both Matins and Evensong, psalms are chanted and hymns are sung. At Matins are also sung the VENITE, the TE DEUM (or, at certain seasons, the BENEDICITE), and BENEDICTUS (or sometimes the JUBILATE); and at Evensong, the MAGNIFICAT and NUNC DIMITTIS .

From this it will be seen that, at its best,

# Choir or Chorus

Any group of singers; or that part of a cathedral in which the services are celebrated (the same as the chancel in a parish church).

A 'mixed voice choir' is one which contains both men and women, arranged S.A.T.B. (Soprano, Alto, Tenor, Bass). But there can also be women's choirs (S.S.A., usually) and male voice choirs (T.T.B.B., or some similar combination). A 'double choir' is one that can be divided into two equal choirs in order to sing choral passages that 'answer' each other.

Music for a 'chorus' is usually less complex than that written for a choir – as, for example in an opera, where the singers are required to move about and act as well as sing.

**Chorus** (*above*) This cartoon of Berlioz conducting a chorus is by the 19th-century French artist, Gustave Doré. Church music is sung by this 15th-century French choir *right* gathered around a lectern.

the cathedral choirboy's life is that of a professional singer. The voice-training (and training in other aspects of music), together with his ordinary school work, help to make it a thorough and interesting form of education. And it is not perhaps surprising to find that so many great composers have begun their careers in choir schools. (→ **Church service**)

The average range for a boy's trained voice is shown on the right. Soloists, of course, can go a little higher.

**Chopin** → page 86

**Chopsticks** A simple waltz tune that children enjoy playing on the piano, using the sides of their forefingers in a kind of wood-chopping motion. Its origins are obscure, but in France and Germany it goes under the name of 'Cutlets waltz'. In 1880 a number of Russian composers (including Borodin and Rimsky-Korsakov) wrote a set of variations on a version of the same tune.

**Chorale** The Protestant chorale is a type of German hymn-tune dating from the time of Martin Luther (1483–1546) and the Reformation of the German church. Chorales came into being as simple tunes which could be sung by the whole congregation in German (as opposed to the Latin used by the Catholic church). A few of them were composed for this purpose, but most were adapted from existing tunes – including plainsong and folksong.

**Choirboys at King's College, Cambridge** All-male choirs are now mostly confined to cathedrals, but until fairly recently they were a feature of ordinary parish churches.

Chorales came to occupy such an important position in the Lutheran church that many composers (in particular J. S. Bach) made use of them in their own choral and instrumental pieces – rather as if, by making them the basis for new music, they were performing an act of worship and underlining the religious meaning of their work.

Chorales can be found in Bach's cantatas and Passions: sometimes arranged in four-part harmony, and sometimes embedded in more complicated textures – as a kind of strand of special religious significance.

He also based whole instrumental compositions on them – such as the Chorale Preludes for organ. These were intended as introductions to chorales, to be played before they were sung by the congregation.

**Choral symphony** Three kinds of composition are called by this name:
1. An orchestral symphony which makes some use of voices – as Beethoven's ninth does in the last movement.
2. A symphony mainly for voices, with orchestral support – as in Britten's *Spring Symphony*.
3. A symphony entirely for voices – as in Malcolm Williamson's *Symphony for Voices*.

**Chord.** → **Harmony** – and for particular chords see also *Chromatic chords, Diminished seventh, Dominant discords,* and *Leading seventh*.

# Chopin

**Frédéric François Chopin** 1810–1849

**Piano lesson** (*above*)
This caricature of 1844 by Maurice Sand shows Chopin criticizing the piano style of the singer, Pauline Viardot.
**Recital** (*below*) Chopin at the piano in Prince Anton Radziwill's salon, Berlin, 1829.

Frédéric François Chopin. Born in Żelazowa Wola, near Warsaw, in 1810 and died at Paris in 1849. Chopin was by birth half French and half Polish, his father being a Frenchman who had settled in Warsaw and his mother a Pole, but he always looked upon himself as a Pole and throughout his life acted as a very patriotic one.

His father, who was a schoolmaster, seeing early proofs of musical talent, provided him with good teachers and he was able to play a piano concerto at a public concert when he was only eight years old. He made good progress in composition and when he was 14 some music of his was published.

At the age of 20, being well advanced in his art, he decided to go out into the larger world. He gave a series of farewell concerts in Warsaw and then set off on a tour, performing in various cities in Germany and Austria and working his way through to Paris. Whilst he was on this journey he heard the news that the Russians had taken Warsaw, which distressed him to the point of despair.

In Paris, where there was much sympathy for the oppressed Polish nation, he was well received. There were then in the city a great many eminent musicians of different nationalities (Cherubini, Liszt, Meyerbeer, Berlioz, and others), and they recognized the newcomer's striking gifts and were friendly to him. He gave piano lessons and sometimes played in public. His playing had a style of its own – and so had his compositions, which were what he almost exclusively played.

His health had never been very good, and in 1837, when he was 27 years old, he decided to go to England to consult a certain doctor as well as to attend to some business with a London music publisher. On this occasion he lived very quietly, saw few people, and did not play in public.

On returning to Paris he now became more and more involved with the novelist George Sand (whose real name was Aurora Dudevant). Chopin had loved other women, and had even been engaged to a young Polish girl Maria Wodzinska until her family, alarmed at the rumours of his ill-health, broke it off. But Mme Sand could do as she liked and the pair were soon living together.

In 1838 Chopin's health gave real cause for alarm and he went with Mme Sand and her family to Majorca, believing that the warmer climate would help him. At first it did, but soon things took a turn for the

worse, and from now on his decline was slow but steady.

Back in Paris he resumed his teaching ('my treadmill', he called it) and continued also to compose. His life with Mme Sand, however, was stormy, and in 1847 they parted.

The last two years of his life were considerably eased by the devotion of a Scottish pupil, Jane Stirling. Thanks to her he spent most of 1848 in England and Scotland, where his playing and his music were much admired. His health grew worse, and on returning to Paris he was scarcely able to teach or compose. Miss Stirling tried to give him £1,000 anonymously, but he found out and could only be persuaded to accept part of the gift. He lingered through the summer of 1849 and, on October 29th, he died of tuberculosis.

Though Chopin wrote a certain amount of music which includes other instruments (two Piano Concertos, for example), it is through the piano that he spoke with real authority. Indeed, he changed the whole art of piano writing (and playing), introducing a singing style which greatly resembles the best of Italian opera. Some of these ideas he owed to the Irish composer John Field, but he was able to explore them more thoroughly and with a much greater depth of feeling.

His music is so easy to listen to that it is sometimes forgotten that he was a great innovator in the field of harmony and used chromatic discords with daring and imagination. And while on the one hand his music could be poetic and seem to dream (the *Nocturnes* are an example), on the other it could be intensely rhythmic and full of fire (the *Polonaises* are like this).

It is sometimes said that he was only happy when writing music on a small scale. This is not wholly true. Though some people say his two Piano Concertos are not very convincing, his four *Ballades* are remarkable examples of sustained musical thought.

Along with Berlioz, Mendelssohn and Schumann, Chopin may be claimed as one of the great Romantics.

Chopin's music includes: 54 Mazurkas; 25 Preludes; 27 Studies (Etudes); 14 Waltzes; 19 Nocturnes; 10 Polonaises; 4 Ballades; 4 Impromptus; 4 Scherzos, and 3 Sonatas.

**Cittern** This example was made for the Archduke Ferdinand of Tyrol in 1754. The cittern was exceedingly popular in 16th- and 17th-century music.

**Chord clusters** In 20th-century music, composers often employ chords that consist of a 'cluster' of adjacent notes, such as cannot be analysed in the traditional way, but nevertheless make an agreeable effect.

**Chordophone** → page 88

**Chromatic** A word derived from the ancient Greek, meaning 'coloured'. Used to describe notes which do not belong to the prevailing scale. Thus in C major all sharps and flats are 'chromatic' notes. Chords which contain such notes are known as 'chromatic chords'. The CHROMATIC SCALE is the scale which contains all 12 semitones available to Western music. (→ **Harmony**)

**Chromatic chords** → page 88

**Church service** → page 90

**Ciaccona** → **Chaconne**

**Cimarosa, Domenico** Italian composer, 1749–1801. He wrote his first opera in 1772 and thereafter won great renown as an operatic composer whose works were popular throughout Europe. In 1787 he became Chamber Composer to Catherine II of Russia, and later succeeded Salieri as Director of Music to the Austrian court in Vienna. It was here, in 1792, that he wrote his most famous opera *The Secret Marriage*. His last years were somewhat clouded, for, having returned to Naples, he became involved in politics and went to prison for expressing too great an enthusiasm for Napoleon. On being released he set out for St Petersburg once more, but died in Venice. There was some suspicion that he had been poisoned, and the government went to great lengths to have the rumour denied.

**Cimbal, cimbalom** → **Dulcimer**

**Citole** A medieval instrument, the ancestor of the Renaissance **Cittern** → . It is thought to have been invented in Italy. It had a flat body, a short neck, and four brass or steel strings that were plucked with a quill. By 1550 the word had disappeared, cittern being used instead.

**Cittern** A member of the guitar family. Shaped rather like a fig, with a flat back. It has a fretted fingerboard and wire strings –

# Chordophone

Any instrument in which the sound is produced by the vibration of a stretched string. For example, violins, harps, pianos. The following instruments, all described in this book, are all chordophones: Balalaika, Banjo, Baryton, Cello, Chitarrone, Cimbalom, Cittern, Clavichord, Double bass, Dulcimer, Fiddle, Guitar, Harp, Harpsichord, Kit, Lira da braccio, Lira da gamba, Lute, Lyre, Mandolin, Pandora, Piano, Psaltery, Rebec, Sharnisch, Spinet, Tambura, Theorbo, Tromba marina, Ukelele, Vina, Viol, Viola, Violin, Virginals, Zither.

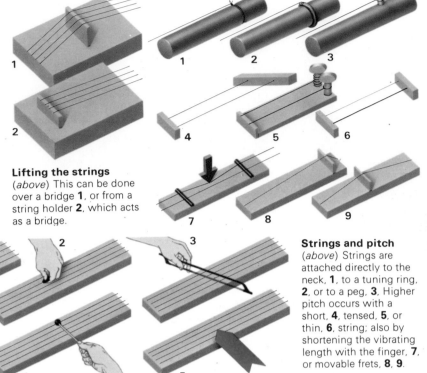

**Lifting the strings**
(*above*) This can be done over a bridge **1**, or from a string holder **2**, which acts as a bridge.

**Sounding the strings**
(*right*) Most chordophones are played by plucking with either the finger, **1**, or a plectrum, **2**, or by bowing, **3**. Some zithers are played with hammers **4**, (the piano is an example) and the strings of the aeolian harp, **5**, are sounded by the wind.

**Strings and pitch**
(*above*) Strings are attached directly to the neck, **1**, to a tuning ring, **2**, or to a peg, **3**, Higher pitch occurs with a short, **4**, tensed, **5**, or thin, **6**, string; also by shortening the vibrating length with the finger, **7**, or movable frets, **8**, **9**.

# Chromatic chords

When a passage of music is written in a particular key, the chords are usually made up from the notes of that key. But it is also possible to introduce chords that borrow notes from other keys. Such chords are said to be CHROMATIC. The most common chromatic chords are those built on:

1. The supertonic of the scale. These are either ordinary triads, or sevenths:

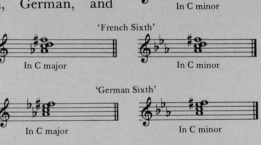

Major chords on the Supertonic

In C major    In C minor

Chord of the Supertonic Seventh

2. The flattened supertonic of the scale:

Major chords on the Flattened Supertonic

In C major    In C minor

When this chord appears in its first inversion it is known as the NEAPOLITAN SIXTH.

3. The flattened sixth of the scale. These are augmented chords, for they also contain the sharpened fourth of the scale. There are three kinds, called, respectively, Italian, German, and French Sixths:

'Italian Sixth'
In C major
In C minor

'French Sixth'
In C major    In C minor

'German Sixth'
In C major    In C minor

The same chords can also occur on the flattened supertonic:

In C major

4. The tonic of the scale. In particular the chord of the minor seventh:

Chord of the Tonic Minor Seventh

Chromatic chords do not bring about modulation (though they can be used for that purpose), but, as their name suggests, they lend 'colour' to the harmonies and make it more interesting.

usually four pairs. Descended from the medieval CITOLE, the cittern became very popular during the 16th century as it could be made cheaply and was relatively easy to play. The larger, bass cittern is called a PANDORA.

**Clappers** Any kind of instrument that consists of two pieces of the same material (wood, bone, metal, etc.) that can be struck together. Instruments of this kind have been known for thousands of years and in every part of the world. Such folk-instruments as the SPOONS and BONES are clappers.

**Clarinet family** → page 92

**Clarke, Jeremiah** English composer, 1670–1707. He was a chorister in the Chapel Royal under John Blow, and later became organist of Winchester College and then St Paul's Cathedral (1695). He became mentally deranged (it is said through hopeless love) and shot himself. He wrote anthems and services, a certain amount of theatre music, and various pieces for harpsichord, one of which, *The Prince of Denmark's March*, is well known as the *Trumpet Voluntary* and often wrongly attributed to Purcell.

**Clàrsach** This is the ancient small harp of the Scottish Highlands. It fell out of use almost entirely and was then revived during the 20th century.

**Clavecin** (Fr.) Harpsichord.

**Claves** Two short round sticks of hardwood. One is held in such a way that the hollow of the hand acts as a resonating cavity to amplify the sound. The player then taps this stick with the other one. Claves are used a great deal in Latin-American dance music, or in music that imitates this style.

**Clappers** *Left* This Moroccan dance troup use metal clappers as well as a drum.

**Clappers** These decorative instruments – hand, lotus, bowl and pomegranate shaped – date from ancient Egyptian and early Christian times.

# Classical

This is a troublesome term because it has different meanings according to whoever is using it. For example, historians use it to describe the music of the period 1760–1827 (approximately), when it is felt that all art aspired to ideals of balance and moderation – such as were believed to have been practised by the ancient Greeks. Music of this kind (that of Gluck, Haydn, Mozart, and, to some extent, Beethoven) places great emphasis on logical form, and though it can be very expressive seldom allows the emotional side to get out of hand. By contrast, the art of the 19th century was felt to be 'Romantic', and to be more interested

**Classical architecture** These Greek columns typify the form and balance of classical ideals.

in exploring the emotions and inner feelings of the artist than in the construction of perfectly proportioned forms. The greatest care must be taken in interpreting these terms, however – for it would not be true to say that all 'classical' music is without emotion, or all 'romantic' music is formless!

The word is also used to describe music that seems to have a lasting quality – as opposed to something that is pleasing for a time and is then forgotten. Certain music is therefore spoken of as 'classical', or 'serious' – but again there is no reason why 'classical' music should not be cheerful, or why 'pop' should not have a lasting, 'classical' quality.

# Church service

The word 'service' has many meanings in the English language, one of which is 'the meeting of a congregation for worship'. To musicians, however, it also means the musical settings of the various parts of the liturgy that are used on such occasions.

Until the time of the Reformation it was the liturgy of the Roman Catholic Church that most concerned the musicians of Western Europe. Thereafter their allegiance split, according to whether their country remained Catholic or embraced some version of the reformed faith. In the case of England, Protestantism became the official church.

## 1. Music in the Catholic Church

There are two principal classes of service: the *Office*, and the *Mass*. Each has a collection of appropriate plainsong chants, handed down from the time of Pope Gregory the Great (c. 540–604) but much older in origin. These were always sung in Latin.

Certain parts of the liturgy, however, attracted the attentions of composers, who made their own often very elaborate settings. These include the Mass itself, and certain hymns from the various Offices – as for example the MAGNIFICAT, which is sung during Vespers. In addition to this, composers found a further outlet in writing MOTETS, which, though not an essential part of the liturgy, were allowed at certain points (for example, at the Offertory, during the elevation of the Host).

There are eight OFFICES, or CANONICAL HOURS. They are celebrated mainly in monasteries and cathedrals, and represent the cycle of prayer that is part of the routine of a religious institution. They are:

| | |
|---|---|
| Matins | before daybreak |
| Lauds | at sunrise |
| Prime | at 6am, the first hour of the working day |
| Terce | 9am |
| Sext | midday |
| None | 3pm |
| Vespers | at sunset |
| Compline | 7pm |

The musical features of the Offices are: the chanting of psalms, the singing of hymns and canticles, and the chanting of lessons from the scriptures. From the musical point of view the most important Offices are

**Salzburg Cathedral** Musicians, seen in the balconies to left and right, take part in this church service of 1682 to mark the enthronement of the Archbishop of Salzburg.

**St Andrew's Church, Plymouth** This engraving of 1830 shows a simple Anglican service. The organ in the background of the picture provided the accompaniment to hymns.

MATINS, LAUDS, and VESPERS. Vespers is the most important of the three, for it was the only Office that officially allowed polyphonic music.

The Mass is the principal service of the Catholic Church. It can be celebrated at any convenient and appropriate time of day, either as LOW MASS (in which the words are spoken by the priest, and the congregation remains silent), or HIGH MASS (which is sung or spoken aloud). From the composer's point of view the important texts are the five invariable sections which form the basis of the ORDINARY OF THE MASS:

Kyrie
Gloria
Credo
Sanctus and Benedictus
Agnus Dei

It is these sections that have been set to music over and over again. (→ **Mass**)

The music of the Catholic Church is now undergoing radical changes, however. The Second Vatican Council (1962–65) declared that services should be conducted in the language of the country and not in Latin. The old settings have therefore been replaced by modern compositions suitable for congregational singing – some adapted from plainsong, some totally new. These changes affect what may be called the 'public' church; monasteries, etc., keep to the traditional ways.

## 2. Music in the Anglican Church

The details of the Anglican Church Service were first laid down in the 'Book of Common Prayer' (1549). There are three main services:

The Office of the Holy Communion
Morning Prayer
Evening Prayer

Each is based on the ritual of the Catholic Church. The Office of the Holy Communion is the equivalent of the Mass; Morning Prayer corresponds to Matins, and Evening Prayer (often called Evensong) corresponds to Vespers.

The portions of the Communion Service that may be sung are: the *Kyrie, Gloria, Credo,* and *Sanctus* (without *Benedictus*). In Elizabethan days the service consisted only of the *Kyrie, Credo,* and *Sanctus*; but in the middle of the 19th century the *Gloria* was admitted, and later still (1892), the *Benedictus* and *Agnus Dei* were permitted to those who wanted them.

The musical parts of Morning Service are the five CANTICLES (biblical hymns): the VENITE (Psalm 95: 'O come, let us sing unto the Lord'); the TE DEUM ('We praise Thee, O God'), or at certain times the BENEDICITE ('O all ye works of the Lord'); and the BENEDICTUS ('Blessed be the Lord God of Israel'), or at certain times the JUBILATE (Psalm 100: 'O be joyful in the Lord, all ye lands').

Evening Prayer has two main musical sections, each with an alternative: the MAGNIFICAT ('My soul doth magnify the Lord'), or sometimes the CANTATE DOMINO (Psalm 98: 'O sing unto the Lord a new song'); and the NUNC DIMITTIS ('Lord, now lettest Thou thy servant depart in peace'), or sometimes the DEUS MISEREATUR (Psalm 67: 'God be merciful unto us and bless us').

In addition, both services may have psalms (chanted or spoken), congregational hymns, and an *Anthem* sung by the choir.

A complete setting to cover all three services is known as a **Full Service**. All the music is in the same key and it is customary to refer to the setting by the key and the composer: for example, 'Stanford in B flat'.

Elizabethan composers (the first to be faced with the problem of writing music for the new Church) wrote two kinds of setting: the **Short Service**, in which each syllable was set to one note of music, so that the words could be clearly heard and understood; and the **Great Service**, which was contrapuntal and very elaborate.

Service music is often sung unaccompanied, but since the 18th century composers have preferred to make their settings with an obligatory organ accompaniment.

Like the Church of Rome, the Protestant Church has in recent years made sweeping changes in the structure and content of its liturgy. New translations of the old texts have been made, and in consequence new musical settings are being composed. But the old texts and their accompanying music are still widely used.

**Muzio Clementi**
1752–1832

**Clog-dancing** This dancer performs a Lancashire clog-dance during a summer festival.

**Clavicembalo** (It.) Harpsichord. Often abbreviated to 'cembalo', a term that is also used in modern Germany. The word is derived from the Latin *clavis*, a key, and *cembalo*, a dulcimer, which aptly describe what the instrument is – a keyed dulcimer.

**Clavichord** → page 93

**Clavier** Another word for 'keyboard'. Thus it often means a keyboard instrument (clavichord or harpsichord) and in German today (generally spelt *Klavier*) the piano.

### Clef → Notes and notation

**Clementi, Muzio** Italian composer and pianist, 1752–1832. He was trained in Rome and his first compositions were heard when he was 12 years old. When he was 14 he was brought to London by a rich Englishman. He continued his studies and then, in 1773, took musical England by storm.

His reputation as a pianist, composer and teacher spread throughout Europe and he wrote a great deal of music to demonstrate the special qualities of the pianoforte which was at that time displacing the harpsichord as a popular instrument. When he was about 60 he became a music publisher and a manufacturer of pianos. His sonatas, sonatinas and studies are well worth playing.

### Clocks, Musical → Mechanical instruments

**Clogs and Clog-dancing** The sound of marching or stamping feet has been used throughout history and all over the world as a simple form of music. Clogs, the carved wooden shoes formerly used by working men and women in the North of England, have proved to be excellent 'instruments' to accompany a very intricate type of folk dancing still practised today. The dancers, eight men to a team, line up in two files. Each man carries a 'sling' – a length of cotton, stuffed with bits of material – with which he makes elaborate swinging circles. The step is brisk, rather like a march. Originally the dance was performed in spring time – it may have once had some pagan religious significance.

**Close harmony** When used in the general sense, this term describes any harmonization of a tune in which the notes of the harmony are kept close together. Many hymn-tunes are harmonized in this way.

# Clarinet and Clarinet family

The modern orchestral clarinet is usually said to have been 'invented' by the German instrument maker Johann Christoph Denner (1655–1707) some time towards the very end of the 17th century. In fact what he did was to take an already existing instrument, the CHALUMEAU, and improve it by adding two keys which brought into play a number of extra notes. In the 1840s the Boehm system of keys was applied to the clarinet and, with a few modifications over the years, the instrument became the agile, expressive member of the orchestra it is today.

The clarinet, like the chalumeau, is a single-reed instrument. This reed, which is made of thin cane, is fixed to a mouthpiece by a metal ligature. When the player blows through the mouthpiece the reed vibrates and . causes the air in the body of the instrument to vibrate in turn, thus producing the note. The tone is very smooth and pleasant.

All modern clarinets are transposing instruments. That is to say, their music is written out at a different pitch from the sounds actually required (→ **Transposing instruments**). The two most common orchestral clarinets are in B flat and A, and their music is written a tone and a minor third higher, respectively. The military band uses a high E flat clarinet called the

ALTO CLARINET. A BASS CLARINET in B flat can be found in certain larger scores, and many 18th-century scores call for a BASSET HORN, which is a tenor member of the clarinet family. Even large, contrabass clarinets exist, but seldom find their way into orchestral scores. The **Wind band →**, however, makes use of several sizes of clarinet.

**Brazilian uruas** These primitive instruments are related to the clarinet.

**Clarinet family** The clarinet is used most often in symphony orchestras, military bands and dance bands. It also features as a solo instrument and in chamber music. Here you can see the principal members of the clarinet family and their 'sounding lengths': (*left to right*) sopranino clarinet in E flat 48 cm; soprano clarinet in B flat 66 cm; alto clarinet in E flat 96 cm; basset horn (in F) 107 cm; bass clarinet in B flat 140 cm; and contrabass clarinet in B flat 269 cm.

# Clavichord

This keyboard instrument was popular before the piano was invented and from the end of the 19th century it has gradually come into use again among people who like to play music on the instruments for which it was written. There are now a great many clavichord-makers again – some even sell 'kits' from which, with a little patience and skill, you can make your own instrument.

The clavichord is a small instrument. Sometimes it is simply an oblong box which can be placed on a table; but more often it has its own legs and stands on the floor.

**Clavichord** *Above* This 16th-century Flemish painting shows a young woman at the clavichord.

*Right* Keyboard and strings of a clavichord of 1790. The clavichord was much used from the 16th to the 18th century.

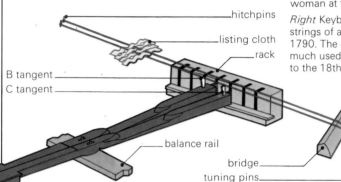

hitchpins
listing cloth
rack
B tangent
C tangent
balance rail
bridge
tuning pins

The tone of a note on the piano is made by a hammer hitting the string, after which it drops away. The tone of a clavichord is made by a small piece of metal hitting the string and then remaining there as long as the player holds the key down. This piece of metal is called a TANGENT.

The clavichord has a very quiet voice. It is no use in a concert hall, but ideal in an ordinary room. It is also a very sympathetic and personal sort of instrument to play.

But the term also describes a particular style of group singing in which the tune appears in the middle voices, with harmonies above and below it, all bunched closely together and often moving in parallel chords.

Close-harmony groups, singing arrangements of popular songs, were a feature of American student life at the end of the 19th century. They often called themselves Glee Clubs (even though they did not necessarily sing glees), and it is probable that, originally, they modelled themselves on this particularly English form of amateur music-making (→ **Glee** and **Glee Club**). Such groups consisted entirely of male singers, but groups of female close-harmony singers have also come into existence. In the 1970s close-harmony singing again became extremely popular – this time in the world of entertainment, through the example of the King's Singers.

Singing in close-harmony has also been a feature of 'pop' music – either as a manner of presenting a complete number, or as a background to a soloist.

**Coates, Eric** English composer, 1886–1957. After training at the Royal Academy of Music he became known as a fine viola player in both chamber music groups and major London orchestras. Later he became widely known as a composer of light music – the

**Samuel Coleridge-Taylor** 1875–1912 One of his most celebrated works was *Hiawatha*, three cantatas first performed in 1900. It was based on the narrative poem about American Indian life by Henry Longfellow. The work was regularly performed at the Royal Albert Hall before the last war.

'Knightsbridge' march from the *London Suite* (1933) is a good example of his tuneful style.

**Coda** (It.) Tail. A passage added to the end of a piece of music to round it off effectively.

**Codetta** (It.) Little tail. A shorter version of the coda. In fugues, however, it has the special meaning of a short passage in the middle of an Exposition section which is neither Subject, Answer, nor Counter-subject. (→ **Fugue**)

**Col, Coll', Colla** (It.) Forms of 'with the', found in such directions as:
  **Col basso:** 'with the bass'
  **Colla voce:** 'with the voice' (a warning to accompanists to follow the singer)
  **Coll' arco:** 'with the bow' (after a pizzicato passage)
  **Colla punta d'arco:** 'with the point of the bow'
  **Col legno:** 'with the wood of the bow'

**Coleridge-Taylor, Samuel** English composer, 1875–1912. He was of mixed parentage, his father being a native of Sierra Leone and his mother a native of England. He studied at the Royal College of Music under Stanford and began to make his mark as a composer as early as 1895 (there is a splendid Clarinet Quintet of this date).

Public success came in 1898 when the first part of his 'Hiawatha' triology, *Hiawatha's Wedding Feast*, was performed at the Royal College. He thereafter received a steady stream of commissions, but found it hard to make an adequate living as a composer.

Of all his many works, only *Hiawatha* (a setting of Longfellow's poem for chorus and orchestra) has remained a favourite – which is a pity, for delightful as it is, it does not show him at his best. His music is always colourful and immensely tuneful – he might be described as an English Dvořák.

**Coloratura** Derived from the German word *Koloratur*, the term describes the florid ornamentation (runs, trills, and arpeggios, etc.) found in certain kinds of vocal music, particularly operatic. The correct Italian term is 'fioritura' – literally 'flowerings'. A coloratura soprano is one who can sing this kind of music easily. A good example of coloratura writing occurs in Mozart's opera *The Magic Flute*, in the two arias of the Queen of the Night.

**Comic opera** A general term which embraces many different types of opera, all of which have an amusing plot – for example, Rossini's *The Barber of Seville* (1816), or Puccini's *Gianni Schicchi* (1918). Operettas are usually comic, but they always have spoken dialogue (some 'comic operas', *Gianni Schicchi* for example, are sung throughout).

**Common chord** → **Harmony**

**Community singing** This describes almost any occasion when a considerable number of people begin singing together. The expression seems to have arisen in the USA during the First World War, when definite occasions of this kind were organized in army camps – the singing being led by an official 'Song Leader'. After the war the idea spread, and whole concerts were organized – the audience providing its own entertainment, as it were. Special song books for community singing have been published. They contain a mixture of national songs, music-hall favourites, and the popular tunes of the day (and even a few 'classics', such as 'Land of Hope and Glory' – a song adapted to the tune of Elgar's 'Pomp and Circumstance' March, No 1). To be effective, community songs have to be bold and simple, and, of course, easy to remember.

**Comodo** (It.) Convenient. Thus *tempo comodo* means 'at a comfortable (convenient) speed'. Note that the word is spelled with one 'm'.

**Comic opera** Rossini's *The Barber of Seville*, one of the best-known and most popular of comic operas, was hissed on its first performance in 1816.

# Composition

In French 'poser' means 'to put'. And 'com' at the beginning of a word generally means 'together'. So to 'compose' is to 'put things together' – for instance words and ideas, as in the 'compositions' we write at school.

In music 'to compose' means to put together sounds in such a way that other people understand the logic of what we have done. For music, like all the arts, is a form of language – a way of conveying thought or feeling from one person to another. If it does not have this quality of 'meaning' then it is not music in the generally understood sense of the word. It is, however, quite another matter to say exactly what a piece of music 'means'.

Composers learn to compose simply by composing. Usually they start by imitating the music of those composers they most admire. The more practised they become, the more they shake free of these models and are able to do things in their own way. We recognize the truly great composer by the fact that he has established his own way of doing things – that he has his own *personality*, so to speak.

When they are students, composers will, of course, exercise their musical minds by studying harmony and counterpoint and orchestration. But this is no more than breaking down into easy stages what other composers have done and making 'rules' about it.

People who are not composers often find it hard to imagine where musical ideas come from. If they come from anywhere it is from what other composers have done in the past. Think of it like this: from the moment a 'composer' is born, his mind responds to every musical impression that comes its way. Whether he knows it or not he stores away these impressions, so that his mind gradually becomes a vast Reference Library of musical ideas.

**Compass** The range of a voice or instrument, from its lowest note to the highest. The highest note will, or course, vary sometimes with the ability of the performer.

**Compound Binary Form** → **Sonata Form**

**Compound intervals** → **Intervals**

**Compound time** → **Notes and notation**

Everybody does this, of course – to a greater or lesser degree. But the composer has a very special type of mind. He 'creates' new ideas out of old ideas.

For example: imagine that Beethoven is considering the possibility of writing a second symphony. Two perfectly common-place ideas float to the surface. One is a D major chord:

The other is a little decorative figure:

Neither are very interesting in themselves. Both have been used a thousand times before. But in Beethoven's mind they come together and are linked inextricably. They become, in fact, a new and very original, very Beethovenish idea, quite sufficient to launch the first movement:

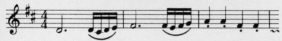

All this takes place in the unconscious mind. The composer does not sit down and say 'I will take this commonplace idea and combine it with that commonplace idea and thereby make something that will astonish everybody'. But his unconscious mind does something of the sort for him and presents his conscious mind with the result. His conscious mind then considers what is being offered very critically. If it approves and recognises that this is an idea it can do something with, then the laborious business of 'composition' begins.

Many composers find it helpful to use a piano at this stage – Haydn did, Stravinsky did. But others prefer to work out all the details in their head – as Mozart and Britten did. Either way is good (if the results are good!) – it is simply a matter of taste. But the composer who uses a piano does *not* sit at the keyboard fishing for notes. Rather he uses it as a stimulus to musical *thought*, and as a means of testing his ideas.

For all composing takes place in the mind. The composer has a musical idea and he knows how to write this down on paper (just as he can look at a piece of music and hear it in his head). This seems a difficult thing to do, but really it is not. It is all a matter of training the memory – just as we all train ourselves to read and recognize the sound of words.

Many composers begin by making a general 'sketch' of the work they are composing. They can then go back over this and work out the details, changing things as they please. Some like to do this on paper. Others, as we have said, can do it in their heads.

Composing, therefore, is a matter of painstaking hard work – of gradually assembling all the ingredients needed for a particular piece of music and making them work together in a logical, effective way. But there is a mysterious something which we may, perhaps, call 'inspiration'. And this would seem to be the capacity that composers have of visualizing what the finished composition should be like and of recognizing the ingredients that will make it.

Why some people should have this capacity, nobody can say. Or why some should have it for a few years, or a few compositions, and then lose it. Or why the truly great composers can go on growing – for ever evolving new ideas, new ways of expressing themselves. Or why it is that only some composers can endow their music with a sense of personality and originality. All these are mysteries and are likely to remain so.

**Computer** An electronic calculator. It has entered music through the work of electronic composers, and is used to translate whatever 'programme' is fed into it into a series of impulses on a tape-recording. This pro-gramme will include information about every aspect of music (pitch, duration, intensity, etc.), including many that cannot be achieved by ordinary human means. The programme eventually emerges through loudspeakers as sound, and the computer is therefore both an instrument and a device for composition. Composers using computers need to know a great deal about mathematics and electronics.

**Concert grand** A large grand piano, suitable for use in a concert hall. The modern concert grand is usually about 3 m long and has a compass of seven and a half octaves.

# Concertina

A portable free-reed instrument (→ **Reed organ family**) invented by Sir Charles Wheatstone and patented in 1829. It consists of a small bellows with a keyboard at each end that holds several rows of buttons. As the player expands or contracts the bellows (squeezing or pulling it between the palms of his hands) he presses the buttons, which allow air to pass through the appropriate reed and produce a sound.

There are three main types of concertina, all English in design and origin:

1. **The English concertina** which is made in treble, tenor-treble, bass, baritone, and contra-bass sizes, and has four rows of buttons on each side, arranged in vertical lines. This instrument produces the same note whether the bellows are pushed or pulled, and the notes of the scale alternate between the two keyboards.

2. **The Duet concertina** which operates on the same principle as the English concertina, except that all the high notes are on the right-hand keyboard, and all the low notes on the left. This means that a melody can be played with one hand and accompanied with the other.

3. **The Anglo concertina** which is a cross between the other two. Each button, however, produces two notes – one for the push and one for the pull. Again, the high notes are on the right and the low notes on the left.

The keyboard ends of the concertina are usually eight or twelve-sided. Cheaper models have six sides. All these instruments

can produce a very fine and powerful effect, and are much in demand for accompanying Morris dancing. A so-called German concertina can also be found, but it is merely a poor copy of the Anglo concertina and not a type in its own right. The concertina should not be confused with the **Accordion →**.

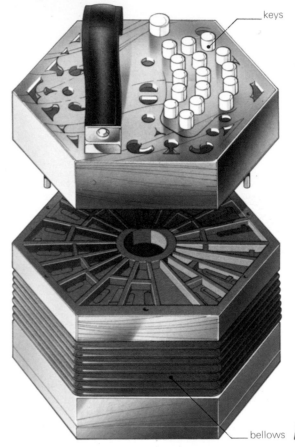

keys

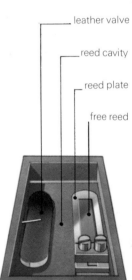

*Left* The hexagonal-bodied concertina has never made an impact on the concert hall, but has always been popular for accompanying Morris dancing and other folk dances.

leather valve

reed cavity

reed plate

free reed

bellows

---

**Concert master** The leader of the orchestra. A term used in the USA, and in Germany: **Concertmeister**.

**Concerto** → page 98

**Concert overture** → **Overture**

**Concert pitch** → **Pitch**

**Concerts** → page 97

**Concertstück** (Ger.) It means

1. A CONCERT-PIECE – that is, suitable for playing at concerts.

2. The more common use of the word – A CONCERTED PIECE – that is, one in which a solo instrument has other instruments to play with (really a short concerto).

**Conducting** → page 100

**Conjunct motion** → **Motion**

**Conservatory** A place where things are 'conserved' or protected – for instance plants. In Italy in the 16th, 17th, and 18th centuries orphanages were called by that name (*conservatorio*) because boys or girls were kept and looked after there. Then it was found that many of the boys and girls could be trained as musicians and thus could earn their living when they left.

Gradually, then, *conservatorio* became the Italian word for a school of music and the French adapted the word as *conservatoire* and the British and Americans as Conservatory (but in Britain the word is still not much used except to mean 'greenhouse').

# Concerts

The idea of a 'concert' in the modern sense of a public performance at which an audience pays for the right of admission seems to have begun in England in 1673, when John Banister began to hold meetings with 'musick performed by excellent Masters' in his London house. Banister had just lost his job as leader of King Charles II's Band of Twenty-four Violins (he upset the King by saying that English violinists were every bit as good as French, if not better!), and was having to earn a living as best he could.

These concerts were modelled on the kind of casual entertainment to be found in any common tavern or alehouse. But in this case the audience paid to come in, and the accent was on the music rather than the drinking. Even so, the musicians insisted on being hidden behind a curtain – presumably because they didn't want to be mistaken for mere tavern musicians.

A more famous series of concerts began in 1678, the year in which Banister's venture came to an end. These were organized by Thomas Britton, a keen musical amateur who sold charcoal for his living and was known throughout London as 'the musical small-coal man'. These became very popular and were attended by poets and scholars, noblemen and musicians – Handel among them. Soon, concerts on similar lines began to flourish all over London.

Concerts of this kind, however, were more like the meetings of a Music Club. Not everybody could afford to attend them, and the kind of music they offered was addressed to people already 'in the know'. Similar but even more exclusive societies were founded in the 18th century. For example, there was the *Academy of Antient Music*, founded in 1710 for the specific purpose of avoiding modern music – by which they meant Handel, who had just arrived in London. There was the

**Vauxhall Gardens** concert in the late 18th century.
*Below* **St James's Hall**, a 19th-century choral concert.

**Henry Wood Promenade Concert** The last night of the Proms at the Royal Albert Hall.

*Philharmonick Society* (1728), which was really an amateur orchestra. A third society was founded in 1776. It too was called the *Concerts of Antient Music* – which meant Handel, who was now safely dead! Only one of these old institutions still survives. It is the *Royal Philharmonic Society* and it was founded in 1813.

Rather nearer our own ideas of a public concert were the performances that took place in the various London Pleasure Gardens (Vauxhall, Ranelagh, etc.) throughout the 17th and 18th centuries.

It was also customary at this time for musicians to organise independent concerts of their own – hiring the hall and the performers, taking all the risks and pocketing all the profits. The concerts that Salomon organized for Haydn's London visits are examples of this.

Concerts as we know them really began in the 19th century. Conductors with a flair for showmanship, such as Louis Antoine Jullien, gave mammoth Promenade Concerts at Drury Lane Theatre, charging comparatively small entrance fees and providing popular programmes designed to attract large audiences of ordinary people. In 1855 August Manns began a rather more sedate series of concerts at the newly erected Crystal Palace. A few years later (1858) a series of Saturday and Monday 'Pops' (Popular Concerts) were started at the St James' Hall. Henry Wood's Promenade Concerts began at Queen's Hall in 1895 and still continue to this day in the Royal Albert Hall.

It is on foundations such as these, for which parallels can be found throughout the world, that the great concert industry of our own day was raised. Gramophone records and broadcasting, despite gloomy forecasts in the early days, have actually increased the popularity of concert-going.

---

**Consort** This is the old way of spelling 'concert'. It has been used in music to describe any group of musicians performing together, and in particular to describe a group of viols. A typical 'consort of viols' might consist of two trebles, two tenors, and two basses. A 'consort' consisting entirely of strings was called a WHOLE CONSORT. A BROKEN CONSORT was one that included wind instruments, with the strings.

**Broken consort** This late 16th-century German consort is a 'mixed' one.

**Continuo** →**Figured bass**

**Contralto** → **Voice**

**Contrapuntal** The adjective of the word 'counterpoint' (see that word), and a **contrapuntist** is a person who is skilful at writing counterpoint.

**Contrary motion** → **Motion**

# Concerto

If we say that a number of people are working 'in concert', we mean that they have agreed to work together. And it was in this sense that the Italian word *Concerto* was originally used. It described any piece of music that involved several players working together. Gradually, however, it came to be applied to a very distinct kind of composition: one in which a soloist, or small group of soloists (the *concertino*), showed off their skill against an orchestral accompaniment (the *ripieno*). Music of this kind falls into three distinct types and periods:

1. During the first half of the 18th century a very popular type was the CONCERTO GROSSO. Such works consisted of a number of contrasting movements, arranged like a suite. Each movement had a different character – fast, slow, lyrical, dance-like, etc. – and it was this chain of contrasts that gave the work a sense of variety and interest. There was no special limit to the number of movements, but from three to five is the average.

In at least some of these movements a group of two or three soloists were set apart from the orchestra. As the movement progressed they would play together with the orchestra, or by themselves, or against its accompaniment. This alternation gave what is known as the 'concerto style' – that is to say: a pattern of contrasts, between solo and orchestra, loud and soft sounds, etc.

The pattern also gave a special shape to these movements. For almost always each movement would begin with a bold statement from the orchestra. This set the mood of the movement and announced the main musical material. From time to time during the movement the orchestra would return with this idea, either wholly or in part. Between these orchestral outbursts the soloists would make their contribution.

Music operating on this plan is bound to have a distinctive pattern. We say that it employs a *ritornello* – something which 'returns' again and again. The typical Concerto Grosso movement, therefore, may be said to employ a 'Ritornello System'. The main orchestra in such movements is usually referred to as the *ripieno* section (*ripieno* is Italian for 'full'), and the group of soloists as the *concertino* (the 'small group' playing 'in concert').

The most important masters of the concerto grosso are: Corelli, Vivaldi, Bach,

**Piano concerto** Daniel Barenboim conducts with the maestro Artur Rubinstein at the piano.

**Yehudi Menuhin,** one of today's most famous violinists, plays a violin concerto.

and Handel. But thousands of composers contributed to it, for it was a very popular form of music and came at a time when public concerts were being born. It was also a time when virtuoso soloists were beginning to come into their own, and we find that in certain cases the concertino group consists merely of one player. It is out of this idea of a star soloist that the concerto of the second half of the 18th century was born.

2. We call the concerto of Mozart's day the CLASSICAL CONCERTO. It had three movements (almost invariably) and a single soloist.

Moreover, the shape of the movements were different from those of the concerto grosso. At least one, the first movement, adopted the new **Sonata Form** $\rightarrow$ plan. The middle movement was usually slow and lyrical, and the Finale very brisk and cheerful – often in Rondo Form.

The Sonata Form of the first movement, however, is very interesting because, lurking behind it, so to speak, you can see the remains of the concerto grosso's Ritornello System. Thus: it always began with a bold statement of ideas by the orchestra. Only when this was over would the soloist enter. Moreover, at each important point in the unfolding of the Sonata pattern, the orchestra tended to return with a fairly hefty outburst of its own. For example: at the end of the Exposition section, the end of the Development, and immediately after the Cadenza (see below). The effect of these orchestral outbursts is very similar to that made by the returns of the Ripieno section in the typical concerto grosso movement.

The first movement plan, however, must be described as a Sonata Form with a Double Exposition. The first 'Exposition' is, as we have seen, for the orchestra alone. It gives the main ideas of the movement, but 'exposes' them *in the same key*. The second 'Exposition' repeats the first, but includes the soloist, and *changes key* in the normal sonata manner. Most composers introduce a new idea during this second Exposition, simply for the sake of surprise and variety.

The Development that follows is shared by soloist and orchestra, and so is the Restatement. But just before the end, the orchestra pauses and the soloist is left free to play a CADENZA. Sometimes this was improvised on the spot, and sometimes written down. It was designed to show off the player's skill and whip up excitement with a display of musical fireworks before the orchestra returned to round off the movement with a final flourish.

The great composers of the Classical Concerto are Mozart and Beethoven – more especially Mozart, for Beethoven's concertos are edging towards the new style that became popular in the 19th century.

3. The concerto style favoured by the 19th century was very like the Classical Concerto, but different enough in detail to warrant a new descriptive title: the ROMANTIC CONCERTO.

This retained the shape of the Classical Concerto, but streamlined its details. The Double Exposition of the first movement gave way to a Single Exposition, shared from the outset by soloist and orchestra. And the Cadenza was moved from the end of the Restatement section to the end of the Development. It thus came at the climax of the Development and served as an exciting introduction to the Restatement. Mendelssohn's *Violin Concerto* shows this kind of plan very clearly.

The only other change came as the century wore on and the demands of virtuoso violinists and pianists became more and more extravagant and the public more and more eager to see them do their tricks. The result was to make the opposition between soloist and orchestra, which in Mozart's day had been a polite conversation between equals, more like a pitched battle. The Tchaikovsky piano concertos are good examples of this style. But of course by this time pianos had become larger and stronger, and orchestras (and concert halls) much bigger than in Mozart's day.

4. The only thing that need be said about the concerto in the 20th century is that it is possible to find examples of every type of concerto being written by different composers at one and the same time. Thus, while Elgar and Rachmaninov were quite happy to compose full-scale Romantic concertos, Stravinsky returned not only to the 'balance' of the Mozart concerto, but also to a deliberate exploration of the old concerto grosso style. Composers in the 20th century adopt whichever style they need, and the concerto continues to thrive.

**Coperario, John** English composer, c. 1575–1626. He began life as plain John Cooper, but changed his name during a visit to Italy and, on returning, kept it because the Italian fashion was all the rage. He was a lute and viola da gamba player, and as a composer is particularly important for his string *Fantasies*.

**Copland** → page 101

**Copyright** This is the legal recognition of the fact that the creative artist is the 'owner' of the work he creates and that nobody has any right to perform or publish it unless they enter into a proper agreement with him.

Though this may seem a simple and wholly natural right, it is only during the last hundred years or so that the law has made any serious attempt to recognize it. In Mozart's day, for example, it was common practice for publishers and performers to 'pirate' a composer's music without any thought of payment.

In Britain (since 1911), and in most countries, this is no longer possible. The composer is said to 'own' the music as soon as he puts it on paper. Ownership lasts throughout his lifetime and passes to his heirs for 50 years after his death (the period varies slightly with different countries).

When a composer 'publishes' a piece of music, he enters into a legal agreement with the publisher and therefore *shares* his copyright. This means that he will now get, for example, 10% of the sale price of all printed music, a proportion of any fees that come from hiring out scores or orchestral parts, a share of any fees that come from recordings, etc. In return, the publisher prints his music, advertises it, promotes performances, and generally looks after its welfare.

If the composer is performed frequently enough, he can become a member of the Performing Right Society. He now has a share of the vast sums that are collected throughout the world in granting public places (such as concert-halls) a 'licence to perform music'. His share in this general revenue is worked out on a basis of the number of minutes of his music performed during the period under consideration.

The important thing for ordinary music-lovers to remember is that a composer's music is *his property*. If you write out a copy, or duplicate one on a xerox machine, or copy it by any other means, you are *stealing* from him as surely as if you had broken into his house and robbed him of his last penny.

# Conducting

Although it seems obvious that somebody must always have taken charge of an instrumental or choral performance, the idea of a 'conductor' who not only indicates the basic beat of the music, but also controls the way in which it is 'interpreted' is of comparatively recent date.

In the early days probably all that was needed was for the choirmaster to mark the beat and indicate the entries of the different voices. He would use a short stick, or a roll of paper, or just his hands.

During the 17th and early 18th centuries it was common, particularly in France, for the director of the music to thump out the beat loudly by banging on the floor with a long stick.

The early orchestra however, was more often directed quietly from the harpsichord. For this was the period of the 'continuo', and it would be sensible for the player (who was in any case supplying the basic harmony in an orchestra that had not yet settled into a pattern of self-supporting strings, brass and woodwind) to be in command of the whole situation.

Later in the 18th century, when the 'continuo' began to go out of use, the lead tended to pass to the first violinist (even now called the 'leader' in England and the 'concert master' in the USA), who would indicate with his bow what was to be done.

Conducting with a baton, as in modern times, seems to have begun in Germany, but it only became the general practice during the first half of the 19th century. Among the earliest conductors to use a baton was the composer Spohr (who introduced the method to London in 1820)

It was, of course, necessity that brought this about. For orchestras were growing larger, music was becoming more complicated, and composers were deliberately searching out expressive and colourful effects that could not be left to chance. By the second half of the century, conducting had become an art in itself, and the conductor had emerged as a special type of musician.

What, then, is his job? Primarily he must indicate the beats – which he does by a series of universally recognized movements (see centre column). At the same time as spelling out the beats he can control the speed, suggest loud or soft effects, and to some

**Conductors** *Above* This 18th-century conductor uses two rolls of paper to direct his musicians.
**A modern conductor** *Right* Daniel Barenboim b.1942.

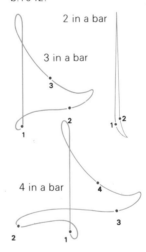

2 in a bar
3 in a bar
4 in a bar

**Orchestra's guide** This cartoon by Hoffnung takes a light-hearted view of the conductor's request for pizzicato.

extent indicate the kind of phrasing.

For example: a large beat would suggest a loud sound, and a small, neat beat, close to the body, would suggest the need for quietness. A brisk, angular kind of beat would suggest a very different kind of interpretation from the same beat made in a soft, flowing way. All these gestures are usually carried out with the right hand.

The conductor's left hand can be used to bring in different instruments, give warning signs about the dynamics and speeds, etc. His whole face, and especially his eyes, are equally important in suggesting to the players what he expects of them.

The conductor must study the score until he knows its every detail, and he must find a way of suggesting his interpretation to the performers. But this interpretation must be as near to what the composer has asked for as possible. There is bound to be some variation, because different personalities are involved. But ideally the conductor must 'get under the skin' of the composer. Though he must master the orchestra, he must be the servant of the music.

What we see at a concert, however, includes a great deal of showmanship – put on for the benefit of the audience, who expect conductors to be somewhat larger than life. The real work is done at the rehearsals, not when he is on parade.

# Copland

Aaron Copland, b. 1900. He is one of America's most outstanding composers – as highly regarded abroad as he is in his own country.

He studied first in America and then (1921–24) in France under Nadia Boulanger, where he also came under the influence of Stravinsky's music. Even at this time, however, he was anxious to write music 'that would immediately be recognized as American in character'. Inevitably, he was much influenced by jazz and various forms of popular music, but he did not turn to folk music for inspiration until the 1930s. Twenty years later his interests moved on again to include the possibilities of serialism.

Copland's career therefore falls into a number of distinct 'periods'. In the first, up to about 1929, his music was highly rhythmic and rather jazzy (*Concerto for Piano and Orchestra*, 1927). In the second, 1930–36, he began to write a rather more austere kind of music, still very rhythmic, but rather bare and angular (*Statements*, for orchestra, 1934). Then came the influence of American folksong and the beginnings of a much more colourful, tuneful, popular style. Works of this period have had a wide success. They include the ballets *Billy the Kid* (1938), *Rodeo* (1942), and *Appalachian Spring* (1944); the orchestral *El Salón México* (1936), and the *Concerto for Clarinet and*

**Aaron Copland**
This composer is well-known outside the USA as a champion of American music. He often conducts his own music.

*Strings* (1948); the unaccompanied choral work *In the Beginning* (1947), and the song-cycle, *Twelve Poems by Emily Dickinson* (1950). In 1950 Copland began to experiment with a modified version of serialism (*Quartet for Piano and Strings*) and his work consequently became once more rather austere and intellectual.

Besides being a composer of great importance in the history of American music, Copland has been an influential teacher, an excellent conductor and pianist, and has written several books about music.

---

**Cor** This is *really* the French word for 'horn' but it forms part of the names of several instruments that are not really horns at all – for instance the COR ANGLAIS.

**Cor anglais → Oboe family**

**Corant, Coranto → Courante**

**Corda** Italian for 'string' and **corde** is its plural.

So *una corda* means 'one string'. In the older grand pianos most of the notes had two strings, but if you used the soft pedal the keyboard moved so that only one was struck. The grand piano now has three strings for most of the notes, of which two are sounded when the soft pedal is used, but the old expression is still retained. Thus whenever *una corda* is seen the soft pedal is to be depressed.

When the soft pedal is to be released again the sign is, in older music, *due corde* ('two

**Arcangelo Corelli**
1653–1713

strings'), or, in more modern music, *tre corde* ('three strings'), or it may be *tutte le corde* ('all the strings').

**Corelli, Arcangelo** Italian composer and violinist, 1653–1713. He was famous throughout Europe as a virtuoso violinist and spent time in France and Germany before settling in Rome (c. 1685), where he began to add to his reputation by publishing his own compositions.

Although he did not write a large quantity of music, the quality of what he wrote is so fine that he must be considered one of the most important composers of his day. It was largely his example that helped to establish the new 'sonata' and 'concerto grosso' styles. He published four sets of 12 Trio Sonatas, and a set of 12 Solo Sonatas. After his death a set of 12 Concerti Grossi (Op 6) were published, but they had, of course, become famous in his lifetime.

Corelli appears to have been a very amiable man, an ardent collector of fine paintings, and very modest, despite his great fame. Handel, however, who admired him as a musician, did accuse him of being rather tight-fisted!

**Cornelius, Peter** German composer, 1824–74. He was a close friend and champion of Liszt and Wagner. Though he wrote a number of very fine songs and part-songs, he is now remembered only for his comic opera *The Barber of Bagdad* (1858).

**Cornet** A small valved instrument in B flat, something like a trumpet, but actually developed from the old post-horn. It is used primarily in brass bands and military bands, but its tone is less noble and thrilling than that of the trumpet.

**Cornett** A woodwind instrument with a cup-shaped mouthpiece (as in a trumpet or trombone). It was very popular in the 16th and 17th centuries, though its origins seem to go back to at least the 13th century. There were three main sizes: treble, small treble, and tenor – the treble being the most popular. Cornetts are made in two main shapes: a straight tube, and a curved tube (like a shallow S). Though cornetts were virtually extinct by 1850, they have been revived in recent years for the purpose of playing early music.

**Corranach** or **Coronach** A song of lament sung at funerals by a minstrel to his own harp accompaniment in the Scottish Highlands.

**Cotillion** A popular ball-room dance of the 19th century. It had no special music of its own, but borrowed from waltzes, mazurkas, etc.

**Cottage piano** A small upright piano, developed during the first half of the 19th century and sold very cheaply in large quantities to people with limited space in their houses.

**Countersubject → Fugue**

**Countertenor** Though this voice is sometimes confused with that of the male alto (which is usually a baritone singing *falsetto*), it is in reality a high natural voice that makes great use of the head resonances.

It was very popular up until the end of the 18th century, and has been revived again in recent years. Composers have even begun to write for it again (as Britten did in the opera *A Midsummer Night's Dream*), and, of course, it

# Counterpoint

1. Counterpoint is the art of combining two or more melodic lines. The lines must not only be interesting in themselves, as melodies, but also fit together well. A piece of music written with these considerations in mind is said to be CONTRAPUNTAL.

The difference between Harmony and Counterpoint is really a matter of approach. In writing harmony we are concerned with fitting notes together to make chords. In counterpoint we are concerned with fitting melodies together. Nevertheless, good counterpoint must always make good harmony. But good harmony need not necessarily contain evidence of good counterpoint.

For example: here is a hymn-tune. It makes good sense as harmony, but, apart from the tune, the individual lines are not very interesting.

Hymn-tune 'Hold the Fort' [P.P. Bliss]

But here is a hymn tune harmonized by J. S. Bach. Not only do the harmonies make good sense, but each line is a tune in itself. The individual parts are, in fact, 'in counterpoint' with each other:

Old German hymn-tune:'Ein feste Burg'

2. **Strict Counterpoint** is a type of contrapuntal writing that follows very strict

**Cornett** *Left to right* 17th-century tenor, alto and treble cornetts.

is now possible to perform earlier music, such as Purcell's, in the way that was intended.

**Country and Western →** page 104

**Country dance** A type of English dance that was very popular in the 17th century. When taken up in France its name was roughly translated into *Contredanse* (in Germany it became the *Kontretanz*). In these new continental versions it lost some of its rustic character and became an elegant ball-room dance. One well-known English country dance is *'Sir Roger de Coverley'*.

rules. It is particularly useful as a method of teaching students, step by step. The student is given a melodic line (referred to by the Latin name CANTUS FIRMUS, 'fixed song'), and then adds his own part, or parts, above, or below it.

Tradition lays down five steps in practising this art. They are called the FIVE SPECIES of counterpoint. The first four deal with one problem at a time, but in the fifth all four steps are combined.

The FIRST SPECIES deals with the problem of adding one note for every note in the Cantus Firmus (C.F.):

First Species

The SECOND SPECIES asks for two notes against each note of the Cantus firmus:

Second Species

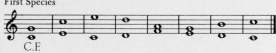

In the THIRD SPECIES, four notes are set against each note of the Cantus Firmus (or three notes against it, if it is a dotted note):

Third Species

The FOURTH SPECIES is concerned with suspensions and syncopation:

Fourth Species

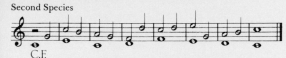

And the FIFTH SPECIES combines the other

four, in any order:

Fifth Species

3. **Invertible Counterpoint** This occurs, as its name suggests, when contrapuntal lines are written in such a way that they can be changed about – an upper part becoming a lower one, while the lower part takes its place. Here is a simple example:

Hymn-tune: 'St Gertrude'                                    [Sullivan]

If two parts can be inverted, as above, they are said to be in DOUBLE COUNTERPOINT. If there are three parts, and they can all be inverted, in any order, then we have TRIPLE COUNTERPOINT. If there are four parts, then we have QUADRUPLE COUNTERPOINT – which would allow for twenty-four possible permutations!

4. **Imitation** When one part repeats what another part has just given out, 'imitation' is said to have taken place. In the following example, the bass line imitates the first few notes of the soprano part:

From Handel's 'Messiah'

**Couperin, François** French composer, 1668–1733. He came of an illustrious family of musicians who were active in Paris over a period of two hundred years. At least seven of them occupied the important post of organist in the Church of St Gervais, as he in his turn did.

François, known as 'Couperin the Great', was much admired by King Louis XIV, both as a composer and as a virtuoso performer on the organ and harpsichord. He wrote a considerable quantity of church music, a number of trio sonatas, and a vast amount of

**François Couperin**
1668–1733

music for the harpsichord. These keyboard pieces were assembled in collections, known as *Ordres*. All the pieces have individual poetic titles – 'The Bees', 'Sister Monica', 'The Nightingale in love', 'The little Windmill', etc – and are delicately written, with delightful ornamentation. You will find one such piece, 'The Harvesters', printed in this book under the heading 'Rondo', where it is analysed in some detail.

**Couplet** Two notes of equal value slurred together (♩♩). The second note is made to sound a little shorter than its written value.

# Country and Western

The general name for white American folk music, which developed out of European (particularly British) folk music brought over by the early settlers. From these songs grew a number of new musical forms and styles, including the 'hillbilly' and 'bluegrass' music (mountain ballads), Western (cowboy) songs, religious songs associated with the many revivalist movements and rival religious sects, and work songs of all kinds. As it developed, this music was influenced by the spirituals and blues styles of black America, and later by jazz and commercial music generally. It is usually played on stringed instruments (such as

**Country music** This American group gives an outdoor performance.

guitar, banjo, fiddle, etc.), and therefore differs from jazz, which uses wind and percussion almost exclusively.

Country music flourished in America because the pioneer communities were often very isolated and had to provide their own entertainments – in the form of hoedowns, barn-raising, quilting parties, and so forth. It became more widely known after 1925, when the radio station WSU, in Nashville, Tennessee, began a weekly country music programme, *Grand Ole Opry*. By the 1960s it had become part of the commercial music scene, combining with jazz and rock styles, but never quite losing its 'folk' flavour.

The term is also found in French *Rondos* of the early 18th century where the 'episodes' that separate the returns of the main rondo tune are sometimes called 'couplets'.

**Courante** A dance of French origin, popular in the 17th and 18th centuries. Together with the Allemande, Saraband, and Gigue it became one of the standard movements in the 18th-century suite.

The courante is a quick dance in triple time beginning on a quaver up-beat. There are two types: the Italian courante, which is in a rapid triple time (3/8 or 3/4); and the French courante, which mixes 3/4 and 6/8 times and makes a feature of dotted rhythms. The word *courante* comes from *courir* (Fr.) ('to run'), and this gives an idea of the dance itself.

**Covent Garden** To British music-lovers this means only one thing: not the fruit and vegetable market (which in any case has now moved to Nine Elms in the London borough of Wandsworth), but the Royal Opera House that stands at the centre of this area of London.

The original theatre was opened in 1732 under the management of John Gay (who composed the words for *The Beggar's Opera*). It was burnt down twice, in 1808 and again in 1856, when it was rapidly rebuilt as the present theatre and opened two years later.

Though opera has been played there since it first opened, it did not become exclusively an opera house until 1846 – since which time it has staged all the greatest operas and been an important goal for all the greatest singers. The present building is exceptionally beautiful.

Henry Purcell

**Courante** This dance developed from the earlier farandole. It was popular in the court of Louis XIV and the king himself is reputed to have danced it well.

**Covent Garden** This theatre designed by J. M. Barry has had its own resident opera and ballet companies since 1946. Both have attained international standard and attract virtuoso performers from all over the world.

**Coward,** (Sir) **Noël** English composer, playwright, singer and actor, 1899–1974. His brilliant and varied career included the composition of many popular songs – some written for revues (*On with the Dance*, 1925), others as part of operettas and musicals (*Bitter-sweet*, 1929). He was self-taught as a composer and was not always sure how to write his music down, but this did not stop him being one of the most inventive and amusing song-writers of his day.

**Cowell, Henry** American composer, 1897–1965. Though largely self-taught as a composer he gave the first concert of his own music when he was 15. It included his first experiments with 'chord clusters' (*The Tides of Manaunaun*, 1912). He continued to make experiments in music throughout his life – particularly in matters of rhythm. He also explored American folksong and made use of it in his music. Some of his earlier experiments provoked audiences to near riot, but they nevertheless greatly influenced younger composers.

**Cramer, Johann Baptist** German-born composer, 1771–1858. He was a member of an important musical family that settled in London in 1772. He became famous as a pianist and wrote many 'studies' to help pass on his technique. He wrote seven piano concertos, 105 piano sonatas, and many small piano pieces, etc.

In 1842 he founded the music-publishing house of Cramer (originally Cramer, Addison and Beale), which is still in existence. The firm also made pianos.

**Creed** A creed is a statement of what one believes. There are 3 main creeds in use in the Roman Catholic Church and the Anglican Church – the APOSTLES' CREED )which was probably the earliest), the NICENE CREED (drawn up by the Council of Nicaea in the year 325), and the ATHANASIAN CREED.

The Roman Catholic Church has also another Creed – the CREED OF POPE PIUS (1564).

All these creeds are intoned (sung on one note), or else sung to some simple ancient chant, or (sometimes) sung in some elaborate setting by a composer.

**Crescendo** (It.) 'Increasing' or 'growing'. In musical use it means 'getting gradually louder'. The abbreviation *cres.* is often seen.

**Creston, Paul** American composer, b. 1906. Though he had teachers for piano and organ, he is self-taught as a composer. He has written a great deal of music of all kinds, including five symphonies and several concertos for different instruments. His musical style is fairly conservative and only mildly dissonant by 20th-century standards.

**Gordon Crosse** b.1937
His works include
*Symphonies for chamber orchestra*, *Elegy for small orchestra*, and the operas, *Purgatory* and *Grace of Todd*.

**William Crotch**
1775–1847 This engraving shows the composer, a child prodigy, at the age of three. He became Professor of Music at Oxford when he was 22 and the first principal of the Royal Academy of Music in 1822.

**Cristofori, Bartolomeo** Italian instrument maker, 1655–1731. He was a skilled harpsichord maker and was persuaded by Prince Ferdinand, the son of the Grand Duke Cosmo III, to leave his native Padua and settle in Florence. It is there that he seems to have invented the hammer mechanism that made possible the change from harpsichord to piano (1711).

**Croche** ('hook') is the French name for a quaver (*not* crotchet or quarter-note).

**Croft, William** English composer, 1678–1727. He was a chorister of the Chapel Royal under John Blow, and later became its organist, as well as organist of Westminster Abbey (1708). He wrote a number of trio sonatas and harpsichord pieces, as well as music for various theatrical performances. But it is by his church music (anthems, hymns and services) that he is mainly remembered – particularly his fine setting of the burial service.

**Crooning** A style of singing much favoured by American singers of popular music from about 1930. They sing very softly and rely on microphones to build up the tone. The word itself gives a very good idea of what the sound is like. Bing Crosby was a master of this particular art.

**Crosse, Gordon** English composer, b. 1937. He has studied with, among others, Goffredo Petrassi and has written music that reflects an interest in serialism and the methods of medieval composers. But he has also written a more tuneful, traditional kind of music for children to perform – including *Meet my Folks!* (1964) and *The Demon of Adachigahara* (1968). He has written several operas and a striking second Violin Concerto (1969).

**Cross rhythm** This occurs when, by means of syncopation and additional accents, the rhythm that you hear contradicts the basic rhythm of the beat. Sometimes even the notation is altered, so that, for example, a piano piece may suddenly have a passage in which the basic 3/4 accompaniment is 'crossed' against a tune in 2/4 (the crotchets (quarter-notes) of the 2/4 passage become, in effect, dotted crotchets). This kind of rhythmic ambiguity has become a commonplace in 20th-century music.

**Crotch, William** English composer, 1775–1847. His father, a musical carpenter, made him a small organ which he began to

105

play when he was two. When he was four he gave organ recitals in London; when he was 11 he became pupil-assistant to the organist of King's and Trinity Colleges, Cambridge, and when he was 14 he composed an oratorio (*The Captivity of Judah*) which was performed in that city. When he was 15 he became organist of Christ Church College, Oxford.

After this dazzling display of precocity, Crotch settled to a fine career as a composer, performer and teacher. He wrote anthems, piano pieces, several excellent glees, and an oratorio *Palestine* (1812) which is still sometimes played. He was also an accomplished painter in watercolours. Unlike Mozart, however, he did not live up to his early promise.

**Crush-note** or **crushed-note** An English name for the *acciaccatura*. (→ **Ornaments and grace-notes**)

**Crumhorn** A woodwind instrument with a double-reed which is enclosed inside a long wooden cap, in which there is a hole (at the top) through which the player blows. It was popular in the 16th and 17th centuries, and in recent years it has been revived by musicians who like to play their music on the authentic instruments. Crumhorns were made in all sizes: trebles, tenors, and basses – a complete 'consort', in fact.

**Crystal Palace** Built in 1851 to house the Great Exhibition. It was designed by Sir Joseph Paxton and constructed like a gigantic greenhouse, of iron girders and glass. It occupied 20 acres of Hyde Park. After the Exhibition it was taken down and re-erected at Sydenham. At the suggestion of Sir George Grove it soon became a popular place for concerts – August Manns being the most important conductor associated with it. The building was destroyed by fire in November 1936.

**Cuckoo** This is really a children's toy (→ **Toy Symphony**). It has, of course, merely the two notes of the bird after which it is named. Cuckoo clocks have such an instrument inside them, which they play to mark the hours.

**Cue** In music this is found in the individual parts which orchestral and chamber music players use. Cues are short passages of music (printed in small notes) inserted towards the end of any lengthy passage of rest-bars. They serve as warnings to the player who is about to come in, just in case he has not counted his bars of rest correctly.

**Crystal Palace** at Sydenham *c*.1855

**Crumhorn**

**Cymbals** *Right* This cartoon by Hoffnung looks at the hazards of playing a large pair of cymbals. Cymbals were important in the religious and ceremonial music of ancient times.

**Cui, César** Russian composer, 1835–1918. He was partly of French origin and trained as an army officer, eventually becoming a general. He wrote 11 operas, a number of choral works, four orchestral suites, a small quantity of chamber and piano music, and a great many songs. He was a member of the group of Russian Nationalist composers known as 'The Five', whose cause he helped in his writings as a music critic.

**Curtall** The English name for the early form of bassoon (16th to 18th centuries).

**Cymbals** These are dishes of brass with leather handles. They can be clashed together, or rattled together at their edges, or one of them can be hung up and struck with a drumstick, or have a roll played on it with two drumsticks.

Sometimes, in brass bands, one is fixed to the side of the big drum and the other held in the hand and clashed against it.

**Czárdás** This is one of the national dances of Hungary. It has two parts; a slow part, called *Lassù*, and a quick part called *Friss*. These two parts alternate.

**Czerny, Carl** Austrian piano teacher and composer, 1791–1857. He was a pupil and friend of Beethoven. He became famous as a teacher of the piano and a composer of dozens of books of studies for the instrument. At one time everyone who was learning to play the piano played Czerny studies.

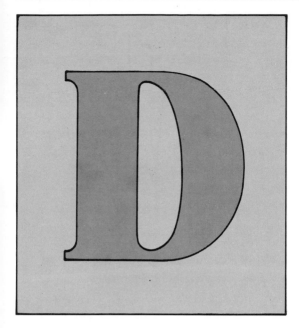

**Da capo** (It.) 'from the head'. That is to say, 'from the beginning'. A direction to a performer that a piece, or a section thereof, must be repeated. Often shortened to D.C.

This term is usually found in compositions that fall into three sections, of which the third is the same as the first – for example, the **Minuet →**. It saves having to write out, or print, the entire section again. A frequent direction is **da capo al segno**: 'from the beginning to the sign' (the sign being the symbol ⅜, which indicates where to stop). **Da capo al fine** ('from the beginning to the word fine (end)') means the same thing.

Sometimes a **Coda →** is included, which is to be played after the repetition. The direction will then be **da capo e poi la coda**: 'from the beginning and then the coda'.

**Dallapiccola, Luigi** Italian composer, 1904–75. He studied in Graz, Trieste and Florence and later came to know Alban Berg, whose music, together with that of Schoenberg and Webern, made a deep impression. His own early compositions were more or less tonal and neo-classical in style (for example, the orchestral *Partita*, 1932), but he began to move towards serialism in the *Divertimento* for soprano, flute, oboe, clarinet, viola and cello (1934). By the time he had completed what is probably his masterpiece, the opera *Il Prigioniero* (1944–48), he was using a very free version of serialism. Later works, such as the *Quaderno musicale di Annalibera* for piano (1952) are much more strictly serial.

Of all the Italian composers to use serial techniques, Dallapiccola was one of the most successful – partly because he never abandoned his natural Italian lyricism, and

**Walter Damrosch**
1862-1950

**Danse macabre** This 15th-century woodcut depicts the Dance of Death, a popular theme in medieval art and music.

partly because, as his opera shows, he had a strong sense of theatrical effect. He is one of the most interesting and important composers of his generation.

**Dal segno** (It.) 'From the sign'. This tells the performer to go back to the place where he sees the sign ⅜ and repeat the music from that point until he arrives at the word *fine* ('end'), or at a double bar with a pause sign (⌒) above it.

**Damp, to** To check the vibrations of an instrument by touching it in some way. For example, the plucked strings of a guitar or harp will continue to vibrate unless stopped. So will the skin of a kettledrum, and the plate of a cymbal.

**Dämpfer** (Ger.) Mute. **Mit Dämpfern**, 'with mutes'. **Dämpfung**, 'muting'.

These expression apply equally to (1) the muting of bowed and wind instruments (2) the use of the soft pedal of the piano. (**→ Mute**)

**Damrosch, Walter** American composer and conductor, 1862–1950. He was one of a musical family of German origin. His father, Leopold (1832–85), was a doctor who eventually became a noted violinist and conductor. His brother, Frank (1859–1937), founded what eventually became the Juilliard School of Music. He himself was much admired as a conductor, founded an opera company, and wrote several operas – including *The scarlet Letter* (1896) and *Cyrano de Bergerac* (1913). His music, not surprisingly, is rather Germanic in style and owes much to Wagner – there is nothing very 'American' about it.

**Dance →** page 108

**Danse macabre** Composers have been fascinated by the medieval idea of Death leading a dance in which every human being

# Dance

As long as there have been men on earth, it is fairly safe to assume that there has been some kind of dancing. For dancing is direct physical action, and physical action is the simplest and most forceful way for a human being to express himself.

Dancing, as such, probably came into existence when a whole group of people were caught up in some event that made them want to express themselves in the same way. For example, the excitement of a successful hunt might have led them to 'dance' their pleasure, each imitating the other until a pattern emerged out of their movements.

As soon as people begin to do things together, the satisfaction in what they are doing becomes stronger and the effect more powerful. And so dancing became an important way for a whole community to express itself. It is no surprise to find that in

**Devil Dance** This brilliantly costumed and masked dancer performs an ancient ritual in Bhutan, a small kingdom on the southern slopes of the East Himalayas.

**Cherokee Eagle Dance** This is part of a modern out-door drama which re-enacts the history of these North American Indians from the Smoky Mountains of North Carolina.

primitive societies dancing is important as an expression of general emotion (a War Dance, say), and as an expression of religion (a Rain Dance, say).

Moreover, the rhythmic patterns of such dances must have forced a pattern on the grunts and shouts that inevitably accompanied them, turning them into a kind of music. Indeed, it soon becomes hard to think of music and dancing as being separate things – so closely are they linked as activities.

It seems likely that in primitive societies, dancing was always connected in some very direct way with the daily life of the community. Only when societies became relatively civilized (free, that is, of the struggle to keep alive on a day-to-day basis) was there leisure to indulge in dancing for its own sake.

When this happened dances became tidy and more formal, fixing themselves into set patterns and losing much of their spontaneity.

In sophisticated societies, there seems always to be a tendency for dances to move away from the peasantry and pass into polite society. Even in the late 18th century it was possible for 'polite' society to take over the Austrian peasants' Ländler and turn it gradually into the ballroom waltz. Whenever this kind of thing happened, the dance gained enormously as music, but lost

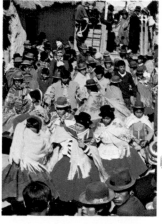

The Charleston

The Waltz

something of its vitality as dance. Nearly all formal dances began life in this way.

Dances are also important for the way they have influenced instrumental music. The 18th-century suite is a particularly striking example of this. Beginning as a collection of contrasted dances, it soon became the basis of the concerto grosso, the solo concerto, the early overture, and the symphony.

Even in the 20th century we find dances exerting a profound influence on music in general – the rhythms of jazz are one example.

In recent years there has been a strong tendency for dancing to return to a less formal way of expression – nearer, in fact, to the style of primitive tribes: a direct expression of personal feelings. Jitterbugging, jive, rock'n roll, etc., are all informal and spontaneous, and far removed from the stately patterns of ballroom dancing. Such dances are sometimes condemned as immoral, but it is worth remembering that nearly all dances, at some time or another, have run into this criticism.

Dances, like all popular forms of self-expression, tell you a great deal about the society that uses them. And so whether it be in the primitive rituals of a tribe, the stately patterns of an 18th-century minuet, the languorous swirl of the 19th-century waltz, or the jerkiness of today's popular dances you get a clear picture of the kind of life and values of the people that danced them.

**Different types of dance** The Branle, **1**. Was originally a French peasant dance but was taken up by the court in the 16th century. Tap-dancing was popularized in the 1930s and 40s through films starring Fred Astaire and Ginger Rogers, **2**. In South America dancing is used on social and ceremonial occasions, **3**. The flamenco is the best known of Spanish dances, **4**. Indian dancers make much use of body and arms, **5**. This is a Kenyan fertility dance, **6**.

must sooner or later join, and some have written music to express this. For example: Liszt: *Todtentanz*, for piano and orchestra, 1849; and Saint-Saëns: *Danse macabre*, symphonic poem, 1874. The Dance of Death can be seen vividly illustrated in a famous series of woodcuts by Holbein (1538).

**Dargomizhjsky, Alexander** Russian composer, 1813–69. Though he began to compose at 11 he became a civil servant and only took up music seriously at the age of 21. He was encouraged by Glinka, but was almost completely self-taught. He was particularly interested in the problems of setting the Russian language to music and his operas contain many important and influential experiments in recitative. His most famous works are the operas: *Rusalka* (1856) and *The stone Guest* (produced in 1872).

**Darmstadt** A city in West Germany, just south of Frankfurt. Of some small importance in the 18th century when it housed the court of the music-loving Margrave Ernst Ludwig, it is now world-famous for an annual series of musical events which take place in July. They began in 1946 and have been an important advertisement for the latest avant-garde experiments. Special courses are held for young students. Old music is not entirely neglected, but even here the emphasis is on the unusual.

**Davies,** (Sir) **Henry Walford** Welsh composer, 1869–1941. Usually called Walford Davies, he studied at the Royal College of Music and later held many important organist, academic and administrative posts. He was the Royal Air Force's first director of music (1917) and wrote their famous *March Past*. He pioneered the idea of schools' music broadcasts (1924) and began a series for adults in 1926. He was appointed Master of the King's Musick in 1934. His anthems and services are still played, but most of his music,

**Miles Davis** b. 1926. One of the most important of post-war jazz musicians. His style, as a composer and performer, is polished and sophisticated.

**Peter Maxwell Davies** b. 1934 *Below* This scene is from the composer's opera *Taverner*, first produced at the Royal Opera House, Covent Garden in 1972. Davies also wrote the libretto about the 16th-century composer, John Taverner, who was imprisoned as a Protestant heretic.

including a once famous cantata *Everyman* (1934), is now forgotten. One piece, the *Solemn Melody* (1908), is genuinely popular – at funerals.

**Davies, Peter Maxwell** English composer, b. 1934. He studied at the Royal Manchester College of Music, where he helped to form the Manchester New Music Group, for whom he wrote a number of works (*Five Pieces for Piano*, 1956). In 1957 he went to Rome to study with Petrassi. His works at this time showed the influence of serialism, total serialism, and the rhythmic experiments of Olivier Messiaen (for example, his first important orchestral work: *Prolation*, 1958). From 1959 to 1962 he was Director of Music at Cirencester Grammar School, and from 1962 to 1964 he worked in America at Princeton University. His music, in the meantime, had become much influenced by medieval methods of composition (*Alma Redemptoris Mater* 1957, *Ricercar and Doubles* 1959). On returning from America he went to live in Dorset and shortly afterwards set up an ensemble known as the Fires of London for whom he, and other composers, wrote music which often contained a strong theatrical element (*Eight Songs for a Mad King* 1969, *Miss Donnithorne's Maggott* 1974). Since 1971 he has lived on the remote island of Hoy, in the Orkneys, and his music now reflects the bleak but stirring quality of life there (*Stone Litany: Runes from a House of the Dead*, 1973; and the opera *The Martyrdom of St Magnus*, 1977). He has also written music for films by Ken Russell (*The Devils,*) and an important opera *Taverner*, produced at Covent Garden in 1972.

**D.C.** is short for **Da capo →**.

**Davis, Miles** American jazz trumpeter and composer, b. 1926. Though he began as a student at the Juilliard School of Music he soon found his way into the jazz world and in 1948 formed his own band in New York. He helped to create what is known as 'cool' jazz – something more restrained and thoughtful than the exaggerated 'bebop' style of the 1940s. His composition *Miles ahead* (1957) is an example of this fruitful crossing of jazz and 'classical' methods.

**Debussy** → page 112

**Début** This French word means 'first appearance'. For instance, when a musical performer first appears before the public that is called his or her 'début'.

# Delius

Frederick Delius, 1862–1934. He was born in Bradford, the son of a wealthy wool-merchant of German origin.

Although his father was fond of music and allowed him to study the violin, he insisted that his son joined the family business. Delius's efforts to become a wool-merchant were not very convincing, and in 1884 he persuaded his father to set him up as an orange-grower in Florida.

Once in America, however, he let the oranges look after themselves and settled down to teach himself how to compose. Fortunately he met an organist, Thomas Ward, who was able to direct his studies and he began to make progress. He began, also, to be noticed locally as a violinist and was later able to set himself up as a teacher of that instrument.

By this time he had also contrived to hand over the orange-grove to his brother Ernest. Outwitted, his father now gave in and in 1886 Delius returned to Europe ready to study composition at Leipzig.

He did not make a good student – he was too determined to go his own way. But he did meet Grieg and received considerable help and encouragement from him. He also completed his first large-scale work, the orchestral suite *Florida* (1886), and heard it played.

From 1888 to 1896 Delius lived in Paris, helped and encouraged by his uncle Theodor. Here his musical life began in earnest and works began to pour from him. He made friends with poets and painters and soon fell in love with one of them – a German girl named Jelka Rosen. They lived together and later married.

In 1897 Delius and Jelka went to live in a small village some 48 km south of Paris: Grez-sur-Loing. This was to become his home. Though he made occasional visits to England he never lived there again.

Delius's music first made its way in Germany, and to some extent in France. It was not until Sir Thomas Beecham began to champion it (1908 onwards) that it made any impression in England.

In 1924 symptoms of blindness and paralysis began to affect his health. Gradually his condition grew worse and it seemed as if he would have to stop composing. But in 1928 a young musician, Eric Fenby, offered to act as his amanuensis,

**Frederick Delius**
1862-1934

*Above* Scene from *Hassan* for which Delius wrote the incidental music. *Below* Score cover for the opera *Fennimore and Gerda*. *Right* Delius, in wheelchair, with his wife and the composer Percy Grainger.

writing down the music as Delius dictated it to him. Painfully, note by note, they managed to set down on paper a number of fine new works. In this way, Delius was able to continue composing almost until the end of his life.

The most striking thing about Delius's music is its use of harmony. Chords of the 7th, 9th, 11th etc, are used rather as Debussy uses harmony – for the sake of their 'colour' rather than in the classical sense of logical harmonic progression. It is always sumptuously orchestrated (for very large orchestras), and is filled with a kind of melancholy. It is not always to everybody's taste, however. Some people find it rather shapeless and inclined to wander. Others claim that this 'rhapsodic' style is a positive virtue. But one thing cannot be denied: it is intensely personal – once heard, never forgotten.

Among Delius's works the following are outstanding: the opera *A Village Romeo and Juliet* (1901); the choral works *Appalachia* (variations) (1902), *Sea Drift* (1903), *A Mass of Life* (1905), *Songs of Sunset* (1907), *Requiem* (1916), and *Songs of Farewell* (1932); the orchestral works *Brigg Fair* (1907), *Summer Night on the River* (1911), *On hearing the first Cuckoo in Spring* (1912), and *North Country Sketches* (1914). He also wrote several concertos, some chamber music, and a number of fine songs.

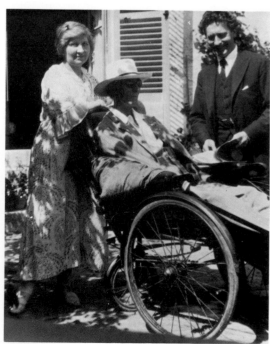

# Debussy

Claude Achille Debussy. Born near Paris in 1862 and died in Paris in 1918.

## 1. Debussy's life

Though Debussy was born at St Germain-en-Laye, he was, to all intents and purposes, a Parisian, for his parents abandoned the small china shop they ran there and returned to Paris in 1864. He seems to have received very little ordinary schooling, but when he was ten began to show a definite talent for music. A pupil of Chopin (Mme Mauté de Fleurville) helped prepare him for the entrance examination to the Paris Conservatoire, and he enrolled as a student in 1873.

He studied there for 11 years – first the piano and general theory, and then composition with Ernest Guiraud and Massenet. He seems to have been a rather impatient pupil, with strong ideas of his own about music. But he won a number of prizes, including the important Prix de Rome (1884).

Already, however, he had travelled quite widely, for in 1880 Mme Nadejda von Meck, Tchaikovsky's wealthy patron, had engaged him to go to Moscow as tutor to her children. There he met most of the leading Russian composers. He also accompanied her family on their holiday travels in France, Austria and Italy.

He spent only three of the four years his Rome Prize entitled him to in Italy, and none of the works he wrote there were much admired by his professors in Paris. Only his setting of Rossetti's 'Blessed Damozel' poem (in translation), *La Damoiselle élue* (1888), earned any kind of praise.

But by now Debussy was beginning to develop a style of his own. He began to feel that music was too enslaved to the major-minor diatonic system and that harmony could be treated in a much freer way. To his ear harmonies were 'colours' to be used almost as a painter might use them – that is to say, put together according to taste and instinct rather than according to 'rule'. He began to take an interest in oriental scales, and in scales made up of whole tones. He began, in short, to abandon what the textbooks told him were the 'correct' ways of using harmony and trusted more and more to his ear. If what he wanted to write 'sounded' right, then it must be right – even if there was no rule to explain it.

**Claude Achille Debussy** 1862–1918. Painting by Marcel Baschet, 1884.

**Pelléas et Mélisande** A scene from Debussy's opera first performed in Paris in 1902.

The first mature Debussy work to attract serious attention was the String Quartet in G minor. It was performed in 1893 and disconcerted almost everyone who heard it. But in the following year an orchestral piece, the *Prélude à l'après-midi d'un Faune*, reversed opinions. It was now clear that a new and highly original composer had come into existence.

He was still very poor, however, and depended largely on the generosity of his publisher, Georges Hartmann. Even so, he got married in 1899.

In the meantime he was at work on the opera *Pelléas et Mélisande*, over which he laboured for nine years. It was produced in 1902 and, together with the three orchestral *Nocturnes* which had been very successful in 1900, immediately placed him in the forefront of modern music generally and French music in particular.

His private life, however, was not so successful. Having fallen in love with Emma Bardac, the wife of a wealthy financier, he left his own wife (who tried to commit suicide), obtained a divorce and eventually married Mme Bardac (1905). In doing so, he not only added to his financial problems, but upset many of his friends.

From about 1908 he was in demand as a pianist and conductor and travelled to London, Vienna, Budapest, Moscow, Rome, Amsterdam and elsewhere to perform and supervise performances of his own music, which was now very highly thought of. But he was a sick man. An operation for cancer was unsuccessful. Even so, he continued to work. He died in the last year of the 1914–18 war, while German long-range guns bombarded his beloved Paris.

7ᵐᵉ Saison des Ballets Russes

## 2. His music

Many of Debussy's closest friends were painters and poets and he was much influenced by their artistic beliefs. One of the things that most interested them was the idea of 'Impressionism'. Its aim was to portray the 'impression' we receive of an object or an event, rather than the object or event itself. Thus, for example, when we look at a lake we do not see just a stretch of water of a particular shape, but a stretch of water that is also a myriad flashes of light and colour. And we see it also through a 'mood' that changes with the time of day, the weather, and even our own feelings.

Painters such as Pissarro, Monet, Degas, Renoir and Whistler all sought a way of suggesting these effects. They abandoned firm, hard outlines and concentrated instead on trying to capture the changing lights and colours they saw.

Debussy's music attempts something similar. Instead of the hard outlines of classical music (with its clear-cut tunes, carefully developed themes, balanced phrases, and harmonies that lead the ear forward in a steady procession) he used soft, delicate harmonies, chosen for their 'colour'; vague, wandering melodies that are

**L'après-midi d'un Faune** Design by Léon Bakst for the dancer Nijinsky as the Faun, 1912 in Diaghilev's ballet to Debussy's prelude.

**Debussy conducting** A contemporary sketch.

**Pelléas et Mélisande** This scene is from the 1969–70 production of the opera at Covent Garden featuring George Shirley as Pelléas and Elisabeth Söderström as Mélisande.

difficult to pin down; and, above all, a careful mixture of orchestral effects — shimmering and flashing, like the points of colour in an impressionist painting.

The result of all this was profoundly important for European music. Up to this time musicians had tended to think that music *had* to be written in the way that the great German composers had written it. Debussy proved that it was possible to think of harmony, melody and orchestration in quite a different way, and yet produce music that not only made sense but was extremely beautiful.

Though he never made much of a fuss about what he was doing, Debussy managed to change the whole face of music. He is therefore one of the most important and revolutionary artists of his time.

## 3. Summary of Debussy's main works

(a) Opera:

| | |
|---|---|
| *Pelléas et Mélisande* | 1892–1902 |

(b) Choral music includes:

| | |
|---|---|
| *L'Enfant prodigue* | 1884 |
| *La Damoiselle élue* | 1888 |

(c) Orchestral music includes:

| | |
|---|---|
| *Prélude à l'aprés-midi d'un Faune* | |
| *Nocturnes* | \|1892–94 |
|   1. Nuages | 1893–99 |
|   2. Fêtes | |
|   3. Sirènes | |
| *La Mer* | 1903–5 |
|   1. De l'Aube à midi sur la Mer | |
|   2. Jeux de Vagues | |
|   3. Dialogue du Vent et de la Mer | |
| *Images pour orchestre* | 1906–9 |
|   1. Gigues | |
|   2. Iberia | |
|   3. Rondes des Printemps | |

(d) Chamber music includes:

| | |
|---|---|
| String Quartet in G minor | 1893 |
| Sonata for cello and piano | 1915 |
| Sonata for flute, viola and harp | 1916 |
| Sonata for violin and piano | 1917 |

(e) Piano music includes:

| | |
|---|---|
| *Suite bergamasque* | 1890–1905 |
| *Estampes* | 1903 |
| *Images I* | 1905 |
| *Images II* | 1907 |
| *Children's Corner* | 1908 |
| *Twelve Préludes*, Book i | 1910 |
| *Twelve Préludes*, Book ii | 1913 |
| *Twelve Études*, Book i | 1915 |
| *Twelve Études*, Book ii | 1915 |

Debussy also wrote many fine songs.

**Deciso** (It.) With decision.

**Decrescendo** (It.) Gradually getting softer.

**Degree** By this we mean simply a step of a scale. For instance we may speak of 'the next degree' (higher or lower), meaning the note next (above or below) to the one which we are considering. Or we may speak of the 'fourth degree' of the scale, etc.

**Delibes, Léo** French composer, 1836–91. After studying at the Conservatoire he held various organist posts in Paris and later became accompanist at the Opéra (1863) and a chorus master (1865). He was very successful as a composer for the theatre, and his work includes serious opera: *Lakmé* (1883); opéra-comique: *Le Roi l'a dit* (1880); operettas, and the ballets: *Coppélia* (1870), and *Sylvia* (1876). His music is very tuneful, lively, and colourfully orchestrated.

**Delicato** (It.) Delicate. Also the superlative **delicatissimo**, 'very delicate', the adverb **delicatamente**, 'delicately', and the noun **delicatezza**, 'delicacy'.

**Delius →** page 111

**Dello Joio, Norman** American composer, b. 1913. He studied first with his father and then with Hindemith and later earned his living as an organist and choirmaster. He has also directed his own jazz band and a ballet company, appeared as a solo pianist, taught composition, and been a baseball player. His music is neo-classic in style and quite tuneful. It includes several short concertos, a number of choral works (e.g. *The Mystic Trumpeter*, 1943) and two operas: *The Trial at Rouen* (1955) and *Blood Moon* (1961).

**Denner, Johann Christoph** German instrument-maker, 1655–1707. He came of a family of musical instrument makers that settled in Nuremberg, and became famous for the quality of his flutes, and for the fact that he is said to have invented the clarinet.

**Dent, Edward J.** English musical historian, 1876–1957. He was educated at Eton and Cambridge, where he eventually became Professor of Music in 1926. He is principally known for his work on opera, including the translation of many libretti, and four important books: *Alessandro Scarlatti* (1905), *Mozart's Operas* (1913), *Foundations of English Opera* (1928), and *Feruccio Busoni* (1933). He helped to organize the International Society for Contemporary Music, and was a director of Sadler's Wells Opera House.

**Johann Christoph Denner** An 18th-century clarinet (chalumeau) by this famous flute-maker. Nuremberg, c.1700.

**Descant** This word has several meanings, according to the musical period you are dealing with. As used today it usually refers to the practice of singing a free soprano part above a hymn-tune – the tune itself being sung by the rest of the choir, or by the congregation.

Other meanings include:
an extemporized part sung by one singer against a written part sung by another singer; the art of composing or singing part-songs; the soprano part in choral music. In the 12th to 14th centuries 'descant' meant the art of writing almost any kind of polyphonic music. And a little later it came to mean the highest part in such a composition.

**Destro** and **Destra** (It.) Right. **Mano destra** means 'Right hand'.

**Détaché** (Fr.) Detached. In music for strings it implies that the playing is to be *staccato*.

**Deux** (Fr.). Two. **À deux** (literally 'at two'), as part of the title of a composition, usually means that the music is for two voices or two instruments, but sometimes the same expression is short for **deux temps** (see below).

In orchestral music *à deux* has two (opposite) meanings: (*a*) What have previously been two separate instrumental parts are now merged into one; (*b*) What has previously been one instrumental part is now divided into two.

*À deux mains* means 'for two hands', as distinct from *à quatre mains*, 'for four hands', that is, the two expressions signify 'piano solo', and 'piano duet', respectively.

**Deuxième** (Fr.). Second. So we get the expression **deuxième fois**, second time.

**Deux temps** In $\frac{2}{2}$ time. But a *Valse à Deux Temps* is (*a*) a quick one in which there are only two steps in each bar, or (*b*) one with two 'times' going on together, for instance, with a melody in $\frac{3}{2}$ time and an accompaniment in $\frac{3}{4}$ time, the accompaniment having thus two bars for every bar of the melody.

**Development → Sonata Form**

**Diatonic** and **Chromatic** By a Diatonic Scale we mean an ordinary major or minor scale, made up of tones and semitones (steps and half-steps), as distinct from the chromatic scale, which is made up entirely of semitones (half-steps).

So diatonic intervals, diatonic chords (or diatonic harmonies), and diatonic passages are such as are made of the major or minor key in use at the moment, as distinct from chromatic intervals, chromatic chords (or chromatic harmonies), chromatic passages, which have some notes not forming part of that key.

In the key of C the semitones E–F and B–C are diatonic semitones; whereas F to F♯ or B to B♭, or C to D♭, or G to F♯, and other semitones which include a note not in the key, are chromatic semitones.

**Diabelli, Anton** Austrian composer and publisher, 1781–1858. He was a friend of Haydn and Beethoven and pupil of Michael Haydn. He became a popular teacher of piano and guitar and wrote many simple pieces for the piano, as well as easy masses suitable for use in the less ambitious churches. Having thus prospered, he set up as a publisher, first in partnership (1818) and then under his own name (1824).

He is remembered today, however, as the man who wrote the waltz tune that Beethoven used for his *Diabelli Variations*. Diabelli intended a publicity gimmick – inviting various composers to write one variation each. Beethoven's set of 33 far exceeded his expectations!

**Diamond, David** American composer, b. 1915. He studied at the Eastman School of Music and later in Paris with Nadia Boulanger. His early music was neo-classic in style and somewhat influenced by Stravinsky. Later works were more romantic, but by 1958 (*Quintet for Woodwinds*) he had begun to use a 12-note technique. He has written music of all kinds, including many symphonies and concertos; and has also made something of a name as a painter.

**Dibdin, Charles** English composer and dramatist 1745–1814. Mainly self-taught, he began his London career in 1762 as a singing-actor, graduating to author-composer in 1764. He wrote the words and music of many successful short operas, including *The Padlock* (1768), *The Ephesian Matron* (1769), *The Waterman* (1774), and *The Quaker* (1775). He later toured England with his 'Table Entertainments' (one-man shows), and then wrote a book about his adventures: *The Musical Tour of Mr Dibdin* (1788).

During the Napoleonic wars he wrote a number of stirring 'sea songs' ('Tom Bowling' is still sung). These helped to recruit a good many unsuspecting sailors, and he was rewarded with a pension by a grateful government. Dibdin was at various times a

**Léo Delibes** 1836-1891 His work is noted for its grace and lightness.

**Anton Diabelli** 1781-1858 As a music publisher he was concerned with issuing the works of Schubert and Beethoven.

**Charles Dibdin** 1745-1814 A choirboy at Winchester Cathedral, and then a shop assistant, he later became an actor-singer. He wrote novels, musical textbooks and autobiographies, but his fame rests on his 600 or more songs.

publisher, a theatre manager, a theatre owner, a novelist, poet, and autobiographer. He was frequently successful, and just as frequently bankrupt.

**Diction** This term (from Latin *dictio*, 'saying') really means the words in which a thought is expressed, so that good diction and bad diction mean, respectively, clear expression and unclear expression of thought.

But singing teachers and elocution teachers have given another meaning to the term, and with them 'good diction' and 'bad diction' mean clear utterance of the words in singing or unclear utterance of them.

**Dièse** (Fr.) Sharp (♯)

**Dies Irae** ('Day of Wrath'). This is a poem by Thomas of Celano (13th century). It forms part of the Requiem Mass and many composers have set that mass to elaborate and often dramatic music (including the *Dies Irae*).

**Dilettante** A lover of music or one of the other arts who is not very serious but rather amateurish and trifling.

**Diminished intervals** → **Intervals**

**Diminished seventh** As an interval the diminished seventh is a semitone less than the minor seventh. We meet it most frequently in a certain chord which is, therefore, called the *chord of the diminished seventh*. This chord has the leading note as its bottom note: for instance in key C it consists of the notes B–D–F–A♭.

It is a chord which is very useful for modulating, because by just changing its notation we are taken into another key. For instance:

Remaining in Key C — Modulating to A minor — Modulating to A major

All this cannot be gone into fully here but readers who are taking lessons in harmony will find an explanation of the chord and its uses in their textbooks.

**Diminished triad** → **Harmony**

**Diminuendo** (It.) Diminishing, in the sense of getting gradually softer. Can be abbreviated to **dim.**, or **dimin**.

**Diminution** This means changing a passage into shorter notes (perhaps half the time-value of what they were before). The corresponding term for the reverse treatment is **Augmentation** →

## d'Indy → Indy

**Direct** This is a sign sometimes used in old music at the end of a page to show what the next note or notes will be when we turn over. Sometimes it is even used at the end of a line.

From a Fugue by Dr. Chas. Burney (1751)

End of line 3    Beginning of line 4

## Div. → Divisé

**Divertimento** This usually describes a light-hearted suite of contrasted movements, meant, as the term implies, to be easy to listen to – a 'diversion', in fact.

The word can also be used for a collection of favourite airs from an opera, or some other extended work. Nowadays we should probably use the word 'medley' or 'selection'.

**Divertissement** In music this can describe (1) a short work in popular style made up from tunes taken from another source (i.e. an opera), (2) an *Entr'acte* in a French opera.

It can also be used to describe a short, cheerful ballet, a series of songs and dances inserted (as a 'diversion') in French opera of the 18th century, or an episode in a ballet which has nothing much to do with the main plot.

**Divisé** (Fr.) and **Divisi** (It.). Divided. These terms are used where (for instance) the first violin in an orchestral composition shows double notes and the players, if not warned, might think they were intended to play them in double-stopping, instead of which they are to divide into two groups, one playing the upper notes and the other the lower.

A frequent abbreviation is *Div.*

**Divisions** The long runs in many of the vocal solos of Bach, Handel, and other composers of the 18th century are called by this name.

The name was also given in the 17th century to a type of variation in which the notes of the original tune were split up into groups of shorter notes.

## Do and Doh → Sol-fa

**Dixieland** An early jazz style, established in New Orleans at the beginning of the 20th century. It was named after a group called the 'Original Dixieland Jazz Band' – Dixieland (or Dixie) being the popular name

**Original Dixieland Band** This was the first group to make jazz recordings, first with Victor in 1917 and later with Columbia.

for the southern states of America (probably named after Mason and Dixon's boundary line, which separated the free state of Pennsylvania from the slave-owning states of Virginia and Maryland).

**Dodecaphonic** A word artificially derived from ancient Greek. It is simply an impressive way of describing 12-note music.

**Dohnányi, Ernö** Hungarian composer, 1877–1960. He made a name as a composer, concert-pianist, conductor and teacher, but had the misfortune to be known to most music-lovers by a single work: the *Variations on a Nursery Song*, for piano and orchestra (1916). He settled in America in 1947.

**Dolce** (It.) Sometimes shortened to **dol**. sweet (implying also 'soft'). The superlative is **dolcissimo**, very sweet. There are also an adverb **dolcemente**, sweetly and a noun **dolcezza**, sweetness.

**Dolente** (It.) Sorrowful. Also **dolentissimo**, very sorrowful and **dolentemente**, sorrowfully.

**Dolmetsch, Arnold** French-born musician, naturalized British, 1858–1940. He came from a long line of musicians and learned piano-making from his father and organ-building from his grandfather. After studying in Brussels and at the Royal College

**Dolmetsch workshops** These skilled craftsmen are at work in the harpsichord section. The carefully designed, hand-made instruments are exported in large numbers to all parts of the world.

of Music, London, he became violin master at Dulwich College (1885). His interest in old music led to a determination to revive the kind of instruments and methods of performance necessary for its proper appreciation. He made his first clavichord in 1894, and his first harpsichord a year later.

After working in America (1905–9) and Paris (1911–14), where he learned more about instrument-making, he returned to England and settled in Haslemere (Surrey). There he set up workshops, particularly for the construction of recorders and viols, and in 1925 established the first of his annual Festivals of early music.

A Dolmetsch Foundation was set up in 1928 to further his work, which by now had attracted widespread attention and admiration. His work has been successfully continued by his third wife, Mabel (1874–1963); his sons, Rudolph (1906–42), and Carl (b. 1911); his daughters, Cécile (b. 1904), and Nathalie (b. 1905); and various grandchildren, the sons and daughters of Carl Dolmetsch.

**Doloroso** (It.) Sorrowfully.

**Dominant** The fifth degree of the major or minor scale. It is the most important degree of the scale, next to the tonic.

**Dominant discords** These are chords of the seventh, ninth, eleventh, and thirteenth, built up from the dominant of the scale. The most important is the DOMINANT SEVENTH. Like all discords, it must be resolved: the third of the chord rises one degree, and the

Gaetano Donizetti 1797–1848 A self-caricature of 1821.

seventh falls one degree on to the appropriate notes in the next chord:

In C major    In C minor    In C major    In C minor

Dominant Ninths, Elevenths, and Thirteenths are created by piling up thirds on top of the Dominant Seventh. In four-part harmony they have to be used in an incomplete form, with certain notes left out. For example, the Dominant Ninth often appears without its root.

**Donizetti, Gaetano** Italian composer, 1797–1848. With Bellini he represents a type of Italian opera that employed romantic stories, set to music of great melodic beauty. The main emphasis is on the human voice, the orchestra acting mainly as a discreet accompaniment.

His first opera appeared in 1818 and was followed by a string of 70 or more, most of which enjoyed considerable success. His masterpieces include two romantic tragedies: *Lucrezia Borgia* (1833), and *Lucia di Lammermoor* (1835); and two sparkling comedies: *The Daughter of the Regiment* (*La Fille du Régiment*) (1840), and *Don Pasquale* (1843).

Donizetti's last years were clouded by mental illness. His operas were enormously popular in the 19th century, and now, after a brief lapse from favour, are once more being successfully revived by singers with the vocal technique to do them justice.

# Double bass

The largest member of the string family. It was developed in the 16th century from the largest member of the viol family – the VIOLONE, or double bass viol. The modern double bass is just over two metres high. Most orchestral players sit on a high stool to play it, but players in dance and jazz bands often stand (probably because they are mostly required to play *pizzicato*). It has four strings, tuned in fourths to $E_1$, $A_1$, D, and G. Some instruments have a 'C-string attachment', which is a device that allows the E-string to be lengthened mechanically. Because of the depth of the notes, double-bass music is written an octave higher than it sounds.

The practical playing range of the double bass is shown above.

sounding an octave lower

Orchestral double bass player (*right*), who is usually seated on a high stool.

Jazz musician Charles Mingus (*left*) stands to play *pizzicato* i.e. pluck the strings.

**Doppio** (It.) Double. *Il doppio movimento* means 'double speed' (that is, twice as fast).

**Dorian mode** → **Modes**

**Dot, Dotted note** A dot placed after a note makes it half as long again (→ **Notes and notation**).

But in some of the older music, such as that of Bach and Handel, the addition to the note was not necessarily exactly half, and the performer was allowed to exercise, to some extent, his personal taste and common sense. Thus if the right hand had ♩♪ and the left hand a triplet ♪♪♪ the right-hand part would be made to fit the left-hand part ♩♪

We now use not only single dots but double dots, the second dot being half the value of the first one. Thus ♩.. means the same as ♩ ♪♪

Mozart was the first great composer to use the double dot and it was his father (himself a fine musician) who invented it. The reason he did so was that in slow movements when ♩. ♪ was used it was generally intended that the first note should be longer than is shown and the second note shorter. To notate this correctly he suggested ♩.. ♪ , and this practice was gradually taken up, though Beethoven, Schubert and Weber still often used the old method. It was not until the early Romantic composers Mendelssohn, Schumann and Chopin that 'accurate' notation as we know today was firmly established.

When in a Bach or Handel slow movement we see ♩. ♪ we should generally imagine it written as Mozart would have written it, ♩.. ♪ , and play accordingly.

**Double** A word that has a variety of meanings in music. Here are some of them:
1. In French keyboard music of the 17th and 18th centuries it indicates a particular type of variation, in which the harmony remains unchanged but the melody is embellished with ornamentation (notes often being 'doubled' by halving their value). The term is found in the music of other countries (for example in Bach's 'English' Suites), and in England, where the normal term would have been 'Divisions'.
2. Bass instruments that play an octave lower than the ordinary bass of their class are often called 'double'. For example, the DOUBLE BASS is the larger version of the cello, and the DOUBLE BASSOON, a larger bassoon.
3. In stringed instruments the term DOUBLE

STOPPING means playing on two adjacent strings at the same time.
4. DOUBLE COUNTERPOINT is invertible counterpoint – two lines of music that will sound well whichever is above or below the other.
5. A DOUBLE CONCERTO has two solo instruments instead of the usual one, for example: Brahms's Double Concerto for violin, cello and orchestra (1887); or else may be for two orchestras, for example: Tippett's Concerto for Double String Orchestra (1938–9). Triple Concertos, such as Beethoven's for violin, cello and piano, are also possible, but somewhat rarer.
6. A DOUBLE FUGUE is one with two 'subjects', the second of which may have its own exposition (→ **Fugue**) or may simply be introduced during the working out of the principal subject.

Most other usages of the word (Double Reed, Double Flat, etc.) explain themselves.

**Double bass** → page 117

**John Dowland** 1563-1626 This page is from the composer's *First Booke of Songs or Ayres*.

**Dowland, John** English composer and lutenist, c. 1563–1626. Little is known of his early years and education, and he may have been of Irish origin. It is clear, however, that he soon became an accomplished performer on the lute, eventually becoming famous throughout Europe.

Dowland spent much of his time abroad, probably because he was a Catholic at a time when that religion was frowned upon in England. He worked in the courts of Brunswick, and Denmark (1598–1606), and travelled in Italy. Though somewhat neglected by his fellow-countrymen, he was at last given a court appointment in 1612, as one of the King's Musicians for the Lutes.

He published three books of 'Songs or Aires' (1597, 1600, and 1603), an instrumental work, *Lacrymae, or Seven Teares, Figured in seven Passionate Pavans* (1604), and a final volume for lute and viols called *A Pilgrimes Solace* (1612). His songs show a marvellous sensitivity to the English language, and are remarkable for the flexibility of the lute accompaniment. Such was his fame during his lifetime that his music was published not only in London, but also in Paris, Antwerp, Cologne, Nuremberg, Frankfurt, Leipzig, Hamburg, and Amsterdam. He is rightly considered one of the greatest song composers of all time.

**Doxology** The Greek *doxa* means 'glory' and *logos* means 'discourse'. So a doxology is a discourse that gives Glory to God.

The most common doxologies are *Gloria*

*Patri* ('Glory be to the Father', etc.) or the *Gloria in excelsis* ('Glory to God in the Highest').

The *Gloria Patri* has an English version, as a metrical verse 'Praise God, from whom all blessings flow', etc.), and this is often what is meant by the Doxology.

**D'Oyly Carte Opera Company** Founded in 1876 by the theatre-impresario Richard D'Oyly Carte (1844–1901) for the purpose of performing and managing the operettas of Gilbert and Sullivan. At that date, however, the company was called the Comedy Opera Company and Gilbert and Sullivan had only collaborated on *Thespis* and *Trial by Jury*. They did not become directors of the company until 1878, whereupon the name was changed. The D'Oyly Carte company mounted all the original G and S productions, toured them widely at the time, and has continued to tour them ever since, not only in Great Britain, but throughout the world.

**Dragonetti, Domenico** Italian double-bass player, 1763–1846. He was renowned as a virtuoso performer and wrote a number of interesting solos for the double bass. He spent most of his life in London, playing at the opera houses and in various orchestras, but his fame was international.

**Drone pipe → Bagpipe**

**Drum → page 120**

**Due corde** (It.) Two strings.

(1) When used in piano music the term has the meaning explained under **corda**.

(2) When used in the music of bowed instruments it means that the notes of the passage to which it is attached are to be played alternately on one string and on the next one, instead of their being played all on the one string. For instance the violin passage below can be played all on the A string and this will give the effect of uniformity of tone. But if uniformity of tone is to be avoided it will be marked **a due corde** and will then be played as if it had been fingered as follows:

**Duet** A duet is a piece for two performers, with or without accompaniment.

**Dufay, Guillaume** Netherlands composer, c. 1400–74. He is first heard of as a chorister at the cathedral of Cambrai, and then

**Domenico Dragonetti**
**1763–1846**

**Guillaume Dufay**
*c*.1400–1474 As a canon of the Church he travelled widely and held posts with the Papal Chapel in Rome and the Court of Burgundy. He was respected throughout Europe and Piero and Lorenzo de' Medici were amongst his admirers.

**Dulcimer**, a Rumanian example. Its most highly developed form appears in Hungary.

appears to have travelled and studied in Italy, entering the papal choir in Rome in 1428. Here his double career as priest and musician (a very usual combination in those days) advanced rapidly and he was granted several well-paid livings in France. He spent the last 30 years of his life in Cambrai.

Dufay commanded the respect of all the musicians of his time, and together with Dunstable must be regarded as one of the greatest musicians of the period. Among the works that have come down to us there are a handful of complete masses, fragments from a great many more, two settings of the Magnificat, nearly 100 motets, and a considerable number of French and Italian *chansons*.

**Dukas, Paul** French composer, 1865–1935. After studying at the Paris Conservatoire he became known as a composer by a series of works, of which the popular orchestral 'scherzo' *L'Apprenti Sorcier* (The Sorcerer's Apprentice) (1897) is best known. From 1910 he worked at the Conservatoire, first as Professor of Orchestration, and then as Professor of Composition.

**Dulcimer** An instrument which belongs mainly to Hungary, Rumania and Czechoslovakia. It consists of a shallow closed box over which wires are strung. These are struck with small wooden hammers, with heads that are clad on either side with hard and soft leather (thus producing loud and soft sounds). There is no arrangement for damping the strings, so the sound is always confused.

The dulcimer probably came to Europe from the near East. It exists, largely as a folk instrument, under several names: CIMBALOM (Hungary and Rumania), SANTOURI (Greece), CIMBAL (Czechoslovakia). In the Appalachian highlands of America it is known as the APPALACHIAN DULCIMER, or MOUNTAIN ZITHER, and here it usually has three strings, one for playing the melody, and the other two for playing a supporting drone.

**Dulcitone** A set of tuning forks of different sizes, arranged inside a miniature piano and struck with hammers worked by a keyboard.

**Dumka** A type of Slavonic folk ballad, basically melancholy, but alternating with passages that are wild and cheerful. There is often a major-minor alternation in the music, also. The term was introduced into concert music by Dvořák, whose *Dumky Trio* for piano, violin and cello (1891) follows this pattern.

# Drums and the Drum family

Drums have been known all over the world for many thousands of years. References to them go back almost to the beginning of recorded history. Primitive peoples considered them to have magical properties. They used them in religious ceremonies to ward off evil spirits and encourage good ones. But they also used them for practical and pleasure purposes.

Drums come in all shapes and sizes (→ **Membranophones**), but they all have one thing in common: a skin or membrane that is stretched tightly over some kind of hollow vessel. This is beaten with a stick, or with the hands. The skin vibrates, and its vibrations are amplified by the hollow vessel beneath.

There is, however, one kind of drum whose sound is made differently. This is the FRICTION DRUM. It too has a skin, but this is pierced by a stick or a string. When the stick is rubbed or pulled, the vibrations communicate with the skin and are in turn amplified by the vessel over which it is stretched.

The drums we use in the orchestra belong to the main category. The following drums are found in the modern orchestra:

1. **The kettledrum** This consists of a metal bowl with a parchment (or nowadays a plastic skin) stretched over the top. This skin can be made tighter (for higher notes) or looser (for lower notes) and thus can be tuned to any note the composer requires. Sometimes this is done by turning handles set round the head of the drum, but in modern drums it is done automatically by pedals operated by the player's foot.

There are always two kettledrums in the orchestra, and more often than not, three. They are tuned to different notes (which can be changed during the course of the performance), and are played by one person. He uses two drum sticks with padded ends.

In orchestral music kettledrums are usually referred to by their Italian name TIMPANI. (→ **Percussion**)

2. **The side drum** Often called the SNARE DRUM. This consists of a wooden or metal cylinder, with a skin stretched over each end. The lower end (opposite to the end the player beats with his wooden sticks) has a series of strings (gut, wire, or nylon) stretched over it. These are called SNARES.

*Right* **Marching drums**
These are specially designed to be relatively lightweight for the marcher. The two largest drums are bass drums, the two smallest ones are side drums, the remaining three, tenor drums.

*Below* **Kenyan drummer**
This cylindrical drum, the body of which has painted patterns, is used in one of the Chaka tribe's traditional ceremonies.

**Drummer from Kerala, south India** *Above*
Different tone qualities are achieved by striking the drum with the whole hand or with several fingers in different places.

*Left* **Korean changgo** This waisted drum has a lacquered wooden body and two laced heads. Drums of this type are found in most of the Far Eastern countries.

**Pop group drummer**
*Left* The late Keith Moon (died in 1978) performs with the celebrated pop group The Who.

**Nigerian 'talking' drum**
*Below* This drummer from the Yoruba tribe plays with a crooked beater. The drum's pitch is varied by adjusting, with the hand, the tension of the drum's densely packed lacing.

**Cylindrical drum** This drummer from the Bastar district of central India wears a bison horn as part of a ceremonial ritual. This type of elementary drum is found in many primitive societies and dates back to Neolithic times.

**Slit drums** These drums from the New Hebrides, Melanesia are made by hollowing out a tree trunk through a narrow slit. They are often used as 'talking' drums to send messages.

**Frame drums** These drums of ancient origin played by Moroccan musicians. The tambourine is a kind of frame drum with jingles.

**Friction drum** This detail from Franz Hals' *The Man with the Rommelpot* shows a 17th-century friction drum. The upright stick through the drum skin is rubbed to produce sound.

They rattle when the drum is beaten and add brilliance to the sound. They can, however, be loosened so that they remain silent. Besides the ordinary wooden drum sticks, there are also wire brushes which can be used for special effects.

The side drum cannot be tuned.

3. **The tenor drum** This is really a larger version of the side drum. Its note is therefore somewhat deeper, but like the side drum it cannot be tuned. It differs from the side drum in that it has no snares.

4. **The bass drum** A very large double-headed drum. The sizes varies from about 61 cm to 102 cm in diameter. The 'shell' of the drum is about 40cm wide. There are no snares, and the two parchment heads are 'tuned' by screw handles set around the rim of the drum. These do not change the note as such, but make certain that the two skins are in resonance with each other. The bass drumstick has a wooden handle and a large felt knob.

5. **The gong drum** Similar in size to the bass drum. It has only one head.

6. **Drums for special effects** Including the TAMBOURINE: which has a single head, stretched over a thin wooden hoop with small metal jingles set in the sides. The TABOR or *Tambourin de Provence*, which is a version of a medieval instrument. It has two heads, the upper one being fitted with a snare, and is beaten with a wooden stick. The BONGO DRUMS: borrowed from Latin-American music, and consisting of two small drums set side by side and tuned to different notes. They are patted with the hands. INDIAN AND CHINESE TOM-TOMS: small drums with pigskin heads over a bowl-shaped shell.

7. **Drums for special occasions** Dance bands and jazz bands all make use of a basic set of drums, played by one performer. It includes: a side drum, a tenor drum, three suspended cymbals, and two hi-hat cymbals (→ **Cymbals**). There is also a bass drum that is beaten by a padded stick operated by the player's foot.

Military bands have their own types of drum (→ **Military band**). Some are carried by the bandsman, slung on his body – either to one side (the side drums and the tenor drum), or directly in front of him (the bass drum). Others (the large kettledrums) are carried on either side of a horse, with the drummer mounted behind.

# Dvořák

Antonin Dvořák. Born near Prague in 1841; died in that city in 1904, aged 62. He was born in the small village of Nelahozeves, the eldest child of a poor innkeeper and pork-butcher who, like most Czech peasants, was also a keen amateur musician. He showed musical talent at an early age and was soon taking part in all the musical activities of the village. Thus, from the very beginning, he absorbed the folk music of his native land.

When he was 12 he was sent to the nearby town of Zlonice to learn German (the official language at this time, as Czechoslovakia was part of the Austrian Empire), and here he received his first important music lessons. Eventually his family found enough money to send him to the famous Organ School in Prague (1857), from which he emerged two years later 'admirably fitted to fulfil the duties of organist and choirmaster'.

His first employment, however, was as an orchestral viola player. In 1862, when his country was granted a measure of independence, he joined the orchestra of the new National Theatre. He also began to compose seriously: first, chamber music and songs, then orchestral music (including two symphonies), and finally an opera (1870).

He was 32 before he achieved real success. This was with a patriotic choral work: *The Heirs of the White Mountain* (1873). He now gave up his orchestral post, married and settled to a life of full-time composition. From now on he developed rapidly. Brahms recommended him to his own publishers, Simrock, and the way was open for him to make a reputation in Germany.

By 1880 he was not only established as a mature composer, but also appreciated as an important one throughout Europe. He made the first of his eight visits to England in 1884. Here his choral music became particularly popular: with the result that he wrote a cantata, *The Spectre's Bride* (1885), and a *Requiem Mass* (1890) for the Birmingham Festival, and an oratorio, *St Ludmilla* (1889) for Leeds.

Honours now began to pour on him. In 1892 he was invited to America to become Head of the National Conservatoire in New York. He remained for only three years, but out of the visit came the 'New World' Symphony, several important chamber works and the Cello Concerto.

The rest of his life was spent in Prague

**Antonin Dvořák** 1841-1904

where, in 1900, he was made Director of the Conservatory and created a member of the Austrian 'House of Lords'.

Dvořák wrote music of all kinds. His ten operas are not often performed outside his own country, but they include masterpieces such as *The Devil and Kate* (1899), and *Rusalka* (1901). He wrote, as we have seen, many fine choral works, including a *Stabat Mater* (1875), a *Mass in D* (1887), and a *Te Deum* (1892). He also wrote a great deal of

*Above* **Dvořák in America** This steamship, the Saale, took the Dvořák family to America in 1892. They were accompanied by a pupil of Dvořák's, J. J. Kovarik, and stayed in the United States for three years.

**Dvořák's operas** *Selma Sedlák* (*The Cunning Peasant*) (*above*), first performed in 1878, was popular on both the Czech and German stage. This scene is from a 1949 production in Prague.

*Čert a Káča* (*The Devil and Kate*) and *Rusalka* (*The Water Nymph*) These posters are for perhaps the most popular of Dvořák's nine operas. *The Devil and Kate* was first performed in Prague in 1899, *Rusalka* in 1904.

chamber music, music for the piano, and many songs. His orchestral music includes a number of symphonic poems based on Czech legends, and, most important of all, nine symphonies.

Though strongly influenced by Czech folk song, Dvořák's music belongs firmly to the German romantic tradition. In style it falls somewhere between that of Brahms and Tchaikovsky. It is as tuneful and colourful as Tchaikovsky's, but not so emotional. It is as well-constructed as Brahms's, but more light-hearted. Indeed, it is this very sense of cheerfulness and spontaneity that sometimes tempts people into taking his genius for granted. Like Haydn (also of peasant origins) Dvořák had a natural sweetness of character and this shows in his music. But he was also a man of considerable intellect, and his music, enlivened by an unfailing flow of melody and a fine sense of orchestral colour, is among the most deeply satisfying of all 19th-century composers.

**Dvořák's symphonies** After Dvořák's death it was discovered he had written four symphonies in addition to the five that had been published. They were early works, but it meant that symphonies 1 to 5 should really be numbered 5 to 9.

Now that all the symphonies have been published and can be performed, it has been thought proper to correct this mistake. Unfortunately the old numbering is still sometimes used. It is therefore very necessary to be absolutely sure which Dvořák symphony you are referring to. The following table gives them first in their chronological order with their 'correct' numbers, their dates, their keys, and then their 'old' numbers.

| No. | Date | Key | Opus number | Old number |
|-----|------|-----|-------------|------------|
| 1. | 1865 | C minor | None | |
| 2. | 1865 | B flat | None | |
| 3. | 1873 | E flat | 10 | |
| 4. | 1874 | D minor | 13 | |
| 5. | 1875 | F | 24, revised as Op 76 | 3 |
| 6. | 1880 | D | 60 | 1 |
| 7. | 1885 | D minor | 70 | 2 |
| 8. | 1889 | G | 88 | 4 |
| 9. | 1893 | E minor | 95 | 5* |

\* This is the 'New World' Symphony.

**Jan Dussek** 1760–1812 a pupil of C.P.E. Bach and a friend of Haydn, Dussek was famous in his own time as a pianist and composer. His music is now used mainly for teaching.

**Dunstable, John** English composer, d. 1453. Though we know little about Dunstable's early life, not even when he was born or where, it is certain that he was regarded throughout Europe as one of the greatest musicians of his time. We know also, from his epitaph, that he was 'an astrologian, a mathematician, a musitian, and what not'. This combination of music and science was not, in those days, unusual; for philosophers believed that music mirrored the ordered system that kept the Universe in motion and that both were governed by mathematical principles.

His contemporaries were impressed by the beauty of his melodic lines and the smooth flow of his harmonies. This quality of sweetness and grace will certainly strike the present-day listener. Most of his existing music consists of motets and settings of the Mass.

**Duplet** This is the reverse of Triplet. A triplet is a group of three notes (or the equal of this in notes and rests) to be performed in the time of two and the *duplet* is a group of two to be performed in the time of three. (→ **Notes and notation**)

Just as the triplet is indicated by the figure 3 placed over three notes so the duplet is indicated by the figure 2 placed over the two notes.

**Duple time → Notes and notation**

**Dur** (Ger.) Major, in the sense of 'major key'. So a Sonata in *A dur* is one in A major.

(The corresponding word for 'minor' is *moll*.)

**Dussek, Jan** Czech composer, 1760–1812. He was celebrated as a pianist and wrote many sonatas, concertos, and individual piano pieces that helped to create a distinctive style for the instrument at a time when it was just coming into its own.

**Dvořák → page 122**

**Dynamic accents** Those which go with the regular rhythm indicated by the time-signature of a piece. (Other accents are **Agogic →**.)

**Dyson,** (Sir) **George** English composer, 1883–1964. Though most of his career was spent in teaching, and then as Director of the Royal College of Music (1937–53), he wrote a number of works that are still popular among amateur choirs – for example, *In Honour of the City* (1928), and *The Canterbury Pilgrims* (1931). His music is an effective mixture of Elgar and Vaughan Williams.

Gottfried von Einem
b. 1918

**Eccles, John** English composer, 1668–1735. He came of a very musical family, but his father, Solomon Eccles (1618–83), eventually became a Quaker and forswore all music. He wrote music for the theatre (which would certainly have annoyed his father!) and was appointed Master of the King's Band of Music in 1700. His setting of Congreve's masque *The Judgment of Paris* (1700) is typical of his tuneful, lively style.

**Écossaise** A type of contredanse (→ **Country dance**) popular in the late 18th century and early 19th. It has nothing to do with Scotland – it is simply the French idea of what a Scottish dance might be like. It is in a quick 2/4 time and often begins with an upbeat. Beethoven, Schubert, and Chopin all wrote piano pieces in this style which they called Écossaises. The German *Schottisch* is a different dance altogether and belongs to the 19th century.

**Effects** Any kind of 'instrument' that imitates a non-musical sound – such as sleigh bells, the sound of horses' hooves, bird whistles, wind-machines, etc. These are usually played by members of the percussion section. (→ **Special effects**)

**Egk, Werner** German composer, b. 1901. He received some training at Augsburg and Munich, but is largely self-taught. He has written several ballets and operas, and a number of very successful radio operas, including *Columbus* (1933). His most successful stage opera is *Die Zaubergeige* (*The Magic Fiddle*) (1935). His music is tuneful, often rather folksong-like, and colourfully orchestrated.

**Einem, Gottfried von** Austrian composer, b. 1918. He studied with Boris Blacher in Berlin, where he was also assistant conductor at the State Opera. He is best known for his opera *Dantons Tod* (Danton's Death) (1947) but he has also written orchestral and chamber music.

**Ein' feste Burg** → **Hymns and hymntunes**

**Electric instruments** → page 126

**Electronic instruments** → page 127

**Elgar** → page 128

**Ellington, Edward Kennedy ('Duke')** American jazz pianist and composer, 1899–1975. He directed bands of his own from about 1918 onwards and, in addition to writing many very popular individual numbers, such as *Mood Indigo* and *Solitude*, experimented with rather longer pieces, such as the *Creole Rhapsody* (1931) and *Green Apple* (1965). Though his music was always personal and distinctive, his way of writing allowed the individual qualities of his players to stand out. Thus, even his scores for 'big band' still retain the intimate quality of true jazz.

**Embouchure** Although in the original French the word is used to describe the actual mouthpiece of a wind or brass instrument, we use it more generally to describe the way in which a performer adapts his lips and mouth in the performance of these instruments. The lips themselves, the facial muscles, and even the teeth play an important part in forming the player's

# Ears and hearing

The human ear has three main working sections:
1. The Outer Ear – which collects vibrations.
2. The Middle Ear – which passes them on to . . .
3. The Inner Ear – which sorts them out and conveys them to the brain.

The Outer Ear consists of the fleshy cup we normally call 'the ear', and a short tube covered at the far end by a membrane known as the EAR-DRUM. The outer cup is ideally shaped to 'collect' vibrations – it acts like a funnel, and is to some extent directional.

The Middle Ear contains a chain of three small bones: the HAMMER, the ANVIL, and the STIRRUP. These act as flexible links which convey the vibrations from the ear-drum, across a gap to the Inner Ear. The Middle Ear also has an important safety-valve known as the EUSTACHIAN TUBE. This emerges in the upper part of the throat and balances the pressure of air on both sides of the ear-drum, so that vibration can take place.

The Inner Ear is an exceedingly complex structure. It contains, among other things, a cavity (called a COCHLEA), spiral in shape like a snail's shell and filled with liquid. Inside this is the BASILAR MEMBRANE. It is attached to the nerve ends that belong to a bundle of fibres that make up the auditory nerve. There are some 24,000 fibres and each responds to a different vibration. The vibrations that pass through the little bones in the Middle Ear activate the liquid in the canal, which in turn stimulates the appropriate fibres. Those that respond pass their message to the brain, which translates them into 'sound'.

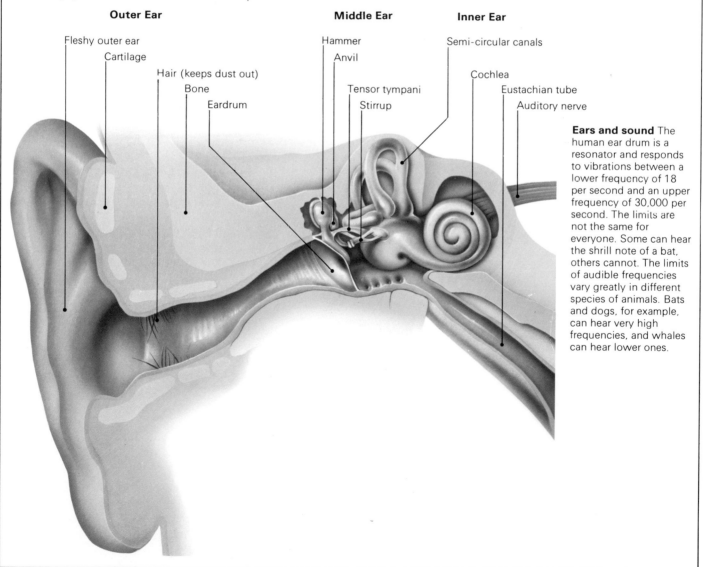

**Outer Ear**

Fleshy outer ear
Cartilage
Hair (keeps dust out)
Bone
Eardrum

**Middle Ear**

Hammer
Anvil
Tensor tympani
Stirrup

**Inner Ear**

Semi-circular canals
Cochlea
Eustachian tube
Auditory nerve

**Ears and sound** The human ear drum is a resonator and responds to vibrations between a lower frequency of 18 per second and an upper frequency of 30,000 per second. The limits are not the same for everyone. Some can hear the shrill note of a bat, others cannot. The limits of audible frequencies vary greatly in different species of animals. Bats and dogs, for example, can hear very high frequencies, and whales can hear lower ones.

# Electric instruments

These may be divided into two groups:
1. Those whose sound is produced by ordinary means, and then modified or amplified by electricity.
2. Those whose vibrations are converted electronically into sound.

In the first category the most important instruments in general use are:

**The vibraphone** which looks like a xylophone, but has a series of resonator tubes beneath its keyboard. These have a small blade at the top. When the note is struck, an electric motor makes the blade revolve. This gives the note a pronounced vibrato.

**The semi-acoustic guitar** which looks like an ordinary guitar, but is connected to an amplification system. It is played in the normal way, but its sounds are amplified electronically. It can, if necessary, be played as a normal acoustic guitar.

In the second category we find:

**The electric guitar** In this instrument vibrations from the strings are converted directly into electrical impulses. These pass through a preamplifier, which has tone and volume controls which can be adjusted to vary the quality of the sound, and then through an amplifier and out through a loudspeaker.

*Top* **Semi-acoustic guitar** which can be played with an amplifier or alone. *Right* Peter Townshend of *The Who* with an electric guitar (*Above*) which has a solid body, i.e. no sound box.

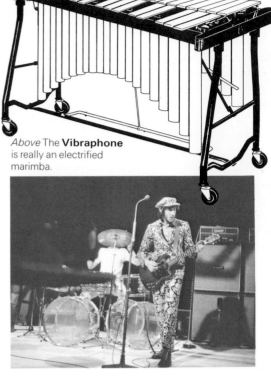

*Above* The **Vibraphone** is really an electrified marimba.

The second category includes:

**The electric organ** This looks like a normal organ, except that it has no pipes. When the keys on the manual(s) are pressed they activate a series of oscillators which produce an electric signal. This passes through a preamplifier, where it is boosted, and then on through an amplifier to the loudspeakers, where it emerges as sound. Organs come in all shapes and sizes, suitable for small rooms, large halls, churches, and so on. They can be built to imitate the sound of any ordinary kind of organ, and some incorporate several types of organ sound in the one instrument. One interesting portable electric organ is the TUBON. It can be carried, slung round the neck, by the performer.

**The electric piano** This works on the same principle as the electric organ, but imitates the sound of the piano (harpsichord imitations are also available). They are very popular with rock bands. The keyboard is so arranged that when the keys are touched gently the sound is soft, but when pressed firmly it becomes loud. The electric piano is much smaller and less weighty than the normal piano and is therefore a very convenient instrument in certain circumstances.

**Electric organs** *Right* This Hammond organ which was invented in the U.S. in 1934, has swell and great manuals, a pedal keyboard and a large number of stops. *Below* Small two-manual electric organs like this are popular with rock musicians because of their versatility and portability. Sun Ra plays the instrument in this example.

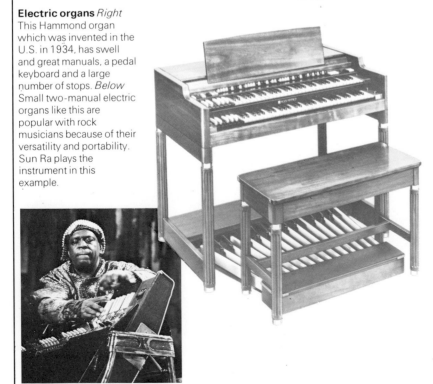

# Electronic instruments and music

Though similar to those electric instruments whose vibrations are converted electronically into sound, these produce a type of sound that does not try to imitate that of conventional instruments. They include:

**Ondes Martenot** An instrument invented in 1928 by Maurice Martenot. It has a keyboard and a bank of oscillators, linked to amplifiers and loudspeakers. The sound can also be varied by a special 'ribbon' device. It produces a strange, rather ethereal, wailing sound – half-way between a hum and a voice singing 'Oo'. Examples of its use can be found in Messiaen's *Turangalîla Symphony* and Honegger's oratorio, *Joan of Arc at the Stake.*

**Ondes Martenot** This instrument, played with a keyboard, sounds only one note at a time.

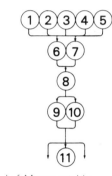

*Left* Moog portable synthesizer. *Above* Oscillators **1**, **2**, **3**, with sound source **4**, and input **5**, pass signals through contour generators **6**, **7**, a filter **8**, and amplifiers **9**, **10**, to speakers **11**. *Below* The world's largest synthesizer.

**The synthesizer** Developed during the 1940s and now used by 'electronic' composers. The synthesizer gives a composer complete control over sound, for the notes it produces can be refined and modified to a degree utterly beyond the scope of any ordinary instrument or player.

A series of oscillators generate the sound – which can be as 'pure' (that is, as free of harmonics) as required, or as 'impure'. It can also generate what is called 'white noise' (a sound very like waves breaking on the shore), which is a kind of indiscriminate mix of all possible sound. All this material can be modified by filters. It can be made louder or softer, given echoes and vibrato, made to taper off gradually, or stop suddenly. It can be given a rhythm, a definite pitch, and every possible tone colour. It can produce a sound that is quite new, or it can imitate the sounds of conventional instruments.

The results are recorded on tape and then performed through loudspeakers as a finished composition.

**Electronic music** Developed during the 1950s in various studios belonging either to Radio Stations (as at Cologne) or Universities (as at Columbia, USA). Composers involved include: Herbert Eimert, Karlheinz Stockhausen, Giselher Klebe (Germany); Henri Pousseur (Belgium), Pierre Boulez (France); Luciano Berio, Bruno Maderna (Italy); Ernst Křenek, Edgard Varèse (USA); and Tristram Carey (Great Britain).

By using the electronic synthesizer the composer has an incredibly precise control over an infinite range of sounds. When eventually he has programmed his apparatus to produce the sounds he wants, the result is recorded on tape and can be played back without further ado. In this way he can by-pass the interpreter and avoid all the accidents that can happen during a 'live' performance. The electronic composer is therefore his own performer, totally in charge of his music from beginning to end.

Electronic compositions can exist in their own right (*Mutazioni*, 1956, by Berio), or be mixed in with live performances (*Gesang der Jünglinge*, 1956, by Stockhausen). They can resemble orthodox music, or be utterly different from it. The possibilities available to the creative artist are, quite literally, endless. The only limitation lies in his artistic imagination.

# Elgar

(Sir) Edward Elgar. English composer, 1857–1934.

Elgar was born at Broadheath, a small village just outside Worcester where his father and uncle ran a music shop. His family and their friends were all musical and he must have begun to absorb musical knowledge almost without realizing it. This was just as well, for there was no money to spare for advanced training at one of the colleges. His first teacher was his father; after that he had to depend upon teaching himself.

When he was old enough, Elgar threw himself into local music-making: playing the violin alongside his father in various orchestras, deputizing for him as organist, helping in the shop, teaching, and generally taking every chance that came his way. He also began to write music for his friends and for local occasions. In short, he learned his trade by doing it.

Elgar's first chance of fame outside Worcestershire came in 1884, when his orchestral piece *Sevillana* was performed at

'The view . . . is inspiring-'

'But . . . writing is always a trial'

'I play over . . . orchestral parts-'

'And consult photographs for effect

**Edward Elgar** *Above* From *The Sketch,* 1903. *Left* Young Elgar (*back centre*) in wind quintet. *Above opposite* Elgar recording.

the Crystal Palace in London. Shortly afterwards a publisher accepted his *Romance* for violin and piano. This decided his future. Though he might have to earn his living as a music-teacher, his aim was now to become a full-time composer. In this ambition he was greatly helped by his marriage to Caroline Alice Roberts in 1889, who proved to be a constant source of encouragement.

In 1890 he was asked to write an orchestral piece for the Worcester meeting of the Three Choirs Festival. The outcome, the overture *Froissart*, made a considerable impression, and not only brought him a major publisher (Novello), but also made other festivals eager for his music. Following the fashion of the time he began to write choral works: *The Black Knight* (1893), *King Olaf* (1896), *The Banner of St George* (1897), *Caractacus* (1898). By the time he was 40, Elgar had made a considerable name for himself.

But on 19 June 1899 his whole life changed, for this was the date of the first performance of the orchestral work the *Enigma Variations* – the first of his works to show his true originality and genius. Within four months he had added a fine song cycle, *Sea Songs*, and by the end of the following year an oratorio, *The Dream of Gerontius.*

*Gerontius*, however, was not a success at its first performance (Birmingham), and it was not until 1901, when it was performed in Germany, that people in England came to realise that it was a masterpiece.

Thereafter, Elgar's career flowed smoothly. Masterpiece followed masterpiece: two symphonies, two more oratorios, two concertos, and many other works. Honours also came his way: doctorates from many universities, a knighthood (1904), the Order of Merit (1911). He was soon generally recognized as the greatest English composer since Purcell.

But in April 1920 Lady Elgar died. Elgar was devastated. He wrote a few trifling pieces, toyed with ideas for an opera, and even completed sketches for a third symphony. But his heart was no longer in his work. In 1924 he was appointed Master of the King's Musick, and in 1931 he was made a baronet. Nothing could rouse his genius, however, and he died a sad and lonely man.

Elgar was important in bringing to English music the realization that it could once more compete with continental masters on their own terms. When speaking of his music he once said 'If you cut it, it would bleed' – meaning that it was red-blooded and full of life. This quality had been absent from English music since 1695, the date of Purcell's death, in fact. And, of course, it is one of the distinguishing qualities of great music.

## Summary of Elgar's main works

1. Choral music includes:

| | |
|---|---|
| *The Black Knight* (cantata) | 1893 |
| *The Light of Life* (oratorio) | 1896 |
| *Caractacus* (cantata) | 1898 |
| *The Dream of Gerontius* (oratorio) | 1900 |
| *The Apostles* (oratorio) | 1903 |
| *The Kingdom* (oratorio) | 1906 |
| *The Music Makers* (choral ode) | 1912 |

2. Orchestral music includes:

| | |
|---|---|
| Variations on an original theme, the 'Enigma' | 1899 |
| 'Pomp and Circumstance' Marches 1–5 | 1901–30 |
| 'Cockaigne' ('In London Town') Overture | 1901 |
| Introduction and Allegro (strings) | 1905 |
| Symphony No 1 in A flat | 1908 |
| Symphony No 2 in E flat | 1911 |
| 'Falstaff' (symphonic poem) | 1913 |

3. Concertos:

| | |
|---|---|
| Concerto for violin and orchestra | 1910 |
| Concerto for cello and orchestra | 1919 |

4. Chamber music includes:

| | |
|---|---|
| String Quartet in E minor | 1918 |
| Quintet for piano and strings, in A minor | 1918 |
| Sonata for violin and piano, in E minor | 1918 |

He also wrote many songs and part-songs, and a number of shorter orchestral pieces.

'embouchure'. And though it can be improved, its existence is largely a matter of being born with the right physical equipment. As the player's embouchure is responsible for the 'tone' he produces from his instrument, it is a matter of vital importance.

**Encore** When the French wish to hear a piece of music repeated, they use the Latin word for 'twice' and shout out *Bis!* The English use the French word *Encore!* ('again') for the same purpose. Sometimes at concerts the orchestra will play another piece, rather than the same one, for variety.

Though flattering to the performer, encores are not always a good thing from a musical point of view. The repetition of an aria in an opera, for example, can seriously hold up the action and even destroy the musical shape of the act as a whole.

**End pin → Tail pin**

**Energico** (It.) Energetic.

**English Hymnal** Published in 1909 by the Oxford University Press, with the Rev. Percy Dearmer as its general editor, and Ralph Vaughan Williams as its music editor, this collection of hymns was offered as 'a humble companion to the Book of Common Prayer'. Its contents were arranged according to the seasons of the Christian year and the details of the Anglican Calendar. In choosing the hymn tunes, Vaughan Williams allowed himself to range very widely – searching out the finest from all periods, adapting folksongs, and adding many remarkable examples of his own (eg. *Sine Nomine*, No 641). Most Anglican churches use either the English Hymnal or the older *Hymns Ancient and Modern* (1861).

**Enharmonic intervals** These are microscopic intervals such as do not exist on a keyboard instrument, for instance the interval from A sharp to B flat or that from B sharp to C. So ENHARMONIC MODULATION is change of key effected by considering, for instance, that an F sharp just performed has now become G flat and treating it accordingly.

**Ensemble** (Fr.) Together. Used in music to describe the playing together of several performers. We speak of 'an ensemble', meaning a collection of performers; and we speak also of a 'good ensemble', meaning that the performers are aware of each other's playing and keep together in such a way as to give a well-balanced performance.

**Entr'acte** Any music performed between the acts of a play or opera can be called by this French name. (→ **Intermezzo**)

**Episode** → **Fugue ; Rondo**

**Equal Temperament** A way of tuning of instruments that is convenient but not quite correct. Thus F♯ and G♭ are really different notes, and so are C♯ and D♭, and B♯ and C♭, and E♯ and F, and so on. All our pianos and organs nowadays are, for convenience in playing and composing, purposely tuned a little incorrectly, making the notes in every pair slightly out of tune. If the F♯ were correctly tuned it would not sound right in a piece which required a G♭, and vice versa, so the tuner makes that note something between the F♯ and the G♭, and it sounds more or less right in pieces that require either of these notes.

Bach wrote two books of Preludes and Fugues to show the advantages of Equal Temperament. Each book has a Prelude and Fugue in every major and minor key, and on his clavichord or harpsichord (which he tuned himself) all sounded equally well in tune – as they do on our pianos today. As there are 12 major and 12 minor keys, the two books make up a collection of 48 Preludes and Fugues, and we often call this collection 'The Forty-Eight'. Bach called the collection 'The Well-tempered Clavier'. (Clavier means 'clavichord' or 'harpsichord'.)

**Equal Voices** A choral composition is said to be for 'equal voices' when it is for several groups of singers of only one kind of voice – for instance, it may be in two or three 'parts', all soprano.

**Espressivo** (It.) Expressive(ly). (→ **Expression**)

**Esquisse** (Fr.) Sketch. A title sometimes given to short instrumental pieces.

**Estampie** Though this began life in the 12th century as a type of song that was also danced, it gradually became a purely instrumental dance. It therefore counts as probably the oldest type of instrumental composition in Western music. In English it is sometimes referred to as 'stantipes'.

**Estinguendo** (It.). Dying away. Also **estinto** – as soft as possible.

**Euphonium** The brass band equivalent of the orchestral tuba, this transposing instrument in B flat has a normal range of three octaves, although some players of ability have been known to attain four octaves. To make it lighter in marching bands it sometimes loses the fourth valve and corresponding tube.

**Ethnomusicology** The study of folk music in relation to the social and cultural conditions of the time and place that has produced it. The subject of such studies is usually outside the normal Western tradition, and concerns the folk music of Africa, India, China, Japan, and similar non-European cultures. Western Europe only began to take such music seriously towards the end of the 19th century. The increased, and increasing sympathy with and understanding of non-European methods of composition, scales, and instruments, has had a considerable influence on contemporary Western music, both serious and 'pop'.

**Étude** (Fr.). Study. A piece of music evolved from a single phrase or idea (melodic or harmonic). It is intended in the first place as a technical exercise for the performer, since it rings all the possible changes on a particular idea (which may, of course, involve a special technical problem). But this does not mean that it is necessarily a purely mechanical piece of music. Chopin's *Études*, for example, are great works of art. 'Studies' of this kind are found particularly in piano music.

**Euphonium** Though sometimes described as a tenor tuba, it is actually a large bugle with three to five valves. The 3m tube, however, is bent round, so that the instrument resembles a tuba, except that its bell points slightly forward. It was invented in Germany in the 1840s and was first used to replace the bassoon in military bands. It is, even now, primarily a military band instrument but it can also be found in brass and wind bands. Its compass is shown on the left, but there are a number of 'pedal' notes taking it down to the low B flat.

**Evensong** → **Nunc Dimittis**

**Exposed fifths and octaves** → **Harmony**

**Exposition** → **Fugue ; Sonata Form**

**Expression** When we speak we 'colour' our words in a thousand different ways, so that those we are talking to hear not only the words themselves, but also the meaning and emotion *behind* them. For example: we may say 'Good morning' cheerfully, or sadly, or in bored tones, or with surprise, or even anger.

We suggest these additional meanings by speaking quickly, or slowly, by raising the pitch of the voice, or dropping it – by making, in fact, a musical phrase out of what we say.

Music itself demands the same degree and variety of 'expression' if it is to have *meaning*. Played without expression, music will sound flat and dead and very boring.

But expression is not something we *put into* music: it is, or should be, something that *comes out of it* through our performance. If we do not ourselves *feel* the music, our audience will not feel it either.

Most pieces of music have 'expression marks' – words and signs to indicate the speeds and the degree of force to be used for particular notes and passages. In the days of Bach and Handel composers added very few instructions of this kind to their music, even when printed. But by the time of Debussy and Elgar scarcely a note is without its attendant mark of expression.

Even so, the performer must add effects of his own if the music is to come alive. These additions must, of course, keep to the spirit of the piece as the composer intended, and they must never be exaggerated or excessive. To apply them correctly calls for a serious study of the music and its composer, a great deal of thought and a great deal of taste.

**Expressionism** A term borrowed from painting, where it describes a style practised around 1912 by such painters as Kandinsky. These painters tried to record their inner experiences – usually very extreme states of mind, bordering on breakdown and madness.

At much the same time, certain composers attempted a similar exploration in music. In order to do so they often turned to extremely jagged and 'unvocal' melodic lines, harsh orchestration, and violently dissonant harmonies. Schoenberg's *Pierrot Lunaire* (1912) is a good example of the style.

**Extemporization → Improvisation**

**Extended mordent → Mordent**

**Eye music** Any music which actually looks on paper something like the idea it is trying to express. Thus, for example, a composer may choose to set a word like 'serpent' to a long, wriggling melodic line. Symbolic devices of this kind were particularly popular in the 16th and 17th centuries.

**Expressionist painting**
*Above* This abstract expressionist work dated 1910 and entitled *Cossacks* is by the Russian-born artist Wassily Kandinsky. *Right The Scream* by the Norwegian early Expressionist painter Edvard Munch. His works frequently deal with anguish, despair and death.

**Eye music** This 15th-century French love song is set in the shape of a heart.

F or **f** stands for **forte** (It.) Loud.

**Fa** or. **Fah** The fourth degree of any major scale (→ **Sol-fa system**). In French and Italian it always means the note F.

**Faburden** or **Fauxbourdon** This word has different meanings at different periods. Here are some of them:

1. In the early 14th century it meant the harmonization of a plainsong melody in *parallel* thirds and sixths. (→ **Plainsong**)
2. In the 16th and 17th centuries it was used to describe the tenor part of a metrical psalm tune – it was the tenor part that carried the melody and not the alto or treble lines.
3. It has also been used to describe a 'refrain' in the verse of a song.
4. It can be used to describe the type of drone bass you find on a bagpipe.
5. Nowadays it is used as an alternative to the word DESCANT.

**Falla, Manuel de** Spanish composer, 1876–1946. He studied composition with Felipe Pedrell and later won a competition for the best national opera with *La Vida breve* (Life is short) (1905). He lived in Paris from 1907–14 and was much influenced by the music of his friends Debussy and Ravel.

The most productive years of his life were spent in Spain (1914–33) where he allowed the rhythms and melodic shapes of folk music to influence his work as he set about the task of creating a truly national style of music. His ballets *El Amor Brujo* (Love the Magician) (1915), and *El Sombrero de tres Picos* (The Three-cornered Hat) (1919) were very successful, as were the three pieces for piano

**Manuel de Falla**
1876–1946 The composer at the harpsichord during a performance of his *Concerto for Harpsichord and Chamber Orchestra*, composed in 1926.

and orchestra *Nights in the Gardens of Spain* (1909–15) and the *Concerto for Harpsichord and Chamber Orchestra* (1926).

Falla's last years were spent partly in Majorca and, after 1940, in Argentina; but he wrote very little music after about 1926.

**Falsetto** All male singers can produce notes beyond their normal range by means of a special technique known as 'singing falsetto'. Very simply it means that instead of allowing the whole vocal cord to vibrate, only the outer edges are allowed to do so.

Though the falsetto notes are usually fairly weak and of poor quality, they can be cultivated and developed. This is what happens in the case of the male alto, whose voice production depends entirely upon falsetto techniques.

**False relation** When a note that bears an accidental is followed immediately, in another part, by the same note without an accidental (or vice versa), the result is said to be a false relation. In music of the classical period this was considered to be incorrect, but nowadays it is quite acceptable – just as it was, for example, among the English madrigalists of the 17th century. Here is an example:

A similar effect can occur harmonically, when notes bearing contradictory accidentals occur in one chord (see left).

**Fancy** An old English word that corresponds to the Italian *Fantasia*. It was used to describe a type of instrumental composition (usually for viols) designed rather like a madrigal or motet.

**Fandango** A lively Spanish dance with three or six beats to the bar. Its speed increases throughout. It also has moments when everything stops and the performers stand motionless.

**Fanfare** A flourish of trumpets, used on ceremonial occasions. Sir Arthur Bliss, for example, wrote a great many splendidly imaginative fanfares for Royal occasions when he was Master of the Queen's Musick. The word comes from the Spanish *fanfarria* ('noisy arrogance'), and the idea of fanfares or 'flourishes' originated in the Army.

In France the word is also used to describe a cavalry band or any kind of brass band.

**Fantasia** In general terms this word means any kind of 'fanciful' composition which sounds almost as if it is being improvised. It can also mean a composition based on a string of tunes from an opera, or some similar larger work.

In the 16th and 17th centuries, however, a Fantasia was an instrumental piece, often for viols, that was contrapuntal in character, like a madrigal or motet. It is thus an early form of chamber music.

The term FREE FANTASIA is sometimes used for the Development section in Sonata Form. (→ **Phantasie**)

**Fantaisie, Fantasie** The French and German equivalents for the Italian *fantasia*.

**Fantastic Symphony** → **Berlioz**

**Farnaby, Giles** English composer, c. 1560–1640. He graduated B.Mus. at Oxford in 1592 and published a volume of 20 *Canzonets* in 1598. Charming and unusual as these are, his real claim to fame lies in his many pieces for virginals (over 50 are included in the Fitzwilliam Virginal Book) – for example: 'Quodling's Delight', and 'Giles Farnaby, his Reste'.

**Fauré, Gabriel** French composer, 1845–1924. He showed signs of an exceptional talent at an early age, and because his parents were very poor he was accepted without payment as a pupil at the École Niedermeyer in Paris (1855–65) where eventually he came to be taught by Saint-Saëns. His first published composition appeared during his school days (1863).

He began his professional career as an organist and teacher, eventually moving to the Madeleine in Paris (as assistant in 1877, and as organist in 1896), and to the Conservatoire in 1896. His life, and his development as a composer, was quiet and

**Fanfare** These fanfare trumpets, hung with heraldic banners, are used in Britain on state and ceremonial occasions.

**Gabriel Fauré** 1845–1924

**Morton Feldman** b. 1926

unspectacular, and it is therefore easy to overlook the fact that he was really a very remarkable musician. His music is equally discreet and gentle: it conceals its art. And yet, by any standards, it is music of exceptional beauty.

Fauré's mature work includes two operas, *Prométhée* (1901) and *Pénélope* (1913), a quantity of church music, including the famous *Requiem* (1887); several important chamber works, and a number of short orchestral pieces, such as the suite *Masques et Bergamasques* (1920), and the *Ballade* for piano and orchestra (1881). Probably his finest music, however, is to be found in his many piano pieces and songs.

**Fauxbourdon** or **Faux Bourdon** → **Faburden**

**F Clef** → **Notes and notation**

**Feldman, Morton** American composer, b. 1926. Much influenced by John Cage, he has experimented with Indeterminacy in matters of pitch, duration, and dynamics in such works as *Projections* (1951). Later works, such as *Durations* (1961), leave the results rather less wholly to chance, but are still, from the purely traditional point of view, highly experimental.

**Feminine cadence** → **Cadence**

**Ferguson, Howard** Anglo-Irish composer, b. 1908. He studied at the Royal College of Music and has pursued a triple career as pianist, composer, and musical editor. Though he has written only a small quantity of music (ceasing altogether after 1959), it is all of excellent quality. His *Octet* for clarinet, bassoon, horn, string quartet and double bass (1933) is his best known work. It is very much in the Brahms romantic tradition.

**Feroce** (It.) Ferocious. **Ferocità**, ferocity.

**Fermata** (It.) Pause. The sign ⌢, which directs that a note or a rest is to be held beyond its written duration. When the sign occurs over a bar line, it indicates that the performer must pause briefly before moving on to the next bar.

**Ferrabosco, Alfonso** Italian composer, 1543–88. Though little is known about his childhood, he probably studied in Bologna with his father, Domenico Ferrabosco (1513–74), who was himself a distinguished composer. Between about 1560 and 1578 he spent many years in England and it seems likely that he was partly employed as a spy on

# Fiddle

Although people are apt to speak of almost any kind of violin as a 'fiddle', the term is only correctly used to describe two basic types of instrument.

1. **The folk fiddle** These are actually bowed lutes. They appear in all shapes and sizes in Africa, Asia, America and Europe. Two types are common: those with long necks (spike fiddles), which are popular in North Africa, Asia, and the Middle East; and those with short necks (short-necked fiddles), which occur in Europe. The neck of the spike fiddle goes straight through the body of the instrument and projects as a spike at the base. The neck and body of the short-necked fiddle are often carved from the same piece of wood. Such fiddles can have one, two, or three strings (though Indian versions of the same instrument have many more). The one-stringed fiddle is very common. Spike-fiddles are held vertically, with the spike resting on the player's knee, or on the floor. Short-necked fiddles are held more or less horizontally, resting against the player's chest, shoulder, or neck. The bows are usually curved.

**Folk fiddles** *Right* The Ethopian Thcira, a spike fiddle with only one string, is used for sustained sound as a background to folk recitation. *Below* This Tibetan fiddle has a bow threaded between the four strings. It produces a thin, melancholy sound which can be very effective.

**Yugoslavian fiddle**
This pear-shaped folk instrument from Dubrovnik is called a 'lirica'.

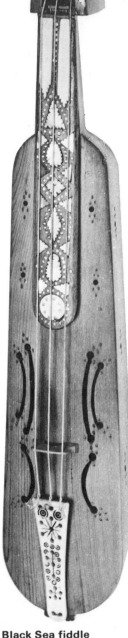

**Black Sea fiddle**
(*above*) This decorative instrument is from Turkey.

**Medieval fiddle** (*right*) This 13th-century Spanish manuscript shows a fiddle (*left*) and a gittern (early guitar).

**Balinese spiked fiddle** (*below*) Simple one- or two-stringed instruments similar to this were known to exist in the East from the ninth century A.D.

2. **The medieval fiddle** These are found under several different names: vielle, fidel, fiedel, fithele, fidula, vigele, etc. They were in use from the 12th to the 14th centuries, after which they were replaced by the various members of the viol family. They were made in many different shapes and usually had three, four, or five strings. The ordinary medieval fiddle had a flat back, but there was a **Rebec →** type which had a rounded back.

behalf of Queen Elizabeth I. His madrigals were much admired by his English contemporaries. His son, Alfonso (1575–1628) also worked in England as a composer and instrumentalist, as did his grandsons, Alfonso (c. 1620–c. 60), Henry (c. 1623–c. 58), and John (1626–82).

**FF** or **ff** stands for **fortissimo** (It.) Very loud. **FFF** or **fff** stands for 'extremely loud'.

**f holes** → **Sound holes**

**Fiddle** → page 134

**Fiddle G** The name sometimes given to the G on the top space of the bass clef.( → **Pitch**)

**Field, John** Irish composer and pianist, 1782–1837. He was the son of a Dublin violinist; he studied with Giordani and made his first appearance as a pianist when he was nine. In 1793 his father settled in London and apprenticed him to Muzio Clementi, who not only taught him but also employed him as a kind of salesman to demonstrate the pianos in the showroom of his London firm.

In 1802 master and pupil visited France, Germany, and Russia. Field's playing made a great impression, particularly in St Petersburg, where he settled as a fashionable teacher and virtuoso performer. He remained successful until about 1833 and made several European tours. But by then he had taken to drink and he spent his last years in decline.

Field wrote seven piano concertos, a small quantity of chamber music, and a number of individual piano pieces. His main claim to fame, however, lies in his 18 *Nocturnes* for piano. These greatly influenced Chopin, and are, indeed, almost worthy of him. Field invented the form and the singing style that is part of it – Chopin, however, perfected it.

**Fife** → **Flute**

**Fifth** → **Intervals**

**Figure** The shortest complete idea in music – thus, any series of notes grouped together to make a recognizable musical shape, or a coherent succession of chords. The first four notes of Beethoven's Fifth Symphony make a musical 'figure' (see right).

In German the equivalent is *motiv*, and in French *motif*. These words convey the importance of 'figures' rather more clearly, for, as the Beethoven example shows, a 'figure' can be the basis from which an entire movement grows. ( → **Sonata Form**)

**John Field** 1782–1837
This portrait shows the composer aged about 18.

**Gerald Finzi** 1901–1956
Although best-known for his vocal works Finzi also wrote instrumental music including a clarinet concerto.

**Figured bass** → page 136

**Film music** → page 137

**Fin** (Fr.), **Fine** (It.) End. Note, however, that *fin* in Italian is short for **fino** →, and means 'as far as'.

**Finale** The last movement of a work, such as a sonata or symphony. In the 18th century finales were usually light-hearted, but from Beethoven onwards they tend to become weightier and form the climax of the whole work.

18th-century operas often had a 'finale' to end each act. It consisted of a string of arias, recitatives, ensembles, and even choruses, all linked together in one continuous movement and forming the climax to the act. The finales of Acts 2 and 4 of Mozart's *The Marriage of Figaro* are particularly striking.

**Fingering** Any recommended system that shows which fingers to use when playing a musical instrument. This is usually shown by numbering the fingers and placing the numbers above the notes in the music. Such numbers would only be printed in books of exercises, but performers often pencil in appropriate 'fingering' in the copies they use for performance.

**Fino** (sometimes shortened to **fin**) (It.) as far as. So **fino al segno** means 'as far as the sign 𝄋'.

**Finzi, Gerald** English composer, 1901–56. Notable mainly for his many songs, in particular his settings of Thomas Hardy's poems. A song cycle, *Let us Garlands bring* (1942), to words by Shakespeare, and a setting of Thomas Traherne's *Dies Natalis* (1939) have become deservedly popular.

Though a 'minor' composer, somewhat in the shadow of Vaughan Williams, Finzi was nevertheless a very fine one. He also did important work in bringing to light music by neglected 18th-century composers, such as John Stanley, Richard Mudge, and Charles Avison.

**Fioritura** An Italian word meaning 'flowering' or 'flourishing', used to describe the ornamental decorations that can be added to a melodic line. For example, it was much favoured by Italian opera singers in the 18th century, who often improvised their 'flowerings' on the spot. But it is also found in 19th-century piano music, particularly that of Chopin, whose 'singing style' was much influenced by opera.

# Figured bass

This is a form of musical shorthand. Instead of writing down a tune, its bass line, and the *complete* harmony, the composer supplies the tune, the bass line, and a series of figures (written beneath the bass line) to indicate which chords he has in mind. Thus, the following tune and figured bass:

could be interpreted to mean:

Note that when there are no figures beneath the bass line, a common chord is intended. If only the figured bass line is given, the performer must make up the tune as well. Thus, the following example is another way of 'realizing' the same information:

Figured bass has been used as a teaching method to help young students (and is still used to a limited extent). But its origins are much more important and involve what is known as the BASSO CONTINUO – or, more commonly, the CONTINUO.

The idea of the continuo begins to creep into music after 1600 – for it is at this period that public performances, of opera and later of orchestral music, begin to become popular. The 'modern' music of this period was less interested in polyphony than in the idea of a bold tune, an equally bold bass line, and a filling of harmony in between. In such circumstances it was perfectly logical for a composer to supply the main ingredients (the tune and the bass line) and merely indicate what harmonies he wanted, leaving the detailed working-out to the performer.

The instruments to which this 'working-out' were entrusted would, naturally, have to be those that could play chords, for example, the harpsichord, or organ, or possibly some such instrument as the lute or guitar.

The continuo instrument of the 17th and 18th centuries was, therefore, primarily a chord-playing one that could be played by *one* person. But the bass line was very important, and it became the custom to add to the continuo another instrument that could play the bass very firmly. Thus the continuo ended up as a partnership between a chord-playing instrument and a bass-line instrument: a cello and a harpsichord, for example.

The continuo group is found not only in chamber music of the period (such as solo and trio sonatas, or songs with instrumental accompaniment), but also in the early *orchestral* music. Here it serves another function: that of holding the performance together and supplying the *complete* harmony. Performances were often directed from the keyboard by the continuo player (acting as a kind of conductor). And because the orchestra had not yet developed into balanced sections of strings, woodwind, and brass, each capable of supplying a complete four-part harmony, it was necessary to have a continuo 'backing'.

In the 18th century a continuo player was expected to be able to read the figured-bass shorthand fluently and to be able to interpret it in an interesting way. Editors of old music often supply 'realizations' of the old continuo parts and print them together with the rest of the music. But it is becoming common practice for musicians to revive the old methods and 'interpret' the figured bass on the spot, during the performance.

# Film music

Music is added to films in order to supply 'atmosphere', or tell the audience something extra about what is happening on the screen.

For example, a sudden and frightening event on the screen can be made all the more terrifying if accompanied by a sudden and frightening sound. A cleverly orchestrated chord can thus seem like a blow on the head. Similarly, it is perfectly possible for music to contradict what is happening on the screen. Thus, if the picture shows a quiet country lane and the director wants you to know that something unpleasant is about to happen, the music can suggest this feeling quite easily.

The importance of music was realized from the very early days of film. In the silent film era, performances were accompanied by the piano – or, in larger cinemas, by a small orchestra. The music was either made up on the spot by the pianist, or selected from a 'library' of suitable pieces.

It began to be realized that the music accompanying a film would be much more effective if specially written, instead of being cobbled together from existing pieces. And so the practice of commissioning composers to write a 'film score' grew up. Eventually even important composers, such as Ralph Vaughan Williams, William Walton, Aaron Copland, and Serge Prokofiev, etc., were tempted into writing for films, and many of the scores they produced went on to find a further life in the concert hall as orchestral Suites. In the case of Vaughan Williams, the music he wrote for the film *Scott of the Antarctic* (1948) became the basis for a whole symphony: the *Sinfonia Antartica* (1952). In writing a film score the composer can adopt two basic approaches. Either he can write music which suggests

**Famous film music**
*Above* Scenes from *War and Peace* (*top*), the Russian film completed in 1964 with music by Shostakovich; *Lawrence*

the *general mood* of each scene, or he can write music which underlines *every detail* of what is happening.

If he takes the first line of approach all he needs to know is the length (in seconds) of each scene and what the mood is supposed to be. If he takes the second line, he will need to know not only the length of each scene, but the exact moment (to the split second) when each event occurs.

The composer will see the film several times and be given a detailed 'cue sheet', showing each 'shot', its length, and the exact moment when events take place. All this can be worked out to the split-second by counting the number of 'frames' (each individual photo-picture) in each scene and working out a timing (the film is projected at a fixed number of frames per second).

The composer can then calculate how many bars of music he needs, what the music should be like, and at exactly which bar his 'musical event' will take place.

For example, if he has 60 bars of music, playing at a metronome speed of 60 beats per minute in 4/4 time, his score will last four minutes (60 bars at four beats = 240 beats; divided by 60 beats per minute = four minutes).

Nowadays the business of writing a film score is taken very seriously. The tendency is to supply only what is absolutely necessary. Some films exist quite happily without music. The bad old practice which you find in films of the 1930s and 40s of pouring music all over a film, rather like glue to keep it together, seems to have gone forever.

*of Arabia* with memorable music by Maurice Jarre (*centre*); and *The Longest Day*, the film about D day released in 1961 with music by Jarre.

**Synchronizing the music** *Far left* Prokofiev's score for Eisenstein's *Alexander Nevsky* is here charted to individual picture frames.
*Left* Vaughan Williams wrote the music for *Stolen Life* (1946).

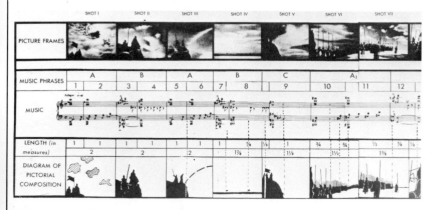

**Fipple flute** A class of flute that is held vertically. The player's breath flows through a narrow slit in the mouthpiece and strikes against a sharp edge (the 'lip') which sets up vibrations that are transmitted to the main tube of the instrument. The 'fipple' is the plug which stops the playing end of the instrument and forms the mouthpiece. To this family of instruments belong the RECORDER, the FLAGEOLET, the BAMBOO PIPE, and the PENNY WHISTLE.

**Fitzwilliam Virginal Book** One of the most important manuscript collections of Elizabethan keyboard music. It is preserved in the Fitzwilliam Museum, Cambridge. The music can now be obtained in printed editions. It includes items by John Bull, William Byrd, Giles Farnaby, and Thomas Morley.

**Fipple flute** (flageolet)

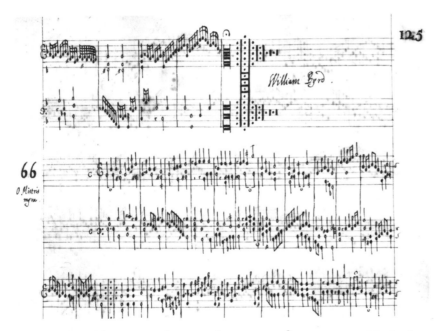

**Fitzwilliam Virginal Book** This page includes the first line of *O Mistress Mine* by William Byrd.

**Five, The** The name given to the group of Russian composers who banded together to further the development of a national style of musical composition. They were: Balakirev, Cui, Borodin, Mussorgsky, and Rimsky-Korsakov. They based their efforts on the example set by Glinka and Dargomihjsky earlier in the century.

**Flageolet** → **Fipple flute; Recorder**

**Flat, Sharp** → **Notes and notation**

**Flotow, Friedrich von** German composer, 1812–83.

He was a nobleman and educated for the diplomatic service, but became a musician and composed about 20 operas, of which *Martha* (1847) is the one best remembered today.

# Flute family

Members of the flute family have been in use for many hundreds of years. There are two chief types: those held vertically and blown through the end (end-blown), like the **Recorder** and **Fipple flute** →; and those held horizontally and blown through a hole cut in the side (side-blown). It is this second type, the **Transverse Flute**, that is found in the modern orchestra.

The transverse flute is a cylindrical tube made of wood or metal, stopped at one end. The player blows across a hole cut in the side of the instrument about two inches from the stopped end.

Different notes are obtained by the player opening and closing a series of holes cut along the side of the tube. These are operated by the system of keys and levers invented by Theobald Boehm in the 1830s.

The flute has a range of about three octaves, starting at middle C. The lower register is dark and mysterious, but the tone gets brighter and more 'silvery' as you go up, until the high register is quite penetrating and shrill.

Flutes, nowadays, are mostly made of silver (there are a few made of gold!). The average-sized orchestra has two flutes. A large orchestra may have three – though one of these may be a bass flute or a piccolo. Flute players are called FLAUTISTS.

The PICCOLO is a small version of the flute, and its pitch is an octave higher. The BASS FLUTE (more properly called an alto flute) is a larger version of the flute and its range is a fourth lower.

The transverse flute was brought into the orchestra around the time of Lully, but many scores of this period still call for the end-blown flute (recorder). By the time of Haydn and Mozart the transverse flute was firmly established as an orchestral instrument. The piccolo joined the orchestra towards the end of Beethoven's life, and the

**Double fipple flute** This recorder-type flute is played by a Yugoslavian musician.

bass flute about thirty years later (in the 1860s).

The FIFE is a very simple type of flute. It is small, side-blown, but has no mechanism to help the fingering. It is found only in Drum and Fife bands.

**James Galway** This Irish flautist was with the Berlin Philharmonic Orchestra before leaving to follow a successful freelance career.

*Above* **The flute family** (*left to right*) C bass, G alto, C concert, G treble and piccolo.

*Above right* **Female consort** This late 16th-century Flemish painting by the painter known as the Master of the Female Half-Lengths shows a singer accompanied by the flute and the lute.

*Above* **Melanesian nose flute** This primitive instrument, 'end-blown' with the nostril instead of the mouth, is still used by the inhabitants of some of the Pacific Islands.

*Left* **Bamboo flutes, Bolivia** The blow holes of these South American flutes have a square-shaped notch. This creates a sharper edge against which to direct the airstream. End-blown flutes are found in every continent but particularly in South America, Africa and Asia.

*Right* **Metal flute, Hungary** Modern folk instruments are more commonly made of wood or bamboo.

**Flue pipe** → **Organ**

**Flügelhorn** → **Saxhorn and Flügelhorn**

**Flute** → page 138

**Folía** or **Follía** Originally a wild Portuguese dance. It was very noisy, accompanied by tambourines, and danced by men dressed as women. The word *folía* means 'madness', and this is how the dance appeared to most onlookers.

One particular 'folía' tune has been used by composers for over three hundred years as a basis for instrumental pieces of the 'theme and variation' type. The best known example is Corelli's 12th sonata for violin and harpsichord.

**Folk rock** A type of 'pop' music that developed in America in the 1960s among such singers as Bob Dylan. The vocal lines imitate folksong, but are presented in a rock style. The words are often concerned with social problems.

**Folksong** → page 142

**Forlane** An Italian dance, particularly popular in Venice among the gondoliers. It is in 6/8 or 6/4 time. There is an example in Bach's *Suite No 1* in *C major*.

**Form in music** → page 143

**Forte** (It.). Strong, loud. Often abbreviated to **F**. Also **fortissimo** (**ff**), very loud; and **fortemente**, loudly. (→ **Notes and notation**)

**Fortissimo** → **ff**

**'Forty-eight, The'** A common abbreviation for Bach's set of *48 Preludes and Fugues* (*Das Wohltemperierte Klavier* – The Well-Tempered Keyboard-instrument) (→ **Equal Temperament**)

**Forza** (It.) Force. **Forzando** (often abbreviated to **fz**) means 'forced'.

**Foss, Lukas** American composer, b. 1922. He was born in Berlin but settled in America when he was 15, after some study in Paris. After studying at the Curtis Institute in Philadelphia he became known as an excellent pianist and conductor as well as a composer. Though his early works are orthodox he began, after 1957, to experiment with Indeterminacy and the use of non-musical effects – in such works as *Echoi* (1961–63) for four soloists. One of his earlier pieces, the *Symphony of Chorales* (1958), is based on Bach's music.

**Folk rock** Bob Dylan *(top)* and Joan Baez *(bottom),* the two most famous American folk singers of the 1960s. Dylan incorporated a pronounced rock beat and backing in a number of his later songs.

# Folk dances

Dancing is as old as human history. It has existed all over the world, and in every age, as an important means of self-expression. It has been closely linked with various forms of social and religious ritual (war dances, rain dances, etc), and has been enjoyed as a simple means of recreation. Wherever human beings have lived together in communities we may safely guess that they have danced, and danced to a purpose.

The dances of ordinary people (which, in general terms, we may conveniently call folk dances) vary according to different parts of the world. In the East, for example, graceful and intricate movements of the hands and arms have played a large part – each gesture being a symbol of deep significance. We seldom find this in the West. In primitive societies dancing has involved energetic movements of the body, wild stamping of the feet and waving of arms – all to the beat of drums. Only in very recent times, with the arrival of rock 'n roll, has Western dancing investigated movement of this kind.

In general terms we may say that when Western man has wanted to dance he has linked hands with his neighbours, and then moved in a very controlled, formal kind of way. The result has been either some form of CHAIN DANCE, which moves forward in a follow-my-leader motion, or a ROUND DANCE, in which the chain becomes a circle moving round some central object (such as a maypole). A variation, or development, of the round dance involves the dancers standing in two lines, facing each other – as if the circle had been broken at both ends. And a further development of this kind of LINE DANCE leads to each dancer pairing off with his opposite number – a PAIRED DANCE.

The ancient reasons for dancing were either *ritual* or *recreational*, and there are certain important differences between the two types of dance. Ritual dances were always seasonal – that is, they were only danced at certain times of the year. They were thought to have magical properties concerned with the raising of crops and other matters of importance to people living close to nature. Moreover, they were only danced by men, for women were not considered suitable for handling 'religious' matters of this kind. Recreational dances, however, could be danced at any time and

**British folk dances**
*Below* **1** North country sword dance. **2** Furry Dance at Helston, Cornwall, a processional dance held on Flora day in early May.

by both sexes. We may call these COUNTRY DANCES.

The folk dances of Great Britain include:

**The Sword dance** This is a ritual dance for mid-winter. It was originally part of a play (now lost) which symbolized the rebirth of the year after its 'death' in winter. It is a group dance (and quite different from the Scottish Sword dance) performed by five, six, or eight men, each carrying a 'sword' (usually made of wood). Each man holds one end of his own sword and the other end of his neighbour's, and goes through a series of complicated movements. At the end of the dance the swords are meshed together in a star-shaped pattern called the Lock, Rose, Glass, or Nut. This is often placed over the head of a 'victim', as if to decapitate him (but he is 'reborn', of course).

**The Morris dance** This is a ritual dance for Whitsun. It symbolizes the purification of the earth and encourages the raising of crops. It is normally danced by six men. They carry a white handkerchief in one hand and a stick in the other, and they have bells strapped to their legs (bells have always been associated with magic, for their sound drives out evil spirits).

**Animal dances** These are usually processional dances in which the dancers, or a dancer, dress up as an animal – as, for example, in the famous Padstow Hobbyhorse dance, or the 'horn dance' of Abbots Bromley in Staffordshire (in which the men wear antlers). The exact significance of

these dances is no longer understood, but they clearly derive from magic ritual.

**Processional dances** In which the dancers join in a long chain and dance through the village, often in and out of the houses – as, for example, at Helston in Cornwall. These differ from the usual ritual dances in that both men and women are involved. Indeed, they lie somewhere in between the true ritual dance and the country dance, and are perhaps best thought of as a form of country dance designed to bring 'good luck'. They are only danced on particular dates.

**The country dance** These include LINE DANCES, in which the men and women face each other in two straight lines; ROUND DANCES, such as the Maypole dance; and SQUARE DANCES, in which the dancers form a square and then pair off across the square. All these dances have relatively simple steps, but involve intricate formations. It is important to remember that they were as eagerly danced at court as on the village green.

**The revival of folk dance** Though folk dancing never died out entirely in the remoter parts of Great Britain, it came close to doing so. It was saved from oblivion by one man: Cecil Sharp. Between about 1899 and 1924 he travelled the country and noted down over two hundred dances and their music. In 1911 he founded the Folk Dance Society. Its activities have prospered and today it is possible for anyone to learn and enjoy the dances of their ancestors.

**European folk dances**
*Right* An Eastern European folk dance, the 'verkhovina', performed by members of the Brest City Dance Co., U.S.S.R.
*Below* The Jota, a Spanish folk dance performed with castanets, Palma, Majorca.

# Folksong

'Folk' songs are those that have grown up among country people and have been handed on from singer to singer, and from generation to generation, without being written down. Nobody knows who actually composed them in the first place, or when they were composed. In a sense, everybody who sings them makes a contribution – for each singer will make, either by accident or design, some tiny variation to the words and the music. A folksong therefore becomes the musical expression of a community.

Folksongs are usually single-line tunes and can be sung without accompaniment. Indeed, if a professional composer decides to add an accompaniment, he must be particularly careful not to produce something that goes against the spirit of the original song. In the 18th century, for example, composers were apt to look upon folksongs as being rather primitive. When they made arrangements of them they tended to clean them up so as to conform to the rules of 'polite' music. It is only in the last 80 years or so that composers have realised that folksongs are 'correct' in themselves.

Folksongs are only fixed for all time when somebody 'collects' them (writes them down and publishes them). Frequently several people 'collect' the same song in different parts of the country. What they write down will vary, often quite considerably, in detail – though it may be recognizably the same song.

The collecting of folksong only began to be taken seriously during the second half of the 19th century. And it only began to be treated as a science during the 20th century. It was much helped by the invention of the

**Irish folk group** The Dubliners, seen here in performance, are one of the best-known of modern folk groups, perhaps as a result of their music for films. Folksong ( and collecting) fascinated serious composers, such as Bartók and Kodály in Hungary, Janáček in Czechoslovakia, Holst and Vaughan Williams in England. The more they studied it the more they absorbed its characteristics into their own music and the more they were able to create a style that not only seemed personal to themselves, but seemed also to belong to their own country.

gramophone, which made it possible for collectors to record their finds on the spot. In England such pioneers as Cecil Sharp and Maud Karpeles were responsible for preserving a great part of the folksong heritage – for they began their collections only just in time, as the old ways of country life were disappearing forever. It is always closely linked with language (words and tunes tend to come into existence together), and imitates its distinctive rhythms and melodic shapes. It is often concerned with daily activities (songs to accompany weaving, threshing, etc.). It often recounts important events in the history of a country, or a small community.

With all these direct links with life as it is lived and felt by millions of ordinary people, it is scarcely surprising that folksong should possess such strengths and virtues.

**Foster, Stephen** American composer, 1826–64. Though born in Pittsburg, he specialized in sentimental and humorous songs on subjects taken from life in the old South – particularly Negro subjects. Most of these were written for Minstrel shows. Foster's music has genuine quality; it can be comic, as in '*Oh! Susanna*' and '*Camptown Races*', or touching, as in '*Beautiful Dreamer*' and '*Old Folks at Home*'. It can also be dreadfully sentimental, as in '*Willie we have missed you*'! And at least one song is worthy of the greatest composer: '*Jeannie with the light brown Hair*'.

**Foxtrot** This dance is still one of the most popular ballroom dances.

**Fourth → Intervals**

**Foxtrot** A ballroom dance that originated in America in 1912. To begin with it consisted of alternating groups of long and short steps, but soon developed many intricate patterns. The Charleston and Black Bottom dances developed as rather jerky versions of the foxtrot.

**fp** stands for **forte-piano** – that is, first loud and then immediately soft.

**Françaix, Jean** French composer, b. 1912. He was a pupil of Nadia Boulanger and has written much music of the tuneful, witty,

# Form in music

In order to be effective, a piece of music must have a shape that is recognizable to the ear. Music that merely repeats the same idea over and over again rapidly becomes boring – as does music that passes from new idea to new idea in an endless stream. The human mind seems to demand a compromise between these two extremes and is only happy when presented with something that contains both CONTRAST and REPETITION.

There are many ways of achieving this in music. And composers have used different methods at different periods of musical history. But when we speak of 'musical form' we generally mean the kind of patterns favoured by composers from about 1650 to 1950.

This was a period dominated by the use of major and minor diatonic scales. And just as the individual notes in these scales stood in strict relation to each other, the keys they formed were also related in a very definite way. Thus in each composition it was possible to establish one key as the *main* key, and then make journeys to neighbouring keys and back.

This movement from a 'home' key to a new key, and back again, proved a very important ingredient in creating a sense of musical form. It was effective because it could be allied to the use of contrasting musical ideas. For example: it was easier for the ear to appreciate a move away from the 'home' key if a *new* musical idea was introduced when the *new* key was reached. The return to the 'home' key would then be underlined by the repetition of the first musical idea.

In this way, using keys and musical ideas, the composer was able to build very effective musical forms. The relationship of key to key was as important as the contrast and repetition of musical ideas.

This kind of musical form is easily appreciated by the ear because it is built up almost like architecture – out of solid blocks of material that can instantly be 'heard' to be alike, or different, as the case may be.

This, of course, is not the only way of giving music a sense of coherence and logic. Music in medieval times used different methods – as does the avant-garde music of today. But it is an extremely effective method, and it is the one used in most of the pieces we hear as part of our daily musical diet.

Explanations of individual musical forms will be found under the following headings: **Binary**, **Ternary**, **Rondo**, **Sonata**, **Sonata-Rondo**, **Air with variations**, **Fugue**.

---

neo-classic kind usually associated with Stravinsky and the Paris of the 1920s. Such works as the *Concertino for piano and orchestra* (1932), and the suite for oboe and orchestra *L'Horloge de Flore* (1961), give a good idea of his elegant style.

**Franck, César** French composer, 1822–90. Though he was born in Belgium (Liège) he became a French citizen and passed most of his life as an organist and teacher in Paris. Though he was famous as an organist, recognition as a composer came rather late in his life and a handful of his works are now very highly regarded. For example: the *Symphony in D minor* (1888), the *Variations symphoniques* for piano and orchestra (1885), and the *Sonata for violin and piano*, (1886). He also wrote a number of fine organ works, and much church music, including the oratorio *The Beatitudes* (1879). His musical style is, romantic, powerful but very chromatic.

**Franz, Robert** German composer,

**César Franck** 1822-1890
A Belgian by birth, he studied at the Paris Conservatory where he later taught. For forty years he was organist at Ste Clothilde. Although admired by his pupils d'Indy and Duparc, his music attracted little notice, until at 68, his *String Quartet* won popular acclaim.

1815–92. Though he was known as an organist, conductor, and teacher, he is now admired as the composer of some 260 songs, the first set of which appeared in 1843. His work was praised by Schumann, Mendelssohn and Liszt and still holds its place in concerts of German Lieder. In his later years he was troubled by nervous disorders and deafness, but devoted much time to musical research – in particular the editing and arranging of works by Bach and Handel.

**French horn → Horn family**

**French sixth → Chromatic chords**

**Free-reed** Found in such instruments as the harmonium, accordion, and harmonica. The reed is a small metal tongue which is attached to a metal plate with a slot in it. When air, from the mouth or from a bellows, passes over the reed, it vibrates freely, back and forth through the slot. The pitch of each reed is determined by the length and thickness of the tongue – the longer and heavier the tongue, the lower the note. (**→ Reed**)

# Fugue

A fugue is a contrapuntal composition that explores the possibilities of one main musical idea.

Within reason a fugue may be for any number of voices (parts). Two is the obvious minimum. Four is the number most commonly found.

Although textbooks usually state that the fugue can be divided into three sections, in practice these divisions are not noticed by the ear. The music flows on from start to finish. However, the three sections are: EXPOSITION: MIDDLE ENTRIES: FINAL ENTRIES.

It is also important to realize that the 'copybook' description which follows is a mere convenience. Most fugues may follow such a plan, but they will never do so *in detail*. The difficulty is that fugue is not so much a form, as a *method* of writing music. Indeed, it might be better if, instead of describing such works as 'fugues', we were to say that they are 'pieces of music *in fugue*'.

In a four-part fugue (that is: a fugue with four 'voices') what happens is something like this:

1. **Exposition** The basic idea on which the piece is built is known as the SUBJECT. This is stated by the first voice, entirely by itself. Subjects are usually fairly brief and always very striking.

Once the Subject has been made clear, a second voice enters and restates it. This time, however, it is in the *dominant* half of the key. In this new tonal region the 'subject' is known as the ANSWER.

The logic of calling the same idea first the Subject and then the Answer may be understood better by following an example:

Bach '48' Book I No. 16 in G minor

The 'Answer' does indeed sound like an answer to the Subject.

An Answer that repeats the Subject, interval for interval, is known as a 'Real Answer'. If it adjusts the intervals very slightly, as in the example above, it is known as a 'Tonal Answer'. These adjustments are made so as to preserve the feeling that the key in which the Fugue began is always present, even though the Answer touches on the dominant regions.

While the second voice states the Answer, the first voice continues against it – playing music that fits the Answer and yet has a character of its own. This new idea is known as the COUNTERSUBJECT.

An important feature of the Countersubject is that it must make good sense both

---

**Frescobaldi, Girolamo** Italian composer and organist, 1583–1643. After working in the Netherlands, where he published his first book of Madrigals (1608), he returned to Rome as organist of St Peter's (November 1608). He was renowned as an organist and his compositions for that instrument helped to create a style of organ music that became very influential. His many *ricercari* and *canzonas* are forerunners of the fugue, and together with his toccatas, etc. they give a very vivid idea of his abilities as a virtuoso.

**Frets** On a stringed instrument these are raised lines across the finger-board showing where the player should put his fingers to

**Girolamo Frescobaldi**
1583–1643

produce each note. The viol, lute, mandolin, guitar, and banjo have frets; the members of the violin family have none.

**Frottola** A kind of simple madrigal very popular in Italy in the late 15th and early 16th centuries. The music is repeated for each verse, and the different voices give pride of place to the soprano line, which carries the tune (in other words, it is not polyphonic in the way that a true madrigal is). Frottola tunes are always very rhythmic and have a strong dance-like pulse.

**Full close → Cadence**

*above* and *below* the Subject (Answer). The two strands are thus in Invertible Counterpoint. (→ **Counterpoint**)

The process is then repeated, with the third voice taking the Subject (in the tonic key) while the second takes the Countersubject and the first continues with new counterpoint. The fourth voice then enters with the Answer (dominant), the third takes the Countersubject, and the other two continue with appropriate counterpoint.

When all four voices have entered, the Exposition is said to be complete. But it slides without a break into:

2. **Middle entries** These consist of entries of the Subject, Answer, and Countersubject, marching purposefully through a series of new keys.

Each entry may perhaps be separated by short EPISODES of related material – moments when, as it were, the intensity of the musical argument is relaxed somewhat.

All kinds of contrapuntal devices may be used to add to the interest of this section. For example, the Subject may be stretched out in long notes (augmentation), or squeezed up in short notes (diminution). And in these versions it may be played against itself in its original form. Entries of Subject and Answer may be made to overlap in what is called STRETTO. Here is an example:

From bars 28–29

At last, however, the tonality moves towards the Tonic key and the Fugue slides smoothly into the:

3. **Final entries** This is a grand climax in which Subject and Countersubject triumphantly reassert the main key of the piece.

This final section frequently makes use of long held notes placed over or beneath the other moving parts. These are known as PEDALS and they add to the feeling of climax and excitement.

Fugues may be written for a group of individual instruments, such as a string quartet, or for voices in a choral piece, or for a keyboard instrument, such as the harpsichord, piano, or organ. Here are some famous examples:

For keyboard: Bach's *48 Preludes and Fugues*.
For voices: Beethoven's *Missa Solemnis*, the passage beginning 'Et vitam venturi'.
For orchestra: Bartók's *Music for Strings, Percussion and Celesta* (first movement).
For quartet: Mozart's *Adagio and Fugue in C* (K.546).
And even in opera: Verdi's *Falstaff* (final chorus).

A great deal of nonsense is talked about fugues. They may be difficult to write, but they are certainly not difficult to listen to. On the contrary, they are some of the most exciting things in the whole of music – amply repaying any slight demands they make on the listener's power of concentration.

**Full organ** When one sees this term on a piece of organ music it means that all the loud stops are to be used (Swell and Great coupled together, and perhaps another manual also).

**Fuoco** (It.) Fire. As in **con fuoco**, with fire.

**Furioso** (It.) Furious, in the sense of energetic and enthusiastic.

**Furore** (It.) Enthusiasm. Used to describe the enthusiastic reaction of an audience to a fine performance. Thus we can say that somebody's performance 'created a furore'.

**Fux, Johann** Austrian composer, 1660–1741. Though admired in his own day

**Johann Fux 1660-1741**
This prolific composer left over 20 operas and 50 masses.

as a Court composer in Vienna – particularly for his operas – he is mainly remembered for his method of teaching counterpoint, step by step, by means of 'species' (→ **Counterpoint**), which he explained (in Latin) in a book called *Gradus ad Parnassum* (1725). This very book *(Steps to Parnassus)*, or books based on it, has been used by most musicians during their years of study, and its usefulness has not diminished over the years.

**Fz.** Abbreviation for **Forzato**, 'forced', that is, strongly emphasized.

## G clef → Notes and notation

**Gabrieli, Andrea** Italian composer, c. 1520–86. Though he travelled extensively in Germany and Bohemia in his early years, he is associated mainly (1566 onwards) with the church of St Mark's, Venice. He wrote many madrigals and sacred works, and is particularly important for his experiments in combining choral and instrumental music. He was a pupil of Willaert and himself taught Sweelinck.

**Gabrieli, Giovanni** Italian composer, 1557–1612. He was Andrea Gabrieli's nephew and chief disciple. After spending several years in Munich he returned to Venice, where he eventually succeeded his uncle as organist of St Mark's (1586). He continued his uncle's experiments with combined choral and orchestral sound. Certain purely orchestral works, such as the famous *Sonata pian' e forte* (1597), are landmarks in the history of music – helping to bring into existence the 'concerto style' that dominated the 17th and early 18th centuries.

**Gade, Niels** Danish composer, 1817–90. He began his career as a violinist, but attracted attention with an overture, *Echoes of Ossian* (1840), and a Symphony in C minor (1841). He was given a government grant which enabled him to study in Leipzig, where he met and was much influenced by Mendelssohn. He wrote eight symphonies, six overtures, a Violin Concerto, and a number of cantatas, some of which, including the charming *Elverskud* (Fairy Spell) (1853), were very popular in England.

**NielsGade** 1817-1890
He was much influenced by Mendelssohn's works.

**Francesco Geminiani** 1680-1762

**Galant** (Fr.) An adjective used, in the sense of 'courtly' or 'polite', to describe a kind of pretty, elegant musical style that flourished in the mid-18th century – in the work of J. C. and C. P. E. Bach, for example.

**Galanteries** Any dances, or other movements, found in 17th- and 18th-century suites, other than the obligatory Allemande, Courante, Sarabande, and Gigue. The Minuet, Bourrée, Passepied, Chaconne, the Sinfonia, Prelude, are all 'galanteries'.

### Galliard → Pavan and Galliard

**Galop** This is a lively round dance of two beats to the bar.

**Gamelan** A type of orchestra found in Indonesia (and to some extent in Siam). The leader plays a RABAB (which has two strings and is related to the viol family), and there is usually a SULING (a type of bamboo flute) and a SELOMPRET (rather like an oboe). The rest of the orchestra consists of percussion instruments. This includes drums, various types of gong and xylophone, and a CHEMELPUNG – a member of the zither family. The effect is rich and intricate and has fascinated many Western composers, for example Debussy. Britten's ballet *The Prince of the Pagodas* (1957) contains passages which imitate the sound of the gamelan.

**Gamelan** These orchestras, which consist largely of tuned percussion instruments, vary considerably in size and composition. They are used in Indonesian state and religious ceremonies and also as an accompaniment to acting and puppetry. All the performers play from memory.

**Gamut**
1. Originally this was the name for one particular note, the G on the bottom line of the bass stave, which is still called 'Gamut G' (→ **Pitch**).
2. Then it came to be used with the meaning of 'scale' (compare French *gamme*).
3. And it also came to mean the whole range of musical sounds, from the lowest to the highest.

**Gardiner, Balfour** English composer, 1877–1950. He studied composition in Frankfurt and later devoted much of his private wealth to furthering the cause of English music. He was a friend of Gustav Holst. His own work was much influenced by folksong. Certain pieces, such as *Shepherd Fennel's Dance* (1911), became very popular.

**Gardner, John** English composer, b. 1917. He studied at Oxford University, then acted as a singing coach at Covent Garden (1946–52), taught at Morley College (becoming Director of Music in 1965) and at St Paul's Girls' School, from 1962. His music, which includes a fine Symphony No. 1 (1947), an opera *The Moon and Sixpence* (1957), and several important choral works, is traditional in style, tuneful, and enlivened by the influence of jazz.

**Gavotte** A French dance, with four beats to the bar. Each phrase begins on the third beat. Though not slow it is rather dignified and was very popular at the court of King Louis XIV. It is said to have originated among the Gavot peasants of the Dauphiné region of France.

Gavottes are frequently found in 18th-century suites. (→ also **Musette**)

**Gay, John** → **Beggar's Opera**

**Gedämpft** (Ger.) Deadened. Used musically to describe all forms of muting.

**Geige** (Ger.) Violin.

**Geminiani, Francesco** Italian violinist and composer, 1687–1762. His remarkable abilities as a virtuoso helped not only to popularize Corelli's concertos and sonatas, but the whole art of violin playing, about which he wrote an important book of instruction. He spent many years in London (1714–28, 1740–59) and Dublin (1728–40, 1759–62). His published work includes five sets of concertos, four sets of sonatas, and a number of trios.

**Gemshorn** Either (1) an organ stop, or (2) an ancient type of recorder made of chamois or goat horn.

**Generalpause** (Ger.) Everybody silent. A warning, often abbreviated to **G.P.**, used in musical scores to show that nobody is playing at that particular point.

**German,** (Sir) **Edward** English composer, 1862–1936. His real name was Edward

**Gemshorns** by Rainer Weber, Bayerbach.

German Jones. He studied at the Royal Academy of Music and then worked as a violinist and conductor in various London theatres. During this time he became known for his incidental music to plays (e.g. *Henry VIII*, 1892). After completing Sir Arthur Sullivan's last operetta (*The Emerald Isle*) he won great fame with operettas of his own, including *Merrie England* (1902) and *Tom Jones* (1907). Among his more ambitious works are two symphonies and a fine *Welsh Rhapsody* (1904).

**German Sixth → Chromatic chords**

**Gershwin →** page 148

**Gesualdo, Carlo** (Prince of Venosa) Italian composer, c. 1560–1613. Despite his noble birth he was a skilled lutenist and composer and between 1594 and 1611 published six books of madrigals, as well as a number of sacred works. Many of the later madrigals are extremely chromatic. His personal life was unhappy and in 1590 he caused his wife and her lover to be murdered – an action which, even at the time, seemed rather excessive.

**Gewidmet** (Ger.) Dedicated – in the sense of 'dedicated' to a particular person.

**Gibbons, Orlando** English composer, 1583–1625. He is the most distinguished of a very musical family and was born at Oxford, though he received his training at King's College, Cambridge. He came to London in about 1604 and was soon appointed organist of the Chapel Royal and, in 1619, became one of the King's private 'musicians for the virginalles'.

In 1623 he succeeded John Parsons as organist of Westminster Abbey. He died in Canterbury, where, as a member of the Chapel Royal, he had gone to await the arrival from France of Henrietta Maria on her way to marry King Charles I.

Gibbons wrote many important anthems, a set of 20 *Madrigals and Motets of five Parts: apt for Viols and Voyces* (1614), a number of fantasias for strings, and a great many dances, sets of variations, fancies, etc., for the harpsichord.

To judge by some of the words he set to music, and the way in which he set them, Gibbons was a melancholy man. His famous madrigal *The Silver Swan* is a good example of this side of his nature:

> *Farewell all joys!*
> *O Death, come close my eyes:*
> *More geese than swans now live,*
> *More fools than wise!*

**Orlando Gibbons**
1583–1625

# Gershwin

George Gershwin. American composer and pianist, 1898–1937. His parents were Russian immigrants living in New York. He began to study the piano seriously in 1912, and in the following years started to write popular songs. By 1919 he had achieved his first 'hit' with the song *Swanee*, which sold over two million copies.

Although he was soon established as a highly successful Broadway composer, Gershwin continued to take lessons in composition – first with Rubin Goldmark (1923), then (1926) with Henry Cowell, and finally with Joseph Schillinger (1932). In the meantime he gradually turned himself into the first composer to combine popular, jazz, and serious symphonic music into a new and convincing style.

Signs of this appear in 1922, with the one-act opera *Blue Monday*. Encouraged by the jazz band leader Paul Whiteman, Gershwin

**George Gershwin**
1898–1937 His only opera *Porgy and Bess*, a story of doomed love, was written for a Negro cast. It is indebted to jazz as well as Negro spirituals. Gershwin died at the age of 39 after an unsuccessful brain operation.

achieved his goal in 1924 with the *Rhapsody in Blue*. It was an instant and lasting success. A *Concerto in F*, for piano and orchestra, followed in 1923, and an orchestral tone-poem, *An American in Paris*, in 1928. His masterpiece, the opera *Porgy and Bess*, appeared in 1935.

Throughout this period Gershwin wrote individual songs, (mostly to lyrics by his brother Ira) music for films, and a number of shorter orchestral and piano works. His Broadway musicals include: *Lady be Good* (1924), *Oh, Kay* (1926), *Funny Face* (1927), *Girl Crazy* (1930), *Strike Up the Band* (1930), and *Of Thee I Sing* (1931).

Gershwin's music, whether it be individual songs like *The Man I love*, or complete symphonic scores, like the *Cuban Overture* (1932), is remarkably resourceful and imaginative. He is undoubtedly one of America's most important composers.

**Gibbs, Armstrong** English composer, 1889–1960. Educated at Cambridge University and the Royal College of Music, he wrote many choral works and songs which achieved considerable popularity among amateurs because of their simple tunefulness. He was particularly skilled in setting the words of Walter de la Mare. One of these settings, the song *Five Eyes* (1917), is still widely sung.

**Gigue** (in French), **Giga** (in Italian), **Jig** (in English).

A lively dance of Italian origin, written in some form of triple time – or even in 4/4, with triplets (the notes of a gigue tend to run along in groups of three). Gigues are usually in Binary Form, and there was a convention that the second part should be an upside-down version of the first – as in the gigue from Bach's Fourth French Suite:

Opening of 1st Section

Opening of 2nd Section

It was usual to end a dance suite with a gigue.

**Gilbert and Sullivan → Sullivan**

**'Dizzy' Gillespie** b.1917 American jazz trumpeter and band leader, with his unique trumpet.

**Gillespie, 'Dizzy'** American jazz musician, b. 1917. He was born in South Carolina and became famous in the 1940s for his brilliant ('dizzy') virtuoso trumpet playing. He formed his own band in 1945 and his style represents the peak of 'bebop'. His harmonic and rhythmic experiments were considerably in advance of their time.

**Ginastera, Alberto** Argentinian composer, b. 1916. He was trained at the National Conservatoire in Buenos Aires, graduating in 1938, and is now recognized as one of the foremost Latin American composers. He has written music of all kinds, including two piano concertos, and a massive choral work, *Turbae ad Passionem Gregorianem* (1974). His operas include *Don Rodrigo* (1964), *Bomarzo* (1967), and *Beatrix Cenci* (1971).

**Giocoso** (It.) Jokingly.

**Gioioso** (It.) Joyfully.

**Giordano, Umberto** Italian composer, 1867–1948. He studied at the Naples Conservatory and became known as an operatic composer of the *verismo* (Italian name for 'realism') school. His best known opera, still often performed, is *Andrea Chénier* (1896).

**Giusto** (It.) Exact. Found mainly in the direction **tempo giusto**, which can mean either 'exact time' or 'appropriate speed'.

**Glass harmonica** Musical glasses. The proper name is **armonica**. Instruments of this type have been known in the middle and far east for centuries, with cups made of pottery or glass. In Europe they were first treated as an amusing scientific toy, but began to be taken seriously in the middle of the eighteenth century. Gluck gave a concert in London in 1746, playing a concerto on 26 glasses; and Mozart wrote a quintet for armonica, flute, oboe, viola, and cello in 1791. The principle (known to any one who has played with empty glasses after a meal) is that if the rim of a good quality glass is gently stroked by a moistened finger it will emit a delicate, flute-like sound. By adding water to the glasses, or using glasses of different sizes and weights, a whole scale of notes can be set up. In about 1761 the American statesman Benjamin Franklin produced an improved version of the armonica, using a series of graded glass bowls fitted to a spindle. These were turned through a trough of water, the player applying his finger as required. Arranged in this way, the glass bowls were easier to get at, and the performance could be that much smoother. It was also now possible to play whole chords.

**Glass harmonica** The American statesman and scientist, Benjamin Franklin, playing his improved version of the musical glasses.

**Glazunov, Alexander** Russian composer, 1865–1936. He studied with Rimsky-Korsakov and produced the first of his eight symphonies when he was only 16. He is now remembered mainly for his ballets, *Raymonda* (1898) and *The Seasons* (1900), the Symphony No 6 in C minor, and the Violin Concerto in A minor.

Glazunov joined the staff of the St Petersburg Conservatory in 1900, became its Director in 1906, and helped to reorganize it as the Leningrad Conservatory after the Revolution. He was declared a 'People's Artist of the Republic' – somewhat prematurely, however, for in 1928 he left Russia, never to return.

**Alexander Glazunov** 1865–1936

**Glee** An exclusively English type of part-song, very popular in the 18th and early 19th centuries. It is unaccompanied and intended for male voices only (the male alto taking the top line), and contains a number of contrasting sections, each with different music. Though the individual parts move about, it is not very contrapuntal in style. Among the most important and interesting

glee-composers are: Samuel Webbe (1740–1816), Jonathan Battishill (1738–1801), William Beale (1784–1854), William Horsley (1774–1858), and Reginald Spofforth (1842–1900).

**Glee club** The first of the many English 'Glee Clubs' was founded in 1787 and met regularly in London until 1857. The gentlemen members and their guests wined and dined, sang glees and part-songs, and generally enjoyed themselves. Ladies were not allowed to attend the meetings. From 1790 the proceedings always began with Samuel Webbe's *Glorious Apollo*. William Byrd's canon *Non Nobis Domine* was always sung immediately after dinner. (→ **Catch club**)

The term was adopted in the 19th century by American university music clubs, and is still used. Their activities, however, now cover a much wider range of music-making, though singing still plays an important part. Many of these clubs originally came together to sing college songs, but gradually expanded their interests. One of the most famous is the Harvard University Glee Club, which began life as an all-male choir.

**Glière, Reinhold** Russian composer, 1875–1956. He studied in Kiev and Moscow (under Ippolitov-Ivanov) and later in Berlin. His first taste of success came in 1908 with a symphonic poem *The Sirens*.

After the Revolution he became very active in the organization and promotion of Soviet music. Many of his compositions reflect a rather narrow patriotism and have therefore not been widely performed outside his own country. He was a fine teacher and Prokofiev and Khachaturian were among his pupils.

**Glinka, Mikhail** Russian composer, 1804–57. He was born into a well-to-do family, studied music in a rather amateurish fashion, composed in fits and starts, and travelled to Italy (1830–33) to luxuriate in the operas of Bellini and Donizetti, whom he greatly admired.

In 1833, however, he began to study seriously and spent a year in Berlin under the celebrated theorist Siegfried Dehn. On returning to Russia he set about the task of creating a truly Russian kind of opera. His first attempt, *A Life for the Tsar* (1836), succeeded admirably and was greeted with enthusiasm. He followed it with an opera that was finer, though less pleasing to the public: *Ruslan and Ludmilla* (1842). These two works are now looked upon as the starting point of Russia's musical development, and Glinka is often described as 'the Father of Russian music'.

After the failure of *Ruslan and Ludmilla*, Glinka travelled in France and Spain, Germany and Poland, writing a number of orchestral works and many songs and piano pieces. He never settled to any work of major importance, however, and it is by his two operas that he is now remembered.

**Glissando** A purely musical term made out of the French verb *glisser* (to slide) and given an Italian ending. The correct Italian word is *strisciando*, but this is not used outside Italy.

A *glissando* is a rapid slide between two notes some distance apart. The notes in between are sounded in passing, but not lingered upon. On a piano or harp (etc.) the glissando takes the form of a rapid scale. On a bowed instrument or trombone, the slide is a genuine one – incorporating the smallest fraction of an interval, as well as the tones and semitones. A similar effect can be obtained with the voice. (→ **Portamento**)

**Glockenspiel** A percussion instrument consisting of a set of steel plates, arranged in a scale, which are struck by hand with small hammers of wood or metal. The sound is like a bell.

The glockenspiel originated in German military bands, where it was carried on a lyre-shaped frame, held on a rod vertically in front of the bandsman. Marching bands still use them.

At the end of the 19th century glockenspiels were improved by being set in a wooden box and provided with a keyboard, like a small piano. In this form the glockenspiel is known as a CELESTA. The first major work to make use of the celesta was Tchaikovsky's ballet *The Nutcracker* (1892), in 'The Dance of the Sugar Plum Fairy'.

**Gluck** → page 151

**Glyndebourne** Founded in 1934 by John Christie and his wife, the soprano Audrey Mildmay, at their manor house in Sussex, Glyndebourne Opera House has become world-famous for the standard of its productions and the excellence of its singers. Its first and most famous conductor and producer were Fritz Busch and Carl Ebert, whose Mozart performances were especially memorable.

**Mikhail Glinka**
1804–1857

**Glockenspiel** A form of keyboard-operated glockenspiel was used in the 18th century, notably by Handel in *Saul* and in Mozart's *The Magic Flute*. It had a harsher sound than the later *celesta*.

**Benny Goodman** b.1909
Although best-known as a jazz musician Goodman has been solo clarinettist with orchestra and chamber music ensembles. Aaron Copland's clarinet concerto and Bela Bartók's *Contrasts* were written for him.

**God Save the Queen** This must be one of the best known tunes in the world, for at least 20 countries have used it for their National Anthem. Great Britain, however, was the first to use it, and the first country ever to adopt a 'National Anthem' of any kind.

Its origins are obscure. It was probably first sung in public on 28 September 1745, at Drury Lane Theatre, as an act of defiance when the news came that the Young Pretender (Charles Edward Stuart, 'Bonnie Prince Charlie') had defeated the English at the battle of Prestonpans. But the tune certainly existed before this, though nobody knows for sure who composed it. In 1796 George Carey claimed that his father, the composer Henry Carey, had written it in 1740.

It makes an excellent National Anthem. It is easy to sing – for it lies within the range of most average voices – unlike the American National Anthem, 'The Star Spangled Banner'. It is out-of-the-ordinary, in that it has unusual phrase lengths: three phrases of two bars for the first half, balanced by four of two bars each for the second half. It is not excessively noisy and military in feeling – unlike the French National Anthem, the 'Marseillaise'. And, most important of all, it is short!

**Gong** → page 152

**Goodman, 'Benny'** American jazz musician, b. 1909. A leading virtuoso clarinet player and bandleader. His recordings of 'swing', made in 1934, helped to launch the new style of jazz playing. He made many successful tours with both large bands and small groups, and eventually became known as the 'King of Swing'. He also played classical music, and various composers wrote works especially for him – for example, Aaron Copland (Clarinet Concerto, 1948).

**Goossens,** (Sir) **Eugene** English composer and conductor, 1893–1962. The only composer member of a famous musical family. His father and grandfather were both conductors, his brother Adolphe was a horn player, his brother Leon is an outstanding oboist, and his sisters Sidonie and Marie are harpists. He himself was highly regarded as a rather avant-garde composer in the 1920s and 1930s, but his music is now seldom played. He went to Australia (1947–56) as Principal of the New South Wales Conservatory of Music and conductor of the Sydney Symphony Orchestra.

# Gluck

Christoph Willibald von Gluck. German composer, 1714–87.

There is some mystery about the details of Gluck's musical education and it seems likely that he was mainly self-taught. In 1737, however, he greatly impressed an Italian Prince who took him to Milan where he became a pupil of Sammartini and began, perhaps for the first time, to study seriously.

By 1741 he had produced his first opera, *Artaserse*, and its success led to invitations to write more. The 10 operas he wrote during the next four years are all in a style typical of Italian opera – that is to say, they are singers' operas, without much dramatic logic.

In 1745 Gluck left Italy and came to London, where he had some success as an opera composer (though not enough to impress Handel, who roundly said that Gluck knew less about counterpoint than his cook!). And in the years that followed he pursued a successful career, working for various theatres in Leipzig, Hamburg, Vienna, Prague, Naples, and Rome. His operas, during the whole of this time, were still conventional and musically un-remarkable.

The change came in 1762 with the production in Vienna of *Orpheus and Euridice*, in which he collaborated with the poet Ranieri Calzabigi. Opinions are somewhat divided about the part that each played in 'reforming' opera – for *Orfeo* signalled nothing less than a revolution in operatic methods – but it is generally thought that Calzabigi was the intellectual force behind Gluck.

The new work differed from the old Italian style of opera in that its plot was simpler and far more 'believable'. The music, too, is less artificial, less designed to flatter the singer's vanity, and much more appropriate to the dramatic action. In the same way, Gluck's orchestral writing is more carefully thought out, and something more than a mere accompaniment to the vocal line. In short: Gluck and Calzabigi made opera a more convincing expression of human emotions than it had been since the days of Monteverdi.

Though he did not immediately continue with his policy of 'reformed' opera, Gluck made a second attempt in 1767 with *Alceste*.

It was enormously successful in Vienna. A third opera, *Paris and Helen*, followed in 1770.

In 1773 Gluck went to Paris and there produced his first French 'reformed' opera, *Iphigenia in Aulis* (1773), only to become unwittingly involved in an artistic battle with Piccinni, who represented the traditional Italian style. His second French opera, *Iphigenia in Tauris*, appeared in 1779 and was very successful, but *Echo and Narcissus* (1779) failed miserably. Gluck, now rather ill, returned to Vienna where, after a series of strokes, he died.

**Christoph Willibald von Gluck** 1714-1787 This painting (1775) of the composer at the clavichord is by the French painter, J. S. Duplessis. Gluck wrote more than 45 stage works as well as instrumental pieces.

# Gong

A percussion instrument of indefinite pitch. It consists of a large metal plate (usually circular) which is hung on a stand and beaten with some kind of mallet (usually covered with felt or leather). Gongs are found all over the world and are of ancient origin. The earliest type consisted of a flat bronze plate, but later examples have a curved surface or a raised central boss. In Asian countries it is customary to have a whole set of gongs hung as a chime, either vertically on a frame, or horizontally in a wooden trough.

Gongs have been used in the orchestra since about the end of the 19th century. Those made in China are usually preferred to Turkish ones, and they vary in size from about 51 cm to 71 cm in diameter (the composer specifying large or small, according to the type of sound he requires). The orchestral gong is usually called by its French, Italian, and German name: the **Tam-tam →**.

**Gong** *Right* An orchestral gong of Chinese origin. It produces a sustained sound of indeterminate, or sometimes definite pitch.

*Below* Gongs in the Indonesian gamelan.

**Gospel song** The Gospel songs, and the particularly fervent style of singing them, were created by the American Negro slaves after they had been converted to Christianity. They are a marriage between nonconformist hymns and the negro's own work-song blues – for it was natural for the negro to sing his master's hymns in his own way, with rhythmic hand-clapping and foot-stamping as an accompaniment to a highly emotional vocal style. Gospel songs are often improvised during the service. A particularly joyful song is known as a 'Jubilee'. Gospel songs are one of the important ingredients that went into the creation of jazz.

**Goss,** (Sir) **John** English organist and composer, 1800–80. He was a chorister of the Chapel Royal and later its organist (1856). He was organist of St Paul's Cathedral (1838–72) and wrote a great many anthems, chants, and psalm-tunes, etc. His anthem, *If we believe*, was written for the funeral of the Duke of Wellington.

**Gottschalk, Louis Moreau** American pianist and composer, 1829–69. He studied in Paris and made an enormous impression as a pianist in a series of flamboyant tours in Europe and America. He organized 'monster' concerts in which he played and conducted his own very colourful com-

**Louis Moreau Gottschalk** 1829–1869

positions. His works were much influenced by Creole and Caribbean music (for example, the Symphony *La Nuit des Tropiques*, 1859). He wrote a very cheerful autobiography, *Notes of a Pianist*, which was published in 1881.

**Gould, Morton** American composer, b. 1913. He came to serious 'concert' music through success in writing 'popular' music for Broadway and the films. He has deliberately cultivated a very 'American' style, much influenced by jazz and blues, as the titles of his works show: *Swing Symphonietta* (1950), *Concerto for Tap Dancer and Orchestra* (1952), *Cowboy Rhapsody* (1944), etc.

**Gounod, Charles** French composer, 1818–93. He studied at the Paris Conservatoire and won the Grand Prix de Rome in 1839. During his period in Rome he composed three masses, and on returning to Paris seriously considered entering the priesthood.

It was, however, the theatre that eventually claimed him. His first opera, *Sapho*, appeared in 1851. His fourth opera, *Faust* (1859), brought him world-wide success and it has remained in the repertoire of most opera houses ever since – it is certainly one of the most tuneful and colourful 'grand operas' ever composed.

After *Faust* he wrote nine more works for the operatic stage, of which *Mireille* (1864) and *Roméo et Juliette* (1867) were the most successful. During the last years of his life, however, he turned once again to religion and devoted himself to the composition of the kind of sacred choral works that were much admired by the British public. Two of these works, the oratorios *The Redemption* (1881) and *Mors et Vita* (1885) were first heard at the Birmingham Festival. One of his masses, the *St Cecilia Mass* (1855), is still often performed.

**G.P.** → **Generalpause**

**Grace-notes, Graces** → **Ornaments and grace-notes**

**Gradus ad Parnassum** → **Fux**

**Grainger, Percy** Australian composer and pianist, 1882–1961. He was first taught by his mother, an excellent pianist but formidable lady who very much directed the course of his career. From 1894 he studied in Leipzig under James Kwast and Busoni. He made his London debut as a pianist in 1902 and thereafter made many successful tours in different parts of the world.

Grainger became known as a composer in 1912, with such popular pieces for string orchestra as *Mock Morris* and *Shepherd's Hey*. Like many of his works they were heavily influenced by folksong, of which he had become an avid collector.

In 1914 he settled in America and there pursued a colourful and somewhat eccentric career as pianist and composer. Many of his works experiment with unusual instruments and unusual ways of writing for orthodox instruments – often with very imaginative results. In 1935, after a successful tour of Australia, he founded a Percy Grainger Museum in the grounds of the University of Melbourne (his native city). Today it contains a vast quantity of objects connected with his life and career – for he preserved literally everything, from manuscripts to old clothes!

**Gramophone** → page 154

**Granados, Enrique** Spanish composer, 1867–1916. He studied in Barcelona and later in Paris, returning to Spain in 1889 to a successful career as a composer and pianist. Though he wrote several operas, he is mainly known for his piano music – particularly the two books of pieces, *Goyescas*, named after scenes from the paintings of the great Spanish artist Goya. In this collection he achieved a truly Spanish style.

**Charles Gounod**
1818–1893

**Enrique Granados** 1867-1916 Spanish composer and pianist, a pupil of Pedrell, he founded a school of music in Barcelona.

Granados and his wife died tragically when the boat in which they were returning from America was torpedoed by German submarines.

**Grandioso** (It.) Nobly.

**Grand opera** Although the term is used very loosely to describe almost any kind of serious opera, it really applies only to a particular type that was developed in Paris during the 19th century. The true 'grand opera' has five acts, and is in every sense spectacular. The subject matter is always tragic, and often based on some historical event. Considerable use is made of the chorus, and there is always a lengthy ballet sequence. Stage sets and costumes are likely to be particularly striking and extravagant, and the solo parts call for a virtuoso technique. Meyerbeer was perhaps the most important composer of this type of opera, and many of his contemporaries felt his influence. The most frequently performed 'grand operas' still in the regular repertoire are Verdi's *Aida* (1871) and Gounod's *Faust* (1859).

**Grand orchestre** (Fr.) Full orchestra.

**Grand orgue** (Fr.) Great organ (as distinct from swell organ, etc.). Sometimes used to describe a pipe organ. ( **Harmonium** → )

**Graun, Carl** German composer, 1704–59. He was the most important of three musical brothers and became Music Director to Frederick the Great in 1740, for whom he established a flourishing Italian Opera company in Berlin.

**Grave** (It., Fr.) Slow and solemn.

**Grazia** (It.) Grace. Also **grazioso**, gracefully.

**Great Stave** If the stave with the treble clef and the stave with the bass clef are pushed closer together it will be seen that one middle line (C) is sufficient to unite them into a series – the Great Stave (see left)
Though all the different clefs can be located on the Great Stave, it is obviously not at all easy to read from. 10 spaces and 11 lines are too many for the eye to take in, so we divide them into groups of 4 spaces and 5 lines.

Separate

United

C Clefs   G Clef   F Clefs

| Soprano Voice | Mezzo Soprano Voice | Alto Voice, Viola, etc. | Tenor Voice, Tenor Trombone, etc. | Soprano Voice, Violin etc. | Baritone Voice | Bass Voice, Cello etc. |

# Gramophone (Record Player)

The first practical machine of this kind was invented by the American Thomas Edison in 1877. It was a 'dictating machine' which recorded spoken messages on a wax cylinder. The process was quite simple: you spoke into a tube, at the end of which there was a membrane that would vibrate in sympathy with the pressure changes caused by the voice. Attached to this membrane was a needle which also vibrated and scratched a wave-pattern on a wax cylinder which revolved, and, at the same time, moved sideways. When the process was reversed, the wax impression of the wave-pattern would vibrate the needle and the membrane, and the recorded sound could be heard again – faint, but unmistakable. The first words that Edison spoke into his invention were 'Mary had a little lamb'!

This kind of recording method, which translated pressure changes into straight wave-patterns cut in grooves on wax, is known as ACOUSTIC RECORDING. It works effectively – but only when the speaker is near enough and speaking loudly enough to agitate the membrane fully.

The next step in Acoustic Recording came in 1888, when Emil Berliner, an American of German origin, patented a way of recording on flat shellac discs which revolved on a turn-table. It now became possible to take any number of copies of a recording, simply by using a master-copy as a 'stamper'.

Although the methods of acoustic recording were refined over the years, they remained more or less as Edison and Berliner had invented them until 1925, when the processes of ELECTRICAL RECORDING came in.

In the meantime, recordings reached a surprisingly high standard, despite the physical problems the method caused. Perhaps the greatest leap forward came in 1913, when the HMV company issued the first recording of a complete symphony. This was Beethoven's Fifth Symphony, played by the Berlin Philharmonic con-

**Early developments** The gramophone was initially regarded as a 'talking' machine and the musical possibilities of the new invention were not fully realized until the 1890s. From then onwards many famous opera singers recorded solos. Music-hall songs and band music were also recorded.

Speaking into the phonograph . . .

. . . and making it talk

Berliner's gramophone

**How a record is made** Separate component sounds from the microphones are recorded on different tracks of a multi-track tape recorder. Up to 24 channels can be recorded on a single tape. This is then fed into a mixing unit, **1** which reduces these channels to the two needed for stereo reproduction. Editing and re-recording is carried out at this stage to get the best possible results. The record is made from this tape which sends electrical signals to the cutting head **2** on the disc. The disc then goes through various production processes **3–10**. The record is then cooled and checked for quality before packaging.

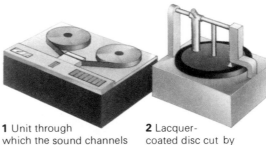
**1** Unit through which the sound channels are mixed' and edited.

**2** Lacquer-coated disc cut by electrically vibrated stylus.

**3** Cut lacquer disc spray sprayed with silver to accept electroplating.

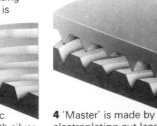
**4** 'Master' is made by electroplating cut lacquer disc.

**5** Master sprayed with colloid separator and nickel stripped off.

**6** 'Positive' replica electroformed from the master.

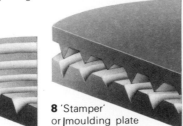
**7** Positive is sprayed with colloid to give a fine separating layer.

**8** 'Stamper' or moulding plate electroformed from positive.

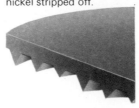
**9** Stamper formed at the centre and edge to fit in the record press.

**10** Another stamper for flip side sandwiches vinyl material.

Phonograph advertisement

ducted by Arthur Nikisch, and it was issued on eight single sides. Records and recording suddenly became a dignified medium for the serious musician – something that neither he nor the music-loving public could treat any longer merely as an amusing toy.

Electrical recording confirmed the importance of the gramophone record. Sounds were now converted into electrical energy, which could be amplified and controlled. Artists no longer had to crowd round a large recording horn and shout down it. Individuals, and whole orchestras, could be placed comfortably and naturally in front of as many microphones as were needed, and the final result could be balanced by skilled engineers.

There was still one problem, however. The standard recording played at 78 revolutions per minute. Each side of the large 12in. record lasted approximately four minutes. A symphony, for example, could only be heard in seven or eight sections – with an interlude between each while the record was turned over or changed.

In 1948 the Columbia Gramophone Company of America introduced the first 'long playing' record. It revolved at a much slower speed ($33\frac{1}{2}$ revolutions per minute) and was recorded in much narrower grooves, called 'micro-grooves'. Each side could now take nearly half an hour's music.

At much the same time, a German invention made during the Second World War, whereby sound was recorded on long strips of magnetized wire, or steel tape (and later on a plastic ribbon coated with metallic oxide), began to come onto the market. This was the TAPE RECORDER. Its advantages are obvious.

The importance of recording can scarcely be over-emphasized. Not only is it now possible to preserve the work of great artists, but, perhaps most important of all, it means that everyone can possess a library of great music from all over the world and from every period of musical history.

Recordings have undoubtedly changed, and improved our standards of performance. And they have certainly raised our standards of appreciation. In less than a hundred years, the record has left its mark on the whole art of music.

**Charles Griffes**
1884-1920

**George Grove**
1820-1900

**Gregorian chant** The name given to the great collection of plainsong used by the Roman Church since early Christian times. It consists of music for the Mass (and for other occasional services, such as Baptism), and music for the daily Hours of Divine Service. It is named after Pope Gregory I (St Gregory, c. 540–604). ( → **Church service**)

**Grieg** → page 156

**Griffes, Charles** American composer, 1884–1920. He studied in Berlin, returning to America in 1907 to teach in New York. He was particularly interested in oriental music and his impressionistic style shows its influence. His music includes the symphonic poem *The Pleasure-Dome of Kubla Khan* (1916), an important piano piece, *The White Peacock* (1915), *Poem for Flute and Orchestra* (1918), and a fine *Piano Sonata* (1918). His early death was a great loss to American music.

**Grofé, Ferde** American composer, 1892–1972. He worked first as a viola player, and then as pianist and conductor in theatres and cafés. He joined Paul Whiteman's band as pianist and arranger, in 1920, and won fame in 1924 when he orchestrated Gershwin's *Rhapsody in Blue*. His own compositions include the popular *Grand Canyon Suite* (1931).

**Ground bass** → page 156

**Group** A term sometimes applied to two or more notes which are joined together by their stems (  or etc).

**Grove, (Sir) George** English musician, 1820–1900. Like a great many Victorians, Grove was an extremely energetic man, interested in a wide variety of things including civil engineering and exploration.

To musicians, however, he is principally known as the founder and editor of Grove's *Dictionary of Music and Musicians*, which first appeared in 1879, as an authority on Beethoven, Schubert, and Mendelssohn, as the first Director of the Royal College of Music (1882), and as the man who, with Arthur Sullivan, unearthed the 'lost' music that Schubert wrote for *Rosamunde*. He was also one of the first musicians to write 'programme notes' – for the Crystal Palace concerts.

# Grieg

Edvard Grieg. Norwegian composer, 1843–1907. He was born in Bergen into a fairly well-to-do family of Scottish descent and received his first lessons from his mother, who was a good amateur pianist.

He began to compose when he was nine, and in 1858, when he was 15, so impressed the famous Norwegian violinist Ole Bull that his parents decided to send him to study at the Leipzig Conservatory.

Though he was not particularly happy in Leipzig he remained there until 1862. On returning to Bergen he gave a very successful concert in which he played his own Opus 1 – a group of four piano pieces. In the following year he went to Copenhagen and began a course of study with the Danish composer Niels Gade.

During his two years in Copenhagen he became engaged to his cousin, the singer Nina Hagerup, whom he married in 1867. He also began to discover the folk music of his own country, and, urged on by an ardent young Nationalist composer Rikard Nordraak, soon decided that his own music should reflect its special qualities. A group of piano pieces, *Humoresques* (1865), was the first fruit of this new attitude to music.

Grieg returned to Norway in 1866, living first in Christiania, (now called Oslo) where

**Edvard Grieg**
**1843–1907**

he conducted the Harmonic Society and gave music lessons. Thereafter his life was a fairly settled pattern of composition, recitals (in which he was partnered by his wife), and the organization and direction of concerts. Little by little his fame grew, not only in his own country, but in Europe generally. He undertook extensive concert tours, including several visits to England.

Certain works brought him great fame – the *Piano Concerto in A minor* (1869) for example, the *Holberg Suite* (1885), and the incidental music he wrote for Ibsen's play *Peer Gynt* (1876). His many piano pieces, which include ten volumes of *Lyric Pieces*, and his songs (he wrote nearly 150), also helped to spread an enthusiasm for his music among amateurs. He may fairly be said to be the first Scandinavian composer to have enjoyed a truly international reputation.

Apart from the Piano Concerto, most of Grieg's music consists of short pieces. Like many Nationalist composers, Grieg used the example of his country's folksong to enable him to break away from the overwhelming influence of German music. In doing so he helped to enrich the whole of music with the flavour of a very distinct and agreeable personality.

# Ground bass

This is a type of variation composition that was particularly popular in the 17th and 18th centuries. In it, the same short bass tune is repeated over and over again, while the music above changes and grows to a climax. On the right is an example from the opening of a Ground by Purcell. A similar method of musical construction is found in the **Chaconne** and **Passacaglia**.

Henry Purcell

**Gruppetto** (It.) Turn. (→ **Ornaments and grace-notes**)

**Guarneri family** The members of this family of violin makers were active in Cremona, and other towns of North Italy, from about 1645 to 1744. The first of them, Andrea Guarneri (c. 1626–98), was a pupil of Nicola Amati (→ **Amati family**). The last, and greatest, of them was Giuseppe Guarneri (1698–1744), who is sometimes called Giuseppe del Gesù, to distinguish him from his father. Guarneri violins, like those of Amati and Stradivari, are prized possessions.

**Ivor Gurney** 1890-1937
He also composed piano and orchestral music.

**Gurney, Ivor** English composer and poet, 1890–1937. He was born in Gloucester and trained at the Royal College of Music. He served as a private in the First World War, but was invalided out in 1917. He resumed his studies, and then tried to make a career as a composer, but suffered a breakdown in 1922 and spent the rest of his life in a mental home. Gurney wrote many fine songs, of which about 80 are published, and a vast amount of poetry, largely unpublished.

**Gusto** (It.) Taste. Also **gustoso**, tasteful; and **con gusto**, with taste.

# Guitar

The Spanish guitar is the best known member of a family of instruments that includes the lute, mandolin, and gittern, etc. It is of ancient origin, and may have come from Egypt. Its shape is similar to that of the violin, but it has a flat back and belly, and is plucked (or 'picked') with the fingers.

The modern guitar has six strings, tuned to E, A, d, g, b, and e[1]. Its music is written an octave higher than it sounds. Owing to the prevalence of the many varieties of electric guitar in the various fields of 'pop' and jazz music, it is perhaps necessary nowadays to refer to the traditional guitar

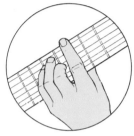

**Fingering** *Above* The classical guitarist stops the sixth string with his index finger (*top*). The steel guitar has a narrower finger board and can be stopped with the thumb (*bottom*).

*Left* **Andrés Segovia** b.1893, the Spanish guitarist who is largely responsible for the revival of interest in the classical guitar during the 20th century.

*Below* **German four-course guitar** of the 16th century.

as the 'Acoustic Guitar', and so avoid misunderstandings. Though electric guitars can sound like acoustic guitars, they also have a much wider range of sound and colour – so much so that they are better considered as a quite new sort of instrument.

In recent years the acoustic guitar has been re-established as a serious concert instrument through the genius of such players as Andrés Segovia (b. 1893). It has always been a favourite instrument of folk musicians, and because of this it played an important part in the early history of jazz. (→ **Electric instruments; Jazz**)

**Acoustic guitar** *Above* American folk-singer John Henry Fortescue, known as 'Guitar Shorty', plays a bottle-neck guitar at Elm City, N. Carolina in 1972.

**Electric guitar** *Left* Jimi Hendrix, American pop musician and guitarist, at a Royal Albert Hall concert, 1967. Hendrix, who died in 1970, was noted for his strident style of singing.

H The German name for the note we call B, the note we call B flat being in the German language called B. (→ **Alphabet pieces**)

**Habanera** A type of song and dance now associated with Spain, though, as its name suggests (Habanera: Havana), it came from Cuba. It is in 2/4 time and has a strong characteristic rhythm: ♩♫♪ | ♩♫♪ As a dance it is slow and rather oriental in character.

**Hadley, Patrick** English composer, 1899–1973. Educated at Winchester College, Cambridge University, and the Royal College of Music. He was Professor of Music at Cambridge, 1946–63. He wrote only a small quantity of music, rather in the style of Vaughan Williams. His choral works, *The Trees so High* (1931), *The Hills* (1946), and *Fen and Flood* (1955), have been much admired.

**Halévy, Jacques** French composer, 1799–1862. He was a pupil of Cherubini and became a very successful operatic composer, working mainly in Paris. His masterpiece, *La Juive* (1835), is a typical 'Grand' opera, but he was equally at home composing in a lighter style – for example, the operatic comedy *L'Éclair* (1835).

**Half close** → **Cadence**

**Half-note, Half-rest** → **Notes and notation**

**Hallé,** (Sir) **Charles** German-born pianist and conductor, 1819–95. He settled in Manchester in 1848 and later formed the famous Hallé Orchestra which gave regular concerts from 1858 onwards. In London,

**Jacques Halévy** 1799-1862 This composer wrote over 30 operas in French and one, *The Tempest*, in Italian. Amongst his pupils was Bizet, his future son-in-law.

**Charles Hallé** 1819-1895

**A caricature of Eduard Hanslick,** 1825-1904.

**Hardanger fiddle** This decorative Norwegian instrument is held under the chin in the same way as the violin.

however, he was best known as a pianist, particularly for his performances of Beethoven sonatas, and Chopin. He also helped to found the Royal Manchester College of Music (1893) and was its first Principal.

**Hallelujah Chorus** Though there are many such 'choruses of praise', *the* Hallelujah Chorus is the one that brings Part II of Handel's *Messiah* to a triumphant close. At its first performance in London (1743), King George II rose to his feet, followed by the entire audience. This practice is still carried out – though whether out of respect for Handel, religion, or royal precedent is by no means clear.

**Halling** A vigorous Norwegian folk dance, which takes its name from the Hallingdal region between Oslo and Bergen. It is something like a Scottish reel, and may be descended from it. The music is generally in 2/4 time and is typically played on the Hardanger fiddle.

**Handbells** → **Bells and bell-ringing**

**Handy, W. C.** American jazz composer, 1873–1958. William Christopher Handy was born in Alabama, where his father was a Methodist preacher and strongly opposed to the idea of a career in music. He trained as a teacher, but learned to play the cornet and eventually formed his own band in 1903. His own compositions include the famous 'Memphis Blues' (1911), and even more famous 'St Louis Blues' (1914). Though he is often called 'The Father of the Blues', he did not invent them, but was certainly a pioneer in composing them as a type of popular song.

**Handel** → page 160

**Hanslick, Eduard** Austrian music critic, 1825–1904. Hanslick lectured at the University of Vienna from 1856, becoming a professor in 1870. In the meantime he was extremely influential as a music critic for the *Wiener Zeitung* (1848–49) and *Die Presse* (1855–64). He wrote many books and became notorious in some circles for his resistance to the 'new music' of Liszt and Wagner. He was, on the other hand, an ardent champion of Schumann and Brahms.

**Hardanger fiddle** The Norwegian folk violin. It is somewhat smaller than the ordinary violin and besides the usual four playing strings (tuned, however, to A, D, A, E, and not to G, D, A, E) it has four sympathetic strings underneath them (tuned to D, E, F♯, A). These vibrate when music is played on the upper strings. It is said to have been invented by a Hardanger schoolteacher in about 1650.

**Harmonic minor scale → Scales**

**Harmonica** A small free-reed instrument commonly called the Mouth Organ. It consists of a small rectangular box with apertures in the sides. The player breathes through these, moving the box from side to side so as to breathe through the right hole, and his breath vibrates a small metal reed set inside the instrument. A sound emerges whether the player blows or sucks. Each aperture leads to two reeds of the same pitch,

**Harmonica** This example is a Blues harmonica.

one of which operates on blowing and the other on sucking. Mouth organs began to be manufactured in Europe in the 19th century, but they were known in Asia and China for many hundreds of years (in China as far back as 1100 B.C.).

**Harmonics** → below

**Harmonium** → page 163

**Harmony** → page 164

**Harp** → page 167

**Harpsichord** → page 168

# Harmonics

Voices and instruments produce their sounds when something is made to vibrate – for example, the stretched string of a violin.

What actually takes place, however, is extremely complex. For not only is there a main vibration (of the whole string), but also a series of lesser vibrations. These are the 'harmonics'.

Thus a string not only vibrates along its whole length, but also in halves, thirds, quarters, fifths, and so on into infinity (at least, in theory). The note we hear is that of the whole vibrating string. But the vibrating halves, thirds, quarters and fifths, etc., also produce their own notes, and though these are largely swallowed up in the sound of the main note, they are sufficiently strong to add 'colour' to it. We call these lesser notes 'overtones' or 'partials'.

This is why we can distinguish between the sounds of different voices or instruments. Each emphasizes different harmonics, and each therefore has its characteristic colour.

Harmonics always follow the same mathematical progression. The whole vibrating length produces the FIRST HARMONIC, or fundamental note. The vibrating halves produce a SECOND HARMONIC, which is always an octave above the fundamental note. The vibrating thirds produce a THIRD HARMONIC, which is always an octave and a half above the fundamental.

Here is the HARMONIC SERIES on the note C:

Note that the common chord (C E G in this case) occurs very early on in the series – one reason why it sounds so natural to our ears.

On certain instruments it is possible to isolate these sounds by damping down the fundamental note. For example, if a violin player bows an open string and touches it lightly at the half way point, the sound of the second harmonic can be clearly heard (as a delicate silvery note) instead of the fundamental. Touched a third of the way along, the same string will produce the third harmonic, and so on.

String players describe harmonics produced from a stopped string as ARTIFICIAL HARMONICS. Those from an open string are NATURAL HARMONICS. In notation a small circle is placed above the note that is to be played as a harmonic.

In the early days of brass instruments, before the invention of crooks and valves, the only notes that could be played were those of the harmonic series appropriate to the length of tube being used. The player picked out these notes by varying the pressure of his breath and the tightness of his lips.

Although the words 'harmonics', 'overtones', and 'partials' are frequently used as if they were the same, they have slightly different meanings. Strictly speaking, 'harmonics' refers to the different vibrating lengths that produce a sound. 'Overtones' and 'partials' are the actual notes. The confusion has come about because string players always refer to their 'overtones' as 'harmonics', and the habit has spread.

# Handel

George Frideric Handel. Born at Halle, in Saxony, in 1685, and died in London in 1759.

## 1. Handel's life

Handel's father was a prosperous barber-surgeon who, as a hard-headed business man, not unreasonably had doubts about allowing his son to become a musician. However, the boy's obvious talent brought favourable comment from the Duke of Saxe-Weissenfels and from 1693 he was able to study with Friedrich Zachow, an organist and excellent all-round musician then in Halle. Three years later he attracted the interest of the Elector of Brandenburg, who wanted to send him to Italy for further study. This time his father refused to co-operate and insisted that the boy should concentrate on his general studies, with a view to becoming a lawyer.

Though Handel's father died in 1697, he still followed his wishes and in 1702 enrolled at the University of Halle as a law student. He remained there for a year – and then his resolution broke. For better or worse he would be a musician.

He went first to Hamburg, where he found employment in the orchestra of Reinhardt Keiser's famous opera house, eventually becoming its conductor. His own first opera, *Almira*, appeared in 1705 with great success and was followed by another, *Nero*, in the same year. It was now clear that Handel was a composer of exceptional talent.

In 1706 he left Hamburg and went to Italy. For a composer anxious to shine in opera this was a natural thing to do, for the Italian operatic style dominated the whole of Europe. He spent four years there, in Florence, Rome, Naples, and Venice. Everywhere he went he triumphed: his operas, in the Italian style, conquered even the Italians themselves.

Having learned everything Italy had to teach him, Handel now returned to Germany (1710) to take up the post of Kapellmeister to the Elector of Hanover – on the understanding that he would be allowed to visit England that year.

He could scarcely have arrived in London at a more favourable moment. Italian opera was all the rage. He was immediately commissioned to write one, and in two weeks had completed *Rinaldo*. It

**George Frideric Handel** 1685–1759 This engraving of the composer by Jacob Houbracken is dated 1738.

**Chapel of the Foundling Hospital, London** Handel, who was a Governor of the Hospital, directed eleven performances of *Messiah* in order to raise money for the charity. The oratorio was first performed at Neal's Music Hall in Dublin in 1742.

was performed in February 1711 and proved a great success.

In June, however, Handel was obliged to return to Hanover and there settled to a rather less exciting musical routine. But in the autumn of 1712 he came back to London – for it was now obvious to him that this was where fame and fortune lay.

As it happened, his first new opera for London, *Teseo* (1713), was not a success. But he was asked to write music to celebrate

Queen Anne's birthday, and later to celebrate the Peace of Utrecht, and was duly rewarded with a pension of £200 a year.

This time he cheerfully overstayed his leave from Hanover, thereby annoying his employer, the Elector. But in 1714 Queen Anne died, and now Georg, Elector of Hanover, became George I of England!

At first he was not disposed to forgive his errant Kapellmeister. But gradually the rift was mended. The pension from Queen Anne was continued, and then doubled. The Princess of Wales also paid Handel a further £200 a year to teach her children. He was therefore a comparatively wealthy

**Handel manuscript** This page is from Handel's score of *Messiah*. The words from the Bible were compiled by Charles Jennens, a Leicestershire squire and friend of the composer's.

**Handel's opera,** *Flavio* This scene from one of the composer's lesser known operas shows the famous Handel singers, Senesino a castrato (*left*), Cuzzoni and Berenstadt. The opera was first performed in London in 1723.

man – or would have been had he not decided to invest in operatic production on his own account.

His first venture was as a member of an operatic company known as the Royal Academy of Music, for whom he quickly wrote a number of successful operas. But by now London had become a battlefield for operatic rivalries. The Italian composer Giovanni Bononcini had been set up as a counter-attraction, and the different singers engaged by the two composers only added to complications. Matters were not improved when, in 1728, John Gay produced his ballad opera *The Beggar's Opera* – a direct and enormously successful satire on the absurdities of Italian opera. By June 1728, the Academy was bankrupt.

Handel promptly decided to become his own manager. After a shaky start he slowly began to retrieve his financial position. It was now, however, that he decided to revive a Masque he had written in 1720 for the Duke of Chandos. It was called *Esther*, and because it was based on a Bible story he decided not to stage it, but give it in concert form. It proved extremely successful, and it now dawned upon Handel that dramatic oratorios were something that the English might prefer to opera.

Though he continued to write operas, he now began to produce oratorios as well. Their success helped to keep him afloat – though in 1738 he came near to being imprisoned for debt.

In 1741 Handel visited Dublin, taking with him a score he had written in the space of three weeks. It was called *Messiah*, and it proved to be enormously successful. From now on he abandoned all attempts to write opera, and concentrated solely on the composition of oratorios – which were themselves a kind of opera, even though they were not staged.

The last years of Handel's life were tranquil, though marred by increasing blindness. When he died he was mourned by the entire nation, which had come to regard him as an English composer, just as he regarded himself as an Englishman.

## 2. His music

Unlike Bach, Handel was a man of the theatre and therefore accustomed to the necessity of making an immediate dramatic impact. Mozart said of him 'When he

strikes, he strikes like a thunderbolt': and this is true. Handel's ideas are always sturdy and bold. They grip the attention immediately. He was able, as certain choruses in the great oratorios show, to command the most monumental effects. Yet he could also write music of extreme delicacy – for example, the 'Nightingale' chorus in *Solomon*. He could write counterpoint as complex and ingenious as Bach's, but he could also write melodies of great power, sweetness, and simplicity.

### 3. Summary of Handel's main works

(a) Operas include:

| | |
|---|---|
| *Almira* | 1705 |
| *Rinaldo* | 1711 |
| *Giulio Cesare* | 1724 |
| *Rodelinda* | 1725 |
| *Berenice* | 1737 |
| *Serse* | 1738 |
| *Deidamia* | 1741 |

(b) Oratorios include:

| | |
|---|---|
| *Israel in Egypt* | 1739 |
| *Messiah* | 1741 |
| *Samson* | 1743 |
| *Belshazzar* | 1745 |
| *Judas Maccabaeus* | 1747 |
| *Solomon* | 1749 |
| *Theodora* | 1750 |
| *Jephtha* | 1752 |

(c) Choral music includes:

| | |
|---|---|
| 11 Chandos Anthems | 1717–20 |
| 4 Coronation Anthems for King George II | 1727 |

Various secular works, such as:

| | |
|---|---|
| *Acis and Galatea* | 1720 |
| *Alexander's Feast* | 1736 |

**Fireworks Music** This structure was built in Green Park, London, for the performance of Handel's Royal Fireworks Music in Celebration of the Treaty of Aix-la-Chapelle in 1749 which ended the War of the Austrian Succession. It was burned down during the performance.

| | |
|---|---|
| *Semele* | 1744 |
| *Hercules* | 1745 |

(d) Orchestral music includes:

| | |
|---|---|
| 'Water' Music | 1717 |
| 'Fireworks' Music | 1749 |
| 12 Concerti Grossi (Op 6) | 1739 |

Handel also wrote many cantatas, oboe concertos, trio sonatas, vocal solos, church music, and music for the harpsichord.

### 4. Handel the man

Handel, as the details of his career suggest, was a man of enormous courage and determination. Like his father, he was shrewd and practical and remarkably independent. At a time when it was customary to lean heavily on patronage, he struck out on his own and, despite many changes of fortune, died a wealthy man.

He is said to have had a lively sense of humour, though he was always too busy to be sociable in the sense of spending a lot of time with friends. He collected paintings, and, it is said, was inclined to over-eat. He spoke four languages (German, Italian, French, and English), and was at home in setting at least three of them to music. He never married – probably because he was too deeply involved in the day-to-day flurry of his artistic life to have time for domesticity. In his own day he was regarded with awe, as being rather larger than life.

**Handel in old age** This painting of the composer by Thomas Hudson was made in 1756, three years before Handel's death.

# Harmonium

A member of the Reed Organ family, particularly popular in the 19th century when it developed through the experiments of a number of makers, of whom the most important was Alexandre Dubain (1809–77). It has a keyboard like that of a piano, and two pedals which work a pair of bellows. These pump air through a set of vibrators made of thin slips of brass or steel, known as 'reeds'. The larger instruments have several sets of reeds which can be brought into use by a series of 'stops', similar to those on an organ. An 'expression' stop cuts out the air reservoir and connects the reeds directly to the bellows, thus enabling the player to modify the tone by the way in which he pedals – increasing or decreasing the pressure to make the sound swell or fade. The dynamics can also be altered by means of a 'knee swell' – a flap of wood which can be moved by the player's knees, and which opens or shuts a venetian blind at the back of the organ. (→ **Organ**)

The AMERICAN ORGAN, or CABINET ORGAN, is very similar to the harmonium, but whereas in the harmonium the air is *blown* through the reeds, in the American organ it is *sucked* through them. The tone of the American organ is somewhat softer and more organ-like than the harmonium, but it has less variety. Early versions were known as melodeons, but the American organ as we know it today dates from 1860.

**American organ** This late 19th-century advertisement is aimed at the domestic market. This instrument was easier to play than the harmonium but had less variety of tone. With the introduction of smaller electric organs its popularity declined.

**Harris, Roy** American composer, b. 1898. He was born in Oklahoma and did not decide to become a composer until he was about 24. He then studied in Los Angeles, and later in Paris with Nadia Boulanger. He began to make an impression in 1934, when his First Symphony was performed.

International success came in 1939 with his *Third Symphony*, which is now recognized as a 'classic' of American music. Harris has written nine symphonies and a *Symphony for Voices* (1936), as well as many shorter orchestral works, concertos, chamber music, and choral works. His musical style is polyphonic, very rhythmic, and largely tonal. He is one of the most important American composers of his generation.

**Harty,** (Sir) **Hamilton** Irish composer and conductor, 1879–1941. He began his London career as an accompanist, but was appointed conductor to Manchester's Hallé Orchestra in 1920, where he remained until 1933. Thereafter he conducted the London Symphony Orchestra and was responsible for introducing the work of many English composers. His own music was romantic and fairly conventional. It includes a tone-poem, *With the Wild Geese* (1910), and a choral work, *The Mystic Trumpeter* (1913).

**Hauptwerk** (Ger.) Great Organ.

**Hautbois, Hautboy** → **Oboe family**

**Hawkins,** (Sir) **John** English musical historian, 1719–89. Though he was a lawyer and a magistrate he is chiefly remembered for his five-volume *History of Music*, which was published in 1776. He was a friend of Handel and Dr Johnson, but was not universally admired, for he appears to have been very quarrelsome.

# Harmony

1. Whenever two or more notes are sounded together they combine to make a vertical effect known as *harmony*.

If the effect is pleasant to our ears and the notes appear to agree with one another, we call the harmony a CONCORD. If the effect is unpleasant and the notes seem to disagree, we say that the harmony is a DISCORD.

It is important to note that there is no *absolute* rule about discords – what is disagreeable to one person may seem pleasant enough to the next. Opinions have also changed very considerably over the centuries – what is acceptable to the 20th century would have been intolerable to 18th-century ears.

There are, however, certain basic facts of acoustics that go some way towards explaining why it is we accept certain combinations of notes as being concords.

When any note is sounded, we know that it contains also the notes of its *harmonic series*. Thus, for example, the note C contains within itself the following notes:

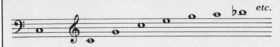

Although we do not hear these notes as individual sounds, but merely as a 'colouring' to the *fundamental note* C, it follows that they all 'agree' with the fundamental note in direct proportion to their closeness to it. Thus the fundamental note and the second harmonic (C and C) are in complete agreement. They form a Perfect Octave, and if we were to compare them we should find that the lower C has a wave-length exactly twice that of the higher C.

The third harmonic produces a G, the fourth another C, and the fifth an E:

Bunch these notes together and we have a simple, satisfying harmony: the kind that text-books call a COMMON CHORD:

It can hardly be an accident that the first steps towards adding harmonies to a melody more or less followed the pattern laid down in the harmonic series.

Very roughly, the progress of harmonization has gone like this: a thousand years ago melodies were sung in unison or harmonized at the octave (→ **Plainsong**). Then it was thought pleasant to add a harmony moving in parallel lines a fifth apart from the melody (→ **Organum**). A little later on the third was admitted as making an agreeable sound. And so the process has continued until, in one way or another, it has been found possible to use hundreds of different combinations of all the twelve semitones available to Western music.

2. What we mean by harmony and the rules of harmony really applies only to the music of a particular period in musical history – the period bounded, roughly, by the careers of Bach and Brahms. During this time there was general agreement about what made a concord and a discord, and how you should handle them both. It was therefore possible to lay down a set of 'rules', and give neat descriptions of all the ingredients you were likely to find in the grammar of music.

Although music written outside this period operates in much the same way, it has done so in a rather less formal fashion and frequently takes heed of other considerations. This is simply because the period we have mentioned was concerned to make its music almost exclusively out of the note-patterns of the diatonic major and minor scales. Other periods have been less exclusive, and so their 'rules' of conduct have been different.

Nowadays, in the most 'advanced' music, the situation is almost totally unpredictable and it is impossible to lay down any generally agreed 'rules' of conduct. Composers using, more or less, the 'old' methods exist alongside composers who work along totally different lines. All that can be safely said is that the human ear, given time, seems able to adjust itself to almost any combination of sounds and any method of musical construction.

3. **Some common terms used in orthodox harmony**

a. A CHORD is a combination of more than two notes, heard together (two notes form an Interval).

b. A chord with only three notes is called a

TRIAD. It consists of any note of the scale, plus the 3rd and the 5th above it. The note upon which the triad is built is called the ROOT of the chord:

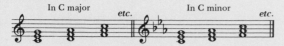

c. If the distance between the root and the 5th is a perfect 5th, the triad is said to be a COMMON CHORD. Common chords can be MAJOR or MINOR, according to whether the distance between the root and the 3rd is major or minor.

If, however, the distance between the root and the 5th is augmented, we have an AUGMENTED TRIAD. If it is diminished, we have a DIMINISHED TRIAD.

d. Major common chords occur on the Tonic, Subdominant, and Dominant degrees of the scale. We describe them as PRIMARY TRIADS. All other triads are SECONDARY TRIADS.

Triads in C major
(Primary shown in white and secondary in black)

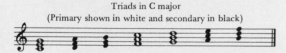

Minor common chords occur on the Supertonic, Mediant, and Submediant degrees of the scale.

The Diminished triad is found on the leading note. The Augmented triad occurs only in minor keys, on the mediant of the scale:

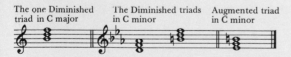

e. The chords we have used so far are said to be in their ROOT POSITION – because their root is also their lowest note.

But we can rearrange the notes of a chord so that its 3rd or its 5th becomes the lowest note. A chord which has its 3rd as the lowest note is said to be in FIRST INVERSION. A chord with its 5th as the lowest note is in SECOND INVERSION.

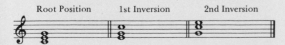

THIRD INVERSIONS are also possible – in a four-note chord, such as the chord of the Dominant 7th:

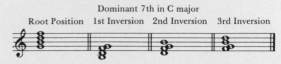

f. A useful shorthand way of describing all these chords is to count up the intervals they contain, starting from the lowest note, and make them into a kind of fraction. A common chord in root position becomes a Five-three ($\frac{5}{3}$) chord; a first inversion becomes a Six-three ($\frac{6}{3}$) chord; and a second inversion becomes a Six-four ($\frac{6}{4}$) chord; and so on.

g. A chord in which all the notes seem to be in agreement with each other is said to be a CONCORD. A chord which seems less restful – as if it needs to be followed by something else – is a DISCORD. We can also say such chords are Consonant (make a consonance), or Dissonant (make a dissonance).

When a discord passes on to something more restful (a concord, in fact), we say it has been RESOLVED. Here are some discords and their resolutions:

h. A FUNDAMENTAL DISCORD is one in which the discordant note forms part of the actual chord – for example, the 7th of a Dominant 7th chord:

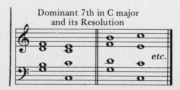

i. But there are other kinds of discord, which arise as a passing effect. For example: a note from one chord may be 'held over' against the notes of the next chord, so that it forms a dissonance for a moment, and then slips into its proper place in the new chord. This type of discord is called a SUSPENSION:

Suspended 9ths          Suspended 4ths

9 8          9 8          4 3          4 3

j. In the case of the suspension, the discordant note *always* resolves downwards, by step. But it is possible to have an upside-down kind of suspension, which resolves upwards by step. This is called a RETARDATION:

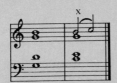

k. Suspensions and Retardations are usually PREPARED – that is to say, the discordant note appears in the *same* part in the previous chord. When a discord occurs without 'preparation' we have an UNPREPARED DISCORD, or Appoggiatura (→ **Ornaments and grace-notes**).

l. PASSING NOTES are notes that do not belong to any harmony, but which form links between the true harmony notes:

Hymn-tune: 'Aberystwyth'

m. PROGRESSION means moving from one note, or chord, to another. The aim in writing harmony is to use chords that form 'good' progressions – that is to say, sound pleasant.

n. DIATONIC HARMONY is that which uses the major and minor chords of the key. CHROMATIC HARMONY introduces chords that involve notes outside the key.

o. PART WRITING is the art of writing music in such a way that each performer (or, in keyboard music, each 'performing finger') has an interesting part to play. The most common form of part writing sets out the music in four parts (corresponding to the four main voices: Soprano, Alto, Tenor, Bass). When triads are used, one note must be doubled.

p. A PEDAL occurs when one note is held, while the other notes of the following chords move against it. Pedals are usually bass notes. A pedal in an upper part is called an INVERTED PEDAL. If two notes are held, we have a DOUBLE PEDAL (usually the tonic and dominant notes of the key).

From the hymn-tune: 'Praise my soul' (last lines of organ accompaniment)

Praise him!  Praise him!  Praise him!  Praise him!

Praise with    us    the    God    of    grace.

# Harp

A very ancient instrument dating back to the earliest civilizations. In all its different forms, the harp has always consisted of a sound-box, held near to the player, and a series of strings that are stretched between it and a 'neck' that projects outwards at an angle. The player plucks the strings with his fingers.

The modern orchestral harp is a very complicated piece of mechanism. It dates from 1810, when the instrument maker Sébastien Érard patented a system of pedals and levers which enabled the performer to get all 12 semitones of the chromatic scale from a limited number of strings.

This kind of harp has seven strings to each octave. There are 47 strings in all, and the range of available notes is:

*Below* **African harp** This arched instrument is of a type still found in Chad. It has a deep pitch because of its flexible 'bow' neck.

**Early harps** *Right* This 12th-century harp, held against the chest, appears in an English Psalter. *Below right* This tomb painting shows an ancient Egyptian arched harp.

*Below left* **Modern concert harp,** played by Myor Rosen of the New York Philharmonic Orchestra. Neglected by many composers it was favoured by the Impressionists.

**Types of harp** *Above* Sumerian arched harp of about 3000 B.C. *Above right* Burmese harp, traditionally tuned pentatonically. *Right* Early 19th-century pedal harp; French pedal harp made about 1785; 18th-century triple harp.

Each string must be individually tuned. The player does this with a special key which fits a series of pins on the right-hand side of the neck of the instrument.

The seven strings are tuned to the unlikely scale of C♭. This is because they are linked to seven pedals, set at the base of the instrument and operated by the player's feet. When a pedal is raised one notch, the string is shortened slightly and its pitch rises a semitone. Thus all the C flats become C naturals. When it is raised a second notch the same process occurs. The C naturals now become sharps. In this way it is possible to obtain all 12 notes of the chromatic scale from seven strings.

Moreover, each string has the possibility of a note in common with the next string. For example: if the C string is raised to C sharp, and the D string left at D flat, the two strings will both sound the same note. By using different pedal combinations the harp player can obtain all kinds of complicated effects.

The harp player changes his pedals during the performance and can do so very quickly indeed.

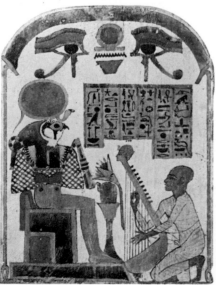

# Harpsichord

A keyboard instrument. The earliest surviving example was made in Italy in 1521, but there are pictures and descriptions that suggest that similar instruments existed for at least a hundred years before that. Though its origins are not yet properly understood, it seems likely that it grew out of the idea of applying a keyboard (such as had existed in organs for many centuries) to some such instrument as the **psaltery** →.

There are three main members of the harpsichord family: the VIRGINALS, the SPINET, and the HARPSICHORD. They have one thing in common: they produce their notes when the player presses a key (as on a piano) and a mechanism causes the string inside the instrument to be *plucked*. Thus they are quite different from the piano – for in the piano the string is *struck* by a padded hammer.

The device that actually 'plucks' the string is called a PLECTRUM. It is usually a small piece of quill attached to an upright 'jack' at the far end of the key which the player presses down. The key acts like a see-saw and pushes the jack past the string, and the plectrum plucks it in passing.

The full harpsichord looks something like a grand piano, only rather more elegant and less heavy. Very often it has two manuals (keyboards), which can be operated independently. It can also have a number of pedals and hand-stops, which bring into play different effects.

The tone of the harpsichord is crisp and clear, and can be very powerful. Its weakness as an instrument lies in its inability to make any *gradual* distinction between loud and soft sounds. Loud and soft sounds can, of course, be made (by using the different stops and pedals), but, unlike the piano, the player cannot control the volume by the force he exerts on the keys.

It was for this reason that the harpsichord went out of fashion at the beginning of the 19th century and the piano took its place. Nowadays, however, it has come back in popularity and many new makers have set up business.

Composers have also begun to write for it again – for example, Poulenc's *Concert champêtre* (1928) for harpsichord and orchestra.

**How it works** When the key is depressed, the jack rises and the plectrum, a wedge of leather or a quill, plucks the string as it passes setting it in vibration. When the key is released, the jack falls back bypassing the string.

plectrum
string
damper
tongue
jackslide
lower guide
jack
key

**18th-century French harpsichord** This instrument was made by the distinguished craftsman Pascal Taskin (1723-93), and is longer and wider than 17th-century models allowing a compass of four to five octaves. Couperin and Rameau wrote for this type of instrument.

*Above* **17th-century Flemish harpsichord** depicted here in Jan Steen's painting *The Music Lesson.*

*Below* **Harpsichord with two keyboards** This 18th-century French example has a range of five octaves

**Hay** or **Hey** This is an old English name which seems to have been given to several different kinds of round dance. (→ **Canaries**)

**Haydn** → page 170

**Haydn, Michael** Austrian composer, 1737–1806. He was the younger brother of Joseph Haydn and as a boy joined him in the St Stephen's choir school in Vienna. He became Music Director to the Archbishop of Salzburg (1762), and was an accomplished composer. His fairly large output includes 24 masses, 30 symphonies, and several operas.

**Heckel, Wilhelm** German instrument maker, 1856–1909. Established the firm of Heckel at Biebrich-am-Rhein in 1831, and there (with Carl Almenraeder) improved the structure and key-system of the bassoon, and later the double bassoon. The firm also invented a number of instruments, such as the Heckelphone.

**Heckelphone** Though rather different in construction from other members of the oboe family, it is, in effect, a baritone oboe. It was patented in 1903 and first used by Richard Strauss in the opera *Salome* (1905).

**Heller, Stephen** Hungarian pianist and composer, 1814–88. After studying in Vienna with Czerny he eventually settled in Paris and pursued a highly successful career as a virtuoso pianist. He wrote a great deal of piano music which, though not so highly thought of as that of Chopin and Schumann, does not deserve the neglect. His Op. 82 collection of short pieces, *Nuits blanches*, make a good introduction to his style.

**Heldentenor** (Ger.) Heroic-tenor. A type of tenor voice which is particularly strong and dramatic. It is needed, in particular, in Wagner's operas.

**Helmholtz, Hermann** German scientist, 1821–94. As Professor of Physiology at the University of Heidelberg he published an influential book on acoustics: *The Sensations of Tone* (1862). It was the first convincing explanation of dissonance and the quality of sounds, and is now recognized as a classic. His system of written pitch notation is still widely used:

C' B' C B c b c' b' c" b" c''' b'''

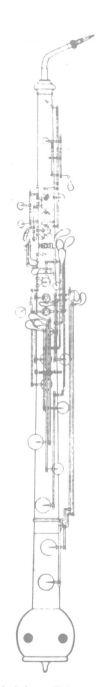

**Heckelphone** This instrument was used by Richard Strauss, Delius, Holst and Hindemith under the name 'brass oboe'. Its pitch lies between the cor anglais and the bassoon.

**Hemiola** (or **Hemiolia**) Literally 'the whole and the half', also used to mean 'the proportion of two to three'.

In the Middle Ages the term was used to describe the interval of the perfect fifth – because this was obtained by stopping a string 2/3rds of the way along its length.

In the 16th century it describes the rhythm we now call triplets – that is to say, three notes played in the time of two.

The word may also be used to describe a change of rhythm in triple time, where a note is tied over, so that two bars sound like one double-length bar:

**Hemidemisemiquaver** → **Notes and notation**

**Hen Wlad fy Nhadau** 'Land of my Fathers'. This fine song is the 'national anthem' of Wales and well known to (and heartily sung by) every man, woman, and child in that country. The words are by Evan James, a weaver of Pontypridd, and the music by his son, James Jones James. They wrote it in January 1856.

**Henze** → page 172

**Herbert, Victor** American composer, 1859–1924. Though born in Dublin, he settled in New York in 1886 as a cellist in the orchestra of the Metropolitan Opera House, later appearing as a soloist.

From 1894 to 1898 he was Bandmaster of the 22nd Regiment of the National Guard of the State of New York, and from 1898 to 1904 was conductor of the Pittsburg Symphony Orchestra. Thereafter he devoted his time to composition and won great fame with his many operettas, including: *Babes in Toyland* (1903), *Mlle Modiste* (1905), *The Red Mill* (1906), *Naughty Marietta* (1910). He also wrote two 'Grand' operas (*Natoma*, 1911, and *Madeleine*, 1914) and several orchestral works, but it is by his operettas that he is remembered.

**Hérold, Louis** French composer, 1791–1833. He studied in Paris at the Conservatoire, winning the Prix de Rome in 1812. He then settled to a successful career as an operatic composer, though he also wrote ballets and a great deal of piano music. His most important operas include *La Clochette* (1817), *La Pré aux Clercs* (1832), and *Zampa* (1831), which is also world-famous for its lively overture.

# Haydn

Joseph Haydn (his full Christian name was Franz Joseph). Born at Rohrau, in Austria, in 1732, and died in Vienna in 1809.

## 1. **Haydn's life**

Haydn's father was a wheelwright, and it seems likely that but for a stroke or two of good fortune his own life would have been passed in similarly poor circumstances.

The first instance of good fortune came in 1738 when a schoolmaster relative, Johann Mathias Franck, noticed how musical the little boy seemed to be and offered to take over his education and upbringing. Young Haydn therefore went to live in Hainburg, where he learned to sing and to play various instruments.

A second instance occured in 1740 when Georg Reutter, the organist of Vienna's famous Cathedral of St Stephen, heard the boy sing. He was on the lookout for good voices and immediately recruited Haydn into the cathedral choir.

Haydn remained a chorister until he was 17, but by that time his voice had broken and he was obliged to leave. He went to live in a small attic room, and managed to find a few pupils. He earned very little, but he was content – for he now had time to teach himself how to compose. He did this by studying the music of other composers, in particular that of J. C. and C. P. E. Bach.

Shortly after this Haydn met the famous singing teacher Nicola Porpora, who took him on as his accompanist. It was interesting work and taught him more about music. It also meant that he began to meet influential people, and they, in turn, noted that he was a reliable and talented young musician.

In 1755 one of these new acquaintances, a young nobleman named Karl von Fürnberg, invited Haydn to stay at his country house. There he kept a small orchestra, and Haydn was able to write music for it.

Four years later, in 1759, Fürnberg recommended him to an even grander nobleman, Count Morzin. This time he was offered an official appointment and a salary – £20 a year. It was enough to live on in those days, and in the following year Haydn got married.

Soon after this, however, Count Morzin ran into difficulties and was obliged to dismiss his private musicians. But Haydn's

**Joseph Haydn 1732-1809** This portrait of the composer is an engraving after a portrait by Guttenbrünn. Haydn wrote about 104 symphonies – the exact number is in doubt. Whatever the number, the astonishing thing is their variety. Haydn seldom does the same thing twice. He was always experimenting. Even his musical vocabulary is full of surprises – sudden changes of rhythm, unexpected turns of phrase, touches of humour.

*Below* **L'incontro improvviso** A scene from Haydn's opera at Esterház in 1775.

luck held, and within six months he had found an even better job.

This time he went to work for Prince Paul Esterházy, who lived in a magnificent palace at Eistenstadt, about 48 km from Vienna. Though Prince Paul died in 1762, his successor, Prince Nicholas, was even more passionately fond of music, and Haydn kept his job.

He served the Esterházy family, as Director of Music, for 30 years.

From about 1780 onwards, when his music began to be published by the Viennese firm of Artaria, Haydn's reputation spread beyond the walls of Esterház. Not only did visiting noblemen, from the Emperor of Austria downwards, admire and encourage him, but the general public also began to take notice of his music. By 1790 he was famous throughout Europe.

But in 1790 Prince Nicholas died. His successor did not care for music and soon dismissed most of the large staff of musicians. Haydn, however, was allowed to retire on a pension. He was now free to accept a pressing invitation to visit London and conduct a series of concerts of his music for the impresario Johann Peter Salomon. His last 12 symphonies, sometimes called the 'London' or 'Salomon' Symphonies, were written for performance in London.

He visited England twice, first in 1791, and again in 1794. Both visits lasted about 18 months and both were enormously successful. He ended up with enough money

to ensure a comfortable retirement.

But retirement was the last thing he wanted. Once back in Vienna he wrote a number of very fine quartets, and then settled to the composition of two major choral works: the oratorios *The Creation* and *The Seasons* – both inspired by the works of Handel he had heard in London.

When Haydn died, the guns of Napoleon's army could be heard bombarding the walls of Vienna. But he was deeply mourned by friend and foe alike. Everybody realized that the world had lost not only a very great master of music, but also a truly noble man.

*Below* **Palace at Esterház**
This grand palace was built by Prince Nicholas Esterházy. Here Haydn found himself in charge of two theatres, a chapel and a court orchestra. He therefore wrote music for every conceivable occasion. It did not worry him that he was a servant and wore a uniform. He simply got on with his work and enjoyed the many different opportunities for writing music.

## 2. His music

Though Haydn did not actually 'invent' the symphony and the string quartet, he did more than any other man to explore their possibilities and turn them into one of the supreme achievements of 18th-century music.

When Haydn began his career, the symphony was little more than a collection of simple movements strung together to form a pleasant entertainment. By the time he had come to write his last great works, it had become a tightly-organized sequence of four contrasted movements in which the musical argument of Sonata Form is carried out logically and with great dramatic effect. A similar development took place in the string quartet.

Haydn's music is also very optimistic and good-natured. And for this reason his is one of the most attractive personalities in music.

## 3. Summary of Haydn's main works

a. Operas include:

| | |
|---|---|
| *L'incontro improvviso* | 1775 |
| *Il mondo della luna* | 1777 |
| *L'isola disabitata* | 1779 |
| *Armida* | 1784 |
| *Orfeo ed Euridice* | 1791 |

b. Choral music includes:

| | |
|---|---|
| St Cecilia Mass | 1772 |
| Nelson Mass | 1798 |
| Creation Mass | 1801 |
| The 'Creation' | 1798 |
| The 'Seasons' | 1801 |

c. Symphonies include:

| | |
|---|---|
| No 45 in F sharp minor (The 'Farewell') | 1772 |
| No 82 in C major (The 'Bear') | 1786 |
| No 92 in G major (The 'Oxford') | 1788 |
| No 94 in G major (The 'Surprise') | 1791 |
| No 100 in G major (The 'Military) | 1794 |
| No 101 in D major (The 'Clock') | 1794 |
| No 103 in E flat major (The 'Drum Roll') | 1795 |
| No 104 in D major (The 'London') | 1795 |

Haydn also wrote many Overtures, Divertimenti, Marches, and Dances; Concertos for Keyboard, Violin, Cello, Horn, Flute, Oboe, Lira →, Trumpet; 83 string quartets, numerous string trios, piano trios, duets, divertimenti for baryton, piano sonatas; songs, canons, folksong arrangements.

## 4. Haydn, the man

Haydn considered his remarkable talents to be a gift from God, and never began a score without first inscribing the words 'In nomine Domini' (In the name of the Lord), and never completed one without the words 'Laus Deo' (Praise be to God). Though proud of his work (as he had every right to be), he was also genuinely humble – as willing in the days of his maturity to learn from Mozart (25 years his junior) as he had been to learn from J. C. and C. P. E. Bach.

He has often been called 'Papa Haydn': and though he was indeed a man of great sweetness of character, this should not lead us to think of him merely as a rather harmless, kindly old gentleman. He was, as his music shows, as capable of fire and indignation as any young revolutionary. And the fact is that he did revolutionize music – but did it quietly and without fuss.

# Henze

Hans Werner Henze. German composer, b. 1926. He was a pupil of Wolfgang Fortner (Heidelberg) and René Leibowitz (Paris) and is now regarded as one of the leading German composers of his time

His early work was much influenced by Stravinsky, but after 1946 he adopted a very free and very effective type of serialism (e.g. the Violin Concerto, 1947). More recently he has written works that express a great interest in left-wing politics (e.g. the 'oratorio' *The Raft of the Frigate 'Medusa'*, 1968) and has felt free to draw on a wide variety of traditional and avant-garde techniques to achieve his ends.

Henze is one of the few contemporary composers who seems able to reach a wide audience, and yet at the same time remains interesting to the specialist. He has written a large quantity of music of all kinds, including six symphonies, a ballet *Undine* (1956), and several important and widely performed operas: *Boulevard Solitude* (1952), *King Stag* (1956) *The Prince of Homburg* (1960), *Elegy for Young Lovers* (1962), *The Young Lord* (1965), *The Bassarids* (1966), and *We come to the River* (1976).

*We Come to the River Above* This scene is from the first performance of Henze's opera *We Come to the River* at the Royal Opera House, Covent Garden in July 1976. The libretto was by the English playwright, Edward Bond.

**Hans Werner Henze** b.1926 In addition to his work as a composer Henze also conducts and produces opera.

**Heterophony** A term used to describe a musical texture made up of the simultaneous performance, in several parts, of what is essentially the same melody (even though the rhythms and time-values may be altered). Textures of this kind occur in Oriental and African music, and in the folk music of certain European countries.

**Hey** → **Hay**

**Hindemith** → page 173

**His Master's Voice ('H.M.V.')** The famous 'trade-mark' picture adopted by The Gramophone Company, who accordingly changed their name to 'His Master's Voice', is a portrait of 'Nipper', a dog who seemed to recognize the recorded sound of his dead master's voice and was therefore painted in an attitude of intelligent appreciation by his master's brother, Francis Barraud. Nipper was first painted listening to a cylinder-gramophone, but as these were going out of fashion the painter up-dated his picture and thus attracted the attention (and the cash!) of the record company.

**H.M.V.** The Gramophone Company, later to become H.M.V., was responsible for the first opera ever recorded in 1903. It was also the first company to introduce albums of entire symphonies and string quartets.

**History of Music** → page 174

**Hocket** Literally a 'hiccough'. This device is found in medieval music (such as that of Machaut) and consists of a melodic line broken up into individual notes, or very short phrases, with rests in between them. This is carried out regardless of the fact that the words being sung are also broken up into separate syllables. The device has been reintroduced by certain avant-garde composers in recent times.

**Hoddinott, Alun** Welsh composer, b. 1929. He was educated at the University College of South Wales (where he is now head of the Music Department), but began writing music at an early age. He attracted serious attention with his First Symphony (1955) and is now regarded as the leading Welsh composer of his generation. His Fifth Symphony (1973) is a highly imaginative and ingenious work and has been much admired. Though Hoddinott often uses 12-note techniques his music is basically tonal. It is marked by a strong rhythmic sense and can at times be grim and powerful. Lighter

# Hindemith

Paul Hindemith. German composer, 1895-1963. He was born in Hanau. His parents did not wish him to make a career in music, so he left home, when he was 11, and earned his living by playing the violin in café and dance bands. He then studied at Hoch's Conservatory in Frankfurt. From 1915 to 1923 he was leader of the Frankfurt Opera orchestra. Later he became well known as a viola player, in particular with the Amar-Hindemith String Quartet.

During this same period he also began to win recognition as a composer much interested in polyphony and the 'neo-classic' style. He was particularly attracted by the idea that a composer ought to write 'useful' music, suitable for children and amateurs to play, and not merely try to express himself through works which only professional musicians could tackle. In later years, rather in deliberate opposition to Schoenberg's system of atonality, he set out his own belief that harmony should be firmly based on the laws of acoustics in an influential book: *The Craft of Musical*

**Paul Hindemith** 1895-1963 *Below* Hindemith with his wife and children as a string quartet. This sketch is from a family Christmas card.

*Composition* (1939). In a second important book, *A Composer's World* (1952), he explained his beliefs about the nature of composition and the composer's relation to society.

From 1927 to 1935 Hindemith taught composition at the Berlin High School for Music, but his works were banned by the Nazi Party in 1934 and he was soon obliged to leave the country. In 1939 he settled in America, and in 1942 became Head of the School of Music at Yale University.

Hindemith wrote a great deal of music of all kinds, including operas: *Cardillac* (1926, revised 1952) and *Mathis der Maler* (1938); symphonies: *Mathis der Maler* (1934), based on the opera and *Harmonie der Welt* (1951); concertos for violin (1939), cello (1940), piano (1946), and horn (1950); chamber and orchestral works, including the very fine *Symphonic Metamorphoses on themes by Weber* (1945); and choral works, including an oratorio *Das Unaufhörliche* (1931) and an 'American Requiem': *When Lilacs last in the Doorway bloomed* (1946).

works, such as the suite of *Welsh Dances* (1958), have become very popular.

**Holbrooke, Josef** English composer, 1878–1958. He studied under Sir Frederick Corder at the Royal College of Music and came into prominence with a symphonic poem *The Raven* (1900). This was followed by further large-scale works such as *The Bells* (1906) and *Apollo and the Seaman* (1908), both for chorus and orchestra. He then devoted himself to the composition of a trilogy of Wagnerian-style music dramas based on Welsh legends: *The Children of Don* (1912), *Dylan, Son of the Wave* (1914), and *Bronwen* (1929).

Though successful up to about 1920, Holbrooke was always considered somewhat eccentric. The last years of his life were marred by deafness and the almost complete neglect of his music.

**Holst** → Page 177

**Homophonic, Homophony** A term used to describe musical textures in which all the parts move 'in step' with one another and do not show the kind of rhythmic independence you get in **Polyphony** →. Good examples can be found in most hymn-tunes.

**Arthur Honegger,** 1892-1955, seen here in a car with his wife.

The homophonic style began to dominate music after 1600 and is largely responsible for the rapid exploration of unusual harmonies in the 18th and 19th centuries. In homophonic textures the tune and bass line are prominent, and the harmony forms a kind of sandwich in between them.

**Honegger, Arthur** Swiss composer, 1892–1955. After studying in Paris and Zurich he became known as a very prolific composer of rather sensational music – including such orchestral pieces as *Pacific 231* (1923), which describes a locomotive in action, and *Rugby* (1928), which describes a football match. His 'dramatic psalm' (a kind of opera) *King David* (1921), and his stage oratorio *Joan of Arc* (1935) have also enjoyed considerable popularity, as has the very attractive orchestral *Pastorale d'été* (1920). From 1923 onwards Honegger also wrote scores for many films. He was one of the group of French composers known as 'Les Six'.

**Hook** (of a note) The black line attached to the stem (or 'tail') of all notes of less value than the crotchet (quarter-note).

# History of Music

We study the 'history' of the different arts in order to understand and enjoy them as fully as possible. For example, we may get great pleasure from a Mozart symphony without knowing who Mozart was, or when he lived, or what the conditions of music-making were like in his day, but our enjoyment and understanding will be increased beyond measure if we have even the most general idea of such matters.

A really detailed knowledge of musical history will, of course, only come after long study and a great deal of careful listening. But knowledge at this level is not really necessary unless you plan to make a career in music. The important thing is to fix a clear outline of what has happened to Western music during the past 1000 years. This can then be used as a basic framework for further investigations. Here, in very simple terms, is such a skeleton outline.

## 1. Music of the early Christian Church, 800–1100

Modern Europe began to take shape about a thousand years ago. Although music must have played a part in people's daily lives, we know very little about it, for at this period it was never written down. What has come down to us is really the music of the Church, for it was only the monks who were able to write. To begin with, then, we must accept that our view of music is somewhat lopsided.

The music of the early Christian Church consists mainly of the simple tunes it used for chanting the various parts of the Services (**→ Plainsong**). At first these tunes were sung in unison and were thus pure melody – self-supporting and without any accompanying harmony.

Such music was built on Modal scales (**→ Modes**) and some of it may have been borrowed from very ancient sources (Greece and Rome, for example). It was, and still is, singularly beautiful and expressive.

Gradually the church musicians began to find a way of enriching their music by weaving together several melodic lines. This process is known as **Polyphony →**. At first it was carried out in a very simple way, merely by doubling the existing tune at a different pitch – at the octave, say, or the fifth throughout (**→ Organum**). But soon the added part was allowed to take on a shape of its own, wandering off in different

*Above* 11th-century musical notation from a Spanish manuscript. The notes, or 'neumes' indicate the rise and fall of the melody as well as the rhythm.

*Above* An illuminated letter from a medieval manuscript showing typical musical instruments of the period, harp, chimes, rebec, panpipes and medieval viol. *Below* An illustration from a manuscript from Florence, 1450, showing festivities about to take place. In the centre is a musician playing an early form of guitar, employed to entertain the guests.

directions from the original melody and thus becoming a melody in its own right.

This process was greatly helped when, in about the year 900, ways of writing down music began to be developed.

## 2. Music in the Middle Ages, 1100–1400

After about 1100 we begin to hear a little more about music outside the Church. There were songs and dances, written and performed by general entertainers such as the Jongleur, and later, in the 12th and 13th centuries, rather more subtle songs from the TROUBADOURS and TROUVÈRES (**→ Minstrels**) of France. Gradually, from about 1350 onwards, we find secular music being written by professional musicians (such as Landini and Machaut) who were mainly employed by the Church itself.

Indeed, not only does the music of the Church become more complicated and intricately polyphonic during this period, but there was an increasing demand for music to entertain the noblemen who were beginning to settle down in elaborate courts and palaces. And so, alongside the elaborate and beautiful polyphonic settings of the Mass, we find composers writing music for everyday use.

## 3. Music in the Renaissance, 1400–1600

By 'Renaissance' we mean that period in the history of Western Europe when men began to explore the world, both by travel and through science, and began also to think about themselves – exploring, as it were, through the arts.

It is therefore not surprising to find that the interest in secular music began to increase, until, by about 1500, great strides were being made in the composition of music for instruments as well as for voices.

*Left* The Moresca was a Moorish dance which did not carry any settled rhythm or style. This 16th-century German illumination shows the courtiers of Maximilian I dancing, accompanied by the pipe and tabor.

*Below* The harp is played by plucking the strings with the fingers causing them to vibrate. This miniature from Boccaccio's *Des Cleres et Nobles Femmes*, a French manuscript of 1470, shows an elegant lady playing an early form of the instrument
*Bottom* An evening concert given by the Jena Collegium Musicum in 1744.
By this time music written for entertainment had overtaken music written for the Church. It is interesting to note the layout of the orchestra compared to that of today.

Although most composers still worked mainly for the Church, others can be found working for wealthy music-lovers.

Nevertheless, Church music was still very important and the polyphonic vocal style may be said to reach its height during this period. Such composers as Josquin des Prés, Orlandus Lassus, William Byrd, and Palestrina are rightly regarded as supreme masters of this art.

## 4. Baroque music, 1600–1750

Several great changes occurred in the 17th century that revolutionized the whole art of music. They were:

a. The fact that music for entertainment gradually overtook, both in quantity and quality, music written for the Church. By 1700 several distinct instrumental forms had come into existence – for example, the SOLO SONATA, the TRIO SONATA, the DANCE SUITE, and the CONCERTO GROSSO, and even the early 'overture' type of symphony.

b. Modal scales began to give way to the diatonic major and minor scales (the traditional scales with which we are all familiar) – thus making possible the art of modulation, and therefore a whole new way of giving music a sense of form and coherence. Without this development large-scale instrumental forms would have been impossible.

c. The invention of opera and oratorio in Italy (1600) meant that composers began to write for solo voices in a new way (→ **Monody**, **Opera**, **Recitative**). The interest was now concentrated on a single melodic line supported by a firm bass line, with blocks of harmony in between the two (→ **Homophony**). From this moment polyphony began to decline in importance.

The great composers of the period include Monteverdi, Purcell, Bach, Handel, Lully and Rameau.

## 5. Classical music, 1750–1827

Instrumental music now dominates the scene, and so does the idea of giving music a kind of 'architectural' shape by means of contrasting, repeated and varying recognizable passages and themes, linked together by a carefully worked out scheme of modulations. The prime example of this method is the Sonata Form – the musical shape that is at the root of the two main types of instrumental music popular at this time: the SYMPHONY and the CONCERTO.

Instruments themselves were greatly improved during this period and began to be grouped together into regular orchestras. The idea of public concerts also took root, and composers began to break away from the private patronage of the Church and the Nobility and fend for themselves by appealing directly to a paying audience.

The great names of the period, Haydn, Mozart, Beethoven, and Schubert, constitute a kind of Golden Age when music reached a point of perfect balance between expressiveness and satisfying formal shape –

There are so many outstanding composers in the 19th century that an adequate list is scarcely possible. But certain names stand out – they are: Schumann, Chopin, Mendelssohn, Brahms, Berlioz, Dvořák, Tchaikovsky, Liszt, Wagner, Verdi, Bruckner, Mahler, Strauss, Elgar, and Debussy.

like a perfectly proportioned Greek temple. This is why we describe it as a 'Classical' period.

## 6. Romantic music, 1827–1914

Using the ingredients developed in the Classical period, the Romantic composers began to search for ways of making music more and more expressive. Their music increasingly became a kind of autobiography that reveals their personalities and inner emotions.

The symphony and concerto grew grander in scale, and sometimes sought to tell stories or paint pictures in terms of music. This new element is called PROGRAMME MUSIC, and it reached a high point of development in a new form: the SYMPHONIC POEM.

At the same time, music, in its search for expressiveness, became more complex. Extremes of dissonance were now explored, and chromatic notes found their way increasingly into 'diatonic' scales. By the end of the century it no longer made sense to talk about diatonic scales. Modulation was often so swift and so frequent that the listener could no longer be sure which key the music was in. And when this happened, TONAL music had all but given way to ATONALITY.

Orchestras, too, grew bigger and better and there were an increasing number of public concerts. Composers now depended almost wholly on what they could earn at the box office. The old forms of private patronage gradually died out.

Though the great names of the period are predominantly German, other countries began to make an important contribution to music. Some of them deliberately sought to create a distinctive National style – usually deeply influenced by folksong. This tendency also helped to undermine the 'Classical' conception of music.

*Above* Chamber music was originally defined as music 'not intended for the church, theatre or public concert rooms.' It excludes music for soloists or orchestras, but is now performed publicly. This painting of 1799 *Chamber Music in a Schloss* shows typical instruments, flute, violin, cello and harpsichord.
*Right* Franz Liszt, 1811-86, composer and pianist, caricatured in *La Vie Parisienne* of 1886.

## 7. 20th-century music

The main problem that 20th-century music has had to face is whether to continue with some version of 18th- and 19th-century musical grammar, or whether to search for some new method of giving music a sense of logic and coherence.

Composers who have continued to explore more or less traditional methods include: Bartók, Stravinsky, Vaughan Williams, Prokofiev, Shostakovich, Copland, and Britten.

Others have been more ruthless – in particular Schoenberg and his disciples – in cutting their way through to an entirely new concept of music. This process gained speed after the 1939–45 war, until today certain experiments are really experiments in the manipulation of sound – so far are they removed from the music of previous ages. (→ **Serialism, Atonality, Electronic music, Aleatoric**)

*Below Jeux 2* composed by Roman Haubenstock-Ramati in 1968, in a new notation for aleatory music. This differs greatly from conventional notation, which would not suit the ideas or instruments of electronic or a eatoric music.
*Below right* Cornelius Cardew's *Treatise*, written in 1967, uses a combination of conventional and graphic notation.

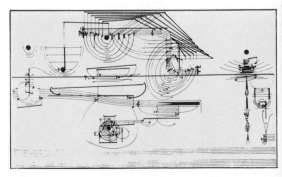

# Holst

Gustav Holst. English composer, 1874–1934.

His family came originally from Sweden, but his grandfather settled in Cheltenham as a music teacher, and his father carried on the tradition. He himself began composing when he was 12, and eventually (1893–98) went to the Royal College of Music to study under Parry and Stanford.

On leaving college Holst had a struggle to earn a living, for unlike his friend and fellow-student Ralph Vaughan Williams he had no money of his own. He managed by playing the trombone in various orchestras. Despite many hardships he was able to marry in 1901 and gradually began to find publishers and performances for his music.

During this period he began to study the literature, religion, and philosophy of India, and even taught himself to read Sanskrit. Several important works grew out of this interest, including the chamber opera *Savitri* (1909) and the four sets of *Choral Hymns from the Rig Veda* (1908–12).

Equally important was his interest in folksong. Together with Vaughan Williams he studied it carefully and allowed it to influence his own music. In this way they both learned how to write music that was distinctly 'English' in character.

In 1905 Holst was appointed Director of Music at St Paul's Girls' School, and two years later took charge of music at the

**Gustav Holst**
1874–1934 His suite of seven orchestral tone poems, *The Planets*, was based on astrological associations. The fourth and fifth suites represent Jupiter (*below top*) as Bringer of Jollity and Saturn (*below bottom*) as Bringer of Old Age.

Morley College for Working Men and Women. These posts were important to him as a composer, even though they took up a great deal of his time and energy, for they taught him how to be practical and write music, such as the *St Paul's Suite* for strings (1913), that was simple and effective for young people and amateurs to play.

Real fame as a composer did not come to Holst until 1918, when his friend Balfour Gardiner financed a performance of the orchestral suite *The Planets*. It made a deep impression, which was later confirmed by the first performance of the choral work *The Hymn of Jesus* (1920). He was now recognized, along with Vaughan Williams, as an important new composer on the English scene.

Fame, however, did not bring money, and Holst was obliged to teach and lecture for the rest of his life. Undoubtedly the strain of this work undermined his health and made it impossible to write as much music as he would have liked. Nevertheless, several important works were completed, including the operas *The Perfect Fool* (1923), *At the Boar's Head* (1925), and *The Wandering Scholar* (1934); two major works for chorus and orchestra, *Ode to Death* (1919), and the *Choral Symphony* (1924); and a number of orchestral works, including the fine overture *Egdon Heath* (1927).

---

**Hook, James** English composer, 1746–1827. He studied with the organist of Norwich Cathedral and then made a very successful career in London as an organist, piano teacher, and composer of popular vocal and instrumental pieces for the Vauxhall Pleasure Gardens. He had a great capacity for writing attractive tunes, such as *The Lass of Richmond Hill.*

**Hootenanny** A folk singers' jam session (performance). The word seems to have been first used in 1941 at a folksong gathering in Seattle, Washington.

**Horn family** → page 178

**Hornpipe** An almost exclusively British dance, dating back to at least the 16th century. Early hornpipes were in triple time, but later ones adopted a 2/4 rhythm. As the dance required no partners and was concerned mainly with intricate footwork it

**Hornpipe** Both Purcell and Handel composed music for this popular dance.

naturally became popular with sailors in the cramped space available aboard ship. Hornpipes can be found in some suites.

**Hovhaness, Alan** American composer, b. 1911. Of partly Armenian descent, he has often turned to oriental subjects for inspiration and to oriental methods of composition (monody, heterophony, etc.). He studied at the New England Conservatory and has written a large amount of music of all kinds, including many symphonies. His *Symphony for Metal Orchestra* (1963), for six flutes, three trombones, and percussion is typical of his constant search for unusual effects.

**Howells, Herbert** English composer, b. 1892. He studied first with the organist of Gloucester Cathedral, and then with Stanford at the Royal College of Music. He has written music of all kinds, including many

# Horns and the Horn family

Simple versions of the horn have been known all over the world and throughout recorded history. The earliest were fashioned either from an animal horn, or from a large, suitably shaped sea shell. The most common were end-blown, but a few types exist that were blown through a hole cut in the side. Horns of this simplicity could produce only a few notes, but they were useful both for signalling and for playing during ceremonies and rituals.

So far as Europe is concerned, horns have also been known since the earliest times. In the Middle Ages they were associated with hunting and the battlefield. The earliest were made of horn, and some few examples exist most beautifully carved from ivory. Metal horns did not come into existence until about the 14th century. They were made of brass (as most horns are nowadays), copper and occasionally of silver, and consisted of a slender tube anything from 2 m to 6 m in length, coiled in several circles and ending in a flared 'bell'. They were played through a special mouthpiece shaped like a deep cone, and they too were capable of producing only a handful of notes.

Simple hunting horns of this kind found their way into the earliest orchestras, playing simple 'hunting horn' passages, but they did not become a regular feature in orchestral music until the beginning of the 18th century.

The story of the orchestral horn is largely the story of how instrument makers discovered ways of overcoming the limitations of the hunting horn. These, as we have seen, were simple tubes which could be made to produce a few notes when the player blew into a mouthpiece, forcing his lips to vibrate. These vibrations communicated with the sounding length of the tube and, by changing the pressure of his breath and the tension of his lips, allowed the player to pick out many of the notes of the harmonic series (→ **Harmonics**) that the tube could produce. The problem was: how to get notes that did not occur in the harmonic series of that particular tube?

The first orchestral horns were 'natural' instruments, identical to the hunting horn, but more elegantly shaped. In the early part of the 18th century the natural horn came to be provided with a series of extra lengths of

**Hunting horn** *Left* This intricately carved horn dates from medieval times.

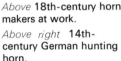

*Above* **18th-century horn makers at work.**
*Above right* **14th-century German hunting horn.**

**Practical range**
(actual sounds)

*Above* **Coiled hunting horn of the 17th century.**

**Modern French horn**
*Right* This orchestral horn with rotary valves is able to play any note of the chromatic scale. The hand in the bell is used to alter pitch or mute sound.
**Below** Hoffnung makes fun of the French horn player.

tubing called 'crooks'. These could be added to, or subtracted from the main tube quite quickly. And because they altered the *total* length of the instrument, they allowed the player to move to a different harmonic series and thus pick out the note he wanted. The only difficulty was that however adept the player became in changing from one crook to another, it still took time, and composers had to leave a sufficient number of bars' rest in their scores for this to be done.

The answer came in the 19th century with the invention of valves. These allowed the instrument maker to coil several lengths of 'extra' tubing alongside the main tube, and these could be brought into use as soon as the appropriate valve was pressed down. The credit for the invention of valves should probably go to Heinrich Stölzel who, together with Friedrich Blühmel, took out a patent for them in 1818.

The present-day orchestral horn is known as the French horn in F – even though the most up-to-date are really horns in F and B flat (the two types being accommodated on a single instrument, thus making upper notes easier to play). Because it is in F ( → **Transposing instruments**) its music has to be written five notes higher than it actually sounds – the note C, for example, has to be written as G.

The French horn has about 6m of tubing. Its range is shown on the left. Soloists may go a little higher. In the hands of a good player the French horn is an agile instrument, full of colour and variety (see, for example, the horn parts in any of Richard Strauss's scores). But even the best of players can 'crack' a note, for everything depends in the end on his lips.

**19th-century horns**
Before the invention of valves in about 1815 crooks of various lengths, and even mouthpieces which could be moved from tube to tube, had been used to alter pitch.

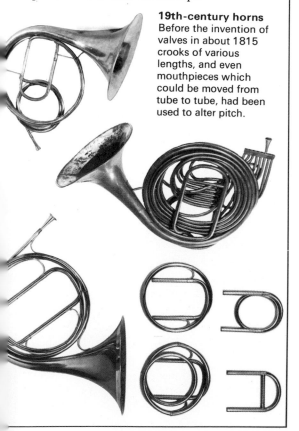

**J. N. Hummel**
1778–1837 A child prodigy pianist, he was a pupil of Clementi. He became musical director to the Esterházy family, a post held earlier by his former teacher, Haydn. Czerny was one of his piano students.

**Engelbert Humperdinck**
1854–1921 His opera *Hansel and Gretel* is often performed for young audiences.

anthems and services. Certain early works, such as the two piano concertos (1913 and 1924), were well received, but he was then rather ignored as a composer and only came into prominence again when his choral work *Hymnus Paradisi* was heard at the 1950 Three Choirs Festival.

**Hullah, John** English composer and educationist, 1812–84. He became known as a composer by his music to Charles Dickens's opera *The Village Coquettes* (1836), the score of which, however, perished in a theatre fire. In 1841 he opened a school to instruct day and Sunday school teachers in an important system for teaching sight-singing, and it is for this work that he is now remembered.

**Humfrey, Pelham** English composer, 1647–74. He was a chorister of the Chapel Royal and had the pleasure of hearing his Anthems sung there before he was 18. Charles II sent him to France and Italy for further studies. He remained abroad until October 1667. In 1673 he was appointed as one of the Composers in Ordinary for the Violins to His Majesty. His anthems, songs, and two Choral odes for the King's Birthday are still much admired.

**Hummel, Johann Nepomuk** Hungarian composer, 1778–1837. A pupil of Mozart, he made his first appearance as a pianist in 1787 at one of Mozart's concerts. Thereafter he toured extensively in Bohemia, Germany, Denmark, and England. On his return to Vienna in 1793 he devoted himself more to composition, and this alternation of composing and touring continued throughout his career. Though he wrote much music of all kinds, he is mainly remembered as one of the founders of modern piano technique.

**Hum note** → **Bells and bell-ringing**

**Humoreske** (Ger.) (or **Humoresque**, Fr.) A title used by Schumann, and others, for short, lively pieces of music – not so much humorous as good-humoured.

**Humperdinck, Engelbert** German composer, 1854–1921. He assisted Wagner at Bayreuth during the preparation of *Parsifal* (1880–81), and then, after travelling in France, Italy, and Spain, lived in Germany and was much respected as a teacher. His fairy-tale opera *Hansel and Gretel* was produced in 1893 and instantly became popular. Later operas were less successful.

**Hurdy gurdy** → page 180

**Hymns** → page 181

**Hypoaeolian, Hypodorian** → **Modes**

# Hurdy gurdy

A mechanical instrument much favoured in medieval times, when it was called an ORGANISTRUM, or ROTA. It looks something like a viola with a handle at one end. When this is turned, a wheel revolves under the strings and sets them in vibration. It is, in fact, a kind of endless bow.

A small keyboard attached to the side of the instrument enables the play to stop the strings as required.

The hurdy gurdy is thus a cross between a bowed instrument and a keyboard instrument. There are usually four to six strings, and two are always given over to a continuous fixed DRONE, while the others can be used to play the tune.

**Hurdy gurdy players**
*Above* This 15th-century Italian miniature shows an angel with a hurdy gurdy *Left* Medieval English player depicted in the 14th-century Luttrell Psalter *Right* This Spanish manuscript of the same period shows a pair of hurdy gurdies. This instrument, widely played in the Middle Ages, still survives as a folk instrument in France.

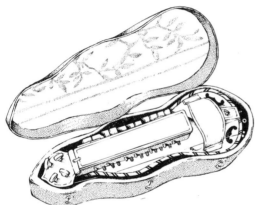

**Child's decorative hurdy gurdy**, of French origin, in its original small case.

**Types of hurdy gurdy**
*Above* Traditional French hurdy gurdy of the early 19th century.
*Right* An 18th-century hurdy gurdy opened to reveal the keys.
*Left* Hurdy gurdy player of the 17th century by the French painter, Georges de la Tour. The instrument, called a *vielle* in France, was exceedingly popular in that country in the later 17th and early 18th centuries. Both Haydn and Mozart wrote music for the hurdy gurdy.

The description 'hurdy gurdy' is commonly applied to street barrel-organs and piano-organs, but this is incorrect and probably arose simply because the Italian street musicians of the early 19th century actually used the hurdy gurdy proper, and only gradually gave it up in favour of the more powerful mechanical organs and pianos.

# Hymns and hymn-tunes

In the very earliest days of the Christian Church almost anything sung in praise of God could be called a hymn, and it was not until the fourth century A.D. that hymns came to be regarded as a special class of religious song. But in those days, and for many centuries afterwards, hymns were written in Latin and sung to plainsong melodies. They were therefore not the kind of popular music we think of nowadays as a hymn, but something that could be sung and understood only by the trained priests and clerks of the church. The *congregational* hymn, which could be sung and enjoyed by anyone, belongs to the Reformation period and after.

When the 16th-century Reformation of the Churches came, it had two main branches – that of Martin Luther, in Germany, and that of John Calvin in France and Switzerland (and later, England and Scotland). Both men thought it important that ordinary people should be able to sing their praises in their own language and to simple tunes that were easy to learn. Luther wrote many hymns himself, and adapted (and sometimes composed) all kinds of popular tunes (and even plainsong) to fit them. Calvin and his followers preferred to sing psalms, but they made verse arrangements of them which were easier to remember and could be fitted to simpler tunes.

The Lutheran type of hymn came to be known as the CHORALE (*Ein' feste Burg* – 'A safe stronghold our God is still' – English Hymnal No 362, is an example), while Calvin's were known as METRICAL PSALMS (for example, the 'Old Hundredth' – 'All people that on earth do dwell' – English Hymnal No 365).

Hymn singing rapidly became popular wherever the reformed churches took root, and from that time on the words and music of thousands of new hymns, suitable for all occasions, were written. Examples can be seen in the work of Nahum Tate and Nicolas Brady (17th–early 18th century): 'While shepherds watch'd their flocks by night'; Isaac Watts (18th century): 'When I survey the wondrous cross'; Charles Wesley (18th century): 'Jesu, Lover of my soul'; Bishop Heber (18th–early 19th century): 'Holy, holy, holy, Lord God Almighty!'; and John Mason Neale (19th century): 'Jerusalem the Golden'.

During the 19th century a great many hymns were written on behalf of social reforming movements – to encourage people not to drink and gamble, etc. These are not to everyone's taste today, but, in their time, they undoubtedly did much good. The American Revivalists, Dwight Moody and Ira D. Sankey were particularly prominent in this field.

Composers have continued to write fine hymn-tunes in the 20th century. Vaughan Williams in particular included several excellent examples of his own in his edition of the English Hymnal (1904). In the second half of the century experiments have been in writing hymn tunes in a 'pop' style, accompanied by guitars and all the paraphernalia of commercial music. Though some of these efforts have been admired, few have proved memorable as yet.

**The Village Choir** This painting by Thomas Webster (1847) depicts singers in a country church accompanied by clarinet, bassoon and cello.

## Hymn-tunes of various periods

**1** *A 16th-century Genevan psalm tune* The melody from the Genevan Psalter of 1551. In the churches of Geneva they used to sing in unison without any organ. These harmonies belong to a later period.

**2** *A German chorale Valet will ich dir geben* (a hymn of farewell to the 'false and evil world'). The tune is by Melchior Teschner (1613), and this is Bach's harmonization of it for four-part choir, 150 years later.

**3** *An 18th-century tune Rockingham* by Dr. Edward Miller, Organist of Doncaster Parish Church, as it appeared in his *The Psalms of David* (1790). He altered it from a slightly earlier tune by some other composer.

**4** A typical, sturdy mid 19th-century hymn-tune composed by the Rev. John Bacchus Dyke (1823-76).

**5** Vaughan Williams's famous *Sine Nomine*, No 641 in The English Hymnal.

1 THE OLD HUNDREDTH

2 VALET WILL ICH DIR GEBEN

3 Largo con affetto

4 MELITA

5

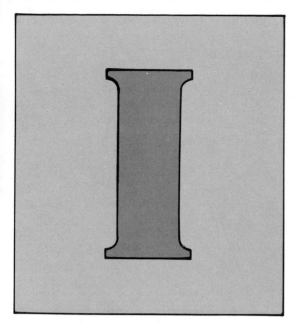

**Iambic** →**Metre**

**Ibert, Jacques** French composer, 1890–1962. Studied at the Paris Conservatoire, winning the Prix de Rome in 1910, and later (1937) becoming Director of the Rome Academy itself. He wrote music of all kinds, including many operas (*Angélique*, 1927) and ballets (*Diane de Poitiers*, 1937), and much choral, orchestral, and chamber music.

**Idée fixe** (Fr.) A term used by Berlioz for a musical idea that not only describes something, but which occurs in each movement of an extended work – as, for example, the theme that dominates his *Fantastic Symphony*. Musically, this theme helps to bind the symphony's five movements together, even though each deals with a different aspect of the 'story'. At the same time it represents the woman the poet loves, around whom the symphony's story is built.

The notion of using musical themes to represent definite ideas or characters in a story-telling symphonic work was very popular in the 19th century. Variants of the device can be found in Liszt's *Metamorphosis of themes* and Wagner's **Leitmotiv** →.

**Idiophone** → page 184

**Imitation** → **Counterpoint**

**Imperfect cadence** → **Cadence**

**Impetuoso** (It.) Impetuous(ly).

**Impressionism** → page 185

**Impromptu** We use the French adverb meaning 'unprepared' to describe things said or done on the spur of the moment. And in music it describes a piano piece which,

though written down, sounds as if it has just been improvised. In other words, impromptus are written in a rather free-and-easy style.

Chopin's four *Impromptus* are probably the best-known examples of this kind of music, but other composers, such as Schubert, Schumann, and Fauré, have also used the title.

**Improvisation** To improvise means to play without notation, making up the music as one goes along. Extemporization (to extemporize) is an alternative word for the same thing.

Improvisation has always played a part in music. At certain periods it has developed into a very testing art. For example, singers in 18th-century operas were expected to add decorations to the tunes of their arias. The soloist in an 18th-century concerto would decorate his part in a similar way – the Cadenza section, in fact, was usually made up on the spot. Improvisation was less popular in the 19th century, except among organists. Jazz musicians, however, have always relied on improvisation. It has now crept back into concert music in the form of Indeterminacy.

**In Alt, in Altissimo** → **Alt**

**Incalzando** (It.) Pressing forward. In music it means working up the speed and force.

**Incidental music** Any music that occurs during a play or a film is said to be 'incidental' to the performance.

Sometimes the music is part of the action – for example, a song sung by one of the characters, or a fanfare to announce the arrival of someone important. But it can also be *background music*, designed to create a particular atmosphere – an approaching storm, say, or a feeling of mystery. Pieces played before the play begins, or between the scenes and acts (overtures, interludes, etc) are also 'incidental' music.

Music has always played an important part in the theatre. Shakespeare's plays, for example, frequently call for it. And many important composers, such as Purcell and Beethoven, have made contributions to the plays of their times. Indeed, some of their efforts have been so distinguished that we now play them as independent pieces in the concert hall – Beethoven's overtures to *Coriolanus* and *Egmont* are examples. Other composers have deliberately arranged suites of concert music from pieces they originally wrote for the theatre. Grieg's music to Ibsen's

**Jacques Ibert** 1890-1962

# Idiophone

All instruments made of some material that produces a sound from itself alone are classed as idiophones. They are classified according to the way in which they are made to produce their sound – by stamping, shaking, beating, clashing together, rubbing, scraping, and plucking.

Examples of idiophones: Bells, Castanets, Celeste, Clappers, Claves, Clogs, Cymbals, Glockenspiel, Gong, Glass Harmonica, Jew's Harp, Jingles, Maracas, Metallophone, Musical Glasses, Rattles, Scrapers, Steel Drum, Stamping Stick, Tam Tam, Triangle, Washboard, Wood Block, Xylophone.

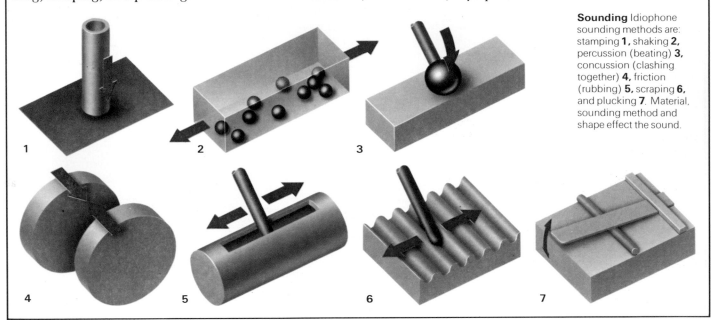

**Sounding** Idiophone sounding methods are: stamping **1**, shaking **2**, percussion (beating) **3**, concussion (clashing together) **4**, friction (rubbing) **5**, scraping **6**, and plucking **7**. Material, sounding method and shape effect the sound.

play *Peer Gynt* is often heard in this form.

Economic circumstances make it difficult for the modern theatre to use large orchestras, but incidental music is still commissioned for plays, even though it must now be scored for a few instruments. With films, however, these limitations do not apply and this form of incidental music still flourishes.

But whether it is written for theatre or film, for large orchestras or small ensembles, incidental music makes its greatest impact when it is applied sparingly. If there is too much, it will simply become a nuisance and a distraction and ruin the main point of the evening's entertainment – which is the performance of the play itself.

**Inciso** (It.) Incisive. In music it indicates that a strong, clear rhythm is required.

**Indeciso** (It.) Undecided. In music it indicates that the speed must vary according to the performer's artistic feeling.

**Indeterminacy** A term first used by the American composer John Cage in the early 1950s to describe music which does not employ a fixed notation, but leaves certain events to chance.

**Indeterminacy** A section from the score of David Bedford's *With 100 Kazoos* (1975). In this piece, Bedford used the principle of indeterminacy invented by John Cage. The performers improvise in response to the pictures.

# Impressionism

A term borrowed from late 19th-century French painting. It describes a style of music mainly associated with Debussy and those composers who were influenced by him – such as Ravel, Bax, Delius, etc.

Impressionist painters, such as Manet, Monet, Pissarro, Degas, and Renoir, realized that things change their appearance according to the conditions under which we see them. For example, a tree seen in the mid-day sun appears quite different from the same tree seen at twilight. They tried therefore to capture the 'impression' of things at a particular moment.

To do this they made an intense study of the effects of light and colour. They saw that a tree was not merely something with a tree-like shape, but a tree-shaped area of many different colours. They therefore painted what they saw in terms of thousands of minute touches of colour, rather than as patterns of hard outlines. Looked at close to, such paintings appear a jumble of colours. Step away, and the colours merge into a shimmering impression not only of the object, but of the very atmosphere under which the painter first saw it.

Just as impressionist painting differs from the painting of earlier times, impressionist music approaches composition from a new point of view. Instead of the hard outlines of contrasting themes, which are then made into a logical musical argument (which is

**Impressionist painting**
*Above Gare St Lazare, Paris* by Claude Monet, perhaps the greatest of the Impressionist artists whose painting *Impression, Sunrise* (1872) gave its name to the movement.

*Below Boulevard Montmartre, Night Effect* by Camille Pissarro who, with Monet, was one of the great Impressionists.

what we find in, say, Beethoven), we have small scraps of musical ideas, merging, changing, and creating an 'impression'.

If we try to listen to such music in the way that we listen to a Beethoven symphony, we shall hear only a muddle of details. But if we, so to speak, 'step back', the details will blend and a powerful overall mood will emerge.

Impressionist composers, such as Debussy, treated harmonies and orchestral effects in much the same way as impressionist painters treated light and colour. In particular they explored the different 'colours' of harmony. They began to use each harmony for the sake of its particular colour, without regard for its place in the classical system of harmonic progression. For example, in 'classical' music a discord is always followed by its proper resolution. But in impressionist music a discord could stand as an effect in its own right – without preparation or resolution.

This new attitude to harmony and orchestral colouring did much to undermine the traditional ways of thinking about music. It opened up a vast new territory of possibilities for composers, even though they were not necessarily impressionists themselves.

Examples of musical impressionism can be studied in Debussy's orchestral music, such as the *Prélude à l'après-midi d'un Faune, La Mer, Nocturnes, Images*. (→ **Debussy**)

# Indian music

Although music has existed in India for thousands of years and has been developed into a very complex and extremely impressive art-form, it has no 'history' in the sense that Western music has. The Indian 'composer' is always a composer-performer, and he is interested not in writing down his music so that future generations may study and enjoy it, but in improvising around a number of set themes. He creates *as he plays* – and then moves on to something else. In India the whole art of the composer lies in the study of 'how' to create music, and not in the amassing of an array of 'complete works'. This knowledge of how to compose is passed on from master to pupil in direct contact with each other.

Indian music also differs from Western music in that it is concerned exclusively with melody. Harmony, in the Western sense, does not exist. What matters is melody, and the composer shows his skill by the way in which he elaborates and decorates it. The theory of composition and performance is also very closely associated with religion – for the Indians believe that man was originally taught by the Gods themselves.

As the voice was the first instrument available to man, pride of place is always given to vocal music. And though instrumental music exists in great quantity, it is believed that its sound should be as *vocal* as

**Indian musical instruments**
*Above* The **sitar**, a long-necked lute, now familiar in the West through the music of Ravi Shankar, the Indian sitarist, composer and teacher. His works include a concerto for sitar and orchestra and scores for such films as *Pather Panchali, Conrad Rooks* and *Chappaqua. Below left* The modern **vina** with large gourd. This increases the resonance of the instrument. *Below right* The **sarangi**, an Indian fiddle, has three main strings which are played with a bow and some 40 or 50 sympathetic strings.

possible. It is for this reason that melody is so important.

Indian musical theory divides the octave into a basic scale (SAPTAK) of seven notes – roughly corresponding to the Western scale. But it also allows the octave to be divided into a series of steps that are much smaller than the semitone. As many as 66 of these **Microtones** → are possible in theory, but in practice only 22 are used. These small intervals are known as SRUTIS. At first hearing, the Western listener is likely to regard them as no more than ordinary notes played slightly out of tune, but, with a little patience, he may eventually come to appreciate their beauty.

Using these scales as a basis, the art of Indian music is concerned with what are called RAGAS. These are patterns of notes which the composer uses as material for his composition. Each raga is partly a scale, partly a melody, and partly a source of ideas for improvisation. The nearest thing to it in Western music is the Tone Row in Serial music ( → **Serialism**).

Thousands of ragas have been created by Indian musicians and handed down to their successors, but of these only 132 are considered essential for general use. Each, however, has its special meaning and corresponds, among other things, to a particular mood or emotion, and to a particular time of day and season of the

year. No composer would dream of using a raga that was not appropriate to the mood of the moment, or went against the time of day and the season of the year. Here is an example of a 'morning' raga:

Todi

Besides the raga, which gives the Indian composer his melodic material, there is also the TALA. This is a rhythmic pattern which is used in conjunction with the melody. There are many of them, but about 40 are in general use.

The third element in Indian composition is the KHARAJA – the *drone*. This is the only

**Tabla** These small-sized Indian drums are part of the classical ensemble.

'harmony' in Indian music, and it forms a continuous background to each composition. In Western music a similar effect is found with bagpipes.

When the Indian composer-performer creates his music, what he is doing is exploring a particular mood – gradually establishing the mood he wishes to explore. And then the 'variations' begin, gradually becoming more and more intricate. At first the explorations are purely melodic, but then the percussion instruments join in and the rhythms of the tala are added to the composition. If all goes well, a really 'inspired' composition may last for an hour or more.

It is perhaps rather misleading to speak of an individual composer-performer as 'creating' the composition. For although one man may act as leader, the performance (and the 'creation') is actually carried out by a group of musicians. But, as with the finest jazz improvisations, the understanding between the musicians is such as to make them play as one man – each sharing the other's thoughts and moods and reacting accordingly.

Indian music makes use of four groups of instruments: the TANTU (strings), SUSIR (wind), AVANADA (percussion), and GHANA (gongs, bells, and cymbals). Among the most important of these are the **Sitar** →, the **Sarangi** →, the **Tambura** →, the **Shanai** →, and the **Tabla** →.

**Indian musicians** *Left* The classical Indian ensemble consists of the tabla, the tambura and the sitar. *Below* Large gilt trumpets form part of this Indian village band.

**Snake charmers** play a pungi. It is, however, the swaying movement of this reed instrument, not the music, that hypnotizes the snake.

# Instruments

All musical instruments are mechanical devices designed to create the kind of controlled vibrations that our ears interpret as musical 'sounds'. Most of them consist of a COUPLED ACOUSTIC SYSTEM – that is to say, something that sets up and sustains the initial vibrations *coupled* to something that responds by vibrating in sympathy, controls and amplifies these vibrations and then transmits them through the air to our eardrums. Only the very simplest instruments consist of a single system.

**Idiophones** Instruments in which sound is produced by the body of the instrument itself. They are classified according to how they are sounded. Simplest are the stamping idiophones; these produce their sound by banging, either on another hard surface or on the ground. Stamped idiophones work on the reverse principle. Rattles and jingles are typical examples of shaken idiophones. Friction idiophones are sounded by rubbing, and plucked idiophones have a flexible tongue as in the jew's harp. Concussion idiophones, such as the cymbals, are sounded by the clashing together (concussion) of two similar objects, whereas percussion idiophones are struck to produce their sound. This last group is the largest and includes gongs, xylophones and clapper bells.

**Chordophones** (stringed instruments) These consist of a series of stretched strings, coupled to some kind of hollow box that amplifies their vibrations. It is these that produce the sound. There are various ways of making the strings vibrate; a bow can be drawn across them, as with the violin and viol families, or they can be plucked by the player's fingers, as with the harp and guitar. Others are hammered or plucked

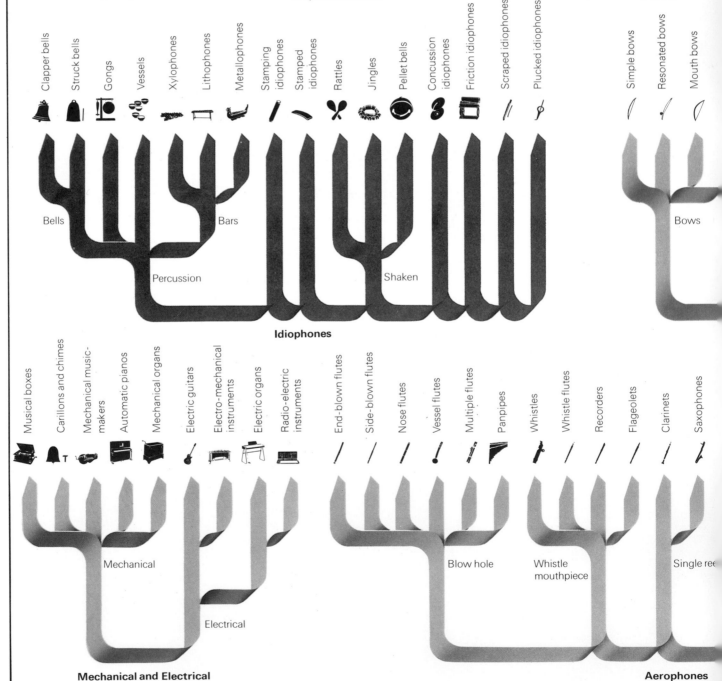

mechanically by means of a keyboard. Examples of this include the piano, clavichord, harpsichord and spinet. Different notes are produced either by employing a series of strings of different fixed lengths as on a harp or a piano, or by employing a few strings that, firstly, are tightened or slackened to the required pitch and then 'stopped', (made shorter) by the player's fingers, to raise the pitch.

**Mechanical and electric instruments** In some mechanical instruments, like the hurdy gurdy, the strings are stopped and selected physically but sounded mechanically; a musical box, however, is completely automatic. Most electric instruments produce their sound totally by electronic means, though a few, such as the electric organ, use an electric mechanism but produce their sound in the normal way.

**Aerophones** (wind instruments) These are instruments in which the sound is produced by the vibration of air. The vibrations are started either by the player blowing through a reed – a double reed in the case of oboes and bassoons and a single one in clarinets – or by the player's breath hitting the sharp edge of a hole. In a flute, for instance, the player blows across the hole; in the case of horns, trumpets and trombones, he or she blows downwards onto it. The initial vibrations are taken up by the rest of the instrument. This consists of a tube that can be shortened or lengthened, either by opening or shutting holes cut in the side (woodwind) or by adding new lengths of tube by means of valves or slides (brass). This allows the tube to produce notes other than its so-called fundamentals.

**Membranophones** Instruments which produce their sound from a tightly stretched membrane. A drum is sounded by beating with the hand or drumsticks. The tension of the skin (and the size of the instrument) controls the pitch of the note; the tighter the tension the higher the note. Another type of membraphone is the mirliton, whose skin is vibrated by humming.

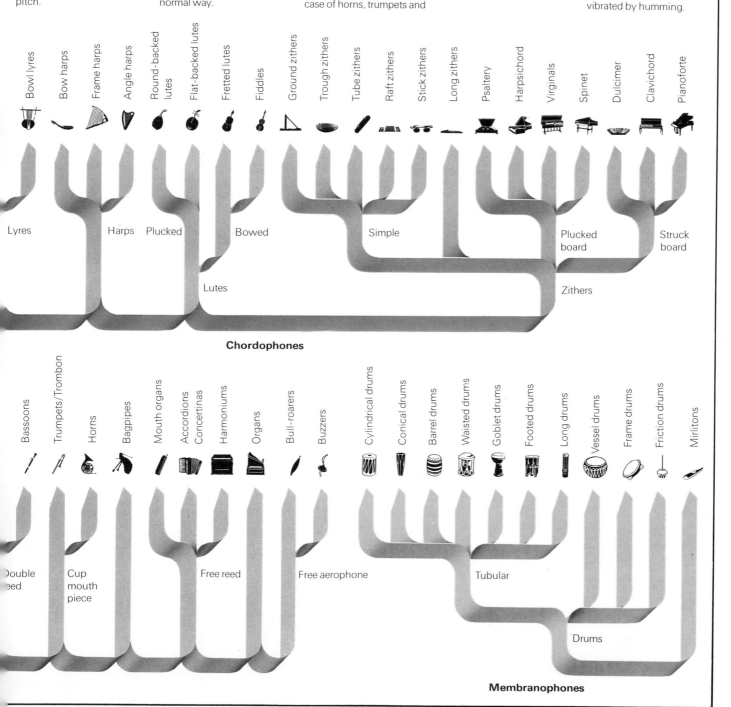

189

For example, the performers may be given a series of short musical ideas and told to play them in any order. Or they may be given an 'instruction' that is not actually musical notation in the ordinary sense, but more like a graph or a picture to which they are expected to respond in a creative, musical way.

Indeterminacy is a reaction against the idea of a composer rigidly laying down the law about a particular composition. It came into existence probably because certain 20th-century systems of composition (such as SERIALISM and TOTAL SERIALISM) were too rigid and dictatorial. Composers who practice it usually quote Oriental philosophies (particularly Zen Buddhism) as their justification – the idea that happiness and peace of mind lie in not trying to control events.

Unfortunately, this belief is also a perfect recipe for avoiding responsibility. Though there are a few composers of this kind of music

**Vincent D'Indy**
1851–1931 This composer was a great admirer of Wagner and also defended Debussy at a time when his work was derided by the public.

who truly understand what they are doing, there are a great many more who are merely deluding themselves and their public.

**Indy, Vincent D'** French composer, 1851–1931. He was a pupil, friend, and biographer of César Franck, and possessed a similarly earnest attitude of mind. This led him to help found the Schola Cantorum in Paris (1894), which had a strong religious and moral side to its teaching. His own music, which includes operas, symphonies, and tone-poems is not often heard nowadays outside France. The symphonic variations *Istar* (1896), and the three descriptive orchestral pieces *Jour d'été à la Montagne* give a fair idea of his style.

**Inflexion** (**Inflection**) The raising or lowering of a note by means of an accidental (a sharp or flat).

**In modo di** (It.) In the manner of.

**In Nomine** A type of English instrumental

# Intervals

The distance between two different notes is called the 'interval'. Thus, the distance between C and G is the 'interval of a fifth' (C d e f G). The distance between C and G is also a fifth, and so is that between C♯ and G, C and G♯, C♭ and G♭, etc. It is the alphabetical name that gives us the interval number.

But we have not described an interval completely until we have indicated its *quality*. This is shown by the number of semitones included in the interval. Thus, the distance between C and E is a third. But if this distance includes 4 semitones (C to E) we say that it is a MAJOR THIRD. If it has only 3 semitones (C to E♭), we call it a MINOR THIRD. A major interval always has one more semitone than its corresponding minor interval.

All 2nds, 3rds, 6ths, and 7ths are either major or minor. But we use the special name PERFECT to describe the unison, octave, 5th and 4th.

If a major interval is chromatically increased by a semitone it becomes AUGMENTED. Thus, C to A is a major sixth, but C to A♯ is an AUGMENTED SIXTH.

We have seen already that when a major interval is reduced by one semitone it becomes a minor interval. If a minor interval is reduced by one semitone it is said to be DIMINISHED. Thus, G to B♭ is a minor

third, but G♯ to B♭ is a DIMINISHED THIRD.

By adding or subtracting a semitone, Perfect intervals can be made Augmented or Diminished.

Any interval of more than an octave is known as a COMPOUND INTERVAL. For example:

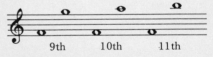

An interval is said to have been INVERTED when the position of one of its notes is changed by an octave – the changed note, as it were, leap-frogging the fixed note. When this happens, all perfect intervals remain perfect, but major intervals become minor, minor become major, augmented become diminished, and diminished become augmented. To find the new number of the interval we must subtract the original number from *nine*. Thus, a 2nd becomes a 7th, a 6th becomes a 3rd, a 4th becomes a 5th, etc. For example:

Maj. 3rd    Min. 6th

Intervals are either CONCORDS or DISCORDS. All perfect intervals and all major and minor sixths are concordant. All other intervals are discordant. ( **→ Tritone**)

composition, written usually for a consort of viols, but also found for keyboard or lute. It is contrapuntal in style and one part always plays the plainsong *Gloria Tibi Trinitas Aequalis* in long notes. (→ **Plainsong**)

The first instrumental *In Nomine* was written by John Taverner. It was identical with a passage of music in his Mass *Gloria Tibi Trinitas* (based on the plainsong) which occurs in the Benedictus at the words 'In Nomine Domini'. Other composers of music in this style adopted the title and the plainsong out of respect for Taverner.

**Inner parts** Any part, or line, in music other than the highest or lowest. Thus, in a four-part choral piece for mixed voices, the alto and tenor lines are 'inner parts'.

**Instrumentation** The term is sometimes used to describe a general knowledge of orchestral instruments, without including the additional knowledge of how to make use of them in orchestration. (→ **Orchestration**)

**Instruments** → page 188

**Interlude** Any short piece of music intended to be performed between ('inter') the acts or scenes of an opera or play, or between the main movements of a large work.

**Intermezzo** This Italian word has the same meaning as **Interlude**, and applies particularly to a short orchestral piece played between the acts or scences of an opera.

The word, however, also has two very special meanings. In the 17th century it meant a brief comic opera designed to be performed between the acts of a serious opera, as light relief.19th-century composers such as Schumann and Brahms it is used as a title for short piano pieces.

**Interpretation** Although the composer writes his music down on paper, it does not exist *as music* until someone else performs it. However carefully he may have expressed his wishes, he must also leave a great deal to the performer's common sense and musical feeling. The performer, in fact, must 'interpret' what the composer has written.

For example, certain bars may need to be played *accelerando*. But the composer cannot possibly say exactly how the speeding up is to take place. He may state that the music is to be played *piano* – but there is no rule to say exactly how soft a soft passage should be. These decisions must be left to the performer, for they are all matters of interpretation.

What the performer (or conductor) must do is study the composition in detail and try to grasp it as a whole. He must do his best to get inside the composer's skin and *feel* how he intended the music should sound. The more he knows about the composer and his work, and indeed of the historical period in which he lived, the more he is likely to interpret his work effectively.

No two performers, however skilful and artistic, will ever interpret a work in exactly the same way. Nor will one performer necessarily interpret a work in the same way on two different occasions.

Although we say that the composer 'creates' the work and the performer 'interprets' it, it is clear that there is a strong element of 'creation' in the art of 'interpretation'. Perhaps the word 'recreation' would give a better idea of what actually happens.

Interpretation is only good if it is done with a true respect for the music. If a performer is too anxious to make the music express his own personality, then he is bound to harm it. Instead of an interpretation, we get a distortion.

**Interrupted cadence** → **Cadence**

**Intervals** → page 190

**Intonation** The word used to describe whether a performance is properly in tune or not. Thus we may say that a singer's intonation is 'good', or 'bad'.

**Intone** To sing on one note – as may be done when reciting the Creed in church. Pitching the words to a particular note helps the voice to carry.

**Introduction** A term used mainly in connection with symphonic music, where it can mean anything from a few chords to a short movement (usually slow) that prepares the way for the main body of the work (usually quick). 'Slow introductions' can be found in the first movements of most Haydn symphonies.

The word is also used to describe short movements placed at the beginning of a suite, or some other collection of movements. It can also describe the opening instrumental section of an aria, or some similar piece.

In all these meanings there is the sense that the introduction is merely a preparation for something more important that is to follow.

**Introit** This is a passage, generally an **Antiphon** → with a verse of a psalm, sung in the Roman Catholic Mass at a certain point.

In the Anglican Church it means much the same thing, but in some other Protestant Churches it means a short piece of choral music used for opening a service.

**Invention** Bach wrote 15 short keyboard pieces in two parts (or 'voices') which he called by this name. Each piece begins with a scrap of tune out of which the piece is gradually woven.

He also wrote 15 similar pieces in three parts (or 'voices') and today we call them his *Three-part Inventions*. But he himself called them symphonies.

**Inversion** This word has several meanings:

1. For INVERSION OF INTERVALS → **Intervals**

2. For INVERSION OF CHORDS → **Harmony**

3. For INVERSION OF TWO OR MORE 'PARTS' (that is, Invertible Counterpoint) → **Counterpoint**

4. INVERSION OF A MELODY is much the same as Inversion of Intervals. We often find it in Bach, as in the following Gigue from the 6th French Suite, which begins:

and then continues:

**Ionian** → **Modes**

**Ireland, John** English composer, 1879–1962. He was the son of two well-known authors, Alexander and Anne Elizabeth Ireland, and studied at the Royal College of Music under Stanford, where he later became a composition teacher himself (1923–39).

Though he wrote a number of important orchestral works, including *The forgotten Rite* (1913), the symphonic rhapsody *Mai-Dun* (1921), and a very popular Piano Concerto (1932), he is mainly remembered as the composer of a number of very pleasant songs and piano pieces.

**I.S.C.M.** The International Society for Contemporary Music. It was formed as the result of a festival of new music given by young Viennese composers in Salzburg, 1932. It now meets every year in different cities for the express purpose of giving new and unusual music a hearing.

**Isorhythm** This is a compositional device

found in the motets and masses by 14th- and 15th-century composers such as Guillaume de Machaut.

It means that a short rhythmic pattern has been applied to a melodic line and repeated over and over again, regardless of the melody's natural, original rhythm. For example, this is now *The Bluebells of Scotland* would sound if the following isorhythmic pattern: were applied:

**Italian sixth** → **Chromatic chords**

**Ives, Charles** American composer, 1874–1954. He was born at Danbury, Connecticut, and received his first music lessons from his father, who was a bandmaster and teacher. Later he studied under Horatio Parker at Yale University.

Realizing that he had no interest in writing orthodox kinds of music, and therefore had little hope of being able to earn a living from composition, he became an insurance agent.

Until he retired from business (1930), Ives composed only in his spare time. He wrote music of such daring originality that it was seldom performed and nearly always misunderstood. His true genius only began to be appreciated after 1947 when he was awarded a Pulitzer Prize for his Third Symphony.

His work is original because he wanted to capture the effect of music as it is heard under everyday circumstances. For example, if you walk down a street past the open windows of people who are all playing different things on pianos, violins, and radios, etc., what you hear will be a strange muddle of conflicting sounds, *and yet* you will accept the mixture as a perfectly natural thing. Ives's music deliberately explores and exploits these contradictions, mixing all manner of incongruous materials in a highly original way.

Examples of his extraordinary imagination can be heard in such works as *Variations on a National Hymn ('America')*, 1891; *General Booth enters into Heaven* (1914), the 'Concord' Sonata for piano (1915), and his four great symphonies (1898, 1902, 1911, and 1916).

**John Ireland** 1879 – 1962

**Charles Ives 1874–1954**
This unassuming American composer shunned fame and publicity. He printed his music at his own expense, often years after the works were written and rarely went to concerts of his works.

**Jam session** An occasion when jazz players improvise together. The word 'jamming' means 'to improvise'. Jam sessions are always very informal, and may take place with or without an audience – the musicians are really playing just for the pleasure of it.

**Janáček** → page 194

**Janissary music** The Janissaries were a famous corps of Turkish soldiers whose music greatly intrigued 18th-century Europe. As a result, Turkish military musicians were engaged by European military bands. They brought with them kettledrums, side drums, cymbals, triangles, tambourines, and all manner of fascinating pieces of equipment, such as the 'Jingling Johnny' (a decorated pole with bells on it).

Orchestral composers were also attracted by the new sounds and began to imitate them in their music. Side drums, bass drum, triangles, and cymbals, etc., began to appear in their scores in works such as Haydn's *Military Symphony* (1794) and the Turkish interlude in the finale of Beethoven's Ninth Symphony. It was a craze and soon passed, but it proved very beneficial to the development of the orchestra's percussion department.

**Jannequin, Clément** French composer, c. 1475–1560. Though little is known about his life and career, Jannequin is remembered as a composer who specialized in descriptive choral music: four-part Chansons with such titles as *The Hunt, The Song of the Birds, The Chattering Women, The Battle of Marignan*.

**Japanese fiddle** A one-stringed instrument sometimes played by street musicians.

**Jew's harp** This detail is from an early 16th-century woodcut.

**Jingling Johnny** This particular example has an interesting history. It was captured by the French from the Turks in the mid 18th century. They later added the Napoleonic eagle, but in 1812 it was taken by a British regiment, the Connaught Rangers, at the Battle of Salamanca.

Instead of the usual sound-box it has an amplifying horn. (→ **Stroh violin**)

**Jaques-Dalcroze, Émile** Swiss composer and educationist, 1865–1950. After training in Paris, under Delibes, and in Vienna, under Bruckner, he became Professor of Harmony at the Geneva Conservatory, where he began to evolve a system of co-ordinating music and bodily movement in order to develop a sense of rhythm in young students. This system of EURHYTHMICS proved very influential, and schools for teaching it were set up in many parts of the world. He also wrote music in a folksong style for use in schools, but his more ambitious works made little impression.

**Järnefelt, Armas** Finnish composer, 1869–1958. After studying in Berlin and Paris he became known as a conductor, first in Germany and then in Sweden. He became a naturalized Swedish subject in 1910. His fame as a composer rests upon two charming light orchestral pieces: the *Berceuse* and *Praeludium*.

**Jazz** → page 196

**'Jerusalem'** This famous choral song was composed by Sir Hubert Parry in 1918, to words by the great poet-painter William Blake (1757–1827). It has been adopted by the National Federation of Women's Institutes as their own special song.

**Jew's harp** The English name of this instrument may be a corruption of its Dutch name: *Jeugdtromp* (child's trumpet). It has no special connection with the Jewish people.

It consists of a small metal frame shaped, in outline, like a bottle. A small metal tongue runs through the centre of the shape, projecting out of the 'neck' end. The player holds the neck end between his teeth and twangs the metal tongue with his fingers. By changing the shape of his mouth, and thus changing the shape of the air cavity it makes, the player is able to produce different notes.

Instruments of this kind are found all over Europe, and in Asia. Though it has its limitations, it has produced a number of virtuoso performers. Composers, however, have not generally been inspired by its possibilities, and it is now hardly ever seen.

**Jig** → **Gigue**

**Jigg** A form of entertainment popular in England, and to some extent Holland and Germany, from about 1550 to 1750. It consists of a short comedy for several characters, sung in verse to well-known

# Janáček

Leoš Janáček. Czech composer, 1854-1928. Though Janáček's early career includes several periods of intensive study, at Brno, Prague, Leipzig, and Vienna, it was not particularly distinguished, for he developed very slowly. He was 40 when he began his first truly significant work, the opera *Jenůfa*, and over 60 before he came to be appreciated by the musical world in general.

Indeed, his originality might never have been recognized but for a series of accidents that led to the production of *Jenůfa* in 1916. It was successful. Suddenly he felt confident of his own genius, and in the remaining twelve years of his life he produced a stream of masterpieces – including five great operas, two symphonic poems, a splendid *Sinfonietta*, and the highly original *Glagolithic Mass* (1926).

One of the reasons why Janáček's music sounds unlike that of almost any other composer is because he was keenly interested in the rhythmic patterns and melodic shapes that lie behind ordinary speech and everyday events. For example, he noticed that there are many different melodic shapes hidden behind a simple greeting such as 'Good morning!' They vary according to the emotion you put behind the greeting. A happy 'Good morning!' has a different 'tune' and a different rhythm from a sad one, or a bored one. He listened also to the 'melodies' behind such things as the wind in the trees, the sound of running

**Leoš Janáček**
**1854–1928**

*The Cunning Little Vixen* Janáček's opera, which uses both human and animal characters, was first produced in Brno in 1924. These costume designs by Rosemary Vercoe were for the 1975 Glyndebourne production of the opera.

water, the song of the birds, and the hum of insects. All these things he noted down with scrupulous care and used them as raw materials for his own work.

Added to this, of course, was his own deep love and knowledge of folksong.

Though Janáček's music looks, on paper, shapeless and repetitive, it proves, in actual performance, to be extremely effective. It *is* repetitive – in the sense that short phrases are repeated over and over again. But as they are repeated they gradually change shape, put out new shoots and develop. Janáček's repetitions always have a purpose.

Janáček's operas are much admired. They are not only beautiful and theatrically effective, but also extremely moving as dramas. Janáček firmly believed that life was a precious and glorious thing. All his major works celebrate this belief, and are, in consequence, among the most optimistic statements ever made about human beings and the fact of living.

Janáček's operas include: *Jenůfa* (1894–1903), *Katya Kabanova* (1919–21), *The Cunning Little Vixen* (1921–23), *The Makropoulos Affair* (1923–25), and *From the House of the Dead* (1928). Orchestral works include the six *Lachian Dances* (1890), the symphonic rhapsody *Taras Bulba* (1918), and the *Sinfonietta* (1926). He also wrote two important string quartets, and a remarkable song cycle (really a miniature opera): *The Diary of One who Vanished* (1916–19).

tunes, with lively dances in between the various sections of the story.

**Jingles** 1. Instruments consisting of a number of small bells or rattling objects (such as nuts, or shells), sometimes attached to a stick or frame and shaken, but more often strung together and worn on a dancer's body so that he provides his own accompaniment. They are a very ancient form of music-making. In the modern orchestra the main jingles are sleigh bells and the tambourine.
2. A short, catchy piece of music, sung to equally catchy words and used by commercial radio and television stations as a means of advertising the sponsor's products.

**Jingling Johnny** or **Turkish crescent** A stick-jingle used by British and German military bands since the 18th century, when it was borrowed from the Turkish Janissary bands (→ **Janissary music**). It consists of an ornamental pole, hung with tiny bells.

**'John Brown's Body'** A marching-tune that became immensely popular during the American Civil War (1861–65). It started life as a hymn, probably composed by William Steffe in the 1850s, which was adopted by the 'Tiger' Battalion of the 12th Massachusetts Regiment as a march. Doggerel words about a fanatical Kansas Abolitionist (campaigner against negro slavery) (John Brown) were added as time went on.

The tune later became famous as the 'Battle Hymn of the Republic', when Mrs Julia Ward Howe wrote the splendid words 'Mine eyes have seen the glory of the coming of the Lord' (1861).

**Jolivet, André** French composer, b. 1905. After some success in literature and painting he settled to composition, eventually evolving an advanced style that was largely atonal. He has been much concerned with the idea of music as a 'magical' force, able to cast a spell over an audience. Examples of this kind of music include the *Five Ritual Dances* (1939) and the orchestral prelude *Cosmogonie* (1938).

**Jongleur** → **Minstrels**

**Joplin, Scott** American jazz pianist and composer, 1869–1917. He was more or less self-taught and spent many years (1885–93) in St Louis playing in honky-tonks and developing a style of piano music known as RAGTIME. He continued this occupation in Chicago where he met the publisher John Stillwell Stark, who brought out his *Maple Leaf Rag* in 1899 with huge success.

In all, Joplin published some 39 piano

**Scott Joplin**
1869-1917

**Josquin des Prés**
*c.*1440–1521 He was a pupil of Ockeghem and then seemed to have travelled a great deal in Italy. Like many musicians of his time he took Holy Orders.

**Juke Box** *Above* This coin-operated record player of 1948 uses the 12 inch disc with 78 rpm. One side played a complete song. *Right* A typical southern 'juke', Moore's Cafe, at Yazoo City near the Mississippi. A dance floor is at the side of the building.

rags. He also wrote a ragtime opera, *A Guest of Honour*, in 1903, but the manuscript has been lost. He completed a second opera, *Treemonisha*, in 1911, but this does not employ ragtime exclusively. It received a single unsuccessful performance during his lifetime. The disappointment probably helped to bring about the mental collapse that led to his early death. It was, however, revived in 1976 and has since been recorded. (→ **Ragtime**)

**Josquin des Prés** Netherlands composer, c.1440–1521. Though the details of his career are not clearly known, he seems to have joined the Papal Chapel, Rome, in about 1486, remaining with it until 1494. He afterwards entered the services of King Louis XII of France. In 1503 he was appointed Director of Music to the court of Ferrara, but seems to have returned to France in the following year.

Josquin's compositions were included in many 16th-century printed collections and occur in many manuscript copies of the period. We know of about 18 masses, 100 motets, 70 chansons, and a number of other secular works.

He was regarded by his contemporaries as the 'Father of Musicians' and the 'best of the composers of our time'. Now that scholarship has made his work available once more, we can see that he was indeed one of the greatest composers of all times.

**Jota** (Pronounced 'Hota') A dance of Northern Spain. It is a type of fast waltz in 3/4 time. It is sometimes sung by the dancers.

**Juke box** An automatic machine for playing 'pop' records, found in public houses and cafés, etc. Originally called a nickel-odeon (because, in America, it cost a nickel to operate the machine), the juke box spread throughout America after 1933 when the laws prohibiting the sale of alcohol were repealed, and then throughout the rest of the world. The name 'juke' comes from a certain type of drinking place found in southern black America.

# Jazz

So many ingredients have gone into the making of jazz that it is almost impossible to give a clear account of its history and development. In origin it is really a type of folk music; and like all folk music it evolved at the hands of countless men and women who felt the need to express themselves through song and dance. Some of them were black – negro slaves imported from Africa to work in the cotton fields of North America's Southern States, and on the railroads. Some were white – professional musicians, and amateurs, of many different racial origins. Each brought some important element of his native musical culture, and it went into the melting pot.

To begin with, the most important contribution came from the negro slaves. As Africans they were accustomed to use song and dance for every occasion. Work-songs were particularly important to them – for, like the sailor's **Shanties** →, they ensured that a whole group could exert themselves at the same moment and thus get the work done more quickly and efficiently. Many of them were of direct African origin.

A second ingredient was the song the negro sang in order to express his personal feelings. Many of these took the form of **Blues** →. They are true folk songs: some happy, many sad – all a record of daily life

and deep emotion. Most blues are built on the same strict basis: three lines of poetry to twelve bars of music, with a simple, unvarying pattern of harmonies. There were two main types: the quiet, meditative 'country' blues, sung by wandering minstrels to a guitar accompaniment; and the harsher, noisier 'city' blues, sung in places of entertainment against an instrumental backing.

Religious music also played a vital part in the life of the negro slave. Again there were two main types: the **Gospel song** →, which is the white man's nonconformist hymn sung in a blues style; and the **Spiritual** →, which is the negro's own musical interpretation of the Christian message. Both were encouraged by the strong revivalist movement that swept America during the early part of the 19th century.

There is one other type of popular music which is related to the Negro: the songs of the **Minstrel shows**. But this is really the white man's version of the way the slaves sang, for the performers were in fact white men with blackened faces. The singing was accompanied by instrumentalists – the banjo and drums being particularly important. The shows included all the popular songs and dances of the day, some borrowed

**Early jazz bands** *Below left* This mixed band of black and white musicians from Lutcher, Louisiana, typifies the American jazz band at the turn of the century. *Below* Fate Marable's Riverboat Band of 1918. The great jazz trumpeter Louis Armstrong is seated immediately left of the pianist, Fate Marable. Riverboat bands gave many jazz musicians their first professional engagement.

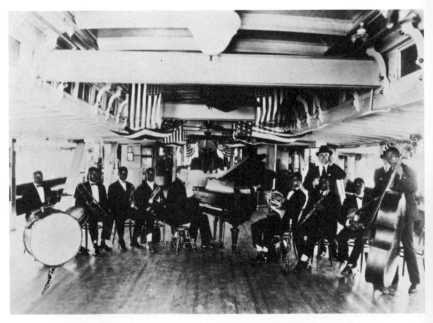

*Left* **Cakewalk** This dance which originated in the Negro plantations was later danced to ragtime music.

direct from negro slaves, some written in imitation of their music.

Another ingredient of jazz in which white musicians played an important part was **Ragtime** →. It flourished for about 20 years (1896–1917) as a form of piano music, composed and written down and eventually highly commercialized. Its steady basic rhythm was probably borrowed from the military march, but the tunes were syncopated and owe something to a popular dance of the time – the 'Cakewalk'.

If we add to these main ingredients the influence of music from other countries – that of the French and Spanish Caribbean islands, for example – something of the strange mixture that went into making jazz begins, perhaps, to become clear.

It is generally accepted that these elements began to be fused into a new style by the American negro musicians of New Orleans, round about 1900. These first jazz performers played entirely by ear. They expressed themselves through free improvisation, using the syncopated rhythms and Ragtime and the melodic style of the Blues, and thus creating a very powerful kind of music. Their bands were quite small: a rhythm section (string bass, drums, guitar, banjo, or piano), and a melody section (one or two cornets, clarinet, and trombone).

Such bands were similar to the kind that the Negroes used to accompany funeral processions – themselves a development of the military band.

What is now sometimes called the 'Jazz Age' began after the First World War, when jazz began to spread internationally and become extremely popular. This growth was enormously helped by the rise of the gramophone industry, the arrival of sound broadcasting, and, in 1927, of the talking film. The first jazz recordings were made in 1917, by the Original Dixieland Jazz Band (a white group).

The centre of jazz moved from New Orleans, however, when its notorious Storyville district (a gambling and brothel area) was closed down in 1917. The jazzmen moved up river, and in the 1920s Chicago became an important centre. Here a mixture of black musicians, such as Louis Armstrong and King Oliver, and white, such as Bix Beiderbecke, began to develop the style of jazz playing. One of their inventions was **Skiffle** →, another was **Boogie-woogie** →. And though spontaneous improvisation played as important a part as ever, more and more jazz now came to be written down.

*Below left* **Jazz Age bands** *Top* Bix Beiderbecke and his all white band, the Wolverines, were popular in the 1920s. *Bottom* 'King' Oliver's Creole Jazz Band in the early 1920s in Chicago. It was one of the most important jazz bands for the many talents it nurtured. Here, 'King' Oliver plays the cornet, Louis Armstrong the trumpet, Johnny Dodds, the clarinet, 'Baby' Dodds, the drums and Lil Harden (Mrs. Armstrong) the piano.

*Above* **Jazz band of the 1940s** The Bunk Johnson Band was formed in 1945 and played with numerous changes in its members until 1948 when Johnson suffered a stroke. He died the following year.

By the 1930s jazz had developed very considerably. The centre was now New York, and the public favoured **Big Bands** →, such as those of Duke Ellington, Count Basie, Benny Goodman, etc., and a bouncier style of playing known as **Swing** →. A further development, **Bop** →, emerged in the early 1940s, and with it the influence of the Big Bands waned and there was a return to smaller jazz groups.

The 1950s were notable for the introduction of COOL JAZZ, a style which used small groups and was much more relaxed and elegant in its approach. Miles Davis and Dave Brubeck were particularly important innovators in this field. At the same time, West Coast jazz men (often working for the Hollywood film industry) began to make experiments with musical ideas brought in from straight music. East Coast (New York) musicians also experimented with classical ideas (such as fugue and canon) but insisted always that the emotional content of the music should be strong. By the 1960s there was a flourishing school of 'New Wave' jazz composers, such as John Coltrane and Ornette Coleman, making use of all available style of music – classical, jazz, atonal, modal. And, as a revolt against this 'intellectualizing' of what had once been a matter of spontaneous improvisation, such jazz-types as **Rock** → and **Soul** → came into existence. In short, jazz continued, and continues, to flourish and develop.

It also continues to influence the 'straight' musician, and it is no exaggeration to say that jazz ingredients have been some of the most important additions to 20th-century music. Such composers as Ravel and Stravinsky, Milhaud and Kurt Weill, Hindemith and Křenek, Gershwin and Copland, Walton and Vaughan Williams have all felt its influence. Jazz is now accepted as a subtle and important art form.

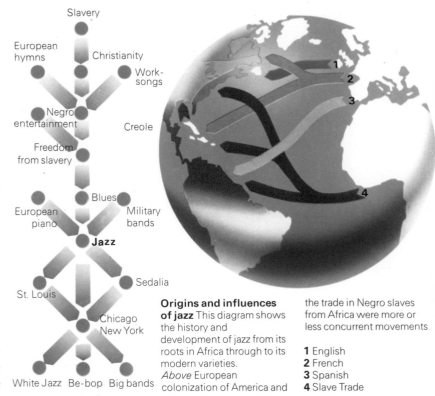

**Origins and influences of jazz** This diagram shows the history and development of jazz from its roots in Africa through to its modern varieties. *Above* European colonization of America and the trade in Negro slaves from Africa were more or less concurrent movements.

1 English
2 French
3 Spanish
4 Slave Trade

**Piano rags** This sheet music front cover is for 'Original Rags' selected by the pianist and composer, Scott Joplin. This first publication of Joplin's music appeared in 1899 and thereafter he became well-known as interest in ragtime spread from the Southern States to Chicago and the East. The son of an ex-slave, Joplin's music has enjoyed a revival in the 1970s largely because it was featured in the popular film, *The Sting*.

Above **Charles Mingus**, the jazz bass-player at a rehearsal. *Right* **Charlie Parker**, alto-saxophonist, was perhaps the first 'modern' jazz composer. His distinctive rhythmic style coupled with the emotional power of his music has yet to be surpassed by imitators. *Far right* The pianist **Thelonius Monk**, whose unconventional style includes off-beat harmonies.

## Jazz terms

| | |
|---|---|
| *Arrangement* | a jazz composition. |
| *Beat* | the basic pulse in jazz. |
| *Book* | a jazz band's repertoire. |
| *Break* | a passage for solo instruments, without rhythmic backing. |
| *Blue note* | the flattened 3rd or 7th of the scale. |
| *Changes* | the harmonic progressions in a composition. |
| *Chase* | passages played by several players, each taking a few bars in turn. Often called 'splitting eights' or 'splitting fours' – meaning that each player takes eight bars, or four bars, etc. |
| *Combo* | a small group of instruments (as distinct from a Band). |
| *Cool* | the West Coast jazz style of the 1950s. |
| *Dirty* | a particularly harsh, aggressive style of playing. |
| *Front man* | the band leader. |
| *Funky* | very 'dirty' sounds – distorted and wild. |
| *Gig* | a playing job. |
| *Horn* | any wind instrument – sometimes any instrument. |
| *Jam session* | the occasion when players meet to improvise. |
| *Side men* | jazz players, other than the 'front man'. |
| *Shake* | an extreme form of vibrato. |
| *Trad* | the Dixieland/New Orleans style of jazz. |

*Left* **Duke Ellington** and his band, probably the best known of all big jazz bands. *Above* **John Coltrane** plays the soprano sax with tenor slung ready to hand.

*Above* **Miles Davis**, a jazz trumpeter with prodigious technique, developed with others the elegant and relaxed style of 'cool' jazz.

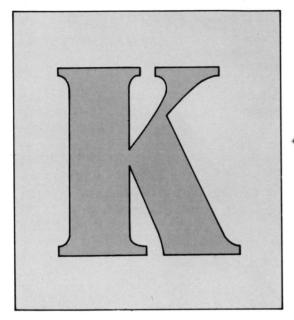

**K**, followed by a number (e.g. K 459) is the catalogue reference for Mozart's complete works. (→ **Köchel**)

**Kabalevsky, Dmitry** Russian composer, b. 1904. Studied at the Moscow Conservatory, where he later became a professor of composition. A straightforward lyrical style and a fluent technique have enabled him to produce the kind of music that Soviet authority prefers. His opera *The Craftsman of Clamecy* (1937), based on the novel *Colas Breugnon* by Romain Rolland, has been much admired, as have his three piano concertos and Concerto for Violin and Orchestra (1948).

**Kapellmeister,** or **Capellmeister** (Ger.) Though nowadays we use this German word to describe any kind of conductor, it was originally applied to the choirmaster in a court chapel. During the 17th and 18th centuries, and even into the 19th, the job of 'Master of the Chapel' was one that most composers aspired to – for it meant financial security and the opportunity to write music. (The Italian term was *Maestro di cappella.*)

**Kazoo** A member of the MIRLITON family. It consists of a short tube (nowadays usually made of plastic) with a small hole in the side which is covered with a membrane. When the player blows through the tube, the membrane makes a buzzing sound. The player makes the notes himself, the 'instrument' merely adds a different quality to their sound. The kazoo is used primarily as a toy instrument, often in primary schools, but it is of ancient origin.

**Kazoo** This instrument, sometimes known as Tommy Talker, is used mostly in folk music although in the 1930s kazoo bands were popular in some parts of Europe.

**Jerome Kern** Ethel Merman as Annie Oakley in the Broadway production of *Annie Get Your Gun* in 1946. This was one of the composer's most popular musicals.

**Aram Khachaturian** 1903–1978 The son of a book-binder, he showed no interest in music until he was nineteen.

**Kern, Jerome** American composer, 1885–1945. After studying in New York he used his considerable melodic gifts to write a series of first-rate musical comedies, beginning with *The red Petticoat* (1912) and continuing through *Very Good Eddie* (1915), *Oh, Boy!* (1917), *Sally* (1920), etc., to his masterpiece, *Show Boat* (1927). Later works, such as *Roberta* (1933), were also very successful. All these shows contain songs that became immensely popular in their own right (*Smoke gets in your Eyes, Ol' Man River*, for example). The complete shows are important in the history of the American musical because they set a higher standard of dramatic logic and musical coherence than was usual in those days.

**Kettledrum** → **Drums**

**Key** → page 201

**Key** This is also the name given to the levers on wind instruments which enable the player to open and close the soundholes mechanically.

Early wind instruments had no 'keys', and therefore, like the recorder, could only have the same number of soundholes as there were fingers to cover them. The gradual addition of keys in the 18th and 19th centuries made it possible for instrument makers to put their soundholes in exactly the right place and add as many as were needed for a complete chromatic scale.

On keyboard instruments, the 'keys' are the levers the player must press in order to make the instrument sound.

**Key-note** → **Key 1**

**Key signature** → **Key 3**; and also **Notes and notation**

**Khachaturian, Aram** Russian composer, 1903–78. He was born at Tiflis (now Tbilisi) in Georgia and studied composition in Moscow under Alexander Gnesin and Myaskovsky. Some of his music, which is bold, rhythmic, and tuneful, has become very popular. It includes ballets, such as *Gayaneh* (1942) and *Spartacus* (1954), as well as several symphonies, a Piano Concerto in D flat (1936), and a Violin Concerto in D minor (1940). Many of his works draw upon folksong, particularly that of his native Georgia. In Britain, he is best known for *The Sabre Dance* and music from the ballet *Spartacus* which has been made into the signature tune for a T.V. series called 'The Onedin Line'.

# Key

All music written in accordance with the major and minor diatonic scales is said to be 'in a key'.

Music written in accordance with the Church Modes (that is, music written before about 1600) is not in a key, nor is the music of countries such as India or China. Moreover, many composers have now abandoned the idea of key altogether, and write their music according to other principles, such as atonality.

Key is therefore not an essential element in music. It is simply an aspect of one particular kind of music – the music written in Europe after about 1600.

1. **The principle of key** Tunes which are written in a key are 'controlled' by a note which is felt to be more important than any other. We call this the KEY-NOTE or TONIC. The other notes also have fairly definite qualities. Some seem almost as important as the key-note, others seem to lead up to it, and others seem very distant. A key is therefore a network or relationship between a series of different notes, one of which, the key-note, is felt to be all-important.

For example, in the following tune the note C dominates all the others – they seem to spring from it, and then make their way back to it at the end. C is the key-note of this tune:

Many tunes begin on their key-note, and still more end on it. And if a tune has been harmonized, the last note in the bass part is nearly always the key-note. The key-note, in fact, has a restful effect. If we were to stop the tune on any other note, the effect would be less satisfying.

2. **Major and minor scales** If we take that tune and arrange its notes in order, beginning and ending with the key-note, we shall get:

This is a SCALE. The word comes from the Latin *scala*, meaning 'a ladder', and that is exactly what the scale is: a ladder of notes arranged in ascending order.

A scale is a kind of chart or outline of a key. It sets out, in their correct order, all the notes that go to make up that key. All other notes, such as F♯ or B♭, do not belong to that particular key – but they do belong to other keys, as we shall see.

The scale we have illustrated is made up from a series of whole-steps and half-steps – tones and semitones:

When these steps appear in these positions, the scale is said to be a MAJOR scale, and it represents a Major key. (Note that it has a major 3rd, C-E, and a major 6th, C-A).

If we change the original tune slightly, its whole character will alter:

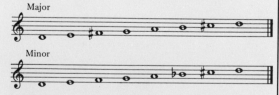

The scale that corresponds to these notes is:

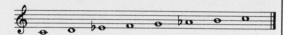

The arrangement of tones and semitones has now become:

C  D  E♭  F  G  A♭  B  C

This is a MINOR scale, representing a Minor key. (Note that it has a minor 3rd, C-E♭, and a minor 6th, C-A♭).

Both forms of the tune were in the Key of C – but one was in C *major* and the other in C *minor*. We could, however, put the tunes into a different key, higher or lower than C.

For example, if we take D as the key-note, our major and minor scales will be:

Major

Minor

The tones and semitones are still the same.

And if we now write our tunes in the scale of D (major and minor), they will appear:

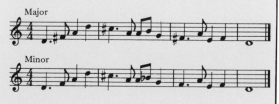

The tunes in D are the same as the tunes in C – they have simply been lifted up one degree. If we want, we can put them down one degree:

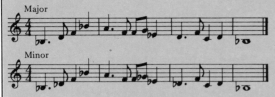

B♮ is now the key-note, and our tunes are in the key of B♭ (major, and minor).

As there are 12 semitones in every octave (twelve different notes), it is obvious that we can start a scale on every one of them:

This brings a total of 24 scales: 12 major, and 12 minor.

3. **Key signatures** As it would be cumbersome always to add accidentals in front of the notes that require them, we collect them together and add them to the beginning of each line of music in the form of a KEY SIGNATURE:

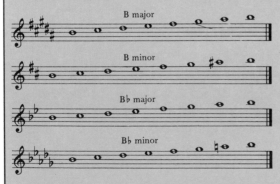

It will be noticed that the minor form of the scale still needs one accidental. Though the key signatures could have been written:

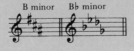

this is never done, because the accidental on the seventh note is not always required.

If we take the whole series of keys and arrange them in order of sharps and flats, their key signatures are:

4. **The cycle of keys** If we compare the key-notes of each key in the order of their sharps and flats, we shall find that each is five notes away from the other. The order of the sharp keys goes *up* in fifths. The order of the flat keys goes *down* in fifths. Thus:

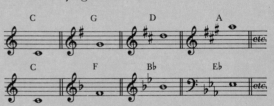

This pattern of fifths is called a CYCLE, and it shows how all the keys are related to each other. Each key requires *one* accidental more, or less, than its neighbour – which means that neighbouring keys have only a one-note difference.

5. **Modulation** Only the very shortest pieces of music stay in one key all the time. Most move into another key at some point, and then return to the original key at the end of the piece. Indeed, the piece may make several such moves before it eventually returns to the original key. These changes of key are called MODULATION.

For example, we might extend our original tune like this:

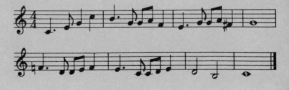

In bar 3 a sharp has been added to the F, and so, for a moment, until the sharp is cancelled by a natural in bar 5, the music is in G major – the key with one sharp.

It is worth noting, however, that not all accidentals in a piece of music necessarily mean that a modulation has taken place. Some are introduced merely as a passing decoration, as for example:

None of these accidentals destroys the feeling that C is still the key-note of the piece.

6. **The naming of compositions** The key of a composition is often included on its title-page. For example: *Sonata in A major*. This is merely so that we can distinguish the piece from any other of that same kind that the composer may have written. The first and last movements of extended works are usually in the same key, and it is this key that is used to describe the whole work. If a composer has written a number of similar works in the same key, further means of identification have to be included – as, for instance, *Sonata No 2 in A major*.

Kit An engraving by Le Bas after Covot depicts an 18th-century dancing master instructing a pupil. In his hand is a kit, virtually a pocket violin.

**Zoltán Kodály** 1882–1967 A composer who drew on the richness of his country's folksong. Collaborated for a while with Bartók in collecting and editing folksong. His music reveals a strong national flavour. He studied at the Conservatory of Budapest which he later joined as a teacher of composition.

**Kirbye, George** English composer, c. 1565–1634. Most of his life was spent in his native Suffolk, and it seems likely that he was employed as music master in the house of Sir Robert Jermyn, near Bury St Edmunds. He wrote a number of motets, and two dozen fine madrigals.

**Kirkman, Jacob** German harpsichord and piano maker, 1710–92. He settled in England in the 1730s and became well known as a maker of harpsichords, and later (from about 1775) of pianofortes. The firm of Kirkman continued its activities until about 1810. Its instruments are now highly prized.

**Kit** A small violin, developed in the 16th century from the rebec. It was particularly popular in the 18th and 19th centuries with dancing-masters, who could carry it around easily and use it to provide music for their lessons.

**Klangfarbenmelodie** (Ger.) Tone-colour-melody. A term invented by Schoenberg to describe a melody that depends on different tone colours rather than different pitches. For example, the third movement of his *Five Orchestral Pieces* (1909) makes use of single, sustained chords whose colour changes as different instruments are added and taken away.

**Klebe, Giselher** German composer, b. 1925. He is a pupil of Boris Blacher. His music has been much influenced by that of Webern (see, for example, the *Symphony for 23 Strings*), but he has also been active in the field of electronic music (e.g. *Interferenzen*, for tape, 1956). He is now regarded as one of the leading German composers of his generation.

**Klavier** → **Clavier**

**Köchel, Ludwig von** German scientist, 1800–77. He was a botanist and mineralogist, but won musical immortality in 1862 when he published a Chronological Thematic Catalogue of Mozart's music. In it he gave each work a number according to its date of composition. Thus it has become easy for musicians to identify the music, even though there may be several similar pieces in the same key. For example, we can now distinguish between Mozart's G minor Symphony of 1773 and the G minor Symphony of 1788 simply by quoting their 'Köchel' numbers: K.183, and K.550.

**Kodály, Zoltán** Hungarian composer, 1882–1967. Together with Bartók he was largely responsible, not only for the thorough exploration and preservation of Hungarian folk music but also for the creation of a genuine national style of music.

Kodály was trained at the Budapest Academy of Music and began to study and collect folksongs immediately after graduating in 1904. He came into prominence as a composer in 1910. Later works, such as the *Psalmus Hungaricus* (1923) and the opera *Háry János* (1926), brought him world-wide fame.

Kodály wrote a great many choral works, including a fine *Te Deum* (1936). A number of orchestral works, such as the *Marosszék Dances* (1930) and the *Dances of Galánta* (1933), reflect his interest in folk music.

Besides his work in collecting and studying folksong, Kodály spent much time in setting up a method of training young musicians and children through sight-singing (known as the Kodály method). He has probably had a greater influence over the teaching of music in his native country than any composer has ever enjoyed anywhere or at any time.

**Koechlin, Charles** French composer, 1867–1951. He studied at the Paris Conservatoire under Massenet and Fauré and became known as the composer of a series of elaborate and rather unusual works – such as his setting of *Three Poems from Kipling's Jungle Book* for chorus and orchestra (1910), and the *Seven Stars Symphony* (1933), which celebrates a group of film stars.

Though his music was often extremely complex and experimental, it is seldom played nowadays – perhaps because he wrote an immense amount and never settled to any one style.

**Korngold, Erich Wolfgang** Austrian composer, 1897–1957. He was the son of a famous Viennese music critic, Julius Korngold (1860–1945), and became famous when he was only 11 when his pantomime *The Snowman* was performed at the Vienna Court Opera. The works which followed, including two one-act operas, *The Ring of Polykrates* and *Violanta* (1916), established him as one of the most remarkable prodigies of all time. This impression was confirmed by a three-act opera *Die tote Stadt* (The Dead City) (1920) which achieved enormous popularity.

Thereafter, however, his amazing talents failed to develop and later works suggest he was merely repeating himself. This was perhaps all the more noticeable because his music was extremely romantic and therefore at odds with the austere music of his contemporaries.

Korngold was forced to leave Vienna in

1938, because of Nazi persecution. He settled in Hollywood and became much admired as a composer of lavish film music.

**Koto** The Japanese form of zither. Since the 17th century it has been a national instrument of great importance. It consists of a long box, with 13 strings passing over movable bridges. It is placed on the ground, or on a low table, and played with three plectra worn on the thumb, index and middle fingers of the right hand.

**Koto** The most famous of Japanese musical instruments, the koto is played entirely by ear. Its music is at first startling to Western ears because of its combination of sharp sounds, continuous tones and sudden silences. Its music is precisely codified in 17th-century Japanese manuscripts.

**Ernst Křenek** b.1900 He composed, among other things, a choral work *Santa Fe Time-Table* on the names of American railway stations. His first wife was Mahler's daughter, Anna, and his second, Berta Hermann, the well-known actress to whom he dedicated his successful opera *Johnny Strikes Up*.

**Křenek, Ernst** Austrian composer, b. 1900. He was born in Vienna where he studied with Franz Schreker, whose expressive romantic style he at first copied. Gradually, however, he began to experiment with atonality and then with jazz. His opera *Jonny spielt auf* (Johnny strikes up) (1927) was a sensational success – partly because of its jazz, and partly because the story was considered rather shocking.

In the 1930s Křenek turned once more to atonality, this time adopting Schoenberg's principles wholeheartedly. The chief work of this period was the opera *Karl V* (1933), which unfortunately fell foul of the Nazi party and was not produced until 1938. In the meantime Křenek had left Vienna for Los Angeles. He became an American citizen. His later music, though still often harsh, is less strictly atonal, and he has experimented with electronic techniques (in, for example, the opera *Der goldene Bock*, 1964). His output is large, and includes six symphonies, four piano concertos, and a great many chamber works.

**Kyrie Eleison** (Greek) Lord have Mercy. The opening words of the mass and communion service.

**La** or **Lah** The 6th degree of the major scale, and in the Tonic Sol-fa system the 1st degree of the minor scale ( → **Sol-fa system**). On the continent, however, it stands for the note A, whatever degree of the scale it may happen to be.

**Lacrimoso** (It.) Tearful.

**Lalo, Édouard** French composer, 1823–92. After studying in Lille and at the Paris Conservatoire he made his mark as a composer of songs. His first great success came in 1874 when the violinist Sarasate played his *Violin Concerto in F minor*. An even more popular work followed in 1875, the *Symphonie espagnole* for violin and orchestra. Lalo's graceful, tuneful style and flair for colourful orchestration is seen at its best in these works, though his masterpiece is probably the opera *Le Roi d'Ys* (1888).

**Lambert, Constant** English composer, 1905–51. The son of a well-known painter, he studied at the Royal College of Music under Vaughan Williams. While still a student he was commissioned to write a ballet for Diaghilev, *Romeo and Juliet*, (1926). Other ballets followed: *Pomona* (1926), *Horoscope* (1937), and *Tiresias* (1951). In the meantime he developed as a music critic and conductor, even though these activities left him less time for composition. Nevertheless, certain works made a great impression – the brilliant, jazzy *Rio Grande* (1927) for piano, chorus and orchestra, for example. He completed his most ambitious work, the choral *Summer's last Will and Testament*, in 1935. His book *Music Ho!: a Study of Music in Decline* (1934) is regarded as a classic.

Édouard Lalo 1823-1892 One of his finest works is his ballet *Namouna*.

**Ländler,** danced here by Viennese laundry girls.

Francesco Landini 1325–1397 This illustration from a 15th-century manuscript shows the composer playing a portative organ. Landini was also a poet, philosopher and skilled astrologer.

**Lament** In Scottish and Irish folk music certain tunes are played at a death or some other calamity. These are 'laments' and they are always very beautiful. Most clans have their own special lament. They are usually played on the bagpipes.

**Lamentoso** (It.) Mournfully.

**Lancers, The** A type of quadrille with its own particular figures, danced by 8 or 16 couples. It came into existence in about 1819.

**Ländler** A country dance popular in Austria and Bavaria. It is similar to the waltz, only somewhat slower and much less sophisticated. Mozart, Beethoven, and Schubert all wrote *ländler*.

**Land of my Fathers** → **Hen wlad fy nhadau**

**Landini, Francesco** Italian composer, 1325–97. Most of his life was spent in Florence, where he was much admired as a virtuoso organist as well as an excellent performer on other instruments, such as the lute and rebec. His music includes a number of madrigals and dance-songs of great beauty. His skill as a musician is all the more remarkable for the fact that he was blind from childhood.

**Langsam** (Ger.) Slow.

**Languido** (It.) Languid(ly).

**Lanner, Joseph** Austrian composer and conductor, 1801–43. In 1818 he formed a small band in Vienna to play dance music. He was joined by the elder Johann Strauss, who eventually broke away (1825) to form a rival orchestra. Like Strauss, Lanner wrote a series of splendid waltzes, polkas, quadrilles, galops, and marches, etc. Some people consider them to be more imaginative than Strauss's.

**Largamente** (It.) Broad and spacious, but not slower than the prevailing tempo.

**Larghetto** (It.) Slow and dignified, but not so slow as *Largo*.

**Largo** (It.) A very slow tempo.

**Larsson, Lars-Erik** Swedish composer, b. 1908. He studied in Stockholm, Leipzig, and Vienna (under Alban Berg), and has written a considerable quantity of music in the neo-classic style. Certain pieces, such as the tuneful *Pastorale Suite* (1938), have become very popular.

**Lassus, Orlandus** (**Orlando di Lasso**) Netherlands composer, 1532–94. He is regarded as one of the greatest composers of 16th-century vocal polyphony, and his music was admired as much in his own day as now.

He began his career as a choirboy at Mons, and his voice attracted so much attention that he was kidnapped three times by rival choir-masters! The third kidnapping brought him into the service of the Viceroy of Sicily, who took him to Italy. In due course he became a choirmaster in Rome, but later travelled|in France and the Netherlands.

In 1577 he joined the chapel of the Duke of Bavaria in Munich and eventually became the Kapellmeister. Though he remained in this post for the rest of his life, he was able to travel in France, Germany, and Italy. Everywhere he went his music was greatly admired and he was soon generally accepted as one of the most outstanding composers of the day. His music was published from about 1555 onwards and was performed throughout Europe.

Lassus wrote nearly 1,000 works, including a great many fine Italian madrigals.

**Last Post** This is a British Army bugle call. In the old days the 'First Post' at 9.30 p.m. called the men back to barracks, and the 'Last Post' at 10 p.m. ended the day.

The call is also used at military funerals as a final summons to rest.

Though confined to a few notes (the bugle has no valves and can only play the notes of one **Harmonic series**) it is a powerful tune of great beauty:

(→ **Harmonics; Horn family**)

**Orlandus Lassus**
1532–1594 This portrait of the composer is from his *Livre de chansons nouvelles*, 1571. As well as French songs Lassus composed over 500 Latin motets.

**Jean Marie Leclair**
1697–1764 In his early career he was associated with ballet and in his twenties took the post of ballet master at Turin.

**Leadbelly** (Huddie Ledbetter) An ex-convict, he learnt the blues from Negro street musicians and in the brothels of Shreveport, Louisiana. He was perhaps the greatest of the early blues singers.

**Lawes, Henry** English composer, 1596–1662. He wrote music for a number of masques, including Milton's *Comus* (1634), as well as many aires and anthems. He was admired as much in his own day as now.

**Lawes, William** English composer, 1602–45. The brother of Henry. He wrote vocal and instrumental music, including a series of very interesting Fantasies, before being killed at the siege of Chester during the Civil War.

**Lay clerk** One of the singing men in an Anglican Cathedral choir. Originally the lay clerk was in holy orders, but nowadays they are simply professional or amateur musicians who join the choir for the services and then supplement their meagre pay by doing some other work – often teaching at the cathedral's choir school, should it have one.

**Leader** The first violin player of a string quartet or the principal first violin player of an orchestra (in the U.S.A. the latter is called the 'concert-master').

**Leading motif** This is a musical theme which is used in an opera, oratorio, programme symphony, or symphonic poem to represent a particular person or idea, thus enabling the composer to 'tell a story' in terms of music.

We find the device used most extensively in Wagner's music dramas. The German word is **Leitmotiv.**

**Leading note** The seventh note of the diatonic scale. It is a semitone below the tonic and has a feeling of wanting to rise to it – 'leading' in, as it were. In minor scales it can occur in two forms: with an accidental, so that it is a true leading note; and without an accidental, in 'flattened leading note' form, which, of course, no longer has the 'rising to tonic' quality.

**Leclair, Jean Marie** French composer, 1697–1764. Mainly famous as a violinist. He also wrote a number of important solo and trio sonatas which helped to extend violin playing technique. He was murdered on his own doorstep, but nobody has ever found out why.

**Ledbetter, Huddie** American jazz composer, 1885–1949. Known as 'Leadbelly', he was born in Louisiana and became known as a remarkable blues singer and performer on the 12-string guitar. He was sentenced to death for murder, but, after many years in prison, was reprieved in 1925. He is particularly important for his knowledge of the old Negro work songs, and he kept alive a folk tradition that other jazzmen were then able to learn from.

**Ledger lines** or **Leger lines** Short lines added above or below the stave to accommodate notes which lie too high or too low to be written on the stave itself. They correspond to the line/space arrangement of the stave.

**Legato** (It.) Smooth. A style of playing in which the notes of a phrase feel as if they are flowing into each other. **Legatissimo** means 'very smooth'.

**Leggiero** (It.) Light. **Leggerissimo**, very light. Do not confuse with *Legato*.

**Legno, Col** (It.) With the wood. A direction used in music for strings, to indicate that the player must turn his bow over and tap 'with the wood'.

**Lehár, Franz** Hungarian composer, 1870–1948. He studied in Prague and began his career as a conductor of military bands, but soon became famous as a composer of operettas in the Viennese style. Many are still performed and are generally considered to be the best of their kind since those of Johann Strauss. The most famous are: *The Merry Widow* (1907), *The Count of Luxembourg* (1909), *Gypsy Love* (1910), *Frasquita* (1922), and *The Land of Smiles* (1923).

**Leid** (Ger.) Sorrow. Do not confuse with *Lied*.

**Leigh, Walter** English composer, 1905–42. He studied at Cambridge University and in Berlin with Hindemith. His music includes pieces for amateurs, and several operettas somewhat in the style of Sullivan's – for example: *Jolly Roger* (1933). He also wrote music for several revues, and a very agreeable *Concertino for Harpsichord and Strings* (1936). He was killed in action in the Libyan desert during the Second World War.

**Leise** (Ger.) Soft, gentle.

**Leitmotiv** (Ger.) → **Leading motif**

**Lento** (It.) Slow. **Lentamente**, slowly. **Lentissimo** or **Lento di molto**, very slowly.

**Leoncavallo, Ruggiero** Italian composer, 1858–1919. He studied at the Conservatory

Ruggiero Leoncavallo
1858-1919

in Naples and won international fame in 1892 with a two-act opera *I Pagliacci*. This is now usually performed with Mascagni's one-act opera *Cavalleria Rusticana* (the two are often referred to as 'Cav' and 'Pag'). Though he wrote many more operas, including a very interesting version of *La Bohème* (1897), none achieved the success of *I Pagliacci*.

**Léonin** French 12th-century composer. Little is known of his life, beyond the fact that he was in charge of music at the church which eventually became Notre-Dame de Paris. He was regarded as the leading composer of that type of early composition called **Organum** →. He is one of the first great composers in the history of Western music.

**Leonora overtures** → **Beethoven**

**L.H.** is short for Left Hand. Found in piano music when, for example, something written in the right hand's stave has to be played by the left hand.

**Liadov, Anatol** Russian composer, 1855–1914. He studied under Rimsky-Korsakov at the St Petersburg Conservatory, at which he later became a professor. He became known as a composer of delicate piano music, somewhat influenced by Chopin, but still very Russian in style. His busy life as a teacher left little time for composition and he wrote few large-scale works. His symphonic poems *Baba Yaga*, *The Enchanted Lake*, and *Kikimora* are still very popular.

**Liberamente** (It.) Freely, in accordance with the performer's feelings.

**Libretto** (It.) Little book. Used to describe the book of words of an opera, oratorio, operetta or musical comedy. A writer who specializes in such works is known as a LIBRETTIST.

**Licenza, Con alcuna** (It.) With some freedom. (→ **Liberamente**)

**Lied** (Ger.) Pl. **Lieder** Song. Used in particular to describe the kind of song developed by Schubert, Schumann, Brahms, Hugo Wolf and Richard Strauss – that is to say, songs in which the vocal line, piano accompaniment, and poem are treated as having equal importance and are welded into an artistic whole. Great care is taken in the musical interpretation of the poem being set, with the result that many of these songs are miniature dramas. The term 'art song' is sometimes used to describe such settings, and it suggests the general seriousness of the composer's approach (though the song itself may, of course, be light-hearted).

A set of songs intended to be sung one after the other may be called a *Liedercyklus* (song cycle), *Liederkreis* (song circle), or *Liederreihe* (song series). Such songs are grouped together because they either tell a complete story (each song being, as it were, a new chapter), or evoke a similar mood.

Mendelssohn used the term *Lied ohne Worte* (Song without Words) to describe some of his short piano pieces.

### Ligature

1. The SLUR used in vocal music to show that several notes are to be sung to one syllable.
2. The TIE used to link two notes over a bar line.
3. The metal band used to fasten the reed to the mouthpiece of a clarinet, etc.
4. In medieval music it is a form of notation that shows that two or three notes (or more) must be sung to one syllable.

### Ligeti, György

Hungarian composer, b. 1923. Like many Hungarians he left his native land after the 1956 uprising. He lived first in Germany, and then in Vienna where he became an Austrian citizen. His music is very experimental. For example, he has been stimulated by the sounds that electronic instruments can make into asking singers and instrumentalists to produce similar effects. Such pieces as *Atmospheres*, *Apparitions*, *Requiem*, *Clocks and Clouds* make use of 'sound-clusters', arranged in a kind of beautiful chaos that is, nevertheless, very carefully calculated.

### Lilburn, Douglas

New Zealand composer, b. 1915. He is New Zealand's best known composer. He studied at the Royal College of Music with Vaughan Williams and is now on the music staff of Victoria University in Wellington. His music includes the *Aotearoa Overture* (1940) and several symphonies, of which the Third (1961) is probably the most popular. Besides these fairly traditional works he has experimented with electronic music.

### Lilliburlero

A 17th-century dance tune, which may possibly have been composed by Purcell. It was adopted in the 19th century by Irish Orangemen (supporters of Protestantism in Ireland), with new words ('Protestant Boys') added. The original words poke fun at the appointment of General Talbot to the Lieutenancy of Ireland in 1687.

**György Ligeti b.1923** This composer's works include music-theatre pieces *Adventures* and *New Adventures*, *Articulation* for recorded tape, and *Symphonic poem* for 100 metronomes.

**Lira da Braccio** This is one of the earliest European bowed instruments and is shown here in a detail from Raphael's painting *Il Parnaso*.

**Lira da gamba**, an early 17th-century example.

### Linley, Thomas

English composer, 1732–95. He worked first as a singing master in Bath, but settled in London in 1776 as manager of Drury Lane Theatre. He wrote a great many stage works of the **Ballad opera** → variety. The most famous and successful was *The Duenna* (1775), to words by his son-in-law the great playwright and manager R. B. Sheridan. His daughter Elizabeth (1754–92), Sheridan's wife, was famous for her beauty and her soprano voice. His son Thomas (1756–78), who wrote some of the music for *The Duenna*, was a promising composer, much admired by Mozart. He died in a boating accident before his gifts could mature.

### Liturgy

This word nowadays means a fixed and official set of forms for religious services. There have been many Christian liturgies. In the more important services of these churches great parts of the liturgy are set to music. Until very recently the Roman Catholic liturgy was in Latin. The Anglican liturgy has been in English since Henry VIII's day.

### Lira da braccio, Lira da gamba

These are Italian stringed instruments of the 15th and 16th centuries. The LIRA DA BRACCIO had seven strings and was played, like a violin, at shoulder level. The LIRA DA GAMBA was a bass instrument, held between the knees. It could have anything from 11 to 16 strings.

### Lira organizzata

A type of hurdy gurdy combined with a miniature organ, the bellows of which is operated by the same wheel that 'bows' the strings (→ **Hurdy gurdy**). Haydn wrote a number of works for the instrument, to please the King of Naples, who was an expert performer.

### Liszt → page 209

### L'istesso tempo

(It.) 'The same time'. Very often found when the value of the beat changes, but the duration remains the same. For example, the beat may change from crotchets (eighth-notes) to dotted crotchets, but both are to have the same duration value.

### Locatelli, Pietro

Italian violinist and composer, 1695–1764. He was a pupil of Corelli and, like his master, became famous as a virtuoso violinist and composer of solo and trio sonatas, and concerti grossi. He spent most of his working life in Amsterdam. Unlike Corelli, however, he sometimes allowed his music to degenerate into mere display.

### Locke, Matthew

English composer, 1630–77. He was a chorister at Exeter

# Liszt

Franz Liszt. Hungarian composer and pianist, 1811–86.

In some respects Liszt was one of the most remarkable musicians of his day. He was a brilliant pianist, a fine conductor, a highly original composer, and a great friend and champion of other musicians. But there was also something about him – a touch of calculated showmanship and vulgarity – that has made historians hesitate when it comes to deciding how 'great' he really was. Even now, opinions differ.

He was born at Doborján (now Raiding, Austria), where his father worked as a land steward on the estates of Prince Nicholas Esterhazy (→ **Haydn**). Though he was a delicate child it soon became apparent that he had extraordinary musical gifts. His father taught him all he could, and then organized a series of concerts that so impressed the local nobility that they provided the money to send him to Vienna to study with Carl Czerny.

His progress was remarkable. By the time he was 15 he was completely self-supporting and recognized as one of the greatest pianists of the day. He also began to draw attention to himself as a composer. Many of the pieces he wrote were designed to show off his brilliant technique, but he also wrote music of greater depth – such as the *Twelve Transcendental Studies* (1838, revised 1851).

Liszt's greatest years as a pianist fell between 1839 and 1847. During this time he toured Europe in triumph, enjoying the kind of reception that 'pop' stars are given by their fans today. He also became

**Franz Liszt** A photograph of the great pianist and composer.

This silhouette shows Liszt at the piano. From the 1850s when he turned to religion his compositions took a religious trend. He was a generous supporter of younger musicians and a particular champion of Wagner who married his daughter, Cosima.

notorious for his many love affairs, in particular for those with the Countess Marie d'Agoult and the Princess Carolyne Sayn-Wittgenstein.

In 1847 he retired from the concert platform and settled in Weimar, where there was an excellent orchestra and a fine opera house. Here he was able to help other composers, such as Berlioz and Wagner, and Weimar soon came to be regarded as the centre for 'modern' music. His own music blossomed during this period. In particular he began to explore the possibilities of descriptive music, both in the form of the **Programme symphony** and the **Symphonic poem** (which he invented).

In the late 1850s, however, various personal tragedies and disappointments plunged him into despair and in 1861 he went to Rome and began to make preparations towards becoming a priest. He became an Abbé in 1865, but was never a priest in the fullest sense.

Liszt spent his last years in Weimar, composing steadily (often making extremely daring experiments), teaching, and generally enjoying his position as Europe's most famous and notorious musician.

He wrote about 1,300 works, including three piano concertos, two symphonies (*Dante*, 1855–56, and *Faust*, 1854–57), thirteen symphonic poems (including *Les Préludes*, 1854; *Orpheus*, 1854; *Mazeppa*, 1851–54), two oratorios (*Christus*, 1866, and *St Elizabeth*, 1857–62), and a vast quantity of piano music.

Cathedral and seems to have become composer to King Charles II. He composed a number of anthems and instrumental pieces, but is mainly famous for his theatre music, which includes the masque *Cupid and Death* (which he wrote with Christopher Gibbons), and contributions to *The Siege of Rhodes* (1656), which is often spoken of as the first English opera.

**Loco** (It.) Place. The word occurs in music when there has been some sign directing that the performance shall be an octave higher or lower than printed, and the normal 'place' of the notes is now to be resumed.

**Loder, Edward James** English composer, 1813–65. A member of a very musical family

from Bath. To make money he was forced to compose popular songs, but deserves to be remembered as the composer of several operas which are far superior to those his fellow countrymen were writing at this time. For example: *The Night Dancers* (1846), and *Raymond and Agnes* (1855).

**Loeffler, Charles** American composer, 1861–1935. He was born in Alsace, spent some time in Russia and France and settled in America in 1881. To begin with he earned his living as an orchestral violinist, but retired to a farm in 1903. His best known works are the symphonic poems *The Death of Tintagiles* (1905) and *Pagan Poem* (1906).

**Loewe, Carl** German composer, 1796–1869. Although he wrote a great deal of music of all kinds, including five operas and 16 oratorios, he is remembered as the composer of over 300 **Lieder** →, many of which are fine enough to be ranked alongside those of Schubert and Schumann.

**Loewe, Frederick** American composer, b. 1904. He was born in Vienna, but emigrated to America in 1923 where he earned a precarious living as a serious musician. In 1942 he began to collaborate with the writer Alan Jay Lerner and in 1947 they achieved considerable success with a musical, *Brigadoon*. In 1956 they produced a record-breaking musical: *My Fair Lady*, based on the play *Pygmalion* by George Bernard Shaw. It was equally successful as a film.

**Lontano** (It.) Distant, faint.

**Lortzing, Albert** German composer, 1801–51. Besides his work as a composer he was also a talented actor, singer, librettist, and operatic producer. Though not quite so skilful as Sullivan, he occupies a similar place in German operatic history. His most famous opera is *Tsar and Carpenter* (1837).

**Loure** A type of bagpipe found in many parts of France, but especially in Normandy. Also used to describe a peasant dance (a kind of slow gigue, in 6/4 time) accompanied by such a bagpipe. In the 18th century the word came to be applied to any passage of music in the style of the old bagpipe dances – as, for example, in the sixth movement of Bach's *French Suite, No 5 in G major*.

# Lute

One of a family of stringed instruments of Persian-Arabian origin that came to Europe at the time of the Crusades. It became particularly important during the 16th century, and is the first instrument for which we find a really large quantity of written music.

The body of the lute resembles a pear – split along its length, so that it has a curved back and a flat belly. The neck usually has frets, and can run either straight back, or be bent at an angle where the pegbox begins. The number of strings varies according to the period and country, but they are arranged in pairs (called 'courses'). There is usually a single treble string – the 'chanterelle'. A typical renaissance lute might have 19 strings: nine double courses and one chanterelle.

Lutes were made in various sizes, from the large **Chitarrone** → and **Theorbo** → to the small MANDORA.

Lute music is not written in notation but **Tablature** →. A lute player is called a LUTENIST (or Lutanist).

In recent years, guitarists such as Julian Bream and John Williams, have brought the lute and its music back into popularity.

**Vietnamese lute** *Above* This instrument has a long neck.

**Nigerian lutes** *Right* These have long necks.

**16th century lutenist** *Below* Painting by an anonymous 16th-century artist.

**Modern lute** *Left* The British guitarist, Julian Bream, playing the lute.

**Arabic lute** *Below left* An Egyptian lute player, from a 14th-century miniature.

**Lully, Jean-Baptiste** French composer, 1632–87. He was Italian by birth, but was taken to Paris when he was about ten. There he learned to play the violin. A stroke of good fortune brought him to the notice of King Louis XIV, who first appointed him to his orchestra and then created an orchestra especially for him to lead.

Lully was not only a gifted musician, but an intelligent man, a very hard worker, and a born intriguer. He pleased the King so much that he was soon chosen to compose music for the court ballets – in which he also danced, to great acclaim.

As time went on he gradually acquired more and more control over the court's music. He collaborated with the writer Molière in a series of comédie-ballets, but broke away to produce true operas of his own. In due course he established a French style of opera to rival the Italian style that was so popular at the time.

Despite his success, and the great fortune he was able to amass, Lully was not much liked. He established a virtual dictatorship over French music and was quite unscrupulous in the way he held down his rivals. Nevertheless he must be regarded as one of France's greatest and most influential composers.

**Lungo, Lunga** (It.) Long. **Lunga pausa** means 'pause'.

**Lur** The ancient bronze trumpet of Scandinavia. Some fifty examples have been found, the earliest dating from about 1,000 B.C. Lurs were made in pairs, twisting in opposite directions so that they look like the

**Jean-Baptiste Lully** 1632–1687, the 'father' of French opera.

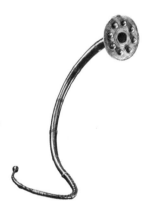

**Lur** This ancient bronze instrument, one of a pair, was found in Denmark.

horns or tusks of an animal. The twisted stem of the instrument ends in a flat disc. The lur has a cup-shaped mouthpiece, similar to that of the modern trombone.

**Lusingando** (It.) In a coaxing manner.

**Lute** → page 210

**Lutoslawski, Witold** Polish composer, b. 1913. He is one of a number of Polish avant-garde composers who came into prominence after the 1939–45 war. His music combines elements of folksong with serial and, more recently, aleatory techniques. His *Funeral Music for Strings* (1958) made a profound impression, for it combines a very strict construction (based on canon and variation) with a very deep sense of emotion. Before studying music at the Warsaw Conservatory, Lutoslawski had been trained as a mathematician. His *Concerto for Orchestra* (1950–54) is very popular.

**Luther, Martin** 1483–1546. Besides being a great religious reformer, he was an enthusiastic amateur musician and it is thought that he may have composed the music for at least some of the many hymns (**Chorale** →) he wrote. He published his German version of the Mass in 1525, and collections of his hymns began to appear from 1524 onwards.

**Luthier** (Fr.) A lute maker. But the word has also come to mean a maker of stringed instruments in general.

**Lydian mode** → **Modes**

**Lyric piece** A lyric is a short poem suitable for singing. Grieg adopted the word as a title for some of his short piano pieces (*Lyric Pieces*, Books 1–10, 1867–1901).

# Lyre

A stringed instrument known to have been in existence since Sumerian times (3000 B.C.). It was popular with the Egyptians, but is particularly associated with Greece.

The lyre has four sides, consisting of a soundbox, two arms, and a crossbar. The strings vary in number, but are fastened to the front of the soundbox and run over a bridge to the crossbar, where they are fastened with tuning-pegs. It was plucked.

In medieval times lyres were popular in Northern Europe, where they were usually carved from a solid piece of wood. The Welsh and Swedish versions of the lyre (the CRWTH, and the TALLHARPA) were played with a bow.

**Ancient Egyptian lyre** This instrument depicted on a wall painting dates from about 1,000 B.C.

**Ethiopian lyre** Bowl-shaped lyres like this 18th-century example are still found in Ethiopia today.

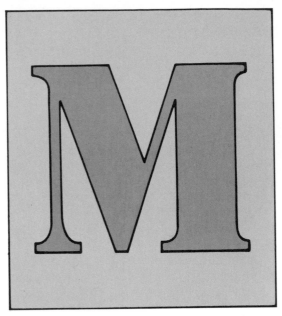

# M

**McCabe, John** English composer, b. 1939. After studying at the Royal Manchester College of Music and in Munich, he began to emerge as a composer of importance in the early 1960s, with such works as the orchestral *Variations on a Theme of Hartmann* (1962) and the *First Symphony* (1963). In 1970 he reached a much wider audience with a singularly beautiful symphony song-cycle *Notturni ed Alba*. An orchestral work, *The Chagall Windows* (1975) also made a very great impression. He has written music for children, including a delightful opera *The Lion, the Witch, and the Wardrobe* (based on the novel by C. S. Lewis) (1971), and is known as a fine recital pianist.

**MacCunn, Hamish** Scottish composer, 1868–1916. Studied at the Royal College of Music with Parry and Stanford. An exceptionally fine overture, *The Land of the Mountain and the Flood* (1887) brought him early fame. He wrote similar descriptive overtures on Scottish scenes and stories, as well as many choral works, and two operas: *Jeanie Deans* (1894) and *Diarmid* (1897). His last years were spent as a conductor with the Carl Rosa Opera Company.

**MacDowell, Edward** American composer, 1861–1908. From 1876 he studied in Europe, at Paris, Stuttgart, and Wiesbaden. In 1881 he joined the staff of the Darmstadt Conservatory, but later moved to Frankfurt to teach piano privately. In the meantime he became known as a concert pianist. He returned to America in 1889 and settled in Boston. From 1896 to 1905 he was Professor of Music at Columbia University, New York,

**Edward MacDowell** 1861–1908 This photograph of the composer was taken when he was about 20. He died at the age of 46 from a brain disease.

**Guillaume de Machaut** c.1304–1377, composer, poet and priest. He was the last of the French troubadour poets to write not only the words but also the music of his songs. He wrote numerous compositions, both sacred and secular.

**Bruno Maderna** 1920–1972 Experimentalist and follower of Webern. He was also a conductor.

but his health failed and he eventually went mad.

MacDowell's work includes three symphonic poems, two important piano concertos (No 1 in A minor, 1885; No 2 in D minor, 1890), orchestral music, a number of delicate songs, and a large quantity of piano music – including four sonatas. He was the first American composer to gain an international reputation, though his style was deeply indebted to German models.

**Machaut, Guillaume de** French composer, c. 1304–77. He was a poet as well as a composer. He became secretary to John of Luxemborg, King of Bohemia, in about 1323. Later patrons included Charles, King of Navarre, Charles VI, King of France, and the Duc de Berry. Most of his music has been preserved, for he took the precaution of having copies prepared for his princely admirers. It includes 23 motets, many of which make use of **Isorhythmic** → and **Hocket** → techniques, and a great many secular polyphonic songs, often to his own words. Only one Mass, the *Messe de Notre-Dame*, has survived, however. It may have been written for the coronation of Charles V at Rheims in 1364. He is one of the most important composers of the 14th century, as well as a poet of great distinction.

**Maderna, Bruno** Italian composer, 1920-72. After achieving fame as a boy conductor, he studied with the influential Italian composer Malipiero. He began his composing career much under the influence of Webern, though he carried out his serial techniques in conjunction with complicated mathematical calculations. He later became involved with experiments in electronic music, working with Luciano Berio at the Studio di Fonologia in Milan. Since then he has written works which involve both live music and electronic effects, as well as 'actions' to be carried out by the performers. For example, in the 'opera' *Hyperion* (1964) one of the chief 'characters', a flute player, spends the first ten minutes of the performance quietly unpacking his instruments.

**Madrigal** → page 213

**Maelzel, Johann Nepomuk** (1772–1828). → **Metronome**

**Maestoso** (It.) Majestic.

**Maggiore** (It.) Major.

# Madrigal

A vocal composition for several un-accompanied voices. The words are always secular, but can be serious as well as light-hearted.

The earliest type of madrigal belongs to 14th-century Italy, and such composers as Landini. It was an unaccompanied vocal song for two or three voices. It usually had several stanzas, for which the music was repeated.

What we usually mean by 'madrigal', however, originated in 16th-century Italy. It too is an extended vocal setting of secular words, but it can be for three, four, five, or more voices. It is contrapuntal and unaccompanied.

There are three main kinds of madrigal:

1. The AYRE, which has a tune in the top voice, accompanied by the other voices. All the verses have the same music.

2. The BALLET (pronounce the 't'; sometimes the spelling is 'Ballett'), which is much the same as the Ayre, but with a dance lilt and a 'fa-la' refrain.

3. The MADRIGAL proper, which does not

**Madrigal singers** This 16th-century woodcut shows German madrigal singers around a table.

repeat the same music for the different verses and which is 'contrapuntal', that is, the voices weave in and out with one another all the time. It usually has a good deal of 'imitation' – one voice giving out a scrap of tune and then another voice taking it up, and so on.

Usually, in any sort of a madrigal each 'part' (treble, alto, tenor, bass, if it was a four-part madrigal) was sung by only one voice, but nowadays such music is some-times sung by a full choir.

The madrigal comes from Italy, but in Queen Elizabeth's day English composers took it up and composed many beautiful specimens. Some of the greatest English madrigal composers were Weelkes, Wilbye, Byrd, Gibbons, Morley, Tomkins, and Bateson. The great age of the madrigal ended about 1630.

There is a very famous book of madrigals in praise of Queen Elizabeth called *The Triumphs of Oriana*. Twenty-six different composers contributed to it.

---

**Magnificat** This is the hymn of the Virgin Mary (*My soul doth magnify the Lord*) as given in St Luke's Gospel.

It is sung in the Roman Catholic Church at Vespers and in the Anglican Church at Evensong. It may be sung to plainsong, or in the Anglican Church to an Anglican Chant, or, in either church, to a setting by some composer.

Very beautiful settings exist by Palestrina, Bach, and others, and many by English composers of various periods.

**Mahler** → page 214

**Main** and **Mains** (Fr.) Hand, hands. As in:
  **Deux mains**, Two hands.
  **Main droite** (or **m.d.** ), Right hand.
  **Main gauche** (or **m.g.** ), Left hand.
  **Quatre mains**, 'Four hands' (i.e. piano duet).

**Malagueña** A Spanish dance in 3/4 or 3/8 time, named after the town of Malaga. It is often sung as it is danced. Some malagueñas make use of a particular pattern of har-monies, consisting of chords based on the first, seventh, sixth and fifth degrees of the scale.

**Mandolin** This Neopolitan singer, sculptured in the early 20th century by Anatole Dubois, plays a mandolin.

**Mancando** (It.) Fading away.

**Mandoline**, or **mandolin** A small stringed instrument shaped like a lute. It is played with a PLECTRUM. There are two types of mandolin: the Neapolitan, which has four pairs of strings, tuned g, d, a, e; and the Milanese, which has five pairs, tuned g, b, e, a, d, e.

The serenade in Mozart's opera *Don Giovanni* is to be played on a mandolin, and several composers (Mahler and Verdi, for example) have used it as an orchestral instrument.

**Malinconia** (It.) Melancholy. **Malin-conico**, 'in a melancholy fashion'.

**Malipiero, Gian Francesco** Italian com-poser, 1882–1973. He studied in Vienna, Venice, and Bologna. Although he began as a rather romantic composer, he became very interested in 17th- and 18th-century music (he edited many of Monteverdi's and Vivaldi's works). This experience prompted him to try to bring a rather more serious spirit into Italian music. He wrote a number of operas, and, rather surprisingly for an Italian, a large number of symphonic works. He was much respected as a teacher.

# Mahler

Gustav Mahler. Austrian composer, 1860–1911. Although Mahler's childhood was far from happy, his parents encouraged his musical talent. He was sent to study in Prague when he was ten, and entered the Vienna Conservatory five years later. He was, however, very poor and had to support himself by giving piano lessons. He gained his diploma in 1878, and for a time continued to teach. He was already composing fluently.

In 1880 he was offered a conducting post in a rather out of the way place in Upper Austria. It was only a summer job, but he enjoyed it and discovered that he had a natural talent. During the next few years further opportunities presented themselves and gradually he built up a reputation as a skilful operatic conductor. His first really important post came in 1888, when he was appointed chief conductor of the Budapest Opera.

Mahler remained in Budapest until 1891, when he was offered an even more important position at the Hamburg Municipal Theatre. He stayed in Hamburg for six years.

This now became the pattern of Mahler's life. He earned his living as a conductor, and was regarded as a very great one indeed. And in the long summer holidays, when the opera houses were closed, he wrote music. Little by little his importance as a composer began to be recognized.

Mahler's most important conducting appointment dates from 1897 when he became Kapellmeister to the Royal and Imperial Opera House in Vienna. He schemed to get the job, even renouncing his Jewish religion and becoming a Roman Catholic. He remained in charge until 1907, and his term there has become a legend for operatic perfection. In 1898 he added to his conducting triumphs by being elected conductor of the Vienna Philharmonic.

The last years of Mahler's life were overshadowed by ill health. In 1907 he went to New York for one year as conductor of the Metropolitan Opera House. He returned again in 1909, this time adding the New York Philharmonic Society's orchestra to his list of appointments. The experience was not wholly satisfactory, however, for his dictatorial ways did not go down well with some musicians. Moreover, he was now very

**Gustav Mahler** 1860–1911 This photograph of the composer was taken about three years before his death when still at the Court Opera House, Vienna.

**Mahler's summerhouse** at Toblach in the South Tyrol. Here, during the summers of 1908, 1909 and 1910 Mahler worked on *Das Lied von der Erde*, the Ninth Symphony and the unfinished Tenth Symphony.

**Silhouette of Mahler conducting** He took up conducting as a career in 1880 to obtain the time and money for his symphonic compositions. Although tyrannical he was utterly dedicated and was one of the great conductors of his day.

ill indeed. His second New York Philharmonic season opened in November 1910, but he was unable to complete it. In February 1911 he collapsed and had to return to Europe. On May 18th he died.

Though Mahler's music includes a number of very important song-cycles, such as *Songs of a Wayfaring Lad* (1884), *Songs from 'Des Knaben Wunderhorn'* (1899), *Kindertotenlieder* (1904), and the *Five Rückert Songs* (1902), it is his symphonies and the 'song-symphony' *The Song of the Earth (Das Lied von der Erde)* (1909) that form the bulk of his achievement.

There are nine symphonies, and they span the whole of his creative life:

| | |
|---|---|
| Symphony No 1 in D major | 1884–88 |
| Symphony No 2 in C minor | 1888–94 |
| Symphony No 3 in D minor | 1895–96 |
| Symphony No 4 in G major | 1899–1900 |
| Symphony No 5 in C sharp minor | 1901–02 |
| Symphony No 6 in A minor | 1903–05 |
| Symphony No 7 in B minor | 1904–05 |
| Symphony No 8 in E flat major | 1906–07 |
| Symphony No 9 in D major | 1909–10 |

There is also a Symphony No 10 in F sharp minor, but it was left unfinished at his death. In 1964 the English musicologist Deryck Cooke brought out a 'completed' version of such skill and understanding that most musicians have now accepted it as authentic and totally satisfactory.

The song-symphony *Das Lied von der Erde* (The Song of the Earth) is a work for alto, tenor, and orchestra – a setting of poems from the Chinese. As several of Mahler's symphonies (2, 3, 4, and 8) make use of solo voices and chorus, it is reasonable to regard this as a symphony too. It certainly has the 'weight', and to some extent the construction of a symphony.

Mahler's music is typical of German late romanticism. With Elgar and Richard Strauss he shared a passion for vast orchestras and works of great length. His music is highly emotional, full of contrasts and contradictions – sudden changes of mood. It is also very intricate – the music of a very subtle mind. Though for many years it was considered by some musicians to be unacceptable (too long-winded, too emotional, too extreme altogether), it is now much admired.

**Mannheim Orchestra, The** When Duke Carl Theodor held his court at Mannheim, between the years 1743 and 1778, he employed an orchestra that came to be admired throughout Europe. It was formed by Johann Stamitz, and later enlarged and perfected by Christian Cannabich. Both were excellent composers as well as being fine string players.

The Mannheim Orchestra not only set new standards of playing and conducting, but also explored methods of writing effectively for the orchestra. Its composer-performers helped to establish the early form of symphony. They are sometimes referred to as the 'Mannheim School'.

**Mano** (It.) Hand. As in:
  **Mano destra** (or **m.d.**), Right hand.
  **Mano sinistra** (or **m.s.**), Left hand.

**Manual** → **Organ; Harpsichord**

**Maracas** A Latin-American percussion instrument. It consists of two medium-sized gourds, mounted on sticks, and held one in each hand. There are dried seeds inside the gourds which rattle when shaken.

**Marbecke** → **Merbecke**

**Marcando**, and **Marcato** (It.) Marked. Used in the sense that the notes must be well-accented; and also to indicate that a melody (or inner part) must be brought out strongly.

**March** → page 216

**Marcia** (It.) March. As in **alla marcia**, in a march style.

**Marenzio, Luca** Italian composer, 1553–99. His working life was passed mainly in Rome and Venice. He was famous throughout Europe as a composer of madrigals, of which he published more than 200, in nine collections, between 1580 and 1599. His works were introduced into England in 1588 in a collection entitled *Musica Transalpina*. Its popularity encouraged English composers to write madrigals of their own, and thus brought into existence the great English Madrigal School.

**Marimba** → **Xylophone**

**Marseillaise** → **Rouget de Lisle**

**Martelé** (Fr.) **Martellato** (It.) Hammered. Used mainly in music for bowed instruments, to indicate that the playing is to be done by short, sharp strokes of the bow. This is usually done with the point of the bow, unless otherwise indicated.

**Maracas** This singer in a Trinidadian calypso band is playing maracas.

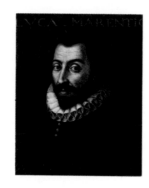
**Luca Marenzio** 1553–1599 As well as madrigals, he also wrote a mass and other church music.

**Frank Martin** 1890-1974 A Swiss composer and pianist who lived in Holland, he wrote choral, orchestra and chamber music.

**Martin, Frank** Swiss composer, 1890-1974. His early works were French in spirit and showed the influence of Franck and Fauré, and to some extent Ravel. From about 1930, however, he began to study serialism and soon developed his own modified version of its techniques which allowed a certain 'tunefulness'. Such works as the popular *Petite Symphonie Concertante* for harpsichord, harp, piano, and strings (1945) show this very clearly. Much of his music is deeply religious – for example, the oratorios *In terra pax* (1944), and *Golgotha* (1948). His opera *The Tempest* (1956) is one of the more successful attempts to set Shakespeare's play.

**Martinů, Bohuslav** Czech composer, 1890–1959. He trained first as a violinist and was largely self-taught as a composer. In 1923 he settled in Paris, but had a hard struggle to make a living from music. Certain works, such as the *Concerto Grosso* (1938), brought him a degree of success, but in 1940 he had to leave Europe because of the war and start again in America. He was not able to return to his native land until 1946. His work includes operas and ballets, six symphonies, and 20 concertos, as well as a great deal of chamber music. His style is basically neo-classic, but also employs elements of folksong. It is strongly nationalistic in spirit.

**Marziale** (It.) Martial. Found in such terms as **allegro marziale**.

**Mascagni, Pietro** Italian composer, 1863–1945. He leapt to fame in 1890 when he won first prize in a competition with his one-act opera *Cavalleria Rusticana*, which immediately achieved a sensational popularity. Though he wrote operas throughout his life, many of them far finer than 'Cav', as it is familiarly known, he never achieved a similar success. Nowadays it is always performed with another short opera by Leoncavallo, *I Pagliacci*. *L'amico Fritz* (1891) and *Iris* (1898) are two of his later operas.

**Mason, Daniel Gregory** American composer, 1873–1953. He studied at Harvard University and at Boston, and taught on the music staff of Columbia University (1910–40). He wrote three symphonies and a great deal of chamber music, some of which makes use of folksong. His best known work is probably the *Chanticleer Overture* (1928). He also wrote a number of important books on music.

# March

Soldiers march better if they have a band and music to help them keep in step. Marches therefore originate with the Army. As they must set up a 'left-right, left-right' rhythm, they can only have two or four beats in a bar – they must therefore be in 2/4, 4/4, 6/8, or 12/8.

The first military marches were drum marches – simple drum-beat patterns. Tunes were added in the 16th century, usually played on fifes. Marches of this kind became so popular that we find them transcribed for keyboard. There are several in such collections as the *Fitzwilliam Virginal Book* (1562-1612).

Military marches, and military music generally, flourished in the 18th century, particularly in France and Germany. Regiments began to adopt favourite tunes as their own special regimental marches, sometimes borrowing them from works that were far from being military – such as Handel's operas and oratorios. An added stimulus to military music came with the Napoleonic Wars.

Nowadays the British Army has two main types of march: a SLOW MARCH, at 70 beats per minute (according to the metronome), and a QUICK MARCH, at 120. The quick march speeds vary a little from regiment to regiment. For example, Highland regiments march at 110 beats, and Light Infantry regiments at 140.

Though most composers have written marches, some have had a special knack. The American John Philip Sousa, and the Englishman Kenneth Alford are two such composers. Sousa's remark that 'a march should make a man with a wooden leg step out', just about sums up the particular quality that is needed.

Marches for the concert hall are also popular, but they are often so complicated that they are not much use on the parade ground. The intention in this case is to conjure up a spirit of pageantry – something which Elgar's five *Pomp and Circumstance* marches do particularly well.

---

**Masque** This is the English version of a type of court entertainment known in Italy as the *trionfo* ('triumph') and in France as the *ballet de cour* ('court ballet'). It was mainly popular during the 17th century.

The masque is a spectacular entertainment which uses song and dance, costumes and scenery, to tell a simple story which is usually designed to flatter the aristocratic audience for which it is intended. Often members of the Court itself took part, particularly in the dancing. In England these entertainments reached a peak of artistry and extravagance in the work of the poet Ben Jonson and the designer Inigo Jones. Their works cost many thousands of pounds to mount, for they were masterpieces of elaboration and ingenuity.

One famous masque was *Comus* (1634) by John Milton, with music by Henry Lawes. It is still read for its fine poetry. A very late example is Arne's *King Alfred* (1740), remembered for the song 'Rule, Britannia!'

**Mass** → page 217

**Massenet, Jules** French composer, 1842–1912. He studied at the Paris Conservatoire, winning the Prix de Rome in 1863. Though he wrote a certain amount of orchestral music and some fine songs, his fame rests on a series of lyrical operas that

**Jules Massenet** 1842–1912, best remembered for his popular light operas.

**Mastersingers** A 16th-century engraving of the famous mastersinger Hans Sachs.

achieved enormous popularity and are still often performed. The best known are *Manon* (1884), *Werther* (1892) and *Thaïs* (1894).

**Master of the Queen's Musick** There is some evidence of a musician being in charge of music in the royal household as far back as 1483, when Richard III came to the throne. But it is not until Charles I's time that any one man is officially referred to as 'master of the music'. This was Nicholas Lanier, and the date, 1623, is usually held to be the start of the office.

Nowadays the position is largely honorary it offers little financial reward and makes few demands. Certain Masters, however, have delighted in producing music for Royal occasions – fanfares for weddings and coronations, etc.

A few holders of this office have been genuinely distinguished composers, such as William Boyce, William Shield, Sir Edward Elgar, Sir Arnold Bax, and Sir Arthur Bliss, but some, whom we shall not name, have been painfully dull. The present Master, since 1976, is the Australian-born composer Malcolm Williamson.

**Mastersingers** A type of musician active in Germany from the 14th century onwards, though declining in the 18th century and

# Mass

So far as composers in general are concerned, the important parts of the Mass are the five parts of the Roman Catholic liturgy called the 'Ordinary of the Mass' – that is to say, the five parts that remain the same, regardless of the day or season. These have been set, in Latin, over and over again, by composers of all styles and periods, and, it may be added, by composers who are not necessarily Roman Catholics.

The five sections are:

**Kyrie** 'Lord have mercy'
**Gloria** 'Glory be to God on high'
**Credo** 'I believe in one God, the Father Almighty'
**Sanctus** and **Benedictus** 'Holy, Holy, Holy' and 'Blessed is He that cometh in the name of the Lord'
**Agnus Dei** 'Lamb of God, that takest away the sins of the world, have mercy on us'

These texts may, of course, be sung to the traditional plainsong tunes, but they have always attracted the attention of composers, and still do, even though Latin is no longer in use in church services. The variable parts of the Mass – called the 'Proper of the Mass' – are sung to the traditional plainsong.

In the long history of setting the Mass to music, the greatest period is probably that from the 13th to the end of the 16th century. During that time it can be considered the most important art form in music.

By the 18th century, however, other musical forms (such as opera and the symphony) had displaced it, and the attitude of those composers who did make settings had also begun to change. The settings themselves may have contained splendid music, but it was not always suited to the needs of the church service. This tendency reaches its height in the 19th century, when such masterpieces as

Beethoven's *Missa Solemnis* (1823) are essentially works for the concert hall.

One form of Mass for a particular occasion that composers have frequently set to music is the Mass for the Dead – the *Requiem Mass*. The text is similar to that of the Ordinary of the Mass, but it omits the joyful sections (*Gloria* and *Credo*) begins with the Introit 'Requiem aeternam' ('Rest eternal'), and includes the Sequence 'Dies Irae' ('Day of wrath, day of judgement'). Notable settings include those of Mozart (1791), Berlioz (1837), Verdi (1874), and Fauré (1887).

The Protestant equivalent of the Mass is the Office of Holy Communion. Those parts of it that are set to music, in English, are: the Kyrie, Credo, Sanctus, and Gloria. Again, many settings have been made – though most composers, whether Protestant or Catholic, believers or non-believers, seem to prefer the Latin. On the whole it is the texts of the evening canticles, the *Magnificat* and *Nunc Dimittis*, that have proved more attractive to Protestant composers.

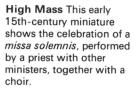

**High Mass** This early 15th-century miniature shows the celebration of a *missa solemnis*, performed by a priest with other ministers, together with a choir.

eventually dying out in the 19th. They took over the art of the aristocratic Minnesingers, forming themselves into local guilds and writing their poetry and music according to very strict rules. The members were mostly tradesmen and craftsmen. The story of Wagner's opera *The Mastersingers of Nuremberg* (1868) concerns their work, and one of its characters, Hans Sachs, actually existed (1494–1576). They

are sometimes classed as **Minstrels** →, but they are more like members of a club.

**Matins** This is the name of the first of the 'Canonical Hours' of the Roman Catholic Church and also of the service of Morning Prayer in the Anglican Church.

**Mazurka** A Polish national dance, usually sung to a bagpipe accompaniment. In triple time, with accents falling on usually the second but sometimes the third beat. It was adapted for the ballroom in the 18th century, and became particularly important in the 19th when Chopin used its rhythms as a basis for an important part of his piano music.

**Measure** (1) This means the same as 'bar', in the sense of the music that lies between two bar-lines. (2) It is also an old English word for any sort of dance tune.

**Mediant** The name for the third note of the major or minor scale. It is so called because it lies midway between the chief two notes of the scale, the tonic and the dominant.

In the major scale the mediant is a major third above the tonic or key-note, and in the minor scale a minor 3rd above it.

**Megaphone** A large speaking-trumpet, used to amplify the voice.

**Melodic minor scale** → **Scales**

**Melodic sequence** → **Sequence**

**Melodica** A 'free-reed' instrument, developed from the mouth organ. It consists of an oblong box with either a miniature keyboard, or a similar row of buttons, which when pressed allows the player's breath to pass over the reeds and make a sound. The player holds the instrument in the left hand, blows down a tube at one end, and operates the keyboard with his right hand. (→ **Free-reed**)

**Melodrama** Although the word has come to mean any sort of play that is exciting and sensational, it was originally used to describe that part of a play, or opera, in which the words were spoken against a musical background. An example can be found in the 'Wolf's Glen' scene in Weber's opera *Der Freischütz* (1821). Richard Strauss's *Enoch Arden* (1902) is also a melodrama. It consists of Tennyson's famous poem, which is read to the accompaniment of a piano score that underlines its meaning and changing moods. The use of background music in films is really a development of the idea of melodrama, though it is never described as such.

**Melody** → page 220

**Membranophone** → page 220

**Memory in music** → page 221

**Melodica** Held like a recorder, this chromatic harmonica was invented by Matthias Hohner in the second half of the 19th century.

# Mechanical instruments

The idea of musical instruments that play by themselves goes back several centuries. It reached a height of ingenuity in the late 18th and early 19th centuries, but there are examples dating from before this time. King Henry VIII, for instance, owned a mechanical virginals, driven by clockwork and operated by a barrel set with pins.

Besides self-playing instruments, inventors have also delighted in making mechanical dolls that appear to 'play' instruments. One such device, a whole mechanical orchestra, was assembled by Johann Maelzel (→ **Metronome**) He called it the PANHARMONICON, and even persuaded Beethoven to write a work for it – the so-called 'Symphony' *The Battle of Vittoria* (1813).

Here are some of the best known mechanical instruments, with a brief explanation of how they work:

1. **Musical clocks** (or 'Flute Clocks') were once very common. They had bellows and pipes inside them and were really little barrel organs (see below), but had no handle, being played by the clockwork.

2. **Barrel organs**, played by turning a handle, were once to be found in dozens of English churches and homes. When the handle was turned a 'barrel' (a metal cylinder) inside revolved. It had little pins on it and these caught levers that opened the pipes for the various notes. (After the barrel organ went out of use it was forgotten and people applied the name to the street instruments that had then come in, which were not organs at all but had strings and hammers and really ought to have been called 'barrel pianos' or 'street pianos'.)

3. **Musical boxes**, large and small, are still a common sort of mechanical instrument. Thousands of them are made every year in Switzerland, for export all over the world.

Like the barrel organ they have a revolving drum set with pins, but the pins pluck the teeth of a small metal comb. The teeth are of different lengths and so produce different notes.

4. **The pianola** was once very popular in Europe and America. It had a long roll of paper for every piece of music. The paper had holes in it corresponding to the different

notes and when the instrument was played these allowed air to pass through tubes (one for every note) and the air then made the piano's hammers strike the strings. In some instruments of this kind the owner of the instrument could, by means of little hand levers, control the speed and the 'expression'. Many popular rolls recorded the performance of some great pianist and reproduced his performance very exactly.

5. **The carillon** (→ **Bells and bell-ringing**) is, of course, often played mechanically.

6. The commonest mechanical instrument of today is the **Gramophone** →.

**Fairground organ** *Right* This instrument is operated from a steam traction engine, along with many other amusements and roundabouts found at a fair.

**Musical box** *Below* This Swiss 'symphonium', dated about 1905, depicts 'pussies at play' and uses a revolving metal disc to produce the sound.

**Carillons** Bell-ringer (*right*) at the controls of a carillon. A system of cables and levers leads directly to the bell-clappers (*below*). Ringing is achieved either by direct manual operation or by setting in motion a drum with a pre-determined sequence which is automatically operated.

**Barrel organ** This London street scene of 1905 shows children gathered around what is, strictly speaking, a street piano. This instrument is said to have been invented in England in the early 19th century but the manufacturers and performers of them were almost exclusively Italian. They were a common sight in London streets up until the 1920s but are now a rarity.

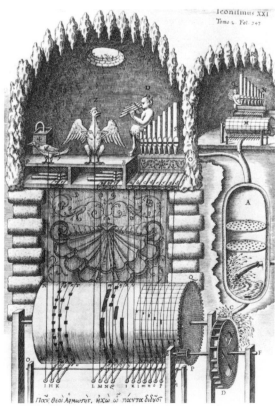

**Water organ** *Right* This instrument from Kircher's *Musurgia Universalis* of 1650, is operated by water power diverted from a stream. It sounds in response to studs on the barrel connected to lines opening the pipes. The birds, also connected by lines, move at the same time.

**Automatic self-playing violin** *Left* This German Hupfeld Phonoliszt-Violina of about 1912 uses pneumatic power to play three violins. However, each violin has only one operating string which comes into contact with a rotating bow. A piano accompanies the violin and the resulting sound is that of a piano-violin duet.

# Melody

Any series of notes that makes musical sense to the listener can be called a MELODY. Next to rhythm, melody is the oldest ingredient in music – for harmony, as we know it today, did not arrive on the musical scene until comparatively recently (about 900 A.D.).

The words 'melody' and 'tune' are sometimes used as if they were the same. Up to a point they are. But it is perhaps safer to say that a 'tune' is a melody that is complete in itself, whereas a 'melody' may be part of a larger work.

Even so, in order to be recognizable as such, a melody must be fairly extensive. A mere group of three or four notes, however melodious, is better described as a 'melodic idea', or a 'theme', or 'motif'. Musical ideas of this kind are really only the beginnings of much larger compositions: they are, as it were, the individual bricks of a building, and a great many must be put together before the whole can take shape.

Exactly what causes a melody to make musical sense is almost impossible to explain. For one thing, the qualities of a good melody vary throughout musical history. The requirements of a plainsong melody, which is not dependent on the idea of harmonies moving beneath it, are quite different from those of, say, a Beethoven melody, which is closely dependent on the accompanying harmonies. And the requirements of an atonal melody are different.

However, in very broad terms we may say that all good melodies have an overall curve that is *shapely* – the notes moving purposefully towards some sort of climax, and then falling away with an equal sense of purpose. Within the melody, individual phrases balance one another satisfactorily. There is repetition of ideas and phrases, but also contrast and variation. Rhythm plays an important part in giving a melody its definition. It too must be carefully organized, so that there is repetition, contrast, and variation. When a melody is constructed with harmonies in mind (as in the 18th and 19th centuries), then the sequence of harmonies must not be commonplace – though they can be simple. And in all these matters there must always be an element of surprise – some twist that lifts everything out of the predictable and yet seems exactly right.

# Membranophone

Any instrument in which the sound is made by the vibration of a stretched skin, or some kind of membrane. The most important members of this family are the drums, but there is a lesser branch called **Mirlitons →**.

Drums have been in existence for at least four thousand years, and have been used to accompany singing and dancing, for sending messages and on the field of battle, and in ritual ceremonies (to ward off evil spirits, etc).

Membranophones described in this book include: Bass drums, Bongo drums, Kazoo, Kettledrums, Nakers, Side drums, Tabor, Tambourine, Timpani, and Military drums.

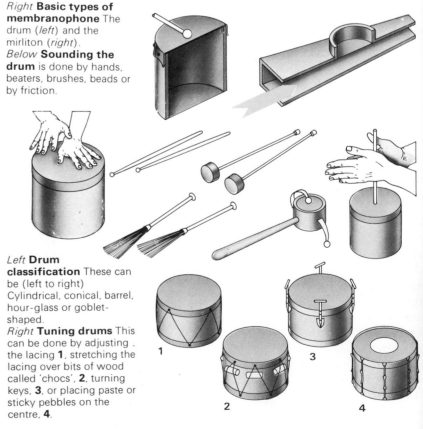

*Right* **Basic types of membranophone** The drum (*left*) and the mirliton (*right*).
*Below* **Sounding the drum** is done by hands, beaters, brushes, beads or by friction.

*Left* **Drum classification** These can be (left to right) Cylindrical, conical, barrel, hour-glass or goblet-shaped.
*Right* **Tuning drums** This can be done by adjusting the lacing **1**, stretching the lacing over bits of wood called 'chocs', **2**, turning keys, **3**, or placing paste or sticky pebbles on the centre, **4**.

## Memory in music

Memory plays an important part both in the performance and composition of music.

Some performers and conductors prefer to memorize a whole concert. They feel that it enables them to get more deeply 'under the skin' of the music, and thus give their whole attention to the performance. There have been many examples of the most amazing feats of memory, but it would be an extremely self-confident person who could claim that his memory would never let him down!

Composers use memory in a slightly different way. During the very act of composing they must rely on being able to turn over their ideas in their heads, before putting them down on paper. Some even compose the entire work in their heads and only write it down when it is complete. Mozart worked in this way. Others use their memories to a lesser extent and like to write down their ideas as they go along – as Beethoven did.

Even the listener must use his memory if he is to get any real satisfaction out of music. He will only be able to appreciate the *shape* of a piece if he can remember at least something of what he has heard and so link it in his mind with what is happening at the moment and what is to come. In a funny kind of way we use our memories to enable us to 'see' what we hear.

So far as instrumentalists are concerned there are three types of memory: MUSCULAR, VISUAL, and AUDITORY MEMORY.

**Muscular memory** means that the fingers, having found a habit of playing a particular passage, can repeat that passage ever after. **Visual memory** means memory of the look of the music copy. Some have this very strongly, so that as they play they are mentally turning over each page as they come to the end of it. **Auditory memory** means that you can remember the actual *sound* of a piece of music.

Most people who memorize use a combination of all three types of memory. Even so, they have to take great care that mistakes do not creep in. It is so easy to believe you have learned something correctly, when all you have done is to learn a mistake!

**Mendelssohn** → page 222

**Mendelssohn scholarship** Mendelssohn was always a great favourite with the British people, and when he died, in 1847, they collected money to found a valuable scholarship in his honour, so that some young performer or composer could pursue his studies at home or abroad (it is now awarded only to composers).

Sir Arthur Sullivan was the first 'Mendelssohn Scholar'.

**Meno** (It.) Less. As in **meno mosso**, slower (less moved).

**Menotti, Gian Carlo** American composer, b. 1911. He was born in Italy and only settled in America in 1928, by which time he was already composing fluently. His first opera, *Amelia goes to the Ball*, was produced in 1937 and established him as one of the most successful operatic composers of the day. Though his music is always theatrically effective, it can, however, sometimes fall into sentimentality. His most admired operas include the two one-act works, *The Medium* (1945) and *The Telephone* (1947), the three-act opera *The Consul* (1950), and the 'Christmas' opera *Amahl and the Night Visitors*

**Olivier Messiaen** b.1908
Shown here collecting bird-song, Messiaen has imitated these sounds in various works, notably *The Awakening of the Birds* for piano and orchestra.

(1951), which was originally written for television.

**Merbecke, John** English composer, c. 1510–85. He was organist of St George's Chapel, Windsor, but was tried and condemned for heresy in 1544. He was eventually pardoned, and with the establishment of the Protestant Church as the Church of England he devoted himself to making the first setting of the English liturgy, adapting the old plainsong (sung in Latin) to the rhythms of the English language. The results were published in 'The Booke of Common Praier Noted' (1550).

**Messiaen, Olivier** French composer, b. 1908. As a child he taught himself to play the piano and compose, and began to study seriously at the Paris Conservatoire when he was 11. He rapidly became a star pupil.

In 1931 he was appointed organist at the Trinité in Paris, and in the same year made a deep impression with his first orchestral work: *Les Offrandes oubliées*. By the end of the Second World War he had become accepted as a leading French composer, whose ideas, however, often caused controversy.

Messiaen's theories include the possibility

# Mendelssohn

Felix Mendelssohn (full name Jacob Ludwig Felix Mendelssohn-Bartholdy). Born at Hamburg in 1809 and died at Leipzig in 1847.

Good fortune attended Felix Mendelssohn at almost every stage of his career. He was the son of a wealthy banker, and his grandfather had been a famous philosopher. He was brought up in Berlin, surrounded not only by luxury, but in an artistic and intellectual atmosphere that encouraged children to develop their gifts. He studied with the best teachers, became a fine pianist, and gave his first public concert when he was nine. He also wrote music fluently. In his 12th year, for example, he wrote five symphonies for strings, nine fugues, several piano pieces and songs, and two operettas! And as the Mendelssohn family and their friends were all musical, he was able to get them together as a little orchestra and practise conducting.

His father, however, was not convinced that a musical career was the right thing. After all, the boy was talented at almost everything he did. Perhaps music should be a hobby? And anyhow, music was not considered in the 19th century to be a fit career for a gentleman.

Fortunately Abraham Mendelssohn decided to consult the most important musician he knew: Luigi Cherubini. The verdict was favourable, and Felix Mendelssohn was set on his way as a composer.

Cherubini was right. Mendelssohn was probably one of the most talented and precocious composers there has ever been. When he was only 16 he completed a masterpiece of chamber music, the *Octet* for strings. And in the following year he added a masterpiece to the world's orchestral repertoire: the overture *A Midsummer Night's Dream*.

He was also greatly interested in the music of the past, and in particular that of J. S. Bach. In 1829 he organized and conducted the first performance of the *St Matthew Passion*, and in so doing forced the whole of Europe to admit that a composer who had more or less been ignored since his death in 1750 was, in fact, one of the world's great masters.

If there was any flaw in Mendelssohn's upbringing it was that he was surrounded by too much family love and protection. But

**Felix Mendelssohn** 1809–1847 He wrote important works for all forms except opera (although he left an early one and a later unfinished work). He was also one of the first composers to write concert overtures.

in 1829 he took the first steps towards independence. He set out for London on the first stage of a Grand Tour designed to complete his education and make him a polished man of the world.

Everything in Britain delighted him, and he delighted everyone he met. He returned not only assured of success as a composer (for he had conquered a foreign land with his music), but also with ideas for two important works: a descriptive overture *The Hebrides*, and a symphony, the 'Scotch'. Both had been inspired by a visit to Scotland.

The second stage of his Grand Tour took him to Italy (1830), and this too gave him musical ideas – in particular for an *Italian Symphony*.

**Birmingham** This pen drawing by Mendelssohn was executed in 1846 when he produced his oratorio *Elijah* at the Birmingham Festival. He died the following year. As well as a composer, Mendelssohn was also a talented artist.

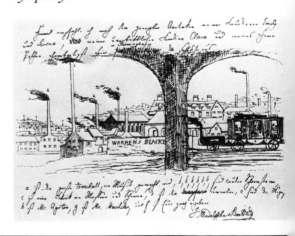

The remainder of his career is marked by an almost unbroken line of successes. He returned to England nine times, for he had become a favourite with all music-lovers including Queen Victoria herself. He conducted his works, and wrote music for English institutions – for example, the oratorio *Elijah* (1846) for the Birmingham Festival.

But he also had work to do in Germany. From 1833 to 1846 he took charge of the Lower Rhine Festival of Music. In 1834 he became conductor of Leipzig's famous Gewandhaus Orchestra. In 1841 he became Director of the Berlin Academy of Arts. In 1843 he established and taught at a Conservatory of Music at Leipzig. In short, he set about working himself to death.

Although he had married very happily in 1837, Mendelssohn was particularly devoted to his sister Fanny. He had just returned from England when the news came of her sudden and totally unexpected death. His health began to fail and within six months he too was dead.

Mendelssohn's music is elegant, melodious, and completely charming. It is not perhaps the most powerful music of the 19th century (though there are some remarkably strong moments, in, for example, *Elijah*), but it is always satisfying. Unlike many 19th-century composers he retained something of the 'classicism' of the 18th century. And so, even when he is being poetic and descriptive, as in the *Hebrides Overture*, there is a strong feeling for balance and proportion that never lets the imaginative side of his genius race ahead out of hand.

His music includes several choral works: the oratorios *St Paul* (1836) and *Elijah* (1846), and the 'symphony-cantata' *The Hymn of Praise* (1840). There are a number of symphonies, including No 3 in A minor ('*The Scotch*'), 1842; No 4 in A ('*The Italian*'), 1833; and No 5 in D ('*The Reformation*'), 1832. Several overtures are still very popular: the *Midsummer Night's Dream* (1826), *The Fair Melusine* (1833), *Calm Sea and Prosperous Voyage* (1832), '*Hebrides*' (1832), and *Ruy Blas* (1839). He wrote a great deal of chamber music, including several fine string quartets, piano music, including the famous set of *Songs without Words*, songs, and several concertos, including the *Violin Concerto in E minor* (1844).

**Metallophone** This instrument, early types of which date from about 900 A.D. is frequently found in the Indonesian orchestra, the gamelan. Here, it accompanies the performance of a shadow puppet play.

**Metronome** This instrument is normally used as a guide to the speed at which a composition should be played. Sometimes metronome marks are given by the composer or editor of a piece but as an aid not a rule for determining the tempo. The Brazilian Villa-Lobos has composed a work using three metronomes ticking at different speeds.

of constructing new scales on alternating tones and semitones, the use of complex rhythmic patterns to give shape to music, the use of extremely complicated chromatic chords, and melodic shapes derived from a study of birdsong and other natural sounds.

The practical result of these theories is music that sounds like an intricate, slightly exotic version of Debussy. He is a devout Catholic, and most of his works have a strong religious element; for example, the series of nine Christmas 'meditations' for organ called *La Nativité du Seigneur* (1935). He is also a master of orchestral colour – as can be seen in the enormous *Turangalîla Symphony* (1948). His piano music, such as the *Vingt Regards sur l'Enfant Jésus* (1944) and the *Catalogue des Oiseaux* (1959), is extremely difficult to play.

**Mesto** (It) Sad.

**Metallophone** Similar in general appearance to a xylophone, but has metal bars instead of wooden ones, arranged on a frame and beaten with small hammers, usually by hand. Different shapes and sizes of metallophone are found all over the East ( → **Gamelan**), and are of very ancient origin.

**Metrical psalms → Hymns and hymn-tunes**

**Metronome** A mechanical device for fixing the speed at which a piece of music is to be played.

The simplest consists of a tape with a weight on the end, which is allowed to swing backwards and forwards. The longer the tape, the longer the swing – and thus the slower the speed. The tape can be marked off so that different speeds can be judged from its different lengths.

The most popular metronome is the clockwork one, patented by Johann Maelzel (1772–1838). The mechanism swings a small metal rod backwards and forwards, ticking like a clock. A weight is attached to the rod and can be slid up and down it. The higher up the rod the weight goes, the slower the ticking motion. The rod is engraved with numbers that correspond to the number of beats per minute. So a metronome set at ♩= 100 will beat 100 crotchet (quarter-note) beats a minute.

Nowadays there are more sophisticated metronomes on the market. They include small clockwork metronomes shaped like a watch, and electric (transistorized) metronomes that work off a battery. Some electric metronomes merely tick (a 'bleep', really); others include a light that flashes on and off.

The metronome is best used to set the speed before playing. If we try to play *with* it, the result tends to become too mechanical.

**Metropolitan Opera House** The 'Met' is New York's chief opera house. It was opened in 1883 and has long enjoyed a reputation as one of the world's great opera houses, attracting the finest singers, conductors, and producers of the day. The original building, on Broadway and 39th Street, gradually became out of date, and eventually, in 1966, the Metropolitan Opera Association moved to a splendid new building in the Lincoln Center.

**Mezzo** (It.) Half. As in **mezzo forte**, half-loud; **mezzo piano**, half-soft; **mezza voce**, half-voice (i.e. not using the full power of the

**Metropolitan Opera House** This photograph shows the proscenium and auditorium in the new complex at the Lincoln Center.

voice). A **mezzo-soprano** voice lies half way between a soprano and a contralto. The direction **mezzo staccato**, half-detached, is shown in music by slurs being placed over the staccato dots, or by a *tenuto* dash and a dot.

**M.F.** is an abbreviation of **mezzo forte**.

**M.G.** is an abbreviation of **main gauche** (Fr.), left hand.

**Microtones** These are intervals that are smaller than a semitone, such as quarter-tones and sixths-of-a-tone. They are found in folk music, and in Oriental and Indian music. Some 20th-century composers have experimented with them (Alois Hába, for example), but the results tend to sound merely out of tune to Western ears. Quarter-tones can be played easily on such instruments as a violin, or a trombone. But

# Meyerbeer

Giacomo Meyerbeer. Germany, 1791–1864. The son of a wealthy banker, he began his career as a prodigy pianist. He soon turned to composition, however, and in 1812 wrote his first opera.

Though he achieved early operatic success in Italy (changing his name from Jakob to Giacomo, to help things along), his claim to fame lies in the 'Grand' operas he wrote for Paris, beginning with *Robert le Diable* (1831), and continuing through *Les Huguenots* (1836) and *Le Prophète* (1849) to his final work *L'Africaine*, (1865).

With these operas he became one of the wealthiest and most famous composers of his day. They were designed as massive

**Giacomo Meyerbeer** 1791–1864 *Below* A scene from the first performance of Meyerbeer's *L'Africaine* in Paris in 1865. This was revived at Covent Garden in 1979 with notable success.

entertainments, to be sung by the greatest singers of the time, and staged with all manner of spectacular effects. They have been criticized as being merely sensational and devoid of any real meaning (Wagner was particularly scornful of them), but this is not a fair judgement, for they contain many moments of genuine beauty and imagination and are never less than expertly written. They have not been performed so regularly in the 20th century, simply because they are so expensive to put on the stage. But signs of a definite revival of interest have occurred in recent years, and singers have once again begun to recognize their undoubted qualities.

*Above* A scene from Meyerbeer's first successful opera, *Il Crociato in Egitto*. He was invited to see it produced in Paris in 1862 and thereafter lived most of his life in France.

instruments with a fixed tuning cannot be used for them. For this reason special quarter-tone pianos have been constructed, but they are very rare and very expensive.

**Milhaud, Darius** French composer, 1892-1974. As a member of the group *Les Six* he amused Paris with a number of witty ballets, such as *Le Boeuf sur le Toit* (The Ox on the Roof), 1920, *La Création du Monde* (The Creation of the World), 1923, and *Le Train bleu* (The Blue Train), 1924. All these works were much influenced by jazz and popular music.

His output since then has been enormous and varied. It includes large-scale operas, such as *Christophe Colomb* (1928), and *Bolivar* (1943), symphonies, concertos, chamber music, songs, piano music, and music for many films. He has drawn upon all kinds of techniques and styles, old and new, but is probably at his best when writing light-hearted tunes, set to spicy harmonies and brilliantly orchestrated – as, for example, in the *Suite Provençale* for orchestra (1937), and the wind quintet *La Cheminée du Roi René* (The Path of King René), 1939.

**Military Band → page 226**

**Military calls** 'Calls' are signals – commands to be acted upon as soon as heard. They can be made on the drums alone, or on the trumpet or bugle. They have simple

**Darius Milhaud**
1892–1974 He collaborated with Claudel, the poet and dramatist, on *Christophe Colomb* in which the spoken voice is used with the orchestra or percussion instruments.

rhythms and tunes. Each is distinctive and easily learned. And because they are played on powerful instruments they can be heard at a great distance, and above the noise of battle. They are, in short, a very effective means of telling soldiers what to do.

Trumpet and bugle calls are made up of only a few notes, chosen from the instrument's basic harmonic series. Nevertheless, this handful of notes has provided an enormous variety of distinctive melodies. Some are brief, like the command 'Fall in':

Some are lengthy, like the 'Warning for Parade':

# Military drums

**How drums are carried**
Military drums are carried in three ways: by marching men, slung slightly to the left-hand side of the body (*left*); by marching men slung directly in front and resting against the chest, as with the bass drum (*below*); and by the drum-horse mounted on either side of the saddle, as with the kettledrums (*right*). Drums have been used for military purposes since the earliest times. The tabor and artillery drum are early types.

*Above* 16th-century German soldiers: drummer and standard-bearer.

# Military band

By this we mean the kind of band used by the armed forces of the world, Army, Navy, and Air Force. Though their precise constitution varies from country to country, they all consist of a mixture of brass, woodwind, and percussion instruments.

The origin of military bands is somewhat obscure, but musical instruments have been used by armies for as long as armies have existed. Both drums and trumpets were used for giving out orders on the field of battle; and drums have always provided a steady beat to accompany men on the march. It is also worth remembering that musicians attached to royal courts would be expected to provide music not only for entertainment but also for military occasions, using those instruments that could be played effectively out of doors. By the end of the 16th century royal bands might contain some combination of recorders, flutes, shawms (early oboes), cornetts, curtalls (early bassoons), and sackbutts (early trombones). Similar bands of instruments were used by town minstrels. ( → **Waits**)

It is not until the 17th century and the rise of France as a great military power, that military bands begin to develop distinct characteristics. During this period armies became better organized, and the idea of pomp and pageantry became more important to them. The first regular military bands appeared in the middle of the 17th century. They consisted of oboes and bassoons – both powerful and effective in the open air. As their popularity spread, other instruments were added: first, horns and trumpets, and the clarinets. By 1770 the basis of the modern military band had been established, and many regiments could boast:

2 trumpets
2 horns
2 bassoons
4 oboes or clarinets
Drums

If an 18th-century regiment was particularly wealthy, it might also have 'Turkish percussion' – that is to say, bass drums, cymbals, triangles, and the 'Jingling Johnny'. The craze for these instruments began when the Sultan of Turkey presented the King of Poland with a full military band of the corps of Janissaries, which contained not only fifes and shawms, but a vast array

**Early military bands**
*Above top* Detachment of foot soldiers led by a band parade the colours through the courtyard of St James's Palace c.1790. *Above* This painting by Wojcieck Kossak dated 1893 shows the band of the Austrian

Imperial and Royal 13th Infantry Regiment led by their drum major. *Above right* This 18th-century Turkish military band is mounted on horse and camel. *Below* British band of the Marines, 1825, tune their instruments. *Bottom*

This engraving of 1805 shows a mounted squad from the French National School of Military Music, Versailles. The instruments they are playing are (*left to right*) bassoons, oboes, horns and trumpets.

of percussion. Europe was fascinated, and soon every self-respecting regiment felt it necessary to have Turkish instruments of its own. Even the music of the concert hall was affected, and the new sounds crept into such works as Mozart's opera *Die Entführung aus dem Serail* (1782), and Beethoven's *Ninth Symphony* (1825). (→ **Janissary music**)

During the 19th century military bands grew bigger and better. The instruments themselves were improved, and new instruments were added. Bands were also better organized and instead of being merely musicians hired for the purpose, they began to develop as soldier-musicians – an integral part of the army, and trained by it in both military and musical skills. The first example of a special training school for military music came with the opening of Kneller Hall, near London, in 1857.

The basic modern military band contains the following instruments:

Flute and piccolo
E flat clarinet
Oboe
B flat clarinets
E flat clarinets
E flat alto saxophone
B flat tenor saxophone
Bassoon
Horns
B flat cornets
Tenor trombones
Bass trombone
Euphonium
String basses (but not on the march, of course!)
Percussion

Bands vary in size, but in England the average regimental band will consist of about 30 players.

The sound that a military band can make is varied and very interesting, and it is perfectly adapted to playing all kinds of music, and not just routine marches. Composers, however, have been rather slow to take advantage of its possibilities: comparatively few important pieces have been written for it. The enormous popularity of the MARCHING BAND in American schools and colleges has opened up new possibilities for the military band proper – the two types of band are very similar (→ **Wind bands**) and can therefore borrow each other's music.

**Mirliton** French Eunuch-flute *c.* 1800.

**Minstrels** → page 228

**Minuet** → page 229

**Mirliton** Though they are classed as part of the family of membranophones, because they contain a skin which vibrates, they are very different from the rest of the family – the drums. In mirlitons the skin is used to modify a sound made in some other way – usually by blowing or singing against it. The simplest mirliton is the tissue paper and comb, but there are also **Kazoos** →.

Similar instruments can be found among primitive peoples, and Europe in the 17th and 18th centuries had the so-called Eunuch Flute.

**Mirror music** Any piece of music that will sound the same when played backwards (starting at the end and working back to the beginning) as it does when played in the normal way is said to be in 'mirror' form. Another name for such a composition is a PALINDROME. Bach, and other ingenious composers, sometimes constructed canons in this way.

The same description is given to a piece of music in which two parts (or even two pairs of parts) are arranged so that they appear simultaneously upside down and the right way up. For example:

A mirror fugue is one that treats its subject and countersubject in this way, first stating it normally and then turning it upside down.

**Misterioso** (It.) Mysterious.

**Misura** (It.) Measure, in the sense of:
1. a bar
2. regular time – as in: **alla misura**, in strict time; **senza misura**, in free time.

**Mixolydian** → **Modes**

**Mixture stops** → **Organ**

**M.M.** Maelzel's Metronome. Found in old printed music to show that the metronome mark is to be measured by one of Maelzel's machines – thus: M.M.♩ = 120.

**Moderato** (It.) Moderate, in the sense of speed. Found also with other adjectives, as in **andante moderato**, moderately slow; **allegro moderato**, moderately quick.

# Minstrels

In every age and every country there have been musicians who have wandered about the countryside and moved from town to town making music for money. We give them the general title 'minstrel', though, as will be seen below, there are several types:

1. **Jongleurs** These were travelling entertainers, found all over Europe in the 11th, 12th, and 13th centuries. They moved about in troupes which included musicians, jugglers, acrobats, and dancers – rather like a small-scale version of the modern circus.

2. **Troubadours** These, in the 11th, 12th and 13th centuries, were poet-musicians of a superior class in Provence, in the south of France, and in neighbouring countries (northern Spain and Italy). Many, but not all, were of noble birth. A considerable quantity of their songs and lyric poetry remains.

**Minnesingers** (*above*) Frauenlob, one of the best known Minnesingers, here conducts players with shawm, fiddles, nakers, bagpipes, pipe and tabor.

*Right* **14th-century Italian minstrels** at a wedding.

3. **Trouvères** They were very similar to the Troubadours, but lived mainly in central and northern France and wrote in French. They began and ended their activities about fifty years after the Troubadours.

4. **Minnesingers** The German equivalent of the Troubadours.

# Modes

These are the scale systems used in Western music before the idea of KEY came to be accepted (by about the year 1600). They are sometimes called Church Modes, but this does not mean that they were only used in church music.

In any *major* scale, the tones and semitones always occur in exactly the same place, thus:

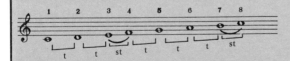

Each major scale therefore sounds like any other, except that it is at a different pitch.

Each mode, however, arranges its tones and semitones in a different order.

Here are the six main modes, first as they occur on the white notes of the piano, and then as if they all commenced on C. Each has a name borrowed from the ancient Greek modes. The first and last notes of each mode are called the FINAL (not the Tonic), but the fifth or sixth note is the DOMINANT (marked F and D below).

Modes written out as above, so that they run from Final to Final, are said to be AUTHENTIC MODES. But if a composer wished to write music that went outside the simple octave, he would have to make use of the PLAGAL MODE – that is to say, the same mode beginning four notes below the Final. The name of the mode remains the same, but the word 'Hypo' is added to the beginning – as in Hypodorian, Hypophrygian, etc. Thus:

# Minuet

A dance in 3/4 time that was immensely popular in the 17th and 18th centuries.

Minuets generally consist of two sections: a MINUET, and a contrasting TRIO. Both sections are normally in Binary Form, and the Minuet is usually repeated after the Trio – giving an overall form of: MINUET, TRIO, MINUET. The following example is the opening of Purcell's First Harpsichord Suite.

**Minuet's evolution**
Having started life as a dance, the minuet also became a standard part of every instrumental dance. In the 18th-century it found its way into sonatas, symphonies and quartets as the third movement. This illustration from an 18th century instruction book shows the end of the dance, the presenting of both arms.

Melodies could fall wholly within the Authentic Mode, or wholly within the Plagal Mode. A melody which extended into both was said to be in a MIXED MODE:

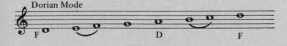

Modes are also commonly referred to by number: All authentic modes have odd numbers, and all plagal modes have even numbers.
Mode I = Dorian
Mode II = Hypodorian
Mode III = Phrygian
Mode IV = Hypophrygian
Mode V = Lydian
Mode VI = Hypolydian
Mode VII = Mixolydian
Mode VIII = Hypomixolydian
Mode IX = Aeolian
Mode X = Hypoaeolian
Mode XI = Ionian
Mode XII = Hypoionian

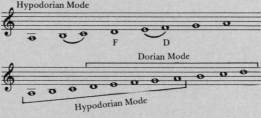

As time went on, changes crept into the way composers used the modal system. Notes began to be flattened here and there, or sharpened, until gradually all modes came to resemble two main modes – the Ionian and Aeolian: the forerunners of the Major and Minor diatonic scales.

The modal system, as we have seen, was largely out of favour by the 17th century. In the 20th century, however, composers rediscovered the possibility of writing music in modal scales. This was often because they had been influenced by their native folksongs, which still maintained the modal tradition.

In bringing back modal techniques and using them alongside diatonic methods, such composers have helped to enlarge the scope of modern music.

# Modulation

This term belongs to the system of composing music in major and minor keys. It will not be found in music that uses **Modes→**, nor in atonal music (**→ Atonality**). It is the art of moving smoothly from one key to another.

If a composition of any length were to remain always in the same key, it would inevitably become boring. But if it begins in one key, and then gradually moves through a series of different keys until it eventually returns to the original key, the music quite literally has a sense of 'movement', and the effect is refreshing.

Here is a short hymn-tune. It modulates several times before returning to the home key of G major. Each modulation is marked:

In order to bring about a modulation it is necessary to introduce notes that are present in the new key, but foreign to the old one. Thus, in the example above, the modulation to E minor in bars 4–5 begins at the point where the D sharp appears – for this is the leading note of E minor, but does not appear at all in G major.

The most common harmonies used in modulation are some form of DOMINANT of the new key, followed by the TONIC of the new key. And the most common modulations take place between those keys that have the greatest number of notes in common. All these keys are said to be 'relative' to one another. For example, the near relatives of C major are A minor (which shares the same key signature but has a G sharp) G major (which has an F sharp), and F major (which has a B flat). F major, however, is less closely related to G major because they have two different notes (F sharp and B flat).

Each key, therefore, has six related keys: TONIC, DOMINANT, and SUBDOMINANT, plus their RELATIVE MINORS (or RELATIVE MAJORS, if the original keys were themselves minor).

Rather than let the modulation take place too suddenly, composers usually make sure that the modulating chords are preceded by one (or more) that can be thought of as belonging to either key. In other words, they are chords that do not contain a note which is characteristic of either the old key or the new one. Here is a modulation from G major to D major. The modulation begins to take place when the C sharp is introduced. But the chord before that contains neither a C sharp (which is characteristic of D major), nor a C natural or F sharp (which are characteristic of G major). It is a chord on G, and we can think of it either as a tonic chord in G major, or as a subdominant chord in D major. It is therefore ambiguous, and we can approach it as if it were in G major, and leave it as if it were really in D major:

ENHARMONIC MODULATION occurs when the notation of a chord (or part of a chord) is changed, without changing the pitch. For example, a major chord on F sharp could be thought of as a major chord on G flat: the notation is different, but the sounds are the same.

**Moeran, Ernest John** English composer, 1894–1950. He is usually spoken of as E. J. Moeran. He was of Irish descent and studied at the Royal College of Music and later with John Ireland. His music was considerably influenced by folksong (which he collected) and includes a number of fine songs and part-songs, as well as effective larger works, such as the *Symphony in G minor* (1937) and the *Sinfonietta* (1948).

**Moll** (Ger.) Minor – in the sense of a minor key.

**Molto** (It.) Very, or much. Used in such phrases as **molto allegro**, very fast. **Moltissimo** Means 'extremely', or 'most'.

**Moment musical** A term used by Schubert, and others, as a title for short pieces, usually for piano. Collectively, *Moments musicaux*.

**Monody** A word derived from two Greek words meaning 'single' and 'song'. It is applied to the musical style that became important at the end of the 16th century when the first operas came into existence in Italy.

The monodic style means a kind of music that concentrates on a single melodic line which is supported by a series of simple harmonies. The typical monodic melody follows the natural rise and fall of speech, and its rhythm. The background harmonies are built up on a **Figured bass →**.

Music of this kind obviously allows words to be heard much more clearly than is possible in a polyphonic style, and thus, of course, it is very suitable for opera.

**Monothematic** A piece of music that is constructed from a single musical idea is said to be monothematic. It is perfectly possible to have a monothematic Sonata Form – both first and second subjects may use the same musical idea, provided that they present it in the correct keys.

**Monteverdi** → page 232

**Moore, Douglas** American composer, 1893–1969. He studied at Yale University, and in Paris with Vincent d'Indy and Nadia Boulanger, and later in Cleveland with Ernest Bloch. He is best known for his operas on American subjects, such as the one-act *The Devil and Daniel Webster* (1939) and the three-act *The Ballad of Baby Doe* (1956). He has also written orchestral music on American subjects, such as the *Pageant of P. T. Barnum* (1924) and *Moby Dick* (1928).

Moresca This dance was often performed in grotesque costumes representing animals or savages. This miniature, dated 1400, is from Froissart's *Chronique d'Angleterre, France et Espagne*.

Thomas Morley The title page of *The Triumphs of Oriana* which Morley edited and also wrote for.

Ferdinand 'Jelly Roll' Morton, 1885-1941

**Morbido** (It.) Soft, gentle, delicate.

**Morceau** (Fr.) Piece – a 'piece' of music.

**Mordent** In addition to the forms set out in **Notes and notation →**, there are others to be found in music of various dates. These, however, are usually explained by the editor and set out in full.

**Morendo** (It.) Dying, in the sense that the music gets softer and softer.

**Moresca** An ancient Moorish dance introduced into Europe by the Moors in Spain. It became very popular in the 15th and 16th centuries. The English 'Morris Dance' is probably derived from it; in both dances the dancers have small bells tied to their legs. ( **→ Morris dance**)

**Morley, Thomas** English composer, 1557–1603. He was organist of St Paul's Cathedral and was made a Gentleman of the Chapel Royal in 1592. He wrote a considerable number of madrigals and ayres, as well as anthems and services and music for the virginals. His madrigals, particularly the cheerful balletts and canzonets, are among the finest of their time. Morley also wrote a text book called *A Plaine and Easie Introduction to Practicall Musicke* (1597) which gives us an invaluable glimpse into Elizabethan music-making, as well as suggesting that he himself was a most likeable person.

**Morris dance** → page 233

**Morton, 'Jelly Roll'** American jazz pianist and composer, 1885–1941. Ferdinand 'Jelly Roll' Morton was one of the leading New Orleans ragtime pianists. He later (1923) went to Chicago and there established himself as a Blues singer of great power and imagination. He is one of the musicians who helped to turn jazz into a genuine art form. He also made a considerable contribution of jazz history by recording a series of illustrated interviews for the Library of Congress in 1938.

**Mosso** (It.) Moved. So **più mosso** means 'more moved' (that is, quicker).

**Moszkowski, Moritz** German pianist and composer, 1854–1925. After a successful career in Berlin as a piano teacher and concert pianist he retired to Paris (1897), but there fell on hard times and died very poor. His piano music is very attractive, and his two books of *Spanish Dances* are still played.

# Monteverdi

Claudio Monteverdi. Italian composer. Born at Cremona in 1567. Died in Venice, 1643.

He was the eldest child of Baldassare Monteverdi, a physician. He must have shown an early talent for music, for after studying with Marc' Antonio Ingegneri (the musician in charge of music at the Cathedral of Cremona), he published his first compositions – even though he was still only 15. Two books of madrigals soon followed (1584 and 1587), and thus by the time he was 20 Monteverdi was already established as a composer of considerable achievement.

His first important appointment came in 1590 when he joined the musical staff of the Duke of Mantua, Vincenzo Gonzaga I. Mantua was famous throughout Italy as one of the wealthiest and most artistic courts of the time. To a young and talented musician it offered every opportunity, even though the Duke was also well-known for a certain meanness when it came to paying his servants their wages!

By 1607 Monteverdi had published five books of madrigals and was famous throughout Italy. He was, however, extremely interested in new ideas – in particular the idea that words could be set to music in a way that was dramatic and expressive. His madrigals had already shown that he was a master of this kind of effect. He now wanted to go further and try his hand at the newly-invented combination of drama and music: opera.

The chance came when the Duke ordered his Chancellor, the poet Alessandro Striggio, to prepare an operatic entertainment. Monteverdi was chosen to write the music. What emerged on 22nd February, 1607, was a setting of the story of Orpheus and Euridice: *Orfeo*. It was an enormous success. In one stroke Monteverdi had proved that he knew better than anyone else how opera should be written.

He was not happy in Mantua, however. His wife died in 1607 and shortly afterwards he asked to be released from his contract. The Duke refused, and promptly offered him a life pension. In the end it was only the Duke's death, in 1612, that gave him the chance he needed. In the following year he set out for Venice and the post of Maestro di cappella to the Cathedral of St Mark's.

**Claudio Monteverdi** 1567–1643 Recognized as an outstanding musician in his own time, Monteverdi also occupies a place of great importance in the history of music for his harmonic invention, his rich orchestration and as the first major composer of operas.

**Choir of St Mark's Cathedral, Venice** (*left foreground*) in a procession around the Cathedral square. From 1612 Monteverdi was musical director of St Mark's, which had long been famous for the splendour and magnificence of its music. Great composers, such as Giovanni and Andrea Gabrieli, had worked there. Here Monteverdi continued to compose until he died in Venice, aged 76.

Monteverdi's work there involved writing music for St Mark's itself, but he was also able to publish further collections of madrigals. And after 1637, when the first public opera house was opened, he was able to write works for the stage once more. Unfortunately only two of these operas have survived, both of them masterpieces.

He continued to write fine music almost to his dying day, for he was one of those fortunate composers whose work got better and better. When he died, the whole of Venice went into mourning.

Like Bach, Monteverdi was able to make use of all the musical styles available in his day and weld them into something that was new and very remarkable. He was able to invent melodic shapes and rhythmic and harmonic effects that would instantly conjure up the meaning of whatever words he chose to set to music. As an opera composer he had that essential gift of human sympathy that enabled him not only to understand the characters he was writing about, but also to bring them to life in terms of music. He is also the first great operatic composer.

Monteverdi's published works include nine books of madrigals, several important religious works, including the Mass and Vespers of 1610, and the collection *Selva morale e spirituale* (1640), which contains a mass written in 1631, 2 magnificats and some 30 motets. His surviving operas are:

| | |
|---|---|
| *Orfeo* | 1607 |
| *The Return of Ulysses* | 1641 |
| *The Coronation of Poppea* | 1642 |

There is also a beautiful 'Lament', part of a lost opera *Ariadne* (1608).

# Morris dance

This is an old English dance which was once performed at Whitsun, probably to help make the crops grow.

Its name comes from the word 'moorish', and it is thought that the dance itself originated with the Moors. Morris men often blackened their faces with soot (to look like Moors?), and tied small bells to their legs (which is something that is done in certain Moorish dances).

Morris dancers wore their everyday clothes and added as many coloured ribbons as they could afford. They also decked their hats with flowers.

**Modern morris dancing**
In the two basic dances the performers carry either handkerchiefs or sticks, as here, and execute a series of complex patterns. The music is a strong 2/4, 4/4, or 6/8 rhythm and traditionally played on a violin. Morris dancing was almost defunct at the beginning of this century but was saved from oblivion by the Folksong and Dance Society. It is currently enjoying a revival all over Great Britain.

**Motet** The motet has existed, in varying forms, from the 13th century. Until Bach's day it was always an unaccompanied vocal setting of religious words (usually in Latin).

The medieval motet was always based on plainsong, but after about 1450 composers began to allow themselves much more freedom. The high point of motet development came in the 16th century, with such composers as Palestrina and William Byrd.

Motets were of less importance in the 17th and 18th centuries, though Bach wrote six magnificent examples. Thereafter the word tends to be used rather loosely, and though many composers still continued to apply it only to unaccompanied settings of religious texts, others used it for works in which there was an instrumental accompaniment.

Motets are used in the Roman Catholic service during the Offertory and at the Elevation of the Host, and also at various other moments for which the liturgy does not require any particular text to be sung. They are, in fact, a sort of Protestant Anthem.

**Motif or Motive** This means a tiny group of notes out of which a tune or passage or whole composition is developed.

**Motion** A term used in music in various ways, thus:

1. CONJUNCT MOTION and DISJUNCT MOTION = progression of a melodic part by step and by leap, respectively:

2. SIMILAR MOTION and CONTRARY MOTION = progression of two parts ('voices') in the

**Mouth organ from Laos** This instrument, called a khen, has up to 16 bamboo pipes, the longest of which can be 3 m. or more. The mouth organ has been in existence in the Far East since about 1100 B.C.

same direction and in opposite directions, respectively:

3. OBLIQUE MOTION = progression of one part up or down whilst the other stands still:

4. PARALLEL MOTION = progression by similar motion, the two parts running parallel:

**Moto** (It.) Motion. So **con moto** means 'with motion', 'quickly', and **moto perpetuo**, 'perpetual motion'. (→ **Perpetuum mobile**)

**Motto theme** A short theme usually presented at the opening of a work, which then returns at appropriate moments during the movement (or movements). In this way it dominates the whole work, for the music is constantly referring back to it. Examples include Elgar's Symphony No 1 in A flat, and Tchaikovsky's Fourth and Fifth Symphonies. A similar device is Berlioz's **idée fixe** →.

**Moussorgsky** → **Mussorgsky**

**Mouth organ** → **Harmonica**

# Mozart

Wolfgang Amadeus Mozart. Born at Salzburg, Austria, in 1756 and died in Vienna in 1791.

## 1. **Mozart's life**

Mozart was lucky in that his father, Leopold, was an excellent musician – a violinist in the court orchestra of the Archbishop of Salzburg. He recognized his son's extraordinary talent and began to teach him to play the harpsichord and violin. By the time he was five he was already composing quite respectable pieces of music, and as a performer he could outshine musicians many times his age.

There were two children in the Mozart family. Anna (known as Nannerl), Mozart's older sister, was also a fine musician. It was therefore not long before Leopold Mozart realized that his children could bring fame to the family, and money. In 1762 he decided to show the world just how talented they were.

He took them first to Munich, to play before the Elector of Bavaria and his court. The visit was a great success. In September 1762 they went to Vienna to play before the Empress of Austria. Here they were even more successful. In the following year they undertook a complete tour, through Germany and then on to Brussels, Paris, and London. Everywhere they went the audiences marvelled and paid well to hear them play. The little Mozarts were famous.

These travels continued for several years. A particularly important tour took them to Italy in 1770. In Rome the Pope conferred the Order of the Golden Spur on the little boy. A few weeks later the Accademia Filarmonica of Bologna tested his skills and, completely satisfied, admitted him as a member, even though he was far too young to join in the normal way.

Throughout this period Mozart was writing music. Not just small pieces, but sonatas, symphonies, and even operas. By the time the Italian tour had been completed he had written well over 100 works – and he was still only 15!

Leopold Mozart has been criticized for exhibiting his two children as if they were monkeys in a zoo. And though neither of them seems to have disliked the experience, their life cannot have been easy.

But, perhaps without realizing it, Leo-

**Wolfgang Amadeus Mozart** 1756-1791 This portrait of the composer in 1789 is by Doris Stock.

**String quartets** The title page of Mozart's six string quartets (K. 387, 421, 428, 458, 464 and 465) dedicated to Haydn and published in Vienna in 1785.

**The Magic Flute** This costume design for Papageno was for a Berlin production of 1816.

pold was giving his son the finest musical education that any musician has ever had. By the time he was 16, Mozart had met every composer of any importance and had studied their work at first hand. As each new influence struck him, he made use of it in his own music. He could scarcely help learning. He wrote, and his music was performed. He competed with his elders on equal terms. He learned, in fact, in the best way possible: by actually practising his craft.

But he was also a young man of genius and no mere imitator. Unlike so many infant prodigies, who burn brilliantly for a few years and then fizzle out, Mozart got better and better.

Eventually, of course, he had to settle to a regular job. Touring was all very well, but it was much more difficult for a 16-year old to impress an audience than it had been for a child. To begin with he worked in Salzburg, alongside his father.

Unfortunately, in 1772 a new Archbishop came to power. Mozart found that he could not stand him. He hated being treated like a servant – for, of course, this was what all musicians were in those days. He took as many opportunities to tour as possible. During one visit to Paris, in 1778, he had a heartbreaking experience – his mother, who had accompanied him, died in his arms.

If anything, life in Salzburg grew worse after this, and in 1781, after a series of particularly bitter scenes with the Archbishop and his officials, he decided to leave.

He went to Vienna, and there began the long struggle to earn a living. He taught, he gave concerts, he looked for patrons to support his music and help in its publication. He wrote operas, in both German and Italian (he spoke the languages fluently, as well as French and some English). To begin with he was successful enough, and in 1782 he was able to marry. But despite many triumphs, things began to go wrong and his last years were spent in comparative poverty.

No one knows exactly where Mozart is buried. There was only enough money for the cheapest funeral, and so he was placed in an unmarked grave. Strangely enough, the tide in his affairs was turning at the moment of his death. His opera *The Magic Flute* (1791) was beginning to draw the crowds and awaken an interest in the rest of his music. Within a few years it was generally acknowledged that he was one of the world's greatest composers.

2. **His music** On the surface Mozart's music may seem merely to be elegant and pretty and no different from the kind of thing the average 18th-century composer turned out all the time. And it is indeed true that he was content to use the musical language of his times. He was not interested in revolutionizing the *ingredients* of music. But he was revolutionary in what he caused those ingredients to *say*.

Mozart's music *is* elegant and pretty, but it is also deeply emotional, and it is this that sets him apart from all his contemporaries save one – Joseph Haydn.

We can see his capacity for emotion most clearly in his operas, for in them he does not merely provide delightful music for his singers, but gives them music that makes the characters they portray *come alive*.

Add to this his extraordinary technique – so fluent that he could carry out the most complicated musical task with the greatest ease – and the immensity of Mozart's genius soon becomes apparent. He is one of that select band of composers whose work seems to achieve perfection.

3. **Summary of Mozart's main works**
a. Operas include:

| | |
|---|---|
| *Idomeneo* | 1781 |
| *The Seraglio* (German title: *Die Entführung aus dem Serail*) | 1782 |
| *The Marriage of Figaro* (Italian title: *Le nozze di Figaro*) | 1786 |
| *Così fan tutte* | 1787 |
| *Don Giovanni* | 1787 |
| *The Magic Flute* (German title: *Die Zauberflöte*) | 1791 |
| *La Clemenza di Tito* | 1791 |

b. Church music includes:

| | |
|---|---|
| 'Credo' Mass | 1776 |
| 'Coronation' Mass | 1779 |
| Solemn Vespers | 1780 |
| Requiem Mass | 1791 |

c. Symphonies: there are 41, including:

| | |
|---|---|
| Symphony in D major, K. 385 ('The Haffner') | 1782 |
| Symphony in C major, K. 425 ('The Linz') | 1783 |
| Symphony in D major, K. 504 ('The Prague') | 1786 |
| Symphony in E flat major, K. 543 | 1788 |

**Leopold Mozart and his children** Wolfgang and his elder sister Maria Anna or 'Nannerl' with their father as they appeared before the public in 1763. This painting by Carmontelle is dated 1777.

**Above** This unfinished portrait of Mozart by Joseph Lange was made about eight years before his death.

| | |
|---|---|
| Symphony in G minor, K. 550 | 1788 |
| Symphony in C major, K. 551 ('The Jupiter') | 1788 |

(the last three were written in the space of six weeks!)

d. Concertos include:
27 for piano and orchestra
5 for violin and orchestra
4 for horn and orchestra
2 for flute and orchestra
1 each for bassoon and clarinet

e. Chamber music includes:
26 string quartets
42 violin sonatas
7 string quintets

Mozart also wrote music for piano, including 17 sonatas, and light music (*Divertimenti, Cassations, Serenades,* etc.) of all kinds, such as the *Eine kleine Nachtmusik*. The complete catalogue of his works comes to over 600 titles.

4. **The man** Though Mozart was loved by his friends, he made many enemies. He was impatient with fools, and found it hard to disguise his contempt for musicians who pursued a successful career without a proper foundation of talent. He admired Haydn, and was happy to acknowledge his indebtedness to him. And Haydn, though his senior by more than twenty years, returned the compliment. But lesser men sometimes felt the edge of his wit, and their hatred did not make his career any easier.

Although he was lively and cheerful, there was a melancholy side to his nature. Even as a young man of 31 he was able to write to his father '... death is the key which unlocks the door to our true happiness. I never lie down at night without reflecting that, young as I am, I may not live to see another day.' It is this side of his character that constantly shines through his music. Even at its most light-hearted there is a sense that grief and tragedy are not far below the surface.

Mozart's marriage was happy, though he and his wife managed their daily affairs rather badly and often had to borrow from friends. He might have made a complete success of his career as a free-lance composer had he been willing to write the kind of music that would always please the public. But he preferred to be true to his inspiration, and the music he wrote was sometimes too difficult for his audiences.

**Movement** Many long compositions are made up of several shorter ones, and these shorter ones are called *movements*. So we speak of (say) 'the slow movement of a sonata', or of the allemande as 'one of the usual movements of a Suite'.

Naturally the composer takes care to contrast the movements making up such a piece (→ **Sonata**, **Suite**, and **Symphony**). Presumably it is the variety of speeds that a composer plans for the different sections of his sonata or symphony, etc., that has led to their being called 'movements'.

**Mozart** → page 238

**Mp** Abbreviation of the Italian term, **mezzo piano**, 'half-soft'.

**M.S.** or **m.s.** Abbrevation of the Italian term **mano sinistra**, left hand.

**Munday, John** English composer, c. 1566–1630. He was the son of William Munday, Gentleman of the Chapel Royal and a minor composer of some distinction. He became organist of Eton College and St George's Chapel, Windsor Castle. He published a set of *Songs and Psalmes, composed into 3, 4 and 5 parts for the use and delight of such as either love or learne Musicke* (1594). A number of his keyboard pieces appear in the *Fitzwilliam Virginal Book*, among them a delightful fantasy describing '*Faire Wether*', '*Lightning*', '*Thunder*', '*Calme Wether*', and '*A Faire Day*'.

**Musette** This word has two meanings in music:
1. It is a type of French bagpipe, very popular during the 17th and 18th centuries among the aristocrats, who liked to play at being simple shepherds and shepherdesses.
2. It is an air in 2/4, 3/4, or 6/8 time which imitates the sound of the bagpipe by holding a bass note throughout. This held bass is either the tonic or dominant (or both) of the piece. It corresponds to the drone found on most bagpipes.

Musettes are rather like gavottes in style.

**Musgrave, Thea** Scottish composer, b. 1928. She studied at Edinburgh University, and in Paris with Nadia Boulanger. Early successes include the *Triptych* for tenor and orchestra (1959), and the *Colloquy* for violin and piano (1960). She has written several concertos and a great deal of chamber music, and has made a particular mark with her operas, which include *The Voice of Ariadne* (1974), and *Mary, Queen of Scots* (1977).

Thea Musgrave b. 1928 As well as chamber music and opera, she has also written incidental music for films and T.V.

Musette This musette is by J. S. Bach and is from his Third English Suite.

**Musica Britannica** A national collection of British music, carefully edited by experts. Publication began in 1951 with three volumes: 1. *The Mulliner Book* (a collection of keyboard music dated c. 1550), 2. *Cupid and Death* (a masque by Christopher Gibbons and Matthew Locke), 3. *Comus* (Milton's masque, with music by William Lawes). The collection now embraces music from many different periods and styles, including chamber music, concertos, opera, and choral music.

**Musica ficta** A Latin term meaning 'feigned music'. It describes the accidentals that were used in modal music. At this period, accidentals were usually inserted by the singers, who knew what was expected of them, and not actually written into the scores as we do nowadays.

**Musical box / clock** → **Mechanical instruments**

**Musical comedy** A term used between about 1890 and 1930 to describe a sentimental, humorous play with plenty of light music in it. Such works have a similarity

# The Musical

A type of play with music. It evolved in America in the 1920s, and may, perhaps, be thought of as an improved kind of **musical comedy** →. The musical (short for 'musical play') tends to have a much stronger plot and its music is also more vigorous and adventurous. The first really important musical was Jerome Kern's *Showboat* (1927).

Though other musicals predate *Showboat*, it set a new standard. Kern's example was followed by Gershwin (*Strike up the Band*, 1930; *Of Thee I Sing*, 1932), Cole Porter (*Anything Goes*, 1934; *Kiss Me Kate*, 1948), Irving Berlin (*Face the Music*, 1932; *Annie get your Gun*, 1946); the partnership of Richard Rodgers and Lorenz Hart (*On your Toes*, 1936; *Pal Joey*, 1940) and Rodgers and Hammerstein (*Oklahoma!*, 1943; *South Pacific*, 1949; *The King and I*, 1951), Leonard Bernstein (*On the Town*, 1944; *West Side Story*, 1957), Harold Arlen (*House of Flowers*, 1954), Frank Loesser (*Guys and Dolls*, 1950; *The most happy Fella*, 1956), Frederick Loewe (*My Fair Lady*, 1956), and Stephen Sondheim (*A little Night Music*, 1973).

Without losing any of its vitality, the American musical has gradually become a very sophisticated form of musical expression, such works as, say, Bernstein's *Candide* (1956), and Sondheim's *A little Night Music* (1973) attaining a complexity that brings them very close to operetta.

*Right* Scene from Jerome Kern's *Showboat*. *Below* Marlon Brando, Jean Simmons, Frank Sinatra and Vivian Blaine in the film version of Frank Loesser's *Guys and Dolls*. Alan Jay Lerner wrote the lyrics for this musical. *Below right* Yul Brynner and Deborah Kerr in the film of Rodger's and Hammerstein's *The King and I. Bottom* Dancers from the film of Leonard Bernstein's immensely popular *West Side Story* which was based on *Romeo and Juliet. Bottom left* Sumptuous dance sequence from *Footlight Parade*, 1933, by Busby Berkeley.

# Music criticism

The idea of someone making a career out of commenting on music and the way it is performed is comparatively new in the history of music. Two things were necessary before it could become a profession:

1. There had to be a reasonable number of newspapers and magazines which were widely read by people who were interested in music and the arts.

2. There had to be sufficient concerts open to the general public.

Both concerts and newspapers began to flourish in the 18th century, and turned into industries during the 19th. Music criticism followed a similar pattern of development.

Criticism can be divided into two kinds:

1. The day-to-day commentary on music and musical performances. This is the kind we read in our newspapers.

2. The carefully considered commentary on music, new and old, such as occurs in books or in the pages of serious monthly or quarterly magazines.

Of these, the second has the longest and most honourable history. Discussions about the nature of music were printed in the 18th century, and so were informed commentaries about particular composers' works.

Music criticism in the daily press seems to have begun in the early years of the 19th century with J. K. F. Rellstab's contributions to the Berlin newspaper *Vossische Zeitung*. The first English newspaper to employ a regular music critic seems to have been *The Times*. Other papers followed suit, and by the middle of the century the professional music critic was a common fact of musical life.

Though there have been some men who can still be regarded as great critics (the German Eduard Hanslick, and the Englishman Ernest Newman, for example), and a few men who have been employed as music critics and have then turned into great writers (such as George Bernard Shaw), and even a number of composers who have added to their incomes by acting as critics (such as Berlioz and Debussy), it has to be admitted that most critics have faded into oblivion rather more quickly than the music they praised or condemned.

The critic who writes for a monthly or quarterly magazine, or better still writes a book, has the best chance of making a worthwhile contribution to our understanding of music. For he at least has time to consider what he has to say. But the critic writing for a daily paper must make up his mind immediately after a performance and then telephone his report through to the paper before it is printed that same night. No wonder that his opinions occasionally prove faulty!

All critics should have one aim: to help the general public understand and assess performances, performers, and the music that is being performed.

---

to operetta, but the music is usually much lighter in style and much less ambitious in construction. A musical comedy, for example, seldom ventures into the kind of 'ensemble' you find in operetta: it remains content with catchy solo songs and the occasional simple duet.

The type flourished in both England and America (European composers tending to stick more closely to varieties of operetta). In some respects the English contribution is the most typical. Some of the better examples include: *The Arcadians* (1909) by Lionel Monckton and Howard Talbot, *Chu Chin Chow* (1916) by Frederick Norton, and *Bitter Sweet* (1929), by Noël Coward. Faced with competition from the much more vigorous American 'musical', musical comedy gradually died away, the last, weak examples coming from the pen of Ivor Novello (*Glamorous Night*, 1935).

**Musical glasses** → **Glass harmonica**

**Music drama** → **Opera**; **Wagner**

**Musicology** 'Logy' at the end of a word generally means 'knowledge of a subject'. For example, Theology means 'knowledge of God', Astrology means 'knowledge of the stars', Criminology means 'knowledge of crime', and so on.

Musicology therefore means 'knowledge of music' and it is now applied to the scientific study of music in all its aspects.

A musicologist is both a scientist and an historian. He must examine and try to understand music in as exact a way as possible, but he must also convey his findings to other people in such a way that they may make use of them.

In some ways he is like an archaeologist, for

it is often necessary to dig deep in libraries and other public and private records for the information he needs. His discoveries will tell us about the lives of composers, and the way in which music was performed in the past. He may also track down lost manuscripts, and examine others that have been ignored for centuries. Part of his job will be to make such discoveries fit for modern performance.

Musicology has only become an exact science in the last hundred years or so. Its disciplines are now systematically taught at universities. And because of it, more and more beautiful music becomes available to us every year.

## Musicians' Union, The
A registered British Trade Union formed in 1921 from two earlier independent Trade Unions in order to protect the interests of musicians and ensure that they are paid fair wages and offered reasonable terms of employment.

## Musique concrète
A type of music established by the composer Pierre Schaeffer in 1948 at the Paris Radio Studios. It consists of recorded sounds, which are then treated electronically and used to make musical compositions. The final composition exists, of course, on tape. Such music differs from other electronically contrived works in that the original source of the sound is a *natural* one

**Modeste Mussorgsky**
1839-1881. This portrait of the composer is by the artist Repin. The costume design by Fedorovsky is for Prince Khovansky in Mussorgsky's unfinished opera *Khovantschina* (1886).

(for example, the sound of a bell, or a human voice). The treatment, however, will change the nature of the sound out of all recognition (for example, it may be played backwards, or faster than it was recorded, etc.).

## Mussorgsky, Modeste
Russian composer, 1839–81. He was the youngest son of a wealthy landowner, and though he showed musical talent at an early age he was sent into the Army. Later (1863) he became a civil servant. Throughout this time he continued with his music and after 1858 began to compose seriously.

Unfortunately the necessity of earning a living away from music, coupled with a tendency to drink too much, meant that he was never able to concentrate sufficiently to make the most of his genius. Many of his works remained unfinished.

Nevertheless, his finest music shows that he was not only the most important and influential of the 'Russian School' of composers, but also a man of powerful imagination. His greatest works include the opera *Boris Godunov* (1868–72), an orchestral piece, *Night on the Bare Mountain* (1867), the piano suite *Pictures from an Exhibition* (1874), and two fine song cycles: *Sunless* (1874) and *Songs and Dances of Death* (1877).

## Mutation stops → Organ

---

# Mute

In music this has several meanings, all connected with quietening and softening the tone:

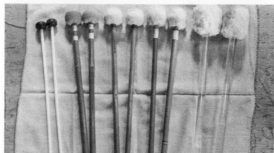

*Left* The mute in brass instruments is a pear-shaped cone that is pushed into the bell of the instrument to soften the tone. If the instrument is blown very hard when the mute is in place, however, the tone becomes harsh. *Below* With the piano the muted effect is obtained by putting down the left-hand pedal – the soft pedal which puts felt pads on the strings.

*Above* In the violin and similar instruments a small clamp that can be fixed quickly to the bridge makes the tone muted, soft and silvery.

*Right* With timpani the muted effect is obtained by using drumsticks with soft sponge heads.

**Nachtmusik** (Ger.) Night music, or serenade. A type of music, usually in the form of a suite, suitable for performance in the open air in the evening. (e.g. Mozart: *Eine kleine Nachtmusik*, A Little Night Music)

**Nakers** The medieval name for small kettledrums of Arabian origin. They were introduced into Western music at the time of the Crusades and are the ancestors of today's orchestral timpani. They can still be found in North Africa, Turkey, Egypt and similar countries – small metal or wooden bowls covered with a skin, used in pairs. The smallest sizes can be held in one hand, but larger versions are often mounted on the back of a camel, etc.

**Nardini, Pietro** Italian composer, 1722–93. He studied with Tartini and soon became known as one of the finest violinists of the day. He worked mainly in Stuttgart, and then, after 1667, in Italy. His compositions include concertos and sonatas for violin, and six string quartets.

**Nares, James** English composer, 1715–83. He was organist of York Minster (1734–56), and then of George III's Chapel Royal, of which he became Master of the children in 1757. He published many canons, catches, and glees, as well as music for the harpsichord and organ, and a number of anthems. His harpsichord music is well worth playing.

**National Anthems** It seems very likely that Great Britain was the first country to adopt a patriotic song as a 'national anthem'. The piece in question, 'God save the King', was first sung in London in 1745 (→ **God save the Queen**), but it does not seem to

**Nachtmusik** This group of 17th-century student musicians performs before a town house in Leipzig.

**Nakers** This example is from a 14th-century Flemish manuscript.

**Carl Nielsen** 1865 – 1931

have been accepted as a 'national' anthem until about 1820. Other countries soon followed Great Britain's example–some even borrowing her tune!

In many ways 'God save the Queen' is the ideal anthem. It is short, dignified, easy to remember, and easy to sing.

Next to the British National Anthem, the most admired tunes are probably those of France (whose *Marseillaise* expresses great revolutionary fervour), Austria (a hymn written by Haydn in deliberate imitation of 'God save the King'), and both the old and new Russian National Anthems. The American National Anthem (borrowed from the English composer John Stafford Smith) is also fine in its way, but rather too long – it also has a very wide range and is therefore rather difficult for most people to sing.

**Natural** This word is used in two ways:
1. For a note that is neither sharpened nor flattened. Thus the scale of C is sometimes spoken of as 'the natural scale'.
2. For the sign (♮) which restores a note to that condition after it has been sharpened or flattened. (→ **Notes and notation**)

**Neapolitan sixth** The first inversion of the major common chord on the flattened supertonic. Thus in C major it will be the first inversion of the chord built on D flat.

Here are a few more examples:

Keys: G major    F major    A major    A minor    C minor

The name probably comes from the fact that such chords were much used at final cadence points by the composers of the Neapolitan School of opera in the first part of the 18th century (Alessandro Scarlatti, etc.). The sudden touch of sadness which the chord suggests was greatly admired.

**Neck** The projecting part of a violin, etc., which has the finger-board on it, and the peg-box at the end.

**Neo-classicism** A movement that emerged in the 1920s as a reaction against the over-romantic music of the late 19th and early 20th century. Composers tried deliberately to recreate the mood of Bach and Mozart in modern terms, often borrowing old forms (such as the Concerto Grosso) and imitating typical 18th-century melodic patterns. The effect sometimes suggests Bach and Mozart with 'wrong notes', but at its best it helped to clarify musical thought. Typical neo-classical composers include Stravinsky, Prokofiev, Poulenc, and Lennox Berkeley.

**Neuausgabe** On German title-pages, this means 'new edition'.

**Neums, Neumes** → **Notation**

**Nicene creed** → **Creed**

**Nicolai, Otto** German composer, 1810–49. After studying in Berlin and Rome he made a successful career as a conductor in Vienna, Rome, and Berlin. He wrote several operas, but is remembered by only one of them – *The Merry Wives of Windsor* (1849) – regarded now as one of the great German comic operas.

**Nielsen, Carl** Danish composer, 1865– 1931. He was born near Odense, and his parents were so poor that he began life as a shepherd boy. Such was his musical talent, however, that friends and neighbours raised enough money to send him to the Royal Conservatory in Copenhagen (1884), where he studied under Niels Gade.

He afterwards earned his living as a violinist, and then (1908–14) as conductor of the Royal Opera in Copenhagen. He was for a short while Director of the Royal Conservatory.

In the meantime he had become famous as a composer. His first symphony was completed in 1894, and in the five that followed it he gradually evolved a very individual and adventurous style. These six symphonies are among the most important written in the 20th century, and Nielsen himself must be counted alongside Sibelius as one of the greatest of Scandinavian composers.

Nielsen wrote two operas: a serious one, *Saul and David*, in 1902, and a comedy, *Maskerade*, in 1906. He wrote concertos for violin (1911), flute (1926) and clarinet (1928), a great deal of chamber music, and many choral works.

**Niente** (It.) Nothing. Sometimes used after a diminuendo sign to indicate that the music must fade into silence. The direction **quasi niente** (almost nothing) is also found.

**Nightingale** A toy instrument. A type of whistle that imitates the song of the nightingale. The lower part of the whistle is held in a glass of water, which gives it its bubbling sound.

**Ninth** → **Intervals** A 'chord of the ninth' is a common chord with a seventh and ninth added.

**Nobile** (It.) Noble. **Nobilmente**, nobly.

**Nocturne** Literally a 'Night Piece' – the kind of music that would be in keeping with a calm moonlit night. This poetic title was first used by the Irish composer John Field for some of his piano pieces. They are mostly rather melancholy.

The finest *Nocturnes* were written by Chopin (in imitation of Field); here is the opening of one by Field himself:

**Noh** This classical heroic drama was developed in the 14th century. The performers wear elaborate costumes and masks.

**Luigi Nono** b.1924 A pupil of Maderna and Scherchen, he was a follower of Webern and many of his compositions involve mathematical calculations.

**Noh** The ancient type of Japanese play with music. It contains solo and choral singing, and is accompanied by drums and flutes.

**Noire** (Fr.) Black. The name given to the crotchet or quarter-note.

**Nonet** A piece of chamber music for nine instrumentalists, usually a mixture of strings and woodwind. There are comparatively few nonets, Spohr's, for violin, viola, cello, double bass, flute, oboe, clarinet, bassoon and horn, being a good example.

**Nono, Luigi** Italian composer, b. 1924. Born in Venice and largely self-taught, he emerged in the 1950s as a twelve-note composer with strong left-wing political ideals. His opera *Intolleranza* (1960) made a deep impression.

**Nota cambiata** (It.) Changing-note. A melodic figure common in polyphonic music from medieval times. ( → **Changing notes**)

**Notation** → page 242

**Note** This word has three musical meanings:
1. The written sign showing pitch and duration of a sound to be sung or played.( → **Notes and notation**)
2. A finger-key on the pianoforte or other keyed instrument.
3. Any single sound made by voice or instrument. In America a note is sometimes a 'tone'.

# Notation

The idea of writing music down came into existence comparatively recently in the history of music. In Western Europe, for example, it was not until the seventh century that any attempt was made, and not until the 11th century that the attempts became reasonably effective. And even then it was only the monks who knew how to write music down and had the time and opportunity to do so.

Before these dates, and for the uneducated for many years after, music had to be learned by rote – a singer or instrumentalist passing on his stock of tunes to a younger man, and so on down the centuries. Hundreds of tunes were remembered in this way, but an equal number must also have been lost for all time ( → **Folksong**). Even today there are societies, in Asia and Africa, where music is handed down from generation to generation.

Music that depends on memory alone is apt to be very simple. It was not until some form of notation had been invented that composers could begin to develop their art. Imagine how impossible it would be for a man to think up a symphony, teach each part to an orchestra, and then hope that the performers could play it together from memory!

One very early form of simple notation consisted of giving each note a different letter of the alphabet. In fact we still do this, naming the notes of our scales from A to G.

But the first step towards notation as we know it came when musicians began to add signs above the words they were to sing which gave a general indication of whether the melody went up ´ , or down, ` or both ^ . Signs of this kind are still used in certain languages (French, for example) and they tell you how to pronounce the word. Slightly more complex signs were also invented to stand for certain fixed groups of notes – we still use some of them to indicate a trill or a turn.

This early form of notation is really little more than a reminder to performers of something they had already learned by rote. Signs of this kind are called NEUMES.

Gradually composers took to placing the neumes at different heights above the words that were to be sung. A neume placed high above a word would remind the singers to

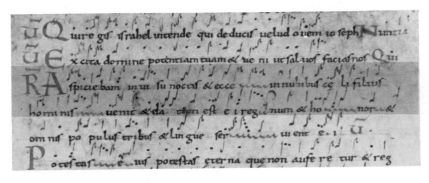

**Earliest form of notation**
*Above* This example of an 11th-century French antiphon shows 'unheighted' neumes, the most simple of aids to performing musicians.
*Right* The antiphon transcribed into modern notation.

R(esponsoriu)m

**Heighted neumes** *Left* This 11th-century manuscript from southern France demonstrates how neumes placed at different heights above the words formed a visual guide to the melody's changes of pitch. *Below left* The modern transcription of this notation.

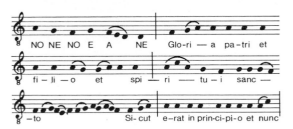

raise their voices to a higher pitch than they had used for a neume placed immediately above a word. The pattern that the neumes made was like a rough outline of the melody.

**Staff system** This piece of medieval liturgical music, shown with its modern transcription, uses lines coupled with a clef or key indication to define exact pitch.

Eventually someone thought of drawing a horizontal line to represent one particular note. Neumes placed above the line represented higher notes, neumes placed below it were lower notes. The first note to be singled out in this way was **F**, and the horizontal line was usually coloured in red.

Shortly after this another line was added, to represent **C**. This was usually yellow. Then another, and another until there was a four-line grid. Each line and each space in between the lines could stand for a different note of the scale, and thus singers could see exactly which note they had to sing. We use the same system nowadays, though the four-line grid has become a five-line affair, which we call a STAVE.

As it was rather expensive and complicated to make each line a different colour, it soon became the practice to add a letter of the alphabet to one or other of the lines to show what its pitch was meant to be. This letter was a 'clue' or 'key' to the grid, and we still use the French word CLEF (key) to describe the very same thing in our own music. In the following table you can see how our modern clefs have developed out of old ways of writing the alphabet:

F F ♯:    C c 𝄡    G ♮ 𝄞

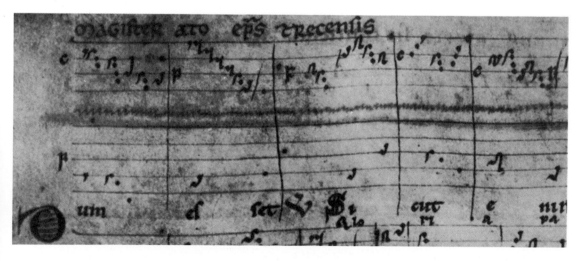

**Clef** *Left* This 14th-century piece of music clearly makes use of clefs – the upper line indicating G (the treble clef), the lower, F (bass clef). Our modern symbols evolved from the different forms of writing these letters. *Below* This music is here transcribed into modern notation.

Magister ato episcopus trecensis

All that was needed now was for someone to invent a way of showing how *long* the different notes were. The simple neumes began to change shape, some developing 'heads', and others being replaced by the kind of squares and diamonds that were easy to write with a quill pen. In time, these grew into the rounded shapes of modern minims, crotchets, and quavers (half-, quarter-, and eighth-notes).

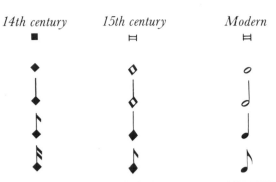

*14th century*     *15th century*     *Modern*

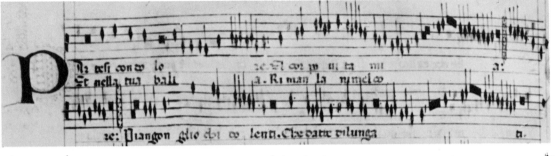

**Time-value of notes** This 14th-century manuscript makes use of black notes of differing shapes to indicate the length of time the note should be held. *Below* The modern transcription of this music into modern minims, crotchets and quavers is not so very different from the original.

**15th-century notation**
*Left* The use of white or void notes along with black notes was a further step in the development of musical notation. Black heads were used for indicating changes of values or rhythms. *Below* The modern transcription of this French song of the 15th century.

Notation of this kind provided most of the basic instructions needed for the performance and preservation of music. As music became more complicated and sophisticated, more information was added: signs to indicate the speed, or the degrees of loudness and softness required, and so on.

But even with all the signs and symbols available to us today, music remains something of a mystery. For nobody has been able to invent a notation to cover the way in which performers must 'feel' the music – the way in which 'expression' must be added if the music is to come alive. Thus, no two performances will ever be the same.

In recent years composers have added a great many new signs to stand for the many new ways of playing instruments that have been developed. Electronic instruments, in particular, demand new notations. Unfortunately their experiments have not yet settled down into a universally accepted system. Performers therefore have to 'learn' the notation of many avant-garde pieces before they can play them. Here are some of the signs you might find in such a score:

**Avant-garde score** This is part of the score of *December Hollow*, a 'musical' composition by the British composer Peter Zinovieff. The score, a series of visual patterns, attempts, like the music, to convey emotional states of mind.

Besides the notations we have described, there are others in daily use – the **Sol-fa system →** in vocal music and the system known as **Tablature →**

**Novellette** Schumann introduced this word as the title for eight of his piano pieces. He said that each could be taken as a sort of 'romantic story' in music. Other composers have since used the term.

**Novello & Co** A famous London music publishing firm established in 1811 by Vincent Novello (1781–1861), the son of an Italian emigrant. The firm prospered particularly when his son, Joseph Alfred Novello (1810–96), took over in 1829 and it became famous for its cheap editions of the standard classics. The Novello editions of choral music by Handel, Mendelssohn, and many other composers helped to popularize the idea of massed choral singing in Great Britain.

In 1844 Novello's began to publish a music magazine, *The Musical Times*, which is now the oldest of its kind still in existence.

**Novello, Vincent** English composer and organist, 1781–1861. He was a pupil of Samuel Webbe and became organist of the Portuguese Embassy Chapel in London. He wrote many glees, anthems, and hymn-tunes, and was a pioneer in editing old music. His publishing firm (see above) rapidly became one of the most prosperous and influential in Great Britain.

**Nuance** A word used in music in the same way as it is used in everyday speech – to express any slight change: of speed, dynamics, tone-colour, etc.

**Nunc Dimittis** This is the Song of Simeon, in St Luke's Gospel ('Lord, now lettest Thou Thy servant depart in peace'). It is sung in the Roman Catholic Church at Compline and in the Anglican Church at Evensong.

It has an ancient plainsong, but in the Anglican Church is often sung to an Anglican Chant. There are also innumerable settings by church composers of all periods.

**Nut** 1. A ridge on the fingerboard of a stringed instrument, just below the pegboard. The sounding-length of a string is measured from the nut to the bridge.
2. A small piece of ebony, or ivory, fitted to the end of a bow to hold the horsehair. It moves in a groove when a screw is turned, thus enabling the player to adjust the hair of the bow to the correct tension for playing.

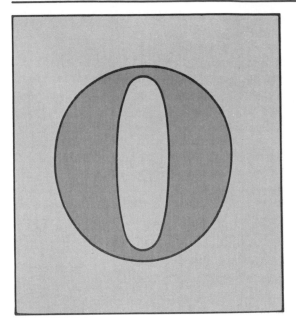

**Johannes Ockeghem 1425–1495** As a boy he was a chorister in Antwerp Cathedral and as a young man in the Chapel of the Duke of Burgundy. In the photo, he is the old man standing in front of the lectern.

**O** A small 'o' placed over a note in music for strings means either that the note must be played on an open string, or as a harmonic – the context will make this clear. In harp music, 'o' always indicates a harmonic.

**Obbligato** (It.) Obligatory. When found in a part for a particular instrument, this direction *should* mean that the instrument is essential and must not be omitted. Unfortunately, some composers have used the word in the very opposite sense – to indicate an optional part. For example, an ordinary song with a piano accompaniment may also have a part for 'violin obbligato' which need not necessarily be played. Common sense will tell us which of the two meanings is intended.

**Oberwerk** (Ger.) Swell organ. Sometimes abbreviated to **Obw.**, or **O.W.**

**Oblique motion** → **Motion**

**Oboe family** → page 247

**Oboe d'amore** Somewhat larger than the oboe, but smaller than the cor anglais, this member of the oboe family was developed in Germany in the early part of the 18th century. It has a bulbous bell, and its reeds are fixed in a short brass crook. It is pitched in A, and its notes are therefore written a minor third higher than they sound. The oboe d'amore was a favourite instrument of J. S. Bach, but it went out of favour in the 19th century. A few modern composers have used it – for example, Richard Strauss (*Domestic Symphony*), Ravel (*Bolero*), Debussy (*Gigues*).

**Obrecht, Jacob** Flemish composer, c. 1453–1505. He worked as a church musician

**Oboe d'amore** This instrument was used by Telemann in compositions dated 1722 and for the first time by J. S. Bach a year later. It was pitched a minor third below the oboe. Its part in the performance of old music is often taken by the ordinary oboe.

in the Netherlands and in Italy (where he died of the plague). His music includes chansons, motets, masses, and an early example of Passion music (St Matthew).

**Ocarina** A member of the family of 'vessel' flutes, found all over the world and dating from the beginnings of civilization. The vessel flute gets its name from the shape of its body, which is globular, or pear-shaped. The ocarina (shaped like a pear), has a mouthpiece projecting from one side, and holes cut in the body which can be opened and closed with the fingers to produce different notes. The player blows into the mouthpiece in the way that he would blow into a whistle.

**Ockeghem, Johannes** Flemish composer, 1425–95. He was a pupil of Dufay and entered the service of the French King Charles VII in 1452. His music, which includes chansons, motets, and masses, was famous for its contrapuntal ingenuity.

**Octave** In Western music this is the interval of eight notes up or down the scale, as from C to the C above or below. Within an octave there are 13 notes separated by 12 semitones.

**Octet** Any group of eight performers, or any piece of music composed for such a group. A STRING OCTET consists of four violins, two violas, and two cellos.

**Octuplet** A group of eight notes played in the time of six.

**Oeuvre** (Fr.) Work. Used in the same sense as **Opus** →.

**Offenbach, Jacques** French composer, 1819–80. Though he was born in Germany, but settled in Paris as a young man and to all intents and purposes became French. He trained first as a cellist, and after earning his living variously as an orchestral player, conductor, and theatre manager, he took over a small theatre, re-named it the Bouffes-Parisiens, and produced a string of enormously successful operettas. They range from short one-act pieces to full-scale three and four-act works. The most famous of them are: *Orpheus in the Underworld* (1858), *La Belle Hélène* (1864) *La Vie parisienne* (1866), *The Grand Duchess of Gérolstein* (1867) and *La Périchole* (1868). His only 'serious' opera, *The Tales of Hoffman*, was produced after his death in 1881.

**Offertory** Music sung, or played on the organ, whilst the priest is preparing the bread and wine of the Communion Service.

# Oboe family

The instruments of this family are wooden tubes with a DOUBLE REED in the mouthpiece. This reed consists of two thin slices of cane, bound close together. When the player blows through them they vibrate and make a squeaking noise. These vibrations are caught up by the rest of the instrument and transformed into a pleasant musical sound. Different notes are obtained in the usual way: by opening and closing the holes cut along the side of the tube and thus changing its sounding length.

Early double-reed instruments include **Shawms** →, which date back to the ancient civilisations of the Middle East and are common in the folk music of Europe, Asia, and Africa. Shawms look rather like the modern oboe (which is directly descended from them), but their sound is harsher and has a pronounced 'buzz'. They are essentially outdoor instruments. In ancient Greece the double-reed instrument was known as the AULOS, and in ancient Rome as the TIBIA.

Shawms played an important part in the music of renaissance Europe. They were made in several sizes: treble, alto, tenor, bass, and sometimes great bass (or POMMER). In some cases the reeds were protected by a *reed-cap*, and therefore, unlike the modern oboe, were not placed directly in the player's mouth. Among the most popular members of the shawm family were the **Crumhorn** →, **Curtall** →, and **Rackett** →.

The modern oboe family was developed from the shawms during the 17th century. They were particularly popular in France at the court of Louis XIV, where their transformation into the present-day sweet-voiced instrument was largely due to the efforts of one maker, Jean Hotteterre (1648–1732). They became part of the regular orchestra in the 18th century, and in the 19th were much improved by the addition of a complex key mechanism.

The chief instruments of the modern oboe family are:
Treble: The **oboe** itself.
Alto: The **cor anglais**.
Tenor: The **bassoon**.
Bass: The **double bassoon**.

Most orchestras have two oboes and two bassoons. The cor anglais and double bassoon are sometimes included (in the larger scores of the late 19th century) as separate instruments, but more often as instruments to be played by the second oboist and second bassoon as required.

The name 'oboe' is derived from the French *hautbois* – meaning, literally, 'high wood' (a treble instrument made of wood). The English first borrowed the word almost exactly: HAUTBOY, and then gradually changed it into oboe.

Oboe

Bassoon

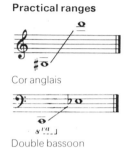

**Practical ranges**

Cor anglais

Double bassoon

**Cor anglais and oboe** (left) The cor anglais has a range from E below Middle C upwards for about two octaves. It was rarely used before the 19th century but is now a common orchestral instrument. The oboe is pitched a fifth higher than the cor anglais. Both are blown through a double reed (*right*).

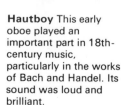

**Hautboy** This early oboe played an important part in 18th-century music, particularly in the works of Bach and Handel. Its sound was loud and brilliant.

**Old Hundredth** Hymn No 365 in *The English Hymnal*: 'All people that on earth do dwell.' This is also sung to the words 'Praise God from whom all blessings flow.' The melody was adapted from the Genevan Psalter of 1551.

**Ondes Martenot** An electronic instrument invented by Maurice Martenot in 1928. The notes are produced by oscillators, controlled from a keyboard. The sound has a curious singing quality, rather like that of a musical saw. Works that employ this instrument include Honegger's oratorio *Joan of Arc at the Stake*, and Messiaen's *Turangalîla* Symphony.

**Op.** Short for **Opus →**. **Op. posth.** means 'posthumous work' – one that was first published after the composer's death.

**Open harmony → Harmony**

**Open string** Any string on an instrument that is allowed to vibrate along its whole length, without being stopped by the player's finger.

**Opera buffa** The Italian form of comic opera. It is important to realize, however, that many such operas are also great art and the term does not imply mere farce. Rossini's *The Barber of Seville* is an opera buffa, as is Verdi's *Falstaff*.

The French equivalent is *Opéra Bouffe*.

**Opéra comique** This French term does not mean 'comic opera', but describes any opera that has spoken dialogue, whether the story is comical or serious. In its original form Bizet's tragic opera *Carmen* was an example of 'opéra comique'.

**Operetta** This word sometimes means a short opera, but is more often used to describe light opera with spoken dialogue. The Savoy Operas of Gilbert and Sullivan are operettas.

**Opera seria** The Italian for serious opera, applied usually to those of the 17th and 18th centuries, for example Mozart's *Idomeneo*.

**Ophicleide** The largest member of the now obsolete key-bugle family of instruments. It was invented in 1817, but within fifty years had been overtaken by the tuba.

**Jacques Offenbach 1819–1880** This immensely popular composer produced nearly 90 operettas but died three months before the Paris premiere of his major opera *The Tales of Hoffman* in 1881.

**Opera buffa** This magazine cover marks the first production of Verdi's comic opera, *Falstaff*, in 1893. The term 'opera buffa' applied particularly to the type of 18th-century Italian opera represented by Pergolesi's *The Servant as Mistress*. The term was adopted in 19th-century France to describe the more farcical approach of Offenbach and others. Mozart's *Don Giovanni* is another example of opera buffa.

# Opera

The idea of using music during a play goes back to the very beginnings of drama. But the idea of using music *throughout* a play and singing everything that would normally be spoken is of comparatively recent origin. For that is what opera is: a form of sung drama. And the first examples appeared in Italy around about the year 1600.

The basic ingredients of any opera are:

1. A LIBRETTO – that is to say the words. (Originally from Latin a 'book' of words.) This is like a play, but must be written in such a way as to leave plenty of scope for the music. The person who writes the libretto is called a librettist. A few composers have written their own (Berlioz, for example, and Wagner).
2. SINGERS – some who take solo parts as the main characters in the drama, some, perhaps, to act as a chorus.
3. An ORCHESTRA to accompany the singers and provide a continuous background of music.
4. A STAGE, COSTUMES, SCENERY, and all the equipment of an Opera House specially designed for the purpose. Also a producer to direct the production, and a conductor to manage the orchestra.
5. A great deal of money to pay all the orchestral players, singers, stage-hands, etc., etc., etc!

When writing an opera, the first thing a composer must do is to decide exactly how he is going to satisfy the conflicting needs of the words and the music, the drama and the stage itself. For if the opera is to be a success, one thing is certain: each will have to give way from time to time to the needs of the others.

For example: there will be moments when the audience must be informed about what is happening in the story. At such times the composer may hold the music back a little *as music*, thus allowing the words to come over as clearly as possible. But there will also be moments when the characters have to express their emotions as forcibly as possible. For this to happen the music must be allowed to flower into a beautiful melody, even if it means that the words have to take second place.

In the early days of opera, composers made a very clear distinction between these two kinds of approach to the words and music. Moments when the words mattered most were sung in RECITATIVE – a form of 'musical speech'. It was simple and not melodious in the ordinary sense, and the accompaniment behind it was also very straightforward. Moments when the emotions mattered most were expressed by an ARIA – a full-blown melody with an elaborate formal accompaniment. (→ **Recitative; Aria**)

In this way the recitative enabled the story to move forward quickly and efficiently, while the aria brought it to a standstill from time to time in order to give the emotions full play.

As time went by, however, the clear-cut division into recitative and aria was abandoned in favour of a continuous sort of music which was sometimes a little like the old recitative and sometimes a little like the old aria – in other words, it would vary in intensity according to the needs of the story.

The composer must also decide how far he wants his orchestra to help in telling the story and revealing the thoughts and emotions of the characters. He may decide to do as early 18th-century composers did and keep it as a simple accompaniment to the voices. He may, on the other hand, decide to do as Wagner did and give it a great deal of work – so that the orchestral background is really a kind of Symphonic Poem which describes in detail everything that happens on the stage. Or again, he may decide to steer a course somewhere in between these two extremes.

**18th-century opera singer** This caricature of 1801 shows the famous English singer Mrs Billington. Her voice had a range of three octaves and she is said to have earned £4000 in one season at Covent Garden.

*Below left* **18th-century Italian opera** This illustration is of an opera performance at the Teatro Regio, Turin. *Below* **Marriage of Figaro** Beaumarchais's comedy, first published in 1785, was the basis for Mozart's opera and for Rossini's *The Barber of Seville*.

But however he decides to solve the problems (and these are only a few of them!), he has embarked on a difficult, but exciting task.

## A brief history of opera

The idea of 'opera' came into existence in Florence just before the year 1600. The men who invented it (→ **Camerata**) were trying to re-create the way in which they thought the ancient Greeks had performed their dramas, and they believed that the story ought to be presented in a sung form, using what we now call Recitative.

Within a very few years, however, composers began to introduce more tuneful passages into their operas – arias, in fact. They also added choruses, orchestral interludes, and dances: so that the whole thing became a varied and exciting entertainment. The first great master of this type of opera was Monteverdi.

During the 17th century the idea of opera spread throughout Italy, and then into France and Germany and elsewhere in Europe. Opera became so popular that it turned into a kind of industry, and composers were forced to adopt a rather simpler style in order to produce their operas quickly enough to satisfy the demand. Arias and recitatives came to be constructed along regular, conventional lines (→ **Aria**); the stories that were set to music were also rather stereotyped. At the

same time, singers became more and more important, so that operas had to be designed to show off their voices.

Only in France did opera remain rather more sober. It was here that Lully and Rameau worked. In England, Henry Purcell shared something of their method.

In the second half of the 18th century two important composers managed to change opera back into something more serious and artistic. One was Gluck, who deliberately set out to 'reform' opera. The other was Mozart, who turned it into great art simply because he was both a great musician and a great musical dramatist.

Opera in the 19th century developed in two main ways. First, there was the type that preferred to give the greatest importance to the voice, keeping the orchestra more as an accompaniment. And second, there was the type that reduced the importance of the singers and allowed the orchestra to dominate the proceedings. The first type could be described as OPERA OF VOCAL MELODY. You can find examples in the work of Rossini, Bellini, Donizetti, and, of course, Verdi. The second type is really SYMPHONIC OPERA. Wagner is its most important exponent.

The 19th century also enjoyed operas that were full of exciting situations, spectacular costumes and scenery, and rather flamboyant music. Meyerbeer, Verdi, and even Wagner (in his early days) wrote operas of this kind (→ **Grand opera**). And in the second half of the century many operas were distinctly 'nationalistic', using historical stories and legends and the kind of music that reflected the influence of folksongs and dances.

During the 20th century composers have tended to steer a course somewhere between the two extremes of 19th-century opera. Such great masters as Puccini, Richard Strauss, Janáček, Prokofiev, and Britten have felt free to adopt whatever style and approach best suited the story they wished to tell. And opera, though increasingly expensive to put on the stage, is as popular and alive as ever.

The operas in the following list are representative of their composers and the various points made in this article. For a more complete list, the articles on individual composers should be consulted.

*Right* **Verdi's** *Otello* This was one of three operas that Verdi wrote on Shakespearean themes (*Macbeth* and *Falstaff* were the others), and it was first performed at La Scala, Milan in 1887. The play also inspired a similar work by Rossini produced in Naples in 1816.

**Mussorgsky's** *Khovantschina (The Kjovansky Affair) Above* Costume *(top)* and set designs *(bottom)* by Federovsky for a later production of the opera first staged in St. Petersburg in 1886. The work was unfinished by Mussorgsky but completed by Rimsky-Korsakov. A later version by Shostakovich is more faithful to the composer's style.

*Left* **Verdi's** *Aida* This 'Grand opera', is set in ancient Egypt.

### 17th-century opera
| | |
|---|---|
| Monteverdi | *Orfeo* |
| | *The Coronation of Poppea* |
| Purcell | *Dido and Aeneas* |

### 18th-century opera
| | |
|---|---|
| Handel | *Giulio Cesare* |
| Gluck | *Orfeo e Euridice* |
| Mozart | *Don Giovanni* |
| | *The Marriage of Figaro* |
| | *The Magic Flute* |

### 19th-century opera
| | |
|---|---|
| Rossini | *The Barber of Seville* |
| Donizetti | *Lucia di Lammermoor* |
| Bellini | *Norma* |
| Verdi | *Don Carlos* |
| | *Otello* |
| | *Falstaff* |
| Wagner | *The Mastersingers of Nuremberg* |
| | *Tristan and Isolde* |
| | *The Ring of the Nibelung* |
| Bizet | *Carmen* |
| Mussorgsky | *Boris Godunov* |

### 20th-century opera
| | |
|---|---|
| Puccini | *Madam Butterfly* |
| Strauss | *Ariadne auf Naxos* |
| Janáček | *The cunning little Vixen* |
| Berg | *Wozzeck* |
| Britten | *Peter Grimes* |
| Stravinsky | *The Rake's Progress* |

**Puccini's** *Turandot* This fantastic Chinese opera, completed by Alfano after the composer's death, was first produced in Milan in 1926. The story is based on Carlo Gozzi's 18th-century version of a widespread and ancient tale about a cruel Chinese princess eventually conquered by love.

**Ophicleide** This now obsolete instrument which was used by Berlioz, Mendelssohn and Verdi, was superseded by the tuba.

**Carl Orff** b. 1895 As well as a composer Orff has been an influential teacher, conductor and editor of the works of Monteverdi and others.

**Opus** is Latin for 'work'. Many composers have a practice of numbering their compositions (Opus 10, Opus 121, etc.) Unfortunately some have done this unsystematically or carelessly, so that the number, though useful as a means of identification, does not tell us, as it should do, to what period of a composer's output a particular work belongs – that is, a low number does not *always* indicate an early work or a high number a late work.

A frequent abbreviation for Opus is OP., and for the plural we often find OPP.

**Oratorio** A setting of a religious libretto for soloists, chorus, and orchestra. It is performed without stage setting, costumes, or action. So far as its music is concerned it is rather like opera (with arias and recitatives), but it gives much greater scope to the chorus, who sing much more elaborate music than you would find in any opera. Indeed, in some oratorios the chorus is the main 'character' in the drama – in Handel's *Israel in Egypt*.

Works of this kind began to appear, first in Rome, at roughly the same time as the first operas (1600). Since then, hundreds of composers have written oratorios, among them Handel, Haydn and Mendelssohn.

**Orchestra →** page 253

**Orchestration →** page 255

**Orff, Carl** German composer b. 1895. He studied at the Munich Academy of Music and became internationally famous as a composer in 1937 when his *Carmina Burana* was performed at Frankfurt. This is a choral work accompanied, ideally, by mime and dancing. It is a setting of 13th-century poems and is written in a very simple style, with bold tunes and a vigorous, swinging rhythm. The *Catulli carmina* of 1943 employs similar methods. Orff has also written several operas, of which the second, *Die Kluge* (The Clever Girl) (1943), has enjoyed a great success.

Between 1930 and 1933 Orff also produced a series of teaching pieces and a 'method' of teaching music to children, using recorders and percussion instruments.

**Organ →** page 256

**Organistrum → Hurdy gurdy**

**Organum** This is a way of adding harmony to the traditional church melodies used by musicians in the 11th and 12th centuries. The harmonizing voices move in parallel lines with the original melody, always keeping a fifth or a fourth or an octave apart. Often the lines move in parallel octaves *and* fifths.

**Ornaments and graces** These are decorative figures that are not given in full in the notation, but indicated by signs that the performer is expected to understand.

During the 18th century, singers and instrumentalists frequently decorated the music they performed according to their own tastes and without consulting the composer. By the end of the century, however, composers had begun to indicate exactly what ornamentation they expected. (→**Ornaments and grace-notes**)

**Orpheus** The tragic story of Orpheus' love for Euridice has been used by many musicians as a subject for their own compositions. Examples include Liszt's symphonic poem *Orpheus* (1854), Offenbach's comic opera *Orpheus in the Underworld* (1858), and two great serious operas: Monteverdi's *Orfeo* (1607), and Gluck's *Orfeo ed Euridice* (1762).

**Oscillator** An electronic device that transforms electrical energy into audible sound. These sounds can be 'pure' – that is to say, free of the overtones that are present in ordinary man-made sounds. There is no limit to the variety of sounds, pure and impure, that an oscillator can produce, and they are used by composers of electronic music instead of (or even in conjunction with) the sounds of ordinary instruments.

**Ossia** (It.) Or. Used in music to indicate an alternative passage, often somewhat easier than the original one.

**Ostinato** (It.) Obstinate, or persistent. Used in music to describe any figure or short phrase that is repeated over and over again. The most usual forms of ostinato are the arpeggio type of accompaniment known as the **Alberti bass** →, and the basso ostinato or **Ground bass** →.

**Ottava** (It.) Octave. Often abbreviated to 8va., and found in such expressions as:

**All' ottava:** 'at the octave' (to be played an octave higher than written).

**Ottava bassa:** 'octave below' (to be played an octave lower than written).

**Coll' ottava:** 'with the octave' (to be played in octaves – the notes as written and the octave above).

**Overtone** → **Harmonics** An overtone is the same as a harmonic.

**Overture** → page 255

**Orpheus – Legend in music** The legendary Greek poet Orpheus, the son of Apollo and Calliope, could move animals, and even plants and stones with his music. The most famous legend concerning him is his descent into Hell to persuade Pluto to allow his wife, Euridice to return to earth. However, Orpheus broke the condition the god set by turning round to look at her and she was lost to him for ever.

# Orchestra

Although we may suppose that as long as there have been musical instruments they have been played together, the orchestra as we know it today began to come into existence only at the beginning of the 17th century. For what makes an orchestra an *orchestra* is the fact that the instruments are grouped together in standard families and are not merely a chance collection of whatever happens to be at hand.

The modern orchestra has four families of instruments:

**Strings**
**Woodwind**
**Brass**
**Percussion**

1. The **stringed instruments** comprise:
   1st and 2nd violins (the same instruments, but performing different 'parts')
   Violas
   Cellos
   Double basses

In the average orchestra today you may expect to find perhaps 16 first violins, 14 seconds, 12 violas, 10 cellos, and 6 double basses – or thereabouts.

2. The **woodwind instruments** comprise:
   Flutes (and perhaps a piccolo)
   Oboes (and perhaps a cor anglais)
   Clarinets
   Bassoons

The standard orchestra has two of each of these, and very often three–especially when a piccolo, a cor anglais, a bass clarinet, and a double bassoon are required.

3. The **brass instruments** consist of:
   Horns
   Trumpets
   Trombones
   Tuba

There are usually 4 horns, 2 (or possibly 3) trumpets, 3 trombones, and 1 tuba.

4. The **percussion section** contains:
   Timpani (3 managed by 1 player)
   Side drum
   Bass drum
   Glockenspiel, xylophone, triangle, cymbals, tambourines, bells, etc.

Add to these basic instruments on occasion one or two harps, and even sometimes a piano, and it will be seen that the modern

orchestra is an elaborate affair capable of producing an immense variety of different sounds.

## The history of the orchestra

A standard orchestra only became necessary when a great many people in different parts of the world wanted to hear the same kind of music. If a German composer wrote a symphony and hoped to hear it played in Paris, or London, or Vienna, it was obviously to his advantage to know that he could expect to find the same kind of orchestra in those cities as he could in his native land. When you have a commodity that everybody wants, it makes sense to pack it in standard sizes. And that is exactly what happened to music during the 17th century – it suddenly became something that everyone wanted to hear. Concerts and operas became the fashion, and if you wanted to hear them you had to make sure that your own city could provide the kind of instruments that were needed to perform them adequately.

In 1600, however, there were no generally agreed standards to say what an orchestra should or should not contain. The operas and oratorios of the period were accompanied by whatever instruments happened to be to hand. There would probably be strings (viols *and* violins), flutes and oboes, cornetts and trombones, harps, harpsichords and organs, and various types of drum.

During that century these groups of instruments began to sort themselves out and by the time of Bach and Handel you might reasonably expect an orchestra to

*Above* A German painting, circa 1775, showing musicians rehearsing a Cantata.

contain:
  Flutes
  Oboes (and probably 'oboes d'amore' a type of small oboe)
  Trumpets and drums
  Strings (1st & 2nd violins, violas, cellos)

This kind of orchestra, however, was held together by a keyboard instrument, usually a harpsichord, playing a BASSO CONTINUO (→ **Figured bass**).

In the meantime, instruments began to improve and new ones were invented. It soon became possible to dispense with the basso continuo, for the strings had become a confident, self-contained group capable of playing a solid four or five-part harmony. Thus by 1800, the year of Beethoven's First Symphony, the orchestra had become much as we know it today:
  2 flutes
  2 oboes
  2 clarinets
  2 bassoons
  2 horns
  2 trumpets
  Drums
  Strings: 1st & 2nd violins, violas, cellos, and double basses.

All that remained for the 19th century to add was more wind and brass and a variety of percussion instruments. And at the same time, of course, these instruments improved and became more efficient – as did the players who played them. By the end of the century it was possible to find really enormous orchestras. A typical Richard Strauss score of around 1890 might very well demand:
  3 flutes and a piccolo
  3 oboes and a cor anglais
  2 clarinets, 1 soprano clarinet, 1 bass clarinet
  3 bassoons, and a double bassoon
  8 horns
  5 trumpets
  3 trombones
  1 tenor tuba, 1 bass tuba
  Timpani, side drums, bass drum, military drum
  Cymbals, triangles, glockenspiel, tubular bells, and gong
  2 harps
  Strings – in enormous quantities!

*Above* This diagram shows a typical seating plan for a standard orchestra. The different families of instruments, strings, woodwind, brass and percussion, are grouped together. This basic configuration, or variations of it, has existed from the early 19th century. *Left* Otto Klemperer conducts the National Philharmonic Orchestra at the Royal Festival Hall. *Below* The comparative compass of the range of the different instruments in the orchestra in relation to the piano keyboard.

Though such orchestras are still common, composers nowadays prefer to write for more modest forces. This is partly because the style of music has changed, and partly because a large orchestra is a very expensive thing to use. It is also interesting to note that composers have begun to write for unusual combinations of instruments once more. And so although the standard orchestra continues to exist, it does so largely to play music written from about 1770 to 1920. Before and after those dates you cannot be absolutely sure what the composer will have decided to include in his 'orchestra'.

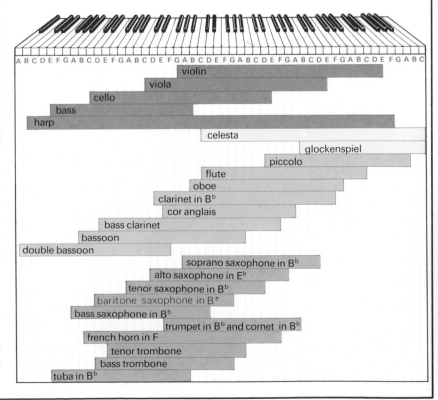

# Orchestration

The art of arranging music for an orchestra.

The orchestrator needs to know, among other things:

1. The range of each instrument (so that he does not write notes that cannot be played)
2. What sounds most effective on each instrument
3. The sound that instruments make when they combine together
4. The relative power of different instruments (so that a naturally quiet instrument, such as the flute, is not swamped by a naturally powerful instrument, like the trombone).

He must also bear in mind the different problems that arise in playing each instrument.

All these matters can be learned by a careful study of the instruments themselves, and by studying the scores of other composers and analysing how the different effects have been obtained.

Orchestration only began to become an important aspect of musical composition in the middle of the 19th century. It was only then that composers began to make use of the particular colours and personalities of the different instruments. Much of the music written before that time could be played with equal effect on any group of instruments.

The most important developments in orchestration took place in the 19th century in the music of the Romantic composers (such as Weber and Berlioz) who wanted to make music as descriptive as possible. Once this had happened, orchestration became an integral part of composition itself – that is to say, composers did not 'arrange' their music for the orchestra, but thought of it right from the beginning in terms of orchestral sound. A composition by Berlioz or Richard Strauss, or indeed by any of the great masters of the 19th and 20th centuries, scarcely ever sounds as effective when played by a different group of instruments from those the composer intended.

# Overture

Literally an 'opening' piece. The term is first used to describe an instrumental movement played at the beginning of an opera or oratorio. Later it came to be applied to single-movement orchestral works intended for the concert hall.

The very earliest operatic overtures were short, fanfare-like pieces. These gradually became more elaborate until overtures of this type could be found in two forms:

1. The **Italian overture**, which began with a quick movement (often fugal in style), continued with a slow movement, and then ended with a lively dance.
2. The **French overture**, which began with a slow movement (often in dotted rhythm), and usually ended with a quick fugal section, sometimes incorporating a return to the style of the opening movement.

The history of this early type of overture is made complicated by the fact that they were also called Sinfonias. Moreover, composers also used both terms to describe works of a similar pattern that were written purely for the concert hall. Thus it can be seen that the early overture (Sinfonia) is the ancestor of the **Symphony** → itself.

As orchestral music developed, the basic plan of the overture gradually changed, so that by the end of the 18th century it had become a single movement work in **Sonata Form** →.

Though operatic and oratorio overtures written in the 19th and 20th centuries often followed the sonata form plan, other, less carefully constructed types can be found. Some were simply a string of tunes out of the work to come; others were short pieces, more properly called *Preludes*.

But during this period composers also began to use the one-movement sonata form for CONCERT OVERTURES – that is to say, overtures intended purely for the concert hall, such as Mendelssohn's *Hebrides Overture*. These, like certain operatic overtures were often descriptive of some scene or story and therefore helped to bring the true **Symphonic poem** → into existence.

Overtures can also be found as part of the incidental music to plays (e.g. Mendelssohn's *A Midsummer Night's Dream* overture), but nowadays these are usually played as concert overtures.

# Organ

Throughout its long history the organ has consisted of a series of pipes connected to a wind supply which is controlled from some form of keyboard.

There are two basic types of organ pipe:
1. FLUE PIPES – which produce their sound in the same way as a whistle-flute, and consist of a tube with a mouthpiece and nothing else.
2. REED PIPES – which have a thin strip of metal inside the mouthpiece, which vibrates when the air passes over it.

Flue pipes, however, can be 'open' or 'stopped' (closed at one end). The 'stopped' pipe sounds an octave lower than an open pipe of the same length.

Organ pipes vary in length from miniatures of a few centimetres to giants of over 64 ft. The smaller the pipe, the higher the sound. Flue pipes and reed pipes produce different kinds of sounds, thus giving the organ its range of colours.

*Right* **How the organ works** Each stop on the organ controls a set of pipes by means of a slider, **1**. When a key is depressed it opens a flap, **4**, allowing air to pass from the reservoir **2**, through the wind chest, **3**, and open pallet holes into selected pipes, **5**. The lower diagram shows the interaction of keys, **Y** and stops, **X**. When the stop is pulled out it connects the wind chest to the pipes. Thus, any key can be depressed and that note will sound through the selected pipe. If all the stops are out then the same note will be played by all pipes of the same pitch.

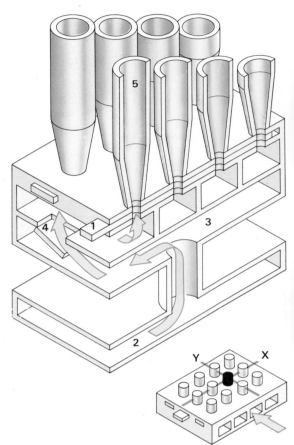

**Medieval organ** *Left above* This instrument has bellows but no keys and relies solely on sliders to change pitch. This would have been sufficient for the needs of the time when the organ was used as an accompanying instrument usually playing long, held notes.

**Royal Festival Hall organ, London** This three manual installation is an electrostatic instrument and one of the most successful of its kind to date. It has an astonishing range of tone and effects, one of which overcomes unsatisfactory architectural acoustics by regulating the period of reverberation.

The various keyboards of an organ are controlled from the Console, which in a modern organ (operated by electricity) may be placed some distance away from the pipes. Keyboards designed to be played by the hands are known as MANUALS; while those that are played by the feet are called PEDAL BOARDS. An organ may have several manuals (five, on really big organs), but only one pedal board.

Each keyboard is linked to a number of rows of pipes. These are brought into action by pulling out a series of stops. Each stop has a name (such as Flute, Trumpet, etc.) to indicate the kind of sound, and a number (8 ft, 4 ft, etc) to indicate the length of the pipe and therefore the pitch of the note. The standard length of pipe is the 8 ft, which produces notes that correspond in pitch to those of the piano keyboard. The same note played on a 4 ft stop will sound an octave higher, or an octave lower with a 16 ft stop.

Many organs have MUTATION STOPS. These produce harmonics and are used to add colour and brilliance to already existing notes. For example, a mutation stop labelled a *Twelfth* will produce the third harmonic of whatever note is played on the keyboard – i.e. when C is played it will produce the sound of G twelve notes higher.

There may also be a MIXTURE STOP, which brings several mutation stops into play at the same time.

Large organs may also have COMPOSITION PEDALS which enable the player to operate several pre-selected stops at the same time, without having to pull out each stop individually.

Organ manuals have different names, according to their different functions and capabilities:

**Solo:** which is used for playing solo tunes, accompanied by another manual.

**Wurlitzer theatre organ** This electronic organ has four manuals and an imposing array of stops and controls. It has no pipes or wind; all the mechanism is contained in the console which is connected by cable with a power cabinet. Sound is created by electrical vibration combinations. Organs of this type were a popular feature in many cinemas from the 1930s to the 1950s.

**Baroque organ** *Left* This splendid example from Amorbach, Bavaria, is typical of the instrument for which Bach and his contemporaries wrote.

**Swell:** on which the notes can be made louder or softer as they are played, by means of opening and closing the shutters of a Swell Box.

**Great:** which operates the Great Organ (the main part of the instrument).

**Choir:** which operates the softer-sounding Choir Organ.

The manuals can be linked to each other, and to the pedal board, by means of a COUPLER STOP. In this way the stops belonging to one manual can be played from the manual of another part of the organ.

The oldest type of organ dates from about 250 B.C. and is called the Hydraulis, because its air-pressure was controlled by means of a reservoir of water. In the early type of organ the air was admitted to the pipes by means of sliders at the base of the pipe. The idea of linking these to a keyboard came somewhat later and did not reach the form we know today until about 1580.

Organs came in different sizes. Small PORTATIVE ORGANS were popular from about 1100 to 1650. They were played by one person, operating a bellows with the left hand and playing the keyboard with the right hand. Later CHAMBER ORGANS were somewhat larger, with a bellows system that had to be pumped by a second person. The modern organ is pumped by an electric motor. Its stops and manuals are also operated by electricity, and therefore do not employ the complicated system of levers used by the old pre-electric organ.

**Positive organ** *Right* This early 16th-century French tapestry shows a positive organ, so-called because it was of fixed position, standing either on the floor or on a table. It was popular from the 10th to the 17th centuries but continued to be made until the 19th century for use in small churches.

**Portative organ** On page 81 you can see a picture of St. Cecilia with a portative organ.

**P** is short for (1) **piano** (It.) Soft. (2) **pedal** (the sustaining pedal on the piano.)

**Pachelbel, Johann** German composer, 1653–1706. Famous as an organist, he worked mainly in Eisenach, Erfurt, Stuttgart, Gotha, and Nuremberg. His organ fugues and chorale variations had a considerable influence on Bach. His son Wilhelm (1685–1764) was also admired as an organist and composer.

**Paderewski, Ignacy Jan** Polish pianist and composer, 1860–1941. Perhaps the most admired and successful pianist of his day. He began his recital career in 1887 and thereafter toured the world in triumph. He wrote a number of successful compositions, including an opera, *Manru* (1901), a symphony, and a piano concerto. He was also an able politician and from 1919 to 1920 served his country as Prime Minister.

**Paganini, Niccolò** Italian violinist and composer, 1782–1840. Though he made a successful debut when he was nine, his professional touring career began in earnest in 1797. His private life was somewhat disreputable, but this only added to his public reputation, and his mastery of the violin was such that he was commonly supposed to be in league with the devil! He wrote a considerable amount of music for the violin, notably the *24 Caprices* for solo violin and the three violin concertos, which greatly extended playing techniques.

**Palestrina, Giovanni Pierluigi da** Italian composer, c. 1525–94. When he was 18 he became organist and choirmaster at the cathedral of his native town (from which he

**Ignacy Jan Paderewski** 1860–1941 This portrait of the pianist and composer is by Edward Burne-Jones.

**Niccolò Paganini** 1782–1840

**Pandora** This large wire-strung instrument was popular in the 16th and 17th centuries as a continuo instrument.

**Panpipes** This primitive set of pipes is played by an inhabitant of the Solomon Islands.

took his name: 'Giovanni Pierluigi *of* Palestrina'). In 1551, however, the Bishop of Palestrina was appointed Pope, and Palestrina was invited to become choirmaster of the Julian Chapel at the Vatican. He remained in Rome for the rest of his life, serving the Vatican for various periods (as Popes came and went, musicians tended to fall in and out of favour!), and working in other important churches.

His fame as a composer of church music spread throughout the civilized world, and his advice was sought when the Council of Trent met (1545–63) to reform and simplify the music of the Catholic Church. He is generally regarded as one of the greatest composers of Church music of all time.

**Pandora** or **Bandora** A bass cittern. It has a flat back, wire strings, and frets. Instead of the smooth, pear-shaped outline of the ordinary cittern, however, it has three pronounced bulges.(→ **Cittern**)

**Panpipes** A set of graduated whistle-flutes, bound together like a raft. Each pipe produces only one note (there are no finger-holes), and the sound is made by blowing across the open end. Panpipes have been known for more than two thousand years. The ancient Greeks called them the SYRINX, and said that they were invented by the god Pan out of a bundle of reeds.

**Panufnik, Andrzej** Polish composer, b. 1914. He studied at the Warsaw Conservatory, and with Weingartner in Vienna. He became conductor of the Warsaw Philharmonic in 1946, and began also to make a reputation as a composer of 'advanced' music. After a series of political upheavals he left Poland and settled in Great Britain (1954), where he has since continued his career as a conductor (City of Birmingham Orchestra, 1957–9) and composer. His *Sinfonia Rustica* (1948) and *Sinfonia Sacra* (1963) show him to be a very powerful symphonic composer.

**Parameter** A term borrowed from mathematics and much used by avant-garde composers. It describes those aspects of musical sound that can be varied, but which impose a limit on composition. In music played by ordinary instruments, the main parameters are: PITCH, VOLUME (loudness), DURATION (the length of notes), and TONE COLOUR. The composer sets down on paper what he wants and the performers do the best they can within human limits.

In electronic music, however, the sounds

are created by machine, and the composer can therefore control virtually every aspect (parameter) of sound, to a degree that is quite beyond the human performer or traditional instrument.

**Parallel motion → Motion**

**Paris Opéra** The official title of this famous French theatre is 'Académie de Musique', but it is familiarly known as the 'Opéra'. As an institution it has existed since 1669, but the present luxurious building dates from 1875. It has an international reputation.

**Parker, Charlie** Jazz musician and composer, 1920–55. He was born in Kansas City and, during the 1940s, became widely known as a saxophonist of great skill and imagination. Together with the trumpet player Dizzy Gillespie, he helped to create the jazz style known as Bebop. He was a creative genius, but addiction to drugs brought about his early death. He is usually referred to by his nickname, Charlie 'Bird' Parker. (**→ Bop**)

**Parker, Horatio** American composer, 1863–1919. He studied in Munich, and worked as an organist and choirmaster in New York and Boston before becoming professor of music at Yale University (1894). He became widely known for his choral music – in particular the oratorio *Hora Novissima* (1893). His musical style was based on that of the German classics and is not in any way 'American'.

**Parody** In the general sense this can simply mean the imitation of someone else's style, or the style of another period. In music it is also used to describe works that make use of previously existing themes – as, for example, in the 15th-century Parody Mass, which often made use of secular material.

**Parry, (Sir) Hubert** English composer, 1848–1918. His father was a wealthy Gloucestershire landowner and skilful amateur painter. He was educated at Eton and Oxford, studied composition with Sterndale Bennett, and made his name as a composer in 1880 with a piano concerto and a choral work: *Scenes from Prometheus Unbound*. He was appointed Director of the Royal College of Music in 1894, and Professor of Music at Oxford University in 1900. He was knighted in 1898 and made a baronet in 1903.

Though he wrote five symphonies and much chamber music, Parry is mainly known as a composer of choral music and songs. His ode *Blest Pair of Sirens* (1887) is one of the

**Andrzej Panufnik**
b.1914

**Charlie Parker**
1920–1955 His nickname Charlie 'Bird' Parker is derived from his close association with the New York jazz club 'Birdland'.

**Sir Hubert Parry**
1848–1918

**Harry Partch**
1901–1974 The composer is shown with percussion instruments of his own invention – gourd, bee and cane gongs.

finest English choral works and an excellent example of his dignified, noble style at its best. He was very sensitive to the English language – as his 12 volumes of songs (*English Lyrics*), his choral works, and his part-songs show. His six motets, *Songs of Farewell* (1916–18), are especially fine.

Together with Sullivan and Stanford, Parry stands at the beginning of the revival in English musical genius that was to lead to Elgar, Vaughan Williams, Delius, and Holst. He was a highly intelligent musician (his books are well worth reading), and the example of his music and his personal life did much to make the profession of 'composer' a respectable one in English eyes.

**Part** An individual line in music – as, for example, the violin 'part' in a string quartet or symphony.

The term 'part-writing' is used in composition to describe music that is made up of distinct strands of melody which are not, however, so independent of each other as to qualify as counterpoint. The four parts (for Soprano, Alto, Tenor, and Bass voices) of a hymn-tune give a good idea of this style of writing.

**Part-song** A vocal composition in which words are set to music for several voices or groups of voices. The voices, Soprano, Alto, Tenor, Bass, can be mixed (S.A.T.B.), or all female (S.S.A.), or all male (T.T.B.B.). Part-songs developed during the 18th century and were particularly popular in the 19th. They are something like madrigals, but much less contrapuntal.

**Partch, Harry** American composer, b. 1901. A self-taught composer, he was the first American musician to reject European ideas about music and proceed to write entirely according to his own intuition. He has used microtones and constructed instruments to play them. Much of his music involves some form of 'visual' presentation, anticipating the work of John Cage.

**Parte** (It.) Part. As in such expressions as:
  **Colla parte:** 'with the part' (the accompanist must take his speed from the soloist).
  **A tre parti**: 'in three parts' (as in a three-part fugue, or a vocal trio).

**Partials → Harmonics.** A note and its harmonics constitute the partials of that note. The note itself is called the 'lower partial' and the harmonics are the 'upper partials'.

**Partita → Suite**

**Passacaglia, Passecaille → Chaconne**

**Passage work** Any portion of a composition that is not particularly important in itself, but serves to link important ideas. Like a passage in a house, a 'passage' in music leads from one thing to another. The term 'passage work' is sometimes used in a derogatory sense to describe sections of music that are mere 'padding'.

**Passamezzo** An Italian dance which became popular throughout Europe in the late 16th century. It is a type of pavan, but its music consists of a number of variations over a repeated bass line.

**Passepied** A dance that is said to have originated among the sailors of Brittany. It was introduced into the court ballets of Louis XIV and is frequently found in the dance suites of the period. Like the minuet, which it resembles, it is in triple time, but is played much faster.

**Passing note → Harmony**

**Passion music** From very early times the Christian Church has had the custom of reading or reciting, during Holy Week, the biblical account of the Passion of Christ (that is, the story of the crucifixion).

From the 15th century onwards, composers have often set this story to music so that it could be sung. Some settings, such as those of Heinrich Schütz, are in the style of an oratorio, while others come very near to being religious operas. The finest and most moving settings, however, are those of J. S. Bach – the *St John Passion* (1723), and the *St Matthew Passion* (1729) – both of which use recitatives, arias, massive choruses, and chorales to give a powerful account of the gospels as told by St John and St Matthew.

**Pasticcio** (It.) Pie. A word used to describe an opera, or some other composition, made up from scraps of other operas. Such works were very prevalent in the 18th century, when the demand for new operas often outstripped the composers' ability to supply new works.

**Pastorale** A vocal or instrumental composition in compound triple time which imitates the sound of a shepherd's pipe and may be built on a drone bass.

**Pastoral** A dramatic composition, or opera, on a pastoral subject, e.g. Handel's *Acis and Galatea*.

**Passion music** Its origins lay in the Holy Week miracle plays and the dramatic recitals in church of the suffering and crucifixion of Christ, depicted in this late 15th-century German stained glass. It reached its' highest development in J. S. Bach's *St Matthew Passion*.

# Percussion

Any instrument whose sound is produced by striking or hitting may be classed as a percussion instrument, though some are **membranophones →**, and others are **idiophones →**.

Percussion instruments such as drums and bells must be among the first instruments known to man, and their origins go back to the dawn of human history. Though such instruments have been used in Western music throughout its history, their use in the modern orchestra dates from comparatively recent times, and even then they were admitted only gradually.

The first to enter were the side drums and timpani – both borrowed from military music, along with the trumpets. A craze for 'Turkish percussion' towards the end of the 18th century brought in such exotics as the triangle, cymbals, and bass drum as special effects. But it was not until the end of the 19th century that percussion instruments were to be found in all orchestras on any really large scale, and not until the twentieth that their true musical possibilities began to be thoroughly explored. Nowadays, composers are happy to write whole compositions for percussion alone.

Percussion instruments are described individually in this book under their own names. They fall into the following main categories:

**Drums** and **tambourines**
**Cymbals** and **triangles**
**Bells** and **gongs**
**Dulcimers** and **pianos**
**Castanets** and **rattles**

In the modern orchestra, the percussion section may contain:

**Timpani** (usually 3)
**Bass drum**
**Side drum**
**Tubular bells**
**Glockenspiel**
**Xylophone**
**Cymbals**
**Triangles**
**Tam-tam**

and a variety of 'special effects' →, such as sleighbells, the whip, various Latin-American drums, temple bells, wood blocks, etc.

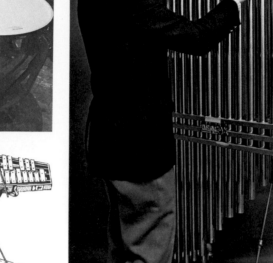

**Timpani** *Above* The modern symphony orchestra usually contains three kettledrums tuned to a definite pitch either by handles on the rim or mechanically, using pedals.

**Glockenspiel** *Right* Its tuned metal bars are played with hammers.

**Bass drum** *Above* This is of low but indefinite pitch. It was sometimes called the 'Turkish drum'.

**Triangle** *Below* Its tinkling sound is without definite pitch.

**Tubular bells** *Above* These chimes, which hang on a frame, are played with small wooden hammers. They have a scale of about an octave.

**Xylophone** *Right* These tuned wooden bars are played with two hard sticks.

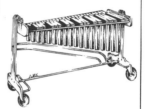

**Scoring for percussion** This is part of a score for percussion instruments from Edgard Varèse's *Hyperrism* (1924).

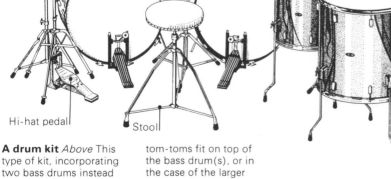

Cymbals | Bass drums | Snare drum | Tom-toms | Bongos

Hi-hat

Hi-hat pedal | Stool

**A drum kit** *Above* This type of kit, incorporating two bass drums instead of one, is commonly used in rock music. The bass drums are struck by padded beaters worked by pedals. The drummer sits on a stool opposite the snare drum. A lever on one side of the drum operates the snare. The

tom-toms fit on top of the bass drum(s), or in the case of the larger ones, stand on adjustable legs. The pair of bongos are differently tuned and often played with the fingers. The cymbals, including the hi-hat, vary in size and number according to the style of the drummer.

**Pop music percussion** *Right* Led Zeppelin's instruments include a bass drum, snare drum, tom-toms, cymbals and, notably, a large gong.

**Patter song** A comic song which is sung so quickly that the words 'patter' out in the shortest possible time. Several fine examples occur in the Gilbert and Sullivan operettas – e.g. 'My name is John Wellington Wells' (*The Sorcerer*).

**Pausa** (It.) Rest ( ♩ ♪ etc). The Italian word for 'pause' (⌢), however, is *fermata*.

**Pause** The sign ⌢, which indicates that the note, chord, or rest over which it is placed is to be prolonged.

**Pavan** and **Galliard** Two renaissance court dances, generally linked as a pair. The pavan is slow and stately, with two beats to the bar; the galliard is quick and lively, with three beats to the bar. Such dances are also found in English 16th-century virginal pieces.

**Peal** A set of church bells. → **Bells and bell-ringing**

**Pearsall, Robert Lucas de** English composer, 1795–1856. He studied in Germany, and after inheriting family estates, lived mostly abroad, finally settling in the castle of Wartensee on Lake Constance. He wrote a number of part-songs and church pieces, but is mainly famous for his madrigals.

**Pedal** → **Piano**, **Organ**, **Harmony**, **Drums**

**Pedale** (It.) Pedal. Found in piano music as **Con pedale**, or **con ped.**, with pedal .

**Peg-box** (of a violin, etc.) This is the name of the part of the instrument in which the pegs for the strings are inserted.

**Penderecki, Krystof** Polish composer, b. 1933. He studied in Cracow and is now regarded as one of the most important Polish avant-garde composers. His music is very complex and often makes use of unusual ways of playing instruments (glissandi, extreme harmonics, slapping and tapping the instrument, etc.), as well as unusual sounds (such as whispering). He makes use of electronics, as well as orthodox serial techniques. His music is very theatrical, and often shows a strong political conscience, e.g. the *Threnody for the Victims of Hiroshima* (1960).

**Penny whistle** → **Recorder**

**Pentatonic scale** → **Scales**

**Pepusch, J.C.** (1667–1752) → **Beggar's Opera**

**Percussion** → page 260

**Pavan** This stately dance originated in the 16th century in Italy.

**Peg-box of a violin** This is inserted with four pegs (*top*), and, with the neck and head, is carved from a solid piece of hard wood.

**Krystof Penderecki** b.1933

**Giovanni Pergolesi** 1710–1736 This caricature of 1734 is by the Italian artist, Leone Ghezzi.

**Percussion band** → **Rhythm section**

**Perdendosi** (It.) Dying away.

**Perfect cadence** → **Cadence**

**Perfect intervals** → **Interval**

**Performing Right Society** A body set up in London in 1914 to protect the interests of composers and publishers and to collect and distribute performing fees (→ **Copyright**) gathered in from all over the world. Most countries have similar societies, as for example the American Society of Composers, Authors and Publishers (A.S.C.A.P.).

**Pergolesi, Giovanni** Italian composer, 1710–36. During a very brief life he composed some 15 operas, several oratorios and masses, and a quantity of instrumental music. The charming comic opera *La Serva Padrona* (1733) and the beautiful *Stabat Mater* (1736) are still frequently performed and are typical of his tuneful, elegant style.

**Peri, Jacopo** Italian composer, 1561–1633. A member of the Florentine Camerata, a group of composers whose experiments brought opera into existence. His *Dafne* (1592, the music now lost), and *Euridice* (1600), written in collaboration with the poet Ottavio Rinuccini, are the first operas ever to be composed.(→ **Camerata**)

**Pérotin** French composer, c.1160–1220. He followed Léonin at the cathedral of Nôtre-Dame in Paris, and is one of the first 'named' composers in the history of western music. Like Léonin he wrote *Organa* and motets and helped in the early development of polyphony.

**Perpetuum mobile** This is Latin for 'perpetually in motion', and is a name sometimes given by composers to a quick instrumental piece that, without pausing, goes on and on in short notes, all of the same value.

Sometimes the Italian form of the expression, *moto perpetuo*, is used.

**Pesante** (It.) Heavy. Notes marked in this way must be played in a decisive manner.

**Petrassi, Goffredo** Italian composer, b. 1904. He studied in Rome with the influential composer Casella, and though his early works were neo-classic in style he has since incorporated 12-note techniques in his music. He is much admired as a teacher.

**Phantasie** (Ger.) Fantasy, or **Fantasia**.

# Phrase and sentence

When we read a passage in a book we take care not only to pause slightly between paragraphs, but also between sentences, and, to a lesser extent, at the punctuation marks within the sentences. We also vary the stresses we put on the different words. We do this in order to reveal the meaning of what we read. Were we to run the sentences together, ignore the punctuation and give each word an equal weight, it would be difficult to follow the meaning.

In the same way, and for the same reasons, music must be given a sense of shape and direction. This is done by means of 'phrasing'.

A phrase is a group of notes that may be considered to belong together. Several such phrases make up a 'sentence'. Phrases may be long or short, and there may be many, or only two, in a sentence.

Phrases are shown by means of a curved line drawn above the notes. For example:

The three phrases make up a complete statement, so the six bars make a sentence.

Phrases commonly contain 2, 4, or 8, bars, but 3, 5, and 7 bar phrases are perfectly possible – and, indeed, often make a nice change from the regularity of twos and fours.

A composer may also wish to phrase his music in very great detail, by means of legato slurs and staccato dots, and so forth. 'God Save the Queen' could be treated:

This kind of detailed phrasing becomes particularly important in music for instruments – for it shows how the strings must bow the notes, and how the woodwind and brass must tongue them.

---

**Philharmonic** A word made from two Greek words meaning 'music loving'. One of its first uses was in the title of the Philharmonic Society of London, founded in 1813. It is now used by many orchestras and music societies throughout the world.

**Phonograph** (Amer.) Gramophone.

**Phrygian cadence → Cadence**

**Piacere** (It.) Pleasure. Found mainly in the direction *a piacere*, 'at pleasure' – according to the performer's taste and feelings.

**Piacevole** (It.) Pleasant(ly).

**Piangevole** (It.) Sad(ly).

**Piano** (It.) Quiet. But it is also the common abbreviation for **Pianoforte →**

**Pianissimo** (It.) Very quiet.

**Piano → page 264**

**Pianola → Mechanical instruments**

**Pibroch** (pronounced Peebrok) A Gaelic word (in full, *Piobaireachd*) for a type of Highland bagpipe music in the style of a theme and variations. They are often warlike in character, and many have names (such as 'The Raid of Kilchrist') which commemorate historical or legendary events.

**Piccinni, Niccolò** Italian composer, 1728–1800. He studied in Naples and began

**Jacopo Peri** 1561–1633 Virtuoso singer as well as composer, he is depicted here as Arion in an early comedy, *La Pellegrina*.

**Pipe and tabor** The melody and rhythm provided by these popular instruments of the Middle Ages and Renaissance was ideal for dancing.

a very successful career as an opera composer in 1754. In 1776 he went to Paris and was much admired by those music-lovers who disliked Gluck's attempts to 'reform' opera. He returned to Naples in 1789 when the Revolution broke out in France, but his last years were plagued by money troubles and illness. He wrote at least 120 operas, of which *La buona Figliuola* (1760), and *L'Olimpiade* (1768) were especially successful.

**Piccolo → Flute**

**Pick** A common folk expression for plucking the guitar. American folk singers often speak of 'guitar picking'. The word can also be used for 'plectrum'.

**Pijper, Willem** Dutch composer, 1894–1947. One of the most distinguished Dutch composers of his generation. He was influenced by French music, Stravinsky, and the folksong of his own country. His music includes three symphonies and five string quartets. He was a fine teacher.

**Pipe** This is a poet's name for any of the smaller wind instruments.

In PIPE AND TABOR it means a small flute (blown at the end, not through a hole in the side) accompanied by a small drum. A single player plays both instruments – one with each hand.

In Scotland 'pipes' is short for 'bagpipes'.

# Piano (Pianoforte)

Inventions seldom spring out of thin air: they usually come about when things that are already in existence are combined in a new way. Thus the strings and hammers of the piano were already being used in such instruments as the dulcimer, while the keyboard could be found in any harpsichord. The credit for combining the two must go to the Italian instrument maker Bartolomeo Cristofori, who produced what he called a *Gravicembalo col piano e forte* (a 'harpsichord with soft and loud') in Florence in 1709.

The point about this cumbersome title was that here at last was a keyboard instrument that could produce a whole range of loud and soft sounds at a touch. This was possible because the strings were struck by a padded hammer which immediately fell away from the string, leaving it free to vibrate. The strength of the sound depended directly upon the force applied to the keyboard by the player's fingers.

The mechanism of the 'piano' is thus very different, and rather more complicated than

*Below* **The action of the upright piano** The yellow areas of the drawings show the fixed parts of the mechanism. **A**. When a key, **1**. Is pressed down the other end is forced upwards, tilting the lever, **2**, which moves on a pivot. **B**. The right end of the lever moves upwards, pushing the jack, **3**, out of the notch, **4**, and against the hammer, **5**, which is propelled towards the string. The left end of the lever moves downwards, pushing the damper spoon, **6**, against the damper lever, **7**. This swings on a pivot to release the damper, **8**, from the string, **9**. Here, these movements are shown by arrows.

that of the harpsichord or clavichord. In the harpsichord the strings are *plucked*, and the variation in dynamics is provided by strings of different registers ( → **Harpsichord**). In the clavichord the strings are struck by a metal tongue, but this remains in contact with the string and there is very little variation in loudness or softness.

Cristofori's invention was explored more fully in Germany by the organ builder Gottfried Silbermann, and other instrument makers were quick to copy his improvements and make refinements of their own. By 1745, or thereabouts, the new instrument was being accepted by musicians everywhere.

Since that date the history of the piano has largely been concerned with:
1. making the striking mechanism as responsive to the touch as possible.
2. developing the kind of framework that would withstand the enormous pressure of longer and heavier strings (because longer and heavier strings produced a more sonorous note).
3. finding ways of making small pianos that would fit into small houses.

And while all these things were happening, composers were busy finding out how to write music that would bring out the best in the instrument – for it was generally agreed that here was an instrument of quite exceptional versatility and convenience.

Pianos have come in different shapes and sizes over the years. They often have different names and different qualities.

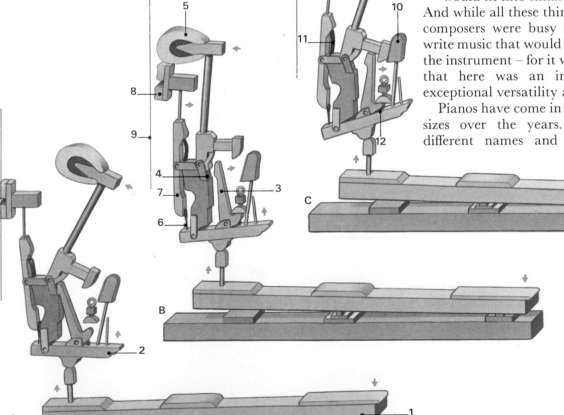

**C**. As the key is fully pressed down the hammer hits and rebounds from the string, producing a note. The check, **10**, prevents it springing back against the string. When the key is released, the damper spring, **11**, returns the damper against the string, and the jack spring, **12**, returns the jacks into the notch.

Nowadays we prefer, if possible, to play our music on the kind of instrument the composer had in mind. Here are a few of the main types. It would be well worth listening to the many gramophone records now available that illustrate the very different sounds these instruments make.

**The fortepiano** This is the early name for the piano. The fortepiano differs from the pianoforte in that it has a wooden frame, thin strings set at a fairly low tension, and small leather covered hammers. The fortepiano can resemble either a harpsichord, with strings stretching away from the keyboard, or a clavichord, with strings running from left to right across the keyboard. The first type is known as a 'grand' fortepiano, and the second as a 'square' piano.

**The square piano** This was probably invented by Johannes Zumpe for the

**The square piano** This painting by Johann Zoffany, dated 1775, shows the Cowper and Gore families, one member of whom plays the so-called square piano (it is, in fact, really oblong). In this instrument the strings run at right angles to the finger keys. Although popular in the late 18th and early 19th centuries examples of the square piano are rarely seen today.

*Right* **The grand piano** Both treble and bass strings, **1**, and **2**, are made of steel, with three strings to each treble note; bass strings have two, while the lowest notes have one. The keys, **3**, are linked to the hammers, **4**, which strike the strings to give a note when a key is pressed. The dampers, **5**, are faced with felt and fall to deaden the sound when the key is released. Each string's tension and pitch is altered by turning the tuning pins, **6**. An iron frame, **7**, is needed to support the total string tension. This is fixed to the wooden sounding board, **8**, which amplifies the sound.

*Below* **Grand piano sizes** The concert grand (*right*) can be three metres long, while the baby grand (*left*) does not usually exceed two metres.

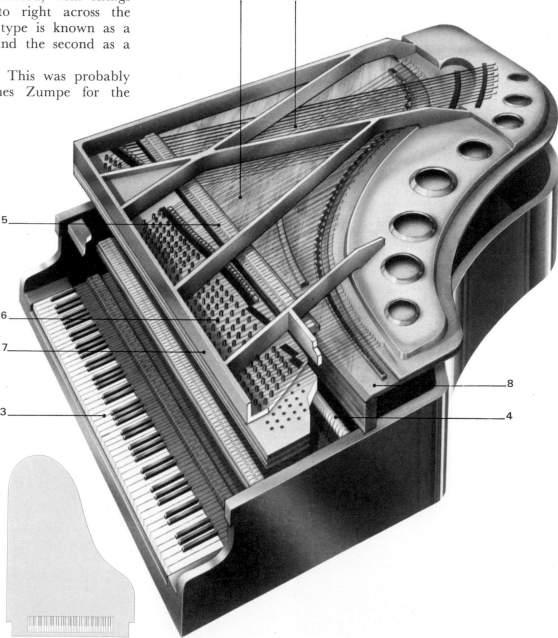

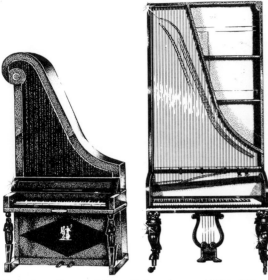

**Early pianos** The giraffe piano (*far left*) and upright grand (*left*) were more expensive and unwieldy than the square piano (*below*), which was internationally popular.

**The upright piano** Towards the end of the 18th century experiments were made with the piano's mechanism so that it could be placed upright on a stand, thus taking up less floor-space. But these 'cabinet' pianos were rather cumbersome, and it was not until 1811 that anything like the modern upright appeared. This was the 'Cottage Upright', patented by a London maker.

These are the main 'historical' types of piano. The modern piano comes in two main shapes: the 'grand' and the 'upright'. Both come in different sizes, so that we can speak of *concert grands* and *baby grands*, *upright grands* and *cottage pianos*.

London firm of Shudi in about 1760. The 'square' was the first type of cheap, small domestic instrument. It was popular until about 1840, by which time it had been displaced by the cottage upright.

**The pianoforte** Fortepianos gradually became pianofortes when ways were found to strengthen the framework – first with metal braces, and later, from about 1825 onwards, with frames cast entirely from iron. This added strength allowed makers to increase the number of notes and use longer and heavier strings. The tension on the framework was, of course, much increased (on a large modern grand it can come to something like 30 tons!). Hammers were made larger and heavier and were padded with felt. All these improvements gave the pianoforte a much 'rounder' and more sonorous sound and a much greater range of loud and soft effects.

*Above* **Experimental piano** John Tilbury performs by running a baby's rattle across the strings of a piano. His other compositions include the use of egg beaters, bolts, paper clips and insects in a piano allied to distorted and amplified sound.

**Emil Gilels at the piano** This Russian virtuoso gained an international reputation after the Second World War.

The final important thing about pianos is that they employ DAMPERS. These are small pads which are lifted off the strings as the notes are struck, and then, when we lift our fingers from the key, fall back and stifle the sound. Just how vital they are can be judged if you hold down several adjacent notes one after the other – the jangle is intolerable.

We can also make *all* the dampers stay away from the strings by putting down the right foot pedal. This is called the SUSTAINING PEDAL (and not the 'Loud Pedal'!). When this happens the sound of the notes we happen to be playing not only lasts longer, but is fuller and richer because all the strings vibrate in sympathy.

Pianos also have a 'SOFT' PEDAL. This shifts the hammer slightly to the right and reduces its contact with the strings, thus making the tone softer.

**Pipe organ** In America the real organ is called by this name, to distinguish it from the 'cabinet organ'.

**Piston, Walter** American composer, 1894–1976. He trained first as an artist, but then studied music at Harvard, where he later returned as professor (1951–60), and with Nadia Boulanger in Paris. His music is neo-classical in style, with some influence of jazz. He was mainly an instrumental composer and wrote eight symphonies (1937 to 1965), two violin concertos (1939 and 1960), and a great deal of chamber music. His writings on music include handbooks on *Harmony* (1941), *Counterpoint* (1947), and *Orchestration* (1955) which are widely used by students.

**Pistons** In brass instruments these are little buttons which are pressed down to enable the

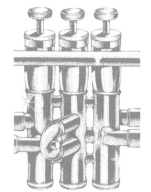

**Piston** These valves greatly increase the range of brass instruments.

player to sound different notes. In the organ there are often 'thumb pistons' which bring into action selected groups of stops.

**Più** (It.) More. As in the direction **più mosso**, 'more moved' – that is to say, 'quicker'.

**Pizz.** An abbreviation for **pizzicato**.

**Pizzetti, Ildebrando** Italian composer, 1880–1968. He studied at the Parma Conservatory, where he later taught. He also held important teaching posts in Florence, Milan, and Rome. He wrote music of all kinds, including several early film scores, but is best known for his operas – in particular *Debora e Jaële* (1922). One of his aims was to 'reform' Italian opera, so his style is much more restrained than that of his contemporaries.

# Pitch

The height or depth of a note. Of course notes are not really 'high' or 'low', but everybody understands when we say that one note is 'higher' or 'lower' than another.

Sound is caused by vibrations (pressure-changes) in the air. The 'pitch' of a note is measured by the number of vibrations that take place in a second. The lower the note, the fewer (and slower) the vibrations. For example, the lowest note on the piano involves about 30 vibrations per second; and the highest note about 4000. We call the rate of vibration the *frequency* of a note, and nowadays there is a general agreement throughout the civilized world as to what the frequency of all notes should be. For example, the A that is used for tuning (second space in the treble stave) has been fixed at 440 vibrations per second. This means that instruments and orchestras tuned to this pitch (known as CONCERT PITCH) will be the same the world over.

This was not always the case. The pitch in use at different periods and in different countries has varied a great deal. For example, in Elizabethan times the organ was tuned to a slightly higher pitch than the virginals (which had a weak frame that might crack if the pitch – and therefore the tension of the strings – was too high).

When tuning an instrument, musicians get the correct pitch either from a TUNING FORK, a PITCH PIPE, or a specially designed electronic gadget. Once the pitch of one note is fixed, all the rest can be found from it.

Certain notes have been given names, and these can be very useful when you wish to describe which octave you are in. The most frequently met with are:

a. **Tenor C:** the lowest note on the 'tenor violin', i.e. the viola.
b. **Middle C:** the note that lies between the treble and bass clefs, and more or less in the middle of the keyboard.
c. **Treble C:** which lies near the middle of the treble clef.

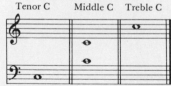

C above the treble clef ('high C') is said to be 'in *Alt*': and the C above that is said to be '*in Altissimo*':

Many musicians claim that they have 'absolute pitch', by which they mean that they carry an accurate sense of pitch in their memories and can therefore tell if a note is being played out of tune. Others, more modestly, claim only a sense of 'relative pitch' – which simply means that they can relate notes to one another by reference to one fixed note. They would therefore know if the notes of a piano were out of tune with one another, but might not realize if a piano had been tuned to something other than concert pitch.

**Pizzicato** (It.) Pinched. Found in music for bowed instruments and means that the strings are to be plucked with the fingers. When the bow is to be used again, the word **arco** (bow) is written in the score.

The plural of **pizzicato** is **pizzicati**.

**Plagal** → **Cadence; Modes**

**Plainsong** or **Plainchant** The name given to the collection of ancient tunes to which, for centuries, various parts of Christian Church services have been sung.

Plainsong is in free rhythm (like English prose), not in metrical rhythm (like verse), and therefore cannot be written out in bars. It is sung in unison, and not harmonized, and it is usually sung without accompaniment. Plainsong uses Modal scales.

**Plectrum** A small piece of ivory, wood, or metal used to pluck the strings of such instruments as the guitar and banjo.

**Pleyel, Ignaz** Austrian composer, 1757–1831. He was a pupil of Haydn, but also studied in Italy. He was organist of Strasburg Cathedral for some time, but later settled in Paris as a music publisher. In 1807 he founded the piano factory which still bears his name. He wrote a vast amount of music, including 29 symphonies.

**Poco** (It.) Little. For example: **poco a poco**, little by little . Also: **pochetto**, very little ; **pochettino**, very little indeed ; and **pochissimo**, as little as possible .

**Poi** (It.) Then. As in *poi la coda*, 'then the coda' (meaning 'now play the coda section').

**Point** of the bow. The end opposite to that which is held.

**Point d'orgue** (Fr.) Organ point. It has several meanings:
a. The pause sign ⌢ .
b. A **cadenza** → in a concerto.
c. A harmonic pedal ( → **Harmony**).

**Polacca** → **Polonaise**

**Polka** A lively dance from Czechoslovakia that was taken up in the ballrooms of Vienna and Paris in about 1840 and soon spread all over Europe. It is in a quick 2/4 time and very rhythmic. Examples can be found in Smetana's symphonic music.

**Plectrum** *Top* This detail from a Japanese print shows a large plectrum of the type used to play a shamisen. *Bottom* Plectra, like these are used for guitars *(left)* and some eastern zithers *(right)*.

**Polka** This Bohemian dance which originated in the early 19th century and reached the height of its popularity in Europe in the 1840s was used by the Czech composer Smetana in his opera, *The Bartered Bride*.

**Polonaise** or **Polacca** A Polish dance which began life among the peasants, but was later adopted by the ballroom. Although strong and rhythmic it is also magnificent and stately, with something of the procession about it.

The polonaise appears as a dance in most 18th-century instrumental suites and was later much used by Chopin for elaborate and highly patriotic piano pieces.

**Polyphony** We use this Greek word (which means, literally, 'many sounds') to describe music in which several strands of independent melody move along together at the same time. Such music is also said to be contrapuntal. ( → **Counterpoint** )

Until the beginning of the 17th century nearly all music was written in this way. After that date composers begin to think more in terms of the opposite approach: *homophony* – music that moves in block chords, like a hymn-tune.

However, it would be wrong to think that *all* music written before 1600 was polyphonic, and all music written afterwards was homophonic – far from it. Here is an example of Bach's polyphony:

and an example of his homophony:

**Polytonal** Music written in several keys at once is said to be 'polytonal' – that is to have 'many tonalities'.

Polytonality appears frequently in 20th-century music. Sometimes it is used only as a passing effect, but sometimes whole movements are constructed in this way. An example can be found in Holst's *Terzetto* for flute, oboe, and viola (1924), in which the flute plays in A major, the oboe in A flat major, and the viola in C major.

**Ponticello** (It.) Little bridge. The word used for the bridge of a stringed instrument. The direction **sul ponticello** means that the bow is to be placed as near to the bridge as possible when playing. This produces a strange, rather husky sound which, especially when played with a *tremolo*, is very effective in creating a sense of mystery and suspense.

**Pop** Short for 'popular'. A term applied in the 20th century to any kind of music that has been deliberately designed for instant popularity. 'Pop' music can be in any style – jazz, swing, ballad, rock, folk, anything – provided that it can be made into a commercial product. Clever publicity, or the voice of a currently famous 'pop' star or group, can turn a 'pop' song into a 'hit' that will sell thousands of records – until it is displaced by the next 'hit'.

The tendency in writing 'pop' music is to make it conform to whatever the current fashion in 'hits' happens to be. In this way it becomes easy to remember, and therefore easy to sell – but equally easy to forget! Of the thousands of 'pop' numbers that get a hearing each year, only a very few prove to have lasting qualities. The best of these 'pop classics' (for example, many of the Beatles' songs) invariably have touches of individuality that raise them well above the rather predictable standards of routine commercial 'pop'.

**Portamento** (It.) Carrying. In vocal or string music, this direction means that the performer must 'carry' the sound from note to note without a break. In other words, the line must be smooth.

When the word is used in piano music, however, it means that a half-staccato effect is required.

**Porter, Cole** American composer, 1892–1965. He studied at Yale, Harvard, and the Schola Cantorum in Paris and then settled down to become a highly successful composer of musical shows. He wrote his own extremely witty and sophisticated words, matching them with equally ingenious and memorable music. His greatest success was *Kiss Me Kate* (1948) – (the story of a production of Shakespeare's *The Taming of the Shrew* containing some scenes from it.)

**Porter, Quincy** American composer, 1897–1966. He studied with Horatio Parker at Yale, and then with Vincent d'Indy in Paris. He held various important academic posts, but was also well known as a viola player in various quartets. His music includes

**Posthorn** This print of 1834 shows the sounding of the posthorn as the Royal Mail arrives at Temple Bar, London.

**Francis Poulenc** 1899–1963 Influenced by Erik Satie and a friend of the poets Cocteau and Apollinaire (many of whose works he set to music).

eight string quartets and a great deal of other chamber music. It is elegant and graceful, but some have judged it not very profound.

**Position** A term used in connexion with stringed instruments when, in playing, the left hand is moved from time to time so that the fingers fall on a different set of places on the fingerboard and thus produce a different set of notes. Each of these placings is a 'position' ('first position', 'second position', etc.).

**Possibile** (It.) Possible. Found in such expressions as **il più forte possibile**, as loud as possible .

**Posthorn** In the days of mail coaches the guards used to have long brass instruments on which they could blow a few notes as they came to a town or village so that people would know that the coach was arriving. These instruments were called 'posthorns'.

Sometimes they were coiled, but generally they were just long straight tubes.

**Posthumous** A word which sometimes appears on the title-page of a piece of music, meaning 'after death', that is, not published during the composer's lifetime.

**Postlude** The opposite of a **Prelude** →, that is, something played *after* a main event – for example, the organ voluntary after a church service.

**Pot-pourri** A medley, or string of tunes played one after the other – perhaps a selection of the best known arias from an opera.

**Poulenc, Francis** French composer, 1899–1963. He was perhaps the most talented member of the group **Les Six** →, and wrote music which is very elegant, tuneful, and witty. His style was neo-classical, full of unexpected twists and delightful 'wrong-note' harmonies, as well as echoes of the music-hall and sentimental drawing-room ballads. He is a good example of the rare kind of composer who can be both light-hearted and serious at the same time.

Poulenc's music includes a great many fine songs, piano pieces, and chamber music, as well as a number of important larger works, such as the *Concert champêtre* for harpsichord and orchestra (1928), the Organ Concerto (1936), the Piano Concerto (1949), and the Sinfonietta (1950). He wrote several ballets, including *Les Biches* (1923), an opera-bouffe *Les Mamelles de Tirésias* (1944), and a serious opera *Dialogues des Carmélites* (1957).

**PP** or **pp** The abbreviation for **pianissimo**, very soft . **PPP** means very, very soft . (Verdi even has *ppppppp* – presumably out of desperation at never hearing orchestras play his *ppp*'s quietly enough!)

**Preambule** A preamble, or prelude.

**Precentor** The 'chief singer'. In English cathedrals the member of the clergy who is in charge of the music is given this title.

**Precipitoso, Precipitando** (It.) Impetuously.

**Prelude** A piece of music intended as an introduction to another piece, or pieces. For example, Bach's *48 Preludes and Fugues*. Chopin, however, used the title for 24 piano pieces that were complete in themselves, and other composers have followed his example.

**Presto** (It.) Quick. **Prestissimo**, 'very quick'.

**Prick song** An old English term (found, for example, in Shakespeare's plays). It means any printed song, as distinct from one sung from memory, or extemporized. Printed (or hand-written) music was said to have been 'pricked out'.

**Prima, Primo** (It.) First. As in *Prima donna*, the most important female singer in an opera, *Prima volta*, first time, *Tempo primo*, first speed – the speed in force at the beginning.

**Primary triads** → **Harmony**

**Principal subject** The first subject in a Sonata Form, or a Rondo Form. (→ **Sonata Form**)

**Printing and engraving** → page 271

**Prix de Rome** The 'Rome prize' is the principal scholarship for young composers (and other artists) in France. The winner is sent to Rome for four years, to study and compose at leisure. The second prize is a gold medal. Berlioz and Debussy both won the prize, but not at their first attempt and Ravel failed, after numerous attempts, to win at all. All this perhaps goes to suggest that men of genius and imagination are not always good 'academic' material!

**Prodigy** We use this word to describe any child who shows surprising gifts, as Mozart

Giacomo Puccini
1858-1924. The caricature
is by Lindloff.

did when he began composing at the age of four.

A great many children have shown such astonishing gifts, both as composers and performers, and many parents have been tempted to exploit them by arranging concert tours. Unfortunately not all of them grow up to be men of genius – artists like Mozart and Mendelssohn are rare.

It is true to say, however, that most great artists show definite talent at an early age, though many of them develop very slowly indeed (Verdi and Vaughan Williams, for example). And it sometimes seems as if those who develop very quickly, burn themselves out. Some die young, as Mozart did; others stop composing, or, even worse, go on composing even though they no longer have anything to say.

**Programme music** Any music which deliberately sets out to 'tell a story' or 'paint a picture' is said to have a 'programme' and can therefore be described as programme music. The term was first introduced in the middle of the 19th century by Liszt to describe his symphonic poems, but descriptive music had been written long before.

Early examples occur in the 17th century – William Byrd's set of virginal pieces *The Batell* is an example. Byrd printed descriptive headings over each section of the music so that performers would know exactly what each was intended to represent:
1. March before the Battle
2. The Soldiers' Summons: March of the Footmen
3. March of the Horsemen
4. Now followeth the Trumpets
5. The Irish March
6. The Bagpipe and the Drone
7. The Flute and the Drum
8. March to the Fight
9. The Retreat. Now followeth a Galliard for the Victory.

Beethoven, two centuries later, wrote a similar work for orchestra: *The Battle of Vittoria* (1813). It celebrates one of Wellington's victories.

The fact that Byrd added his descriptive headings underlines one curious aspect of all 'programme music', which is that it is very difficult to guess what a piece of music 'means' unless you are given some verbal clue. You may easily tell if the music is sad or cheerful, calm or lively, but exactly what it is being sad or lively about is another matter.

Programme music and all the musical devices for story-telling and picture-painting

# Printing and engraving music

Until a way of printing music was invented, copies had to be made by hand – a laborious and slow process.

The first attempts seem to have been made in about 1480. Notes and staves were carved out of a single block of wood. When this was inked, the parts where the wood had been chipped away came out as white spaces on the paper, while the remaining raised-up parts of the wood printed notes and staves. The method worked, but the results were rather clumsy.

The next step was the invention of music type, which could be moved about and rearranged at will. By 1501 such printers as the Venetian Ottaviano Petrucci were able to produce very elegant scores by this method, even though it meant assembling hundreds of different pieces of type for each page – like a complicated jigsaw puzzle.

A German, Alois Senefelder, is thought to have invented the process of *lithography* in about 1796. He discovered that a certain kind of stone had a natural affinity for grease, would absorb water, and would

*Above* **Engraving music** The musical notation is cut onto a copper plate working from right to left in mirror writing so that the right impression is left on the paper.

**Woodblock printing** Notes and staves were carved out of a single block of wood which was then inked. This remarkably fine example was printed by Antico in the 16th century. *Left* **Music type** This meant assembling hundreds of different pieces of type for each page. This is a 17th-century example.

react to various chemicals. He took flat, dry, polished stones of this kind and wrote music on them with a special greasy ink. This marked the stone in firm, clear lines. He then covered the surface with water, which settled everywhere except where the greasy marks were drawn. Next, he rolled the moist stone with ink. This stuck only to the greasy marks and transferred to the printed page. Like the engraver, he had to write his music backwards.

Although this process worked very well (and could be used for printing books and pictures), it was clumsy. The stones were heavy and cracked easily. Fortunately in 1805 he discovered a method of using metal plates instead. This process, known as METAL-PLATE LITHOGRAPHY, soon became the basis of all music printing. It is still in use today, but is now linked with engraving and photography in a process known as PHOTO-LITHOGRAPHY.

Various new methods have almost completely replaced engraving, however. Mostly they are photographic processes, starting either with a manuscript neatly written out by hand, or put together by some form of Lettraset, or printed by a music typewriter. The results are then followed by the modern form of lithography.

And, of course, it is now possible to have a small photo-copying machine in your own home so that all you need do is learn how to write music clearly and neatly.

# Puccini

Giacomo Puccini. Italian composer, 1858–1924. He came from a long line of musicians of Lucca in North Italy. After studying at Milan Conservatory he began a highly successful career as an opera composer with a one-act piece, *Le Villi*, in 1884.

He was a master of theatrical effect, and though subjects were often sentimental they made good entertainment. His most popular operas are: *Manon Lescaut* (1892), *La Bohème* (1896), *Tosca* (1900), *Madam Butterfly* (1904), *The Girl of the Golden West* (1910), and *Turandot*, completed by Franco Alfano and produced in 1926.

**Madam Butterfly** This is one of Puccini's most popular operas. He wrote only 12 operas, but at least six of them became the mainstay of every opera house in the world and he died almost a millionaire. His first opera, *Le Villi*, was a one-act piece completed in 1884. He wrote three other one-act operas (*Il Tabarro, Suor Angelica* and *Gianni Schicchi*, 1918) which are intended to be performed in one evening under the title *Il Trittico*.

received a great boost during the 19th century. **Symphonic poems** and **Programme symphonies** were very popular types of orchestral music, and certain composers (such as Richard Strauss) excelled in writing music that is extremely descriptive.

Music that has no 'programme', but simply exists for itself as music in its own right, is known as **Absolute music →**.

**Progression → Harmony**

**Prokofiev, Sergey** Russian composer, 1891–1953. He began composing when he was five years old and after studying composition privately went to St Petersburg to study at the Conservatoire. He was still only 13. By 1912, a year before completing his studies, he had made a name both as a composer and as a pianist when he performed his First Piano Concerto in Moscow.

His career proceeded smoothly and successfully until 1917, when the Revolution intervened. In 1918 he left for a tour of America, after which (1920) he settled in Paris. He made several European and American tours, but grew homesick for Russia and in 1933 finally decided to take up Soviet citizenship.

Prokofiev's music is basically *neo-classical* (**→ Neo-classicism**) in style. It is very tuneful, highly rhythmic, and brilliantly orchestrated. Some of it is simply pretty and entertaining, but many works are very powerful and profound, and Prokofiev must be regarded as one of the most important composers of his generation.

He wrote seven symphonies, five piano concertos, two violin concertos and a cello concerto, nine piano sonatas, and a great deal of chamber music, besides music for films and plays. His eight operas include: *The Love of Three Oranges* (1919) and *War and Peace* (1942); and his ballets include: *Romeo and Juliet* (1935), and *Cinderella* (1944). To audiences generally he is best known as the composer of *Peter and the Wolf* (1936).

**Promenade concerts** A promenade concert is one at which at least part of the audience is standing up and can walk about. Such events were popular in the Pleasure Gardens of 18th-century London, and similar concerts took place in various London theatres during the nineteenth century. Promenade concerts were started at Queen's Hall by Sir Henry Wood in 1895. When that hall was destroyed during the war they were transferred to the Royal Albert Hall (1941),

**Sergey Prokofiev**
1891 - 1953 This photograph of 'the composer was taken two years before his death.

# Purcell

Henry Purcell. Born in London 1658 or 1659 and died there in 1695.

1. **Purcell's Life**

Henry Purcell came of an exceptionally musical family. Both his father and uncle were Gentlemen of the Chapel Royal and members of the King's Band of Music. His brother Daniel became a noted organist and a successful composer, and his own son and grandson also became musicians. Thus for nearly 150 years the Purcell family lived and breathed music. But of all of them Henry was the most remarkable and is rightly regarded as one of the greatest musicians of his time.

It is fairly certain that he was the son of Henry and Elizabeth Purcell and that when his father died in 1664 he was adopted by his uncle, Thomas Purcell. We know very little about his early years. He was certainly born in London, possibly in Westminster. The year was probably 1659, but the month is quite unknown. He grew up in troubled times. 1665 saw not only a great Plague in London, but also the beginnings of war with Holland. 1666 was the year of the Great Fire of London. In short, he was lucky to survive childhood at all!

When he was about eight years old, young Purcell became a chorister of the Chapel Royal. Here he came under the guidance of Captain Henry Cooke, and later of Pelham Humfrey and John Blow – both excellent composers. We know next to nothing of his career as a chorister, but with musicians of this calibre around him he must surely have received an excellent training.

By December 1673 Purcell's voice had broken and he had left the choir itself. But he had already become assistant to John Hingeston, the Keeper of the King's Instruments, so his musical education continued. He seems also to have been expected to tune the organ at Westminster Abbey and to act as one of the Abbey's music copyists.

In 1677 he succeeded Matthew Locke as composer-in-ordinary to the King's Violins, and in September of the same year his first compositions appeared in print. Two years later, at the age of only 20, he became organist of Westminster Abbey. He was now safely embarked on his career and in 1681 he felt able to marry.

**Henry Purcell** 1659 – 1695
*Below right & bottom* **The Fairy Queen** This was based on Shakespeare's *A Midsummer Night's Dream.* These scenes are from the English Music Theatre Company's production, 1977.
*Below* **King Arthur** This scene is from the English Opera Group's production in 1970. This was really an 'extravaganza' by the playwright, John Dryden, to which Purcell wrote a great deal of music. King Arthur and other leading characters do not sing.

By now music had begun to pour from him. In 1680 came the four-part Fantasias for strings. In 1681 he began to write music for the theatre. In 1683 the *Sonattas of III parts* were published, and several Odes and Welcome Songs for royal occasions appeared. This became the pattern for the rest of his life: Anthems, Songs, Choral Odes and Welcome Songs, instrumental pieces, incidental music for plays, operatic entertainments – all came flowing out as part of the daily routine of a composer prepared to serve music in whatever way was demanded of him.

Perhaps most interesting of all his works were the series of 'operas' that began in 1689 with *Dido and Aeneas*, and ended in 1695 with *The Tempest*. Of these, only *Dido and Aeneas* was a true opera, sung throughout. The rest were 'semi-operas': that is to say, they had spoken dialogue and were really plays with a great deal of music.

Purcell wrote works of this kind because that was what English theatre-goers wanted. The idea of opera in English, sung throughout, was not popular. *Dido and Aeneas* came into existence almost by accident – as an end-of-term entertainment for a girls' school. Even so, it is a masterpiece and proves, as in their own way the semi-operas do, that Purcell was a truly great musical dramatist.

He crammed an enormous amount of work into the last years of his life. In 1694 he wrote some magnificent music for Queen Mary's funeral. And when he died, in the following year, they played it at his own memorial service. He was buried in Westminster Abbey, beneath the organ he had played for more than 15 years. He was, we read, 'much lamented'.

2. **Summary of Purcell's main works**

a. Operas:

| | |
|---|---|
| *Dido and Aeneas* | 1689 |
| *The History of Dioclesian* | 1690 |
| *King Arthur* | 1691 |
| *The Fairy Queen* | 1692 |
| *The Indian Queen* | 1695 |
| *The Tempest* | 1695 |

Incidental music to more than 40 plays.

b. Choral music includes:

| | |
|---|---|
| Welcome to all the pleasures | 1683 |
| (*Ode for St Cecilia's day*) | |
| Come ye sons of Art | 1694 |
| (*Ode for Queen Mary's birthday*) | |
| Swifter Isis, swifter flow | 1681 |
| (*Welcome Song for Charles II*) | |
| Sound the Trumpet | 1687 |
| (*Welcome Song for James II*) | |

There are 14 odes and 8 welcome songs, besides many anthems, services, hymns, etc.; sacred songs, secular songs, and secular cantatas.

c. Instrumental music includes:

| | |
|---|---|
| 3 fantasias in three parts | 1680? |
| 9 fantasias in four parts | 1680 |
| 12 sonatas in three parts | 1683 |
| 10 sonatas in four parts | 1697 |

besides a considerable quantity of harpsichord music (e.g. *Musick's Hand-Maid*, 1689).

2. **The man** Though we have so few biographical details to call upon, we can get some idea of Purcell's character from the numerous poems that appeared, mourning his early death. Seldom has any musician been so praised by his colleagues and friends. He must surely have been not only a supremely talented musician, but also a singularly likeable man.

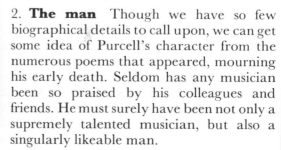

where they continue to be held during the summer of each year. The 'Proms' are now so popular that some of the season's concerts take place in other buildings – such as St John's, Smith Square, and Westminster Cathedral. Promenade Concerts are a feature of the musical life of many great cities, e.g. New York holds a regular series in the Lincoln Center.

**Psalm** The Book of Psalms is the oldest song-book still in use. Some of the psalms are said to have been written by King David, about a thousand years before Christ.

Psalms are poems, but in their original language they are not metrical. Each verse consists of two balancing phrases, linked together. Metrical translations were made by the various European churches, and this is how they are now sung – in the Anglican Church, for example, to Chants.

**Psalter** Book of psalms and psalm-tunes.

**Psaltery** A type of **dulcimer** →. It consists of a sound box (sometimes square, sometimes triangular) above which run the strings, from side to side over one or two sets of bridges. There are often two or more strings to each note, and the tuning pins are usually set on alternate sides of the instrument.

The psaltery is held either on the lap, or resting against the chest, and plucked with the fingers and a small plectrum. The psaltery was developed from a similar Middle Eastern instrument and was particularly

**Proms** This last night audience at the 1952 season of the Henry Wood Promenade Concerts is conducted by the late Sir Malcolm Sargent. Audience participation in the singing of 'Land of Hope and Glory' and other songs is a traditional part of the last night ritual.

**Psaltery** King David is shown playing this instrument in the 14th-century English illuminated manuscript, the Luttrell Psalter. This kind of psaltery is usually called a 'pig's head' psaltery.

popular in Europe from the 14th to 16th centuries.

**Publishing music** The business of publishing music grew up alongside the development of printing (→ **Printing music**) towards the end of the 15th century. One of the first great publishers was Ottaviano Petrucci, who settled in Venice and obtained an exclusive right to print music in 1498. Since that date music publishing has spread and prospered, reaching a peak at the end of the 19th century when it became possible to issue music cheaply and in large quantities.

In return for a share in the composer's **copyright** →, the publisher agrees to print and promote his music. In certain cases he may not actually print the music to sell it, but simply have copies made that can be hired out (for he may judge that the work is unlikely to sell in sufficient quantity. Providing that a work is properly publicized and promoted, the fact that it exists simply in the Hire Library does not matter – indeed there are certain advantages, since you know exactly when it is to be performed and who will perform it and can therefore be sure of getting the appropriate fee.

Though some composers have quarrelled with their publishers, and some publishers have behaved in a very underhand way towards their composers, most have managed to pursue a very happy relationship. A good publisher is a composer's best friend, for he relieves him of all the tedious work connected with getting his work performed. A good composer, however, is the publisher's bread-and-butter.

**Puccini** → page 271

**Pulse** Usually means the same as 'Beat', but in certain cases a distinction is made between them. In 'simple' times, beat and pulse are the same thing; but in 'compound' times, the larger time-divisions are called beats and the smaller ones, pulses. For example:

Compound Duple

6/8   6 'Pulses' grouped into 2 'Beats'

Compound Triple

9/8   9 'Pulses' grouped into 3 'Beats'

Compound Quadruple

12/8   12 'Pulses' grouped into 4 'Beats'

**Pult** (Ger.) Desk–the music stand that two orchestral players share.

**Punta** (It.) Point. As in **punta d'arco**, 'at the point of the bow'.

**Purcell** → page 272

**Quadrille** A dance that was extremely popular at the beginning of the 19th century. It was a type of 'square' dance (the dancers formed up in a square), and consisted of five different sections, alternating 6/8 and 2/4 time. The music was often borrowed from operas popular at the time, though a few composers (such as Johann Strauss) wrote original music for it.

The *Lancers*, invented in Paris in 1856, is a type of quadrille.

**Quadruplet** → **Notes and notation**

**Quadruple time** → **Notes and notation**

**Quail** A toy instrument that imitates the sound of the bird. ( → **Toy Symphony**)

**Quantz, Johann** German composer, 1697–1773. He was a virtuoso performer on the flute, and after travelling and playing extensively in Europe he entered the service of Frederick the Great (1741), with whom he remained until his death. Frederick, who was also an accomplished flautist, is said to have played Quantz's 300 or more concertos in strict rotation, year in year out. His treatise on flute-playing, published in 1752, has been very influential.

**Quarter note** and **quarter rest** → **American musical terms**

**Quarter-tone** An interval that is half the size of a semitone. There are therefore four quarter-tones in every tone. Such intervals are found quite naturally in folk music, particularly in the East, but sound strange to the average concert-goer. 20th-century composers have sometimes made use of quarter-tones (and pianos have even been specially

**Johann Quantz** 1697–1773 He not only wrote a treatise, *The True Art of Flute Playing* (1752), but also improved the instrument by adding a second key and inventing the sliding top for tuning the instrument.

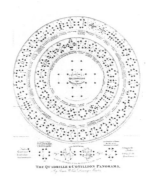

**Quadrille** Plan by Thomas Wilson (1819)

**Roger Quilter** 1877-1953 He set many of Shakespeare's poems to music.

constructed to play them), but the results have never proved very popular.

**Quartet** Any group of four performers, and any music written for such a group to play.

A vocal quartet for 'mixed' voices consists of a SOPRANO, CONTRALTO (or ALTO), TENOR, and BASS – often called, for short, **s.a.t.b.** A male-voice quartet might consist of an alto, two tenors, and a bass; or two tenors and two basses. A quartet of female voices consists usually of two sopranos and two altos. Music for any of these combinations may, or may not, have an instrumental accompaniment.

A STRING QUARTET consists of two violins, a viola, and a cello. The violins each play a different line of music, and are therefore referred to as 1st and 2nd violins.

Quartets that consist of three strings and some other instrument always take their name from the other instrument. For example, a PIANO QUARTET (piano, violin, viola, cello), a FLUTE QUARTET, etc.

**Quasi** (It.) As if. Found in such expressions as **quasi allegretto** 'allegretto-ish'.

**Quaver** → **Notes and notation**

**Quilter, Roger** English composer, 1877–1953. He studied at Frankfurt and became well known as a composer of many fine songs. His light opera *Julia* was produced at Covent Garden in 1936, and one of his light orchestral works, *Children's Overture* (1914), based on nursery-rhyme tunes, became very popular.

**Quintet** Any group of five performers, or any music written for such a group to play.

A VOCAL QUINTET usually consists either of two sopranos, contralto, tenor, and bass, or soprano, contralto, two tenors, and bass.

A STRING QUINTET usually consists either of two violins, two violas, and a cello, or two violins, viola, and two cellos. Very occasionally two violins, viola, cello, and double bass may be found.

A quintet that consists of four strings and some other instrument takes its name from the other instrument. For example, a PIANO QUINTET (piano, and string quartet), a CLARINET QUINTET, etc.

**Quodlibet** This Latin word, meaning 'what you please', is used to describe a collection of tunes played either at one and the same time, or one after the other without a break (the end of one becomes the beginning of the next). In either case the effect is intended to be amusing.

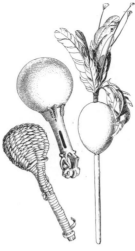

**Rattles** These South American examples are (*left to right*) a Peruvian basket rattle; a clay rattle from Chiriqui; and a gourd rattle of the Baniwa tribe.

**Rackett** An early woodwind instrument with a double reed, used particularly in France and Germany in the 17th century. It came in four sizes: soprano, tenor, bass, and double bass. It made a very distinctive sound which had a kind of buzz to it. Racketts are now being made again so that music of the period may be played more authentically.

**Radio** → **Broadcasting**

**Raga** A type of Indian melody, used by Indian musicians as a basis for subtle variations. Each Raga has its own meaning and is appropriate to different moods and different times of day. (→ **Indian music**)

**Ragtime** → page 277

**Rainier, Priaulx** South African composer, b. 1903. She studied at the Royal Academy of Music in London, and then with Nadia Boulanger in Paris. Her first important work, the String Quartet No 1, dates from 1939. She has written much chamber music and a number of very fine songs. Her largest orchestral works are *Phalaphala* (1961), the suite *Aequora Lunae* (1967), and the Violin Concerto (1977). She has lived in England since her student days, but some of her music makes use of African materials.

**Rakhmaninov** → page 277

**Rallentando** (It.) Slowing down. As with *rallentare*, *rallentato* (It.) and *ralentir* (Fr.), it indicates that the music must gradually get slower.

**Rameau, Jean-Philippe** French composer, 1683–1764. He was taught first by his father, who was an organist at Dijon, and

**Rackett** This instrument, popular from the 16th to the 18th century, was also called a 'sausage bassoon'

**Jean-Philippe Rameau** 1683–1764 At the age of seven Rameau could read any piece of harpsichord music put before him.

soon made great progress as a harpsichord player, organist, and composer. After publishing several books of harpsichord pieces and an important *Treatise on Harmony* (1724), he settled in Paris and became a fashionable teacher and composer.

When he was 50 he suddenly turned to opera and ballet and wrote a series of highly successful works that continued and developed the style laid down by Lully. These, like his harpsichord pieces, proved immensely important in the history of French music. Rameau's operas include: *Castor et Pollux* (1737), *Dardanus* (1737), and *Zoroastre* (1749); and his ballets: *Les Indes Galantes* (1735), *Platée* (1745), and *Les Paladins* (1760). His textbook on harmony formed the basis for the teaching of that subject for the next two hundred years.

**Rattle** A type of percussion instrument (→ **Idiophones**) used all over the world for thousands of years. The simplest rattles are dried gourds or pods containing seeds which rattle when shaken. Others are fashioned out of clay, or wood, or leather, etc., filled with small pellets. Rattles are often used in magic rituals by primitive peoples. They are found in the orchestra as a 'special effect', and play an important part in Latin-American dance music.

**Ravel** → page 278

**Ravenscroft, Thomas** English composer, 1590–1633. He was a choirboy at St Paul's Cathedral, and then music master at Christ's Hospital School in London. His memory is kept alive by his rounds and catches and a very famous book of hymn-tunes.

**Rawsthorne, Alan** English composer, 1905–71. He was born in Lancashire and received his training at the Royal Manchester College of Music. His first important compositions appeared in 1938 (Theme and Variations for two violins) and 1939 (Symphonic Studies, for orchestra). But his career was interrupted by the War, and he served in the Army from 1941 to 1945.

Rawsthorne wrote music of all kinds, but is best known for his orchestral works, which include a lively overture *Street Corner* (1944), two piano concertos, two violin concertos, and three symphonies.

**Real** and **Tonal** → **Fugue**

**Rebec** A type of stringed instrument popular in Medieval and Renaissance times – one of the ancestors of the violin. It was evolved from an Arab fiddle, the REBAB, and

# Ragtime

A type of American popular music which, along with **Blues** →, helped to bring **Jazz** → into existence.

Ragtime became popular in the 1890s, but died out after 1918 – though a revival of interest began in the 1940s and became particularly strong in the 1970s.

The main feature of ragtime is that its melodies are strongly syncopated, against a steady beat in the accompaniment. The word 'rag' itself suggests music with a 'ragged' edge (i.e. syncopated, and unlike the smooth melodies of ordinary music).

This style of playing, which sprang up among the Negro street bands of New

Sheet music cover for *Wall Street Rag* by Scott Joplin, the 'king of ragtime writers'.

Orleans, Memphis, and St Louis, was probably derived from the banjo-songs played by blackface minstrel troupes, and a type of dance called the 'cakewalk' which became popular in the 1880s.

The most famous name associated with the rise of ragtime is that of the pianist and composer Scott Joplin, whose *Maple Leaf Rag* (1899) has had a lasting success. In 1908 he published a set of six exercises, called *The School of Ragtime*, to show pianists how genuine rag should be played. Another important composer of piano-rags was Jelly Roll Morton.

# Rakhmaninov

**Sergey Rakhmaninov** 1873–1943 The music of this expatriate composer and pianist was banned in Russia in 1931 for its 'decadence'. Nevertheless he remained Russian in outlook and his death was deeply mourned in the Soviet Union.

Sergey Rakhmaninov. Russian composer, 1873–1943. He trained at the St Petersburg and Moscow Conservatories and on leaving (1892) began the first of his many concert tours as a virtuoso pianist. His career prospered and he soon became world-famous, both as a pianist and as a composer of highly romantic music. The Russian Revolution (1917) forced him to leave his native land. He spent the rest of his life abroad, living in Switzerland and America.

Rakhmaninov wrote a considerable amount of music of all kinds, including operas, choral works, and many fine songs. But it is for his piano and orchestral music that he is best known. His orchestral works include three symphonies (1895, 1907, 1936), a symphonic poem *The Isle of the Dead* (1907), four piano concertos (1891, 1901, 1909, 1927), and a *Rhapsody on a Theme by Paganini* for piano and orchestra (1934).

appeared in Europe in the 13th century. Unlike the fiddle, which was popular at the same time, the rebec had a rounded back. Its body was pear-shaped, and the tuning pegs were set in the side of the neck. Most rebecs had three strings, tuned in fifths. It was played either resting on the shoulder, or held lower down against the chest. By Renaissance times, rebecs were being made in families of different sizes. The largest of these were played like a gamba, held between the knees.

**Recapitulation** → **Sonata Form**

**Recit.** Short for **Recitando**, **Recitative** →

**Rebec** A similar instrument is still in use today in parts of Greece, Anatolia and the Aegean Islands under the name of *lyra*.

**Recital** A concert, usually given by one person – as, for example, a piano recital. Certain instruments, however, usually call for an accompanist (i.e. a violin recital).

**Recitando** (It.) Reciting. Meaning that the performance is to be like speech rather than song. Also **recitato**, 'recited'.

**Recitative** This describes a type of vocal music that has no 'tune' in the ordinary sense, but which sets words in a way that imitates the natural rise and fall and the rhythm of speech.

# Ravel

Maurice Ravel. French composer, 1875–1937. He studied music at the Paris Conservatoire, but failed to win a Prix de Rome. This was all the more surprising because by 1898 he had already become known and admired as a composer. His life was quiet and comfortable, for he had private means and preferred to live in comparative seclusion. He served in the Air Force during 1914–18 war, and made several tours in Europe and America, conducting his own works. He was an excellent teacher, but took only a select number of private pupils.

Ravel's music includes two operas: *L'Heure espagnole* (1907), and *L'Enfant et les Sortilèges* (1925); four ballets, of which *Daphnis et Chloé* (1912), *Ma Mère l'Oye* (Mother Goose) (1908), and *La Valse* (1920)

Dessin d'Aline Fruhauf.

*Above* A contemporary caricature of Ravel. *Right* Set design by Bakst for Ravel's ballet, *Daphnis et Chloé*.

are the most famous; several large orchestral works, including the *Pavane pour une infante défunte* (1899), *Le Tombeau de Couperin* (1917), and *Bolero* (1927); two piano concertos (both 1931); chamber music and many fine songs and piano pieces. In style, his music is highly romantic, yet very elegant and precise.

---

It was first used in the early operas and oratorios in about 1600 and is an important part of the Monodic style (→ **Monody**) that came into existence at that time.

Recitative is sometimes accompanied by a few chords on a harpsichord (the CONTINUO), and sometimes by the orchestra. Examples can be found in 18th-century operas and oratorios (Handel's, for instance), where most arias are preceded by a short recitative.

**Reciting note → Anglican chant**

**Recorder** Sometimes called the English flute. It is a type of flute, blown at the end instead of at the side. It has eight holes, by which different notes can be obtained.

Recorders come in CONSORTS (families): sopranino, descant, treble, tenor, bass, and double bass. They were much in use from the 16th to 18th centuries, but then died out as orchestral music came into fashion. They can in fact be traced back to the 12th century, but no early examples still exist. (→ **Flute**)

Interest in the recorder revived at the end of the 19th century, through the work of such enthusiasts as Arnold Dolmetsch. Now they are the instruments most commonly learnt by children in school and composers have begun to write for them again.

**Reed → page 279**

**Reed organ family** All instruments that have separate reeds to sound each note may

**Maurice Ravel** 1875-1937

**Max Reger** 1873–1916

be considered as part of the same family. They include:

a. the **Mouthorgan**, or **Harmonica** →
b. the **Accordion** →
c. the **Concertina** →
d. the **Melodica** →
e. the **Harmonium** →

**Reel** This ancient dance is common in Scotland and Ireland, and it may be of Celtic origin. The music is quick and whirling and generally in 4/4 time, though examples in 6/4 time can be found. The Irish reel is played much faster than the Scottish. In Scotland it is usually danced by two couples who stand face to face and then go through a series of figures of eight. The early settlers took the reel with them to America, where it flourished in various forms of its own – such as the 'Virginia' reel.

**Regal** A small organ with reed pipes, invented in about 1460 in Germany. It could be carried easily from place to place and was therefore not only used in churches, but also in private houses for general entertainment.

**Reger, Max** German composer, 1873–1916. Though famous as a pianist, conductor, and teacher, Reger also wrote an immense amount of music, much of it very contrapuntal and ingenious. He was considered to be a very daring harmonic innovator, but, apart from his organ works, his music is seldom performed nowadays.

# Reed

The part of a woodwind instrument that produces the first vibrations. It is cut from a type of grass or reed, known as *sativa*, that grows in the south of Europe. Many people refer to it as 'cane', but it is not quite the same as real cane. The name 'reed' is also given to the same device in certain organ pipes, though these reeds are made of metal.

Woodwind reeds are either SINGLE (as in the clarinet), or DOUBLE (as in the oboe and bassoon). They are very thin, and when the player's breath passes through them they vibrate (you can get the same effect by blowing through a blade of grass).

Oboe reed

Clarinet reed

Bassoon reed

reed plate
aperture
reed

ligature mouthpiece reed

*Left* **Types of reed** Both the oboe and the bassoon have double reeds. The clarinet is a single-reed instrument.

*Above* **Clarinet reed**, here fixed to the mouthpiece by a metal ligature. *Left* **Free-reed** Air vibrates through the metal tongue which is riveted over the aperture.

**Reggae** A type of Jamaican popular music, not unlike 'rock', but even more heavily rhythmic and aggressive. The words of reggae songs are often protests against social and political injustice and closely linked with the religious cult of Rastafarianism, which preaches that the Jamaicans will eventually return to their true home, Ethiopia. The former Emperor of Ethiopia, Haile Selassie, whose original name was Ras Tafari, is worshipped as a god. Reggae was adopted, to a limited extent, by performers outside the West Indies in the 1970s, but few were able to achieve a really convincing rhythmic style. The most outstanding Jamaican performer and composer is Bob Marley.

**Register**, or **Stop** → **Organ**

**Related keys** → **Modulation**

**Relative major and minor** → **Modulation**

**Relative pitch** → **Pitch**

**Repeat marks** → **Useful abbreviations**

**Répétiteur** Someone who teaches musicians their parts – particularly someone who teaches singers in an opera house. This French word is regularly used in England, even though the term 'coach' is just as good!

**Replica** (It.) Repeat. As in **senza replica**, 'without repetition'.

**Reprise** Any repetition in music may be described as a 'reprise', but the term is most often found in musical comedies when songs heard in one act are repeated in another. The 'recapitulation' section in sonata form is sometimes called a 'reprise'.

**Recorder** This instrument, much used from the 16th to the 18th centuries, has been extensively revived in this century.

**Reggae** Bob Marley with his band, the *Wailers*, has popularized reggae music outside Jamaica.

**Requiem** This Latin word means 'rest' and is the first word in the Mass for the Dead. Though that Mass has its traditional plainsong, the words have often been set by composers – including, Palestrina, Mozart, Berlioz, and Verdi.

The word is sometimes used for works of a similarly serious nature which are not actual settings of the Mass for the Dead. For example, Brahms' *German Requiem* (a setting of German words), and Delius's *Requiem* (a setting of words by Nietzsche).

**Resolution** (of Discord) → **Harmony**

**Respighi, Ottorino** Italian composer, 1879–1936. He studied in Bologna, St Petersburg, and Berlin. In 1913 he settled in Rome and there became famous for a series of colourful symphonic poems, orchestrated with great brilliance. The most famous of them, *The Fountains of Rome* (1917), and *The Pines of Rome* (1924) are still played and admired.

**Responses** In the church service these are the replies of the congregation (or choir) to the **Preces** and **Versicles** of the priest. In the Anglican Church the music is an adaptation, made by Thomas Tallis at the time of the Reformation, of ancient plainsong. Two forms are available: FESTAL RESPONSES (with the plainsong in the tenor part), and FERIAL RESPONSES (with the plainsong in the treble).

**Rests** → **Notes and notation**

**Retardation** → **Harmony**

**Retrograde motion** → **Canon**

**Reubke, Julius** German composer, 1834–58. His father was an organ builder,

# Rhythm

That aspect of music that is concerned with time. It includes the different lengths of notes and rests, the way in which certain notes are accented while others are stressed less heavily, and the way in which we group notes into regular patterns.

We cannot say that notes are long or short unless we imagine that behind them (either heard or felt) there is some basic unit of time, ticking steadily away, against which they can be measured. We call this unit of time a BEAT. It may be slow or fast, but it is always *regular*.

Instinct makes us group these beats into patterns – either of twos or threes, or some combination of both. In music we show this grouping by arranging our notation in BARS, each containing the same number of beats.

What tells us whether the beats are grouped in twos or threes, etc., is ACCENT – the feeling that certain notes are more strongly stressed than others. For example, six equal notes could be aranged as:

The first arrangement is by twos, and is therefore DUPLE time. The second is by threes, and is in TRIPLE time. (→ **Notes and notation**)

There is no end to the kind of groupings we can make, using the different note-lengths as basic units of time. Plain twos, threes, and fours are common, but irregular groupings of five $(3+2$, or $2+3)$, and seven $(3+4$, or $4+3)$, and so forth are equally possible.

Rhythm also shows itself in other ways. Though the beat behind a piece of music may be regular, the melodic lines themselves may have a rhythm of their own. Few melodies follow the beat as closely as this:

Melodies are much more likely to have notes of different lengths, and therefore a rhythm of their own, even though the basic beat can still be felt in the background:

A more subtle way of adding to rhythmic interest is the device of *syncopation*. This means that the accent may suddenly be displaced, so that it really does seem to contradict the basic beat:

Whatever the method employed to produce interesting and effective rhythms, one thing is certain: rhythm is the very life-blood of music.

and he himself a skilful organist and pianist. He was a favourite pupil of Liszt, but his early death meant that he only left one really important work – the organ sonata *The Ninety-fourth Psalm*. It is not only remarkable in itself, but encouraged other composers to write descriptive organ music – it is a kind of symphonic poem.

**Reveillé** This word (pronounced 'revally') comes from the French *reveil*, which means 'awakening'. In the Army it is the bugle call that awakens the soldiers in the morning.

**Rezniček, Emil von** Austrian composer, 1860–1945. He studied at the Leipzig Conservatory and worked as a theatre

**Rhythm and blues**
Features a solo voice and an electric guitar. The American musician, Chuck Berry, is shown here.

conductor, and later as a military bandmaster. In 1902 he settled in Berlin. He is best known for his operas, and in particular the comic opera *Donna Diana* (1894), the overture of which is still frequently played.

**Rf** and **rfz** Short for *rinforzando*.

**R.H.** Short for 'right hand'. Found in piano music, etc.

**Rhapsody** A title used in the 19th century, by such composers as Liszt and Brahms, for compositions of a fairly loose structure, often containing a string of different tunes. Later composers have also used the term, often for compositions that are based on folksong (e.g. Vaughan Williams's *Norfolk Rhapsodies*).

# Rimsky-Korsakov

Nikolay Rimsky-Korsakov. Russian composer, 1844–1908. Though he showed a very early talent for music, his aristocratic parents would not allow him to make it his profession. Instead, he entered the St Petersburg Naval College and then served as a Naval Officer until 1873.

He continued to study music privately, however, and in 1865 made a great impression with his First Symphony. In 1871, though he was still officially in the Navy, he was appointed Professor of Composition to the St Petersburg Conservatory.

Rimsky-Korsakov proceeded to teach himself as thoroughly as he taught others. He was particularly noted for his brilliant and imaginative orchestration. He published an excellent book on the subject in 1908. He was a leading member of the nationalist group known as *The Five* and did everything he could to further the cause of Russian music. His own compositions were strongly influenced by folksong.

He wrote music of all kinds, including 15 operas, of which *Sadko* (1898), *Tsar Sultan*

**The Golden Cockerel**
This set design by Gontcharova was for an early production of the opera first produced in St Petersburg in 1909. The work was banned because of its seditious nature and was performed after the composer's death.

(1900), and *The Golden Cockerel* (1909) are the most famous. His orchestral music includes three symphonies, a splendid symphonic suite *Scheherezade* (1888), a colourful *Russian Easter Festival* overture (1888), and orchestral suites from several of his operas.

---

**Rhythm** → page 280

**Rhythm and blues** A type of 'pop' music that combines the main elements of blues and jazz. It developed in America in the late 1940s, mainly as dance music. The melodic lines reflect the blues style, while the accompanying rhythm has a heavy, driving quality borrowed from certain kinds of jazz. It is usually performed on electronically amplified instruments. Both **Rock 'n roll** → and **Soul** → can be considered developments of the rhythm and blues style.

**Rhythm section** The name given to the percussion and double bass section of any jazz group, because these instruments supply the basic beat.

**Ricercare** This word was used in the 16th and 17th centuries to describe the early form of **Fugue** →.

**Rigaudon** (or **Rigadoon**) A lively dance from the South of France, which became popular in England at the end of the 17th century. It has two or four beats to the bar and is characterized by a leaping step. The music generally begins on the third or fourth beat of the bar.

Nikolay Rimsky-Korsakov, 1844-1908.

**Rigoroso** (It.) Rigorously – in exact time and firm rhythm.

**Rinforzando** (It.) Reinforcing. **Rinforzato**, 'reinforced'. In the sense of emphasizing the notes or chords so marked. Usually abbreviated to **rf** or **rfz**.

**Ring of the Nibelung** → page 282

**Ripieno** (It.) Full. A term used to describe passages that are to be played by the full orchestra, as distinct from those that were played by soloists. In the concerto grosso the main orchestra is known as the RIPIENO section, and the soloists as the CONCERTINO.

In British brass bands the first cornet is known as the RIPIANO CORNET (note the spelling). In the score it shares a line with the Flügelhorn. Its job is to supplement the solo cornets.

**Risoluto** (It.) Resolute.

**Rit.** Short for **ritardando**.

**Ritardando** (It.) Holding back. A gradual process, unlike **ritenuto** which is immediate.

# The Ring of the Nibelung

Here is a general outline of the main events:

**Das Rheingold** (The Rhinegold)

At the bottom of the river Rhine there lies a hoard of gold, watched over by the Rhine Maidens. On learning that it will bring him unlimited power, the dwarf Alberich steals the gold and fashions it into a ring.

Wotan, the chief of the gods, has given Freya, the goddess of youth and love, to the giants Fafner and Fasolt as payment for their labour in building Valhalla, the home of the gods. But without Freya everything grows old. Wotan therefore steals the ring from Alberich and offers it to the giants in exchange for Freya. They accept. But Alberich has cursed the ring, and Fafner immediately kills Fasolt. The gods enter Valhalla.

**Die Walküre** (The Valkyrie)

Wotan is the father of two children, Siegmund and Sieglinde, who have been brought up on earth in ignorance of each other. Sieglinde has married Hunding, but when she meets Siegmund they fall in love. Fricka, Wotan's wife, demands that Siegmund should be punished, and Wotan reluctantly agrees. Brünnhilde, Wotan's favourite daughter, tries to protect Siegmund, but Hunding kills him. She is able to protect Sieglinde, however, and carries her away to safety so that she may give birth to a hero-son, Siegfried.

Wotan must now punish Brünnhilde. He strips her of her Valkyrie state and makes her mortal. He then places her on a mountain surrounded by magic fire, to sleep on until someone heroic enough can be

Wagner's four epic music dramas were composed between 1853 and 1874. The story is based on old Scandinavian and German legends. The first complete production of the Ring was at Bayreuth in 1876. *Above* **Das Rheingold** The opera's first scene shows the Rhine Maidens watching over the gold. *Above right* **Die Walküre**, Act II, scene 5 Sieglinde watches as her husband, Hunding kills Siegmund, her brother. *Below left* **Siegfried**, Act III, scene 3 The sleeping Brünnhilde is woken by Siegfried *Below right* **Götterdämmerung**, Act III, scene 2 The body of the dead Siegfried is carried to a funeral pyre.

found to rescue her.

**Siegfried**

Since the death of his mother, Siegfried has been brought up by the dwarf Mime, who has taught him to be a blacksmith. Siegfried remakes his father's broken sword and slays a dragon (really the giant Fafner in disguise). But a drop of the dragon's blood touches his lips and enables him to understand the language of the birds. From them he learns the secret of the ring, and also that Mime is now planning to kill him in order to steal it. Siegfried kills Mime, and guided by the birds makes his way to the mountain to wake the sleeping Brünnhilde, whom he marries.

**Götterdämmerung** (The Twilight of the Gods)

Siegfried leaves the ring with Brünnhilde and goes in search of adventure. At the court of Gunther and his sister Gutrune, he meets Hagen, Alberich's son. Hagen gives Siegfried a magic potion which causes him to forget Brünnhilde and fall in love with Gutrune. Siegfried offers Brünnhilde to Gunther as a suitable bride. Unable to understand his action, Brünnhilde now sides with Hagen in seeking revenge. Hagen kills Siegfried.

Siegfried's body is placed on a funeral pyre. Brünnhilde now understands what has happened. She seizes the ring and throws herself into the flames. Hagen and Gunther also die in the struggle for the ring, which, as Valhalla itself is consumed in the spreading flames, now sinks back into the Rhine and the safekeeping of the Rhine Maidens.

# Rock

A type of 'pop' music that developed in America in the 1950s, and soon spread throughout the world. It began as a mixture of country music and rhythm and blues, played, very loudly, on electric guitars. At first it was mainly black music, but its popularity was much increased by a white singer, Elvis Presley, whose recordings broke many sales records in the 1960s. British groups, such as the Beatles and the Rolling Stones, helped to increase its world-wide influence. Various dance styles also came to be associated with 'rock' (its original name, 'rock 'n roll', aptly describing the way in which such performers as Presley would move their hips while playing the guitar). These included the Twist, and the Shake – both of which involved the dancer moving his body in time to the highly rhythmic music.

The main feature of rock is its heavy, driving rhythm. This is based on eight quavers (eighth-notes) to the bar, with accents often on the second and fourth main

**The Rolling Stones**
Lead singer, Mick Jagger, and lead guitarist, Keith Richards.

beats. Harmonies can be complex and dissonant, but whole pieces are often based on one or two chords. Melodic lines are often quite adventurous, frequently using irregular phrase-lengths, and sometimes borrowing from modal scales. Unusual methods of performance are also sought out – including extreme vocal ranges, falsetto singing, shouting, and speaking.

In the 1960s various offshoots of rock began to develop. For example, the singer Bob Dylan specialized in 'folk rock' – which, as its name implies, had a strong folksong quality and made use of texts that dealt with social and personal problems. 'Hard rock' is rock with a very strong beat. 'Raga rock' makes use of oriental instruments (such as the Indian sitar) and imitates some of the methods and styles of oriental music. 'Acid rock' uses electronic instruments to create unusual sounds and atmospheres that remind its admirers of their experiences when on the drug L.S.D. ('acid').

**Ritenuto** (It.) Held back. Often abbreviated to **rit.** and **riten**.

**Ritmo, Ritmico** (It.) Rhythm, rhythmic.

**Ritornello** (It.) Literally a 'small repetition'. The word is used to describe, among other things:
1. a short instrumental passage played between the scenes of a 17th-century opera, or even between different sections of the same scene.
2. a short instrumental passage played between the different vocal phrases of a song or anthem.
3. the orchestral *tutti* passages, i.e. passages for the whole orchestra, in a Concerto Grosso or solo concerto.

**Rock 'n roll** A type of popular music of the 1950s, derived from **Rhythm and blues** →. ( → **Rock** )

**Rococo** A term used to describe a highly decorative, but very formal style of architecture, furniture, etc., found in the second and third quarters of the 18th century. Music of the same period (J. C. Bach, C. P. E. Bach and early Haydn and Mozart, for example) is sometimes similarly described.

**Rodgers, Richard** American composer, b. 1902. He studied at Columbia University,

**Elvis Presley** 1935-1977 the King of Rock 'n Roll.

where he met Lorenz Hart and began to write musical shows. Their first fully professional collaboration came in 1927 with *A Connecticut Yankee*. Important musicals and revues followed in rapid succession, including: *On your Toes* (1936), which contains a remarkable ballet *Slaughter on Tenth Avenue, Babes in Arms* (1937), and *Pal Joey* (1940). Their partnership ended in 1942 with *By Jupiter*, and Hart died in the following year. They had written 29 shows and a total of over 400 songs, many of which had become enormously popular.

Rodgers then went into partnership with Oscar Hammerstein II and proceeded to even greater success with *Oklahoma!* (1943), *Carousel* (1945), *South Pacific* (1949), *The King and I* (1951), and *The Sound of Music* (1959). Hammerstein died in 1960.

Without doubt, Richard Rodgers is one of the most successful and talented of 20th-century light music composers. His tunes cover a very wide range of types, all instantly memorable and yet never hackneyed.

**Roman, Johan Helmich** Swedish composer, 1694–1758. He began his career as a violinist and oboist, playing in the court orchestra at Stockholm. He was sent to London to study, but in 1720 returned to Stockholm to direct the court music.

# Romantic music

Every so often the artistic world seems to undergo an important change of style and attitude. In the 18th century, for example, composers wrote beautiful and expressive music. But when we listen to it, one of the qualities that really strikes home is its sense of elegance and beauty of form. We say that this kind of beauty is a 'classical' one. And we describe such composers as Haydn and Mozart as **'Classical'** →.

The 'Romantic' attitude in music belongs to the 19th century. What composers then wrote was, of course, still well-organized and satisfying as musical form, but it was also much more colourful and extravagant.

Romantic music seems full of emotion, and full of the power to tell stories and paint pictures. The work of such composers as Weber, Mendelssohn, Schumann, Chopin, Berlioz, Liszt, and Wagner has this quality, and we therefore call them 'Romantics'.

The Romantic Movement began first in literature and philosophy, towards the end of the 18th century. The first signs appeared in France, with the writer Jean-Jacques Rousseau (1712–78), and then in Germany, among such poets as Schiller (1759–1805) and Goethe (1749–1832). English authors of the 19th century, such as Byron, Shelley, Wordsworth and Coleridge, and above all Sir Walter Scott, helped to spread its influence. Music and the other arts soon followed suit.

It was, in part, a political movement–the

**Romanticism in Art**
*Above Avalanche in the Alps* by P. J. de Loutherboug. *Below* Scene from Gounod's *Faust*. Romanticism as a philosophy preached revolt against the constraints of classicism. It argued for a return to 'nature' and 'natural' behaviour, for liberty and self-expression.

French Revolution owed much to Romantic ideals. It believed that it was better to trust the emotions rather than the intellect.

Typical types of 'romantic' music are the short piano pieces of Mendelssohn, Schumann, and Chopin. Each usually has a descriptive title: 'Song without Words', 'Novellette', 'Nocturne', and so on. Each seems to capture a particular mood and to express something outside music itself.

This discovery of how to make music describe non-musical ideas (emotions, moods, pictures, stories) is at the root of the romantic attitude. And two new musical forms of the period, the Symphonic Poem and the Programme Symphony, were designed to allow composers to do precisely this kind of thing.

Because the Romantics were eager to make their music expressive, it is not surprising to find that both harmony and orchestration became extremely important.

---

Roman is often called 'the father of Swedish music'. He wrote 21 symphonies, several concertos, 82 motets, and a mass, as well as many harpsichord suites and trio sonatas. He was much influenced by such composers as Handel, and though he cannot be said to have developed a very distinctive style his music is very attractive.

**Romance** A rather vague term, used to describe short pieces of music that are full of tender sentiment.

**Romberg, Sigmund** American composer, 1887–1951. He was born in Hungary, but settled in America in 1909. He became famous as a composer of romantic operettas such as *Maytime* (1917), *Blossom Time* (1921) (based on Schubert's melodies), *The Student Prince* (1924), *The Desert Song* (1926), and *The New Moon* (1928).

**Richard Rodgers**
*The King and I,* starring Herbert Lom and Valerie Hobson.

**Rondo** → page 285

**Root, Root position of a chord** → **Harmony**

**Rosalia** → **Sequence**

**Rossini** → page 286

**Rouget de Lisle** French poet, composer, and soldier, 1760–1836. In 1792, when stationed with his regiment at Strasburg, he was inspired to write the words and music of a patriotic song which was soon taken up by all France and was eventually adopted as the National Anthem. The *Marseillaise* (so called because it was sung with immense success at a patriotic banquet in Marseilles a few months after it had been heard in Strasburg) is an exciting piece of music, full of revolutionary fervour. It caught the spirit of the French Revolution exactly. But it was the only piece

# Rondo

A Rondo is a musical form which develops the idea of contrast and repetition which we find in **Ternary Form** →. The Rondo opens with a lively tune (or 'subject'), and this returns several times during the course of the movement. Contrasting passages (called 'episodes') separate the various returns of the main tune. The main tune always returns in the same key. The episodes modulate to different keys. The form can therefore be described as an **A B A C A D A** form.

Movements of this kind are frequently found in the keyboard music of the 17th and 18th centuries, and as last movements in sonatas and symphonies by Haydn and Mozart. The last movements of solo concertos are also frequently in Rondo form. A development of Rondo form is the **Sonata-Rondo Form** →, which, as its name implies, combines features of both forms. Beethoven's rondo movements usually have this added complexity.

that its composer wrote that achieved any success, and the rest of his life was spent in comparative obscurity.

**Round** → **Canon**

**Round dance** (1) A dance in which those taking part move in a ring or, sometimes, (2) A dance in which the performers keep turning round.

**Roussel, Albert** French composer, 1869–1937. Though he showed a considerable talent for music, he trained first as a naval cadet and then served as an Officer in the French Navy until 1894. In 1896 he became a pupil of Vincent d'Indy at the newly founded Schola Cantorum in Paris.

Roussel began to attract attention as a composer around about the year 1900. He wrote music of all kinds, including the ballets *The Spider's Banquet* (1912) and *Bacchus and Ariadne* (1930), an opéra-bouffe *Le Testament de la Tante Caroline* (1933), and an opéra-ballet *Padmâvatî* (1918). He wrote four symphonies (1906, 1921, 1930, 1942), chamber music of all kinds, and many fine songs. His music is rather intricate and polyphonic, and somewhat influenced by Prokofiev and Stravinsky.

**Royal Albert Hall** → **Albert Hall**

**Royal Festival Hall** Opened in 1951 as part of the Festival of Britain. It seats 3,000 people. Two smaller halls, the Purcell Room and the Queen Elizabeth Hall, were later built alongside it.

**Royal Philharmonic Society** Founded in London in 1813 as a concert-giving society. Its concerts are open to the public, but 'membership' is restricted to the musical profession. Many famous musicians have

**Albert Roussel 1869-1937** A member of the Impressionist school, his style was influenced by his travels in the East.

**Royal Festival Hall** Built on the south bank of the Thames, it was scientifically designed for favourable acoustics.

conducted its concerts, including Mendelssohn, Wagner, and Elgar, and almost every great conductor of the day.

Since 1871 the Society has presented a Gold Medal nearly every year to some musician of distinction.

**Rubato** or **Tempo rubato** There are very few pieces of music that should be performed in a steady clockwork time that never varies. Nearly all pieces call for a little lingering or hastening here and there, slight pausing on a note or slight hurrying from it, and so on.

The composer cannot show this in his notation and, indeed, it is a part of the performer's personal expression, so that in a particular piece no two performers might linger or hasten in just the same places and just the same way. All that is what we call *rubato*. The word is Italian for 'robbed' and the idea is that of taking a little time from one note or passage and adding it to another note or passage.

Chopin's music is an example of music which calls for a good deal of *rubato*, and he himself used to play it in this way.

**Rubbra, Edmund** English composer b. 1901. His parents were very poor, so he had to work first as a railway clerk. His music, however, attracted the attention, and help, of the composer Cyril Scott and in 1919 he won a scholarship to Reading University. Here, and afterwards at the Royal College of Music, he was able to study composition with Holst.

Rubbra began to make his way as a composer in the 1930s. His first symphony appeared in 1936 and others have followed at regular intervals and he has now completed nine. He has also written much chamber music, including three fine string quartets, and a great deal of church music, including

# Rossini

Gioacchino Rossini. Italian composer, 1792–1868. He was born in Pesaro, where his father was Town Trumpeter and Inspector of Slaughter Houses. When Napoleon invaded Italy, Rossini's father was suspected of sympathizing with him and was promptly put in prison. His mother took him to Bologna and earned a living as an opera singer. By the time he was ten, however, the young Rossini was able to help his parents by playing and singing.

In 1806 he began to study at the Conservatory of Bologna and within four years had produced his first opera: *The Marriage Market* (1810). International success came in 1813, when he produced, among other things, an amusing opera buffa, The Italian Girl in Algiers (*L'Italiana in Algieri*), and a tragic opera, *Tancredi*.

For the next 16 years he wrote operas without ceasing – sometimes, as in 1812, 1816, 1817 and 1819, as many as four a year! Some were comic: The Barber of Seville (*Il Barbiere di Siviglia*) (1816), *Cenerentola* (Cinderella) (1817), *The Count Ory* (1828). Some were tragic: *Otello* (1816), *Semiramide* (1823). And one, his last opera, was in the new style of Grand Opera that was to sweep Europe in the 1830s: *William Tell* (1829). They were all, or nearly all, enormously successful, and Rossini soon became a very wealthy man.

But he also suffered greatly from ill-health and frequent bouts of depression, and in 1829, in spite of the success of *William Tell*, he decided to retire – nobody quite knows why. Perhaps it was because of sheer

*Above* **The Barber of Seville** Rolando Panerai as Figaro in this most popular of Rossini operas. The plot is that of Beaumarchais's French play *Le Barbier de Seville* (1775).
*Above right* **Cinderella** (La Cenerentola) This opera was first produced at Rome in 1817.

**Gioacchino Rossini**
1792-1868

exhaustion – for he had written over 40 operas. Perhaps it was because he felt that his music had become a little out of date – for it was, in spirit, very much of the 18th century.

He did not stop writing music altogether. He wrote a great many short piano pieces – some of them for his dog's birthday! And he wrote two fine religious works: the *Stabat Mater* (1832) and the *Petite Messe solennelle* (1863) – which is neither 'short' nor 'solemn'.

Rossini's music is lively and witty, beautifully orchestrated, and well thought out for the theatre. And it is, above all else, *tuneful*: full of the kind of tunes that singers love to sing, and audiences cannot help remembering. As a composer he was immensely popular and successful, and was admired even by musicians who were quite different from him in character and music – men such as Beethoven and Wagner. His music shows no signs of fading.

---

the *Missa Cantuariensis*.

In style, Rubbra's music is conservative. It is tonal and polyphonic and owes much to 16th-century counterpoint. He has toured extensively as pianist in the Rubbra-Gruenberg-Pleeth Trio, and has been a lecturer in music at Oxford University.

**Rubinstein, Anton** Russian pianist and composer, 1829–94. He first appeared in public when he was ten, and thereafter made successful tours as a pianist throughout Europe. He wrote an enormous amount of music, including 20 operas, six symphonies, and five piano concertos, besides ten string quartets, and many songs and piano pieces. The Symphony No 2 (the 'Ocean') is still sometimes heard, as is the opera *The Demon*

**Anton Rubinstein**
1829–1894 As a pianist he rivalled Liszt in fame and virtuosity.

(1875). He founded the St Petersburg Conservatory in 1862, teaching there 1862–67 and 1887–90.

**Ruggles, Carl** American composer, 1876–1971. After studying at Harvard, he settled in Vermont as a rather eccentric composer and painter. Like Charles Ives, he was a pioneer who insisted on writing music in his own way. His style was polyphonic, chromatic, and sometimes atonal. Important works include: *Angels* for muted brass (1921), *Portals*, for strings (1926), and *Evocations* for piano (1943), and four major orchestral pieces: *Men and Mountains* (1926), *Sun Treader* (1932), *Organum* (1945), and *Affirmations* (1957).

**Rule, Britannia** → **Arne, T.A.**

**Sadler's Wells** A London theatre in Rosebery Avenue, Islington. It began in 1683 as a Musick House and Pleasure Gardens, opened by a Mr Sadler who had discovered an ancient well which was supposed to cure every illness. The Musick House became a theatre in 1765. In 1931 it was taken over by Lilian Baylis as a home for the operatic and ballet side of her 'Old Vic' company. The Sadler's Wells Opera Company moved to the London Coliseum in 1968, and is now called the English National Opera.

**Saint-Saëns** → page 288

**Saite** (Ger.) String. **Saiteninstrumente** are stringed instruments.

**Salieri, Antonio** Italian composer, 1750–1825. He wrote operas for Milan, Venice, Rome, and Paris, but spent most of his successful career in Vienna. He was a friend of Haydn and Beethoven, but seems to have intrigued against Mozart, whom he thought of as a dangerous rival. There is no truth, however, in the rumour that Salieri actually poisoned Mozart!

**Salomon, Johann Peter** German musician, 1745–1815. He was a violinist and concert manager who settled in London in 1781. It was he who persuaded Haydn to visit England in 1790 and 1794, and to write the series of fine symphonies that we now call The London, or Salomon Symphonies (No 7 of the 12 is often called 'The London').He also suggested to Haydn the idea of writing the oratorio *The Creation*.

**Saltando** (It.) Leaping (also **saltato**). The

**Sansa** This example from Rhodesia is encased in a gourd resonator. This instrument is still in use in many parts of Africa today.

**Sarabande** Purcell, Handel and Bach, among others, have written music for this dignified dance.

refercnce is to the use of a springing bow in music for strings – the same as **Sautillé** →.

**Saltarello** A lively Italian folk dance, in 3/4 or 6/8 time. Usually performed by a pair of dancers, who move in circles with a quick, hopping step, while the music gets faster and faster.

**Salzburg Festival** The idea of festival performances of Mozart's works in the town where he was born (and which he rather disliked!), goes back to 1870. But the Festival as we know it today was founded in 1920 by the poet and dramatist Hugo von Hofmannsthal, the composer Richard Strauss, the producer Max Reinhardt, and the conductor Franz Schalk. The festival now takes place each summer, and though Mozart's music forms an important ingredient the works of other composers are included, as well as plays. It is recognized as one of the leading festivals in the world, and maintains the highest possible artistic standards.

**Sämtlich** (Ger.) Complete. As in **sämtliche Werke**, the 'complete works' of a composer: or **sämtliche Ausgabe**, a 'complete edition'.

**Sammartini, Giovanni Battista** Italian composer, 1698–1775. Most of his working life was spent in Milan, but he became famous throughout Europe as a composer of instrumental music. He is regarded as one of the pioneers of the symphony and string quartet.

**Sanctus** → **Mass**

**Sansa** A plucked instrument of African origin. It consists of a number of metal, or cane 'tongues', attached to a wooden board, or box. The tongues are of different lengths and give different notes when the free end is plucked. Sometimes called a 'thumb piano'.

**Sarabande** A graceful dance, dating from the 16th century and probably of Spanish origin. It was particularly popular as a court dance in the 17th century. It is usually slow (though in England a quick variety appeared) and in triple time. Like most dances of the period, it is usually in BINARY FORM. The sarabande was one of the four dances invariably found in instrumental dance suites.

**Sarangi** One of several types of Indian folk fiddles. It has three or four bowed strings, and a number of sympathetic strings that vibrate freely. It has a rather sturdy, oblong shape, and is found in the north of India.

# Saint-Saëns

Camille Saint-Saëns. French composer, 1835-1921. He received his first piano lessons from his mother and showed astonishing musical gifts at a very early age. He made his first public appearance in 1845, and began to study at the Paris Conservatoire in 1848. By this time he was an accomplished composer.

Though some of his early works were orchestral (such as the delightful First Symphony, 1853), Saint-Saëns was fascinated by the theatre. He wrote his first opera, *The Yellow Princess*, in 1872, and five years later produced his operatic masterpiece, *Samson et Dalila* (Samson and Delilah).

His career, both as a virtuoso pianist and composer was successful throughout. He wrote a vast amount of music, including 13 operas, three symphonies, five piano concertos, three violin concertos, two cello concertos, four important symphonic poems, and much choral and chamber music. His most popular piece has always been *Carnival of the Animals*. He was a very fluent composer, but did not always achieve a personal style.

**Camille Saint-Saëns**
1835–1921

*Right* **Samson and Delilah** This illustration shows a scene from the first Paris production of this opera in 1890.

**Sarasate, Pablo de** Spanish violinist, 1844–1908. He trained at the Paris Conservatoire, and won world fame as a skilful and artistic performer. He wrote music for his instrument, and many other composers (such as Saint-Saëns, Lalo, and Bruch) wrote works for him to play.

**Sargent,** (Sir) **Malcolm** English conductor, 1895–1967. He began his career as an organist, but came to the fore in the late 1920s as a conductor. He directed the Royal Choral Society, the Hallé Orchestra, the Liverpool Philharmonic Orchestra, the BBC Symphony Orchestra, and the Promenade Concerts. He was knighted in 1947 and was enormously popular with audiences wherever he went.

**Satie** → page 289

**Sauget, Henri** French composer, b. 1901. He was much influenced by Satie, and began to make a mark as a composer with a ballet, *La Chatte*, which he wrote in 1927 for Diaghilev. Since then he has written music of all kinds, including many film scores and incidental music for plays. His style is graceful and melodious. His masterpiece is

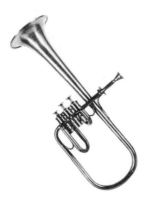

**Erik Satie** 1866-1925

**Saxhorn** This valved bugle was patented in 1845.

probably the opera *Les Caprices de Marianne* (1954).

**Satz** (Ger.) Movement, or piece of music. Also used for 'subject', 'theme', or 'phrase'.

**Sautillé** (Fr.) Jumped. Found in string music to indicate a type of *staccato* bowing in which the bow is made to bounce on the strings. (→ **Saltando**)

**Saw, musical** Any carpenter's saw that is flexible enough to be bent (i.e. not a tenon-saw) can be made to produce a musical note when bowed with a violin bow. The player holds the saw between his knees, bends it slightly, and bows the straight edge of the blade. As he alters the tension (by bending the saw more, or less), the note changes. The sound is rather like that of a wobbly human voice singing 'ah'.

**Saxhorn** and **Flügelhorn** Though invented by the same man, Adolphe Sax, the seven members of the SAXHORN FAMILY should not be confused with the SAXOPHONES. They are not reed instruments, as the saxophone is, but brass instruments working on the same principles as the trumpet. They are found mainly in brass and military bands, and the

# Satie

Erik Satie. French composer, 1866-1925. Of mixed French and Scottish ancestry, he went to the Paris Conservatoire in 1879 and his first compositions appeared in 1887.

Satie lived a rather eccentric life, composing very much in his own style and paying little attention to current fashions. He delighted in musical jokes and in undermining the 'romantic' attitude to music. His own work is full of unexpected and contradictory musical ingredients – plainsong, music-hall tunes, simple harmonies in unexpected combinations, etc. He worked in collaboration with Cocteau and Picasso and was much admired by Debussy and the younger French composers, such as Poulenc and Milhaud, as well as Stravinsky.

Though many people dismissed him as a mere charlatan, Satie's music has proved long-lasting and very influential. He helped very considerably in the general breakaway from 19th-century academic attitudes. His stage works include three important ballets: *Parade* (1916), *Mercure* (1924), and *Relâche* (1924); and his piano works include the *Trois Gymnopédies* (1888)

**Parade** This design by Picasso was for the curtain of Satie's ballet, first performed by the Ballets Russes in 1919. The score included sirens and typewriters and was described as a 'Cubist Manifesto'.

and the *Trois Gnossiennes* (1890), which give a very good idea of his subtle style. Two vocal works are also very important: the choral *Messe des pauvres* (1895), and *Socrate* (1918), a moving setting of Plato's account of the death of Socrates.

complete family consists of:
The E flat sopranino, the B flat soprano, the E flat alto (usually called the SAXHORN), the B flat baritone, the B flat bass (or EUPHONIUM), and the E flat and double B flat basses (or BOMBARDONS).

The FLÜGELHORN is a similar kind of instrument. It is shaped like a cornet, though its tone is similar to that of the saxhorns. In a brass band it plays with the ripiano cornet. In England only the B flat flügel is used, but elsewhere the small E flat soprano and the larger E flat alto members of the family are sometimes found. At least one jazz musician, Dizzy Gillespie, has made use of the flügelhorn.

## Saxophone family → page 290

**Scala, La** Milan's great opera house, the Teatro alla Scala, was completed in 1778 and rapidly came to be regarded as one of the most important operatic centres in the world. It was virtually destroyed by an air raid in the Second World War (16 August, 1943), but has since been rebuilt in exact imitation of the original. It was reopened in 1946. Most of the great Italian operatic composers, from Rossini, Bellini, and Donizetti to

**La Scala** It was originally designed by the architect Piermarini.

**Alessandro Scarlatti** 1660–1725 He composed over 100 operas, many of them now lost.

Verdi and Puccini, have seen their operas premiered at La Scala, and the world's greatest singers and conductors have thought it an honour to work there.

**Scales** → page 291

**Scarlatti, Alessandro** Italian composer, 1660–1725. Perhaps the most outstanding member of a very remarkable family of musicians. He became famous as an operatic composer, working mainly in his native city, Naples. His operas established the basic early 18th-century Italian style, and in particular settled the pattern of the **Da Capo aria**.
He also wrote many chamber cantatas, as well as examples of the early symphony.

**Scarlatti, Domenico** Italian composer, 1685–1757. The son of Alessandro. He also wrote operas, oratorios, and chamber cantatas, but is most famous for his harpsichord sonatas, of which there are some 555 in existence. These works, and his own playing, helped to lay the foundation of modern keyboard technique, and contributed greatly to the development of early Sonata Form. Much of his life was spent in Lisbon and Madrid.

# Saxophone family

The invention of a Belgian instrument maker, Adolphe Sax, in about 1840. It was much used in French army bands and then, about 75 years later, became an important ingredient in jazz bands.

There are 12 members of the sax family, but only the soprano B flat, the alto E flat, the tenor B flat, and the baritone E flat are used with any frequency. The large bass B flat and the small sopranino in F are sometimes called for. Saxophones can be played by clarinettists quite easily, for they produce their notes in the same way as the clarinet, with a reed in the mouthpiece. But they are made of metal, which helps them to produce their distinctive tone-colour.

Saxophones have been used successfully in orchestral symphonic works – such as Richard Strauss's *Domestic Symphony*, Vaughan Williams's *Job*, and Britten's *Sinfonia da Requiem*. ( → **Big band** )

**Saxophone family**
*Above* This jazz group play a range of saxophones: *left to right* contrabass, bass, tenor (2), alto (2), soprano (2). *Right* These four members are the soprano, **1**, the bass **2**, the sopranino **3**, and the contrabass, **4**.

**New and old** *Far left* The modern sax is played here by the jazz virtuoso, Coleman Hawkins. *Left* This engraving shows the instrument patented by Adolphe Sax in 1846.

**Scat song** A type of song that first became popular in America in the 1930s, in which the voices imitate the sound of instruments. Scat singing can be very effective when a well known piece of music, such as a Bach fugue, is treated in this way.

**Scraper** Instruments whose sound is produced by scraping a stick over a series of notches cut in a piece of wood or bone have been used all over the world for many thousands of years. Examples going back to the Stone Age have been discovered. Types in

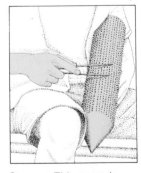

**Scraper** This example from Trinidad is used in folk bands.

use today include the Latin-American GUIRO (a large gourd with notches in the surface), the WASHBOARD ( → **Skiffle**), and the notched stick.

RATTLES, such as those used by excited British football fans are also a type of scraper.

**Scherzetto** (It.) A short scherzo.

**Scherzo** (It.) A cheerful, quick piece of music. The third movements of many sonatas, symphonies, and string quartets etc., are often scherzos. The word comes from the Italian and means 'joke' – hence the playful nature of most scherzo movements.

# Scales

If we take any simple passage of music and arrange its notes in the order of their pitch, the result will be a 'scale'. A scale is therefore a series of notes arranged in their correct ascending, or descending, order.

For example, here is the tune 'Auld Lang Syne':

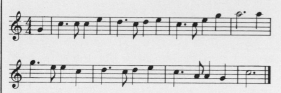

C is obviously the principal note, for it is the note to which the tune constantly returns, and on which it seems to be 'at rest'. The scale of this tune is therefore:

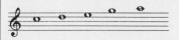

This is a five-note (PENTATONIC) scale. Many simple folk tunes are constructed from Pentatonic scales.

Most Western music, however, prefers a seven-note scale. And for the past three hundred years two main forms of scale have been used: the Major Scale, and the Minor Scale.

The MAJOR SCALE is quite straightforward: it arranges its notes in a strict pattern of tones and semitones (large steps and small steps):

But the minor scale exists in two forms: the HARMONIC and the MELODIC.

The HARMONIC MINOR SCALE is so called because it contains the notes that are likely to be used in making up chords. Besides the large and small steps of the major scale, it also has an even larger step (of *three* semitones) between the sixth and seventh degrees:

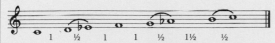

It is to avoid this awkward step that the MELODIC MINOR SCALE came into existence. There are two forms: an upward version, which gets rid of the large step by changing the previous step (between the fifth and sixth degrees):

and a downward version, which makes an adjustment to the octave and seventh degrees:

Either way the awkward gap is avoided, and the scale presents its sequence of notes in a form that is useful for writing melodies.

The third and final form of scale is that which contains all the twelve notes commonly used in Western music. It is called the CHROMATIC SCALE.

There are two ways of writing a Chromatic scale. The first economizes on accidentals and adds sharps when going up, and flats when going down:

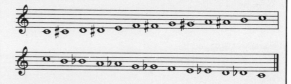

A chromatic scale written in this way is said to be in 'melodic' notation.

The second form of chromatic scale arranges its notes in 'harmonic' notation, mixing sharps, flats, and naturals in the way that they are likely to occur in chords. Both upward and downward forms are the same:

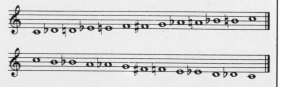

There are, of course, many other ways of forming a scale. Separate articles will be found on: **Microtones**, **Modes**, and **Whole-tone**.

# Schoenberg

Arnold Schoenberg  Austrian composer, 1874–1951. He was born in Vienna, and though he received lessons in violin playing at school, he was self-taught as a composer.

At first, as his father died leaving little or no money, he worked as a bank clerk. But spurred on by a great love for Wagner, Brahms, and Mahler, he continued to compose, eventually so impressing Alexander von Zemlinsky that he agreed to give him lessons. In due course (1897) his First String Quartet was successfully performed. There was little in it to suggest the way he was about to develop.

The first real indication of his originality came in 1899, when he startled the Viennese public with an elaborate string sextet, *Verklärte Nacht*. It was really a symphonic poem (and was later orchestrated), and its musical style began when Wagner left off – in other words, it was extremely chromatic and highly emotional.

The next important works, the *Gurrelieder* for solo, chorus and orchestra (eventually performed in 1913), and the symphonic poem *Pelléas und Mélisande* (1902), confirmed this path of development.

Schoenberg was by now married to Zemlinsky's daughter, and was forced to support himself by doing musical hackwork and teaching. Among his pupils, however, were two young men who were to share his vision of how music should develop: Alban Berg and Anton Webern.

His own music had by now become so dissonant and chromatic that he was forced to recognize that he was no longer using the old 'rules' of harmony and composition. Little by little he was discovering a new kind of music that used all 12 notes of the chromatic scale quite freely and thus admitted entirely new kinds of harmony. Such works as the *First Chamber Symphony*

**Arnold Schoenberg 1874-1951** This self-portrait of the composer is stylistically indebted to the Expressionist painter, Wassily Kandinsky.

**Moses and Aaron** This scene is from a production at the Royal Opera House, Covent Garden. This unfinished opera was first performed in 1957 in Zurich.

(1906), the *Five Orchestral Pieces* (1909), and *Erwartung* (1909) – a kind of opera – were all stepping stones along the path of this gradual development.

By 1923 he had virtually thought out an explanation for what he was doing. His type of composition was, he declared, 'composition with 12 notes related only to one another'. In other words, he had made the revolutionary step of discarding tonality altogether.  In exploring the possibilities of this new type of music he was joined by Berg and Webern, each using the same technique but composing music that expressed their own very different personalities.

Despite his growing fame, Schoenberg was dismissed (as a Jew) from his teaching post at the Berlin Academy of Fine Arts (1924–33) and decided to leave Nazi-dominated Germany. He sailed for America, and eventually settled as Professor of Composition at the University of Southern California (1934–44).

He spent the rest of his life in America – composing, though not always in the 12-note style, writing about musical theory, and teaching. His fame gradually grew, and he came to be regarded as one of the most important composers of the 20th century.

Besides the works already mentioned his music includes an important unfinished (though performable) opera, *Moses and Aaron* (1930), an unfinished (though performable) oratorio, *Jacob's Ladder* (1913), and many fine chamber works, such as *Pierrot Lunaire* (1912) and the four string quartets. Since his death, his method of composition has been widely accepted by many different kinds of composers. And his music, once regarded as wildly revolutionary, now seems but a logical continuation of a great tradition.

**Schmidt, Franz**  Austrian composer, 1874–1939. A late romantic composer who wrote two operas (the first, *Nôtre-Dame* (1914) was very successful), a powerful oratorio, *The Book of Seven Seals* (1937), and four symphonies. His music is not much heard outside Austria and Germany.

**Schnell** (Ger.)  Quick.

**Schottische**  A dance somewhat similar to the polka which was very popular in the 19th century. It has nothing to do with Scotland, but is, rather, a continental idea of what a Scottish dance might be. It is in 2/4 time and very lively. (→ **Écossaise**)

**Schrammel quartet**  A type of Viennese popular music scored for some such combination as two violins, accordion, and guitar. Named after Joseph Schrammel (1850–93), who led such a quartet and wrote music for it.

**Schreker, Franz** Austrian composer, 1878–1934. A leading member of the 'expressionist' school of composition. His highly romantic style is best seen in his nine operas, of which the second, *Der ferne Klang* (The Distant Sound) (1912), was the most successful. He fell foul of the Nazi Party and died in complete isolation and disgrace.

**Schubert** → page 294

**Schuman, William** American composer, b. 1910. He was educated at Columbia University and at the Mozarteum in Salzburg. In 1945 he became President of the Juilliard School of Music. He has written music of all kinds, including eight symphonies, a piano concerto (1942), a violin concerto (1947), several ballets (*Undertow*, 1945; *Night Journey*, 1947; *Judith*, 1950), and a 'baseball' opera: *The Mighty Casey* (1953).

**Schumann** → page 296

**Schumann, Clara** German pianist and composer, 1819–96. One of the most remarkable women pianists of the 19th century. As Clara Wieck she made here concert debut when she was nine and published her first composition when she was 12. After her husband Robert Schumann's tragic death she courageously and successfully resumed her career as a concert pianist. She was a brilliant and influential teacher. Her personality inspired music by both Schumann and Brahms.

**Schütz, Heinrich** German composer, 1585–1672. He studied in Germany, and with Giovanni Gabrieli in Venice (1609–12), where he published a book of madrigals (1611). He returned to Germany in 1613 and, for a while, studied law, but soon devoted himself wholeheartedly to a career in music.

For most of his life Schütz worked for the Court of Dresden, though he seems to have been given leave to visit Copenhagen and Hanover from time to time. He also returned to Italy in 1628.

His importance lay in his ability to combine the serious, polyphonic spirit of German music with the brilliance and drama of the new Italian style of music that began to emerge around 1600. He wrote many madrigals and motets, as well as important early settings of the Passion. His three sets of *Symphoniae sacrae* (settings of Latin texts, for voices and instruments) are also very important.

Schütz was one of the greatest composers of

**Clara Schumann**
1819–1896 One of the most accomplished pianists of her time, she was largely responsible for spreading her husband's reputation as a composer.

**Heinrich Schütz**
1585–1672 Many of his works, particularly his settings of the Passion, anticipate Bach. He also composed the earliest German opera, *Dafne* (1627) which has been lost.

his day, and he laid the foundations that were to support German music from Bach onwards.

**Scordatura** (It.) 'Out-of-tuning'. Used to describe any abnormal way of tuning a stringed instrument – as, for example, lowering the tuning of the lowest string in order to get an extra lower note.

**Score** → page 298

**Scoring** To write music out in full, in all its parts. Orchestration is sometimes called 'scoring', especially when the orchestrator is arranging someone else's music for the orchestra.

**Scotch snap** Many Scottish tunes have a rhythmic peculiarity which consists of a jump from a short note (on the beat) to a longer note (off the beat). As, for example:

COMIN' THRO THE RYE

**Scott, Cyril** English composer, 1879–1970. He was born in Liverpool and studied mainly at Frankfurt. He was an excellent pianist, and many of his shorter piano pieces became very popular. He wrote a great deal of music of all kinds, including a piano concerto (1914), several operas (*The Alchemist* was produced in Essen in 1925), chamber and choral music. His style was somewhat rhapsodic and impressionistic, and he had a great love of rich harmony. In his later years he wrote books on mysticism, philosophy, and natural medicine, as well as two volumes of autobiography.

**Scroll** (of a violin, etc.) That part of the end of the peg-box which is carved into a curl.

**Segno** (It.) Sign. As in **al segno, dal segno**, 'to the sign', 'from the sign'. (:𝄋:)

**Segue** (It.) Follows. A direction sometimes found at the end of a piece, indicating that the next piece must follow immediately (almost without a break).

**Seguidilla** A very old Spanish national dance. It is quick and has three beats in the bar. The performers sing as they dance. A later type of seguidilla is rather more stately and danced to a slower speed.

**Semi** (It.) Half. As in **semibreve, semiquaver, demisemiquaver**. ( → **Notes and notation** )

# Schubert

Franz Peter Schubert. Born in Vienna in 1797 and died there in 1828, aged 31 years.

## 1. Schubert's Life

Like so many great composers, Schubert was born into a very musical family. His father was a schoolmaster, and though he was poor music played a very important part in his life. He taught his young son to play the violin, and then handed him over to an elder brother for piano lessons. Family and friends made a habit of playing together – first as a quartet, and later as a small orchestra. Schubert therefore grew up surrounded by music.

When he was nine he began to study harmony and counterpoint with a local organist, Michael Holzer; and two years later was accepted as a chorister in the Court Chapel of Vienna. It meant that he would now be a scholar of the Imperial and Royal Seminary.

His new school ran an orchestra, and Schubert was not only able to play in it, but was also allowed to conduct it and to write music especially for it to play. It was a perfect way of learning how to be a composer.

By 1811, Schubert had already written a great deal of music – though most of this is now lost. And during the next few years it began to pour out of him. He studied for a time with Salieri, but really he did not need teaching – he seemed to compose naturally and spontaneously.

Schubert's school days came to an end in

**Franz Schubert** 1797 – 1828 He is regarded as the founder of 19th- century German *lied*, and is known to have composed eight in one day. He set the poems of Goethe and Schiller and of other minor poets to music. Schubert's music has a very special quality that can best be described as 'friendliness'. It sounds is if it were written for his friends, rather than for a 'public' in the ordinary sense. For this reason it is very easy to like Schubert – though just as easy to overlook the fact that he was also a very profound composer.

1813. His mother had died in the previous year, and though he longed to devote himself solely to composition he felt obliged to train as a teacher and so help his father. In 1814 he became an assistant at his father's school. Even so, the amount of music he was able to write was remarkable. One song *Gretchen at the Spinning Wheel*, a setting of words from Goethe's *Faust*, is a masterpiece. At 17 Schubert could be considered a mature and original composer.

He remained at his father's school until the spring of 1816. He then applied for a better post, but failed to get it. From this point onwards he never had a regular job. Instead, he earned money where and when he could, and when that failed fell back on the support of a circle of friends who loved him and his music. Between them they managed to see that he had a roof over his head and enough to eat. His own attitude to money was totally happy-go-lucky. All he wanted to do was write music.

From 1821 his works gradually began to appear in print. First they were paid for by private subscription, and then (after 1822) by regular publishers. He was famous in Viennese musical circles and beginning to make a mark on the musical world outside. But in 1828 he caught typhus and, after a few days' illness, died. He was buried in a grave near to Beethoven, whose coffin he had followed only 18 months before. Within a year or so, his name was famous.

**Schubert-Evening** or **Schubertiad** The composer enjoyed these gatherings where he could play his latest works to his friends, who were artists, poets and wealthy bourgeoisie. One of his greatest admirers was his brother, Ferdinand, a minor composer in his own right, who was a firm and loyal supporter.

2. **Summary of Schubert's main works**

a. Operas include:

| | |
|---|---|
| *Alfonso and Estrella* | 1822 |
| *Fierrabras* | 1823 |

b. Choral music includes:

| | |
|---|---|
| Mass in A flat | 1822 |
| Mass in E flat | 1828 |

and many short choral songs with piano accompaniment.

c. Symphonies:

10 in all, but one is lost and two are incomplete. The most important are:

| | |
|---|---|
| No 4 in C minor – the 'Tragic' | 1816 |
| No 5 in B flat major | 1816 |
| No 6 in C major | 1818 |
| No 8 in B minor – the 'Unfinished' | 1822 |
| No 9 in C major – the 'Great C major' | 1828 |

d. Chamber music includes:

| | |
|---|---|
| Piano Quintet in A major – the 'Trout' | 1819 |
| Piano Quartet in D minor – 'Death and the Maiden' | 1824 |
| Octet in F major | 1824 |
| String Quintet in C major | 1828 |

He also wrote 15 string quartets, 14 piano sonatas, and sets of dances and variations for piano, as well as the remarkable 'Wanderer' Fantasy 1822.

e. Songs:

Schubert wrote over 600 songs (sometimes as many as 15 in two days!). They include the two cycles:

| | |
|---|---|
| *Die Schöne Müllerin* | 1823 |
| *Die Winterreise* | 1828 |

3. **The man**

Schubert's music is remarkable not only for its quantity, but for its unfailing inventiveness. He is one of the most prolific composers of melodies there has ever been.

At the heart of Schubert's music are, of course, the songs. They are unlike anything that had been written before. They range from simple tunes, almost like folksongs, with simple accompaniments – *Heidenröslein* (Rose among the heather) is an example – to complex dramatic 'scenes' that are almost like miniature operas – for example, 'The Erl king' (*Der Erlkönig*).

**Semitone** The half-tone or half-step is the smallest interval used in most Western music. The octave can be divided into twelve semitones – as it is on the ordinary keyboard.

**Semplice** (It.) Simple.

**Sempre** (It.) Always. As in **sempre legato**, meaning that a passage is to be played smoothly throughout.

**Sentence** → **Phrase and sentence**

**Senza** (It.) Without. As in the direction found in string music, **senza sordino** 'without mute'.

**Septet** Any group of seven performers, or any piece of music written for such a group. Beethoven's *Septet* (1800) is written for two violins, viola, cello, clarinet, bassoon, and horn.

**Septimole, Septolet, Septuplet** ( → **Notes and notation** )

**Sequence** The repetition of a short passage of music at another pitch. In the following hymn, the soprano and bass parts are repeated three times – 'sequentially':

From the hymn-tune: 'Carlisle'

There are two kinds of sequence: REAL and TONAL. The example given above is a TONAL sequence, because the repetitions are not absolutely exact, semitone for semitone.

In a REAL sequence the repetitions are exact – but this, of course, causes the music to modulate. For example:

Sequences can go up or down. Sequences which go up are sometimes called ROSALIAS – after an old Italian popular song 'Rosalia, mia cara', which began in this way.

# Schumann

Robert Alexander Schumann. Born at Zwickau, in Saxony, in 1810 and died near Bonn in 1856, aged 46 years.

## 1. Schumann's life

Throughout his life Robert Schumann was almost as interested in literature as he was in music. He was brought up among books, in fact; for his father was a bookseller and publisher. At 14 he contributed to one of his father's publications, *The Most Famous Men of all Countries and Periods*: at 17 he was writing poems. But music was his real passion, and he seems to have decided to make it his career at a very early age.

But the way was not smooth. Although he had begun to learn the piano when he was seven, and begun to compose shortly after that, his parents were not convinced that music would provide a safe and solid career. Matters were made worse when his father died in 1826. His mother now felt even more unwilling to take risks.

Accordingly, in 1828, Robert Schumann enrolled at the University of Leipzig – as a law student.

He was not a very keen one. Within weeks of arriving at Leipzig he had sought out the best piano teacher and was devoting his time to constant practice. His teacher's name was Friedrich Wieck, and he had a daughter, Clara, who was nine years old and already a very promising pianist.

This state of affairs continued until 1830. In 1829 he spent a year at the University of Heidelberg – simply because the Professor of Law there was also a fine musician! But by 1830 even his mother had to admit that music had won the day.

Schumann returned to Leipzig to study with Wieck, and live with him as part of the family. At the same time he took lessons in composition from a local conductor, Heinrich Dorn, wrote a great deal of music, and began work on a novel.

He expected to make a career as a concert pianist, but in 1833 he injured his hand when experimenting with a mechanical device that was supposed to strengthen the fingers. It became obvious that he would never now become a virtuoso performer, and so he began to concentrate wholly upon composition.

It was during this period that he realized that he had fallen in love with his teacher's daughter, and that she, Clara, loved him.

**Robert Schumann** 1810-1856 The son of a bookseller and publisher, Schumann retained an interest in literature throughout his life and in 1834 founded a music magazine, the *Neue Zeitschrift für Musik*. He edited it and wrote articles about the music and musicians he admired and the magazine soon became very influential.

Her father was furious. He had planned a career as a concert pianist for her, and not marriage to a penniless composer. The battle between them took many years to settle, and involved several very unpleasant court proceedings. It was not until 1840 that the two were allowed to marry.

Their life together was extremely happy. Moreover, even before marriage Schumann's love for Clara had a remarkable effect on his music. Songs and piano pieces poured out of him and his career prospered.

Shadows began to appear in 1844. He

*Below* Title page of Schumann's **Album for the Young.**

*Below left* **Schumann in 1850** By this time his melancholic fits occurred frequently, and he was often too ill to work. Then, in February 1854, he began to hear imaginary voices, sometimes singing sweet music, sometimes threatening his life. At last he tried to throw himself into the Rhine, but was rescued in time. After this he was sent to an asylum where he died.

had already been subject to sudden fits of depression, but now they became worse. For the next ten years his condition wavered. After a suicide attempt, there was nothing for it but that he should go into an asylum. Two years later he was dead.

## 2. Summary of Schumann's main works

a. Opera:

| | |
|---|---|
| *Genoveva* | 1850 |

b. Choral music includes:

| | |
|---|---|
| *Paradise and the Peri* | 1841 |
| *The Rose Pilgrimage* | 1851 |
| *Scenes from Goethe's Faust* | 1853 |

c. Symphonies:

| | | |
|---|---|---|
| No 1 in B flat – the 'Spring' | | 1841 |
| No 2 in C major | | 1846 |
| No 3 in E flat – the 'Rhenish' | | 1850 |
| No 4 in D minor | | 1851 |
| | originally No 2 | 1841 |

d. Concertos:

| | |
|---|---|
| Piano Concerto in A minor | 1841–45 |
| Cello Concerto in A | 1850 |

e. Chamber music includes:

| | |
|---|---|
| Piano Quartet | 1842 |
| Piano Quintet | 1842 |
| Piano Trio, No 1 in D minor | 1847 |
| Piano Trio, No 2 in F major | 1847 |
| Piano Trio, No 3 in G minor | 1851 |

f. Piano music includes:

| | |
|---|---|
| *Papillons* | 1832 |
| *Davidsbündlertänze* | 1837 |
| *Carnaval* | 1835 |
| *Kinderscenen* (Scenes of Childhood) | 1838 |
| *Faschingsschwank aus Wien* | 1839 |

Songs:

Schumann wrote more than 250 songs, including two very important cycles:

| | |
|---|---|
| *Frauenliebe und -leben* | 1840 |
| *Dichterliebe* | 1840 |

## 3. The man

Schumann was very much a Romantic. More often than not his music was inspired by poetic, descriptive ideas. Much of it was also very autobiographical, reflecting his love for Clara and the strange, rather fanciful way his own mind worked. It is therefore not surprising that his finest music is to be found in his songs and piano pieces – for these were the works in which he could express himself intimately and directly.

**Serenade** This medieval woodcut shows a troubadour, accompanied by his page, serenading his lady love beneath her castle window.

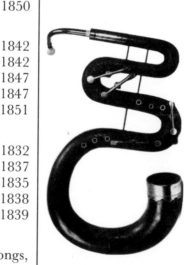

**Serpent** On first hearing this instrument Handel is reputed to have said, 'Vell, *dat* is not the serpent dat tempted Eve.' He used it, however, in his *Fireworks Music*.

**Serenade** A piece of music intended for performance in the open air at nightfall (*sera* (It.), means 'evening'). Despite the romantic picture of a young man 'serenading' his lady, the term is more generally used for instrumental works of the **Divertimento** → kind.

**Serenata** Though the term is used as an alternative for *Serenade*, the serenata was originally either a short vocal **Cantata** →, or an instrumental **Suite** → which always had a march and a minuet as two of its movements. The serenata in both its forms was popular in the first half of the 18th century.

**Serialism** The method of composition explored and established by Arnold Schoenberg during the first part of the 20th century. He decided to treat each of the 12 semitones available to Western music in such a way that none would be more prominent than any other. Thus he would avoid any suspicion of tonality.

For each work, a chosen *row* or *series* presents the 12 semitones in a certain order. No note is repeated within the series, and the first note may not reappear until the twelfth has been heard.

This is the method in its simplest form. There are, however, a variety of ways in which the *series* can be used – transposed, inverted, reversed, etc.

Later composers (from 1950 onwards) have explored the possibility of TOTAL SERIALISM. They have placed rhythms, dynamics, timbre, and texture in *series* form, so that no effect or quality is repeated until the basic set has been used.

**Serpent** An obsolete bass woodwind instrument, shaped like an S – hence its name. It was invented in the 16th century and used by small church orchestras and military bands. It was displaced by the tuba.

**Sessions, Roger** American composer, b. 1896. He wrote an opera when he was 12, entered Harvard University when he was 14, graduated, and then studied composition at Yale University under Horatio Parker. He also studied privately with Ernest Bloch. After travellling widely in Europe he returned to America to teach in various universities, including Princeton and Berkeley, California. His music has developed over the years from a traditional diatonic style to a free kind of serialism. He has written music of all kinds, including eight symphonies, as well as a number of important books about musical theory.

# Score

Music printed in such a way as to show the whole of the composition. For example, an Orchestral Score shows the conductor exactly what each instrument is to play. The following are the main types of score to be met with:

1. a **full score** – shows all the instrumental and vocal parts of a composition. It is usually printed on large paper, for easy reading.

2. a **miniature score** – shows everything that a full score shows, but is printed in a miniature form (usually 14 × 19 cms). A slightly larger version of the miniature score is known as a STUDY SCORE. Both are intended for studying a work at home.

3. a **vocal score** – shows the music of a choral work, an opera, or an oratorio, reduced to an arrangement for piano and voices. It is intended for singers to learn their parts and rehearse from.

4. a **piano score** – is a reduction of an orchestral work to an arrangement for piano. Sometimes arrangements are issued for piano duet.

5. a **short score** – is a reduction to two staves of anything that might normally be written on more staves. For example, the four parts of a hymn-tune are usually printed on two staves. Composers often sketch their works in 'short score' form.

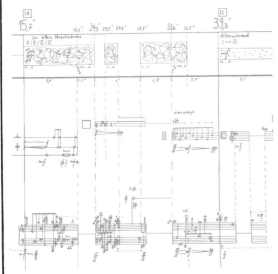

**Stockhausen score** This score for *Kontakte* (1959-60) combines conventional musical notation for percussion and piano with a diagram for electronic sounds.

**The Orchestral full score** (Key)

**1** Title of the work, and the composer's dedication.

**2** Number and title of the individual movement. In this case the title is borrowed from the movement's basic speed 'allegro'. Other movements may be called after their form (*Rondo*, say), or their mood (as in *Scherzo*), or their function in the whole work (*Epilogue*, for example).

**3** The speed at which the music is to be played. This may or may not have a metronome mark to fix it exactly.

**4** Indications of any temporary change in the speed or manner of playing. In this case the first half bar is to be played in a broader manner (*allargando*), but the second half is to be played at the true basic speed (*allegro*).

**5** The direction *a2* shows that both instruments of a pair should play the same line. If only one instrument is needed it is shown as I or II. Compare the directions in the trumpet parts (7).

**6** The Woodwind Family. The Tenor Saxophone is an unusual addition to the normal symphony orchestra.

**7** As in (5), these figures indicate which instrument in a group is to play which line. This is really only necessary when either one instrument of a pair is to remain silent, or when there are more than two instruments to a line. For example, in the bassoon part it is quite clear that each instrument must take one note (since the bassoon cannot play double stopping). Compare this with (12).

**8** The Brass Family.

**9** Besides the normal treble and bass clefs, tenor and alto clefs are also used. Tenor clefs frequently appear in trombone parts; and sometimes in the bassoon and cello parts, when they rise particularly high, as in the first bar and a half of the cellos. Generally speaking, bassoons and cellos remain in the bass clef.

Alto clefs are used by the violas – though in this instance the first bar and a half is placed in the treble clef, to avoid unnecessary leger lines.

**10** The Percussion Family.

**10a** The timpani occupy one line. The figures in brackets indicate the tuning required at this point. Changes are shown as the work proceeds.

**10b** The remaining percussion instruments (as shown in the brackets) occupy one or more lines, according to how many are playing at one and the same time. The xylophone will need a stave to itself, as it is a tuned instrument.

**11** The String Family. *Note:* with the exception of the brass, where, for historical reasons, the horns appear above the trumpets, all these families are arranged in descending order of pitch.

**12** 'Non div.' instructs the players not to divide the two notes between different instruments, but to play them as double stopping (see [7]).

**13** Notice of the date of publication, the name of the publisher, and the important fact that the work is Copyright.

**14** Transposing instruments. Most of these have key signatures that are different from the key of the movement. However, Double Basses and Piccolo keep the key signature of the movement because their transposition is exactly one octave below and above their written notes.

Instruments in B flat (Clarinets, Tenor Sax, Trumpets, in this case) have a key signature that is one tone higher than the key of the movement (A major, instead of G major).

Horns traditionally have no key signature at all. Their music is written a fifth higher (with appropriate accidentals) than it sounds. On the other hand, the Cor Anglais, whose notes are also written a fifth above their actual sound, is given a key signature five notes higher than the key of the piece (D major, instead of G major).

**15** Dynamic markings for each line of instruments go beneath the line in question. Although Vaughan Williams wants each line to play *ff*, you will commonly find that different lines have different markings at one and the same time. For example, the brass may be required to play *pp* as they accompany a tune on the flutes played *mf*. The composer has to take the comparative weight of instrumental sound into account.

**16** In modern scores, bars that are completely empty are usually printed without rests. Bars that are only partly filled with notes are given whatever rests are needed to complete them.

**17** A shorthand way of indicating a rapid reiteration of a single note – each minim is to be played as sixteen demisemiquavers.

**18** Changes in dynamics, in this case a *diminuendo*, go beneath the line of music so affected.

**19** Slurs indicate bowing and phrasing marks. These, together with special accents and marks showing different styles of playing (e.g. *staccato* marks) are placed as near to the note heads as possible.

**20** On later pages of an orchestral score you will find numbers printed at the beginning of a bar, usually above the woodwind, brass, and string sections. These numbers are large, and in bold type, and sometimes have a box or circle around them. They are rehearsal numbers. They appear also in the individual orchestral parts, so that the conductor can use them as references when he wants to go over a particular passage again. Letters of the alphabet are also used for this purpose.

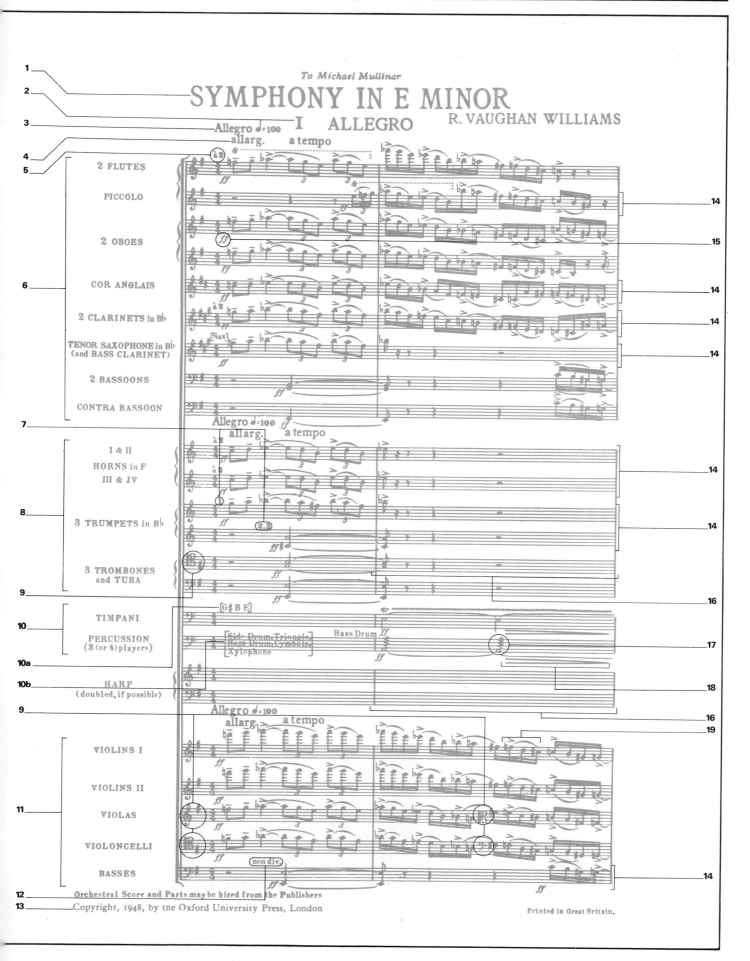

# SYMPHONY IN E MINOR

*To Michael Mullinar*

## I  ALLEGRO

R. VAUGHAN WILLIAMS

Orchestral Score and Parts may be hired from the Publishers

Copyright, 1948, by the Oxford University Press, London

Printed in Great Britain.

**Seven Last Words** The seven last utterances of Christ, as reported by the gospel accounts of the crucifixion. Haydn wrote a set of seven slow movements (1785) to be performed in the cathedral of Cadiz when the 'Words' were read from the pulpit during Lent. Schütz and Gounod, among others, have also made settings of these words.

**Seventh** → **Intervals; Harmony**

**Sevillana** A Spanish folk dance from Seville, similar to the **Seguidilla** →.

**Sextet** Any group of six performers, or a piece of music written for such a group. A STRING SEXTET usually consists of two violins, two violas, and two cellos, but other combinations are possible.

**Sextolet, Sextuplet** → **Notes and notation**

**Sforzando** (It.) Forcing. A note or chord so marked must be given a strong accent. The abbreviation **sfz** is common.

**Shake** → **Ornaments and grace-notes**

**Shakers** A religious sect founded in America in the 18th century by Ann Lee (1736–84), an English-born Quaker. Part of their worship centred around religious dances. Some of their music is particularly beautiful – for example, the hymn 'Simple gifts'.

**Shamisen** (**samisen**) The Japanese long-necked lute. It has a square wooden body, with a belly and bottom made of catskin. It has three strings, plucked with a rather large plectrum, which is used with considerable force. The neck has no frets, unlike the European lute. Shamisens are made in various sizes, and are used mainly to accompany singers.

**Shanai** The Indian folk shawm. Like the oboe it has a double reed. (→ **Shawm**)

**Shanty** A sailor's 'working song', used during the days of sailing ships. It was sung mainly by a Shanty Man, with the other workers joining in the chorus as they pulled together on the ropes, or pushed the capstan round. In this way they were able to keep time together and make their greatest effort at exactly the same moment. Different tasks had different shanties – Halliard Shanties, Capstan Shanties, Short-haul Shanties, etc., all musically shaped to fit the job in hand.

**Shamisen** This Japanese lute bears no relation to the percussion instrument of the same but incorrect name used by Puccini in *Madam Butterfly*.

**Sheng** This ancient Chinese instrument was introduced into Europe in the late 18th century and inspired the creation of the harmonica.

Shanties were never sung aboard Royal Navy ships. They belong to the Merchant Navy and are the folksongs of the sea.

**Sharp, Flat** → **Notes and notation**

**Sharp, Cecil** English folksong collector, 1859–1924. He studied music at Cambridge University, and after working in Australia he became a teacher in London. He began noting down folksongs in 1903, and then devoted his life to their collection and study. He also collected folk dances, and founded the English Folksong and Dance Society (1911).

Sharp's work, together with that of other musicians, such as George Butterworth, Ralph Vaughan Williams, and Sir Richard Terry, helped to preserve English folksong at a time when it was in danger of dying out because of the spread of industrialization. He also collected material in America, in the remote places of the Appalachian Mountains.

**Shawm** → page 301

**Sheng** The Chinese mouth-organ, dating back at least three thousand years. It consists of a wooden windchest, in the top of which a series of bamboo pipes is inserted. Each pipe is of different length and has a finger hole which must be covered if it is to sound. Each pipe also has a brass reed fixed over a small slit towards the bottom of the pipe. This vibrates and causes the air inside the pipes to vibrate in sympathy (if the hole is covered) and thus make their sound. The player blows into the windchest through a hole in the side.

**Shield, William** English composer, 1748–1829. He was apprenticed to a boat-builder, but studied music in his spare time and eventually became a professional violin and viola player. After working in various London theatres he began writing ballad operas, the most famous of which is *Rosina* (1782). In 1817 he was appointed Master of the King's Music.

**Shofar** The ancient Jewish wind instrument, made from a ram's horn. It can make only two notes (a fifth apart) and they are very harsh. It is used to signal the arrival of the New Year in Jewish religious ceremonies.

**Short score** → **Score**

**Shostakovich** → page 301

**Sibelius** → page 302

# Shawm

The shawm is the most important early double-reed instrument. It appeared in Europe in the 13th century, developed out of the folk shawms of the middle East.

The medieval shawm produced a loud, buzzing kind of sound and was best suited to music out of doors. It was made in several different sizes.

*Above* **Shawm family** The Bass Pommer (top) was often made of brass in the early 17th century.
*Below left* the mouthpiece of a Shawm.

*Above* **Renaissance shawm**
*Left* **Egyptian shawm** Still popular in Islamic countries, the instrument was initially used to provide a melodic element in military bands.
*Right* **Tibetan shawms** Although rare in Europe except for parts of Spain, Greece and Italy, the shawm can still be found in many parts of the world.

By the 16th century the shawm family had developed considerably. Not only were there many different sizes and types, but their tone had been somewhat refined (though it never became as smooth as the oboe, the nearest modern equivalent), and was now suited for indoor music. The three most common sizes of renaissance shawm were: TREBLE, ALTO, and TENOR. The BASS SHAWM was less common, and the GREAT BASS (or POMMER) quite rare.

Other types of shawm include the **Curtall** →, the **Crumhorn** →, and the **Rackett** →

# Shostakovich

Dmitry Shostakovich. Russian composer, 1906–75. He was born in St Petersburg (now Leningrad) and studied at the Conservatory (1919–25) under Glazunov. His First Symphony was performed in 1926 with great success, and he was regarded as an important composer.

His career developed smoothly and successfully over the next few years, and he was much admired as a composer and as a pianist. In 1936, however, his second opera *The Lady Macbeth of Mtsensk*, which had been produced in Leningrad in 1934 with great success, was suddenly denounced by the Soviet authorities as 'bourgeois, formalistic, unhealthy, and unintelligible to the people'. Shostakovich was deeply shocked.

In spite of this, his career prospered and he came to be looked upon as the most important Soviet composer of his generation. A sign of how closely he identified himself with his country came during the Second World War in the siege of Leningrad. He stayed behind in the

**Dmitry Shostakovich** 1906-1975. The leading Soviet composer of his day, he attempted in all his work to reconcile his artistic beliefs with official Soviet views. His last years, however, were spent untroubled by party-political interference and his fame was accepted throughout the world. His music, however, tended to become more pessimistic and disturbing. Shostakovich's son, Maxim, is also a pianist, composer and conductor.

beleagured city and, with the guns thundering in his ears, wrote his Seventh Symphony (the 'Leningrad'). It was performed in triumph in 1941.

In 1943 Shostakovich became a professor at the Moscow Conservatory. Five years later (1948) he was again rebuked by the Soviet authorities for writing music that was not sufficiently representative of communist ideals. But he weathered this second storm and in 1954 was named 'People's Artist of the USSR'.

In 1958 a change in Soviet thinking lifted the ban on his *Lady Macbeth* opera, which he later revised under the title *Katerina Izmalova* (1962).

Shostakovich wrote an immense amount of music of all kinds, including concertos, choral works, songs, piano music, film scores, and ballets. His greatest achievements were undoubtedly his 15 symphonies (written between 1926 and 1971), and 15 string quartets. These belong to the great classical tradition and prove him to be an outstanding composer.

# Sibelius

Jean Sibelius. Finnish composer, 1865-1957. He began to take a serious interest in music when he was 15 and soon became a very good violinist. He also tried his hand at composition. In 1885, however, he left school and enrolled as a law student at the University of Helsinki. Within a year he had decided to make music his profession, and in 1886 he began a three-year period of study at the Helsinki Academy of Music.

The next step was to broaden his experience by studying abroad. He went to Berlin, and then in 1890 to Vienna, where he studied under Carl Goldmark.

On returning to Finland in 1891 he became much involved with the patriotic nationalist movement, with the result that he wrote a symphonic poem on a subject from Finnish mythology. This work, *Kullervo*, was performed in 1892 and brought him instant fame.

For the next five years he worked as a teacher and violinist, but continued to compose. Some of these works became very popular – the tone poem *En Saga* (1893), for example, and the *Karelia Suite* (1893). And then, in 1897, he was awarded an annual pension by the Finnish government – one of the most enlightened things any government has ever done. It meant that he could now be a composer full-time.

The rest of Sibelius's life was not eventful, save for the music he wrote. He began his First Symphony in 1898, and it established him as one of the most important symphonic composers of his day. He made occasional visits abroad, to Italy, to America. Major works appeared in a steady stream.

And then, suddenly, in 1929, he stopped composing. From that moment he wrote

**Jean Sibelius 1865-1957**
This drawing is from a photograph of the composer which was taken in 1955, two years before his death from a brain haemorrhage. Sibelius had stopped composing in 1929, despite the fact that he was world-famous, financially secure and in good health. Possibly he felt he had said all he had to say. And perhaps he felt some kind of despair at the way civilization seemed to be going, for his last great work, the symphonic poem *Tapiola* (1955) is remarkably bleak and pessimistic.

nothing – or nothing that he would allow to be performed.

Sibelius wrote seven symphonies. They are:

| | |
|---|---|
| No 1 in E minor | 1899 |
| No 2 in D major | 1902 |
| No 3 in C major | 1907 |
| No 4 in A minor | 1911 |
| No 5 in E flat | 1915–19 |
| No 6 in D minor | 1923 |
| No 7 in C major | 1924 |

He also wrote a number of important symphonic poems, of which *The Swan of Tuonela* (1893–1900), *Finlandia* (1899), and *Tapiola* (1925) are perhaps the best known and most popular.

Among his other orchestral works the most important is probably the Violin Concerto in D minor (1903–5). He also wrote a considerable amount of chamber music, including four string quartets. His songs and choral music are also very fine, but are seldom performed outside Finland – largely because of the language problem.

*Right* Sibelius taking his daily walk outside his home near Helsinki.

# Side drum or Snare drum

A small drum which can be attached to a belt and slung at the side of a player in a marching band.

The orchestral side drum, however, is attached to a stand. The standard size is about 38 cm in diameter, and 15 cm deep. It has two parchment heads, of which the upper is called the 'batter head' (because it is beaten by the wooden drum sticks), and the lower one the 'snare head', because it has a number of gut strings stretched across

it which rattle in sympathy with the vibrations of the batter head. These snares can be loosened, and then the drum gives a dull, hollow note.

The snare drum cannot be tuned. Its note is indefinite, but fairly high. It can be muffled by placing a cloth over the batter head. Wire brushes are sometimes used instead of the usual wooden drumsticks – they produce a whispering sound, very popular in dance bands and 'pop' groups.

**Siciliana** A slowish, swaying dance in 6/8 or 12/8 time, usually written in a minor key. The name comes from a similar dance-song popular in Sicily. The siciliana often occurs as a slow movement in the suites and sonatas of the early 18th century (in Bach, for example), and also as an operatic aria (in Handel, for example). Another dance of the same period, the *Pastorale*, is similar in style.

**Signature**

a. **Key signature** – the sharps or flats placed at the beginning to each stave to indicate the key.

b. **Time signature** – the figures placed at the opening of a piece (or section) to show what time it is in. ( → **Notes and notation**)

**Signature tune** A few bars of music used to introduce the performer in a music-hall act, or radio, or television show (or to introduce a particular programme).

**Similar motion** → **Motion**

**Simile** (It.) Similar. Used after some other instruction to show that a succeeding passage is to be performed in the same way.

**Simple duple time** → **Notes and notation**

**Simple interval** One which is not 'compound'. ( → **Intervals**)

**Simple quadruple time** → **Notes and notation**

**Simple time** → **Notes and notation**

**Simple triple time** → **Notes and notation**

**Sinding, Christian** Norwegian composer, 1856–1941. He studied music in Oslo and Leipzig, and for a time taught composition at the Eastman School of Music, Rochester, New York State. Though widely known as the composer of a piano piece, *Rustle of Spring*, he wrote many more important works, including three symphonies, three violin concertos, and two operas. He was the leader of Norwegian music after Grieg.

**Sine tone** An electronically produced note which is a pure tone – that is to say, it has no overtones. It is the basic material of electronic music.

**Sinfonia** → **Symphony**

**Sinfonietta** Either a short symphony, or a symphony for small orchestra. The word is also used as a title for a small orchestra – for example, the London Sinfonietta.

**Single chant** → **Anglican chant**

**Shofar** In this scene from the siege of Jericho shofars were used as a battle signal.

**Sistrum** This example, dated about 2100 B.C., is from Central Anatolia.

**Les Six** *Left to right* Poulenc, Tailleferre, Durey, Cocteau, Milhaud and Honegger. Auric is missing.

**Singspiel** Literally a 'song-play', this is the name given to the German equivalent of the English Ballad Opera – that is to say, a play with music. The Singspiel emerged in Germany during the 18th century. The two finest examples of Singspiel are Mozart's *Magic Flute* (1791) and Beethoven's *Fidelio* (1805).

**Sinistro, Sinistra** (It.) Left. As in *mano sinistra*, left hand .

**Sistrum** A type of rattle, consisting of a U-shaped frame that carries objects (such as metal discs) that rattle when it is shaken. Examples survive from ancient Egypt, Greece, Mexico, etc.

**Sitar** The Indian lute, invented in about 1300 in Persia. It is now the most popular and important instrument in North Indian music. Nowadays the instrument has between four and seven strings. Melodies are played on one string only, the others serving as a drone accompaniment. Some instruments have extra 'sympathetic' strings. The sitar is plucked with a wire plectrum, worn on the forefinger of the right hand.

**Six, Les** A name given by the music critic Henri Collet to a group of young French composers after a particular concert in 1919. They were in fact linked only by friendship, time, and place, and not by musical aims. To some extent, however, they were held together by the poet Jean Cocteau, who publicized them in a kind of anti-Wagner campaign. The names of *Les Six* are: Georges Auric, Louis Durey, Arthur Honegger, Darius Milhaud, Francis Poulenc, and Germaine Tailleferre.

**Skalkottas, Nikos** Greek composer, 1904–49. He studied at the Athens Conservatory, and then in Berlin (1921) under Schoenberg and Kurt Weill. He remained in Germany for 12 years. On returning to Athens he earned his living as an orchestral player. He wrote an impressive amount of music, but very little of it was performed during his lifetime. He is now regarded as one of the most important Greek composers of his generation. His music was much influenced by Schoenberg's atonality, but is nevertheless very individual.

**Sketch** A name given to some short piano or instrumental pieces. A composer's 'sketch' is his rough draft for a composition that he will later work out in full.

**Skiffle** A type of 'pop' music of the 1950s. Though it could be played by professionals (such as Lonnie Donegan and his Skiffle Group), skiffle appealed very much to amateurs. Skiffle groups consisted of acoustic guitars, backed by such home-made instruments as washboards, tea-chest basses, and kazoos. The music consisted mostly of American folksongs, spirituals, and work songs – played noisily and with enthusiasm.

**Skryabin, Alexander** Russian composer, 1872–1915. He was a brilliant pianist. After studying at the Moscow Conservatory he made many successful concert tours and became known for his piano music. To begin with this was rather in the style of Chopin, but it soon developed a very advanced kind of harmony. Orchestral music followed, some of it very elaborate and very impressive – such as the Symphony No 3 (The 'Divine Poem') (1903), the *Poem of Ecstasy* (1908), and *Prometheus: the Poem of Fire* (1910). He believed that music could release unconscious forces and eventually change the world.

**Slancio, con** (It.) Impetuously.

**Slide trombone** → **Trombone**

**Slide trumpet** → **Trumpet**

**Slur** The name of the curved line used in

**Bedřich Smetana** 1824-1884 In later life he became deaf, suffered from nervous disorders and finally died in a mental asylum.

musical notation for a number of different purposes, as follows:

1. To show which notes fall into one phrase ( → **Phrase and sentence**)
2. To tell the instrumental performer that all the notes it takes in are to be played *legato*.
3. In music for bowed instruments, to show that the notes it takes in are to be played with one stroke of the bow.
4. In vocal music, to show that the notes it takes in are to be sung with one breath, or to one syllable.
5. If combined with dots, to show that the performance of the notes affected is to be *mezzo staccato*.

The same sign is used for the **Tie** → .
( → **Notes and notation** )

**Smith, John Stafford** English composer, 1750–1836. He was the son of the organist of Gloucester Cathedral, and became a chorister of the Chapel Royal. He wrote many pleasant glees, catches, and canons, but is best remembered because his song 'Anacreon in Heaven' was adopted as the tune for the American National Anthem. ( → **Star-spangled Banner**)

**Smorzando** (It.) Extinguishing. The music is to become softer and slower, fading to pianissimo. The abbreviation *smorz.* is often used.

# Smetana

Bedřich Smetana Czech composer, 1824–84. As a boy he was something of a prodigy, learning to play the violin and piano and composing. He was, however, more or less self-taught and had to struggle to make his way as a professional musician.

Some of the difficulties arose because he allied himself with the Czech nationalist cause, and it was not until the 1860s that his country enjoyed any measure of political (and artistic) freedom. When this eventually came about, Smetana was able to express his fellow-countrymen's feelings in a series of operas and symphonic poems which soon became very popular. He is now rightly regarded as the founder of Czech music.

Smetana's operas include: *The Bartered Bride* (1866), *Dalibor* (1868), and *Libuše* (1872). His symphonic poems include a cycle of six, under the general title *Ma Vlast* (My Country), of which the second, *Vltava*, is the most popular. They were completed in 1879.

*Above* **The Bartered Bride** This comic opera was first performed in Prague in 1866. The plot deals with a village intrigue. This popular opera had its first London production in 1895.

**Smyth**, (Dame) **Ethel** English composer, 1858–1944. She studied music at Leipzig and made a considerable name as the composer of a fine mass (1893), and a number of operas that had their first performances mostly in Germany, including *Der Wald* (1898), *The Wreckers* (1906), *The Boatswain's Mate* (1916), and *Fête galante* (1923). She was very active in the cause of women's suffrage and spent some time in prison for her beliefs. She published a series of excellent autobiographical books.

**Snare drum** → **Side drum**

**Soave** (It.) Soft, gentle.

**Soft pedal** → **Piano**

**Solemnis, Solennis** (Lat.) Solemn. As in **Missa Solemnis**, 'Solemn Mass'.

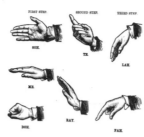

**Sol-fa system** The ascending notes of the scale are here given a singable name. Although this method was popularized by Curwen in the 1840s similar devices had been used by earlier teachers and musicians.

**Solenne** (It.) **Solennelle** (Fr.) Solemn.

**Sol-fa system, The Tonic** A method for teaching sight-singing, popularized in the 19th century by the Rev. John Curwen, whose first book on the subject was published in 1843.

Each note of the scale is given a singable name (*Doh, ray, me, fah, soh, lah, te, Doh*), which can be applied to every key, regardless of the actual note-names, or whether the key is major or minor. Thus in C major, C is Doh; and in E flat major, E flat is Doh, and so on. Sharps are shown by changing the final syllable to 'e' – fah becomes fe, ray becomes re, and so on. Flats are shown by changing the final syllable to 'a' (pronounced 'aw') – ray becomes ra, te becomes ta, and so on. Once this has been learned, the sight-reader

# Sonata

Sonata is an Italian word meaning 'sounded'. It came to be used in the more particular sense of something that is 'played'. And thus, towards the end of the 16th century, it described any piece of instrumental music, simply to distinguish it from the Cantata, which was sung.

During the years that followed the name was used to describe a number of different kinds of composition. The chief of them are:

1. **The Baroque sonata** – 17th century.
   An instrumental work in several movements, arranged like a suite. There were two main kinds: the CHAMBER SONATA (Sonata da camera), which contained mainly dance movements; and the CHURCH SONATA (Sonata da chiesa), which contained mainly abstract movements.

   The Sonatas of this period were all for solo instruments. The most common were: the SOLO SONATA (1 melody part, 1 bass part, and a continuo); and the TRIO SONATA (2 melody parts, 1 bass part, and a continuo). Examples can be found in the music of Purcell, Corelli, Bach, Handel, etc.

2. **The early 18th-century sonata**
   At the beginning of the development of symphonic methods, various types of work were called sonatas. They vary from one-movement pieces, such as the sonatas of Domenico Scarlatti, to collections of several contrasting movements, such as the sonatas of J. C. Bach and C. P. E. Bach.

The actual construction of movements in these sonatas varies somewhat, but they generally employ some version of Binary Form, and all lead towards the development of:

3. **The Classical sonata**
   By this we mean the kind of sonata found in the works of Haydn, Mozart, and Beethoven. Such sonatas are either for keyboard only, or for keyboard and one solo instrument (e.g. Sonata for violin and piano).

   The classical sonata has four contrasted movements, usually arranged in the following way:
   a. A lengthy quick movement, usually in Sonata Form.
   b. An expressive slow movement, probably in an 'aria' form, or perhaps a 'theme and variations'.
   c. A cheerful 'minuet and trio' movement.
   d. A vigorous 'finale', often in **Sonata-Rondo Form** →.

It is important to realize that although the word sonata has always been used to describe some form of chamber music, symphonies, as well as trios, quartets, quintets, octets, etc., are all 'sonatas'. The difference in name is a mere convenience. What binds them all together is the method of composition they all share, which is SYMPHONIC, and best expressed in what we call 'Sonata Form' (see below).

# Sonata Form

This is the form that gradually evolved in the work of countless composers, from Domenico Scarlatti to Mozart, as the perfect answer to the problem of constructing music along TONAL lines. From about 1770, and for most of the 19th century, it came to be the most important and widely used form in music.

The 18th-century composer believed strongly in 'keys' (TONALITY). It was felt that the key you began a movement in was the 'home' key and that it was necessary always to return to it. But to stick to it throughout a movement would, of course, be boring. The problem was how to give a movement variety and contrast and yet remain faithful to the over-riding sense of 'key'. Sonata Form was the answer.

The best way to explain it is to study a very simple example, breaking it up into sections. Here is a movement by Muzio Clementi (1752–1832). It comes from his Sonata in F, Op 36, No 4. If you can play it, you will get an idea of how such movements were constructed. Play it first in sections, and then, when you have read this article, go through the whole movement without a break. Alternatively, study it carefully.

**Clementi's sonata movement**

**Passage 1** *(Key F):*
The FIRST PART of the movement begins with the music on the left.

**Passage 4** *(Key C):* This is a very short passage. It is a 'coda' (a 'tail-piece'), which serves to finish off the section. Notice that the composer now puts the sign :‖ , to indicate that the whole section should be played again.

**Passage 2** *(beginning in Key F and then moving into Key C):* This begins just like the previous one, but goes off to something different. There is really very little that is new in this passage. It is nearly all made out of Passage 1, but it contains a modulation and is obviously leading to something.

**Passage 5** *(various keys):* This begins the SECOND PART of the movement. The music in this section is made almost entirely out of what has gone before. The first three bars are clearly made out of Passage 3. The bass of the next four bars comes from Passage 2 and the treble partly from Passage 3. And so on. We call this process of making new material out of old, DEVELOPMENT. Notice also, as part of the 'development', the music modulates – into D minor and G minor. By the end of the section, however, it returns to the key of F major, ready for the THIRD PART.

**Passage 3** *(in Key C):* This is altogether new. It is different from Passage 1 and forms a contrast to it.

*calando*

**Passage 6** This is the first part over again, but with certain differences. The first part began in F (the key of the whole movement) and ended in C. The third part, however, remains in F throughout, so that the movement may end in the key in which it began.

Each main section of a Sonata Form is known by a special name. First we have the

EXPOSITION consisting of the First and Second Subjects, the Bridge Passage that links them, and the Coda (Passages I, II, III, and IV in our example). Then comes

DEVELOPMENT in which the material presented in the Exposition section is 'developed' – that is to say, worked out and generally explored. And finally we have the

RECAPITULATION in which the material of the Exposition is now 'restated' in the tonic key of the piece.

It is sometimes thought that Sonata Form depends upon the idea of two contrasting themes – the First and Second Subjects. This is not strictly true. Although most Sonata Forms will show such a contrast, what really makes the form 'work' is the contrast of KEY. It is perfectly possible to find a satisfactory sonata form which uses the same musical idea for both First and Second Subjects (the first movement of Haydn's symphony in G major, the 'Oxford', for example). But a Sonata Form does not exist unless contrasting keys are present in the Exposition section.

finds that he has learned to sing in every key. These names are based on the Italian syllables (*do, re, mi, fa, zol, la, si, do*) which are used in countries such as America today.

Curwen's system was based on an earlier method suggested by Miss Sarah Glover of Norwich, which in itself was a modernization of a system in use in the 11th century that was said to have been invented by a Benedictine monk, Guido d'Arezzo.

**Solfeggio** (It.) Exercise. A type of singing exercise, in which the names of the notes are sung. It uses the 'Fixed Doh' system – that is to say, Doh is always C. ( → **Sol-fa system**)

**Solo, soli** (It.) Alone. Used to indicate a single performer (solo), or a group of individual performers (soli). The word 'soloist' has been adopted into the English language.

**Solo manual** → **Organ**

**Somervell,** (Sir) **Arthur** English composer, 1863–1937. He studied at Cambridge University, in Berlin, and at the Royal College of Music. He became Chief Inspector of Music to Schools and Training Colleges in 1901. Though he wrote several large-scale choral and orchestral works, he is now remembered for his songs, in particular the cycle *Maud* (1898).

**Sonata Form** → page 306

**Sonata-Rondo Form** A type of Rondo, very popular with such composers as Beethoven, which is a combination of Rondo and of a Sonata Form

Instead of the normal **ABACADA** pattern of **Rondo Form** →, in which **B**, **C**, and **D** are contrasting sections between the main tune (**A**) which always returns in the same key, we have the pattern **ABA C ABA**. **A** and **B** are the equivalents of First and Second Subjects in a Sonata Form, and **C** is a contrasting section which takes the place of the Development. The sections **ABA** thus stand in place of the Exposition and Recapitulation sections, even though **A** always returns in the same key, just as in simple Rondo Form.

**Sondheim, Stephen** American composer and writer, b. 1930. He was born in New York and studied composition with Milton Babbitt. His talents as a song writer and writer of lyrics for other men's songs emerged very early. His first important commission was to write the lyrics for Bernstein's musical,

*West Side Story* (1957); he then went on to write successful musicals of his own, including *A funny Thing happened on the Way to the Forum* (1962), *Company* (1970), *Follies* (1971), *A little Night Music* (1973), and *Pacific Overtures* (1976). His music, and his lyrics manage to be both ingenious and memorable.

**Sonatina** A short sonata, usually rather simple in style.

**Song cycle** A set of songs that have something in common. For example, they may all be settings of words by the same poet, or the poems themselves may tell a complete story. The songs in a song cycle must therefore be sung in the order laid down by the composer. Examples can be found by Schubert and Schumann.

**Song Form** Another name for **Ternary Form** →, simply because many 18th-century songs and arias followed this pattern. But it is not a very good name, for most songs have different musical shapes to fit in with the words that are being set.

**Song without Words** A term introduced by Mendelssohn (*Lied ohne Worte*) to describe a song-like piano piece (one that has a melody in the top part, with an accompaniment in the lower part).

**Sopra** (It.) Above. As in **come sopra**, as above, and **sopra una corda**, on one string (of a violin).

**Soprano** The highest pitch of human voice. The soprano range, for adult women, is:

A boy's unbroken voice is sometimes called soprano (or treble). And the word is also used in connection with high-pitched instruments – as, for example, the soprano saxophone.

**Sordino** (It.) Mute. **Sordini**, mutes. In string music the expression is **con sordino**, with mute, and **senza sordino**, without mute.

**Sospirando** (It.) Sighing, plaintive.

**Sostenuto** (It.) Sustained.

**Sotto** (It.) Below. As in **sotto voce**, under the voice – that is to say, whispered.

**Soul music** 'Soul' developed among black musicians in America during the 1960s. Musically it is derived from blues and gospel singing (the emotional hymns of the various evangelical churches), mixed in with the driving rhythms of rock. The words nearly always convey the idea of protest – either against some personal misfortune, or, more frequently, against general social injustice. It is sung in a wailing style, and is very rhythmic, with the beats heavily marked.

**Sound holes** These are the holes cut in the belly of the violin (that is, in its upper surface). Often, on account of their shape, they are called 'f holes'.

**Sound post** This is the little wooden stick fixed in a violin, etc., under the bridge to support the belly (that is, the upper surface of the instrument) at the place where there is great pressure on it.

**Sound waves → Acoustics**

**Sousa, John Philip** American composer, 1854–1932. He was trained as a violinist, and after a successful career as leader of the United States Marine Corps band (1880–92) he formed a band of his own which soon became very popular. He wrote a number of operettas, orchestral suites, and many songs, but his fame rests on his marches (he wrote nearly a hundred). Among them are 'The Stars and Stripes for ever', 'The Washington Post', and 'Hands across the Sea'. He once said that 'a march should make a man with a wooden leg step out', and his own are lively enough to do just that.

**Special effects** The percussion section of an orchestra is often required to handle what can only be called 'special effects' – noise-making devices that are not quite instruments in the ordinary sense. These include the ANVIL (hit with a mallet), COW BELLS, CHAINS (which are rattled), THUNDERSHEET (a flexible metal sheet), SANDPAPER BLOCKS

**Special effects** Wind machine. This is used in some musical works, notably in Richard Strauss's *Don Quixote*.

**Gasparo Spontini** 1774-1851 He was musical director to the court in Berlin until 1842.

(which are rubbed together), SLEIGH-BELLS, and WIND MACHINE (a revolving drum, with slats that rub against a sheet of silk).

**Species → Counterpoint**

**Spiccato** (It.) Distinct. A *staccato* effect, which in string music calls for a loose, bouncing movement of the bow.

**Spinet → Harpsichord**

**Spirito** (It.) Spirit, vigour. Also **spiritoso**, 'lively'.

**Spohr, Ludwig** German composer, 1784–1859. From the age of 14 he made many successful European tours as a virtuoso violinist. His compositions were also admired and in 1822 he became the Director of Music at the court of the Elector of Hesse-Kassel.

Spohr wrote music of all kinds, including 11 operas (*Jessonda* (1823) is the most famous), 15 violin concertos, 10 symphonies, 34 string quartets, and several oratorios, such as *The Last Judgement* (1826) and *Calvary* (1835), both very popular in England.

For a time Spohr was thought to be as great a composer as Beethoven, but his music is now seldom played. He had certain tricks of using chromatic harmony that come in over and over again, and these weaken his music. But the present-day neglect is a little unfair, for he was a very capable composer.

**Spontini, Gasparo** Italian composer, 1774–1851. After a successful early career as an operatic composer in Naples and Rome, he settled in Paris (1803) and became very famous indeed. In 1820 he went to Berlin, where he remained until 1842.

Spontini was one of the composers who helped to establish Grand Opera. His most

# Spirituals

The religious folksongs of America. They were not, as is often supposed, the exclusive property of the American Negro.

White spirituals arose out of the religious Revivalist movement of the nineteenth century. Religious ('spiritual') songs played an important part in the 'camp meetings' that were a feature of this movement – meetings of thousands of people in the open air, to hear a preacher, and sing songs of praise. Some of the tunes were new, but many were versions of old tunes that the settlers had brought with them from their countries of origin. The new tunes include

**Negro slave gang** Negro spirituals arose among the Black slave population of America. Most of them were European borrowings but with the Negro's own particular twist. For him the spiritual was not only a means of emotional outlet, it was also a song of religious hope. This is why some are so powerful and moving.

the 'Gospel Songs' of such revivalists as Moody and Sankey.

famous works in this style were *La Vestale* (1807), *Fernand Cortez* (1809), and *Olympie* (1819).

**Sprechgesang** (Ger.) 'Speech-song'. A term used by Schoenberg and his disciples, to describe a kind of singing that is half speech, half song. Examples can be found in his *Pierrot Lunaire*.

**Stabat Mater** A 13th-century Latin hymn which describes the anguish of Christ's mother as she stands at the foot of the Cross. It has its own plainsong, but has also been set to more elaborate music by many composers – including Palestrina, Haydn, Schubert, Rossini, Verdi, and Dvořák.

**Staccato** (It.) Detached. The opposite of **Legato →**. **Staccatissimo** means 'very detached'.

**Staff** or **Stave →** Notes and notation

**Stainer, Sir John** English composer, 1840–1901. He was a chorister at St Paul's Cathedral, and in 1872 became its organist. He studied at Oxford University, later becoming organist at Magdalen College and at the University Church.

Stainer was very active in matters of musical education, and was an expert in musicology – his book *Dufay and his Contemporaries* (1898) is very important. He also wrote a considerable amount of church music and several short oratorios. One of them, *The Crucifixion* (1887), became (and still is) very popular.

**Stamitz, Johann** Czech composer, 1717–57. He settled at the court of Mannheim in 1742 and there directed the famous orchestra that helped to set a standard of playing for the rest of Europe, and whose composers (including Stamitz himself) were important in the development of the early symphony and concerto. He wrote 74 symphonies, besides music of every other kind.

**Stamitz, Carl** German composer, 1745–1801. He was born in Mannheim, the son of Johann Stamitz, and like him became an excellent violinist and the composer of many symphonies, concertos, and chamber works. After playing in the Mannheim Orchestra he toured Europe as a soloist. His brother, Anton Stamitz (1754–1808) was also a violinist and composer.

**Charles Stanford** 1852-1924 His works include seven operas, and among his pupils were Vaughan Williams and Sir Arthur Bliss.

**Johann Stamitz** 1717-1757 As well as a composer he was a noted violinist and composed concertos for this instrument.
This engraving is by Jean-Baptiste Cartier.

**Stamping stick** One of the oldest and simplest types of instrument, still used by primitive tribes. It consists of a length of hollow wood, or bamboo, and is used to produce a rhythm for dancing. It is also used for grinding corn – and then the rhythm helps the work along.

**Stanford** (Sir) **Charles** Irish composer, 1852–1924. He studied at Trinity College, Dublin, Cambridge University, and in Hamburg and Berlin. He taught composition at the Royal College of Music (1883–1924), and was Professor of Music at Cambridge University (1887–1924). Together with Sir Hubert Parry, Stanford helped to raise the standard of English music-making, and was a particularly influential teacher. He wrote an immense amount of music, and is still remembered for his songs and part-songs, and such cantatas as *The Revenge* (1886) and *Songs of the Sea* (1904).

**Stanley, John** English composer, 1712–86. Though blind from the age of two, he made rapid progress as an organist, becoming organist of the Temple Church when only 22. In 1779 he became Master of the King's Band. Much of his music is important, including 14 flute sonatas and six concerti grossi (which are still often performed) but above all, 30 organ **voluntaries →**.

**Star-spangled Banner** This is (since 1931) the official national anthem of the United States. It came to be written in this way.

In 1814 the United States and Great Britain were at war. Francis Scott Key had left Baltimore for the British fleet, under a flag of truce, to carry out certain negotiations. From the British ship on which he was received he anxiously watched the bombardment of Fort Henry till he saw the American flag signalling an American victory over the British.

Key wrote his poem to fit the tune of John Stafford Smith's popular song 'Anacreon in Heaven'. So, despite the outcome of the bombardment, the American National Anthem is the work of a British composer!

**Steel drum →** page 312

**Stem** The line (or 'tail') attached to the head of all notes smaller than a semibreve.

**Stesso** (It.) The same. As in **lo stesso tempo**, 'the same speed'; that is to say that the beats have the same duration, even

# Steel drum

A tuned percussion instrument made by West Indian musicians from Trinidad out of discarded oil drums. One end of the drum is beaten down to form a basin. It is then divided into sections by hammering grooves into the surface with a nail punch. Each section produces its own note when tapped. The drum is heated and then plunged into cold water to temper the steel. Each section is then 'tuned' by further beating with the nail punch.

By tracing different patterns, and dividing the drum-tops into different sections a whole range of instruments can be obtained. The smaller the section, the higher the note. The lower sounding drums are also much bigger in depth.

**Steel band** This colourful steel band performs in Disneyland, near Los Angeles, California. There are six basic types (but with many variations) of steel drum: the rhythm drum which has two sections; the ping pong, with 25 sections; the second pan, with 14; the cello pan, with 8; the guitar pan, with 9; and the bass pan, with 5. Melodies are played on the ping pong, while the guitar pan provides an accompaniment. Steel bands, marching or stationary, are capable of extraordinary virtuoisity.

though they have changed their value (i.e. crotchets (quarter-notes) may have become dotted crotchets). The direction ♩ = ♩. is common.

**Stochasticism** Derived from a Greek word meaning 'to aim at, or guess', this term has been used by composers who work with computers (such as Iannis Xenakis) to describe works that are based on the probability-calculus theories of higher mathematics.

**Stockhausen, Karlheinz** German composer, b. 1928. He trained at Cologne (his birthplace) and Bonn, and studied for a time with Darius Milhaud and Olivier Messiaen. His first important works were written in an advanced form of serialism, partly influenced by Webern and partly by Messiaen – for example, *Kreuzspiel* (1951) and *Kontrapunkte* (1952). Later works, such as *Momente* (1962–4, revised 1972), made use of the idea of 'chance' (→ **Aleatoric**), and then of mixing electronic and natural sounds – as in the *Gesang der Jünglinge* (1956). He has continued to explore new techniques and is widely regarded as one of the most important composers of his generation.

**Stomp** A blues composition in which the beat is very heavily marked. (→ **Soul**)

**Stop** → **Organ**

**Stopping** When the string of a violin, etc., is made shorter by pressing a finger against it, it is said to have been 'stopped'. The note that is produced is a 'stopped note'. Double-stopping involves stopping notes on adjacent strings.

**Karlheinz Stockhausen** b. 1928 The composer rehearses the BBC orchestra in his *Mantra* for two amplified pianos.

**Storace, Stephen** English composer, 1763–96. He was a prodigy violinist and was sent to study in Naples when he was 12. With his sister, the singer Nancy Storace, he spent time in Vienna, where he became a close friend of Mozart. On returning to London (1787) he wrote a series of successful operas. His important *Storace's Harpsicord Collection* included the first publication of some of Mozart's chamber music.

**Stradella, Alessandro** Italian composer, 1642–82. He was a singer, violinist, and composer. His life and career are somewhat obscure, but he was murdered at the instigation of his mistress's brother. He wrote operas, and a number of oratorios, such as *St John the Baptist* (1676), besides being a pioneer of the early symphony.

**Stradivari, Antonio** Italian violin-maker, 1644–1737. He worked in Cremona, and was a pupil of Nicola Amati. His first instruments are dated 1666 and he is thought to have made over one thousand – mostly violins, but also violas and cellos. These are now highly prized and extremely valuable, for he is considered one of the greatest instrument makers of all time.

**Strathspey** A traditional Scottish dance. It is slower than the **Reel** → and makes particular use of dotted notes and the '**Scotch snap**' →

**Strauss family** → page 314

**Strauss, Richard** → page 313

**Stravinsky** → page 316

# Strauss

Richard Strauss. German composer, 1864–1949. He was born into a musical family, for his father was a horn-player in the Munich Court Orchestra, but was not related to the Johann Strauss family. He began to learn the piano when he was four, and to compose when he was six. By the time he was 14 his music had been performed in public, and when he enrolled as a student of the University of Munich (1882) he was already established as a promising young composer.

His talents soon attracted the attention of Hans von Bülow, the great conductor and friend of Wagner, and in 1885 he was appointed his assistant at the Meiningen Orchestra. He remained with von Bülow's orchestra for a year, learning by conducting the great masterpieces of the past and at the same time developing his own style. Wagner in particular began to exert a great influence over his music, and many people thought that the young Richard was preparing to take up where the old Richard had left off.

In 1886 Strauss took up a minor conducting post at the Munich Opera, and remained there for three years. During this time he composed a number of symphonic poems. Two of them, *Don Juan* (1888) and *Tod und Verklärung* (1889), are still regarded as masterpieces. At the time, some critics thought them too dissonant and modern, but it was agreed that a new and great composer had arrived in German music.

For the next few years Strauss worked as a Kapellmeister, first at Weimar (1889–94) and then at Munich (1894–98). He was given time off to conduct elsewhere, however, and between 1895 and 1898 managed to tour most of Europe. He also somehow found time to compose a series of great symphonic poems, including *Till Eulenspiegel* (1895), *Don Quixote* (1898), and *Ein Heldenleben* (1898), as well as many other works. In 1898 he was appointed conductor of the Berlin Royal Opera House.

By 1905 Strauss's life had settled down somewhat. Though he conducted regularly, he spent more time composing. He was now world-famous, not only for his orchestral music, but also for opera – in December 1905, *Salome* caused a sensation.

The appointment at Berlin lasted until 1910, and thereafter Strauss took only one

**Richard Strauss** 1864–1949 This portrait of the composer in 1910 is by Max Liebermann.

*Above* **Salome**, Strauss's first opera. This scene is from the 1977 production at the Royal Opera House, Covent Garden.

**Der Rosenkavalier** First produced in Dresden in 1911, this opera is perhaps the most popular of Strauss's operas. In this scene from the first act the Marschallin, surrounded by servants and suitors, attends to the day's affairs.

major conducting post – at the Vienna State Opera (1919–24) – though he still made many appearances as a guest-conductor.

As a composer, Strauss's life falls into a number of distinct periods. The first, as we have seen, was concerned with symphonic poems and similar orchestral works. He was perhaps the greatest composer of descriptive music there has ever been. The second period concerned opera, and began in 1905 with *Salome*. It continued with great success, with *Elektra* (1909), *Der Rosenkavalier* (1911), and *Ariadne auf Naxos* (1912), all to words by Hugo von Hofmannsthal. After about 1920, however, his music began to seem less powerful and exciting. He was no longer the daring modernist of 1905. The music of Schoenberg and Stravinsky seemed to point the way to the future. Strauss now appeared like a representative of the past.

But towards the end of his long life a remarkable change came over his music. Though it remained as romantic as ever, it suddenly regained the vigour that many people felt it had lost after about 1920. At the age of 80 he began to write a series of masterpieces. They include the operas *Daphne* (1938) and *Capriccio* (1942), concertos for Horn (1942) and Oboe (1946), the *Metamorphosen* for strings (1946), and the beautiful *Four last Songs*, for soprano and orchestra (1948).

What caused this final burst of creative activity we shall never know. Perhaps it was the fact that the Germany he knew and loved had been destroyed by the War and disgraced by the Nazi regime, and that he felt obliged somehow to raise something beautiful out of the ruins – something that spoke of older, happier times.

# Strauss family

Austrian composers and conductors. They lived and worked in Vienna, and, together with Joseph Lanner, made the Viennese Waltz famous throughout the world. The members of the family were:

**Johann I** (1804–49)
and his sons:
**Johann II** (1825–99)
**Joseph** (1827–70)
**Eduard** (1835–1916)
and his son:
**Johann III** (1866–1939)

The most gifted Strauss was Johann II, who became known as the 'Waltz King'.

**Johann Strauss** Austrian composer and conductor, 1825–99. He wrote his first waltz when he was six, but his father refused to allow him to make a career in music and he had to take lessons in secret. In 1844 he formed a small band, which soon rivalled his father's in popularity. On the death of his father (1849) the two bands joined and Strauss now became the undisputed leading composer and conductor of Viennese light music.

**Johann Strauss** 1825-1899 He made many successful tours in Europe and visited England (1869) and America (1876). Beside his many splendid dance tunes, some of which (e.g. 'The Blue Danube' waltz, 1867) are elaborately constructed along almost symphonic lines, he wrote a number of important and successful operettas, including *Die Fledermaus* (The Bat), 1874; *Eine Nacht in Venedig* (A Night in Venice), 1883; and *Der Zigeunerbaron* (The Gypsy Baron), 1885. Together with Offenbach and Sullivan he dominated the world of 19th-century operetta.

**Street cries** These are the musical phrases which were sung by the various hawkers of different goods as they walked the city streets selling their wares. Each 'ware' had its own special words and music – rather like an advertising jingle on today's television programmes! Cries of this kind can be traced back to the 14th century, in Elizabethan times, composers often worked the traditional cries into compositions of their own, making vocal works that are little descriptive pieces depicting a London street-market. Fine examples can be found in the music of Thomas Weelkes and Orlando Gibbons.

**Streichquartett** (Ger.) String quartet.

**Strepitoso** (It.) Boisterously.

**Stretto** (It.) Drawn together i.e. quicker. **Stretto** has a special meaning in **Fugue** →.

**Strict counterpoint** → **Counterpoint**

**Strike note** → **Bells and bell-ringing**

**Stringendo** (It.) Squeezing. In music it means that the notes should get quicker, giving a sense of urgency.

**Stroh violin** A violin that has an aluminium plate and a trumpet bell instead

**Street cries** The songs of street-traders inspired these 18th-century prints.

of the normal wooden body. Invented in 1901 by Charles Stroh for use in the early recording studios, where primitive microphones could only pick up sound aimed directly at them (which, of course, the trumpet bell could do). There are also Stroh violas, cellos, mandolins, and guitars. The German term *Strohfiedel*, however, means a xylophone.

**Strophic song** One in which the same music is repeated for each verse of the poem.

**Stück** (Ger.) Piece.

**Subdominant** The fourth note of the major or minor scale.

**Subito** (It.) Immediately. As in **volti subito** at the end of a page, meaning that it must be turned over quickly (often abbreviated to V.S.). **P subito** and **f subito** mean that the music must suddenly become soft, or loud.

**Subject** The main themes from which a composition is made. A term used in particular in connection with **Sonata Form** →, **Rondo** →, and **Fugue** →.

**Submediant** The sixth note of the major or minor scale.

# Suite

We use this word in everyday speech to describe a *group* or *set* of something – such as a suite of rooms, or a suite of furniture. And by it we mean that everything in the suite 'goes together' and makes a satisfactory whole.

In the same way, a suite in music is a collection of pieces that 'go together' to make an effective overall work.

Suites began in the 16th century. We find composers of the time of Queen Elizabeth I writing keyboard dances in pairs – a slow dance, the PAVAN, followed by a quick dance, the GALLIARD. These composers were simply imitating what happened in actual life on the dance floor, where it made sense to have dances which contrasted with each other in this way. Very often, however, they made their pairs of dances out of the same tune, and so these keyboard dances not only contrasted with each other, but also 'went together' nicely.

Keyboard dances of this kind were the first type of purely instrumental music. As time went by more were added, until in Bach's day a true suite of such movements had come into existence.

The basis of the early 18th-century suite consisted of four dances:

**Allemande** (quick, but serious)
**Courante** (quick and running)
**Sarabande** (slow and solemn)
**Gigue** (quick and cheerful)

Sometimes a PRELUDE was added by way of introduction, and other dances (such as minuets, gavottes, bourrées, hornpipes, etc.) added to give extra variety.

All these movements were originally dances, but soon other kinds of movement were introduced that did not depend on dance rhythms. Arias, fugues, toccatas, marches, and many other types of movement found their way into the suite.

Out of the suite grew the early form of symphony – indeed, the SINFONIA ($\rightarrow$ **Overture**) was really a special kind of suite. In the same way the early form of concerto imitated the pattern of the suite. And so we may say that this simple form of making up an instrumental work came to have a profound effect on the whole of music.

In the days of Purcell, Bach, and Handel all the pieces in a suite were in the same key (or at any rate had the same key signature – as, for example, G major and E minor). With later suites the different movements use a variety of keys.

Sometimes suites appear under different names, such as: *Cassation, Partita, Divertimento, Lesson, Serenade,* and *Overture.*

In the 19th century composers often made suites out of movements, or selections, from some other work, such as a ballet or an opera, or from the incidental music to a play. 20th-century composers do the same thing (e.g. Stravinsky's *Firebird Suite* – from the ballet). When a work is popular, audiences like to have it available in many different forms, and composers have no objection to getting two works for the labour of one, so to speak!

**Subsidiary theme** (**Subject**) Any theme that is less important than the main themes of a composition.

For example, the First and Second Subjects in a Sonata Form may sometimes be divided into a number of themes, of which some are less important than the others.

**Suk, Josef** Czech composer, 1874–1935. He was a fine violinist and one of the founders of a famous string quartet (the Bohemian Quartet, 1892). He studied composition under Dvořák and in 1898 married his daughter. Like Smetana and Dvořák he was intensely patriotic and wrote many works to express this feeling, such as the symphonic poems *Prague* (1904), and *The Legend of Dead Victors* (1919). His earliest works were very romantic and traditional, but he later developed a much more dissonant style.

**Josef Suk** 1874-1935 In this caricature the composer is on the right. Many of his works were for piano.

**Sul, Sull'** (It.) On or over (the). As in such directions to string players as **sul G** on the G string , **sul tasto**, over the fingerboard , and **sul ponticello**, over the bridge – all of which indicate where to place the bow.

**Sullivan** $\rightarrow$ page 318

**Sumer is icumen in** This is a 13th-century song found in a book from Reading Abbey. It may be the work of John of Fornsete, a monk of the Abbey. It is sometimes called the 'Reading Rota' – 'rota' meaning 'round', for the music is a **Canon** $\rightarrow$ for four voices, with two voices singing a short canon below as an accompaniment. It is one of the most elaborate pieces of counterpoint of its period, but it is also very lively and tuneful.

**Supertonic** The second note of the major or minor scale.

**Suppé, Franz von** Austrian composer, 1819–95. He worked in Vienna as a conductor of theatre orchestras and wrote an enormous number of vaudevilles (satirical songs) and operettas, some of which are still remembered by their overtures – for example, *Poet and Peasant*, and *Light Cavalry*.

**Suspension → Harmony**

**Sustaining pedal → Piano**

**Suzuki method** Named after the Japanese teacher Shinichi Suzuki (b. 1897), it trains children from the age of three to play the violin. It begins with an intensive course of ear training, and playing by imitation, and only later proceeds to the use of notation.

**Svendsen, Johan Severin** Norwegian composer, 1840–1911. His father was a military bandmaster, and he too, at 15, enlisted in the army as a musician. On leaving he worked as a theatre musician, but also wrote music. In 1863 illness forced him to give up playing and he went to Leipzig to study seriously.

Svendsen wrote a considerable amount of music, and is generally regarded as being next to Grieg in importance. His style, however, was more 'classical' and less wholly indebted to folksong. His best known works are the *Norwegian Artists' Carnival*, and the two *Norwegian Rhapsodies*.

**Sweelinck, Jan Pieterszoon** Netherlands composer, 1562–1621. He lived and worked mainly in Amsterdam, where he was organist of the Old Church for over 40 years. He was regarded as one of the greatest organists of his day, and his organ works established a style of composition (particularly in fugue) that greatly influenced J. S. Bach. He also wrote many vocal works – both secular and sacred (*Chansons* and *Cantiones sacrae*) – and many pieces for the harpsichord.

**Swell manual → Organ**

**Swing** A type of American popular music of the 1935–45 era, largely associated with the big bands of Paul Whiteman, Benny Goodman, Woody Herman, Glenn Miller, Count Basie, etc. Nobody has ever quite defined the word 'swing', but it is a way of making rhythm come to life by means of subtle *rubato* effects. The swing bands of the

**Shinichi Suzuki** b.1897
He has effected a method of teaching based on imitation which mass-produces child violinists.

**Jan P. Sweelinck** 1562–1621 He introduced independent pedal playing and influenced the art of organ playing and composition throughout Europe.

# Stravinsky

Igor Stravinsky. Russian composer, 1882–1971. Born at Oranienbaum, a town some 48 km west of St Petersburg (now called Leningrad). Though his father was an operatic bass singer, and he was allowed to have piano lessons, his parents seem to have had no desire that he too should become a professional musician. When he became a student at the University of St Petersburg it was to study law, not music.

Nevertheless, it was music that claimed most of his attention, and when his father died in 1902 he felt free to pursue it full-time. He became a private pupil of Rimsky-Korsakov, and gradually became more adventurous in his compositions.

Until 1909 Stravinsky's career was unremarkable. But in that year the ballet impresario Serge Diaghilev heard some of his orchestral pieces and asked him to write the music for a new ballet: *The Firebird*. It was produced in Paris in 1910 and caused a sensation. It was brilliantly orchestrated and extremely effective, and obviously the work of a new and very exciting composer.

In 1911 a new ballet was completed: *Petrushka*. For the first time Stravinsky's flair for exciting rhythms and daring new harmonies was shown in all its glory. Paris, and soon all Europe, was stunned by the work's brilliance.

Stravinsky was now world-famous. But he had no intention of resting on his laurels – he had plans for an even more daring ballet. This was *The Rite of Spring*, and when it appeared in 1913 it caused a riot. Gone was the colourful orchestration of *The Firebird*, gone the pretty folk-like tunes of *Petrushka*. In their place was something wildly dissonant and rhythmically barbaric. The first audiences were not only overwhelmed, they were frightened by the new sounds.

Having scored a resounding success, Stravinsky, throughout his life, seems always to have found the courage to move on to something new. Thus in 1918 he completed a stage work, *The Soldier's Tale*, which turned completely against the gigantic orchestras and lavish effects of the early ballets, and used instead a small group of instrumentalists and an almost bare stage. Instead of the glowing colours of *Petrushka* and the wild, primitive rhythms of *The Rite of Spring*, there were jaunty, jazzy tunes, crisp angular rhythms, and spicy wrong-note harmonies. He had, in short, decided to explore a neo-classic style of composition. (→ **Neo-classicism**)

Works in this vein occupied him until about 1950, and in some respects they are his most powerful and profound pieces.

Then, in 1952, after standing almost in opposition to Schoenberg's method of composition, Stravinsky suddenly decided to explore serialism for himself. During the last years of his life he wrote a series of works that used 12-note methods in a very personal way.

Stravinsky married in 1906, and until 1939 lived mainly in France and Switzer-

*Above* A sketch of Stravinsky in 1920 by Picasso. *Left* The composer with Cocteau, Picasso and Sonia Delauney, Antibes, 1926.

*Below* Design by Bakst for Karsavina's costume in *The Firebird*, 1913. *Bottom* Design by Gontcharova for the backcloth of a 1926 production of *The Firebird*.

land. After the Revolution (1917) he did not return to Russia, save for a brief visit in 1961. He became a French citizen in 1934, but fled to America at the beginning of the Second World War. He settled in California and became an American citizen in 1945. His first wife died in 1939 and he married again in the following year. He was successful throughout his career and died a very rich man. He was buried with great ceremony on the island of San Michele, Venice, in a grave near that of Diaghilev.

## Summary of Stravinsky's main works

Ballets include:

| | |
|---|---|
| *The Firebird* | 1910 |
| *Petrushka* | 1911 |
| *The Rite of Spring* | 1913 |
| *Pulcinella* | 1920 |
| *Les Noces* (The Wedding) | 1923 |
| *Apollo Musagetes* | 1928 |
| *The Fairy's Kiss* | 1928 |
| *Persephone* | 1934 |
| *Jeu de Cartes* (A Card Game) | 1937 |
| *Orpheus* | 1947 |
| *Agon* | 1957 |

Stage works include:

| | |
|---|---|
| *The Nightingale* (opera) | 1914 |
| *The Soldier's Tale* | 1918 |
| ('a story, told, acted and danced') | |
| *Mavra* (opera) | 1921 |
| *Oedipus Rex* (opera-oratorio) | 1927 |
| *The Rake's Progress* (opera) | 1951 |
| *The Flood* (musical play) | 1962 |

Works for chorus and orchestra include:

| | |
|---|---|
| *Symphony of Psalms* | 1930 |
| Mass | 1948 |
| *Canticum Sacrum* | 1955 |
| *Threni* | 1958 |
| *Requiem Canticles* | 1966 |

Orchestral works include:

| | |
|---|---|
| Symphonies of wind instruments | 1920 |
| Concerto for piano and wind orchestra | 1924 |
| Concerto in D for violin and orchestra | 1932 |
| Dumbarton Oaks Concerto | 1938 |
| Symphony in C | 1940 |
| *Danses concertantes* | 1941–2 |
| Concerto in D for string orchestra | 1946 |

Also orchestral suites from the ballets: *Firebird, Petrushka, Pulcinella,* etc.

# Sullivan (Sir) Arthur

(Sir) Arthur Sullivan   English composer, 1842–1900. Sullivan's father was an Army Bandmaster, and he was therefore brought up in a musical atmosphere. In 1854 he won a place as a chorister in the Chapel Royal, and in the following year his first published composition appeared – an anthem, *O Israel*. In 1856 he was awarded the first Mendelssohn Scholarship at the Royal Academy of Music, which enabled him to complete his studies in Leipzig.

At Leipzig (1858–61) he was both successful and popular, and on returning he made an immediate name for himself with a suite of music to Shakespeare's *The Tempest*. By 1864 he was not only Professor of Composition at the Royal Academy, but had written a remarkable symphony (the 'Irish' Symphony). His career might have continued along these lines had he not, in 1867, written a one-act operetta, *Cox and Box*. It then became obvious that he had a flair for the theatre, and in particular for comedy. A larger operetta, *Contrabandista*, followed in the same year, and in 1871 he collaborated with a successful playwright, William Schwenck Gilbert (1836–1911), in yet another operetta, *Thespis*.

Even so, he was still anxious to write 'serious' music, and during this same period he produced oratorios, such as *The Prodigal Son* (1869) and *The Light of the World* (1871), and various orchestral works, including the overtures *In Memoriam* (1867) and *Di Ballo* (1871). And then, in 1875, he collaborated with W. S. Gilbert again. This time they became involved with a brilliantly clever theatrical impresario, Richard D'Oyly Carte. The operetta, a one-act piece, *Trial by Jury*, was an instant success. In the following year D'Oyly Carte took a lease on

Cartoon of Sullivan by Ape, 1874.

*Above* **The Mikado** *Right* **H.M.S. Pinafore** Sullivan remained uneasy about the fame the Savoy Operas brought him. He felt that a 'real' composer ought only to write 'serious' music. But he overlooked the fact that the Savoy Operas were brilliantly constructed, imaginatively orchestrated and full of memorable and very subtle tunes. They have therefore lived, when most Victorian music has perished.

the Opera Comique Theatre and established a company for the express purpose of producing Gilbert and Sullivan operettas.

The works that followed were enormously successful (and still are). In 1881 D'Oyly Carte built a new theatre especially for them. He called it the Savoy, and the operettas henceforth came to be known as 'Savoy Operas'. Here is a complete list of them: *The Sorcerer* (1877), *H.M.S. Pinafore* (1878), *The Pirates of Penzance* (1880), *Patience* (1881), *Iolanthe* (1882), *Princess Ida*(1884), *The Mikado* (1885), *Ruddigore* (1887), *The Yeomen of the Guard* (1888), *The Gondoliers* (1889), *Utopia Limited* (1893), and *The Grand Duke* (1896).

The collaboration between Gilbert and Sullivan was not easy, however, and there were a number of fierce quarrels. But they complemented each other perfectly, and neither was anything like as successful when writing works with other people.

During the Savoy Opera years Sullivan wrote many other works which were successful at the time, though they are seldom performed now. They include oratorios and the opera *Ivanhoe* (1895).

period relied upon written-out orchestrations (often very complex), and therefore approached music rather differently from the jazz band, even though they often played their own versions of jazz and blues. A feature of the big band style was their soloists – men such as Tommy Dorsey (trumpet), Benny Goodman (clarinet), Coleman Hawkins (tenor sax), Fats Waller (piano), Artie Shaw (clarinet), Art Tatum (piano), etc. Many bands also had singers, some of whom – Frank Sinatra, Lena Horne, Peggy Lee, for

**Sword dance** One of the most popular of Scottish traditional folk dances.

example – went on to make names as important soloists.

**Sword dance** Sword dances are traditional in many parts of the world, and their origins are connected with early religious beliefs. (→ **Folk dances**)

The particular kind of sword dance associated with Scotland, in which the dancers perform intricate steps over a pair of crossed swords, is not a group-dance derived from ancient ritual, but a test of individual skill.

# Symphonic poem

An orchestral composition in one continuous movement that 'tells a story', or describes some feeling, idea, or scene. It is therefore an important type of PROGRAMME MUSIC.

The symphonic poem was invented by Liszt, who wrote a series of 12 between 1848 and 1858. It came into existence because of a general tendency in the Romantic period for composers to want to make their music 'mean' something in addition to its purely musical meaning.

Symphonic poems were composed throughout the 19th century, but began to fall out of favour after about 1910. The series that Richard Strauss wrote between 1888 and 1898 show the form at the height of its development. They contain some of the most brilliantly descriptive music ever written.

Many composers found the symphonic poem to be an excellent way of expressing their feelings about their own countries. Nationalist composers of this kind (such as Smetana, Dvořák, Sibelius, etc.) wrote symphonic poems based on legends and historical events.

It is important to realize that a symphonic poem cannot follow *any* story and hope to make musical sense. The story itself must be one that can be turned into a satisfactory musical form. For example, Strauss's *Till Eulenspiegel* not only tells a story, but tells it in the form of a Rondo. In the same way, his *Don Quixote* is really a cunningly worked out 'Theme and Variations'. However descriptive it may be, music must always make sense *as music*.

The other difficulty about all programme music is the fact that music cannot actually *describe* anything in detail. The listener may guess that a piece of music sounds calm. But he could never guess that the 'calmness' was supposed to be the calmness of a clear day on top of a mountain. For all he knows it might as easily be the calmness at the bottom of a coal mine!

For this reason composers not only give their symphonic poems a title, but also supply them with a written explanation of the 'story', to be printed in the programme.

Symphonic poems are sometimes called **Tone poems.** This is a slightly more poetic title. Usually it means that the work is not trying to tell a story, but rather trying to create a particular mood or atmosphere.

---

**Sympathetic strings** Certain stringed instruments, such as the VIOLA D'AMORE, carry a number of strings that are not actually played upon, but which vibrate 'in sympathy' with the playing strings when the note to which they are tuned is sounded.

**Symphony** → page 320

**Syncopation** Any alteration to the normal beats in a bar, made by setting up accents which go against the original beat. This can be brought about by adding accents to unaccented notes:

or by making the longer notes begin on weak beats of the bar:

'Syncopation' is also sometimes used as a general term to describe 20th-century dance- and jazz-band styles, because this kind of music makes great use of syncopated rhythms.

**Karol Szymanowski**
1882-1937 Both composer and pianist, his early work was influenced by Richard Strauss and Debussy.

**Synthesizer** A device that changes electrical impulses into sound. The 'sound' is thus created by entirely artificial means. Every aspect of this sound can be controlled – intensity, tone-colour, quality of attack, durations, variations in dynamics, variations in pitch, etc. The synthesizer is operated from a keyboard, together with a series of switches and variable controls which are 'set' to produce the type of sound the composer wants. The result can be recorded on tape, or played 'live' during a performance. (→ **Electronic instruments and music**)

**Szymanowski, Karol** Polish composer, 1882–1937. Both his parents were very musical and he received his early training from them. Later he studied composition in Warsaw, Berlin, and Leipzig. His mature work dates from about 1910. It includes three symphonies, two violin concertos, and a very fine opera *King Roger* (1926). His music was much influenced by folksong, including that of the Middle East.

# Symphony

This word, which comes from the Greek, really means a 'sounding together'. In music we use it to describe the 'sounding together' of the instruments of an orchestra in a composition in several movements – an orchestral sonata. ( → **Sonata** and **Sonata Form**)

The word was first used in the 17th century to describe almost any kind of instrumental music, simply to distinguish it from *vocal* music. In particular the instrumental interludes in early operas (those of Monteverdi, for example) were called 'Sinfonias' (= 'Symphonies').

The most important instrumental section of any opera, however, was the Overture. And at this period overtures were called SINFONIAS. They followed the pattern of the Dance Suite and consisted of a number of brief, contrasted movements. ( → **Overture**)

Gradually it became the custom to play these pieces in the concert hall, away from the parent opera. And when composers came to write independent pieces especially for the concert hall, they simply copied the style of the existing overtures.

By the middle of the 18th century the operatic sinfonia had taken the name OVERTURE, and the concert sinfonia had changed its name slightly and become the SYMPHONY.

At the same time, this 'symphony' began to develop internally. Each movement of the old suite-like plan began to grow, and each adopted a particular style and musical form. Hundreds of composers were involved in bringing these changes about, but we usually refer to three or four as having had the greatest influence: C. P. E. Bach, J. C. Bach, Haydn, and Mozart.

The 'classical' symphony – that is to say, the form the symphony reached at the end of the 18th century – consisted of a work in four movements, arranged like a sonata ( → **Sonata**, and **Sonata Form**). Thus:

a. A vigorous, quick movement, in Sonata Form.
b. A lyrical, slow movement.
c. A minuet and trio.
d. A cheerful finale, in Rondo or Sonata Form.

From Beethoven onwards, the MINUET movement was replaced by a SCHERZO AND TRIO – a movement less wedded to dance

Here is a list of the most important composers of symphonies:
Haydn (1732 – 1809)
Mozart (1756 – 91)
Beethoven (1770 – 1827)
Schubert (1797 – 1828)
Berlioz (1803 – 69)
Mendelssohn (1809 – 47)
Schumann (1810 – 56)
Bruckner (1824 – 96)
Brahms (1833 – 97)
Tchaikovsky (1840 – 93)
Dvořák (1841 – 1904)
Elgar (1857 – 1934)
Mahler (1860 – 1911)
Sibelius (1865 – 1957)
Nielsen (1865 – 1935)
Vaughan Williams (1872 – 1958)
Prokofiev (1891 – 1953)
Shostakovich (1901 – 75)
Tippett (b. 1905)
Henze (b. 1926)

rhythms and therefore more 'symphonic' in style. And some composers varied the actual style of their movements. Tchaikovsky, for example, makes the last movement of the Sixth Symphony a slow one; and his Fifth Symphony has a waltz instead of either a scherzo or a minuet.

An even greater change came over the *content* of the 19th-century symphony. Whereas Haydn, Mozart, and Beethoven filled their symphonies with purely *musical* argument, 19th-century composers often relaxed this in favour of *description*. In other words, their symphonies 'told a story' and were PROGRAMME SYMPHONIES.

Examples abound: Berlioz's *Fantastic Symphony*, Liszt's *Faust Symphony*, Strauss's *Sinfonia Domestica*. Such works were colourful and exciting, but sometimes rather loosely constructed. Brahms, in particular, disliked this tendency and made sure that his symphonies returned to the practices of Beethoven!

Another tendency at this time was for composers to link the different movements of a symphony by using the same theme (or themes) in each movement. A symphony that does this is said to be a CYCLIC SYMPHONY – César Franck's Symphony in D minor, for example. Sometimes they introduced one special theme which crops up in each movement. This is called a MOTTO THEME – you can find one in Elgar's First Symphony; it first occurs right at the beginning.

At the beginning of the 20th century experiments were made in compressing all the features of a normal symphony into one large movement. Sibelius's Seventh Symphony does this very successfully.

From Haydn and Mozart onwards, many composers have regarded the symphony as the greatest challenge to their powers of imagination and construction. The task of creating a work in which each movement is different and yet fits in with every other movement is formidable indeed.

**Tabla** Indian drums, often used to accompany the sitar. The tabla consists of two drums, tuned to different pitches. One is cylindrical in shape, the other conical. The player squats on the ground and cradles the drums in his lap. He plays them with his hands and fingers. Both drums have skin heads, and often have a paste of flour and iron filings in the centre to improve the resonance. The right-hand drum is known as the TABLA, and the left-hand drum as the BAṄYA, but the instrument's full name (TABLA-BAṄYA ) is not often used.

**Tablature** → page 322

**Table** (of a violin, etc.) The name of the top surface, or 'belly' of the instrument.

**Tabor** An early type of snare drum, used in medieval Europe both as a military and everyday instrument. Tabors came in different sizes, but were always cylindrical. They had two drum heads (of skin), with a snare across the top head (the one that is beaten). Only one drum stick was used, held in the right hand. Tabors were usually slung from the waist, but smaller examples could be held in the left hand. Along with the waist-slung tabor went the PIPE – a small whistle-flute with holes for two fingers and the thumb. One man could therefore play both instruments at the same time.

**Tace** (It.) Silent. A direction which indicates that a particular instrument does not play in the passage where this word occurs. The Latin form, *tacet*, is also frequently used.

**Tafelmusik** During this medieval banquet musicians play from the balcony above.

**Tambourine** As a folk instrument this is often used to accompany dances.

**Tafelmusik** (Ger.) Table music. There are two meanings:
a. music to be performed during a meal, as an entertainment.
b. vocal music to be sung at table after a meal.

**Tail** The 'stem' attached to the head of a minim (half-note), or all smaller notes.

**Tail piece** (of a violin, etc.) The piece of wood at the lower end of the instrument to which the strings are attached.

**Tail pin** or **End pin** The metal rod at the bottom of a cello or double bass, which is pulled out so that the instrument can be set at the correct height for the player.

**Takt** (Ger.) Time (in general), beat, or bar.

**Tallis, Thomas** English composer, c. 1505–85. Not a great deal is known about his life, but he seems to have worked at Waltham Abbey (dissolved in 1540) and then gone to Canterbury, and then become a Gentleman of the Chapel Royal. In 1575 Queen Elizabeth gave him a licence, jointly with William Byrd, for the sole right to print music in England. We may thus safely assume that his gifts were generally admired.

Tallis lived at a time of great religious upheaval. When the Catholics were in power he wrote masses and motets to Latin words. When the Protestants held sway he wrote anthems and services to English words. He was a master of the polyphonic style (there is, for example, a remarkable motet *Spem in alium* in 40 different parts!), but he also mastered the simpler style demanded by the Protestant Church.

Besides his religious music he left a few madrigals, some keyboard pieces, and several '*In Nomines*'.

**Talon** (Fr.) The 'heel' of a violin bow, etc.

**Tambourin** An old French dance from Provence. It was lively and generally in 2/4 time, and played on the equivalent of a pipe and tabor: TAMBOURIN and GALOUBET. 18th-century instrumental suites often imitated the rhythm and sounds of this dance.

**Tambourine** A percussion instrument of very ancient origin (known to the Romans). It consists of a shallow wooden hoop with a parchment stretched across it. This is struck with the knuckles, or rubbed with the thumb. The hoop has small metal plates (JINGLES) which clash together when the instrument is played, or is deliberately shaken.

# Tablature

A form of notation which uses letters, numbers, and other signs, instead of the normal staff notation. Systems of this kind have been used in European music for about seven hundred years – the most notable being for the lute. The two most successful forms of lute tablature came from Italy and France at the beginning of the 16th century. Both used a five or six lined 'stave', which represented the lute strings, the Italian method using numbers to represent the different frets on which the fingers must be placed, and the French method using letters of the alphabet. The length of the notes was shown by 'time-signs' (like the stems and tails of ordinary notation) printed above the 'stave'. Tablatures come near to being a 'picture' of the instrument's strings and where the player must place his fingers. Guitar and banjo tablatures are still in use.

**Early lute tablature**
This 16th-century Italian lutebook uses numbers to indicate which frets must be stopped. The symbols standing above the stave show the rhythm of the piece of music.

**Tambura** A type of Indian lute. It consists of a gourd, which rests on the floor or in the player's lap and acts as a sound box, with a long neck which is held so that it rests against the left shoulder. It has no frets and four strings, which are gently stroked. The pitch can be changed by moving an ivory bridge. The function of the tambura is to provide a continuous drone (in the tonic key).

**Tam-tam** A large bronze gong of Chinese origin. The size varies – anything from 60 cm to 1·5 m in diameter – and the instrument is suspended on a frame and struck with a soft beater. The usual orchestral tam-tam is 71 cm in diameter. The outer rim of the disk is turned down, which prevents the edge from vibrating and increases the rather mysterious sound.

**Tampon** A drumstick with a head at either end. It is held in the middle and used (usually on the bass drum) to produce a roll – by rapidly shaking the wrist so that the two heads strike the drumhead alternately.

**Tango** A Latin American dance, probably of mixed Spanish and Negro origin. It came to Europe as a ballroom dance in about 1915. It is not unlike the **Habanera** →, but is rather slower and more melancholy.

**Tanto** (It.) As much, or too much. As in such directions as **allegro non tanto**, quick, but not too quick.

**Tam-tam** It is notably used by Holst in 'Mars' from his suite, *The Planets*.

**Tango** This Argentinian dance is performed by couples moving at a slow walking pace. It is in two in a bar time, with a dotted rhythm.

**Tanz** (Ger.) Dance.

**Tap dance** A dance in which the feet tap out a rhythmic pattern. Special footwear is often used. Tap dancing became particularly popular in the 1930s, when the American dancer Fred Astaire made a series of Hollywood musicals, but its origins are very ancient indeed, and similar music from stamping feet or tapping shoes occurs throughout musical history. (→ **Clog dance**)

**Tarantella** A dance which takes its name from the town of Taranto in Southern Italy. It is in 6/8 time and is played with ever-increasing speed. It is usually danced by a man and a woman, who may play castanets and tambourines.

It used to be thought that a wild dance of this kind would cure people bitten by the Tarantula spider, but as these spiders are no more dangerous than wasps, the story does not seem very credible.

**Tartini, Giuseppe** Italian composer, 1692–1770. He was the son of a nobleman and came to be regarded as the greatest violinist of his day. He made many improvements to the instrument itself, and was famous as a teacher. His music includes solo and trio sonatas and many concerti grossi. One sonata became famous because Tartini pretended it had been dictated to him in a dream by the devil. It is nicknamed *The Devil's Trill* and is very difficult to play.

**Tasto** (It.) Keyboard (of a piano, etc.). Finger-board (of a violin, etc.).

**Tattoo** Originally a drum 'call' that was played each evening to warn soldiers to return to camp. In this sense it was known as 'beating the retreat'. Later it became a more elaborate ceremony and a fife-tune was added to the drum taps. Certain regiments still perform these attractive ceremonies.

In more recent years the word has been used to describe elaborate military displays, using bands and intricate marching patterns. These are usually performed at night in artificial light and in front of vast audiences. The Edinburgh Tattoo performed at the International Edinburgh (Arts) Festival every year is probably the most famous.

**Georg Telemann**
1681–1767 One of the most prolific of all composers, he wrote, among other works, over 40 settings of the Passion, 40 operas and 600 overtures.

**Taylor, Deems** American composer, 1885–1966. He was well-known as a critic and lecturer on music, and wrote two operas which, for a time, were very popular: *The King's Henchman* (1927), and *Peter Ibbetson* (1931). The orchestral version of his *Through the Looking-Glass* suite (based on Lewis Carroll) also became popular.

**Tchaikovsky** → page 324

**Te Deum laudamus** 'We Praise Thee, O God'. A hymn of rejoicing, dating from the fourth or fifth century and now used as a part of the Christian liturgy. It can be sung to plainsong, but there are also many more elaborate settings – some even using soloists and orchestra (Berlioz, Dvořák, etc.).

**Tattoo** The Edinburgh tattoo is performed by floodlight in the grounds of Edinburgh Castle.

**Taverner, John** English composer, c. 1495–1545. He was a very great composer of polyphonic church music and wrote many fine masses and motets; but when he became a Protestant in 1528 he abandoned music altogether. He then devoted himself to the dissolution of the monasteries. He is now regarded as one of the most important English composers of his time.

**Telemann, Georg** German composer, 1681–1767. He held a number of important musical posts before settling in Hamburg in 1721. He wrote an enormous amount of music. Though not as highly regarded as his contemporaries Bach and Handel were, he was still a very able composer and his music can be played today with considerable pleasure.

# Tchaikovsky

Peter Ilyich Tchaikovsky. Russian composer, 1840–93. Although, even as a child, Tchaikovsky showed unmistakable gifts for music, his parents do not seem to have expected him to make a career of it. Indeed, he was sent to the School of Jurisprudence at St Petersburg (now called Leningrad), and then, in 1859, became a clerk in the Ministry of Justice. But he devoted all his spare time to music, gradually becoming more and more serious about it until, in 1863, he threw up his job and set about the business of becoming a composer.

To begin with he had a hard time of it. His father had lost a great deal of money and could not help him much. He spent two years studying at the new St Petersburg Conservatory, and then went to Moscow where, in due course, he became Professor of Harmony at the Conservatory. Little by little he began to make a mark with his compositions. By 1873, after the performance of his Second Symphony, he was recognized to be one of the most promising of the new Russian composers.

Two important things now happened that were to affect his life in very different ways. His music attracted the attention and admiration of a wealthy widow, Nadezdha von Meck. She decided to help him all she could. At first she commissioned new works, and then, in 1878, she offered him a substantial annual allowance so that he could devote the whole of his time to composition. One of the first-fruits of this generous plan was the Fourth Symphony – dedicated, in gratitude, to 'My Best Friend'.

She made one rule, however. They must never meet! He agreed. And though their friendship continued until 1891, and though they wrote long, intimate letters to each other, they never met face to face – save once, by accident.

In 1876 Tchaikovsky was deeply absorbed in writing an opera, *Eugene Onegin*, in which a young girl is rejected by the man she loves, when he suddenly received a letter from a young student, Antonia Milyukova. She declared that she loved him. More letters followed, each becoming more passionate. Finally she threatened to commit suicide if he did not marry her. In pity he agreed, and the ceremony took place in July 1877.

The marriage was a farce and a disaster.

*Left* **Peter Ilyich Tchaikovsky** 1840–1893 A photograph taken shortly before the composer's death.

*Right* **Puss-in-Boots from The Sleeping Beauty** The last act of this ballet features a number of popular nursery tale characters.

*Below* **Swan Lake** Royal Ballet, Covent Garden, in this most famous of the Tchaikovsky Ballets.

**Tchaikovsky's birthplace** The composer was born in this house in Votkinsk.

*Below* **Bluebird from The Sleeping Beauty** This dancer is one of two bluebirds featured in the composer's ballet, first produced in 1890.

Tchaikovsky tried to kill himself, and before the year was out they had parted for ever. The truth of the matter was that he was homosexual, but longed to lead a 'normal' life. Marriage, he thought, might 'cure' him. But, of course, it could not be, and both he and his wife suffered cruelly.

Even so, the emotional upheaval may very well have helped his music. During the years that followed his works grew deeper and more assured, and it soon became clear that he was a composer of international importance.

The last years of his life were marked by ever-increasing success. He conducted performances of his music all over Europe, and, in 1891, in America. In 1893 he visited England and was made a Doctor of Music by Cambridge University. But, because of his private life, he was an unhappy man. One day, in late October 1893, he brushed aside his friends' warnings and rashly drank a glass of unboiled water. He caught cholera and was dead within a week.

Audiences love Tchaikovsky's music. Everything he wrote expresses some part of his own deepest feelings. His music tells the story of his life, and it is impossible when listening to it not to be deeply moved.

### Summary of Tchaikovsky's main works

Operas and ballets include:

| | |
|---|---|
| *Swan Lake* (ballet) | 1876 |
| *Eugene Onegin* (opera) | 1878 |
| *The Sleeping Beauty* (ballet) | 1889 |
| *The Queen of Spades* (opera) | 1890 |
| *The Nutcracker* (ballet) | 1892 |

Symphonies:

| | |
|---|---|
| No 1 in G minor ('Winter Dreams') | |
| | 1866, revised 1874 |
| No 2 in C minor ('The Little Russian') | |
| | 1872, revised 1879 |
| No 3 in D major | 1875 |
| No 4 in F minor | 1878 |
| 'Manfred' Symphony | 1885 |
| No 5 in E minor | 1888 |
| No 6 in B minor ('Pathétique') | 1893 |

Orchestral works include:

| | |
|---|---|
| Overture 'Romeo and Juliet' | |
| | 1869, revised 1870 and 1880 |
| Symphonic Fantasy 'The Tempest' | 1873 |
| Symphonic Fantasy 'Francesca da Rimini' | 1876 |
| Overture '1812' | 1880 |
| Overture-Fantasy 'Hamlet' | 1888 |

Concertos include:

| | |
|---|---|
| Piano Concerto No 1 in B flat minor | |
| | 1874–5 |
| 'Variations on a Rococo Theme' (cello and orchestra) | 1876 |
| Violin Concerto in D major | 1878 |
| Piano Concerto No 2 in G major | |
| | 1879–80, revised 1893 |
| Piano Concerto No 3 in E flat major | |
| | 1893 |

Other works also include songs, church music, and chamber music.

**Theorbo** This example of the instrument was made by Heinrich Goldt in Hamburg in 1734.

**Tempo** (It.) Time, in the sense of 'speed'. As in **a tempo**, 'in time' (after some change of speed, indicating a return to the original speed). Also:

**Tempo comodo** At a comfortable speed.

**Tempo di ballo** at a dance speed – usually that of the quick waltz.

**Tempo giusto** in strict time.

**Tempo primo** at the original speed (after a change of speed).

**Ten** (It.) Short for **Tenuto** →.

**Tenor C** The lowest note on the viola (the 'tenor' string instrument):

**Tenor clef** → **Notes and notation**

**Tenor drum** → **Drums**

**Tenor voice** → **Voice**

**Tenuto** (It.) Held to the full value of the note. (→ **Ten**)

**Ternary form** → page 326

**Ternary time** Triple time (simple or compound).

**Terzett, Terzetto** → **Trio**

**Tetrachord** A group of four notes. The scale can be divided into two equal tetrachords of tone-tone-semitone pattern. For example, the tetrachords in the scale of C major are C to F, and G to C.

**Tessitura** An Italian term that indicates the general 'lie' of a piece of music. That is to say, whether the majority of the notes lie high up, or low down in the range of the instrument or voice.

**Thematic** Belonging to, or related to the 'theme'. Thus we may speak of a composition's 'thematic material'.

**Theme** A musical idea that returns in one form or another throughout a composition: one of the chief bits of material out of which the piece is made. (→ **Subject**)

**Theorbo** A large member of the lute family, probably invented in Italy towards the end of the 16th century. It had a double neck, with two sets of tuning pegs and two sets of strings. One set of strings could be stopped by the fingers, but the other set were played 'open'

# Ternary Form

Ternary means 'in three parts', and Ternary Form occurs whenever a piece of music can be divided in this way.

One thing is essential, however. The first section and the third section must be alike (or nearly so), and the second section must provide some kind of contrast. Usually the second section is in a different key, and uses different musical material. We describe the overall effect as an **A B A** pattern.

Musical forms of this kind are exceedingly effective. You can find them everywhere, in simple tunes, or in more elaborate movements.

Here is a simple example by Mozart, written when he was eight years old. Section 1 (or '**A**') lasts until bar 8. Section 2, the Middle Section ('**B**'), is from bar 9 to bar 16. Section 3 then repeats the first section and brings the piece to an end. You will see that Mozart does not change key in the middle section, but he has provided a new sort of musical material, to make a contrast.

as a kind of 'drone' accompaniment. It was often used as a continuo instrument, but fell out of use during the second half of the 18th century.

**Theremin** An electronic instrument invented in 1924 and named after the Russian-born scientist Lev Theremin. It looks something like a radio receiver, with a projecting metal rod. As the player moves his hand towards and away from the rod he affects the electric oscillations and thus the pitch of the note. Unfortunately it was only possible to slide from one note to another, and so the instrument's musical capabilities were somewhat limited.

**Thomson, Virgil** American composer, b. 1896. After graduating from Harvard University he studied in Paris with Nadia Boulanger. His music was much influenced by Satie and *Les Six* and is often a curious, and deliberate, mixture of the childlike and the highly sophisticated. His two operas to words by Gertrude Stein (a kind of inspired nonsense) show him at his best. They are: *Four Saints in Three Acts* (1928), and *The Mother of us all* (1947). He is also well known as a critic and has written for, among other papers, *The New York Herald Tribune*.

**Thorough-bass → Figured bass**

**Three Choirs Festival**
Elgar's *The Kingdom* was performed at Gloucester Cathedral during the 1922 Festival. The composer attended this performance.

**Three Choirs Festival** The oldest choral festival in England. It takes place in late August each year and alternates between the three cathedral cities of Gloucester, Hereford, and Worcester. Its records go back to the 1720s, but it probably began somewhat earlier than that. It was intended to raise money for the widows and orphans of the clergy, but gradually developed into an important musical event. The festival is mainly choral, and much of it takes place in the three cathedrals. Many famous composers have written music for it.

**Thunder machine** In the orchestra this usually consists of a large metal sheet which, when shaken, makes a noise like thunder. In theatres, however, a similar effect was obtained by dropping cannon balls into a wooden trough and letting them roll down, or revolving a wooden drum with metal balls inside it. Nowadays, of course, it is simpler to use a tape-recording of real thunder.

**Thunder stick,** or **Bull roarer,** or **Whizzer** An instrument used by the American Indians, the Australian aborigines, the natives of Central Africa, etc. It is a flat piece of wood with a string attached, and when swung rapidly round the head it makes a strange whirring sort of noise – higher or lower, according to the speed.

**Tie** or **Bind** The curved line joining a note and its repetition, showing that they are to be treated as one unbroken long note of the value of the two together.

The reasons for thus 'tying' or 'binding' the note are as follows:
1. A bar-line intervenes, so that the sound required cannot be written as one note:

2. The particular length of sound required is such as no single note could represent:

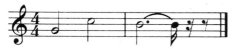

(For other uses of the curved line see **Notes and notation**.)

**Tierce** The interval of the third (→ **Intervals**).

**Tierce de Picardie** The 'Picardy Third' was used by musicians until about the middle of the 18th century to ensure that a piece of music in a minor key ended with a major chord (containing the major third of the scale). The minor third was felt to be too discordant to make a satisfactory ending. The practice was dying out by Bach's time, but some of his pieces still use it:

Ending of a German hymn-tune in D minor, as harmonized by Bach

**Timbre** → **Acoustics**

**Time** → **Notes and notation**

**Time-names** or **Rhythm-names** A French method of teaching time and rhythm. Everything is reckoned by beats and fractions of beats. For example:
A note that lasts one beat is called **Ta**.
A note that lasts two beats is called **Ta-a**.
Two notes, each lasting half a beat, are called **Ta-té**.
And so on.

**Time signature** → **Notes and notation**

**Timpani** → **Drums**

**Tin whistle** → **Recorder**

**Timpani** or kettledrum. This percussion instrument was played by a mounted man in the huge army bands of the Ottoman Empire. By the 16th century it was used in some European cavalry regiments, and by the 17th century it had found its way into the works of Bach and Handel. Today after considerable development, two are an integral part of any orchestra.

**Tippett** → page 328

**Toccata** (It.) Touched. A type of keyboard composition, originating in the 17th century, intended to show off the player's touch and technique. The music of such a 'touch piece' is therefore very quick and brilliant, rather like a showy improvisation. Bach's organ and harpsichord toccatas (e.g. the Toccata and Fugue in D minor) are particularly brilliant. A toccatina is a small-scale toccata.

**Tomkins, Thomas** English composer, 1572–1656. The most important member of a very talented musical family. He was born in Wales (of Cornish descent), and, after studying with William Byrd, became organist of Worcester Cathedral (c. 1596–1646). He was appointed one of the organists of the Chapel Royal in 1621, and would have become Composer in Ordinary to Charles I, had the King not had a sudden change of mind. Tomkins wrote anthems and services of considerable importance, as well as music for viols and virginals. In 1622 he published a fine collection of madrigals (for 3, 4, 5, and 6 voices). His keyboard music, however – he was the last of the 'Elizabethan' school – forms the core of his output.

**Tomtoms** Small drums with double heads and no snares. They vary in size (and pitch) – anything from 30 cm to 45 cm in diameter. The larger varieties are supported on legs, and the smaller versions are often clamped together in pairs on a stand. Though they are of indefinite pitch, the composer will usually specify that he wants a 'high', 'medium', or 'low' sound. They make an excellent substitute for high timpani. Tomtoms with single heads can also be obtained, and their sound is deeper and purer.

**Tonality** The 'tonality' of a piece is its **Key** →.

**Tonal sequence** → **Sequence**

**Tone** The interval of two semitones, as from C to D, E to F sharp, etc. In America, however, the word 'tone' is sometimes used instead of 'note'.

**Tone poem** → **Symphonic poem**

**Tonguing** In playing wind instruments this means interrupting the stream of air by a movement of the tongue, as though the sound T were being made. **Double** and **Triple** tonguing is also possible (t-k, t-k-t).

**Tonic** The first note of the major or minor scale.

**Tonic Sol-fa** → **Sol-fa system**

# Tippett

(Sir) Michael Tippett. English composer, b. 1905. Tippett's musical education began in earnest only when he went to the Royal College of Music in 1923. He had had piano lessons from the age of five, and had begun to compose while still at school, but his experience of music had been limited. He is thus a composer who developed late.

On leaving the College in 1927 he taught at a preparatory school for several years and took part in amateur music-making. But in 1930, a concert of his own music convinced him that he needed to 'start again' as a composer. He undertook a rigorous course of strict counterpoint and did not compose again until he felt technically fluent.

The music which began to build his reputation as a composer dates from the mid-1930s. The most important piece is the Concerto for Double String Orchestra (1939).

The war years (1939-45) brought problems and success to Tippett. He was a convinced pacifist, and spent three months in prison (1943) because of his views. But the war also prompted the composition of an oratorio *A Child of Our Time* (1941) which, when performed in 1944, brought him fame.

His success has since grown steadily and his style has gradually developed. In the 1940s his music, which had always been polyphonic, grew even more luxuriant. In the 1960s, however, it became much simpler and more angular and dissonant.

*Above* **The Midsummer Marriage** This scene is from a 1968 production of the opera. Tippett also wrote the libretto.

*Right* **King Priam** This opera is based on Homer's story of the Greek and Trojan leaders. This scene is from a 1975 production.

**Sir Michael Tippett**
b. 1905

Tippett's work includes four fine symphonies (1945, 1957, 1972, and 1977), three string quartets, a Concerto for Piano and Orchestra (1955), a Concerto for Orchestra (1963), and an extremely complex work for chorus and orchestra: *The Vision of St Augustine* (1965). His four operas, however (for which he also wrote the libretti), probably contain the kernel of his life's work. They are: *The Midsummer Marriage* (1952), *King Priam* (1961), *The Knot Garden* (1969), and *The Ice Break* (1977).

**Tosto** (It.) Rapid. As in the direction **più tosto**, 'quicker'. (But **più tosto** or **più-tosto** followed by another word usually means 'rather'.)

**Toy symphony** A kind of miniature symphony which uses musical toys, such as rattles, whistles, bird-calls, etc. The earliest example dates from 1788 and was thought to have been composed by Haydn, but modern research suggests that it was in fact the work of Mozart's father, Leopold Mozart. Mendelssohn wrote two such works.

**Tranquillo** (It.) Tranquil.

**Transcription** → **Arrangement or Transcription**

**Transition** Either an abrupt modulation, or the 'bridge passage' in **Sonata Form** →

**Transpose** → **Transposition**

**Transposing Instruments** Any instrument whose music is written out at a pitch which is different from the actual sound. The practice arose when instruments and playing techniques were less efficient than they are today – the object being to reduce the number of flats and sharps the player had to cope with. For example, clarinets are made in two main sizes: B flat and A – these are their 'natural' keys, as the key of C is the 'natural' key (i.e. the simplest to play) on the piano. The music for a B flat clarinet is written out a tone higher than it sounds – so a piece in E flat would be written in F, with two less flats to worry about. Music for the clarinet in A is written a minor third higher – so a piece in B would be written out in D, with three less sharps.

# Trombone

A brass instrument of ancient origin. It produces its notes by sliding one length of tube in and out of another. This telescopic arrangement makes it possible for the playing length of the instrument to be varied at will, and thus different sets of harmonics can be brought into action.

The most important members of the family are the tenor and bass trombones. In a large orchestra you would expect to find two tenors and one bass. Their practical ranges are:

**Tenor**     **Bass**

*Below* **Determining the pitch** By moving the U-shaped slide the player can achieve seven notes of different pitch.

There are also treble trombones (found in Purcell, Bach, etc.), alto trombones (found in 19th-century scores, and now replaced by the tenors), and even a double bass trombone, which is said to be very tiring to play.

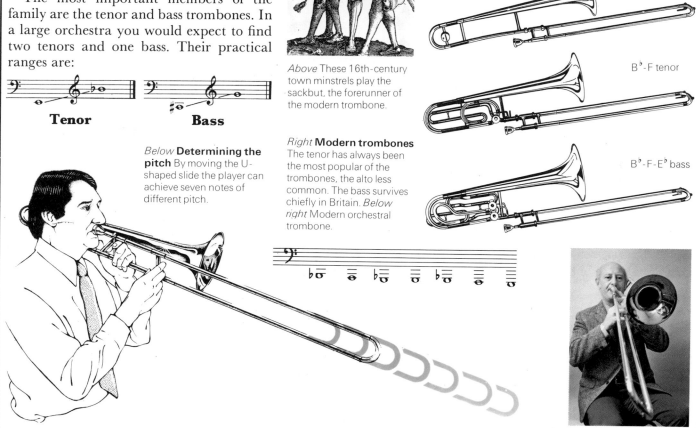

*Above* These 16th-century town minstrels play the sackbut, the forerunner of the modern trombone.

*Right* **Modern trombones** The tenor has always been the most popular of the trombones, the alto less common. The bass survives chiefly in Britain. *Below right* Modern orchestral trombone.

B♭ tenor

B♭-F tenor

B♭-F-E♭ bass

In the orchestra, the main transposing instruments are: the COR ANGLAIS, the CLARINETS, the FRENCH HORNS, and the TRUMPETS. The cor anglais and French horns are pitched in F, which means that their music is written a fifth higher than it sounds (when C is wanted, G must be written). Trumpets are usually in B flat, and clarinets, as we have seen, come in B flat and A (though the B flat clarinet is the most common nowadays).

Certain instruments are 'transposing' instruments in a slightly different way. The double bass, for example, has its music written an octave above its sound; while the piccolo part is written an octave lower. This is simply a convenience that avoids leger lines.

**Transposition** The changing of the pitch of a composition. Each note must be sung or played at the same place in the scale of the new key as it did in the original key. Singers often ask their accompanists to transpose a song into a higher or lower key to suit their particular voice-range.

**Treble** The highest, unbroken boy's voice. The treble clef is used for the upper range of musical notation ( → **Notes and notation**). By treble C we mean the C on the third space up of the treble clef.

**Tremolando** (It.) Trembling. ( → **Tremolo**)

**Tremolo** The rapid repetition of a note, or notes, without measured time value. Particularly effective on strings, where the bow can move up and down very rapidly indeed. Such music is notated (see left) with the direction **trem**, added to show that the repetitions of the note are not measured in any note value.

The term **tremolo** is often used in singing as if it were the same as **Vibrato →**.

**Trepak** A Russian Cossack dance. It is in 2/4 time and very lively.

**Triad → Harmony**

**Triangle** A short steel bar bent into a three-cornered shape. It is struck with a small metal rod. It has no definite pitch, but its note is high and bright.

**Trill → Ornaments and grace-notes**

**Trio** Any group of three performers, or a piece of music written for such a group to play.

A **string trio** usually consists of a violin, viola, and cello. A **piano trio** consists of a piano and two other instruments, such as violin and cello.

The word trio is also used to describe the middle section of the Minuet movement of a symphony, sonata, or quartet. It is usually written for only a section of the orchestra to play, and was originally intended for only a trio of performers. The middle section of a March is also referred to as the trio. In both cases, the trio section makes a contrast with the main part of the movement.

**Triple counterpoint → Counterpoint**

**Triplet** A group of three notes (or notes and rests) to be performed in the time of two. The triplet is shown by a figure 3 placed, with a slur, over the notes. ( **→ Notes and notation**)

**Tritone** The interval of an augmented fourth, containing three full tones – F to B, G to C sharp, etc. In early music it was avoided as the *Diabolus in Musica*, 'The Devil in Music', as it was considered particularly difficult to pitch correctly. It is now used very frequently.

**Triumphs of Oriana, The** An important book of madrigals, probably written in praise of Queen Elizabeth I. It is dated 1601, but was published in 1603, after her death. It contains 29 madrigals by 26 composers, including Morley, Tomkins, and Wilbye.

**Tromba marina** The 'Sea Trumpet' was actually a stringed instrument, very popular in the 15th century, though it had existed since the 12th. It was still in use in Mozart's day, but by then it was a rarity. It consists of a long tapering box (anything up to 2 m in length), with a single string passing over a

**Triangle** This instrument first appeared in Italy in the 14th century but was not used in the orchestra until the 18th century. It is notably featured in Liszt's First Piano Concerto and in Grieg's *Peer Gynt*.

**Triangle** This 15th-century miniature shows an angel playing the instrument.

**Tromba marina** This medieval instrument dates back to, at least, the 12th century. Its loud, brassy sound explains its name 'trumpet', but why it was called 'marine' is still a mystery.

# Trumpet family

The trumpet is an instrument of ancient origin – examples have been found in the tombs of ancient Egypt (those from the tomb of the Pharaoh Tutankhamen, c. 1350 B.C. being perhaps the most famous). But these trumpets were simply long metal tubes, straight or curved, from which only a basic harmonic series could be sounded. The history of the trumpet as an orchestral instrument is therefore bound up with the different attempts that were made to provide a wider range of notes.

*Above* **Side-blown trumpet from Africa** Primitive instruments like this are often associated with ceremonial functions.

*Below* **Conch shell** Used by the Quecho Indians of Peru, like other primitive people, as a basic trumpet.

*Above* **Medieval straight trumpets** These late 13th–century Spanish trumpets are decorated, at the joints in the tubing, with pennants rather like the modern fanfare trumpet.

*Left* Trumpets at a 14th-century jousting tournament.

*Below* **Modern orchestral trumpet** mouthpiece **1**, brace **2**, first valve slide **3**, first valve **4**, second valve **5**, second valve slide **6**, third valve **7**, finger hole **8**, third valve slide **9**, water key **10**, bell **11**. When a valve is depressed it opens a tube which lengthens the air column thereby altering the pitch.

*Above* **Arab kettle-drums and trumpets** These military instruments were often played together in the Ottoman Empire. The practice was adopted in the 15th century in Western Europe.

The trumpet now in everyday orchestral use is the VALVE TRUMPET. That is to say, it has extra lengths of tubing coiled alongside its main tube, and these can be brought into action by pressing down a 'valve'. There are three valves, and by combining them in different ways six different lengths of tubing can be obtained, and therefore six different series of harmonics – in addition to the 'natural' series of the basic instrument. The modern trumpet is pitched in B flat (its music being written a tone higher than it sounds), but C trumpets are also common. It is an agile, flexible instrument – as able to produce soft sounds as it can loud ones.

Valves were added to trumpets in about 1820. Before that time there were several ingenious attempts to provide the NATURAL TRUMPET with a more complete range of notes. For example, from the 17th to 19th centuries trumpets were provided with CROOKS – extra lengths of tubing that could be added by hand. This worked well enough, but required a few moments to make the change from one crook to another. At much the same time experiments were made with SLIDE TRUMPETS, working on the same telescopic principle as the trombone. KEYED TRUMPETS appeared in about 1800, each with from four to six keys set in the body of the instrument and operating like the keys of the woodwind. But all these experiments were made obsolete by the invention of valves.

Alongside the normal orchestral trumpets, there are now instruments of several different sizes. Small 'CLARINO' TRUMPETS, pitched in C, D, and high F, are used to play the high trumpet parts of Baroque music – players of those times used the natural trumpet (which in fact has a much softer, flute-like voice than the modern instrument) and specialized in playing high notes. In recent years composers have begun to write high trumpet parts again (Stravinsky uses a D trumpet in *Petrushka*, 1911). There is also a SOPRANINO TRUMPET in high B flat, which considerably extends the upper range of notes. For the other end of the scale Wagner demanded a BASS TRUMPET (for the 'Ring' cycle), and other composers, such as Stravinsky and Richard Strauss, have occasionally made use of it. The trumpets may therefore now be considered a complete family in themselves.

*Left* **Tibetan trumpet** These straight trumpets are here used to call monks to prayer.

The complete chromatic range of the modern orchestral trumpet.

*Left* **Curved silver trumpets from India** These folk instruments are used in dance rituals and traditional ceremonies.

*Below* **Fanfare trumpets** This 'natural' trumpet can produce notes only of the harmonic series. They are not used in bands or orchestras but for ceremonial purposes.

bridge. It was bowed, but only natural harmonics were used – the player lightly touching the string so as to produce them. Later examples had two strings, and sometimes a number of sympathetic strings mounted inside the box.

**Trombone →** page 329

**Trope** An addition of words or music to traditional **Plainsong** (→) is known as a trope. Such additions began to be made in the ninth century and continued, with varying degrees of enthusiasm, until banned in the 15th century. Some of the additions took on a life of their own, as independent poems and hymn-tunes.

**Troppo** (It.) Too much. As in *allegro ma non troppo,* fast, but not too fast .

**Troubadours → Minstrels**

**Trouvères → Minstrels**

**Trumpet →** page 330

**Trumpet voluntary** An organ voluntary of a kind common in the late 17th century, with a tune for the right hand to play on the trumpet stop on one manual whilst the left hand accompanies on a **diapason stop** on another manual.

**Tuba** This came into existence during the 1820s to provide a good solid bass in military bands, etc. There are several different kinds of tuba, but the one most frequently used in the orchestra is the tuba in F, which has 4 m of tubing at its disposal. Like the trumpet, it is a valve instrument.

Military and brass bands employ a variety of tubas, which go under various names. There is the EUPHONIUM (B flat), the BOMBARDON (or E FLAT BASS), and the DOUBLE (B FLAT BASS). The EUPHONIUM sometimes turns up in orchestral scores under the name tenor tuba.

**Tubular bells** These are also called chimes. They are used with considerable effect in Tchaikovsky's *1812 Overture.*

**Tuba** This instrument comes in different sizes with a variety of musical range. Ravel gave the tuba a well-known solo in his arrangement of Mussorgsky's *Pictures from an Exhibition.*

A special form of E flat and B flat bass is the HELICON, which is so made that it goes right round the player's neck. The type of helicon that does this and then rises in a large bell *above* the player's head is called a SOUSAPHONE. Apart from being used in Sousa's own band, it became very popular in early jazz bands.

The practical playing range of the orchestral tuba is:

**Tubular bells** These are long tubes of metal hanging in a wooden frame, and are sometimes used in orchestras. Each tube plays a different note. The playing is done by striking with drumsticks.

**Tuning fork → Pitch; Acoustics**

**Tutti** (It.) All. In orchestral music, a *tutti* passage is one in which all the instruments play. The same term is used in a concerto to distinguish those passages when the orchestra plays without the soloist.

**Twelve-note music, Twelve-tone music** Alternative terms for **Serialism →**

**Tye, Christopher** English composer, c. 1497 – c. 1573. Not a great deal is known about his life, except that he was closely connected with Cambridge University and Ely Cathedral. He has been called 'the Father of the Anthem', and it is generally considered that he helped to keep the traditions of English choral writing alive at the time of the dissolution of the monasteries. Before this event he wrote a number of fine masses and motets. After it, he wrote equally fine anthems and services.

# Tuning of instruments

If you turn to the article on **Equal Temperament →**, you will see that the modern keyboard instrument is 'tuned' in a way which is only approximately correct. The craft of tuning is a very difficult one, and can only be mastered after long practice and skilled instruction. But it mainly consists of working in a series of octaves, perfect fifths, and perfect fourths. Thus if you start with C, you can then fix the G below it, and from that G go on to D above,

and so on until a whole chromatic scale has been laid out. From that you can proceed to tune the rest of the instrument.

This is a difficult craft, best left to a qualified tuner, although electronic devices giving an exact pitch are now on the market.

**Ukelele** A type of small guitar, developed in Hawaii in the 1870s, it was popular in minstrel shows, music-halls, and jazz bands.

**Unison** Two or more voices or instruments playing 'in unison' – creating sound.

**Up-beat** The last beat of a bar. Many pieces of music start on this beat (for example, 'The Bluebells of Scotland'), rather than the down-beat – the first beat of the bar (for example, 'God save the Queen').

Conductors often begin a piece of music by showing a preparatory up-beat, which gives the players an indication of the speed.

**Upright, Upright Grand → Piano**

**Urtext** (Ger.) The 'original text' – that is to say, an edition which tries to get back to what the composer actually wrote by studying his manuscript, if it still survives, or the first published edition. Over the years many pieces of music become corrupted by various editors, and so an urtext can become very necessary.

**Ukelele** This instrument probably developed from the Portuguese machete, a folk guitar very popular among sailors. It has four strings tuned to B, F sharp, D and A. *Below left* This old time American string band uses a ukelele among other stringed instruments.

**Valen, Fartein** Norwegian composer, 1887–1952. He studied in Oslo and Berlin and developed a very personal atonal style which owed something to Schoenberg. He wrote five symphonies, a violin concerto (1940), and a certain amount of choral and chamber music. Though he was awarded a State Pension in 1932, his music was largely neglected until towards the end of his life. He is now regarded as one of the most important Norwegian composers of his day.

**Valve trombone → Trombone**

**Valve trumpet → Trumpet**

**Vamp** To make up a piano accompaniment for a singer or instrumentalist who has no copy of the music. In music hall and variety concerts the orchestra is often required to 'vamp till ready' when the artiste is going through some comic business routine on the stage. To do this the conductor indicates, in advance, a few bars that can be repeated over and over again until the act is ready to proceed.

**Varèse, Edgard** American composer, 1883–1965. He was born in Paris and studied at the Schola Cantorum (1904–6). After working in Berlin and Prague, and serving in the First World War, he left Europe and settled in America (1916), becoming an American citizen in 1927.

His music explored many new paths, including extreme dissonance and complex rhythms. He later came to believe that electronic methods were best. His works include many pieces for unusual combinations of instruments: *Offrandes*, for soprano, chamber orchestra, and percussion

**Edgard Varèse** 1883-1965 French-born, he studied science in Turin before returning to Paris where he became a pupil of d'Indy and Roussel. In 1916 he moved to New York where he founded The International Composers' Guild which supported modern music. His own work with its extreme dissonance often enraged the audience. He was also a pioneer in taped and electronic music.

**The Vibraphone,** here played by Milt Jackson of the Modern Jazz Quartet, is a percussion instrument whose tuned metal bars are struck with padded mallets. An electrical pulse opens and closes the resonators beneath the bars to produce a vibrato effect. Modern composers such as Berg have used it in their works and it was popular with dance bands of the 1920's and 30's.

(1922); *Octandre*, for wind, brass, and percussion (1923); *Ionisation*, for percussion and two sirens (1931); *Density 21.5*, for platinum flute (the density of platinum is 21.5) (1936). Electronic scores include *Déserts* (1954) and *Poème électronique* (1958).

**Variations → Air with variations**

**Vaudeville** Originally, in the 16th century, this was a type of satirical song popular among the Paris street musicians. Later, the tunes of these songs, with new, topical words, were introduced into the comic plays that were performed during the Paris fairs. These 'comedies with vaudevilles' eventually came to be called simply 'vaudevilles'. Nowadays the word is used to describe some kind of 'variety show'.

The word is also used in opera to describe the kind of finale where each main character steps forward to sing a verse – as for instance, in Mozart's *Die Entführung aus dem Serail*.

**Vaughan Williams → page 335**

**Veloce** (It.) Quickly. **Velocissimo**, very quickly .

**Venite** This is the 95th Psalm, 'O come, let us sing unto the Lord'. In the Anglican Church it is sung as a prelude to the psalms of the morning service, generally to an Anglican chant.

**Verdi → page 336**

**Verismo** The Italian word for 'realism' has been used to describe a type of opera popular from about 1890 to 1920 which made use of very realistic stories. These were often also rather sordid, full of murder and violence. Examples include Mascagni's *Cavalleria Rusticana* and Leoncavallo's *I Pagliacci*, as well as some of Puccini's operas. The first 'realistic' opera of this kind was Bizet's *Carmen* (1875), but it was the Italians who developed the type.

**Verse** and **Full → Anthem**

**Vespers** The seventh of the Canonical Hours, or services of the day, in the Roman Catholic Church. It is normally held at sunset. Many composers (including Monteverdi and Mozart) have written elaborate music for this service.

# Vaughan Williams

Ralph Vaughan Williams. English composer, 1872–1958. He was born in the small Cotswold village of Down Ampney, where his father was the vicar. Most of his childhood, however, was spent at Leith Hill Place in Surrey, for his father died in 1875 and his mother returned to live with her parents. His family background was cultured, intellectual, and wealthy. He began to write music when he was six, but did not begin to study it seriously until he had completed his general education (at Charterhouse School) and went to the Royal College of Music (1890).

On and off, his musical education lasted until 1908. First at the Royal College under Parry, then at Trinity College, Cambridge, and then again at the Royal College (1905) under Stanford. In 1897 he married and spent several months in Berlin studying under Max Bruch. Later, in 1908, he felt obliged to go to Paris to study with Ravel.

Though Vaughan Williams wrote a great deal of music during these years of study, he did not find his own individual style for many years. His early pieces simply echoed the German classics. By about 1910 he was beginning to write the kind of music we now think of as being typical of his style: the song-cycle *On Wenlock Edge* (1909), the choral *Sea Symphony* (1910), and, finest of all, the *Fantasia on a Theme of Thomas Tallis* (1910). At the age of 38 he had at last

**Ralph Vaughan Williams**
1872–1958 In 1903 the composer discovered English folk song and promptly set about collecting and studying it. Gradually he absorbed it into his own music, as for example, in the *Fantasia on 'Greensleeves'* (1934). Many of his works are concerned with the idea of man as a 'pilgrim' enduring and fighting life's difficulties. It is the quality of hope and endurance in adversity that makes his music at times so uplifting to listen to.

*Below* **Job** Backcloth design by Gwen Raverat.

become a mature composer.

Fortunately he had a long life in front of him, and he went on maturing almost to the very end. He served during the First World War in the Medical Corps. He taught composition at the Royal College of Music. He enjoyed a deep friendship with Gustav Holst, whom he met as a student in 1895. He wrote music for every conceivable occasion – great or small – and became, in fact, one of the busiest, best-loved, and most influential composers of his day. His family fortune, and the fortune he made from his music, he left as a Trust to help other musicians and musical projects.

## Summary of Vaughan Williams's main works

Operas and ballets:

| | |
|---|---|
| *Hugh the Drover* (opera) | 1914 |
| | revised 1956 |
| *Sir John in Love* (opera) | 1928 |
| *Job* (ballet) | 1930 |
| *Riders to the Sea* (opera) | 1925–32 |
| *The Pilgrim's Progress* (opera) | 1951 |

Symphonies:

| | |
|---|---|
| A Sea Symphony | 1909 |
| A London Symphony | 1913 |
| | revised 1918, 1920, 1933 |
| Pastoral Symphony | 1921 |
| Symphony No 4 in F minor | 1934 |
| Symphony No 5 in D | 1943 |
| Symphony No 6 in E minor | 1947 |
| Sinfonia Antartica | 1952 |
| Symphony No 8 in D minor | 1955 |
| Symphony No 9 in E minor | 1957 |

Orchestral works include:

| | |
|---|---|
| Norfolk Rhapsody | 1906 |
| Incidental music: 'The Wasps' | 1909 |
| Fantasia on a theme by Thomas Tallis | |
| | 1910 |
| Five variants of 'Dives and Lazarus' | |
| | 1939 |
| Partita for Double String Orchestra | 1948 |

Works for voice or chorus and orchestra:

| | |
|---|---|
| *Toward the Unknown Region* | 1906 |
| *On Wenlock Edge* | 1909 |
| *Sancta Civitas* | 1925 |
| *Benedicite* | 1929 |
| *Five Tudor Portraits* | 1935 |
| *Serenade to Music* | 1938 |
| *Hodie* | 1954 |

Also many songs, song-cycles and folk song arrangements.

# Verdi

Fortunio Giuseppe Verdi. Born at Le Roncole, north Italy, in 1813 and died in Milan in 1901.

Verdi came from a peasant background. His father kept the village shop, which was also the village inn, and the village itself was very poor. Nevertheless, when his parents realized that he had genuine musical talent they did what they could to help. By the time he was 12 he had become organist of the village church – at £4 a year!

In order to broaden his musical experience, his father arranged for him to live during the week at the nearby town of Busseto. Here there was a town band, and a very active Philharmonic Society, whose president, a prosperous merchant named Antonio Barezzi, soon became very interested in the young boy. He offered to take him as an apprentice, and then all but adopted him and made sure he had the best musical education the town could afford.

Verdi proved an apt pupil and in 1831 he won a scholarship to the Milan Conservatory. But when he presented himself, he was told that he was too old.

Disappointed, he was obliged to make do with private tuition with Vincenzo Lavigna, an assistant at La Scala opera house.

The chance came in 1839, when he managed to persuade the management of La Scala to stage *Oberto*, an opera he had written during the previous year. It was a success, and he was offered a contract to write three more operas. The first of these was a comedy, *Un Giorno di Regno* (1840)

It was a complete failure. Perhaps this was not surprising. In 1836 Verdi had married Barezzi's daughter. Two years later both his children died, and in 1840, while he was still working on his 'comic' opera, his wife died too. For a while he was a broken man and gave up composition altogether.

Fortunately the manager of La Scala was determined to encourage him. Early in 1841 he called on Verdi and casually left him the libretto of a new opera. It told the story of the Jews in captivity under Nebuchadnezzar. The words of one chorus, 'Va, pensiero,' caught Verdi's eye. Almost before he knew what he was doing he had set it to music. By October the score was complete, and in 1842 *Nabucco* was produced. It was an immense success. The Italian public identified themselves with the captive Jews

– for Italy was under the domination of Austria at this time. The chorus 'Va, pensiero' became a kind of National Anthem for patriotic Italians, and Verdi was hailed as a national hero.

The operas that followed *Nabucco* increased his reputation, and soon even his name was being used as a patriotic war-cry. 'Long live Verdi!', the crowds shouted. But the Austrians never realized that not only were they praising a great composer, but also using his name to spell out their desire for a king of their own: *Vittorio Emmanuele*

*Right* **The Requiem** This engraving shows Verdi conducting his requiem at La Scala, Milan in 1874.

*Left* **Falstaff** This scene is from Verdi's last and perhaps greatest opera, a masterpiece of comic opera.

*Below* **Aida** A scene from a Royal Opera House production at Covent Garden with Amy Shuard as Aida and Jess Walters as the captured Ethopian King Amonasro.

*Re d'Italia!* (*Victor Emmanuel King of Italy*)
In 1846 Verdi met a singer, Giuseppina Strepponi, and after a while they decided to live together. They did not marry until 1859. By then, of course, he was world-famous. He had written operas for Milan, Rome, Naples, Venice, Paris, and London. And all the while his music had matured. Though it never lost its bold, unforgettable melodies, it became more and more subtle.

After the success of *Aida* (1871), however, it was generally believed that he had retired. It was a masterpiece of Grand Opera, and though it was followed by a masterpiece of religious music, the *Requiem* (1873), Verdi wrote nothing more for the operatic stage. And then, suddenly, in 1885, it was announced that he was at work on a new opera, *Otello*. He was 72 years old!

What had tempted him back to the operatic stage was a libretto, brilliantly adapting Shakespeare's play, by Arrigo Boito – himself a very capable composer. When the work was produced in 1887 the world was amazed to find that Verdi had exceeded all his former triumphs.

But there was one more surprise in store. Boito now prepared a libretto from Shakespeare's *The Merry Wives of Windsor*, and in 1893, at the age of 80, Verdi achieved his last and greatest triumph: *Falstaff*, a comic opera of immense beauty.

In all the history of music there is scarcely a career to compare with Verdi's for length and continuing development. At 80 he was as lively a composer as he had been at 26, but, of course, an infinitely greater one.

Verdi wrote 26 operas, a number of choral works, a handful of songs, and a string quartet (1873). The most important of his operas are:

| | |
|---|---|
| *Nabucco* | 1842 |
| *Ernani* | 1844 |
| *Macbeth* | 1847, revised 1867 |
| *Rigoletto* | 1851 |
| *Il Trovatore* | 1853 |
| *La Traviata* | 1853 |
| *Simon Boccanegra* | 1857, revised 1881 |
| *Un ballo in maschera* (A masked Ball) | 1859 |
| *La forza del destino* (The Force of Destiny) | 1862 |
| *Don Carlos* | 1867, revised 1884 |
| *Aida* | 1871 |
| *Otello* | 1887 |
| *Falstaff* | 1893 |

**Vihuela** This relative of the guitar was the instrument for which the serious 16th-century Spanish player-composers wrote their music.

**Vibraphone** An American development of the glockenspiel. It has a set of steel bars that are played with small mallets. Beneath each bar is a 'resonator' – a tube which is tuned to the note of the bar and therefore vibrates in sympathy with it. At the top of each tube there is a small disc that can be revolved by an electric motor. When this happens the ordinary note becomes rather sweet and vibrating. Vibraphones are much used in dance bands, where they are familiarly called 'vibes'.

**Vibrato** A very slight, rapid fluctuation in pitch. It is thought to make the notes more 'expressive', but it becomes offensive when overdone. The true vibrato is much less pronounced than the **Tremolo →**.

**Victoria, Tomás Lúis de,** Spanish composer, 1549–1611. He was born in Avila and studied in Rome to become a priest, but abandoned his training in 1569 in favour of music. He published his first book of motets in 1572 and soon became recognized as an important composer of polyphonic music.

He remained in Rome until 1585, when he returned to Spain to work as chaplain and choirmaster to the Dowager Empress Maria of Spain, who had retired to Madrid.

Victoria wrote no secular works. His music includes 20 masses and some 45 motets, and with Palestrina and William Byrd it represents a high point in writing for voices.

**Vienna State Opera House** The interior of the present building on Vienna's famous Ringstrasse was almost entirely destroyed in 1945, but has since been restored and remodelled. The original building was opened in 1869. At that date, and until 1918, the Vienna State Opera was the Court Opera. Its history has been remarkable – many of its directors being musicians of international importance, including Hans Richter, Gustav Mahler, Felix Weingartner, and Richard Strauss. It has attracted, and still attracts, singers, conductors, and producers of the highest renown.

**Vierhändig** (Ger.) 'Four-handed', that is, piano duet.

**Vihuela** Though the Spanish word *vihuela* originally meant any type of stringed instrument, it came eventually to be applied to the 16th-century relative of the guitar. The vihuela usually had six strings, tuned like a lute, and was guitar-shaped. It was a plucked instrument, and seems to have been particularly popular with aristocratic amateurs.

**Villa-Lobos, Heitor** Brazilian composer, 1887–1959. Largely self-taught as a composer. He spent several years in Paris before returning to Brazil (1930) to become much involved in establishing new systems of musical education in schools and colleges. He wrote an enormous amount of music (over 2,000 pieces). It shows the influence of jazz, folksong, impressionism, neo-classicism, and nearly every other 20th-century style – often apparently jumbled together. But at his best

Heitor Villa-Lobos

he was capable of powerful and very individual work, and is one of the most important and influential South American composers.

**Vigoroso** (It.) Vigorous.

# Viols and the Viol family

From the 15th to the 17th centuries the viols were the most important bowed instruments in European music. The viol has a soft, delicate voice, much more suited to chamber music in a small room than music in a concert hall. It was for this reason that it was gradually superseded by the Violin family, which began to emerge in the 17th century and by 1700 had firmly established itself.

Though the viol looks rather like the violin, there are important differences. The shoulders of the viol slope downwards (those of the violin are more rounded), and its back is flat (the back of the violin swells out). Its ribs are much deeper, and its sound-holes are usually shaped like a C (the violin's are F-shaped). Its neck is rather broader than the violin's, and it has frets made of gut running across it. The bridge is less arched, and it is therefore easier to play on several strings at the same time. The viol has six strings, which are rather thinner and longer than the four strings of the violin. They are not tuned in fifths, but in fourths and thirds. The viol bow is broader than the violin's and is held differently – with the palm of the hand facing outwards.

Viols came in several sizes, of which the treble, tenor, and bass were the most important. A 'chest' of viols meant a set of six instruments – usually two trebles, an alto, a tenor, and two basses. All were held between the knees, like the modern cello. You also hear the term 'consort of viols' – also meaning the whole viol family.

Interest in the viol and its music began to revive at the end of the 19th century, largely due to the efforts of Carl Dolmetsch, who gave his first concert in London in 1891. It is now a commonplace to hear the music that was written for viols played on the correct instruments, for they are being made again in some quantity.

*Above* **Medieval viols**
These 13th-century Spanish instruments, although different in shape, were an early type of viol.

*Left* **Set of viols** Bass, treble and tenor viols.

*Left* **Consort of viols**
These French musicians of the early 17th century play before Louis XIII.

*Below* **Bass viol of the 18th century** This painting by Jean Marc Nattier shows Madame Henriette, a daughter of Louis XV, playing this instrument. The bass viol was the last of the viols to remain in use well into the 18th century.

*Below* **Music for the viol** This 17th-century engraving is from Simpson's treatise, *The Division Violist*.

# Violin family

Though the precise origins of this important family of bowed instruments is somewhat obscure, it seems to have emerged in the middle of the 16th century from the medieval fiddle, rebec, and lira da braccio. It should not be confused with the family of viols, which is quite different in construction and manner of performance ( → **Viols and the Viol family**). The brilliance of the violin's tone quality, however, meant that it gradually ousted the viols for the performance of instrumental music. By the end of the 18th century it had become the basis of all orchestras and a great influence on the music being written for them.

The violin family exists in various sizes:

1. VIOLIN itself, with four strings tuned to: g, d′, a′, e″.
2. VIOLA, with four strings tuned to: c, g, d′, a′,
3. CELLO (or Violoncello), with four strings tuned to: C, G, d, a.

*(8ᵛᵉ lower)*

*Above* The range of the members of the violin family *(top to bottom):* violin, viola, cello, double bass.

4. There is also the DOUBLE BASS. It was developed out of the double bass viol in the 16th century. It has four strings, and its music is written an octave higher than it sounds.

Some double basses have a fifth string, tuned to the C below the E string.

In the standard orchestra the violin family occupy five lines of music:

**1st violins**
**2nd violins**
**Violas**
**Cellos**
**Basses**

There is no actual difference between the 1st and 2nd violins as instruments, but they play different music. In orchestral scores up until about 1830, the cellos and basses usually played the same line, an octave apart. But after that date they tended to lead a more independent existence.

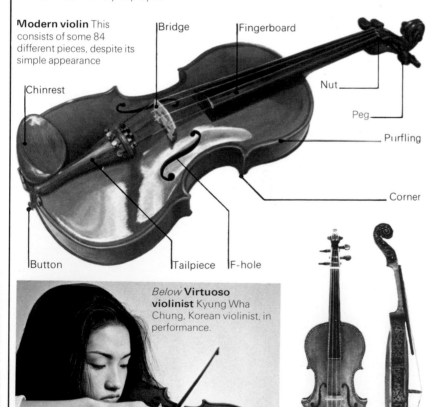

**Modern violin** This consists of some 84 different pieces, despite its simple appearance

Bridge

Fingerboard

Chinrest

Nut

Peg

Purfling

Corner

Button

Tailpiece

F-hole

*Below* **Virtuoso violinist** Kyung Wha Chung, Korean violinist, in performance.

*Above* **Stradivarius** This example of 1683, with inlaid decoration, is by the most famous of violin makers.

*Above* **Folk violin** These Rumanian musicians perform at a Turkish Folk Dance Festival.

*Below* **Violin family** *(left to right)* The violin, viola, cello and the double bass.

# Vivaldi

Antonio Vivaldi. Italian composer, 1678–1741. Born in Venice and spent most of his working life there. From 1704 to 1740 he taught at the Conservatorio dell'Ospedale della Pietà, one of the music-schools for girls. It seems likely that he paid visits to other Italian towns, and other countries in Europe, but he always returned to Venice and he died there. He was a fine violinist and is now remembered and admired for his many concerti grossi. There are more than 400 of these. Some have titles, and are indeed very descriptive – for example, the

**Antonio Vivaldi** |1676 – 1741 A prolific composer, he was admired by Bach.

six concertos that make up Book I of his Opus 8 ('The Trial of Harmony and Invention'):

1. Spring ⎫
2. Summer ⎬ Often played together
3. Autumn ⎭ as *The Seasons*
4. Winter
5. The Storm at Sea
6. Peace

Vivaldi also wrote operas, chamber music (including over 100 sonatas), and church music (e.g. the popular *Gloria* in D major).

# Voice

The voice is an instrument. It therefore has a source of vibration – the air in the lungs, which act like a bellows; something which sets up the initial vibrations – the vocal cords at the back of the throat, which act like the reeds of a wind instrument; and something which amplifies these vibrations – the various hollow parts in the head (the mouth, nose, neck, etc.), which act as resonators.

High notes are made by tightening the vocal cords, and low ones by letting them go slack. Loud notes are made by making the 'bellows' blow hard, and soft ones by letting it blow gently.

The lowest adult male voice is the BASS, then follow the BARITONE, TENOR and COUNTER TENOR:

Bass — Baritone — Tenor — Counter tenor

The lowest adult female voice is the CONTRALTO, then follow the MEZZO-SOPRANO and SOPRANO:

Contralto — Mezzo-Soprano — Soprano

The unbroken boys' voices are ALTO and TREBLE (girls have a similar range of voice, somewhat softer in quality):

Alto — Treble

*Right* **The organs needed to produce the human voice.** Cavities in the mouth, nose and head give resonance to the sound produced. The movement of the jaws, tongue lips and teeth control the sound.

*Below right* The larynx contains vocal cords which vibrate to produce voice sounds, and the pitch depends on the tension of these cords. If they are tightened, the pitch is high, and if loosened the pitch is low.

*Below* The lungs act like bellows, pushing up the air causing the larynx to vibrate. Controlling the amount of air released will determine the strength of sound produced through the mouth.

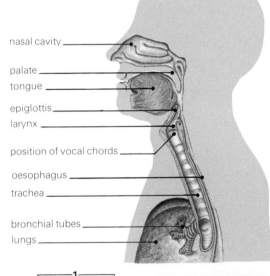

nasal cavity
palate
tongue
epiglottis
larynx
position of vocal chords
oesophagus
trachea
bronchial tubes
lungs

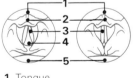

1 Tongue
2 Epiglottis
3 Vocal chords
4 Trachea
5 Oesophagus

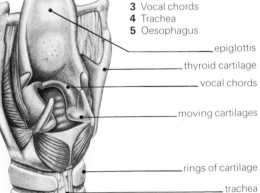

epiglottis
thyroid cartilage
vocal chords
moving cartilages
rings of cartilage
trachea

*Above* An opera singer in full song makes good use of the capacity of his lungs and the potential of his vocal chords.

**Vina** An important and very ancient type of Indian zither. It consists of a long, hollow fingerboard, attached to two gourds which act as resonators. It has seven strings. Four are used for the melody, while the three side strings are used for rhythm and to provide a continuous drone. It is played either horizontally, resting on the ground, or held across the player's body so that the smaller gourd is over the left shoulder. The strings are plucked with a plectrum. The vinas of North India are smaller and more slender (almost like a stick) than those of South India.

**Viol family** → page 338

**Viola** → **Violin family**

**Viola d'amore** A popular bowed instrument of the 18th century, somewhat similar to the treble viol in appearance. It has six or seven gut strings, and a set of sympathetic wire strings lying close to the belly, underneath the gut strings. The gut strings are tuned in thirds and fourths, and the instrument is played like a violin.

**Viola da braccio** In the early days of the violin family, all the smaller members were called 'viole da braccio' ('arm-viols') because, unlike the viols, they were held upwards towards the chin. Later the term was restricted to the alto violin (the viola).

**Viola da gamba** As all members of the viol family were held downwards, resting on or between the knees, when played, they came to be called 'viole da gamba' ('leg-viols'). Eventually only the bass viol was known by this name.

**Violin family** → page 339

**Vina** In this North Indian miniature the instrument is played in a vertical position.

**Viola d'amore** Little music of importance has been composed for this.

**Vivace** (It.) Quick and lively. Also **vivacissimo**, 'very lively'.

**Vivaldi** → page 340

**Vivamente** (It.) In a lively manner.

**Vivo** (It.) Lively.

**Vocal score** → **Score**

**Voce** and **Voci** (It.) Voice, and voices. As in **colla voce**, with the voice (a direction to the accompanist to take his speed, etc., from the singer). Also, **a mezza voce**, at half voice (half strength); **a due voci**, for two voices, **a tre voci**, for three voices, etc.

**Voice** → page 340

**Volta, La** A renaissance court dance which came into fashion in about 1588. The music is in triple time, and though the dance proceeds at a steady speed it is very vigorous – the gentleman helping the lady to leap and turn in the air as he supports her. It is not unlike the galliard. It was considered rather a scandalous dance, for in leaping the lady was often forced to reveal more leg than was felt proper at the time. Queen Elizabeth I, however, is said to have enjoyed the dance.

**Volti subito** (It.) Turn over quickly. Often abbreviated to **V.S.**

**Voluntary** Originally almost any piece of music that was extemporized. But because church organists were often required to extemporize before and after the service, pieces came to be written especially for this purpose and were given this title.

# Virginals

A small domestic keyboard instrument, popular in the 16th and 17th centuries, particularly in England. It has a rectangular box-shaped case, with strings

*Below* Title page of *Parthenia*, the first book of music for the virginals to be printed in England.

running almost parallel to the keyboard. Like the harpsichord, the notes are 'plucked' ( → **Harpsichord**). The range is usually about four octaves.

*Above* This painting by G. de Wedige of 1670 shows a German family gathered around the virginals.

*Below* Title page of *Parthenia*, the first book of music for the virginals to be printed in England.

*Above* This ornately decorated virginal was made in London by Adam Leverside in 1670.

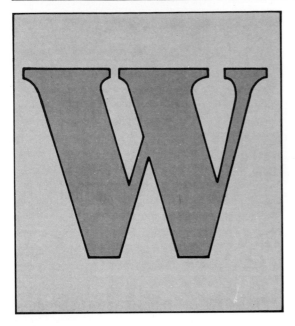

**Wagenseil, Georg** Austrian composer, 1715–77. He studied in Vienna and from 1739 worked as a court composer and music master to the Empress Maria Theresa and her daughters. His music includes many operas, and a number of early symphonies and string quartets.

**Wagner** → | page 344

**Waits** Originally, in medieval times, waits were night watchmen in palaces, castles, and towns, etc. Besides their guard duties, they 'piped watch' upon a musical instrument at certain hours during the night, or in case of alarm, or to awaken individuals by playing soft music outside their doors. They seem to have performed mainly on trumpets and oboes, recorders and, in Scotland, bagpipes. In great houses and palaces they were part of the general musical retinue – minstrels, in fact.

The idea of appointing municipal waits seems to have arisen in the 16th century. These town musicians were responsible not only for watch-keeping, but provided music for entertainment on special occasions (such as a royal visit), and often assisted with their music in the performance of plays. There was no special limit as to the number of waits a town might employ, but the usual number was between four and six. London employed nine waits. They wore fine livery, with a silver collar, badge and chain – many of which can still be seen in museums of city regalia. They were finally disbanded in 1835 by the Municipal Reform Act.

Present-day carol singers are sometimes called 'waits' (presumably because they too perform in the streets at night), but they are

**Waits** This group of 17th-century town waits would have had their own 'signature' tune, usually played on the hautboy but sometimes with brass, woodwind and stringed instruments.

**Washboard** This black washboard band perform with home-made percussion instruments, 1940.

not directly descended from the original musicians.

**Waldteufel, Emil** Alsatian composer, 1837–1915. After studying at the Paris Conservatoire he became famous as a composer of waltzes and other light pieces. Many are still played – for example, the 'Skater's Waltz', Opus 183. He was pianist to the Empress Eugénie, and director of music for the court balls in Paris.

**Wallace, William Vincent** Irish composer, 1812–65. He began his career as a violinist in Dublin, but emigrated to Australia in 1835. Then, after roaming the world, he returned to London and became a successful composer of opera and popular ballads. His greatest success came with the opera *Maritana* (1845).

**Walton** → page 343

**Waltz or Valse** → page 346

**Washboard** This old-fashioned aid to washing clothes consists of a wooden frame which holds a sheet of corrugated metal. In the 1950s it became popular among **Skiffle** → groups as a rhythm instrument, played either by scraping the notched metal surface with a rod, or with thimbles worn on the player's fingers.

**Warlock, Peter** English composer, 1894 – 1930. His real name was Philip Heseltine. Though helped by Delius, he was self-taught and eventually made a reputation as the composer of many fine songs. He wrote very few orchestral works, but his *Capriol Suite* for string orchestra has always been popular. He also worked as a music critic and as an editor of old music. He wrote several books, including one on Delius. He was, however, a strange man. As Philip Heseltine he was gentle and scholarly. As 'Peter Warlock' he was wild and aggressive. Both sides of his nature can be found in his music. But the effort of controlling these two sides of his character eventually proved too much, and in a fit of depression he killed himself.

**Waves (Sound)** → **Acoustics**

**Webbe, Samuel** English composer, 1740–1816. Totally self-educated, he eventually became organist at the Sardinian Embassy Chapel in London. He became famous for his glees and catches, winning no fewer than 27 medals for his compositions.

# Walton

(Sir) William Walton. English composer, b. 1902 in Lancashire, where his parents were both singing teachers. When he was ten he became a chorister at Christ Church Cathedral Choir School, Oxford. He was allowed to become an undergraduate at the exceptionally early age of 16. As a composer, he was virtually self-taught.

Walton was only 21 when he began to make an impression on the musical world – first with a string quartet (1922), and then with *Façade*, an entertainment he wrote in collaboration with the poet Edith Sitwell and her brothers, Osbert and Sacheverell, in 1923. Consisting of a suite of poems, recited (through a megaphone) against the background of Walton's very witty music, this caused a considerable stir, and by the time the overture *Portsmouth Point* (1925) had appeared he was firmly established as an interesting and daringly 'modern' composer. By 1929, with the performance of the Viola Concerto, he was judged to be a composer of major importance.

Thereafter, Walton's career proceeded smoothly. He married in 1948 and settled in Italy, on the island of Ischia. He was knighted in 1951 and made a member of the Order of Merit in 1967.

Though his early music was jazzy, highly rhythmic, and somewhat dissonant, his style has gradually mellowed and he is now regarded as a rather romantic, traditional kind of composer.

Walton has never been as prolific as many of his contemporaries, but has always written carefully and deliberately – with the

**William Walton** b. 1902
*Right* A scene from *The Bear*, a one-act comedy 'extravaganza' first produced in 1967.

*Above* **Facade** This scene is from the Royal Ballet's production at Covent Garden in 1978.

result that nearly all his work has been successful and is now frequently played throughout the world.

Walton's music includes two operas: the three-act *Troilus and Cressida* (1954), and the one-act comedy *The Bear* (1967). There are two Symphonies (1935, 1960), Concertos for Viola (1929), Violin (1939) and Cello (1956); several overtures, including *Portsmouth Point* (1925) and *Scapino* (1941); a fine set of orchestral *Variations on a Theme by Hindemith* (1963); two Coronation Marches (*Crown Imperial*, 1937, and *Orb and Sceptre*, 1953); choral and chamber music, and a splendid oratorio *Belshazzar's Feast* (1931). He has also written important scores for films, including *Henry V* (1944), *Hamlet* (1947), and *Richard III* (1955), all with Laurence Olivier playing a leading role.

Many of them are still great favourites: *When Winds breathe soft, Glorious Apollo*, etc.

His son Samuel (1770–1843) also wrote pleasant glees. He too was an organist, at Liverpool.

**Weber** → page 346

**Webern** → Page 347

**Wedding March** There have been many pieces of music composed for use in church before and after the wedding service. The two pieces most used for this purpose were not specially composed for it. One of these is Mendelssohn's Wedding March, from his incidental music to Shakespeare's *A Midsummer Night's Dream*, and the other is the Bridal Chorus from Wagner's opera, *Lohengrin*.

**Weelkes, Thomas** English composer, 1575–1623. Little is known of his life before his first book of *Madrigals to 3, 4, 5 and 6 Voyces* appeared in 1597. He seems to have been organist of Winchester College, and then (around 1602) of Chichester Cathedral. He wrote many fine anthems and services and published four important books of madrigals. He is widely regarded as the greatest of all English madrigal composers.

# Wagner

Richard Wagner. (Full name Wilhelm Richard Wagner.) Born in Leipzig in 1813 and died in Venice in 1883.

Until about the age of 15, Richard Wagner seemed more likely to become a poet and dramatist than a musician. He had been brought up in a theatrical family, for his father had died when he was a baby and his stepfather, Ludwig Geyer, was a professional actor and dramatist. He too died (1821), but not before several of the Wagner children had decided to go on the stage.

Just as the influence of Shakespeare made him want to write plays, the influence of Beethoven now made him want to write music. Neglecting his school work, he began to teach himself to compose. On Christmas day 1830 he had the satisfaction of hearing an Overture in B flat actually performed in public. It failed badly, and for a few months he undertook a course of strict counterpoint with Theodor Weinlig, the organist and choirmaster (as Bach had been) of Leipzig's St Thomas's Church.

In 1831 Wagner enrolled as a music student at the University of Leipzig. He seems to have spent more time drinking and gambling than actually studying, but he continued to compose and in 1832 not only managed to get a Piano Sonata and a Polonaise published, but also have two new overtures and a Symphony in C performed. In the same year he left the University and began work on his first opera.

Wagner's first musical appointment came in 1833, as chorus-master of the Würzburg theatre. He remained there for only a year, but gained a useful practical knowledge of the operatic stage. In the meantime he completed his own opera, *Die Feen*, but could not persuade anyone to perform it.

He now became musical director of the Magdeburg Theatre Company. It was a third-rate group, but it contained a pretty young actress, Minna Planer. Wagner fell in love with her, and in 1836 they got married.

By now he had completed a second opera, *Das Liebesverbot*. It was produced in 1836, but failed, and did nothing to improve his perilous financial situation. As the debts increased, his relationship with Minna grew worse. Quarrels, separations, reconciliations, further quarrels, all followed in a dreary round – to end only with her death in

**Richard Wagner** 1813–1883 This photograph of the composer was taken in 1864. *Below* A silhouette of Wagner conducting.

1866. He was an exceedingly difficult man to live with.

The need to earn money took Wagner to Riga (1837–39), London, and Paris (1839–42). Though frequently in debt, and often forced to hide from his creditors, he continued to write music and gradually his operatic style matured and grew confident. In 1840 he completed *Rienzi* (a Grand Opera, very much in the style of Meyerbeer) and in 1841 *The Flying Dutchman*. Both were accepted for performance – in Dresden and Berlin respectively. Both were successful. The tide in his affairs had turned, and in 1843 he accepted the post of Royal Kapellmeister to the Court of Dresden.

He spent six years in Dresden – conducting, composing, living luxuriously (and far beyond his means!), and working out schemes for a revolutionary type of opera. He also began to dabble in revolutionary politics. Revolutionary uprisings began to sweep through Europe in 1848, and in the following year Wagner was forced to flee the country. He went to Switzerland, where he remained for 12 years, a political exile.

By now, of course, his reputation had spread far beyond Germany. *Tannhäuser*

**The Ring** *Right* The Rhine Maidens seen from the auditorium at Bayreuth at the first performance of The Ring in 1876. *Below* These 'swimming wagons' carried the Rhine Maidens on stage in this production. Wagner realized that the only way the Ring could be produced according to his ideals would be to build a theatre to accommodate it. Money was raised and Bayreuth opened in 1876.

*Above* Interior of the Wagner Festival Theatre at Bayreuth, designed by Wagner himself. This engraving of 1876 includes, on stage, a scene from *Das Rheingold*.

*Above* This drawing shows the unique orchestra pit at Bayreuth. The curved awning at the top was designed to mingle the sound of the orchestra with the voices.

*Below* **Die Walküre** Gwyneth Jones as Brünnhilde in the 1978 production at the Royal Opera House, Covent Garden. *Bottom* **Gotterdämmerung** This scene is from the last opera in the Ring cycle.

| | 1863-67 | 1868 |
|---|---|---|
| *The Mastersingers of Nuremburg* | | |
| *The Ring of the Nibelung* | | |
| 1. *The Rhine Gold* | 1853-54 | 1869 |
| 2. *The Valkyrie* | 1854-56 | 1870 |
| 3. *Siegfried* | 1854-71 | 1876 |
| 4. *The Twilight of the Gods* | 1870-74 | 1876 |
| *Parsifal* | 1876-82 | 1882 |

had been produced in 1845, and *Lohengrin* followed in 1850. For a time he turned away from music and wrote a series of books and essays explaining his theories about a new and reformed type of opera, which he called 'music drama'. He then began work on the libretto of a colossal cycle of four music dramas, designed to be performed on four consecutive evenings and called **The Ring of the Nibelung →**. He began to write the music in 1853. It was a gigantic undertaking and he did not complete the task until 1874.

In the meantime his life became more and more complicated. He piled up debts, had a series of love affairs, and eventually became involved with Cosima von Bülow, Liszt's daughter and the wife of the great conductor Hans von Bülow. They married in 1870 and, strangely, both Cosima's ex-husband and Liszt remained ardent champions of Wagner's music, despite the scandal his behaviour had caused.

Before that, however, he had enjoyed an amazing stroke of good fortune. In 1864 a new king, Ludwig II, had come to the throne of Bavaria. He was passionately fond of Wagner's music and offered to support the composer in such a way that he could complete his life's work in peace. Though the Bavarian government was not very pleased about this, and though Wagner himself behaved (as usual) very badly towards his patron, the plan went ahead.

| | Composed | Performed |
|---|---|---|
| *Rienzi* | 1838–40 | 1842 |
| *The Flying Dutchman* | 1841 | 1843 |
| *Tannhäuser* | 1843–44 | 1845 |
| *Lohengrin* | 1846–48 | 1850 |
| *Tristan and Isolde* | 1857–59 | 1863 |

## The man and his music

Of all composers Wagner was probably the most selfish and ruthless ever to have written great music. He had immense ambition and a burning conviction that his mission in life was to create a new world of music. He was prepared to go to any lengths to achieve this end, even if it meant misery for the people around him. Yet such was his personality, and the strength of his genius, that people flocked to help him.

Wagner's theory of opera led him to abandon the old pattern of aria-recitative-chorus that had served earlier composers, and still served such men as Verdi. Instead, his 'music dramas' depended on a continuous flow of symphonic orchestral music, made up of many different themes called LEITMOTIFS. Each of these represented a different character, object, idea, or emotion in the story.

Against this continuous flow of orchestral music the singers sing in a kind of melodic recitative. They do not have set-piece arias or duets as they do in the operas of Verdi. In fact they are a part of the orchestral symphony.

Besides developing this new kind of operatic structure, Wagner employed a much larger orchestra and a much more elaborate way of writing for it. He also explored the more extreme kinds of chromatic harmony and gradually developed (especially in *Tristan and Isoide*) a type of music that is constantly modulating. Composers who wanted to go further than Wagner (as Schoenberg did) soon found themselves in a situation where key had been destroyed altogether. The idea of *atonality*, and indeed many of the more extreme developments of modern music, grew directly out of Wagner's discoveries. For he was, in every way, one of the most revolutionary figures in the history of music.

# Waltz, or Valse

A dance in 3/4 time, with usually one harmony to the bar. The bass part almost invariably has the lowest note of the chord on the first beat and the remainder on the other beats, in an 'um-pah-pah' rhythm.

The waltz developed as a ballroom dance out of a peasant dance called the **Ländler** →, which was popular in Austria and South Germany. It swept Europe during the first part of the nineteenth century, reaching the height of its development in the music of the Strauss family. At one time it was felt to be rather immoral, for it was one of the first dances in which you held your partner close to you.

Not all waltzes are for dancing. The waltz rhythm was so infectious that it invaded music meant for concert performance, including the piano music of Chopin, Schumann, and Brahms, and the symphonies of Tchaikovsky.

*Right* **Valse Bleu, 1908** The waltz, with its grace and melodic charm, has remained a popular ballroom dance in this century. *Below* **German and French Waltzing** This engraving is from an instruction book of 1816.

# Weber

Carl Maria von Weber. German composer, 1786–1826. The most outstanding member of a family of German musicians who were Mozart's cousins by marriage. His career began in 1804 when he was appointed conductor of the Breslau opera. Weber remained in Breslau until 1806 and in the following year took a new post at Stuttgart, as Secretary to Duke Ludwig of Württemberg. Unfortunately his father took advantage of his position and pocketed certain sums of money which his son was in charge of. Weber tried to shield his father, with the result that in 1810 both were ordered to leave the country.

For a while they roamed about Europe. His opera *Silvana* was produced at Frankfurt in 1810, and in 1811 the delightful one-act comic opera *Abu Hassan* was given at Darmstadt. During this period Weber made a name for himself as a pianist and wrote much instrumental music, particularly for wind instruments; indeed, his contribution to the clarinet's repertoire is the most important between Mozart and Brahms.

After staying in Prague for two years, he was offered the post of conductor of the German Opera at Dresden (1817). Here he settled, married (1817), and began to write the operas by which he is best known today.

**Der Freischütz (The Marksman)** *Above* Weber conducts his opera at Covent garden Theatre in 1824. *Below* A modern production of this popular opera, the first of the German Romantic operas.

The first of these was *Der Freischütz*, begun in 1817 and completed in 1820. Its success when it was produced in 1821 was overwhelming. Here was a new kind of opera – full of romance and mystery, with emotional and descriptive music to match. It was the beginning of a new style of German Romantic Opera.

*Euryanthe*, which followed in 1823, was also well received. In the following year he was invited to London to compose a work especially for Covent Garden. The outcome was a fairy-tale opera, *Oberon* (1826). It too was successful and earned Weber a very useful and much-needed sum of money. But before he could attempt the journey home he died.

# Webern

Anton von Webern. Austrian composer, 1883 – 1945. He was born in Vienna and studied musicology at the University, taking at the same time lessons in composition from Arnold Schoenberg. On completing his studies in 1908, he began to earn his living as a conductor of theatre orchestras and choral societies. He served in the Austrian army during the First World War. In later years (1929 onwards) he undertook a certain amount of teaching. Two months after the end of the Second World War he was accidentally shot dead by a soldier of the American forces occupying Lower Austria.

Together with Alban Berg, Webern was Schoenberg's most distinguished follower. His life was not an easy one, for his music took Schoenberg's theories to their extremes and was thought to be almost impossible to understand. During the Second World War his music was actually banned in Germany and he was forbidden to teach. His

**Anton von Webern**
1883 – 1945 He wrote mainly vocal and chamber music and his total output in composition can be listened to in about four hours.

importance as a composer only began to be recognized after his death, and then his music began to be taken as a model by avant-garde composers all over the world.

Besides being strictly atonal, Webern's music abandons almost all traces of traditional harmony, melody, and rhythm. It appears instead as isolated points of sound, which are in fact highly organized and often conceal elaborate contrapuntal devices, such as the canon. Many of these works are very short: the *Five Pieces* for orchestra (1913) last only 10 minutes, No 4 consisting of a mere six bars. Nevertheless, the effect is extremely powerful – as if a whole world of feeling has been concentrated into the smallest possible space.

Webern's music includes songs and choral works, various pieces for chamber ensemble, and a few of orchestral works, of which the most important are: *Six Pieces* (1910), *Five Pieces* (1913), *Symphony* for small orchestra (1928), and *Variations* (1940).

**Weill, Kurt** German composer, 1900–50. The first part of his career centred on Berlin where he became known as a composer for the theatre. His greatest success came in 1928 when he collaborated with Bertolt Brecht in a modern version of *The Beggar's Opera – Die Dreigroschenoper* (Threepenny Opera). It was highly satirical, full of catchy, rather jazzy tunes, and brilliantly caught the rather cynical, heartless mood of the times. Similar pieces followed: *Happy End* (1929), *The Rise and Fall of the City of Mahagonny* (1930), etc.

Weill (of Jewish descent) now fell foul of the Nazi Party and in 1933 he left Germany. After working in London and Paris he settled in America (1935). He wrote a number of successful shows for Broadway – including the 'operas' *Street Scene* (1947) and *Down in the Valley* (1948).

Besides his stage works, Weill wrote a certain amount of instrumental music (including two symphonies), and a splendid ballet: *The Seven Deadly Sins* (1933). His wife, the singer Lotte Lenya, was an important interpreter of his work.

**Wesley, Samuel** English composer, 1766–1837. The son of Charles Wesley, the great hymn-writer, and a nephew of John Wesley, the great preacher and founder of

**Kurt Weill** 1900 – 1950 He was involved with the movement for 'Utility Music' which stressed art as a social influence.

**Samuel Wesley** 1766-1837, composer and organist.

Methodism. He was a child prodigy, both as a composer and as an organist, and was later considered to be the finest organist of his day. He wrote a number of fine motets, several large-scale choral works, five organ concertos, five symphonies, three overtures, much chamber music, as well as glees, songs, and music for the piano and organ. One of the first to champion the cause of J.S. Bach in England, he helped to arrange and publish much of Bach's music. This common interest promoted a close friendship between Wesley and the young Mendelssohn.

**Wesley, Samuel Sebastian** English composer, 1810–76. The son of Samuel Wesley. He became a chorister of the Chapel Royal and then pursued an extremely active career as an organist. He was at different times organist of Hereford Cathedral, Exeter Cathedral, Leeds Parish Church, Winchester Cathedral, and Gloucester Cathedral. His services and anthems are among the finest of any English composer. Two of the larger anthems, *The Wilderness* and *Ascribe unto the Lord*, are of particular importance.

**Whistle → Recorder**

**Whole note** The semibreve. The semibreve rest is sometimes spoken of as a 'whole rest'. (**→ Notes and notation**)

**Whole tone** The interval of two semitones – for example, C–D, E–F sharp, etc. A **whole-tone scale** consists entirely of such intervals – for example: C,D,E,F sharp, G sharp, A sharp, C. Debussy made considerable use of such scales in his music.

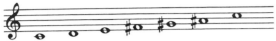

**Whythorne, Thomas** English composer, c. 1528–1590. He was probably an amateur musician, but published an important book of *Songes for three, fower and five voyces* in 1571.

**Widor, Charles** French organist and composer, 1844–1937. He was organist of Saint-Sulpice, Paris, from 1870 and taught organ and composition at the Conservatoire. He was much admired as a recitalist. Though he composed music of all kinds, including several operas, he is remembered for his ten symphonies for organ; the famous 'Toccata' forms the finale of the fifth.

**Wiegenlied** (Ger.) Cradle song. Like *Berceuse* (Fr.), this title is often used for quiet, soothing instrumental pieces.

Adrian Willaert c. 1480-1562 He was one of the first to compose madrigals and to write independent instrumental music.

**Wilbye, John** English composer, 1574–1638. He was a Norfolk man, but settled in Suffolk as chief musician to Sir Thomas Kytson of Hengrave Hall, near Bury St Edmunds. He published two volumes containing 64 madrigals (1598, 1609).

**Willaert, Adrian** Flemish composer, c. 1480–1562. He was one of the many Flemish musicians who went to live and work in Italy. From 1527 he held the post of Maestro di Cappella at St Mark's, Venice. His music includes madrigals, motets, masses, and instrumental pieces. He is said to have invented the idea of using two choirs to answer and echo each other.

**Williamson, Malcolm** Australian composer, b. 1931. He studied at the Sydney Conservatory (1942–49) and then in London, where he decided to live. He rapidly drew attention to himself both as a composer and as a pianist. He has written a great deal of music of all kinds, much of it very tuneful. He is known particularly for his operas, which include *Our Man in Havana* (1963), *The*

# Wind bands

The Wind Band exists in two forms: the basic MARCHING BAND, and the larger SYMPHONIC BAND. The difference between the two is simply that the Marching Band does not use instruments that are awkward to carry, or whose mechanisms are too delicate for work out of doors.

Both may be regarded as a civilian development of the **Military band →**, and differ from it only in the style of playing, which is usually more 'swung', and the variety of music that the Symphonic Band likes to play. Wind Bands are enormously popular in America, where they form a vital part of school and college music-making. Their popularity is now growing in British schools, though they do not yet rival the **Brass band →**.

The instruments of the Wind Band are divided into three families: woodwind, brass, and percussion. In the following tables we have the instruments of the basic wind band, with a separate list of those instruments that will be needed to bring it up to symphonic proportions:

This **Wind band** from Loughton plays at the Epping Forest Show at Chigwell, Essex in 1978.

| Basic instruments | Symphonic instruments |
| --- | --- |
| Piccolo | Oboes |
| Flutes | English horns |
| B flat clarinets | Alto clarinets |
| Bass clarinets | Contrabass clarinets |
| Alto, tenor, and bass saxophones | Bassoons |
| Cornets | Contrabassoons |
| Trumpets | Bass saxophone |
| Horns | Flügelhorns |
| Baritones | Extra tuned and untuned percussion |
| Trombones | |
| Basses | |
| Drums | |

*English Eccentrics* (1964), *The Happy Prince* (1965), and *Julius Caesar Jones* (1966). He was appointed Master of the Queen's Music in 1976, composing the *Mass of Christ the King* for the Jubilee the following year.

**Wirén, Dag** Swedish composer, b. 1905. He studied at the Stockholm Conservatory and in Paris, and afterwards worked as a music critic and as Librarian of the Association of Swedish Composers. Certain works, such as the *Sinfonietta* (1934) and the *Serenade for Strings* (1937), have become very popular. They are bright, tuneful, and elegant, and very much in the neo-classical style. He has, however, written a number of more powerful, sombre works, including several symphonies and concertos.

**Wolf** A dissonant sound heard when certain notes are played on a violin, etc. It occurs when certain parts of the instrument (usually the belly) vibrate in sympathy with one or more notes and cause a howling sound. Most stringed instruments have this defect, but an experienced performer can minimize the trouble. 'Wolf' notes occur also in keyboard instruments, particularly the organ, as a defect in the tuning.

**Wolf, Hugo** Austrian composer, 1860–1903. His father was a keen amateur musician and from an early age he was given violin and piano lessons. From 1875 to 1877 he studied at the Vienna Conservatory, but he was impatient of formal tuition and was eventually expelled. He suffered many hardships in trying to earn a living, but in 1883 was appointed music critic to an influential Viennese newspaper, the *Wiener Salonblatt*.

During his period as critic, he made many enemies, for he was very outspoken and spent much of his time praising Wagner at the expense of Brahms. His attitude irritated many professional musicians, who went out of their way to pour scorn on his early works by way of revenge.

Though Wolf wrote a certain amount of orchestral and chamber music, as well as two operas (*Der Corregidor*, 1895; and *Manuel Venegas* (unfinished), 1897), his real fame rests on his many songs. These were written in sudden bursts of activity – mainly in the years 1888, 1889, 1890, and 1896.

In 1897, however, his health broke down completely and he was placed in an asylum. He seemed to make a recovery, but in October 1898 tried to commit suicide and had to be placed under supervision once more.

**Hugo Wolf** 1860-1903 His songs are based on German translations of Italian and Spanish poems, as well as texts by Goethe.

**Wood block,** about 17.5 cm long with slots cut in it. When struck gives a hard, hollow tone.

Hugo Wolf belongs to the great tradition of German *Lieder* writers that began with Schubert and ended with Richard Strauss.

**Wolf-Ferrari, Ermanno** Italian composer, 1876–1948. As his name suggests, he was of mixed Italian and German parentage. He is mainly remembered as the composer of a number of very effective operas, of which the four-act comedy *School for Fathers* (1906), and the one-act comedy *Susanna's Secret* (*Il segreto di Susanna*) (1909) are the most popular. A 'verismo' (realistic) tragic opera, *The Jewels of the Madonna* (1911), was also very popular at one time. His music is tuneful and lively and very effective in the theatre.

**Wood, (Sir) Henry** English conductor, 1869–1944. He studied at the Royal Academy of Music, and began his career as a conductor in 1889. In 1895 he was engaged to conduct a series of Promenade Concerts at Queen's Hall, which he gradually built up into one of the most important events in the London musical season. The 'Proms', as they came to be called, were transferred to the Royal Albert Hall in 1941, when the original concert hall was destroyed by enemy bombs. He was a noted choral conductor, and made guest appearances with orchestras in many parts of the world. He was particularly active in promoting the cause of British music.

**Wood block** A traditional Chinese percussion instrument, now used in the orchestra. There are two main types. One is T-shaped – the cross-piece consisting of a wooden rod, hollowed out at either end. When the ends are tapped with a hard beater, each gives out a different note (high and low, but not 'tuned' to a definite pitch). The other consists of a small block of wood with a hollow cavity. When struck, this also produces a penetrating 'tock'.

**Woodwind** Flutes, oboes, clarinets, bassoons, etc.; all of which can be made of wood and not brass. (See separate entries)

**Worshipful Company of Musicians** An ancient London Guild, operating originally on a Royal Charter granted in 1604. It claimed to be a successor to an even more ancient London Society of Minstrels. The Charter was revoked in 1636, but the Company continued its activities. A new Charter was granted in 1950. The Company meets and dines regularly, offers various prizes and scholarships, and generally exerts itself on behalf of music and musicians in Britain.

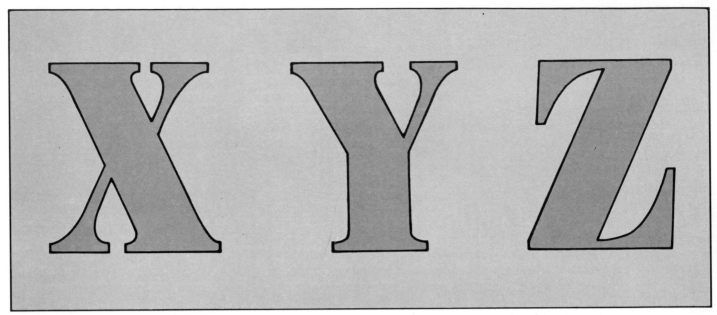

**Xenakis, Yannis** Greek composer, b. 1922. He was born in Athens and trained first as an architect. In this capacity he worked in Paris (1947–59) under Le Corbusier, but took the opportunity to study composition with Honegger, Milhaud, and Messiaen. Many of his compositions, such as *Metastases* (1955),

*Pithoprakta* (1956), and *Achorripsis* (1957), are based on highly complicated mathematical calculations, involving computers (→ **Stochasticism**). He achieves his effects with ordinary instruments, often played in unusual ways, and by electronic means.

## Xylophone

A percussion instrument of ancient origin, known throughout Africa and Asia, which entered the modern orchestra probably with Saint-Saën's *Danse macabre* (1874).

It consists of a series of hardwood blocks, laid out like a keyboard. These are hit with a round-headed mallet and produce a dry, brittle sound—rather reminiscent of bones.

Modern xylophones have resonators fixed beneath each note, and these vibrate in sympathy.

The xylophone, like the marimba, is not often used by the symphony orchestra, but an example can be found in Berio's *Circles*.

*Left* The xylophone played by this Thai musician has bars suspended over a decorative box resonator. *Right* Typical West African gourd-resonated xylophone.

*Below left* This large African log xylophone may be played by several musicians but more usually by three. It can be dismantled after a performance.

*Left* **Marimba** This instrument, played here by a Guatemalan family, is similar to the xylophone but its tone is more mellow and more suitable for melodies. *Below* Modern orchestral xylophone.

**Yankee Doodle** During the war of American Independence (1776–83) this song was popular among British troops, who sang it in derision of the Americans. However, the Americans themselves took it up, and now it ranks as a national song. Nobody knows who wrote the music, or the words, but the tune (in various forms) turns up in several English ballad operas of the 1780s.

**Yodelling** A type of improvised vocal decoration popular among the folk singers of Switzerland and the Tyrol. It alternates the normal chest-voice with falsetto in a series of up and down leaps. No words are used.

**Youmans, Vincent** American composer, 1898–1946. He wrote a number of tuneful musical comedies, of which *No! No! Nanette* (1923), and *Hit the Deck* (1927) were particularly successful. His career was hindered by illness.

**Zandonai, Riccardo** Italian composer, 1883–1944. He was a pupil of Mascagni, and though he wrote a number of orchestral works (including three symphonic poems) he is mainly remembered as a composer of operas. Two were particularly successful – the 'verismo' (realistic) *Conchita* (1911), and the lyrical, romantic *Francesca da Rimini* (1914).

**Zarzuela** A type of Spanish comic opera, usually in one act. It has spoken dialogue and is nearly always satirical. In 1856 a theatre was built in Madrid (Teatro de la Zarzuela) especially for the performance of these works – several being given each evening. The zarzuela is very similar to the Gilbert and Sullivan operetta, and, in Spain, just as popular.

**Zimbalom** → **Dulcimer** (**Cimbalom**)

# Zither

A type of stringed instrument found in many different forms all over the world among both primitive and sophisticated peoples. It is obviously of very ancient origin.

The European zither consists of a flat box which is strung with a variety of different kinds of string (some metal, some gut). The player uses a plectrum to play melodies on the strings nearest to him, while the fingers of the left hand pluck a series of open strings to form an accompaniment. The zither is placed on a table. It is particularly popular as a folk instrument in Bavaria and Austria.

*Above* The German musician J. J. Aberth plays the concert zither. *Above right* This Korean long zither is played either on a low table, horizontally on the floor or across the knees.

*Below* These Indonesian musicians play bamboo tube zithers with palm leaf resonators.

*Below* This decorative Turkish ganun is the ancestor of most European zithers.

*Above* Fretted south Indian vina with a wood body and one gourd resonator.

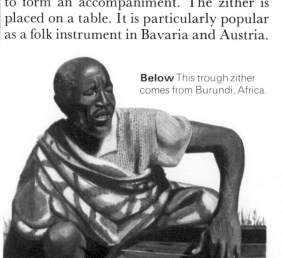

**Below** This trough zither comes from Burundi, Africa.

# Acknowledgements


The publishers are grateful to the following for their permission to use the pictorial and musical illustrations in this book. Every effort has been made to contact copyright holders, but we apologize to anyone who may have been omitted.

**Abel** National Portrait Gallery, London. **Accompaniment** Dobson Books Ltd, London (from G. Hoffnung, *Hoffnung's Music Festival*, 1956). **Accordion** Picturepoint. **Acoustics** p.20: Dobson Books Ltd, London (from G. Hoffnung, *Hoffnung's Acoustics*, 1959) pp.21, 23(b): Charles Taylor, Cardiff. pp.22-3(t): John Wiley & Sons Inc, New York (after L. L. Beranek, *Music, Acoustics and Architecture*, 1962). **Albert Hall, The Royal** Mander and Mitchenson Theatre Collection. **Aldeburgh Festival** Arup Associates; Architects, Engineers, Quantity Surveyors. **Allemande** Bibliothèque Nationale, Paris. **Amati** Ashmolean Museum, Oxford. **Ambrosian chant** Italian Tourist Office. **Anglican chant** Colorific/photo John Moss. **Arabesque** photo Ronald Sheridan. **Armstrong** Camera Press/Universal International. **Arne** National Portrait Gallery, London. **Auber** Caisses National, Paris. **Babbitt** Camera Press. **Bach** p.36: Bettmann Archive Inc; p.37: Museum Geschichte der Stadt Leipzig. **Bagpipe** p.39, 1st row: (c) British Library, London (Add.42130, f.176r); (r) Pitt Rivers Museum, Oxford; 2nd row: (c) British Library, London; (r) Barnabys Picture Library; 3rd row: (l) Alexander Buchner, Prague; (r) Musée Granet, Aix-en-Provence *(Gaspard de Gueidan Playing the Musette* by Hyacinthe Rigaud)/Archives Photographiques. **Balakirev** Novosti Press Agency. **Balalaika** Musikhistorisk Museum, Copenhagen. **Ballad** Mary Evans Picture Library. **Ballet** p.40: (t) Bibliothèque Nationale, Paris/Bulloz; (c) Radio Times Hulton Picture Library; (b) Royal Ballet, Royal Opera House, Covent Garden/photo Leslie E. Spatt. p.41: (t) Mansell Collection; (c) *Dancing Times;* (b) Nikolais Dance Theatre/photo Vartoogian. **Ballroom dancing** (t l, b l) Bild-Archiv, Österreichische Nationalbibliothek, Vienna; (t, b r) BBC Copyright Photographs. **Banjo** Lilly Library, Indiana University, Bloomington. **Bands** p.46(t l, b l), p.47 (t l): Crown copyright, Victoria and Albert Museum, London. p.46 (t r): photo Valerie Wilmer; (c r) Picturepoint; (b r) Burton Historical Collection, Detroit. p.47: (t r) Bettmann Archive Inc; (both c) Picturepoint; (b r) Susan Griggs Agency. **Bartók** (t) Archiv für Kunst und Geschichte, Berlin; (b) Bartók Archives, Budapest. **Baryton** Kunsthistorisches Museum, Vienna. **Basie** Popperfoto. **Bassoon** (t) Deutsches Museum, Munich. **Beatles** Rex Features. **Beethoven** p.53: Historisches Museum, Vienna. p.54 (t, b r), p.55: Beethoven-Haus, Bonn. p.54: (b) Zentralbibliothek Zürich. **Beggar's Opera** Tate Gallery, London/photo A.C. Cooper Ltd. **Bells and bell ringing** p.58, 1st row (c), 3rd row (c): Mansell Collection; 1st row: (r) photo Deben Bhattacharya; 2nd row: Whitechapel Bell Foundry (photos Terry Rand c,r); 3rd row: Whitechapel Bell Foundry (photo Terry Rand r). p.59, top row: (l) Society for Cultural Relations with the USSR; (c) Barnabys Picture Library/photo Georg Sturm; (r) Whitechapel Bell Foundry/photo Barney Burstein. **Bennett** photo Clive Barda. **Berg** Historisches Museum der Stadt Wien. **Berio** photo Clive Barda. **Berkeley** photo Clive Barda. **Bernstein** photo Erich Auerbach. **Birdsong** (l) British Library, London; (r) Mary Evans Picture Library. **Birtwistle** Universal Edition, London. **Bizet** photo Reg Wilson. **Blues** 1st row: Paul Oliver (photo David Gahr, t r); 2nd row: Paul Oliver (photo Jacques Demetre, l). (b) Paddington Press Ltd/Chris Strachwitz, Arhoolie Records (from T. and M. A. Evans, *Guitars*, 1977). **Borodin** Archiv für Kunst und Geschichte, Berlin. **Boulez** photo Eric Auerbach. **Boult** BBC Copyright Photograph. **Brahms** (b) Bild-Archiv, Österreichisches Nationalbibliothek. **Brass band** Popperfoto. **Britten** p.70: (t) Aldeburgh Festival/photo Kurt Hutton; (b) photo Ian Graham. p.71: (t) photo Houston Rogers; (b l) photo Clive Barda. **Broadcasting** p.72 BBC Copyright Photograph. **Brubeck** photo David Redfern. **Bruckner** Bild-Archiv, Österreichisches Nationalbibliothek, Vienna. **Bull** Faculty of Music, University of Oxford. **Bülow** Nationaltheater, Munich. **Byzantine chant** photo Ronald Sheridan. **Cage** (l) photo Erich Auerbach; (r) © 1960, Henmar Press Inc, New York (from J. Cage, *Sonatas and Interludes*, 1956-8). **Calypso** Trinidad and Tobago High Commission. **Cancan** Mansell Collection. **Carnegie Hall** Museum of the City of New York. **Carol** Mary Evans Picture Library. **Cecilia, Saint** Wallraf-Richartz-Museum, Cologne (painting by the Master of the Retable of St Bartholomew). **Cello** photo Clive Barda. **Chamber music** Furstlich Oettigen-Wallerstein'sche Bibliothek und Kunstsammlung, Schloss Harburg. **Chapel Royal** British Library, London (Add.35324, f.31v). **Cherubini** Musée du Louvre, Paris/Giraudon. **Choir** (r) National Széchényi Library, Budapest(lat.424, f.41r) **Choirboys** photo Reg Wilson. **Chopin** (t, b) Archiv für Kunst und Geschichte, Berlin; (c) Mme S. André-Maurois/photo Hachette, Paris. **Cittern** Kunsthistorisches Museum, Vienna. **Clappers** Popperfoto/photo Vincent Brown. **Classical** photo John Agate. **Church service** (t) Museum Carolino Augusteum, Salzburg; (b) Mary Evans Picture Library. **Clarinet** (t) Colorific. **Clavichord** (c) Worcester Art Museum, Massachusetts (*Young Woman Playing a Clavichord* by the workshop of Jan van Hemessen); (r) Deutsches Museum, Munich. **Comic opera** photo Houston Rogers. **Concerts** (t) Crown copyright, Victoria and Albert Museum, London; (c) Mary Evans Picture Library; (b) BBC Copyright Photograph. **Concerto** photos Clive Barda. **Conducting** (t l) British Library, London; (t r) photo Clive Barda; (b) Dobson Books Ltd, London (from G. Hoffnung, *The Maestro*, 1953). **Consort** British Library, London (Egerton 1554, f.2r). **Copland** photo Clive Barda. **Country and Western** Colorific. **Covent Garden** photo Reg Wilson. **Crosse** Oxford University Press, London. **Crotch** Royal College of Music, London. **Crystal Palace** Mary Evans Picture Library. **Cymbals** Dobson Books Ltd, London (from G. Hoffnung, *The Hoffnung Symphony Orchestra*, 1955). **Dance** p.108: (b) Barnabys Picture Library/photo S.Asad. p.109: (t) Bibliothèque Nationale, Paris (lat.873, f.21r); 2nd row: (l) Camera Press; (c) Colorific/photo Tweedie; (r) Mansell Collection; 3 row: (l) Barnabys Picture Library/photo Gerald Clyde; (r) Mary Evans Picture Library; 3rd row: (r) Picturepoint. **Dance Macabre** British Library, London. **Davies** Royal Opera House, Covent Garden/photo Stuart Robinson. **Debussy** p.112: (t) Popperfoto; (b) Bibliothèque Nationale, Paris. p.113: (t l) Snark International/SPADEM; (b) photo Mike Evans. **Delius** (c) Delius Trust Archive; (b r) Grainger Museum, University of Melbourne. **Denner** Bayerisches Nationalmuseum, Munich. **Dixieland** William Ransom Hogan Jazz Archive, Tulane University, New Orleans. **Dolmetsch** Popperfoto. **Dowland** British Library, London. **Drums** p.120: (t l) The Premier Drum Co Ltd, Leicester; (t r) photo Douglas Dickins; (c l) Colorific/photo John Moss; (c r) School of Scottish Studies/photo John Levy; (b l) Rex Features; (b r) Barnabys Picture Library/photo Hubertus Kanus. p.121: (t r) photo Mary Patterson; (b l) Mansell Collection. **Dufay** Bibliothèque Nationale, Paris (fonds.fr.12476, f.98r). **Dulcimer** Tiberiu Alexandru. **Dvořák** (t) Artia, Prague, (from A. Hořejš, *Antonín Dvořák: the Composer's Life and Work in Pictures*, 1955). **Einem** Universal Edition Ltd, London/photo Fayer. **Electric instruments** (b l) David Redfern/photo Andrew Putler; (c) Hammond; (r) David Redfern. **Electronic instruments** (t) John Morton; (b) Electronic Music Studios, London. **Elgar** p.128: Trustees of the Elgar Birthplace/photos Michael Dowty. p.129: EMI Records Ltd, London. **Euphonium** Boosey & Hawkes Ltd, London. **Expressionism** (t) Tate Gallery, London/ADAGP; (b) Oslo Kommunes Kunstsamlinger. **Eye music** Musée Condé, Chantilly (1047, f.11v)/photo Bibliothèque Nationale, Paris. **Falla** Roger-Viollet. **Fanfare** Keystone Press. **Fiddle** (c l) Colorific; (b l) photo Gabrielle Yablonsky; (b c) Alexander Buchner; (b r) Real Biblioteca de San Lorenzo de el Escorial, Madrid (b-I-2, f.39v). **Film music** (b l) Harcourt Brace Jovanovich Inc, New York, (from S. Eisenstein, *The Film Sense*, trans. and ed. Jay Leyda, 1942, 1947); (t, 2nd d) Columbia-Warner; (3rd d) 20th Century Fox; (b r) United Artists. **Finzi** Bassano & Vandyk Studios (incorporating Elliott & Fry). **Fipple flute** Horniman Museum, London. **Fitzwilliam Virginal Book** Fitzwilliam Museum, Cambridge. **Flute** p.139: (t l) Camera Press/photo Les Wilson; (c) Rudall Carte & Co; (t r) Graf Harrach'sche Familiensammlung, Schloss Rohrau/photo Meyer; (c r) photo Gerd Koch. **Folk dances** (t) English Folk Song and Dance Society, London; (c) Radio Times Hulton Picture Library; (b l) photo Douglas Dickins. **Folk-song** photo Brian Shuel. **Foxtrot** Mansell Collection. **Frescobaldi** Bibliothèque Nationale, Paris. **Fux** Österreichisches Nationalbibliothek, Vienna. **Gade** Musikhistorisk Museum, Copenhagen/photo Old Woldbye. **Gamelan** photo Ernst Heins. **Geminiani** Meyer Collection, Paris/photo Zoilo. **Gershwin** Bettmann Archive Inc. **Gillespie** Camera Press/photo Peter Larsen. **Glass harmonica** Bruno Hoffmann, Stuttgart. **Glazunov** Archiv für Kunst und Geschichte, Berlin. **Glinka** Society for Cultural Relations with the USSR, London. **Gluck** Kunsthistorisches Museum, Vienna. **Gong** Indonesian Embassy, London. **Goodman** photo Erich Auerbach. **Gottschalk** Music Division, Library of Congress, Washington, DC. **Gramophone** (t, 2nd r) Mary Evans Picture Library; (c) Science Museum, London; (b)Mansell Collection, London **Griffes** G. Schirmer Inc, New York. **Grove** Royal College of Music, London. **Guitar** (l) photo Erich Auerbach; (c) New York Public Library; Astor, Lenox & Tilden Foundations; (t r, b) photos Valerie Wilmer. **Handel** pp.160, 161(t): British Library, London. p.161(b): Mander and Mitchenson Theatre Collection. p.162(b): National Portrait Gallery, London. **Hanslick** Archiv für Kunst und Geschichte, Berlin. **Hardanger fiddle** Alexander Buchner, Prague. **Harmonica** M. Hohner Ltd, London. **Harmonium** David & Charles Ltd, Newton Abbott (from R. Pearsall, *Edwardian Popular Music*, 1975). **Harp** (t r) Barnabys Picture Library; (c l) photo Max Yves Brandily; (c r) British Library, London (Roy.2.A.XXII, f.14v); (b l) Myor Rosen, harpist in New York Philharmonic, Colorific/photo Don Hunstein; (b r) Musée, du Louvre, Paris/Giraudon. **Harpsichord** (b l) Russell Collection, Edinburgh University; (c r) National Gallery, London; (b r) Conservatoire Nationale de Musique, Paris/Mansell Collection. **Haydn** p.170: (t) Crown copyright, Victoria and Albert Museum, London; (b) Theatremuseum, Munich. p.171: Magyar Nemzeti Múzeum/Corvina Archives, Budapest. **Heckelphone** Wilhelm Heckel KG, Biebrich am Rhein. **Henze** (t) Royal Opera House, Covent Garden/photo Stuart Robinson; (l) photo Werner Neumeister. **Hindemith** photo Erich Auerbach. **His Master's Voice** 'Dog and Gramophone', registered trade-mark EMI Records Ltd. **History of Music** p.174: (t) British Library, London (Add.30850, f.93r); (c) Koninklijke Bibliotheek, The Hague (76.E.11, f.2r); (b) Biblioteca Riccardiana, Florence/photo Pineider. p.175: (t l) Kunsthistorisches Museum, Vienna (PS 5073, f.64r); (c) New York Public Library (Spencer 33); (b) Museum für Kunst und Gewerbe, Hamburg. p.176: (t) Nationalmuseum, Stockholm; (b c) Universal Edition, Vienna (from Haubenstock-Ramati, *Jeux 2*, 1968); (b r) Gallery Upstairs Press, New York (from C. Cardew, *Treatise*, 1967). **Holst** Space Frontiers Ltd (NASA, c). **Hornpipe** Mary Evans Picture Library. **Horns** (t) Archiv für Kunst und Geschichte, Berlin; (2nd row, r) Universitätsbibliothek, Heidelberg (Cod.Pal.Germ.848, f.202r); (3rd row, l) Mansell Collection; (b l) Dobson Books Ltd, London (from G. Hoffnung, *The Hoffnung Symphony Orchestra*, 1955). p.179: (t) Kunsthistorisches Museum, Vienna; (c) Conservatoire Nationale de Musique, Paris; (b) Crown copyright, Victoria and Albert Museum, London. **Hurdy gurdy** British Library, London (Add.34294, f.32r, t), (Add.42130, f.176r, c); (c r) Real Biblioteca de San Lorenzo de el Escorial, Madrid (b-I-2, f.154r); (b l) Musée des Beaux Arts, Nantes/Bulloz; (b r) Metropolitan Museum of Art, New York (Crosby Brown Collection of Musical Instruments, 1889). **Hymns and hymn-tunes** Crown copyright, Victoria and Albert Museum, London. **Impressionism** (t) Fogg Art Museum, Harvard University (Bequest Collection of Maurice Wertheim, Class of 1906); (b l) National Gallery, London. **Indeterminacy** Universal Edition, London (from L. Berio, *Circles*, 1960). **Indian music** p.186: (b l) International Institute for Comparative Music Studies and Documentation, Berlin/photo Jacques Cloarec; (b r) Camera Press. p.187: (t) photo Deben Bhattacharya; (b l) photo Douglas Dickins; (b l) Picturepoint. **Ireland** National Portrait Gallery, London. **Ives** CBS Records/photo W. Eugene Smith. **Janáček** (t) Camera Press; (b) designs by Rosemary Vercoe. **Jazz** p.196: (t l) Duncan Schiedt, Pittsboro; (b l) Mander and Mitchenson Theatre Collection; (r) William Ransom Hogan Jazz Archive, Tulane University Library, New Orleans. p.197 (t l) New York Public Library, Lincoln Center; (b l) Louisiana State University Press, Baton Rouge (from A. Rose and E. Souchon, *New Orleans Jazz; A Family Album*, 1967); (r) Max Jones Files. p.198: New York Public Library (from *Collected Works of Scott Joplin*, i, 1971, ed. Vera Brodsky Lawrence). p.199 (t, both b r) photos Valerie Wilmer; (both c, b l) David Redfern (c l Charles Stewart Collection). **Jingling Johnny** Royal Military School of Music, Kneller Hall, Twickenham. **Joplin** Melody Maker. **Josquin des Près** British Library, London. **Juke box** (c) New English Library, London (from J. Krivine, *Juke-Box Saturday Night*, 1977)/Sotheby & Co, London; (b r) Paul Oliver. **Kazoo** Horniman Museum, London. **Kern** Webb & Bower Ltd, London/Fred Fehl (from Arthur Jackson, *The Book of Musicals*, 1977). **Kit** Kupferstichkabinett, Staatliche Museen Preussischer Kulturbesitz, Berlin. **Kodály** (t) photo Erich Auerbach; (b) Interfoto MTI, Budapest/photo

Károly Gink. **Křenek** Archiv für Kunst und Geschichte, Berlin. **Landini** Biblioteca Medicea-Laurenziana, Florence (Med. Palat. 87, f. 121v)/photo Pineider. **Ländler** Bild-Archiv, Österreichisches Nationalbibliothek, Vienna. **Lassus** British Library, London. **Leclair** Bibliothèque Nationale, Paris. **Ledbetter** Max Jones Files. **Leoncavallo** Archivio Storico Ricordi, Milan. **Ligeti** photo Clive Barda. **Lira da braccio** Stanza di Rafaello, Vatican City/Scala. **Liszt** Archiv für Kunst und Geschichte, Berlin. **Lully** Royal College of Music, London. **Lur** National Museum, Copenhagen. **Lute** (c l) David Redfern; (b l) Bild-Archiv, Österreichisches Nationalbibliothek (Cod.A.F.9, f.42v); (b r) Radio Times Hulton Picture Library. **Lyre** (l) Artia, Prague (from A. Buchner, *Musical Instruments, an Illustrated History,* 1973); (r) British Library, London (Oriental 635, f.19v). **MacDowell** Bettmann Archive Inc. **Machaut** Bibliothèque Nationale, Paris (fonds.fr.1584, f.E). **Maderna** photo Marianne Adelmann. **Madrigal** Kunstsammlungen Veste Coburg. **Mandoline** Mansell Collection. **Mahler** (t) Universal Edition, London; (b) Gesellschaft der Musikfreunde, Vienna. **Marenzio** Schloss Ambras, Innsbruck. **Martin** Universal Edition, London. **Massenet** photo Harlingue-Viollet. **Mastersingers** Stadtbibliothek Nuremberg/photo Armin Schmidt. **Mass** Musée Condé, Chantilly/Giraudon. **Melodica** M. Hohner Ltd, London. **Mechanical instruments** (t r) Picturepoint; (c l) Mansell Collection; (c) Sotheby's Belgravia; (2nd row, r) Belgian State Tourist Office; (3rd row, r) Institut Belge d'Information et de Documentation; (b l) British Library, London; (b r) British Piano Museum Charitable Trust, London. **Mendelssohn** (t) Archiv für Kunst und Geschichte, Berlin; (b) Hamish Hamilton Ltd, London (from W. Blunt, *On Wings of Song,* 1974). **Messiaen** Editions Alphonse Leduc, Paris/photo Mali. **Metallophone** photo Deben Bhattacharya. **Metronone** Dobson Books Ltd, London (from G. Hoffnung, *Hoffnung's Musical Chairs,* 1958). **Metropolitan Opera House** Metropolitan Opera Association Inc/photo Joseph Costa, Sylvania Electric Products Inc. **Meyerbeer** (b l) Mary Evans Picture Library. **Milhaud** Musée des Beaux-Arts, Rouen/Giraudon/SPADEM. **Military drums** (b l) Mary Evans Picture Library; (b r) Trustees of the British Museum, London/photo John Freeman. **Military band** (t) Mansell Collection; (2nd row, l) Bild-Archiv, Österreichisches Nationalbibliothek, Vienna; (2nd row, r) Topkapi Sarayi Müzesi Müdürlüğü, Istanbul (III.A.3593, f.172r); (3rd row) Royal Military School of Music, Kneller Hall, Twickenham; (b) Roger-Viollet. **Minstrels** (l) Universitätsbibliothek, Heidelberg (Cod.Pal.Germ.848, f.399r); (r) Chester Beatty Library, Dublin (W.76.A, f.13v)/photo Pieterse Davison International Ltd. **Monteverdi** (t) Tiroler Landesmuseum Ferdinandeum, Innsbruck; (b) Galleria alla Accademia, Venice/Scala. **Moresca** British Library, London (Harley 4381, f.lr). **Morley** British Library/Fotomas. **Morris dance** Picturepoint. **Morton** Melody Maker. **Mozart** p.234: (t) Musikbibliothek der Stadt Leipzig/Camera Press, photo Len Sirman; p.234(b), p.235(b): Mozart-Museum der Internationalen Stiftung Mozarteum, Salzburg; p.235: (t) National Gallery, London. **Musgrave** Novello & Co Ltd, London/photo Eric Thorburn. **The Musical** (t) photo Reg Wilson; (c l) Samuel Goldwyn; (c r) National Film Archive/20th Century Fox; (b r) Rex Features/Globe/United Artists; (b l) National Film Archive/United Artists. **Mussorgsky** (t) Novosti Press Agency; (b) Senate House Library, University of London. **Mute** photos Mick Baines. **Nachtmusik** Museen für Geschichte der Stadt Leipzig. **Nakers** Bodleian Library, Oxford. **Noh** Japan Information Centre, London. **Notation** p.242: Bibliothèque Nationale, Paris (t, lat.12548, f.217r), (b, lat.1118, f.104r). p.243: (t) Biblioteca Capitolare, Modena (o.I.7, f.102v); Biblioteca del Catedral, Santiago de Compostela. p.244: (t) Biblioteca Laurenziana, Florence (Cod.Pal.87, f.154v); (b) Bibliothèque Nationale, Paris (Rothschild 2973, ff.20v-21r). p.245: from Zinovieff, *December Hollow.* **Oboe** (l) T.W. Howarth & Co Ltd, London; (t r) photo Mick Baines. **Oboe d'amore** T.W. Howarth & Co Ltd, London. **Ockeghem** Bibliothèque Nationale, Paris (fonds.fr.1537, f.58v). **Offenbach** Radio Times Hulton Picture Library. **Opera** p.249: (t) Popperfoto; (b l) Museo Civico, Turin. p.250: (t, b r) Royal Opera House, Covent Garden/photos Houston Rogers; (2nd, 3rd c l) Senate House Library, University of London; (b l) Colorific/photo T. Spencer. **Opera buffa** Richard Macnutt, Tunbridge Wells. **Ophicleide** British Library, London. **Orchestra** p.253: Germanisches Nationalmuseum, Nuremberg. p.254: photo Reg Wilson. **Organ** p.256: (t l) Museo Archeologico Nazionale, Cividale del Friuli/photo Elio Ciol; (b l) Greater London Council. p.257; (t) Camera Press; (c) Bavaria Verlag/photo Emil Bauer; (b) Musée des Tapissiers, Angers/Lauros-Giraudon. **Orpheus** Museo Nazionale, Palermo/Archiv für Kunst und Geschichte, Berlin. **Paderewsky** Royal College of Music, London. **Paganini** Radion Times Hulton Picture Library. **Panpipes** photo Hugo Zemp. **Panufnik** Boosey & Hawkes Ltd, London/ *The Guardian.* **Parker** painting by Roger Law. **Partch** Broadcast Music Inc, New York/photo Richard A. Matthews. **Passion** Cooper-Bridgeman Library. **Penderecki** Schott & Co. Ltd. **Percussion** (t l) photo Mick Baines; (c, t r) Colorific; (music) © Franco Colombo Inc, New York, 1961 (from E. Varèse, *Hyperism,* 1924); (b r) David Redfern. **Pergolesi** Biblioteca Apostolica Vaticana, Rome. **Peri** Biblioteca Nazionale Centrale, Florence. **Piano** p.265: Paul Mellon Collection, Yale Center for British Art, New Haven (painting *George, 3rd Earl Cowper and the Gore Family,* 1775, by Zoffany). p.266: (r) Camera Press/photo John D. Drysdale; (l) photo Clive Barda. **Polka** Trustees of the British Museum London/photo John Freeman. **Printing and engraving music** (t) G. Henle Verlag; (c, l) British Library, London. **Prokofiev** Novosti **Proms** Camera Press **Psaltery** British Library, London (Add.42130, f.149r). **Puccini** p.270: (t) Bottega d'Erasmo, Turin (from L. Frassati, *Il Maestro,* 1967); (b) Archiv für Kunst und Geschichte Berlin. p.271: Royal Opera House, Covent Garden/photo Houston Rogers. **Purcell** (t) National Portrait Gallery, London; (b) photos Reg Wilson. **Quadrille** British Library, London. **Quantz** Kurhessiche Hausstiftung, Kronberg. **Rackett** Bayerisches Nationalmuseum. **Rakhmaninov** Deutsche Grammophon **Rameau** Musée des Beaux-Arts, Dijon. **Rattles** Elanders Boktryckeri Aktiebolag, Göteborg (from K. G. Izikowitz, *Musical and other Sound Instruments of the South American Indians,* 1935). **Ravel** (both c) Roger-Viollet; (r) Musée des Arts Décoratifs/Lauros-Giraudon/SPADEM. **Rebec** Biblioteca Nazionale Marciana, Venice (Lat.I.77 – 2397, f.115r)/Foto Toso. **Recorder** Royal College of Music, London/Cooper-Bridgeman Library. **Reger** Archiv für Kunst und Geschichte, Berlin. **Reggae** London Photo Agency Ltd. **Rhythm and blues** David Redfern/photo Andrew Putler. **Rimsky Korsakov** (t) Senate House Library, University of London/ADAGP; (b) Tretyakov Gallery, Moscow. **Ring of the Nibelung** Mary Evans Picture Library. **Rock** Rex Features/photo Boccon-Sibod/Sipa Press. **Rock 'n Roll** Melody Maker. **Rodgers** photo Houston Rogers. **Romantic music** (t) Tate Gallery, London/photo A. C. Cooper; (b) Victoria and Albert Museum, London/Cooper-Bridgeman Library. **Rossini** (t) photos Houston Rogers; (b) Archives Photographiques, Caisse National des Monuments Historiques, Paris. **Royal Festival Hall** Greater London Council. **Saint-Saëns** (r) Bettmann Archiv Inc; (c l) Archives Photographiques, Caisse National des Monuments Historiques, Paris. **Sarabande** British Library, London. **Satie** p.288; Roger-Viollet. p.289: Musée d'Art Moderne, Paris. **Saxhorn** Spencer Collection, Brighton Art Gallery and Museum. **Saxophone family** (t) Popperfoto; (l) photo Valerie Wilmer; (c) Mansell Collection; (r) Henri Selmer, Paris. **Scala** Museo Teatrale alla Scala, Milan. **Scarlatti** Conservatorio di Musica S Pietro a Majella, Naples/photo Fabrizio Parisio. **Schoenberg** (t) Lawrence Schoenberg/Belmont Music Publishers, Los Angeles; (b) photo Reg Wilson. **Schubert** Museum der Stadt Wien. **Schumann** Robert-Schumann-Haus, Zwickau. **Schütz** Deutsche Staatsbibliothek, Berlin. **Score** p.298: Universal Edition, London (from K. Stockhausen, *Kontakte,* 1966). p.299: Oxford University Press. **Serenade** Österreichische Nationalbibliothek, Vienna. **Serpent** Bate Collection, Faculty of Music, University of Oxford. **Shamisen** Japan Information Centre, London. **Sheng** Museum of Fine Arts, Boston, Leslie Lindsey Mason Collection of Musical Instruments (formerly the Galpin Collection). **Shofar** Biblioteca Apostolica Vaticana, Rome (pal.gr.431.v). **Shawm** (b l) Colorific; (c) National Gallery of Art, Washington, Samuel H. Kress Collection (detail of *Mary, Queen of Heaven,* by the Master of the St Lucy Legend); (r) photo Deben Bhattacharya. **Sibelius** Sibeliusmuseum, Aino/Åbo Akademie. **Side drum** Premier Drum Co Ltd, Leicester. **Sistrum** Metropolitan Museum of Art, New York, Pulitzer Bequest, 1955. **Six, Les** Lipnitzki-Viollet. **Smetana** EMI Records Ltd/photo Angus McBean. **Special effects** L. W. Hunt Drum Co Ltd. **Stamitz** British Library, London. **Steel drum** Popperfoto. **Stockhausen** BBC Copyright Photograph. **Strauss family** Popperfoto. **Strauss, Richard** (t) Royal Opera House, Covent Garden/photo Donald Southern; (c) Franz Strauss, Garmisch-Partenkirche/Archiv für Kunst und Geschichte, Berlin; (b) photo Houston Rogers. **Stravinsky** p.316: (t) drawing by Picasso, SPADEM; (c l) Senate House Library, University of London/SPADEM; (c r) Robert Craft; (b) Crown copyright, Victoria and Albert Museum, London/SPADEM. p.317: photo Erich Auerbach. **Sullivan** Mander and Mitchenson Theatre Collection. **Suzuki** Minaeo Shibata, Tokyo. **Sweelinck** Rijksmuseum, Amsterdam. **Sword dance** Barnabys Picture Library. **Tablature** Newberry Library, Chicago (from the *Capirola Lutebook*). **Tafelmusik** Bibliothèque Nationale, Paris (fr.12574, f.181v). **Tambourine** Palazzo Pubblico, Sienna/Scala. **Tam-tam** Walter Rosenberger, New York Philharmonic/Colorific/photo Don Hunstein. **Tango** Radio Times Hulton Picture Library. **Tattoo** Scottish Tourist Board. **Tchaikovsky** (t l) Society for Cultural Relations with the USSR; (t r, b r) State Theatrical Museum, Leningrad/Robert Harding Associates/photo Victor Kennett; (2nd d) photo Houston Rogers; (3rd d) Tchaikovsky House Museum, Klin. **Theorbo** Crown copyright, Victoria and Albert Museum, London. **Three Choirs Festival** Times Newspapers Ltd, London. **Tippett** (t) photo Houston Rogers; (b) Schott & Co Ltd, London/photo Keith Cheetham. **Triangle** (2nd d) British Library, London (Add.34294, f.31r). **Tromba marina** Historisches Museum, Basel. **Trombone** (b r) Colorific/photo Don Hunstein (Ed Herman, New York Philharmonic). **Trumpet** p.330: (t) British Library, London (Roy.10.E.IV, f.65v); (b) Colorific/photo John Moss. p.331: (t l) Real Biblioteca de San Lorenzo de el Escorial, Madrid (b-I-2, f.286r); (t r) Bibliothèque Nationale, Paris (arabe 5847, f.19r); (c) QED Ltd, London ; (b l) Rex Features/ photo Frilet; (b c) photo Douglas Dickins; (b r) Colorific/photo John Moss. **Tuba** photo Mick Baines. **Ukelele** (b l) Paddington Press Ltd, London/Country and Music Foundation (from T. and M. A. Evans, *Guitars,* 1977); (r) University of Michigan, Ann Arbor. **Vaughan Williams** (t) National Portrait Gallery, London (portrait by Gerald Kelly); (b) Fitzwilliam Museum, Cambridge (design by Gwen Raverat). **Verdi** (t) Museo teatrale alla Scala, Milan (3rd, 4th d) photos Houston Rogers. **Vibraphone** photo David Redfern. **Vihuela** Henry E. Huntington Library and Art Gallery, San Marino. **Vina** Crown copyright, Victoria and Albert Museum, London. **Viola d'amore** Crown copyright, Victoria and Albert Museum, London. **Violin** (b l) photo Clive Barda; (c) Ashmolean Museum, Oxford; (t r) Popperfoto/photo Frances Skinner. **Viols** (t r) Real Biblioteca de San Lorenzo de el Escorial, Madrid (MS b-I-2, f.193v); (2nd d) Musée des Beaux-Arts, Troyes; (b l) British Library, London; (b r) Musée de Versailles/Musées Nationaux, Paris. **Virginals** (l) Wallraf-Richartz-Museum, Cologna; (c) British Library, London; (r) Ashmolean Museum, Oxford/Cooper-Bridgeman Library. **Vivaldi** Biblioteca Apostolica Vaticana, Rome. **Voice** photo Clive Barda. **Waits** Master and Fellows of Magdalene College, Cambridge. **Walton** (t l) Oxford University Press/photo Christina Burton; (t r, b l) photos Reg Wilson. **Washboard** Bettmann Archive Inc. **Wagner** p.344; (t) Radio Times Hulton Picture Library; (2nd d) Archiv für Kunst und Geschichte, Berlin. p.344(t), p.345(t) Richard Wagner Museum, Bayreuth. p.345: Royal Opera House, Covent Garden (2nd d l, photo Reg Wilson), (3rd d l, photo Donald Southern). **Waltz** (l) British Library, London: (r) Mary Evans Picture Library. **Weber** (t) Royal College of Music, London; (b) photo Houston Rogers. **Weill** photo Houston Rogers. **Wesley** National Portrait Gallery, London. **Willaert** British Library, London. **Wind bands** Barnabys Picture Library. **Wolf** Österreichisches Nationalbibliothek, Vienna. **Woodblock** Premier Drum Co Ltd, Leicester. **Xylophone** (t l) Barnabys Picture Library; (t r, b l) photos Peter Cooke; (b c) Popperfoto; (b r) Premier Drum Co Ltd, Leicester. **Zither** (t l) Archiv für Kunst und Geschichte, Berlin; (t r) School of Scottish Studies, Edinburgh/photo John Levy; (c r) Pitt Rivers Museum, Oxford; (b r) Institute for Comparative Music Studies and Documentation, Berlin; (b c) photo Ivan Polunin. **Donizetti** Museo Donizettiano, Bergamo. **Double bass** David Redfern. **Folk rock** Rex Features. **Gibbons** Faculty of Music, University of Oxford. **Mirliton** Pitt Rivers Museum, Oxford. Budapest, photo Attila Károly.